OCR Anthology for Classical Greek AS and A Level: 2024–2026

The following titles are available from Bloomsbury for the OCR specifications in Latin and Greek for examinations from June 2024 to June 2026

Cicero *Pro Caelio*: A Selection, with introduction, commentary notes and vocabulary by Georgina Longley

Juvenal *Satires*: A Selection, with introduction, commentary notes and vocabulary by John Godwin

Ovid *Fasti*: A Selection, with introduction, commentary notes and vocabulary by Robert Cromarty

Letters of Pliny: A Selection, with introduction, commentary notes and vocabulary by Carl Hope

Tacitus *Annals* XII: A Selection, with introduction, commentary notes and vocabulary by Simon Allcock

Tacitus *Annals* XIV: A Selection, with introduction, commentary notes and vocabulary by John Storey

Virgil *Aeneid* II: A Selection, with introduction, commentary notes and vocabulary by Dominic Jones

OCR Anthology for Classical Greek GCSE, covering the prescribed texts by Euripides, Herodotus, Homer and Xenophon, with introduction, commentary notes and vocabulary by Judith Affleck and Clive Letchford

OCR Anthology for Classical Greek AS and A Level, covering the prescribed texts by Aristophanes, Euripides, Herodotus, Homer, Plato and Plutarch, with introduction, commentary notes and vocabulary by Sam Baddeley, Benedict Gravell, Charlie Paterson, Stuart R. Thomson, Neil Treble and Chris Tudor

Online resources to accompany this book are available at bloomsbury.pub/OCR-editions-2024-2026. If you experience any problems, please contact Bloomsbury at: onlineresources@bloomsbury.com

OCR Anthology for Classical Greek AS and A Level: 2024–2026

Selections from

Herodotus, *Histories*, Book 1

Plato, *Republic*, Book 1

Plutarch, *Antony*

Homer, *Iliad*, Books 16 and 24

Euripides, *Hippolytus*

Aristophanes, *Frogs*

With introduction, commentary notes and vocabulary by
Sam Baddeley, Benedict Gravell, Charlie Paterson,
Stuart R. Thomson, Neil Treble and Chris Tudor

BLOOMSBURY ACADEMIC
LONDON • NEW YORK • OXFORD • NEW DELHI • SYDNEY

BLOOMSBURY ACADEMIC
Bloomsbury Publishing Plc
50 Bedford Square, London, WC1B 3DP, UK
1385 Broadway, New York, NY 10018, USA
29 Earlsfort Terrace, Dublin 2, Ireland

BLOOMSBURY, BLOOMSBURY ACADEMIC and the Diana logo are
trademarks of Bloomsbury Publishing Plc

First published in Great Britain 2023

Cover design: Terry Woodley
Cover image: Ancient Greek god of marriage, Hymen, with a musical instrument
© Migfoto/Adobe Stock

A catalogue record for this book is available from the British Library.

A catalog record for this book is available from the Library of Congress.

ISBN: PB: 978-1-3501-5663-0
ePDF: 978-1-3501-5665-4
eBook: 978-1-3501-5664-7

Typeset by RefineCatch Limited, Bungay, Suffolk

CONTENTS

Endorsement statement

The teaching content of this resource is endorsed by OCR for use with specification AS Level Greek (H044) and specification A Level Greek (H444).

All references to assessment, including assessment preparation and practice questions of any format/style are the publisher's interpretation of the specification and are not endorsed by OCR.

This resource was designed for use with the version of the specification available at the time of publication. However, as specifications are updated over time, there may be contradictions between the resource and the specification, therefore please use the information on the latest specification and Sample Assessment Materials at all times when ensuring students are fully prepared for their assessments.

Endorsement indicates that a resource is suitable to support delivery of an OCR specification, but it does not mean that the endorsed resource is the only suitable resource to support delivery, or that it is required or necessary to achieve the qualification.

OCR recommends that teachers consider using a range of teaching and learning resources based on their own professional judgement for their students' needs. OCR has not paid for the production of this resource, nor does OCR receive any royalties from its sale. For more information about the endorsement process, please visit the OCR website.

GENERAL PREFACE

The text and notes found in this volume are designed to guide any student who has mastered Greek up to GCSE level and wishes to read these selections in the original.

The editions are, however, particularly designed to support students who are reading the set texts in preparation for OCR's AS and A Level Greek examination from June 2024 to 2026.

Herodotus, *Histories*
Introduction, Commentary Notes and Vocabulary by Neil Treble
AS: Book 1: 1–6, 8–13, 19–22
A Level: Book 1: 29–45

Plato, *Republic*
Introduction, Commentary Notes and Vocabulary by Stuart R. Thomson
AS: Book 1: 327a–332b
A Level: Book 1: 336b–337a7, 338a4–342

Plutarch, *Antony*
Introduction, Commentary Notes and Vocabulary by Sam Baddeley
A Level: 76–86

Homer, *Iliad*
Introduction, Commentary Notes and Vocabulary by Chris Tudor
AS: Book 16: 20–47, 644–867
A Level: Book 24: 349–595

Euripides, *Hippolytus*
Introduction, Commentary Notes and Vocabulary by Benedict Gravell
AS: 284–361, 391–524
A Level: 601–624, 627–633, 638–662, 664–668, 682–731, 885–911, 914–1028, 1030–1035

Aristophanes, *Frogs*
Introduction, Commentary Notes and Vocabulary by Charlie Paterson
A Level: 1–208, 830–874

Each edition contains a detailed introduction to the context of the ancient work. The notes aim to help students bridge the gap between GCSE and AS or A Level Greek, and focus therefore on the harder points of grammar, word order and idiom. At the end of each edition is a full vocabulary list for all the words contained in the prescribed sections, with words in OCR's Defined Vocabulary List for AS Level Greek flagged by means of an asterisk.

ABBREVIATIONS

acc.	accusative
act.	active
adv.	adverb
adj.	adjective
affirm.	affirmative, affirmation
aor.	aorist
art.	article
causal	causal
clause	clause
collect.	collective, collectively
cm.	common
compar.	comparative
comp.	compound
cond.	conditional
conj.	conjunction
const.	construction
contr.	contracted, contraction
dat.	dative
demonst.	demonstrative
deponent	deponent
dim.	diminutive
emph.	emphatic, emphatically
esp.	especially
f.	feminine
fig.	figurative
freq.	frequently
fut.	future
gen.	genitive
imperat.	imperative
imperf.	imperfect
impers.	impersonal
indeclinable	indeclinable
indef.	indefinite
indic.	indicative
indir.	indirect
inf.	infinitive
interrog.	interrogative
intrans.	intransitive
lit.	literal
locative	locative
m.	masculine
mid.	middle
n.	noun
neg.	negative
neut.	neuter
nom.	nominative
obl.	oblique
opp.	opposed
opt.	optative
part.	particle
pass.	passive
perf.	perfect
pers.	personal
pluperf.	pluperfect
plur.	plural
ppl.	participle
prep.	preposition
pres.	present
pron.	pronoun
refl.	reflexive
rel.	relative
sc.	scilicet
simile	simile
sing.	singular
str.	strong
subj.	subject
subjunc.	subjunctive
subst.	substantive
superl.	superlative
temporal	temporal
trans.	transitive
usu.	usually
v.	verb
voc.	vocative

Herodotus, *Histories*

Introduction, Commentary, Notes and Vocabulary by Neil Treble

AS: Book 1: 1–6, 8–13, 19–22

A Level: Book 1: 29–45

Introduction

The author and his work

Herodotus' life and background

Despite being one of the most famous men of the ancient world, we know surprisingly little about Herodotus and, although there is much that we think we know about his life, there is also considerable uncertainty. One thing which we do know is his place of birth. Herodotus himself, in the opening of his work (which forms part of this selection – *Histories* 1.1), tells us he was a native of Halicarnassus, a Carian city which is now Bodrum in south-western Turkey. Although Carian in origin, by Herodotus' time Halicarnassus was a thoroughly Greek city and was considered part of Ionia, a collection of Greek city-states running along the western coast of Asia Minor. His date of birth is unclear, but he is usually thought to have been born around 480 BCE.

Herodotus' birthplace positioned him at the crossroads of the ancient world. On the one hand, he was a Greek speaker in a Greek city at a time when Greek civilization was flourishing on the Greek mainland immediately across the Aegean. On the other hand, he was an inhabitant of a city which was on the very fringes of the Persian Empire and was subject to its power. Although culturally Greek, Herodotus undoubtedly had a much greater understanding of Persia than his contemporaries living in cities such as Athens or Sparta. The theme of his work, a history of the wars between Greece and Persia, is, therefore, one to which he is ideally suited. The prominence given in his work to the ruler of Halicarnassus, Artemisia, and her interactions with the Persian king Xerxes, also suggests a continued interest in his homeland and its relations with Persia.

In his early life, it seems that Herodotus was politically active in Halicarnassus and may have participated in attempts to remove the Persian nominated tyrant, Lygdamis (Artemisia's grandson), resulting in his exile. From there he embarked on a series of journeys and undertook the research required to write the seminal piece which survives to this day. Herodotus himself suggests that this included travels as far south as Elephantine in Egypt and as far north as the Black Sea, although this is impossible to verify. It is also likely that he was sponsored in the writing of his work by the city of Athens and that the work was reasonably well known by around 450 BCE.

Herodotus probably died around 420 BCE although, again, this is conjecture based on the extent of his writing and the last datable events detailed in the work. He died at Thurii, a Greek colony in southern Italy founded around 443 BCE. Herodotus is said to have been one of the original colonists and had remained there until his death.

The beginnings of history

The development of a literary genre of history did not begin with Herodotus. Indeed, the genre owes a considerable amount to literature dating as far back as the epics of Homer which, even though we do not consider these to be history, set in motion a tradition of storytelling in written form concerning past events. Prior to Herodotus, the Ionian Hecataeus of Miletus (*c.* 550–*c.* 476 BCE) wrote two sustained works of prose: Περίοδος γῆς (*The Journey around the World*) and Γενεαλογίαι (*The Geneologies*), the latter of which is also known as Ἱστορία (*The History*). Both works only survive in fragments (often as quotations found in works by other authors) but the Περίοδος γῆς is clearly a work of geography concerning the cities and peoples of the Mediterranean and Black Sea while Γενεαλογίαι is an exploration of individuals and families who claim descent from mythical or divine beings. While, perhaps, not history in the way we would understand it, Hecataeus' works, as narrative explorations and examinations, were a key component in the development of history.

Herodotus, like Hecataeus, is a key part of this evolution in prose literature. Where Hecataeus' works remain relatively small by comparison, Herodotus took this form of extended prose writing to a new level. A work on a monumental scale, later divided into nine books (traditionally one for each of the Muses), Herodotus' Ἱστορίαι (*Histories*) retains the rational and analytical approach which had developed in the preceding decades and focuses on the exploration of a single theme – the deeds of Greeks and barbarians and why they fought each other.

Herodotus himself presents the material in the following terms:

> μήτε ἔργα μεγάλα τε καὶ θωμαστά, τὰ μὲν Ἕλλησι τὰ δὲ βαρβάροισι ἀποδεχθέντα, ἀκλεέα γένηται
>
> so that great and wonderous deeds, some done by Greeks and others by barbarians, may not be without fame
>
> (*Histories* 1.1)

While his language may feel loaded to us, his work is not designed to be derogatory about non-Greeks. If anything, the emphasis seems to be on the inclusion of others, the achievements of non-Greeks being just as worthy of record as those of Greeks. It is also worth noting that the term βάρβαροι does not carry the same negative connotations as it would do if used by a speaker of English today (although this certainly emerged in the ancient world). Instead, the word is rooted in language, meaning that the language which one spoke denoted one's status. Greeks spoke

Greek, while barbarians did not speak Greek. There is even a suggestion that the word has an onomatopoeic quality (the double *ba-ba* sound representing the incomprehensible nature of a language which one does not speak) but this is heavily disputed.

On the face of it, Herodotus' scope seems extremely broad. The achievements of Greek and non-Greek peoples and δι' ἣν αἰτίην ἐπολέμησαν ἀλλήλοισι ('for what reason they fought each-other') (*Histories* 1.1). However, when Herodotus talks of the achievements of barbarians, by his time this meant particularly those of Median or Persian origin or, more straightforwardly, the inhabitants of the Persian Empire (a large proportion of whom were not Medes or Persians). In this way, Herodotus' work confines itself largely to the achievements and interactions of Greeks and Persians (not the peoples of the whole of the known world). Of course, other cultures and peoples are mentioned (indeed a whole book of the work is dedicated to Egypt) but these digressions, as they are sometimes considered, always form part of the larger narrative about Persia and the Graeco-Persian Wars.

Similarly, 'for what reason they fought each other' also sounds something of a mammoth task – interactions between Greek speakers and those in the land known in Herodotus' time as Persia must have encompassed a significant span of history. While it is true that Herodotus starts from, what he considers, the earliest interactions between the two groups of people, the major focus of the work is the series of conflicts during the fifth century BCE – the Ionian Revolt (499 BCE), the first invasion under King Darius of Persia and the Battle of Marathon (490 BCE), the second invasion under King Xerxes (Darius' son) and the battles at Thermopylae and Salamis (480 BCE), and the final battles at Mycale and Plataea (479 BCE) which led the Persians to withdraw their forces.

That said, Herodotus' work contains so much more. Partly, this is determined by his place in the evolution of history as a genre. While Herodotus sets a theme for his work in the form of a question for discussion, the terms of reference for this discussion had not yet been defined by his time. Where we talk of history, Herodotus (as reflected in the title of the work) talks of ἱστορίη (one of the first words found in the text and in these extracts) and, although this is the origin of the term we use, its meaning was somewhat different. We imagine history to be clear, analytical and, as much as possible, unpartisan. To Herodotus, ἱστορίη was an enquiry, an exploration of the theme and associated ones taking in different viewpoints to be presented to his reader. This is reflected not only in his methods, but also in the text of the finished work containing, as it frequently does, alternate accounts of the same event and numerous digressions into different, if related, topics.

Herodotus also drew on a wide variety of source materials. Certainly, he relied on some written records (he makes specific note of some), but it is also clear that a proportion of his research came from discussions with individuals in the places he visited. He explicitly draws attention to this from the beginning of the text. In 1.1 he talks of Περσέων . . . οἱ λόγιοι (*the Chroniclers of the Persians*) and uses them as the basis of the discussion which follows. He then uses Phoenician sources to provide alternative accounts (*Histories* 1.5) and finally contrasts both with the established Greek version of events. All three accounts are presented to the reader, as if unfiltered, with little to suggest which is the more reliable of the three.

Book 2 also makes direct reference to the use of Egyptian priests as sources from the start:

ὧδε μὲν γενέσθαι τῶν ἱρέων τοῦ Ἡφαίστου τοῦ ἐν Μέμφι ἤκουον

So I heard the story from the priests of the Temple of Hephaestus in Memphis (*Histories* 2.2)

The priests themselves may have been drawing on written records but the information is likely transmitted to Herodotus orally. Through interactions such as these, he gained not just a narrative of events but also local myths and folklore, anecdotes about characters of historical interest, details of prophecies and events of religious importance, information about peoples and customs, even descriptions of the local wildlife. Without a predetermined idea of what constitutes history and viewing his work through the lens of enquiry, it is unsurprising that Herodotus' work is strewn with tangents on topics as diverse as geography, mythology and ethnography. A reader who picks up Herodotus' work will, therefore, not find a history which conforms to modern expectations. Instead, they will find a work which looks to share information, at the same time presenting this in a compelling, entertaining and thought-provoking manner, frequently inviting the reader to draw their own conclusions (at times even including multiple versions of the same event for the sake of completeness). This, then, is the major difference between Herodotus and his successor in the field of history, Thucydides (author of the *History of the Peloponnesian War*). Herodotus poses questions, presents information and offers rival accounts but, when it comes to the events themselves, does not necessarily define the narrative.

The structure of the work

While it may sound as if Herodotus' work lacks structure, despite his tendency to drift from his main theme and to build his narrative from smaller ones, the work (in the form it has come down to us) is arranged in a broadly logical manner which undoubtedly seeks to fulfil the declaration which Herodotus sets out in the introduction to his work. The nine books in which it has come to us (a later division not of Herodotus' choosing) can be divided relatively neatly into groups of three, each of which covers a major aspect of the Graeco-Persian Wars.

- Books 1–3 examine the earliest conflicts between Greek and Asiatic peoples, the rise of Persia, its territorial expansion and the reigns of Cyrus the Great and his son Cambyses. By the end of Book 3, Darius has been installed as king, culminating in his capture of Babylon.
- Books 4–6 detail the reign of Darius, his continued expansion of the empire (particularly his attempt to subdue the Scythians), the Ionian Revolt (an attempt by the Ionic Greeks of the Aegean coast to throw off Persian rule with Athenian support) and the resulting invasion of Greece and the Battle of Marathon.
- Books 7–9 concentrate on the reign of Xerxes, Darius' son, the second invasion of Greece, the battles of Thermopylae, Salamis, Plataea and Mycale.

Book 9 ends with a story of the passion which Xerxes developed for his daughter-in-law and the removal of rope by Athenian sailors from his bridges across the Hellespont to be given as offerings in their temples.

The work is, in its overarching form, chronological (Persia's rise – Darius – Xerxes) and even within the grouping of the books into sets of three, the chronological nature of the narrative continues for the most part. Tangents on which Herodotus embarks may cause him to leap briefly back in time but only for the purposes of adding further information concerning an event within the chronology. Even Book 2 of the work (the so-called *Egyptian Book*), the entirety of which is made up of a digression detailing the history, customs and people of Egypt, fits the overall structure of the work. Herodotus chooses to provide this information only at the point in the narrative when the Persian king, Cambyses, is planning an invasion of the area. The tangents and digressions in Herodotus' work are not random, as it so often sounds when his work is described, but are introduced to the reader at a time which suits the overall structure of the piece and supports his work by providing greater context for his audience.

The role of myth

Notwithstanding the more analytical approach which had developed in prose literature and was adopted by Herodotus, myth and storytelling still play an important part in his work. Undoubtedly there is some attempt by Herodotus to mirror the epic nature of Homer's *Iliad*, the first major clash between Greece and Asia documented in the ancient world (direct reference to the Trojan War is made in *Histories* 1.3 as well as at other moments). Indeed, as a second great clash between the same areas, it would be impossible not to draw parallels of some kind. Likewise, a reader cannot help but feel Homeric influence in Herodotus' introduction, particularly his reference to deeds becoming ἀκλεέα ('without fame') which almost certainly echoes the concept of κλέος ('fame' or 'repute') so often associated with the Homeric heroes.

More than this, however, it often feels as if Herodotus' prose style is emulating the oral tradition of the Homeric epics. On the one hand, direct intervention by a named divinity is not a feature of Herodotus' work. There is no *rosy-fingered dawn* and *bright-eyed Athena* does not appear on the battlefield in the Greek struggle against the Persian invader. Instead, the work exists very much in the physical realm of men. There are, however, some exceptions to this. Most notably, as Pheidippides runs to Sparta to inform them of the Persian invasion (*Histories* 6.105–6.106), Pan appears to him. Likewise, although gods are not normally named directly when examining events on earth, Herodotus commonly refers to 'God' in the context of circumstances which befall individuals, a stark reminder that we are not functioning in a world without divine power. Artabanus (Xerxes' uncle), for instance, cautions Xerxes about the nature of the gods and their tendency to bring men down:

ὁ δὲ θεὸς γλυκὺν γεύσας τὸν αἰῶνα φθονερὸς ἐν αὐτῷ εὑρίσκεται ἐών.

But God, having given a taste of the sweet-life, is often found to be envious in this.
(*Histories* 7.46)

This is not isolated but is an idea which Herodotus introduces much earlier and runs through the work.

> μετὰ δὲ Σόλωνα οἰχόμενον ἔλαβέ ἐκ θεοῦ νέμεσις μεγάλη Κροῖσον . . .
>
> After Solon's departure, great nemesis from God took Croesus . . .
>
> (*Histories* 1.34)

Despite the lack of a named god, therefore, there is clearly a divine force present in Herodotus' work. With this there also comes a moral dimension. Both examples above are given as part of a larger narrative structure but offer a view on the nature of the relationship between gods and men, a theme which is also ever-present in the Homeric works.

More obvious than the presence of a divine power, however, is the storytelling mode which Herodotus adopts, particularly in the earlier books. This has enchanted his readership since ancient times and feels quite reminiscent of the exploits of men related in Homer's works. Most striking is the cunning demonstrated by Themistocles, who employs various stratagems in a manner reminiscent of Homer's Odysseus, to ensure that the events of the war go his way. Ultimately, he tricks the Persians by sending a messenger who pretends to betray the Greeks and urges the Persians to attack while the Greek fleet is, so he says, preparing to flee (*Histories* 8.85). The plan works, forcing the Persians to fight at Salamis, a location which provides them with no advantage despite their superior numbers and ends in their defeat. Other fantastical stories such as Arion riding to safety on the back of a dolphin (*Histories* 1.23–1.24), the cunning thief raiding the treasure-house of the Egyptian Pharaoh, Rhampsinitus (*Histories* 2.121), or the example of extreme devotion shown by Zopyrus' self-mutilation which hastens Darius' capture of Babylon (*Histories* 3.153–160) are littered throughout his work and allow Herodotus, like Homer and in the manner of a true storyteller, to offer his reader moral templates for life and examples of immense cunning, luck or self-sacrifice.

The influence of fate and oracles and the role of hubris

The ever-present influence of the divine is heightened by Herodotus' focus on the impact of fate on human events and the prophecies related to men by oracles. Events of great significance are often foreshadowed or accompanied by a prophecy which invariably comes to fruition, although usually involving some level of ambiguity. Herodotus establishes this pattern very early on in his work through the character of Croesus who experiences the work of fate in a variety of different ways.

Croesus is initially warned of the workings of fate and the impact it can have on men's lives through the arrival of Solon, the Athenian statesman (included in this selection, *Histories* 1.32). Solon's fundamental message is that, despite Croesus' evident wealth and current prosperity, Solon cannot judge him happy since God could remove these at any time. Croesus, however, chooses to dismiss this. Following Solon's departure, Croesus dreams (itself a form of prophecy) of the death of one of his sons (*Histories* 1.34) and takes steps to avoid this happening. Naturally, his actions are futile and the prophecy is fulfilled. Finally, Croesus seeks the favour of the Oracle at Delphi (having first attempted to establish the veracity of its utterances) and asks whether he should invade Persia (*Histories* 1.53). The response given is that, should he choose to, a great empire would fall and, furthermore, that he should show no fear until a mule sits on the throne of Persia. Croesus interprets both statements as positive indicators and proceeds with the plan.

Each of these interactions demonstrates the power of fate and contains lessons about the way in which men should behave in response. Croesus fails to see the truth in what Solon says, questioning how anyone could fail to judge him happy based on his current circumstances. Instead, the truth of Solon's words only emerges when Croesus is about to be executed by Cyrus, King of Persia (*Histories* 1.86). In addition, his attempts to avoid the events of his dream are pointless – regardless of his actions, fate finds a way and Croesus' son dies. Finally, the Oracle at Delphi's prophecy (that of a great empire falling), as any objective outsider would caution, refers not to the Persian Empire but to Croesus' own. To rub salt in the wound, it transpires that Cyrus' mother was Median while his father was Persian – in the ancient world, a crossbreed of sorts just like a mule (*Histories* 1.91).

This is not to say that Croesus is stupid. Although some of his actions appear rash at times (he himself admits his error shortly after the revelation of Cyrus' origins), it is simply that he is not in control of events. Fundamentally, his fate, as described so neatly by Solon, is not in his hands and, as much as he might seek to control events, this is beyond his power. Similar lessons appear repeatedly throughout Herodotus' work. Astyages (the grandfather of Cyrus the Great) dreams Cyrus will usurp him and, in vain, attempts to have him killed as a child (*Histories* 1.108), only for the infant Cyrus to survive and, years later, defeat him in battle (*Histories* 1.128). The Delphic Oracle's prophecy to the Athenians that the wooden wall will not fall (*Histories* 7.141–7.142) is ambiguous and is the catalyst for considerable debate as to how they should defend themselves. Some of the Athenians suggest the prophecy refers to the old wooden fence around the Acropolis, while Themistocles leads others in adopting a less literal view and suggests the wooden wall represents the city's navy. As it transpires, the Persians are beaten back in the naval battle at Salamis and the prophecy is fulfilled. Divine utterances are never wrong, but men's interpretation of them can be deeply flawed. As a result, Solon's view, that which is told to Croesus, also reappears throughout Herodotus' work. Most strikingly, during the Persian conference prior to the invasion, Artabanus (Xerxes' uncle) warns him not to overreach himself, advising that it is always the great buildings and tall trees which God brings down (*Histories* 7.10e). Ultimately, Artabanus' words have no effect and Xerxes (driven on by another unnamed divine force which appears to him in the night) opts to march against Greece and is defeated.

This is not to say that men's actions have no impact on events, simply that those events which are predetermined, or happen through divine will, cannot be avoided. Indeed, on the contrary, men's actions affect events and determine the role of the divine profoundly and Herodotus again chooses to establish this theme in the character of Croesus. Having disagreed with Solon's advice on the nature of the gods and abruptly dismissing him, Herodotus tells us not only that nemesis fell upon Croesus but suggests the reason for this.

> ὡς εἰκάσαι, ὅτι ἐνόμισε ἑωυτὸν εἶναι ἀνθρώπων ἁπάντων ὀλβιώτατον.
>
> so it seems, since he thought himself the most fortunate of all men.
>
> (*Histories* 1.34)

And with this, Herodotus introduces the idea of hubris. Herodotus never actually uses the word when referring to Croesus but, despite being difficult to define (encompassing arrogance, pride, overstepping one's bounds and, above all, outrage against the natural order as determined by the divine), his actions and the inclusion of nemesis, the natural avenger of such acts, show Herodotus' intention clearly. It is precisely because Croesus does not recognize god's power that he is worthy of nemesis and because he thinks his current status and fortune beyond god's reach (otherwise he would have considered Solon's words more carefully). From that moment, he is fated to be brought back down to earth. Croesus' downfall is also part of a much larger cycle of fate (*Histories* 1.13) which determines that vengeance for earlier crimes will be exacted on his dynasty in the fifth generation, neatly coinciding with Croesus' rule. As a result, Croesus is not only blind to the instability of his own position but to the fact that his punishment has already been predetermined by the actions of others. In this way, hubris binds the actions of men and the power of the gods and Croesus, although himself a Lydian, foreshadows what is to come in the character of the Persian king, Xerxes.

Herodotus' Xerxes is a complex character and, at times, paradoxical. Often quick to anger, he can also consider the counsel of his advisors wisely, sometimes restrained he also engages in outbursts of excessive violence. Despite the relatively balanced nature of Herodotus' account, it is Xerxes' shortness of temper and his violent responses, driven by his absolute belief in the dignity of his position and how this should determine the behaviour of others, which is most memorable. The prime example of this comes as Herodotus relates Xerxes' march through Lydia prior to the army's crossing into Europe. At this point, Xerxes is met by a Lydian named Pythius (*Histories* 7.27) who, being wealthy beyond imagination, offers money and food to support Xerxes' campaign against Greece. Xerxes does not accept his offer, instead demonstrating his own generosity in response to the Lydian's. Fast-forward briefly and, buoyed by his apparent favour with the king, Pythius requests that his eldest son be left behind to take care of him rather than joining Xerxes on the war effort. The change of tone is immediate and violent – Xerxes curses him and determines that Pythius can have all of his sons stay with him except the very one he requested: he is to be cut in half and the parts of his body placed on either side of the road for the army to march between as a twisted ritual of sorts (*Histories* 7.39). What motivates Xerxes is his conviction that, since he is king, Pythius has no right to ask anything of him (being a subject makes him a mere slave in Xerxes' eyes) and, regardless of any support Pythius may have previously offered, for him to do so is an outrage of the highest order.

This incident is juxtaposed by two others which show the tremendous depth of Xerxes' hubris. Immediately prior to the Pythius episode, Herodotus details the cutting of a canal through the peninsula containing Mount Athos (*Histories* 7.22–7.25). In theory, the canal is cut to avoid a repeat of a previous naval disaster in the area by providing passage for ships through safer waters and, perhaps to a modern audience, the act is not particularly controversial. In Herodotus' mind it is, however, something rather more than an act of civil engineering, suggesting that Xerxes did it out of mere ostentation:

> ἐθέλων τε δύναμιν ἀποδείκνυσθαι καὶ μνημόσυνα λιπέσθαι
>
> wishing to demonstrate his power and leave something by which he would be remembered
>
> (*Histories* 7.24)

And it is this intent, along with a willingness to turn the inhabitants of the peninsula into islanders (as Herodotus terms it), that makes Xerxes' actions so outrageous. Even for a king of Persia, modifying the nature of the earth is a step too far and creating sea where there was once land smacks of overstepping the mark.

Meanwhile, part way through the Pythius story, Xerxes is shown at his most notorious. Having completed the construction of the canal, engineers are set to work bridging the Hellespont, the narrow strait which separates Asia from Europe (now known as the Dardanelles). In contrast to his actions at the Athos peninsula, where he created sea, at the Hellespont Xerxes, in the form of two bridges, creates land (including soil so that they resemble earth in form and appearance to any animal passing over them). The bridges are, however, broken in a storm and, true to form, Xerxes responds furiously, ordering the Hellespont to be whipped, insulted and symbolically subdued with chains (*Histories* 7.35). As a part of the natural world, Xerxes shows contempt for the divine by his actions and, in doing so, makes himself the tall tree which Artabanus has previously warned him against. These, along with numerous other actions, single Xerxes out for the divine retribution which will come in the form of his final defeat at the hands of the Greeks. It is in Croesus, despite being much earlier in Herodotus' work, that this theme is established.

There are, of course, several other themes which emerge from Herodotus' work, not least the contrast between freedom and slavery depicted through comparison of Greek with Persian society (as exemplified by Xerxes' treatment of Pythius), or the issue of *might vs right* – invasions under both Persian kings, Darius and Xerxes, gathering together unthinkable numbers of troops, are repelled by much smaller Greek forces fighting with conviction for what they believe in. However, particularly with reference to the selection contained here, the issues of fate, the divine and hubris are more potent themes and, importantly, are established from the very beginning of Herodotus' work.

Herodotus' legacy

Despite Herodotus' work being the earliest surviving work of prose history produced in the Western world, he has been subject to a mixed reception both by modern and ancient readers. His title of *pater historiae* (*father of history*) was originally bestowed upon him by the Roman politician and orator Cicero, although Cicero immediately seems to diminish the accolade he has just awarded.

> *quamquam et apud Herodotum patrem historiae et apud Theopompum sunt innumerabiles fabulae.*
>
> although even in Herodotus, the father of history, and in Theopompus (4th-century BCE historian), there are countless stories.
>
> (Cicero, *de legibus*, 1.5)

Although undoubtedly true that Herodotus' work is full of stories, it seems Cicero views it as diminished because of this. Cicero's view of Herodotus as *pater historiae* is likely, to a large extent, motivated by his position as the first writer of such a work and less by his biting, analytical observation.

Similarly, Plutarch (1st–2nd century CE biographer and essayist) in his Περὶ τῆς Ἡροδότου κακοηθείας (*On the Malice of Herodotus*), a critical essay on Herodotus' work, takes a particularly scathing view not just of the work itself, but even of Herodotus the man and his character by comparing him (like Cicero) with both Theopompus and, his rather more well-known successor, Thucydides.

> ἡ δ' Ἡροδότου κακοήθεια λειοτέρα μέν ἐστιν ἀμέλει καὶ μαλακωτέρα τῆς Θεοπόμπου, καθάπτεται δὲ καὶ λυπεῖ μᾶλλον ...
>
> But the malice of Herodotus while certainly being rather lighter and softer than that of Theopompus, it assails and vexes rather more ...
>
> (Plutarch, *On the Malice of Herodotus*, 1)

This passage, taken from the introduction to the piece, sets the tone for what is to follow. The comparison with Thucydides takes an extremely personal tone, stating openly that Herodotus even delights in the misfortunes of others and implying that he is fundamentally unsuited to the writing of history.

> δῆλός ἐστιν ἡδόμενος τῷ κακολογεῖν. ὅθεν ὁ Θουκυδίδης οὐδὲ τῶν Κλέωνος ἁμαρτημάτων ἀφθόνων ὄντων ἐποιήσατο σαφῆ τὴν διήγησιν ...
>
> It is clear that he delights in speaking ill of people. Where Thucydides did not make a clear statement of the faults of Cleon (an Athenian general), despite them being many ...
>
> (Plutarch, *On the Malice of Herodotus*, 2)

The charge relates to Herodotus' methods and the material he chose to include. In Plutarch's mind, Herodotus includes all manner of information, regardless of its usefulness to the wider narrative, while Thucydides shows more restraint – relating all of Cleon's flaws is not, as Plutarch sees it, a relevant addition to his work regardless of Cleon's influence over the events which Thucydides relates to his readers. Plutarch does give credit to Herodotus for his style but in the same breath observes that when admiring a rose, one must beware of the venomous flies (*On the Malice of Herodotus* 43)

This sort of comparison with Herodotus' nearest contemporary historian is, however, only natural and is something which has plagued Herodotus' reputation to the present day. Whether or not Plutarch's criticism was sincere or was simply a rhetorical exercise playing devil's advocate (of the sort often undertaken by students of rhetoric in the ancient world) some of the mud has stuck. In reality, Herodotus and Thucydides are in very different positions and their works should be judged differently because of this.

While Herodotus' work is rooted in the distant past and moves towards more recent events, Thucydides observed contemporary events and wrote about them as they happened. Herodotus, as we have already seen, is reliant on the testimony and records of others and, as such, has little basis on which to make judgements as to which account is more truthful than another. Indeed, he admits as much at times:

> εἰ μέν νυν Ξέρξης τε ἀπέπεμψε ταῦτα λέγοντα κήρυκα ἐς Ἄργος καὶ Ἀργείων ἄγγελοι ἀναβάντες ἐς Σοῦσα ἐπειρώτων Ἀρτοξέρξεα περὶ φιλίης, οὐκ ἔχω ἀτρεκέως εἰπεῖν . . .
>
> Whether Xerxes sent a herald to Argos who said these things and whether Argive messengers went up to Susa to ask Artaxerxes about their friendship, I cannot say precisely . . .
>
> (*Histories* 7.152)

Indeed, in the same section, he states:

> ἐγὼ δὲ ὀφείλω λέγειν τὰ λεγόμενα, πείθεσθαί γε μὲν οὐ παντάπασι ὀφείλω
>
> I am bound to record the things which are said, but I am not bound to believe them in their entirety
>
> (*Histories* 7.152)

Herodotus is clear about his process and open about the results of it – a plainly analytical, history, a true account of events (whatever that might mean) is not his end goal and this should not be the basis for an appraisal of his work

Thucydides, writing about contemporary events at which it was possible for him to be an eyewitness, has a distinct advantage over Herodotus. The Peloponnesian War (431–404 BCE) was unfolding around him as an adult citizen in Athens and he was a part of it, serving as a general in 424 BCE. Indeed, when Thucydides writes about the plague which broke out in Athens in the second year of the war, not only did he see it, he actually caught it. It is no wonder his account of this event is particularly hard-hitting. Furthermore, Thucydides' advantage comes not only from the timing of events (that is, he is alive when they are happening), but also from geography. The Peloponnesian War, although played out over large areas of the Mediterranean, was primarily a war between Athens and Sparta and their allies. While Herodotus is retelling events in Persia, many of which are distant memories, some will also have been distant by many months' march. By contrast, the events in Thucydides' work happened recently and most took place at home or a comparatively short distance away (although not all – the notorious Sicilian Expedition of 415 BCE being a prime example).

Even with these advantages, Thucydides admits his own limitations at times:

> καὶ ὅσα μὲν λόγῳ εἶπον ἕκαστοι ἢ μέλλοντες πολεμήσειν ἢ ἐν αὐτῷ ἤδη ὄντες, χαλεπὸν τὴν ἀκρίβειαν αὐτὴν τῶν λεχθέντων διαμνημονεῦσαι ἦν ἐμοί . . .
>
> As for the speeches that were given, those made when the war was about to begin or those made when it was already in progress, it was difficult for me to remember exactly what was said . . .
>
> (Thucydides, *History of the Peloponnesian War* 1.22)

And so, he goes on to suggest that where this is the case, or where he was not present and others found it hard to recall, he had recourse to what he felt was most appropriate for the speaker to say given the particular circumstances of the occasion.

This, then, is the nub of the matter. The longstanding debates as to whether Herodotus is a *real* historian or whether his style of history is inferior to that of Thucydides are not relevant. It is not a competition between the two. Their methods are different, the resources available to them are different, their aims are different. Where Herodotus looks to preserve the events of the past, Thucydides views his work as something rather grander, a κτῆμά ἐς αἰεὶ ('a possession for all time', *History of the Peloponnesian War* 1.22), a definitive work on the conflict between Athens and Sparta. The result is two works of literature which are not particularly comparable. Each succeeds in its own way but, for many, Herodotus' history is a more open work and its nature (giving both sides, leaving readers to make judgements) provides a deeper insight into the thoughts, prejudices and propaganda of a variety of different peoples throughout the Greek world (and even beyond). Because of this, the experience of reading it is more enriching and the information contained within is more insightful and revealing than Thucydides manages. Herodotus' methods may produce a less analytical style but, for a modern reader, that is often an advantage.

The prescribed text: An overview

This prescription has the distinct advantage of starting at the very beginning of the work (assuming a student studies both extracts) and, as such, requires no additional context. Instead, the student can pick up where Herodotus chooses to begin and view the development of his ideas as intended.

Proem (Introduction) (1.1)

Herodotus begins with a short introduction, setting out who he is, where he comes from (Halicarnassus) and what his aim in writing the work is. Recounting the achievements of Greeks and barbarians and ensuring they are not lost to memory is his theme and, moreover, why the two peoples fought each other.

Myth and history (1.1–1.7)

Herodotus then leaps back in time to the earliest interactions between the people of Greece and Asia and establishes his source material by stating clearly that the opinions given are those of Persian chroniclers. In doing so, he takes one of the objectives laid out in his proem, establishing the causes of the Graeco-Persian Wars, to its furthest possible extent and begins his historical account firmly in the realm of mythology.

He first assigns blame for the conflict, through his Persian sources, to the migration of Phoenicians from the Red Sea to the Mediterranean and their trade in Egyptian and Assyrian goods which led them to Argos. From there he tells us that the Phoenicians abducted Io, the daughter of the Argive king Inachus, and, in doing so, explains how she came to be in Egypt. Thus begins a series of reciprocal abductions, with the Greeks then coming to Phoenicia and abducting Europa (Herodotus assigns blame here to a group of Cretans, potentially, through implication, linking her abduction with the Cretan imagery of bull-leaping and the mythical minotaur). This is immediately followed by an account of the abduction of Medea by the Argonauts (although Herodotus does not mention them directly by name). Herodotus moves to the issue of reparation for the abduction of Medea which the Greeks refuse, having received none for Io.

Alexander (the Trojan Paris) is then inspired, so Herodotus' account goes, to seek a wife for himself by the same means, expecting to suffer no penalty as a result. Having kept the abductions, usually examined in a mythological sense, firmly in the realm of human action, Herodotus doubles down on this with no mention of the famous *Judgement of Paris* or any other interaction usually associated with the abduction of Helen and the beginnings of the Trojan War. The Greeks seek some form of recompense for the abduction of the Spartan queen but are given short shrift by the Trojans.

At this point, Herodotus highlights the turning point in interactions between Greeks and Trojans. The Persians emphasize that, prior to this event, no hostilities had been exchanged but, as a result of the abduction of Helen, the entire Greek world mobilized against Asia. There is some discussion about the merits of such actions but, in the end, the focus is on the fact that the Trojan War, instigated by the Greeks, was the moment when enmity was born.

The style of Herodotus' history becomes increasingly clear at the end of the Persian account as he balances the story told so far with an alternative Phoenician account of the story of Io and how, contrary to Persian statements, she was not taken to Egypt by force but went willingly, having slept with the captain of the ship while they were still in Argos. Herodotus here states his methods directly – ἐγὼ δὲ περὶ μὲν τούτων οὐκ ἔρχομαι ἐρέων ὡς οὕτω ἢ ἄλλως κως ταῦτα ἐγένετο ('I am not going to say about these things that they came about in this way or that'), leaving his reader (although undoubtedly leading them to an assignation of blame) to make up their own mind. Instead, he leaps forward perhaps six centuries leaving the mythical world behind, to a time much more rooted in history, where he can talk with more certainty: Croesus and the Lydian Empire.

Croesus and his background are briefly introduced along with a short description of his territory. More importantly, Herodotus assigns him the dubious honour of being the first foreigner to subdue communities of Greek origin, and thus the first concrete example of hostilities between the two groups. In doing so, he also highlights one of the other, major, subjects of his work, freedom, stating that πρὸ δὲ τῆς Κροίσου ἀρχῆς πάντες Ἕλληνες ἦσαν ἐλεύθεροι ('before the empire of Croesus, all the Greeks were free'). The loss of freedom is particularly poignant when set against the manner of subjection which the Persians endure under their king and which threatens the Greeks during the two invasions of 490 and 480 BCE were they to lose. The theme is established: Greeks are fundamentally a people who yearn for freedom. Herodotus then briefly introduces Candaules, king of Lydia, and the dynasty of Heraclids from which he was descended.

Gyges and Candaules (1.8–1.13)

Having introduced Candaules, the last Heraclid king of Lydia, Herodotus relates the mad passion which he developed for his wife and how, having raved about her beauty to Gyges, the most favoured man in his bodyguard, he contrived a plan by which Gyges could see his wife naked and, in doing so, would be forced to confirm the truth of what Candaules said. Gyges responds badly to this, knowing the inappropriate nature of Candaules' proposal and protests that to do so would deprive Candaules' wife (who remains nameless throughout) of her honour. Gyges is absolutely right in his assertion and his protestations are a warning of the punishment which will certainly befall Candaules for his actions (although undoubtedly Gyges is more concerned with any punishment which might befall him). In a final effort to convince the king not to go through with his plan, Gyges declares wholeheartedly that the queen is the most beautiful of all women.

Candaules, however, pays no attention to Gyges' efforts and reassures him that he is in no danger. He lays out a plan wherein Gyges will hide in the royal chamber prior to their retiring for the night, details the actions which the queen always takes when preparing for bed and suggests that, once Gyges has gazed upon her, he should remove himself from the chamber, being sure that he is not seen. Gyges, seeing that there is nothing else he can do, goes along with the plan but, of course, is seen by the queen. In her mind she understands what has happened and that the contrivance is of her husband but, for the moment, chooses to keep her thoughts to herself. She does, however, determine that her husband should be punished for his outrageous behaviour. Herodotus confirms that it is considered a disgrace for a Lydian, indeed for most foreigners, to be seen naked.

The next day the queen decides to act, gathers her entourage and summons Gyges. He is unsuspecting and comes willingly. On his arrival, he is given a choice: either he must help her to avenge her honour by killing his master and taking the throne of Lydia, along with her hand in marriage, or he himself must die. Gyges again, caught between a rock and a hard place, protests but ultimately chooses self-preservation over loyalty to his master. The queen determines that Candaules should be killed in the bedchamber, the same place as he committed his crime against her, and that Gyges will assume the same hiding place as before. The choice of location creates a certain cyclical, perhaps ironic, quality to the punishment and foreshadows the penalties which will come later in Herodotus' work for acts of hubris. The deed is then carried out: Gyges kills Candaules and takes control of Lydia. The Lydian people are outraged by the treatment of Candaules and take up arms, however, it is agreed that if the Delphic Oracle confirms Gyges in his position, then they will remove their opposition. The oracle does so; however, it also states that the Heraclids, from whom Candaules was descended, will have their revenge in the fifth generation. In mentioning this, Herodotus brings the theme of fate and oracles to the forefront of our minds and returns us to Croesus, who is the fifth generation after Gyges.

The descendants of Gyges and expansion of Lydia (1.14–1.18 – in English only for A Level)

Herodotus then details the offerings of silver and gold made by Gyges to the oracle at Delphi and confirms that he was the first foreigner to do so after Midas, son of Gordias, king of Phrygia (not Midas famed for his golden touch). According to Herodotus, Midas' offering can be seen alongside those of Gyges. Herodotus then details the military conflicts waged by Gyges but quickly moves to his son Ardys and his expansion of territory. He continues by describing the succeeding kings but focuses primarily on Alyattes and his conquest of Miletus. Herodotus describes the tactics used, choosing to destroy only their crops and trees when invading, but leaving their homes unharmed so that they would continue to plant crops around the homes which would then be destroyed again when the Lydian army invaded in the following year. The war went on for eleven years, six years under King Sadyattes and five under King Alyattes, who took up where his father had left off. None of the Ionians assisted Miletus apart from the Chians (the inhabitants of the island of Chios in the Aegean, just off the Ionian coast) who did so because the Milesians had helped them in a previous war.

Thrasybulus tricks Alyattes (1.19–1.22)

In the twelfth year of the war, Alyattes burns the Milesians' crops as usual, however, the fire catches the temple of Athene of Assesos and burns the temple down. Alyattes returns to Sardis with his army and falls sick. The implication is clearly that Alyattes' sickness is a result of the religious outrage caused by the burning of the temple. Alyattes seeks information from the oracle at Delphi which refuses to answer until the temple is restored. Herodotus then adds the additional detail given to him by his Milesian sources. Periander, a friend of Thrasybulus, tyrant of Miletus, informs Thrasybulus of the oracle's reply, or lack of it so, when Alyattes sends a herald seeking a truce to provide time for the temple to be rebuilt, Thrasybulus, despite the poor conditions in Miletus, has gathered all the city's food and arranged a feast in the marketplace. Thus, the herald from Sardis is greeted by a scene of plenty and, having given the message concerning the temple, reports back to Alyattes that the people of Miletus are not suffering as they had believed. Deceived in this way, Alyattes decides to bring the war to an end and, through Thrasybulus' stratagem, the Lydians and Milesians become friends and allies.

Arion and the dolphin (1.23–1.24 – in English only for A Level)

Herodotus, having mentioned Periander, the ruler of Corinth, takes the opportunity to tell the story of Arion and the dolphin. Arion, an outstanding lyre player and inventor of the dithyramb, was a resident of Corinth and of Periander's court but decides to journey to Italy and Sicily. Having done so, he returns to Corinth but, on the return journey, the crew decide to rob him and force him to jump overboard. Arion, having discovered their intention, does one final performance for the crew and then jumps into the sea. The crew continue their journey back to Corinth as intended. Meanwhile, Arion is picked up by a dolphin which carries him to Taenarus from where he makes his way back to Corinth. Periander hears the story but, being unsure of the truth of the matter, keeps Arion under supervision and questions the sailors on their return. The crew say that Arion is still in Italy, at which point Arion is revealed and their lie becomes clear. Herodotus tells us that in Taenarus there is a small monument to Arion in the form of a bronze statue of a man on a dolphin.

Croesus' succession and Lydian expansion (1.24–1.28 – in English only for A Level)

Herodotus returns to the chronology of the Lydian kings and tells us that Alyattes' rule came to an end at his death after fifty-seven years. He also gives details of the offerings made to Delphi. Alyattes is then succeeded by his son Croesus, the introduction of whom led Herodotus to introduce Gyges and Candaules and to relate the stories of the Lydian kings in the preceding chapters. Herodotus informs us of his military exploits against Greeks (again, a theme he has already established previously – having told us Croesus is the first man of Asia to subdue Greeks). Having overpowered Ephesians, Ionians and Aeolians, Croesus sets his sights on the Greek islanders but is swayed from his purpose by a visitor to Sardis who convinces him, by way of an anecdote, that attacking the islands with ships is like the islanders attacking Sardis on horseback (a scenario which favours one party much more heavily than the other). Croesus takes the advice seriously, stops building his fleet and befriends the Greeks on the islands. Croesus, however, continues his campaigns in Asia, consolidating Lydian power and Herodotus provides a list of conquered nations. Sardis reaches the height of its wealth.

Solon, Croesus, Atys and Adrastus (1.29–1.45)

Philosophers from the Greek world begin to arrive in Sardis and, during this time, Solon, the Athenian statesman, arrives at the court of Croesus. Solon had been archon in Athens in 594 BCE and had instituted a series of reforms which paved the way for the democratic reforms in Athens at the end of the sixth century. Immediately after his reforms, he is said to have left Athens for a period of ten years, during which time his reforms were not to be altered. As Croesus' reign in Lydia is believed to have started in 560 BCE, around the time of Solon's death, it is highly unlikely that the meeting between the two men which Herodotus relates ever took place. Nevertheless, it is a compelling story which introduces many of the themes which play out in the remainder of Herodotus' work.

Herodotus tells us that the Athenians were not able to repeal the laws themselves, having taken oaths to this effect, and that Solon had left, fearing possible pressure for him to repeal them. He visits Amasis in Egypt first, then makes his way to Croesus in Sardis. A couple of days after Solon's arrival, Croesus orders that Solon be given a tour of the palace and its riches, after which Croesus asks who was the most fortunate man Solon had ever seen. Croesus clearly intends for Solon to declare him the most fortunate of men, however, he does not do so. The episode instantly displays the differences in perspectives between the two men and sets the scene for the divide between Greeks and the people of Asia minor. Croesus assumes that his wealth equates to happiness and does not consider that Solon may think otherwise. When this is not the case, Croesus simply cannot comprehend Solon's point of view. Book 7 contains a strikingly similar scene when Xerxes, prior to the Battle of Thermopylae, laughs off the suggestion from Demaratus (the exiled king of Sparta who has found his way into Xerxes' entourage) that, despite their vastly inferior numbers, the Spartans will still resist the invasion (7.101–5). Although Xerxes takes Demaratus' advice with good humour, he dismisses it as some kind of joke. This episode between Croesus and Solon goes some way to introducing us to the cultural gulf between Greek and non-Greek which will become evermore apparent in the later books.

Instead, Solon names an Athenian called Tellus as the most fortunate man he has ever known. His reasons are straightforward (he had sufficient income, his children survived, he lived to see his grandchildren born and died a glorious death in the service of Athens). Solon's choice is decidedly not determined by the level of Tellus' wealth. Unperturbed, Croesus asks who is next in line for the title, whereupon Solon names the Argives Cleobis and Biton. They, too, had sufficient wealth and were both accomplished athletes but, moreover, had dragged their mother's waggon to the festival of Hera when the oxen had returned late from the fields. Having earned heightened reputation among the Argives for their achievement, that same night, they had died. The Argives erected statues in their honour.

At this point, Croesus can contain his thoughts no longer and accuses Solon of ignoring his prosperity. Solon explains clearly that Croesus cannot be the most fortunate man whom Solon has ever seen. There are simply too many days of his life remaining and each one of those could see his fortunes overturned. For the moment, Croesus can only consider himself lucky, but certainly not the most fortunate of men. Only if his present run of luck continues to his death would Solon consider making such a judgement. In this, we see the beginnings of the role of fate in Herodotus' work. We, Herodotus' readers, are already aware that the Delphic Oracle has pronounced vengeance on his family line in the fifth generation. Even without this knowledge, though, there is truth in Solon's point of view. Croesus does not know, nor do any of us, what the following days or years will bring. To disregard them, therefore, is foolishness. As it happens, Croesus will have lost his empire to the Persians by 546 BCE.

Croesus declares that Solon is a fool and sends him away. At this point, Herodotus introduces nemesis to his readers by way of a dream which comes upon Croesus in his sleep. Croesus has two sons, one mute and one, Atys, preeminent among his peers. It is the latter whom Croesus sees die in the dream, killed by a spear. Croesus, as is usual in these cases, takes steps to prevent the prophecy reaching fulfilment. He has his son marry, prevents him from leading Lydia's armies and removes the weaponry from the men's apartments.

In the meantime, a Phrygian man (we later learn his name is Adrastus) comes to Croesus' court seeking purification for a blood crime committed at home. Croesus obliges him and, having carried out the appropriate rituals, discovers who the man is and, as Croesus has friendly ties with Adrastus' family, offers him a place in his court.

Suddenly we learn of the arrival of a wild boar ravaging the countryside around Mysia. The Mysians have tried to counter the threat themselves but have failed and now send messengers to Croesus seeking assistance. They, as one might expect considering the nature of Croesus' dream, specifically request that he send his son Atys with a hunting party. Croesus agrees to the request for a hunting party but refuses to send his son. Atys, who enters part way through the conversation, is shamed and demands to know why Croesus will not send him. Croesus comes clean and reveals that his recent actions have been out of concern for his son after the dream. Atys is placated but, nevertheless, persists. As the boar does not carry a spear, it poses no danger (at least in terms of fulfilment of the prophecy) and convinces Croesus (who clearly forgets that the remainder of the hunting party will be armed with spears) to let him go. Having done so, Croesus summons Adrastus, the Phrygian, and orders him, in return for the service which Croesus has done him, to look after his son. Adrastus agrees.

The hunting party arrives at Mount Olympus in Mysia and surrounds the boar. Of course, it is now that the prophecy is fulfilled: the men throw their spears, Adrastus misses and hits Atys, killing him. A messenger is sent to Sardis and Croesus is informed.

Croesus is distraught and all the more angry because his son's death came at the hands of Adrastus whom Croesus had purified and welcomed into his house. He calls Zeus to witness the injustice of the events. The Lydians return with Atys' body and Adrastus surrenders himself to Croesus, asking for death as he is no longer fit to live. Croesus is moved to pity and, at the same time, recognizes the workings of fate and declares that Adastrus was an unwilling participant in a god's plan. Adrastus, however, convinced he is the unhappiest man he knows, kills himself on Atys' tomb. The contrast between the two, Croesus, who could only see his own good fortune (which is already on the decline) and Adrastus who is so blinded by his wretchedness that he kills himself, is striking.

Croesus courts the favour of Delphi (1.46–1.56 – in English only for A Level)

Croesus mourns the loss of his son for a period of two years until Astyages, the last king of the Medes, is overthrown by Cyrus the Great of Persia (550 BCE) also in fulfilment of a dream (see above). Croesus determines to slow the growth of Persian power as much as possible. He sends messengers to various oracles in the Greek and Lydian worlds to test their power before asking whether to make war against Persia.

The test of the oracles was simple. One hundred days after leaving Sardis, the messengers were to ask what Croesus was doing at that time. On their arrival, the Oracle at Delphi instantly utters a bizarre statement about the smell of tortoise and lamb in a bronze pot. Herodotus tells us that the responses from the other oracles have now been lost but that Croesus was most pleased by this as he had indeed been stewing tortoise and lamb in a bronze cauldron.

As a result, Croesus embarks on a mission to win the favour of Apollo (referred to here as the Delphian god), making great sacrifices and commanding the people of Lydia to do the same. In addition, he makes ingots of gold and sends them to Delphi as an offering with a golden statue of a lion which now sits in the Corinthian treasury and two great bowls, one of gold and one of silver, along with various other items. Herodotus provides further insight into these offerings including their current locations, weights, controversy over ownership (in particular a golden vessel which is claimed by the Lacedaemonians) and origins. He also dedicated a golden shield and spear to the oracle of Amphiaraus as it, too, like Delphi, had provided a satisfactory answer to Croesus' riddle, although Herodotus does not know what the answer was.

Messengers bring the offerings to the oracles of Delphi and Amphiaraus and ask the question which was Croesus' original purpose: whether he should attack Persia and whether he should take any allies with him when doing so. The answer from both oracles was that if he were to do so he would destroy a great empire and that he should discover who is the mightiest of the Greeks and befriend them. Croesus is extremely pleased with the response and sends further offerings to Delphi. The Delphians, in turn, give Croesus and the Lydians first right of consulting the oracle along with various other benefits.

Croesus asks one final question of the Oracle at Delphi: whether his reign would be a long one. The reply, that Croesus should only fear when a mule is lord of the Medes, positions him for a fall as Cyrus is of mixed Persian and Median heritage (although Herodotus only informs his readers of this later). Pleased with the outcome of his questions, Croesus sets about discovering who is mightiest among the Greeks and resolves to befriend the Spartans and the Athenians. Herodotus then provides a little detail about the Dorian and Ionic roots of both peoples.

Ancient Persia and the Graeco-Persian Wars

Since the AS and A Level prescribed text focuses on the early part of Herodotus' work, it does not cover what might be considered the main events of the Graeco-Persian Wars. It would be remiss, however, not to include a brief summary of Persia and the conflict to set the selection within the wider structure of the work. All references are to the relevant sections of Herodotus' *Histories*.

The Persians themselves were an ethnic group within modern Iran but came to prominence when Cyrus the Great conquered the Median Empire in 550 BCE (1.128), absorbing the territory of the Medes and establishing the Persian Empire. Cyrus expanded the empire's territory first through conflict with Croesus and the Lydian Empire which fell in 546 BCE (1.86). The Babylonian Empire also fell to the Persians in 539 BCE (1.191). Cyrus continued to reign until 530 BCE when, on his death, his eldest son Cambyses succeeded him.

Cambyses continued the expansion of the empire which had started under Cyrus primarily through an invasion of Egypt in 525 BCE (3.1–11). A revolt in 522 BCE led by his brother, known in Herodotus as Smerdis, or an imposter claiming to be Cambyses' brother (Herodotus claims that Cambyses had killed Smerdis (3.30) on account of a dream), forced Cambyses to leave Egypt (3.61). Before he could return home, however, he died of gangrene in Syria (3.66) leaving Smerdis, or the imposter, on the throne.

In 522 BCE Darius, a Persian noble, along with a group of conspirators then overthrew the imposter, Smerdis (3.78), although it is perfectly possible that the story of the imposter was created to legitimize their seizure of power. He then consolidates his power and expands the territory of the Persians, retaking Babylon (3.159), invading Scythia (4.1) and extending Persian control as far as Thrace in the west and the Indus Valley in the east.

Conflict occurred on the western fringes of the Persian Empire in 499 BCE in the form of the Ionian Revolt. Herodotus claims a variety of causes (5.35–6) although, in reality, the burden of taxation on the surrounding area had likely caused a decline in economic activity. Regardless, the revolt was led by Aristagoras, a Milesian, spread rapidly and, receiving considerable support from the Athenians, made an attempt on the city of Sardis (the local administrative capital). Despite this, the Greeks were beaten back and the territories were reconquered for Persia. Aristagoras was killed while attempting to regroup in Thrace (5.126), bringing the revolt to a close.

Herodotus dramatizes the impact that Athens' involvement in the Ionian Revolt had on the Persian attitude towards the Greek states by characterizing the invasions which follow as a revenge mission in the mind of Darius. It is likely, however, that the Persians, having control of the surrounding areas, had Greece in their sights already. The first Persian invasion was undertaken by sea in 490 BCE under the command of Datis and Artaphernes, Darius's nephew (6.94). The Persians landed in Athenian territory at Marathon and were met by a force of Athenian and Plataean soldiers which, despite being heavily outnumbered, defeated the Persian forces decisively (6.113).

Darius's death in 486 BCE and a revolt in Egypt which occupied his successor, Xerxes, meant that a second invasion did not take place immediately. Herodotus describes Xerxes as initially unwilling to undertake the expedition (7.5) but he allows himself to be persuaded. By the late 480s, Xerxes is gathering his forces and undertaking the march to Greece, this time a land invasion with support by sea. The army crosses the Hellespont (7.55) and marches south through mainland Greece. The first major conflict took place against a small Greek force, led by the Spartans, at Thermopylae in 480 BCE. The geography of the area limited the advantage which the Persians had through their superior numbers and the Greek force held them at bay for a several days before finally succumbing to overwhelming Persian force (7.23–4). Xerxes and his forces then entered and sacked the city of Athens (8.52–3).

The turning point for Xerxes' expedition is undoubtedly, however, the Battle of Salamis. The Athenian navy gathered at Salamis, a small island off the coastline of Athenian territory, and the Persians were induced to engage them there. Again, the narrow straits, like Thermopylae, favoured the smaller numbers of the Greeks and the Persian fleet found it difficult to manoeuvre. The precise details are unclear but the battle resulted in the defeat of the Persian navy (8.91–2) and the withdrawal of Xerxes along with the majority of the Persian forces.

A small force under the Persian general Mardonius remained, in an effort to complete the job, which engaged the Greeks at Plataea in 479 BCE. Again, the Persians were decisively defeated (9.69–9.70). On the same day, so the story goes, a Greek fleet landed at Mycale in Ionia and defeated the Persians stationed there and burnt their camp and ships (9.106). With this, Persian attempts to expand their empire into mainland Greece came to an end.

Ionic Greek: The language of Herodotus

As a native of Halicarnassus, Herodotus' dialect of Greek differs slightly from the Attic Greek which you may be used to. Where useful, this has also been noted in the commentary accompanying the text, but the following points may prove helpful in advance.

Verbs

Verb contraction

Contraction of verbs does not happen in Ionic Greek. In many ways this simplifies things for the reader, but it does mean that verb forms can look unusual:

- καὶ οἰκήσαντας τοῦτον τὸν χῶρον τὸν καὶ νῦν οἰκ**έο**υσι (1.1.1) where the stem in epsilon has been retained rather than Attic οἰκοῦσι.

Alternative verb endings

Third person plural endings -νται and -ντο are often replaced with -αται and -ατο, for example:

- τἄλλα τῶν εἵνεκεν ἀπίκ**ατο** (1.2.2), where Attic would use ἀφίκοντο (see below for the lack of aspiration).

Contracted verb stems

The verbs γίγνομαι and γιγνώσκω are contracted to γίνομαι and γινώσκω, for example:

- βουλοίατό σφι παρ᾽ ἄλλων δίκας **γίν**εσθαι (1.3.2), where Attic would use γίγνεσθαι.

Verbs in -μι

Verbs in -μι sometimes behave like contract verbs, for example:

- Μιλήσιοι δὲ τάδε προστιθ**εῖσι** τούτοισι (1.20), where Attic would use προστιθέασι.

εἰμί

In forms of εἰμί, epsilon is often kept where it would be lost in Attic Greek (generally participles), for example:

- εὑρίσκουσι σφίσι ἐοῦσαν τὴν ἀρχὴν τῆς ἔχθρης τῆς ἐς τοὺς Ἕλληνας (1.5.1), where Attic would use οὖσαν.

Prefixes

Verbs using the prefix εἰς- are shortened to ἐς-, for example:

- δὲ φορτία Αἰγύπτιά τε καὶ Ἀσσύρια τῇ τε ἄλλῃ **ἐσαπικνέεσθαι** (1.1.1) using forms of ἐσαπικνέομαι where Attic would use εἰσαφικνέομαι.

Verbs using the prefix ἀνα- shorten to ἀμ- before verbs beginning with beta or pi, for example:

- ὃ δὲ μέγα **ἀμβώσας** εἶπε (1.8.3), using forms of ἀμβοάω where Attic would use ἀναβοάω.

Augmentation

Sometimes the augment is simply missing from verbs, for example:

- καὶ δύο τε ἀντὶ ἑνὸς νηοὺς τῇ Ἀθηναίῃ **οἰ**κοδόμησε ὁ Ἀλυάττης ἐν τῇ Ἀσσησῷ (1.22.4), where Attic would use ᾠκοδόμησε.

Auxiliary verbs

Herodotus occasionally uses the verbs ἔχω and ἔρχομαι as auxiliaries with participles to create different tenses in a manner not found in Attic Greek, for example:

- νῦν δὲ ἀμφοτέρων με τούτων **ἀποκληίσας ἔχεις** (1.37.2), for the perfect tense ('you have shut me out . . .').
- οὐκ **ἔρχομαι ἐρέων** ὡς οὕτω ἢ ἄλλως κως ταῦτα ἐγένετο (1.5.3), for the future tense ('I am not going to tell . . .').

Nouns

Noun contraction

Like verbs, nouns do not generally contract in Ionic Greek. Again, this simplifies things for the reader as the case endings are more readily apparent, for example:

- ὁμοίως σμικρὰ καὶ μεγάλα ἄστε**α** ἀνθρώπων ἐπεξιών (1.5.3), where Attic would use ἄστη.

Nouns in alpha

Where a noun (or an adjective) in -α would be expected, these are replaced by nouns in -η (like τιμή), for example:

- Ἡροδότου Ἁλικαρνησσέος ἱστορί**ης** ἀπόδεξις ἥδε (1.1.0), using forms of ἱστορίη rather than ἱστορία.

Genitive endings

The genitive singular of first declension masculine nouns is -εω rather than -ου. This is most apparent in names of individuals, for example:

- Κροῖσος ἦν Λυδὸς μὲν γένος, παῖς δὲ Ἀλυάττεω (1.1.6), where Attic would use Ἀλυάττου.

Alternative genitive plural endings in -εων are sometimes used instead of the standard –ων, for example:

- Περσ**έων** μέν νυν οἱ λόγιοι (1.1.1), where Attic Greek would use Περσῶν.

Dative plural endings

Instead of -αις Herodotus uses -ῃσι and instead of -οις he uses -οισι, for example:

- αὐτίκα ναυτιλί**ῃσι** μακρ**ῇσι** ἐπιθέσθαι (1.1.1), where Attic would use ναυτιλίαις and μακραῖς.
- τὰ μὲν Ἕλλησι τὰ δὲ βαρβάρ**οισι** ἀποδεχθέντα (1.1.0), where Attic would use βαρβάροις.

Alternative forms of βασιλεύς and nouns like πόλις

An alternative genitive is used for βασιλεύς in -ος unlike the Attic -ως, for example:

- καὶ δὴ καὶ τοῦ βασιλέ**ος** θυγατέρα (1.1.3) where Attic would use βασιλέως.

While forms of πόλις (and nouns which follow the same pattern) often retain the iota in forms where they would lose it in Attic, for example:

- οὐ καταστροφὴ ἐγένετο τῶν πολ**ίων** (1.6.3), where Attic would use πολέων.

Pronouns

Pronouns often have alternative endings in -ευ or -εο in the genitive, for example:

- τὰ δὲ ἐπ᾽ **ἐμεῦ** ἦν μεγάλα, πρότερον ἦν σμικρά (1.5.4), where Attic would use ἐμοῦ.
- καὶ **σέο** δέομαι μὴ δέεσθαι ἀνόμων (1.8.4), where Attic would use σου.

Reflexive pronouns are often different in form, for example:

- οὗτος δὴ ὢν ὁ Κανδαύλης ἠράσθη τῆς **ἑωυτοῦ** γυναικός (1.8.1), where Attic would use ἑαυτοῦ.

Conventions of spelling

Interrogatives and indefinites

Where Attic Greek would normally use pi for interrogative or indefinite words (**π**οῦ, **π**ότε, ὅ**π**ως etc.), Ionic usually uses kappa instead, for example:

- ποίεε ὅ**κ**ως ἐκείνην θεήσεαι γυμνήν (1.8.2), where Attic would use ὅπως.

Shift in aspiration or lack of aspiration

Where a word contains an aspiration, this can shift position, or be dropped entirely, for example:

- **ἐνθεῦτεν**, διαπρηξαμένους καὶ τἄλλα τῶν εἵνεκεν **ἀπίκατο** (1.2.2) where Attic would use ἐντεῦθεν and ἀφίκοντο.

Alternative spellings

Attic πρᾶγμα becomes πρῆγμα in Ionic Greek, for example:

- τὰ σπουδαιέστερα τῶν **πρηγμάτων** ὑπερετίθετο ὁ Κανδαύλης (1.8.1), where Attic would use πραγμάτων.

Alternative forms

The following words are routinely used instead of the more common Attic form:

- ὦν is used instead of οὖν.
- μιν is used instead of αὔτον or αὐτήν.
- εἵνεκεν is used instead of ἕνεκα.
- ἐς is used instead of εἰς.

This is not an exhaustive list (further information can be found in Morwood's *Oxford Grammar of Classical Greek* for those who would like it) and some variations are not included as they do not appear in the prescribed text. Herodotus is also inconsistent in his usage (possibly as a result of manuscript amendments which attempted to replace Ionic Greek with standard Attic in Herodotus' work).

Further reading

Many significant works have been written about Herodotus and there are a number of translations available, either of the whole work or selections from it. The following should be considered a starting point.

Translations

Penguin currently publishes two translations of Herodotus' work. The Penguin Classics edition, translation by Aubrey de Sélincourt with introduction by John Marincola, is readily available and a clear read (Penguin, 2003), while Penguin Press Ancient Classics has also published a more recent translation by Tom Holland with an extensive introduction and notes which is highly recommended (Penguin, 2014).

For those looking for a slightly lighter introduction to Herodotus, W. A. Johnson's recent condensed version, *The Essential Herodotus* (Oxford Univerisity Press, 2017) contains selections from the text along with an overall introduction and an introduction to each of the selections.

Studies and commentaries

Bristol Classical Press publishes a relatively recent edition (2011) of Sleeman's commentary of Herodotus I which, although longstanding, is extremely thorough.

The influential *Very Short Introductions* series has also produced an edition, *Herodotus: A Very Short Introduction* by Jennifer T. Roberts (Oxford University Press, 2011). This is a brief but academic introduction to Herodotus, his work and the period.

John Hart's *Herodotus and Greek History* (originally published by Croom Helm, 1982, now available by the Self Publishing Association, 1993) is an excellent introduction to Herodotus and contains a particularly useful section on religious beliefs, fate and oracles.

Rosalind Thomas' *Herodotus in Context* (Cambridge University Press, 2000) explores Herodotus' work in the context of the scientific and philosophical beliefs of the time.

Tom Holland's *Persian Fire* (Abacus, 2006) is an excellent introduction to Herodotus and the Persian Wars, to a large extent following the chronology of Herodotus' work.

For a broader overview of the Greek historians, John Marincola's *Greek Historians* (Cambridge University Press, 2008) sets Herodotus alongside the Homeric influence, Thucydides and the later Hellenistic historians.

Fiction

Tim Leach's *The Last King of Lydia* (published by Atlantic books and shortlisted for the 2013 Dylan Thomas Prize) is a fictional work based on Herodotus' account of Croesus and his defeat at the hands of Cyrus the Great.

Text

1

[0] Ἡροδότου Ἁλικαρνησσέος ἱστορίης ἀπόδεξις ἥδε, ὡς μήτε τὰ γενόμενα ἐξ ἀνθρώπων τῷ χρόνῳ ἐξίτηλα γένηται, μήτε ἔργα μεγάλα τε καὶ θωμαστά, τὰ μὲν Ἕλλησι τὰ δὲ βαρβάροισι ἀποδεχθέντα, ἀκλεέα γένηται, τά τε ἄλλα καὶ δι᾽ ἣν αἰτίην ἐπολέμησαν ἀλλήλοισι.

[1] Περσέων μέν νυν οἱ λόγιοι Φοίνικας αἰτίους φασί γενέσθαι τῆς διαφορῆς· τούτους γὰρ ἀπό τῆς Ἐρυθρῆς καλεομένης θαλάσσης ἀπικομένους ἐπὶ τήνδε τὴν θάλασσαν καὶ οἰκήσαντας τοῦτον τὸν χῶρον τὸν καὶ νῦν οἰκέουσι, αὐτίκα ναυτιλίῃσι μακρῇσι ἐπιθέσθαι, ἀπαγινέοντας δὲ φορτία Αἰγύπτιά τε καὶ Ἀσσύρια τῇ τε ἄλλῃ ἐσαπικνέεσθαι καὶ δὴ καὶ ἐς Ἄργος. [2] τὸ δὲ Ἄργος τοῦτον τὸν χρόνον προεῖχε ἅπασι τῶν ἐν τῇ νῦν Ἑλλάδι καλεομένῃ χωρῇ. ἀπικομένους δὲ τούς Φοίνικας ἐς δὴ τὸ Ἄργος τοῦτο διατίθεσθαι τὸν φόρτον. [3] πέμπτῃ δὲ ἢ ἕκτῃ ἡμέρῃ ἀπ᾽ ἧς ἀπίκοντο, ἐξεμπολημένων σφι σχεδόν πάντων, ἐλθεῖν ἐπὶ τὴν θάλασσαν γυναῖκας ἄλλας τε πολλάς καὶ δὴ καὶ τοῦ βασιλέος θυγατέρα· τὸ δέ οἱ οὔνομα εἶναι, κατὰ τὠυτὸ τὸ καὶ Ἕλληνές λέγουσι, Ἰοῦν τὴν Ἰνάχου· [4] ταύτας στάσας κατά πρύμνην τῆς νεὸς ὠνέεσθαι τῶν φορτίων τῶν σφι ἦν θυμός μάλιστα, καὶ τοὺς Φοίνικας διακελευσαμένους ὁρμῆσαι ἐπ᾽ αὐτάς. τὰς μὲν δὴ πλεῦνας τῶν γυναικῶν ἀποφυγεῖν, τὴν δὲ Ἰοῦν σὺν ἄλλῃσι ἁρπασθῆναι· ἐσβαλομένους δὲ ἐς τὴν νέα οἴχεσθαι ἀποπλέοντας ἐπ᾽ Αἰγύπτου.

2

[1] οὕτω μὲν Ἰοῦν ἐς Αἴγυπτον ἀπικέσθαι λέγουσι Πέρσαι, οὐκ ὡς Ἕλληνες, καὶ τῶν ἀδικημάτων πρῶτον τοῦτο ἄρξαι· μετὰ δὲ ταῦτα Ἑλλήνων τινάς (οὐ γὰρ ἔχουσι τοὔνομα ἀπηγήσασθαι) φασὶ τῆς Φοινίκης ἐς Τύρον προσσχόντας ἁρπάσαι τοῦ βασιλέος τὴν θυγατέρα Εὐρώπην. εἴησαν δ᾽ ἂν οὗτοι Κρῆτες. ταῦτα μὲν δὴ ἴσα πρὸς ἴσα σφι γενέσθαι· μετὰ δὲ ταῦτα Ἕλληνας αἰτίους τῆς δευτέρης ἀδικίης γενέσθαι. [2] καταπλώσαντας γὰρ μακρῇ νηί ἐς Αἶάν τε τὴν Κολχίδα καὶ ἐπὶ Φᾶσιν ποταμόν, ἐνθεῦτεν, διαπρηξαμένους καὶ τἆλλα τῶν εἵνεκεν ἀπίκατο, ἁρπάσαι τοῦ βασιλέος τὴν θυγατέρα Μηδείην. [3] πέμψαντά

δὲ τὸν Κόλχων βασιλέα ἐς τὴν Ἑλλάδα κήρυκα αἰτέειν τε δίκας τῆς ἁρπαγῆς καὶ ἀπαιτέειν τὴν θυγατέρα· τοὺς δὲ ὑποκρίνασθαι ὡς οὐδὲ ἐκεῖνοι Ἰοῦς τῆς Ἀργείης ἔδοσάν σφι δίκας τῆς ἁρπαγῆς· οὐδὲ ὦν αὐτοὶ δώσειν ἐκείνοισι.

3

[1] δευτέρῃ δὲ λέγουσι γενεῇ μετὰ ταῦτα Ἀλέξανδρον τὸν Πριάμου, ἀκηκοότα ταῦτα, ἐθελῆσαί οἱ ἐκ τῆς Ἑλλάδος δι᾽ ἁρπαγῆς γενέσθαι γυναῖκα, ἐπιστάμενον πάντως ὅτι οὐ δώσει δίκας· οὐδὲ γὰρ ἐκείνους διδόναι. [2] οὕτω δὴ ἁρπάσαντος αὐτοῦ Ἑλένην τοῖσι Ἕλλησι δόξαι πρῶτον πέμψαντας ἀγγέλους ἀπαιτέειν τε Ἑλένην καὶ δίκας τῆς ἁρπαγῆς αἰτέειν. τοὺς δέ προϊσχομένων ταῦτα προφέρειν σφι Μηδείης τὴν ἁρπαγήν, ὡς οὐ δόντες αὐτοὶ δίκας οὐδὲ ἐκδόντες ἀπαιτεόντων βουλοίατό σφι παρ᾽ ἄλλων δίκας γίνεσθαι.

4

[1] μέχρι μὲν ὦν τούτου ἁρπαγάς μούνας εἶναι παρ᾽ ἀλλήλων, τὸ δὲ ἀπὸ τούτου Ἕλληνας δὴ μεγάλως αἰτίους γενέσθαι· προτέρους γὰρ ἄρξαι στρατεύεσθαι ἐς τὴν Ἀσίην ἢ σφέας ἐς τὴν Εὐρώπην. [2] τὸ μέν νυν ἁρπάζειν γυναῖκας ἀνδρῶν ἀδίκων νομίζειν ἔργον εἶναι, τὸ δὲ ἁρπασθεισέων σπουδήν ποιήσασθαι τιμωρέειν ἀνοήτων, τὸ δὲ μηδεμίαν ὤρην ἔχειν ἁρπασθεισέων σωφρόνων· δῆλα γὰρ δὴ ὅτι, εἰ μὴ αὐταὶ ἐβούλοντο, οὐκ ἂν ἡρπάζοντο. [3] σφέας μὲν δὴ τοὺς ἐκ τῆς Ἀσίης λέγουσι Πέρσαι ἁρπαζομενέων τῶν γυναικῶν λόγον οὐδένα ποιήσασθαι, Ἕλληνας δὲ Λακεδαιμονίης εἵνεκεν γυναικὸς στόλον μέγαν συναγεῖραι καὶ ἔπειτα ἐλθόντας ἐς τὴν Ἀσίην τὴν Πριάμου δύναμιν κατελεῖν. [4] ἀπὸ τούτου αἰεὶ ἡγήσασθαι τὸ Ἑλληνικὸν σφίσι εἶναι πολέμιον. τὴν γὰρ Ἀσίην καὶ τὰ ἐνοικέοντα ἔθνεα βάρβαρα οἰκηιοῦνται οἱ Πέρσαι, τὴν δὲ Εὐρώπην καὶ τὸ Ἑλληνικόν ἥγηνται κεχωρίσθαι.

5

[1] οὕτω μὲν Πέρσαι λέγουσι γενέσθαι, καὶ διὰ τὴν Ἰλίου ἅλωσιν εὑρίσκουσι σφίσι ἐοῦσαν τὴν ἀρχὴν τῆς ἔχθρης τῆς ἐς τοὺς Ἕλληνας. [2] περὶ δὲ τῆς Ἰοῦς οὐκ ὁμολογέουσι Πέρσῃσι οὕτω Φοίνικες· οὐ γὰρ ἁρπαγῇ σφέας χρησαμένους λέγουσι ἀγαγεῖν αὐτήν ἐς Αἴγυπτον, ἀλλ᾽ ὡς ἐν τῷ Ἄργει ἐμίσγετο τῷ ναυκλήρῳ τῆς νέος· ἐπεὶ δ᾽ ἔμαθε ἔγκυος ἐοῦσα, αἰδεομένη τοὺς τοκέας οὕτω δὴ ἐθελοντὴν αὐτὴν τοῖσι Φοίνιξι συνεκπλῶσαι, ὡς ἂν μὴ κατάδηλος γένηται. [3] ταῦτα μέν νυν Πέρσαι τε καὶ Φοίνικες λέγουσι. ἐγὼ δὲ περὶ μὲν τούτων οὐκ ἔρχομαι ἐρέων ὡς οὕτω ἢ ἄλλως κως ταῦτα ἐγένετο, τὸν δὲ οἶδα αὐτὸς πρῶτον ὑπάρξαντα ἀδίκων ἔργων ἐς τοὺς Ἕλληνας, τοῦτον σημήνας προβήσομαι ἐς τὸ πρόσω τοῦ λόγου, ὁμοίως σμικρὰ καὶ μεγάλα ἄστεα ἀνθρώπων ἐπεξιών. [4] τὰ γὰρ τὸ πάλαι μεγάλα ἦν, τὰ πολλὰ αὐτῶν σμικρὰ γέγονε, τὰ δὲ ἐπ᾽ ἐμεῦ ἦν μεγάλα, πρότερον ἦν σμικρά. τὴν ἀνθρωπηίην ὦν ἐπιστάμενος εὐδαιμονίην οὐδαμὰ ἐν τὠυτῷ μένουσαν ἐπιμνήσομαι ἀμφοτέρων ὁμοίως.

6

[1] Κροῖσος ἦν Λυδὸς μὲν γένος, παῖς δὲ Ἀλυάττεω, τύραννος δὲ ἐθνέων τῶν ἐντός Ἅλυος ποταμοῦ, ὃς ῥέων ἀπὸ μεσαμβρίης μεταξὺ Συρίων τε καὶ Παφλαγόνων ἐξιεῖ πρὸς βορῆν ἄνεμον ἐς τὸν Εὔξεινον καλεόμενον πόντον. [2] οὗτος ὁ Κροῖσος βαρβάρων πρῶτος τῶν ἡμεῖς ἴδμεν τοὺς μὲν κατεστρέψατο Ἑλλήνων ἐς φόρου ἀπαγωγήν, τοὺς δὲ φίλους προσεποιήσατο. κατεστρέψατο μὲν Ἴωνάς τε καὶ Αἰολέας καὶ Δωριέας τοὺς ἐν τῇ Ἀσίῃ, φίλους δὲ προσεποιήσατο Λακεδαιμονίους. [3] πρὸ δὲ τῆς Κροίσου ἀρχῆς πάντες Ἕλληνες ἦσαν ἐλεύθεροι. τὸ γὰρ Κιμμερίων στράτευμα τὸ ἐπὶ τὴν Ἰωνίην ἀπικόμενον, Κροίσου ἐὸν πρεσβύτερον, οὐ καταστροφὴ ἐγένετο τῶν πολίων ἀλλ᾽ ἐξ ἐπιδρομῆς ἁρπαγή.

7: As an introduction to the chapters which follow and the story of Gyges and Candaules, Herodotus describes the lineage of Candaules. Candaules was the last of the Heraclids to rule Sardis (a dynasty which Herodotus tells us lasted 505 years) and would be succeeded by the Mermnadae from which family Croesus was descended.

8

[1] οὗτος δὴ ὦν ὁ Κανδαύλης ἠράσθη τῆς ἑωυτοῦ γυναικός, ἐρασθεὶς δὲ ἐνόμιζέ οἱ εἶναι γυναῖκα πολλὸν πασέων καλλίστην. ὥστε δὲ ταῦτα νομίζων, ἦν γάρ οἱ τῶν αἰχμοφόρων Γύγης ὁ Δασκύλου ἀρεσκόμενος μάλιστα, τούτῳ τῷ Γύγῃ καὶ τὰ σπουδαιέστερα τῶν πρηγμάτων ὑπερετίθετο ὁ Κανδαύλης καὶ δὴ καὶ τὸ εἶδος τῆς γυναικὸς ὑπερεπαινέων. [2] χρόνου δὲ οὐ πολλοῦ διελθόντος, χρῆν γὰρ Κανδαύλῃ γενέσθαι κακῶς, ἔλεγε πρὸς τὸν Γύγην τοιάδε. 'Γύγη, οὐ γάρ σε δοκέω πείθεσθαι μοι λέγοντι περὶ τοῦ εἴδεος τῆς γυναικός (ὦτα γὰρ τυγχάνει ἀνθρώποισι ἐόντα ἀπιστότερα ὀφθαλμῶν), ποίεε ὅκως ἐκείνην θεήσεαι γυμνήν.' [3] ὃ δὲ μέγα ἀμβώσας εἶπε· 'δέσποτα, τίνα λέγεις λόγον οὐκ ὑγιέα, κελεύων με δέσποιναν τὴν ἐμὴν θεήσασθαι γυμνήν; ἅμα δὲ κιθῶνι ἐκδυομένῳ συνεκδύεται καὶ τὴν αἰδῶ γυνή. [4] πάλαι δὲ τὰ καλὰ ἀνθρώποισι ἐξεύρηται, ἐκ τῶν μανθάνειν δεῖ· ἐν τοῖσι ἓν τόδε ἐστί, σκοπέειν τινὰ τὰ ἑωυτοῦ. ἐγὼ δὲ πείθομαι ἐκείνην εἶναι πασέων γυναικῶν καλλίστην, καὶ σέο δέομαι μὴ δέεσθαι ἀνόμων.'

9

[1] ὃ μὲν δὴ λέγων τοιαῦτα ἀπεμάχετο, ἀρρωδέων μή τί οἱ ἐξ αὐτῶν γένηται κακόν. ὃ δ᾽ ἀμείβετο τοῖσιδε. 'θάρσεε, Γύγη, καὶ μὴ φοβεῦ μήτε ἐμέ, ὥς σέο πειρώμενος λέγω λόγον τόνδε, μήτε γυναῖκα τὴν ἐμήν, μὴ τί τοι ἐξ αὐτῆς γένηται βλάβος. ἀρχὴν γὰρ ἐγὼ μηχανήσομαι οὕτω ὥστε μηδὲ μαθεῖν μιν ὀφθεῖσαν ὑπὸ σεῦ. [2] ἐγὼ γάρ σε ἐς τὸ οἴκημα ἐν τῷ κοιμώμεθα ὄπισθε τῆς ἀνοιγομένης θύρης στήσω· μετὰ δ᾽ ἐμὲ ἐσελθόντα παρέσται καὶ ἡ γυνὴ ἡ ἐμὴ

ἐς κοῖτον. κεῖται δὲ ἀγχοῦ τῆς ἐσόδου θρόνος· ἐπὶ τοῦτον τῶν ἱματίων κατὰ ἓν ἕκαστον ἐκδύνουσα θήσει καὶ κατ᾽ ἡσυχίην πολλὴν παρέξει τοι θεήσασθαι. [3] ἐπεὰν δέ ἀπὸ τοῦ θρόνου στείχῃ ἐπὶ τὴν εὐνήν κατὰ νώτου τε αὐτῆς γένῃ, σοὶ μελέτω τὸ ἐνθεῦτεν ὅκως μή σε ὄψεται ἰόντα διὰ θυρέων.'

10

[1] ὃ μὲν δὴ ὡς οὐκ ἐδύνατο διαφυγεῖν, ἦν ἕτοιμος· ὁ δὲ Κανδαύλης, ἐπεὶ ἐδόκεε ὥρη τῆς κοίτης εἶναι, ἤγαγε τὸν Γύγεα ἐς τὸ οἴκημα, καὶ μετὰ ταῦτα αὐτίκα παρῆν καὶ ἡ γυνή· ἐσελθοῦσαν δὲ καὶ τιθεῖσαν τὰ εἵματα ἐθηεῖτο ὁ Γύγης. [2] ὡς δὲ κατὰ νώτου ἐγένετο ἰούσης τῆς γυναικός ἐς τὴν κοίτην, ὑπεκδὺς ἐχώρεε ἔξω. καὶ ἡ γυνὴ ἐπορᾷ μιν ἐξιόντα. μαθοῦσὰ δὲ τὸ ποιηθέν ἐκ τοῦ ἀνδρὸς οὔτε ἀνέβωσε αἰσχυνθεῖσα οὔτε ἔδοξε μαθεῖν, ἐν νόῳ ἔχουσα τίσεσθαι τὸν Κανδαύλεα· [3] παρὰ γὰρ τοῖσι Λυδοῖσι, σχεδὸν δὲ καὶ παρὰ τοῖσι ἄλλοισι βαρβάροισι, καὶ ἄνδρα ὀφθῆναι γυμνόν ἐς αἰσχύνην μεγάλην φέρει.

11

[1] τότε μὲν δὴ οὕτω οὐδέν δηλώσασα ἡσυχίην εἶχε· ὡς δὲ ἡμέρη τάχιστα ἐγεγόνεε, τῶν οἰκετέων τοὺς μάλιστα ὥρα πιστοὺς ἐόντας ἑωυτῇ, ἑτοίμους ποιησαμένη ἐκάλεε τὸν Γύγεα. ὁ δὲ οὐδὲν δοκέων αὐτήν τῶν πρηχθέντων ἐπίστασθαι ἦλθε καλεόμενος· ἐώθεε γὰρ καὶ πρόσθε, ὅκως ἡ βασίλεια καλέοι, φοιτᾶν. [2] ὡς δὲ ὁ Γύγης ἀπίκετο, ἔλεγε ἡ γυνὴ τάδε. 'νῦν τοί δυῶν ὁδῶν παρεουσέων, Γύγη, δίδωμί αἵρεσιν, ὁκοτέρην βούλεαι τραπέσθαι. ἢ γὰρ Κανδαύλεα ἀποκτείνας ἐμέ τε καὶ τὴν βασιληίην ἔχε τὴν Λυδῶν, ἢ αὐτόν σε αὐτίκα οὕτω ἀποθνήσκειν δεῖ, ὡς ἂν μὴ πάντα πειθόμενος Κανδαύλῃ τοῦ λοιποῦ ἴδῃς τὰ μὴ σε δεῖ. [3] ἀλλ᾽ ἤτοι κεῖνόν γε τὸν ταῦτα βουλεύσαντα δεῖ ἀπόλλυσθαι, ἢ σε τὸν ἐμὲ γυμνήν θεησάμενον καὶ ποιήσαντα οὐ νομιζόμενα.' ὁ δὲ Γύγης τέως μὲν ἀπεθώμαζε τὰ λεγόμενα, μετὰ δὲ ἱκέτευε μή μιν ἀναγκαίῃ ἐνδεῖν διακρῖναι τοιαύτην αἵρεσιν. [4] οὐκ ὦν δὴ ἔπειθε, ἀλλ᾽ ὥρα ἀναγκαίην ἀληθέως προκειμένην ἢ τὸν δεσπότεα ἀπολλύναι ἢ αὐτὸν ὑπ᾽ ἄλλων ἀπόλλυσθαι· αἱρέεται αὐτὸς περιεῖναι. ἐπειρώτα δὴ λέγων τάδε. 'ἐπεί με ἀναγκάζεις δεσπότεα τὸν ἐμὸν κτείνειν οὐκ ἐθέλοντα, φέρε ἀκούσω, τέῳ καὶ τρόπῳ ἐπιχειρήσομεν αὐτῷ.' [5] ἣ δὲ ὑπολαβοῦσα ἔφη· 'ἐκ τοῦ αὐτοῦ μὲν χωρίου ἡ ὁρμή ἔσται ὅθεν περ καὶ ἐκεῖνος ἐμέ ἐπεδέξατο γυμνήν, ὑπνωμένῳ δὲ ἡ ἐπιχείρησις ἔσται.'

12

[1] ὡς δὲ ἤρτυσαν τὴν ἐπιβουλήν, νυκτὸς γενομένης (οὐ γὰρ ἐμετίετο ὁ Γύγης, οὐδέ οἱ ἦν ἀπαλλαγὴ οὐδεμία, ἀλλ᾽ ἔδεε ἢ αὐτὸν ἀπολωλέναι ἢ Κανδαύλεα) εἵπετο ἐς τὸν θάλαμον τῇ γυναικί. καί μιν ἐκείνη ἐγχειρίδιον δοῦσα κατακρύπτει ὑπὸ τὴν αὐτὴν θύρην. [2] καὶ μετὰ ταῦτα ἀναπαυομένου Κανδαύλεω ὑπεκδύς τε καὶ ἀποκτείνας αὐτὸν ἔσχε καὶ τὴν γυναῖκα καὶ τὴν βασιληίην Γύγης· τοῦ

καὶ Ἀρχίλοχος ὁ Πάριος κατὰ τὸν αὐτὸν χρόνον γενόμενος ἐν ἰάμβῳ τριμέτρῳ ἐπεμνήσθη·

13

[1] ἔσχε δὲ τὴν βασιληίην καὶ ἐκρατύνθη ἐκ τοῦ ἐν Δελφοῖσι χρηστηρίου. ὡς γὰρ δὴ οἱ Λυδοὶ δεινὸν ἐποιεῦντο τὸ Κανδαύλεω πάθος καὶ ἐν ὅπλοισι ἦσαν, συνέβησαν ἐς τὠυτὸ οἵ τε τοῦ Γύγεω στασιῶται καὶ οἱ λοιποὶ Λυδοί, ἤν μὲν δὴ τὸ χρηστήριον ἀνέλῃ μιν βασιλέα εἶναι Λυδῶν, τόν δὲ βασιλεύειν, ἢν δὲ μή, ἀποδοῦναι ὀπίσω ἐς Ἡρακλείδας τὴν ἀρχήν. [2] ἀνεῖλέ τε δὴ τὸ χρηστήριον καὶ ἐβασίλευσε οὕτω Γύγης. τοσόνδε μέντοι ἐπεῖπε ἡ Πυθίη, ὡς Ἡρακλείδῃσι τίσις ἥξει ἐς τὸν πέμπτον ἀπόγονον Γύγεω. τούτου τοῦ ἔπεος Λυδοί τε καὶ οἱ βασιλέες αὐτῶν λόγον οὐδένα ἐποιεῦντο, πρὶν δὴ ἐπετελέσθη.

14–18: Gyges, having become king of Sardis, sends offerings to Delphi which Herodotus details. He also briefly informs us of Gyges' military conquests. Gyges is then succeeded by his son, Ardys, who continues the military expansion during his forty-nine-year reign. Ardys is succeeded by his son Sadyattes and, in turn, by his son Alyattes. Under Alyattes, military expansion continues, including the continuation of Sadyattes' war against Miletus (near modern Balat on the western coast of Turkey). In total, Sadyattes and Alyattes waged war against Miletus for twelve years.

19

[1] τῷ δὲ δυωδεκάτῳ ἔτει ληίου ἐμπιπραμένου ὑπὸ τῆς στρατιῆς συνηνείχθη τι τοιόνδε γενέσθαι πρῆγμα· ὡς ἄφθη τάχιστα τὸ λήιον, ἀνέμῳ βιώμενον ἅψατο νηοῦ Ἀθηναίης ἐπίκλησιν Ἀσσησίης, ἁφθεὶς δὲ ὁ νηὸς κατεκαύθη. [2] καὶ τὸ παραυτίκα μὲν λόγος οὐδεὶς ἐγένετο, μετὰ δὲ τῆς στρατιῆς ἀπικομένης ἐς Σάρδις ἐνόσησε ὁ Ἀλυάττης. μακροτέρης δέ οἱ γινομένης τῆς νούσου πέμπει ἐς Δελφοὺς θεοπρόπους, εἴτε δὴ συμβουλεύσαντός τευ, εἴτε καὶ αὐτῷ ἔδοξε πέμψαντα τὸν θεὸν ἐπειρέσθαι περὶ τῆς νούσου. [3] τοῖσι δὲ ἡ Πυθίη ἀπικομένοισι ἐς Δελφοὺς οὐκ ἔφη χρήσειν, πρὶν ἢ τὸν νηὸν τῆς Ἀθηναίης ἀνορθώσωσι, τὸν ἐνέπρησαν χώρης τῆς Μιλησίης ἐν Ἀσσησῷ.

20

Δελφῶν οἶδα ἐγὼ οὕτω ἀκούσας γενέσθαι· Μιλήσιοι δὲ τάδε προστιθεῖσι τούτοισι, Περίανδρον τὸν Κυψέλου ἐόντα Θρασυβούλῳ τῷ τότε Μιλήτου τυραννεύοντι ξεῖνον ἐς τὰ μάλιστα, πυθόμενον τὸ χρηστήριον τὸ τῷ Ἀλυάττῃ γενόμενον, πέμψαντα ἄγγελον κατειπεῖν, ὅκως ἄν τι προειδὼς πρὸς τὸ παρεὸν βουλεύηται.

21

[1] Μιλήσιοι μέν νυν οὕτω λέγουσι γενέσθαι. Ἀλυάττης δέ, ὡς οἱ ταῦτα ἐξαγγέλθη, αὐτίκα ἔπεμπε κήρυκα ἐς Μίλητον βουλόμενος σπονδὰς

ποιήσασθαι Θρασυβούλῳ τε καὶ Μιλησίοισι χρόνον ὅσον ἂν τὸν νηὸν οἰκοδομέῃ. ὃ μὲν δὴ ἀπόστολος ἐς τὴν Μίλητον ἦν, Θρασύβουλος δὲ σαφέως προπεπυσμένος πάντα λόγον καὶ εἰδὼς τὰ Ἀλυάττης μέλλοι ποιήσειν, μηχανᾶται τοιάδε· [2] ὅσος ἦν ἐν τῷ ἄστεϊ σῖτος καὶ ἑωυτοῦ καὶ ἰδιωτικός, τοῦτον πάντα συγκομίσας ἐς τὴν ἀγορὴν προεῖπε Μιλησίοισι, ἐπεὰν αὐτὸς σημήνῃ, τότε πίνειν τε πάντας καὶ κώμῳ χρᾶσθαι ἐς ἀλλήλους.

22

[1] ταῦτα δὲ ἐποίεέ τε καὶ προηγόρευε Θρασύβουλος τῶνδε εἵνεκεν, ὅκως ἂν δὴ ὁ κῆρυξ ὁ Σαρδιηνὸς ἰδών τε σωρὸν μέγαν σίτου κεχυμένον καὶ τοὺς ἀνθρώπους ἐν εὐπαθείῃσι ἐόντας ἀγγείλῃ Ἀλυάττῃ· [2] τὰ δὴ καὶ ἐγένετο. ὡς γὰρ δὴ ἰδών τε ἐκεῖνα ὁ κῆρυξ καὶ εἴπας πρὸς Θρασύβουλον τοῦ Λυδοῦ τὰς ἐντολὰς ἀπῆλθε ἐς τὰς Σάρδις, ὡς ἐγὼ πυνθάνομαι, δι᾽ οὐδὲν ἄλλο ἐγένετο ἡ διαλλαγή. [3] ἐλπίζων γὰρ ὁ Ἀλυάττης σιτοδείην τε εἶναι ἰσχυρὴν ἐν τῇ Μιλήτῳ καὶ τὸν λεὼν τετρῦσθαι ἐς τὸ ἔσχατον κακοῦ, ἤκουε τοῦ κήρυκος νοστήσαντος ἐκ τῆς Μιλήτου τοὺς ἐναντίους λόγους ἢ ὡς αὐτὸς κατεδόκεε. [4] μετὰ δὲ ἥ τε διαλλαγή σφι ἐγένετο ἐπ᾽ ᾧ τε ξείνους ἀλλήλοισι εἶναι καὶ συμμάχους, καὶ δύο τε ἀντὶ ἑνὸς νηοὺς τῇ Ἀθηναίῃ οἰκοδόμησε ὁ Ἀλυάττης ἐν τῇ Ἀσσησῷ, αὐτός τε ἐκ τῆς νούσου ἀνέστη. κατὰ μέν τὸν πρὸς Μιλησίους τε καὶ Θρασύβουλον πόλεμον Ἀλυάττῃ ὧδε ἔσχε.

23–28: Herodotus digresses briefly, discussing Periander's experience with Arion while he was king of Corinth. Arion, a talented lyre-player and inventor of the dithyramb (a form of music dedicated to Dionysus), voyages from Corinth to Italy and Sicily. On his return journey, the crew of the ship on which he is travelling decide to steal his money and kill him. After an impromptu performance, which the sailors are keen to hear, Arion throws himself into the sea. He is then miraculously conveyed back to Corinth by riding a dolphin. On his arrival, Periander is unsure of the story and questions the sailors who have now arrived in the city. When he reveals Arion, the sailors crack and admit their guilt.

Herodotus returns to the narrative of Alyattes, detailing his death, the offerings he made at Delphi and the succession of his son, Croesus. Croesus continues to make war, attacking Ephesus first and then other Ionian and Aeolian cities. Having subdued the Greeks of Asia, Croesus plans to build ships to attack the Greek islanders. On receipt of advice, Croesus abandons his plans and befriends the Greek islanders while continuing to subjugate other races in Asia. Under him, Sardis reaches the height of its prosperity.

29

[1] ἀπικνέονται ἐς Σάρδις ἀκμαζούσας πλούτῳ ἄλλοι τε οἱ πάντες ἐκ τῆς Ἑλλάδος σοφισταί, οἳ τοῦτον τὸν χρόνον ἐτύγχανον ἐόντες, ὡς ἕκαστος αὐτῶν ἀπικνέοιτο, καὶ δὴ καὶ Σόλων ἀνὴρ Ἀθηναῖος, ὃς Ἀθηναίοισι νόμους κελεύσασι ποιήσας ἀπεδήμησε ἔτεα δέκα, κατά θεωρίης πρόφασιν ἐκπλώσας, ἵνα δὴ μή τινα τῶν νόμων ἀναγκασθῇ λῦσαι τῶν ἔθετο. [2] αὐτοὶ γὰρ οὐκ οἷοί τε ἦσαν αὐτὸ ποιῆσαι Ἀθηναῖοι· ὁρκίοισι γὰρ μεγάλοισι κατείχοντο δέκα ἔτεα χρήσεσθαι νόμοισι τοὺς ἂν σφι Σόλων θῆται.

30

[1] αὐτῶν δὴ ὦν τούτων καὶ τῆς θεωρίης ἐκδημήσας ὁ Σόλων εἵνεκεν ἐς Αἴγυπτον ἀπίκετο παρὰ Ἄμασιν καὶ δὴ καὶ ἐς Σάρδις παρὰ Κροῖσον. ἀπικόμενος δὲ ἐξεινίζετο ἐν τοῖσι βασιληίοισι ὑπὸ τοῦ Κροίσου· μετὰ δὲ, ἡμέρῃ τρίτῃ ἢ τετάρτῃ, κελεύσαντος Κροίσου τὸν Σόλωνα θεράποντες περιῆγον κατὰ τοὺς θησαυροὺς καὶ ἐπεδείκνυσαν πάντα ἐόντα μεγάλα τε καὶ ὄλβια. [2] θεησάμενον δέ μιν τὰ πάντα καὶ σκεψάμενον ὥς οἱ κατὰ καιρὸν ἦν, εἴρετο ὁ Κροῖσος τάδε. 'ξεῖνε Ἀθηναῖε, παρ' ἡμέας γὰρ περὶ σέο λόγος ἀπῖκται πολλὸς καὶ σοφίης εἵνεκεν τῆς σῆς καὶ πλάνης, ὡς φιλοσοφέων γῆν πολλὴν θεωρίης εἵνεκεν ἐπελήλυθας· νῦν ὦν ἵμερος ἐπειρέσθαι μοι ἐπῆλθε εἴ τινα ἤδη πάντων εἶδες ὀλβιώτατον.' [3] ὃ μὲν ἐλπίζων εἶναι ἀνθρώπων ὀλβιώτατος ταῦτα ἐπειρώτα, Σόλων δὲ οὐδὲν ὑποθωπεύσας, ἀλλὰ τῷ ἐόντι χρησάμενος λέγει· 'ὦ βασιλεῦ, Τέλλον Ἀθηναῖον.' [4] ἀποθωμάσας δὲ Κροῖσος τὸ λεχθὲν εἴρετο ἐπιστρεφέως· 'κοίῃ δὴ κρίνεις Τέλλον εἶναι ὀλβιώτατον;' ὁ δὲ εἶπε· 'Τέλλῳ τοῦτο μὲν τῆς πόλιος εὖ ἡκούσης παῖδες ἦσαν καλοί τε κἀγαθοί, καί σφι εἶδε ἅπασι τέκνα ἐκγενόμενα καὶ πάντα παραμείναντα, τοῦτο δὲ τοῦ βίου εὖ

A Level

ἥκοντι, ὡς τὰ παρ᾽ ἡμῖν, τελευτὴ τοῦ βίου λαμπροτάτη ἐπεγένετο· [5] γενομένης γὰρ Ἀθηναίοισι μάχης πρὸς τοὺς ἀστυγείτονας ἐν Ἐλευσῖνι βοηθήσας καὶ τροπὴν ποιήσας τῶν πολεμίων ἀπέθανε κάλλιστα, καί μιν Ἀθηναῖοι δημοσίῃ τε ἔθαψαν αὐτοῦ τῇ περ ἔπεσε καὶ ἐτίμησαν μεγάλως.'

31

[1] ὣς δὲ τὰ κατὰ τὸν Τέλλον προετρέψατο ὁ Σόλων τὸν Κροῖσον εἴπας πολλά τε καὶ ὀλβία, ἐπειρώτα τίνα δεύτερον μετ᾽ ἐκεῖνον ἴδοι, δοκέων πάγχυ δευτερεῖα γῶν οἴσεσθαι. ὃ δ᾽ εἶπε· 'Κλέοβίν τε καὶ Βίτωνα. [2] τούτοισι γὰρ ἐοῦσι γένος Ἀργείοισι βίος τε ἀρκέων ὑπῆν καὶ πρὸς τούτῳ ῥώμη σώματος τοιήδε· ἀεθλοφόροι τε ἀμφότεροι ὁμοίως ἦσαν, καὶ δὴ καὶ λέγεται ὅδε ὁ λόγος· ἐούσης ὁρτῆς τῇ Ἥρῃ τοῖσι Ἀργείοισι ἔδεε πάντως τὴν μητέρα αὐτῶν ζεύγεϊ κομισθῆναι ἐς τὸ ἱρόν, οἱ δέ σφι βόες ἐκ τοῦ ἀγροῦ οὐ παρεγίνοντο ἐν ὥρῃ· ἐκκληιόμενοι δὲ τῇ ὥρῃ οἱ νεηνίαι ὑποδύντες αὐτοὶ ὑπὸ τὴν ζεύγλην εἷλκον τὴν ἅμαξαν, ἐπὶ τῆς ἁμάξης δέ σφι ὠχέετο ἡ μήτηρ, σταδίους δὲ πέντε καὶ τεσσεράκοντα διακομίσαντες ἀπίκοντο ἐς τὸ ἱρόν. [3] ταῦτα δέ σφι ποιήσασι καὶ ὀφθεῖσι ὑπὸ τῆς πανηγύριος τελευτὴ τοῦ βίου ἀρίστη ἐπεγένετο, διέδεξέ τε ἐν τούτοισι ὁ θεὸς ὡς ἄμεινον εἴη ἀνθρώπῳ τεθνάναι μᾶλλον ἢ ζώειν. Ἀργεῖοι μὲν γὰρ περιστάντες ἐμακάριζον τῶν νεηνιέων τὴν ῥώμην, αἱ δὲ Ἀργεῖαι τὴν μητέρα αὐτῶν, οἵων τέκνων ἐκύρησε· [4] ἡ δὲ μήτηρ περιχαρής ἐοῦσα τῷ τε ἔργῳ καὶ τῇ φήμῃ, στᾶσα ἀντίον τοῦ ἀγάλματος εὔχετο Κλεόβι τε καὶ Βίτωνι τοῖσι ἑωυτῆς τέκνοισι, οἵ μιν ἐτίμησαν μεγάλως, τὴν θεὸν δοῦναι τὸ ἀνθρώπῳ τυχεῖν ἄριστον ἐστί. [5] μετὰ ταύτην δὲ τὴν εὐχὴν ὡς ἔθυσάν τε καὶ εὐωχήθησαν, κατακοιμηθέντες ἐν αὐτῷ τῷ ἱρῷ οἱ νεηνίαι οὐκέτι ἀνέστησαν, ἀλλ᾽ ἐν τέλεϊ τούτῳ ἔσχοντο. Ἀργεῖοι δὲ σφέων εἰκόνας ποιησάμενοι ἀνέθεσαν ἐς Δελφοὺς ὡς ἀνδρῶν ἀριστῶν γενομένων.'

32

[1] Σόλων μὲν δὴ εὐδαιμονίης δευτερεῖα ἔνεμε τούτοισι, Κροῖσος δὲ σπερχθεὶς εἶπε· 'ὦ ξεῖνε Ἀθηναῖε, ἡ δ᾽ ἡμετέρη εὐδαιμονίη οὕτω τοι ἀπέρριπται ἐς τὸ μηδὲν, ὥστε οὐδὲ ἰδιωτέων ἀνδρῶν ἀξίους ἡμέας ἐποίησας;' ὁ δὲ εἶπε· 'ὦ Κροῖσε, ἐπιστάμενόν με τὸ θεῖον πᾶν ἐὸν φθονερόν τε καὶ ταραχῶδες ἐπειρωτᾷς ἀνθρωπηίων πρηγμάτων πέρι. [2] ἐν γὰρ τῷ μακρῷ χρόνῳ πολλὰ μὲν ἐστὶ ἰδεῖν τὰ μή τις ἐθέλει, πολλὰ δὲ καὶ παθεῖν. ἐς γὰρ ἑβδομήκοντα ἔτεα οὖρον τῆς ζόης ἀνθρώπῳ προτίθημι. [3] οὗτοι ἐόντες ἐνιαυτοὶ ἑβδομήκοντα παρέχονται ἡμέρας διηκοσίας καὶ πεντακισχιλίας καὶ δισμυρίας, ἐμβολίμου μηνὸς μὴ γινομένου· εἰ δὲ δὴ ἐθελήσει τοὔτερον τῶν ἐτέων μηνὶ μακρότερον γίνεσθαι, ἵνα δὴ αἱ ὧραι συμβαίνωσι παραγινόμεναι ἐς τὸ δέον, μῆνες μὲν παρὰ τὰ ἑβδομήκοντα ἔτεα οἱ ἐμβόλιμοι γίνονται τριήκοντα πέντε, ἡμέραι δὲ ἐκ τῶν μηνῶν τούτων χίλιαι πεντήκοντα. [4] τουτων τῶν ἁπασέων ἡμερέων τῶν ἐς τὰ ἑβδομήκοντα ἔτεα, ἐουσέων πεντήκοντα καὶ διηκοσιέων καὶ

ἑξακισχιλιέων καὶ δισμυριέων, ἡ ἑτέρη αὐτέων τῇ ἑτέρῃ ἡμέρῃ τὸ παράπαν οὐδὲν ὅμοιον προσάγει πρῆγμα. οὕτω ὦν, ὦ Κροῖσε, πᾶν ἐστὶ ἄνθρωπος συμφορή. [5] ἐμοὶ δὲ σὺ καὶ πλουτέειν μέγα φαίνεαι καὶ βασιλεὺς πολλῶν εἶναι ἀνθρώπων· ἐκεῖνο δὲ τὸ εἴρεό με οὔ κω σε ἐγὼ λέγω, πρὶν τελευτήσαντα καλῶς τὸν αἰῶνα πύθωμαι. οὐ γάρ τι ὁ μέγα πλούσιος μᾶλλον τοῦ ἐπ᾽ ἡμέρην ἔχοντος ὀλβιώτερος ἐστί, εἰ μή οἱ τύχη ἐπίσποιτο πάντα καλὰ ἔχοντα εὖ τελευτῆσαὶ τὸν βίον. πολλοὶ μὲν γὰρ ζάπλουτοι ἀνθρώπων ἀνόλβιοι εἰσί, πολλοὶ δὲ μετρίως ἔχοντες βίου εὐτυχέες. [6] ὁ μὲν δὴ μέγα πλούσιος, ἀνόλβιος δὲ δυοῖσι προέχει τοῦ εὐτυχέος μοῦνον, οὗτος δὲ τοῦ πλουσίου καὶ ἀνολβίου πολλοῖσι· ὃ μὲν ἐπιθυμίην ἐκτελέσαι καί ἄτην μεγάλην προσπεσοῦσαν ἐνεῖκαι δυνατώτερος, ὁ δὲ τοῖσιδε προέχει ἐκείνου· ἄτην μὲν καὶ ἐπιθυμίην οὐκ ὁμοίως δυνατὸς ἐκείνῳ ἐνεῖκαι, ταῦτα δὲ ἡ εὐτυχίη οἱ ἀπερύκει, ἄπηρος δὲ ἐστί, ἄνουσος, ἀπαθὴς κακῶν, εὔπαις, εὐειδής. [7] εἰ δὲ πρὸς τούτοισι ἔτι τελευτήσῃ τὸν βίον εὖ, οὗτος ἐκεῖνος τὸν σὺ ζητέεις ὄλβιος κεκλῆσθαι ἄξιος ἐστί· πρὶν δ᾽ ἂν τελευτήσῃ, ἐπισχεῖν μηδὲ καλέειν κω ὄλβιον, ἀλλ᾽ εὐτυχέα. [8] τὰ πάντα μέν νυν ταῦτα συλλαβεῖν ἄνθρωπον ἐόντα ἀδύνατον ἐστί, ὥσπερ χώρη οὐδεμία καταρκέει πάντα ἑωυτῇ παρέχουσα, ἀλλὰ ἄλλο μὲν ἔχει, ἑτέρου δὲ ἐπιδέεται· ἣ δὲ ἂν τὰ πλεῖστα ἔχῃ, αὕτη ἀρίστη. ὣς δὲ καὶ ἀνθρώπου σῶμα ἓν οὐδὲν αὔταρκες ἐστί· τὸ μὲν γὰρ ἔχει, ἄλλου δὲ ἐνδεές ἐστι· [9] ὃς δ᾽ ἂν αὐτῶν πλεῖστα ἔχων διατελέῃ καὶ ἔπειτα τελευτήσῃ εὐχαρίστως τὸν βίον, οὗτος παρ᾽ ἐμοὶ τὸ οὔνομα τοῦτο, ὦ βασιλεῦ, δίκαιος ἐστὶ φέρεσθαι. σκοπέειν δὲ χρὴ παντὸς χρήματος τὴν τελευτήν κῇ ἀποβήσεται· πολλοῖσι γὰρ δὴ ὑποδέξας ὄλβον ὁ θεὸς προρρίζους ἀνέτρεψε.'

33

[1] ταῦτα λέγων τῷ Κροίσῳ οὔ κως οὔτε ἐχαρίζετο, οὔτε λόγου μιν ποιησάμενος οὐδενὸς ἀποπέμπεται, κάρτα δόξας ἀμαθέα εἶναι, ὃς τὰ παρεόντα ἀγαθὰ μετεὶς τὴν τελευτὴν παντὸς χρήματος ὁρᾶν ἐκέλευε.

34

[1] μετὰ δὲ Σόλωνα οἰχόμενον ἔλαβέ ἐκ θεοῦ νέμεσις μεγάλη Κροῖσον, ὡς εἰκάσαι, ὅτι ἐνόμισε ἑωυτὸν εἶναι ἀνθρώπων ἁπάντων ὀλβιώτατον. αὐτίκα δέ οἱ εὕδοντι ἐπέστη ὄνειρος, ὅς οἱ τὴν ἀληθείην ἔφαινε τῶν μελλόντων γενέσθαι κακῶν κατὰ τὸν παῖδα. [2] ἦσαν δὲ τῷ Κροίσῳ δύο παῖδες, τῶν οὕτερος μὲν διέφθαρτο, ἦν γὰρ δὴ κωφός, ὁ δὲ ἕτερος τῶν ἡλίκων μακρῷ τὰ πάντα πρῶτος· οὔνομα δέ οἱ ἦν Ἄτυς. τοῦτον δὴ ὦν τὸν Ἄτυν σημαίνει τῷ Κροίσῳ ὁ ὄνειρος, ὡς ἀπολέει μιν αἰχμῇ σιδηρέῃ βληθέντα. [3] ὃ δὲ ἐπείτε ἐξηγέρθη καὶ ἑωυτῷ λόγον ἔδωκε, καταρρωδήσας τὸν ὄνειρον ἄγεται μὲν τῷ παιδὶ γυναῖκα, ἐωθότα δὲ στρατηγέειν μιν τῶν Λυδῶν οὐδαμῇ ἔτι ἐπὶ τοιοῦτο πρῆγμα ἐξέπεμπε, ἀκόντια δὲ καὶ δοράτα καὶ τά τοιαῦτα πάντα τοῖσι χρέωνται ἐς πόλεμον

ἄνθρωποι, ἐκ τῶν ἀνδρεώνων ἐκκομίσας ἐς τοὺς θαλάμους συνένησε, μή τί οἱ κρεμάμενον τῷ παιδὶ ἐμπέσῃ.

35

[1] ἔχοντι δέ οἱ ἐν χερσὶ τοῦ παιδὸς τὸν γάμον ἀπικνέεται ἐς τὰς Σάρδις ἀνὴρ συμφορῇ ἐχόμενος καὶ οὐ καθαρὸς χεῖρας, ἐὼν Φρὺξ μὲν γενεῇ, γένεος δὲ τοῦ βασιληίου. παρελθὼν δὲ οὗτος ἐς τὰ Κροίσου οἰκία κατὰ νόμους τοὺς ἐπιχωρίους καθαρσίου ἐδέετο κυρῆσαι, Κροῖσος δέ μιν ἐκάθηρε. [2] ἔστι δὲ παραπλησίη ἡ κάθαρσις τοῖσι Λυδοῖσι καὶ τοῖσι Ἕλλησι. ἐπείτε δὲ τὰ νομιζόμενα ἐποίησε ὁ Κροῖσος, ἐπυνθάνετο ὁκόθεν τε καὶ τίς εἴη, λέγων τάδε· [3] 'ὤνθρωπε, τίς τε ἐὼν καὶ κόθεν τῆς Φρυγίης ἥκων ἐπίστιός μοι ἐγένεο; τίνα τε ἀνδρῶν ἢ γυναικῶν ἐφόνευσας;' ὁ δὲ ἀμείβετο 'ὦ βασιλεῦ, Γορδίεω μὲν τοῦ Μίδεω εἰμὶ παῖς, ὀνομάζομαι δὲ Ἄδρηστος, φονεύσας δὲ ἀδελφεὸν ἐμεωυτοῦ ἀέκων πάρειμι ἐξεληλαμένος τε ὑπὸ τοῦ πατρὸς καὶ ἐστερημένος πάντων.' [4] Κροῖσος δέ μιν ἀμείβετο τοῖσιδε· 'ἀνδρῶν τε φίλων τυγχάνεις ἔκγονος ἐὼν καὶ ἐλήλυθας ἐς φίλους, ἔνθα ἀμηχανήσεις χρήματος οὐδενὸς μένων ἐν ἡμετέρου. συμφορήν τε ταύτην ὡς κουφότατα φέρων κερδανέεις πλεῖστον.'

36

[1] ὁ μὲν δὴ δίαιταν εἶχε ἐν Κροίσου, ἐν δὲ τῷ αὐτῷ χρόνῳ τούτῳ ἐν τῷ Μυσίῳ Ὀλύμπῳ ὑὸς χρῆμα γίνεται μέγα· ὁρμώμενος δὲ οὗτος ἐκ τοῦ ὄρεος τούτου τὰ τῶν Μυσῶν ἔργα διαφθείρεσκε. πολλάκις δὲ οἱ Μυσοὶ ἐπ᾽ αὐτὸν ἐξελθόντες ποιέεσκον μὲν κακὸν οὐδέν, ἔπασχον δὲ πρὸς αὐτοῦ. [2] τέλος δὲ ἀπικόμενοι παρὰ τὸν Κροῖσον τῶν Μυσῶν ἄγγελοι ἔλεγον τάδε. 'ὦ βασιλεῦ, ὑὸς χρῆμα μέγιστον ἀνεφάνη ἡμῖν ἐν τῇ χώρῃ, ὃς τὰ ἔργα διαφθείρει. τοῦτον προθυμεόμενοι ἑλεῖν οὐ δυνάμεθα. νῦν ὦν προσδεόμεθά σευ τὸν παῖδα καὶ λογάδας νεηνίας καὶ κύνας συμπέμψαι ἡμῖν, ὡς ἄν μιν ἐξέλωμεν ἐκ τῆς χώρης.' [3] οἳ μὲν δὴ τούτων ἐδέοντο, Κροῖσος δὲ μνημονεύων τοῦ ὀνείρου τὰ ἔπεα ἔλεγέ σφι τάδε. 'παιδὸς μὲν πέρι τοῦ ἐμοῦ μὴ μνησθῆτε ἔτι· οὐ γὰρ ἂν ὑμῖν συμπέμψαιμι· νεόγαμός τε γάρ ἐστι καὶ ταῦτά οἱ νῦν μέλει. Λυδῶν μέντοι λογάδας καὶ τὸ κυνηγέσιον πᾶν συμπέμψω καὶ διακελεύσομαι τοῖσι ἰοῦσι εἶναι ὡς προθυμοτάτοισι συνεξελεῖν ὑμῖν τὸ θηρίον ἐκ τῆς χώρης.'

37

[1] ταῦτα ἀμείψατο· ἀποχρεωμένων δὲ τούτοισι τῶν Μυσῶν, ἐπεσέρχεται ὁ τοῦ Κροίσου παῖς ἀκηκοὼς τῶν ἐδέοντο οἱ Μυσοί. οὐ φαμένου δὲ τοῦ Κροίσου τόν γε παῖδά σφι συμπέμψειν λέγει πρὸς αὐτὸν ὁ νεηνίης τάδε. [2] 'ὦ πάτερ, τὰ κάλλιστα πρότερον κοτὲ καὶ γενναιότατα ἡμῖν ἦν ἔς τε πολέμους καὶ ἐς ἄγρας φοιτέοντας εὐδοκιμέειν· νῦν δὲ ἀμφοτέρων με τούτων ἀποκληίσας ἔχεις, οὔτε τινὰ δειλίην μοι παριδὼν οὔτε ἀθυμίην. νῦν τε τέοισί με χρὴ ὄμμασι ἔς τε ἀγορὴν καὶ ἐξ ἀγορῆς φοιτέοντα φαίνεσθαι; [3] κοῖος μέν τις τοῖσι πολιήτῃσι

δόξω εἶναι, κοῖος δέ τις τῇ νεογάμῳ γυναικί; κοίῳ δὲ ἐκείνη δόξει ἀνδρὶ συνοικέειν; ἐμὲ ὦν σὺ ἢ μέτες ἰέναι ἐπὶ τὴν θήρην, ἢ λόγῳ ἀνάπεισον ὅκως μοι ἀμείνω ἐστὶ ταῦτα οὕτω ποιεόμενα.'

38

[1] ἀμείβεται Κροῖσος τοῖσιδε. 'ὦ παῖ, οὔτε δειλίην οὔτε ἄλλο οὐδὲν ἄχαρι παριδών τοι ποιέω ταῦτα, ἀλλά μοι ὄψις ὀνείρου ἐν τῷ ὕπνῳ ἐπιστᾶσα ἔφη σε ὀλιγοχρόνιον ἔσεσθαι· ὑπὸ γὰρ αἰχμῆς σιδηρέης ἀπολέεσθαι. [2] πρὸς ὦν τὴν ὄψιν ταύτην τόν τε γάμον τοι τοῦτον ἔσπευσα καὶ ἐπὶ τὰ παραλαμβανόμενα οὐκ ἀποπέμπω, φυλακὴν ἔχων, εἴ κως δυναίμην ἐπὶ τῆς ἐμῆς σε ζόης διακλέψαι. εἷς γάρ μοι μοῦνος τυγχάνεις ἐὼν παῖς· τὸν γὰρ δὴ ἕτερον διεφθαρμένον τὴν ἀκοὴν οὐκ εἶναί μοι λογίζομαι.'

39

[1] ἀμείβεται ὁ νεηνίης τοῖσιδε· 'συγγνώμη μὲν ὦ πάτερ τοι, ἰδόντι γε ὄψιν τοιαύτην, περὶ ἐμὲ φυλακὴν ἔχειν· τὸ δὲ οὐ μανθάνεις, ἀλλὰ λέληθέ σε τὸ ὄνειρον, ἐμέ τοί δίκαιον ἐστί φράζειν. [2] φής τοι τὸ ὄνειρον ὑπὸ αἰχμῆς σιδηρέης φάναι ἐμὲ τελευτήσειν. ὑὸς δὲ κοῖαι μὲν εἰσὶ χεῖρες, κοίη δὲ αἰχμὴ σιδηρέη τὴν σὺ φοβέαι; εἰ μὲν γὰρ ὑπὸ ὀδόντος τοι εἶπε τελευτήσειν με ἢ ἄλλου τευ ὅ τι τούτῳ ἔοικε, χρῆν δή σε ποιέειν τὰ ποιέεις· νῦν δὲ ὑπὸ αἰχμῆς. ἐπείτε ὦν οὐ πρὸς ἄνδρας ἡμῖν γίνεται ἡ μάχη, μέτες με.'

40

[1] ἀμείβεται Κροῖσος 'ὦ παῖ, ἔστι τῇ με νικᾷς γνώμην ἀποφαίνων περὶ τοῦ ἐνυπνίου. ὡς ὦν νενικημένος ὑπὸ σέο μεταγινώσκω, μετίημί τε σὲ ἰέναι ἐπὶ τὴν ἄγρην.'

41

[1] εἴπας δὲ ταῦτα ὁ Κροῖσος μεταπέμπεται τὸν Φρύγα Ἄδρηστον, ἀπικομένῳ δέ οἱ λέγει τάδε. 'Ἄδρηστε, ἐγώ σε συμφορῇ πεπληγμένον ἀχάρι, τήν τοι οὐκ ὀνειδίζω, ἐκάθηρα καὶ οἰκίοισι ὑποδεξάμενος ἔχω παρέχων πᾶσαν δαπάνην· [2] νῦν ὤν, ὀφείλεις γὰρ ἐμεῦ προποιήσαντος χρηστὰ ἐς σὲ χρηστοῖσί με ἀμείβεσθαι, φύλακα παιδός σε τοῦ ἐμοῦ χρηίζω γενέσθαι ἐς ἄγρην ὁρμωμένου, μή τινες κατ᾽ ὁδὸν κλῶπες κακοῦργοι ἐπὶ δηλήσι φανέωσι ὑμῖν. [3] πρὸς δὲ τούτῳ καὶ σέ τοι χρεόν ἐστι ἰέναι ἔνθα ἀπολαμπρυνέαι τοῖσι ἔργοισι· πατρώιόν τε γάρ τοι ἐστὶ καὶ προσέτι ῥώμη ὑπάρχει.'

42

[1] ἀμείβεται ὁ Ἄδρηστος· 'ὦ βασιλεῦ, ἄλλως μὲν ἔγωγε ἂν οὐκ ἤια ἐς ἄεθλον τοιόνδε· οὔτε γὰρ συμφορῇ τοιῇδε κεχρημένον οἰκός ἐστι ἐς ὁμήλικας εὖ πρήσσοντας ἰέναι, οὔτε τὸ βούλεσθαι πάρα, πολλαχῇ τε ἂν ἶσχον ἐμεωυτόν.

[2] νῦν δέ, ἐπείτε σὺ σπεύδεις καὶ δεῖ τοί χαρίζεσθαι (ὀφείλω γάρ σε ἀμείβεσθαι χρηστοῖσι), ποιέειν εἰμὶ ἕτοιμος ταῦτα, παῖδα τε σόν, τὸν διακελεύεαι φυλάσσειν, ἀπήμονα τοῦ φυλάσσοντος εἵνεκεν προσδόκα τοι ἀπονοστήσειν.'

43

[1] τοιούτοισι ἐπείτε οὗτος ἀμείψατο Κροῖσον, ἤισαν μετὰ ταῦτα ἐξηρτυμένοι λογάσι τε νεηνίῃσι καὶ κυσί. ἀπικόμενοι δὲ ἐς τὸν Ὄλυμπον τὸ ὄρος ἐζήτεον τὸ θηρίον, εὑρόντες δὲ καὶ περιστάντες αὐτὸ κύκλῳ ἐσηκόντιζον. [2] ἔνθα δὴ ὁ ξεῖνος, οὗτος δὴ ὁ καθαρθεὶς τὸν φόνον, καλεόμενος δὲ Ἄδρηστος, ἀκοντίζων τὸν ὗν τοῦ μὲν ἁμαρτάνει, τυγχάνει δὲ τοῦ Κροίσου παιδός. [3] ὃ μὲν δὴ βληθεὶς τῇ αἰχμῇ ἐξέπλησε τοῦ ὀνείρου τὴν φήμην, ἔθεε δέ τις ἀγγελέων τῷ Κροίσῳ τὸ γεγονός, ἀπικόμενος δὲ ἐς τὰς Σάρδις τὴν τε μάχην καὶ τὸν τοῦ παιδὸς μόρον ἐσήμηνέ οἱ.

44

[1] ὁ δὲ Κροῖσος τῳ θανάτῳ τοῦ παιδὸς συντεταραγμένος μᾶλλον τι ἐδεινολογέετο ὅτι μιν ἀπέκτεινε τὸν αὐτὸς φόνου ἐκάθηρε· [2] περιημεκτέων δὲ τῇ συμφορῇ δεινῶς ἐκάλεε μὲν Δία καθάρσιον μαρτυρόμενος τὰ ὑπὸ τοῦ ξείνου πεπονθὼς εἴη, ἐκάλεε δὲ ἐπίστιόν τε καὶ ἑταιρήιον, τὸν αὐτὸν τοῦτον ὀνομάζων θεόν, τὸν μὲν ἐπίστιον καλέων, διότι δὴ οἰκίοισι ὑποδεξάμενος τὸν ξεῖνον φονέα τοῦ παιδὸς ἐλάνθανε βόσκων, τὸν δὲ ἑταιρήιον, ὡς φύλακα συμπέμψας αὐτὸν εὑρήκοι πολεμιώτατον.

45

[1] παρῆσαν δὲ μετὰ τοῦτο οἱ Λυδοὶ φέροντες τὸν νεκρόν, ὄπισθε δὲ εἵπετό οἱ ὁ φονεύς. στὰς δὲ οὗτος πρὸ τοῦ νεκροῦ παρεδίδου ἑωυτὸν Κροίσῳ προτείνων τὰς χεῖρας, ἐπικατασφάξαι μιν κελεύων τῷ νεκρῷ, λέγων τήν τε προτέρην ἑωυτοῦ συμφορήν, καὶ ὡς ἐπ᾽ ἐκείνῃ τὸν καθήραντα ἀπολωλεκὼς εἴη, οὐδέ οἱ εἴη βιώσιμον. [2] Κροῖσος δὲ τούτων ἀκούσας τόν τε Ἄδρηστον κατοικτείρει, καίπερ ἐὼν ἐν κακῷ οἰκηίῳ τοσούτῳ, καὶ λέγει πρὸς αὐτόν· 'ἔχω, ὦ ξεῖνε, παρὰ σεῦ πᾶσαν τὴν δίκην, ἐπειδὴ σεωυτοῦ καταδικάζεις θάνατον. εἷς δὲ οὐ σύ μοι τοῦδε τοῦ κακοῦ αἴτιος, εἰ μὴ ὅσον ἀέκων ἐξεργάσαο, ἀλλὰ θεῶν κού τις, ὅς μοι καὶ πάλαι προεσήμαινε τὰ μέλλοντα ἔσεσθαι.' [3] Κροῖσος μέν νυν ἔθαψε, ὡς οἰκὸς ἦν, τὸν ἑωυτοῦ παῖδα· Ἄδρηστος δὲ ὁ Γορδίεω τοῦ Μίδεω, οὗτος δὴ ὁ φονεὺς μὲν τοῦ ἑωυτοῦ ἀδελφεοῦ γενόμενος, φονεὺς δὲ τοῦ καθήραντος, ἐπείτε ἡσυχίη τῶν ἀνθρώπων ἐγένετο περὶ τὸ σῆμα, συγγινωσκόμενος ἀνθρώπων εἶναι τῶν αὐτὸς ᾔδεε βαρυσυμφορώτατος, ἐπικατασφάζει τῷ τύμβῳ ἑωυτόν.

A Level

Commentary Notes

Chapter 1

1.1.0

Ἡροδότου Ἁλικαρνησσέος: Herodotus begins his history by introducing himself and his subject matter. Halicarnassus was a Greek city in Ionia on the coast of Asia Minor (present-day Bodrum in Turkey). This style of introduction appears in other ancient Greek texts; Hecataeus and Thucydides both start with a similar format.

ἱστορίης ἀπόδεξις ἥδε: supply the verb 'to be' – 'this is the display of the enquiry of Herodotus of Halicarnassus . . .' The term ἱστορίη does not have the same nuance as the modern term 'history'. It implies knowledge obtained through enquiry.

ὡς: Herodotus commonly uses **ὡς** to show purpose with a subjunctive in present sequence. The clause flows as if he had used a verb in the previous phrase (e.g. 'Herodotus of Halicarnassus here displays his enquiry so that . . .').

ἐξ ἀνθρώπων: literally, 'from men' but more easily translated as 'by men'. Herodotus regularly uses ἐκ where you might expect ὑπό for the agent.

γένηται: the first of two subjunctives following **ὡς** 'so that they might [not] become . . .' The verb is singular with the neuter plural subject.

τὰ μὲν Ἕλλησι τὰ δὲ βαρβάροισι: the central theme of Herodotus' work emerges – the contrast between the Greek and barbarian worlds. The use of the term 'barbarian' is not emotive in its modern sense but refers to non-Greek speaking peoples. Both are datives of agent – 'some by Greeks, some by barbarians . . .'

ἀκλεέα γένηται: the second subjunctive following **ὡς** – 'so that they might not be without fame'.

τά τε ἄλλα καὶ: 'and other things, especially', i.e. 'and more particularly' – **ἄλλα** picks up **τὰ γενόμενα** from earlier.

δι᾽ ἣν αἰτίην: **ἣν** is the relative pronoun 'through which cause' – i.e. 'for what reason (they fought each other)'.

1.1.1

Περσέων μέν νυν: 'of the Persians now', i.e. those contemporary with Herodotus. **Περσέων** modifies **οἱ λόγιοι** which follows.

οἱ λόγιοι: although conventionally translated as 'learned' or 'erudite', λόγιος means specifically a chronicler or annalist. Herodotus is referring to his Persian sources.

Φοίνικας αἰτίους φασί γενέσθαι: this accusative and infinitive construction, dependent on **φασί** ('learned Persians say . . .'), is only the first of a number in this chapter. The Phoenicians were an ancient civilization centred on what is now Lebanon.

τούτους γὰρ: i.e. the Phoenicians. This is a continuation of the indirect statement introduced by **φασί** ('for [they say that] they . . .'). Two participles describe the actions of the Phoenicians (**ἀπικομένους, οἰκήσαντας**) before reaching the first infinitive **ἐπιθέσθαι**. It is undoubtedly more straightforward to treat each as a main verb when translating.

τῆς Ἐρυθρῆς καλεομένης θαλάσσης: 'the sea called Erythraean' / the Red Sea – ἐρυθρός means 'red' and our modern term is a direct translation of the Greek. The Greek term also refers to areas which we would now consider the Arabian Sea around the Persian Gulf.

ἐπὶ τήνδε τὴν θάλασσαν: 'at this sea' – i.e. the Mediterranean.

τὸν καὶ νῦν οἰκέουσι: 'the [country] they inhabit even now' – i.e. the coast of Lebanon.

ἐπιθέσθαι: the infinitive continues the indirect statement ('having arrived . . . having settled . . . they immediately applied themselves to . . .').

ἀπαγινέοντας: Herodotus continues the indirect statement with another participle describing the Phoenicians.

τῇ τε ἄλλῃ: 'elsewhere' – some editions of the text include χώρῃ but the phrase functions adverbially without it. It contrasts with **καὶ δὴ καὶ** which follows ('bringing their Egyptian and Assyrian wares elsewhere they came moreover to Argos.').

1.1.2

τὸ δὲ Ἄργος: Bronze Age Argos, centre of Mycenaean Greece and seat of Homer's Agamemnon. Herodotus is about to launch us into a series of abductions from Greek myth.

τοῦτον τὸν χρόνον: accusative showing duration (*time how long*) – 'for this time'. 'At that time' is a more straightforward rendering in English.

ἅπασι: adverbial – 'in all things' / 'in every respect'

τῶν ἐν τῇ . . . χωρῇ: the genitive **τῶν** follows **προεῖχε** ('Argos surpassed those . . .') while the preposition **ἐν** combines with the article and creates a description ('those in the land'). **νῦν Ἑλλάδι καλεομένῃ** is then sandwiched to complete the phrase ('those in the land now called Greece'). At the time to which Herodotus refers there was no collective Hellenic identity, only individual tribes.

ἀπικομένους δὲ τούς Φοίνικας: Herodotus again picks up the implied indirect statement ('[learned Persians say that] the Phoenicians, arriving . . .') and the Phoenicians remain in the accusative as a result with **διατίθεσθαι** completing the accusative and infinitive construction.

1.1.3

πέμπτῃ δὲ ἢ ἕκτῃ ἡμέρῃ: dative showing time when – 'on the fifth or sixth day'.

ἀπ' ἧς ἀπίκοντο: **ἧς** is the relative pronoun – 'from which they arrived', i.e. after they had arrived.

ἐξεμπολημένων . . . πάντων: genitive absolute – '[almost] everything having been sold', i.e. 'when they had sold almost everything'.

σφι: possessive dative – 'everything to them', i.e. 'everything they had' / 'all their wares'.

ἐλθεῖν . . . γυναῖκας: a further continuation of the indirect statement. This time the women are a new subject ('they say that women came . . .').

ἄλλας τε πολλάς: literally, 'others and many [women]', i.e. 'many other'. **καὶ δὴ καὶ** follows to single out the king's daughter – 'many other women and moreover . . .' / 'many women including . . .'

οἱ: possessive dative – 'the name to her', i.e. 'her name'.

οὔνομα: Ionic form for Attic ὄνομα. This is also the subject of the indirect statement with **εἶναι** – '[They say that] her name was . . .'

κατὰ τὠυτὸ: 'in the same way', i.e. 'the Greeks also say the same thing'. **τὠυτὸ** is crasis for τό αὐτό ('the same').

Ἰοῦν τὴν Ἰνάχου: 'Io, the [daughter] of Inachus' – The use of the patronymic is common in the Greek world. Inachus was a mythical king of Argos (also a river-god) while Io is more commonly said to have been abducted by Zeus. He then famously turned her into a white heifer to protect her from Hera's jealousy.

1.1.4

ταύτας στάσας: i.e the Argive women. Accusative to continue the indirect statement.

κατά πρύμνην: 'near the stern' – The Phoenicians have likely beached the ship with the prow facing out to sea.

τῶν σφι ἦν θυμός μάλιστα: 'the ones of which there was to them a particular longing', i.e. 'the ones which they especially wanted'. **τῶν** refers to **φορτίων** while **σφι** is possessive dative.

τοὺς Φοίνικας: continuation of the accusative and infinitive – '[they say that] the Phoenicians . . .'

ἐπ᾽ αὐτάς: i.e. at the women.

τὰς . . . πλεῦνας: again, the women become the subject of the accusative and infinitive. With the article **πλεῦνας** means 'the majority'.

ἁρπασθῆναι: aorist passive infinitive – 'was carried off'.

ἐσβαλομένους: the Phoenicians become the subject again – '[and they say that they] put them on . . .' The women need to be implied as the object of **ἐσβαλομένους**.

ἐπ᾽ Αἰγύπτου: ἐπί can be used with the genitive to suggest direction – 'for Egypt'.

Chapter 2

1.2.1

οὕτω μὲν: i.e. in the manner which Herodotus has laid out in Chapter 1.

Ἰοῦν ἐς Αἴγυπτον ἀπικέσθαι: accusative and infinitive indirect statement (with **λέγουσι** which follows). Io is usually said to have found her way to Egypt while wandering as a heifer.

λέγουσι Πέρσαι: Herodotus often frames his narratives at the beginning and end with reference to his source material.

οὐκ ὡς Ἕλληνες: as mentioned above, this is not the usual form of the tale in Greek accounts.

πρῶτον τοῦτο ἄρξαι: accusative and infinitive indirect statement – 'The Persians say that Io . . . and that this first began the wrongs', i.e. 'this was the first wrong'.

Ἑλλήνων τινάς: 'certain (of the) Greeks' – accusative for another indirect statement (using **φασὶ** which follows). Herodotus is still narrating what the Persians say.

οὐ γὰρ ἔχουσι: ἔχω here carrying its alternative sense – 'they are [not] able'.

τῆς Φοινίκης ἐς Τύρον: 'Tyre in Phoenicia' – the port city of Tyre in modern Lebanon.

τὴν θυγατέρα Εὐρώπην: Europa was the daughter of the Phoenician king, Agenor. Like Io, in Greek accounts Europa is usually considered to have been abducted by Zeus (this time himself in the guise of a bull).

εἴησαν δ' ἂν οὗτοι Κρῆτες: the optative **εἴησαν** with **ἂν** creates potential, displaying the likelihood of an event – 'these men would have been Cretan'. The Cretans were, at this time, a sea-faring race (although not Hellenic in origin), which potentially gives the statement some merit. In terms of the mythology, Zeus is said to have taken Europa to Crete where she gave birth to King Minos.

ἴσα πρὸς ἴσα: 'equal things to equal things' – i.e. the Greek abduction of Europa from Tyre balances out the Phoenician abduction of Io. 'balanced' or 'tit for tat' may be suitable translations.

Ἕλληνας αἰτίους . . . γενέσθαι: as Herodotus is still narrating the Persian account, a verb of saying needs to be at least implied here to make sense of the indirect statement – '[they, the Persians, say] the Greeks were to blame . . .'

1.2.2

μακρῇ νηί: 'in a long ship', i.e. a ship of war. Herodotus has shifted to an account of Jason and the Argonauts.

ἐς Αἶάν τε τὴν Κολχίδα: 'Aea in Colchis' – Colchis was located at the eastern edge of the Black Sea (modern Georgia) and is famous as the location of the Golden Fleece, the object of the Argonauts' voyage.

ἐπὶ Φᾶσιν ποταμόν: 'to the river Phasis' – ἐπί used with the accusative carries the sense of 'as far as'. The Phasis crossed the territory of Colchis before joining the Black Sea.

διαπρηξαμένους καὶ τἆλλα: 'having accomplished the other things', i.e. the capture of the Golden Fleece. **τἆλλα** is crasis of τά and ἄλλα.

τῶν εἵνεκεν ἀπίκατο: 'on account of which they had come' – **εἵνεκεν** is an Ionic form of the Attic ἕνεκα which is followed by the genitive, **τῶν**. **ἀπίκατο** is pluperfect (third person plural).

ἁρπάσαι: Herodotus continues to narrate the account of the Persians – the infinitive completes the indirect statement.

τὴν θυγατέρα Μηδείην: the third in the series of abductions. Medea, most famous as the eponymous lead in Euripides' play, was the daughter of Aeëtes, the king of Colchis. She fled Colchis with Jason having aided him in obtaining the Golden Fleece. Herodotus' Persian account (limited as it is) does not vary wildly from the Greek mythology.

1.2.3

πέμψαντά δὲ τὸν Κόλχων βασιλέα: all accusative to continue the indirect statement – '[they say that] the King of the Colchians having sent . . .'

αἰτέειν τε δίκας: 'he demanded satisfaction' – **δίκας** here means the result of a judgement, rather than the process itself. **αἰτέειν** is infinitive as part of the indirect statement.

τῆς ἁρπαγῆς: 'of the abduction', i.e. 'for the abduction'.

ἀπαιτέειν: this slightly beefed-up verb includes the idea that the object of your request is rightfully yours to begin with.

τοὺς δὲ ὑποκρίνασθαι: **τοὺς** refers to the Greeks and is a continuation of the indirect statement – 'They [the Greeks] answered . . .'

ὡς: causal – 'since'.

οὐδὲ ἐκεῖνοι . . . οὐδὲ ὦν αὐτοὶ: there is slightly looser pairing of οὐδέ than normal here as the two constructions are not parallel (the second picking up the indirect statement). 'since neither had they [the Phoenicians] given satisfaction . . . they [the Greeks] said nor would they . . .' It may be more straightforward to make both a simple negative – 'since they had not . . . they said that they would not (either)'.

ὦν: Ionic form of οὖν.

Chapter 3

1.3.1

δευτέρῃ . . . γενεῇ: 'in the second generation', i.e. 'in the following generation'. Herodotus often uses δεύτερος (second) to mean 'next' or 'following'.

λέγουσι: as in the previous chapters, this chapter is told exclusively through indirect speech as Herodotus continues to relate the information given to him by the Persians. The accusative and infinitive construction will feature throughout following this single verb of saying.

Ἀλέξανδρον τὸν Πριάμου: Alexander is the Greek name for the Trojan prince, Paris.

ἀκηκοότα: perfect participle in the accusative (agreeing with **Ἀλέξανδρον**) – 'having heard these things'. i.e. Alexander has been influenced by the previous abductions of Io, Europa and Medea.

οἱ . . . δι' ἁρπαγῆς γενέσθαι γυναῖκα: 'for him a wife to happen through abduction'. The construction follows the accusative and infinitive **Ἀλέξανδρον . . . ἐθελῆσαί** ('[they say] that Alexander wanted'). The meaning is clear but requires a little rephrasing in English – '[they say] that Alexander . . . wanted to gain a wife for himself by abduction'. **οἱ** is dative referring to Alexander.

ἐπιστάμενον: 'sure' – although ἐπίσταμαι has the general sense of 'I know,' Herodotus often uses it with the particular nuance 'I am sure' / 'I am certain'.

ἐκείνους: referring to the Greeks.

1.3.2

Ἑλένην: Helen of Sparta (commonly known as Helen of Troy) born of the union of Zeus (while disguised as a swan) with the Spartan queen, Leda. As well as Helen,

Clytemnestra and the Dioscuri, the twins Castor and Pollux, were also born at the same time. Helen and Pollux were thought the offspring of Zeus, while Clytemnestra and Castor were considered the offspring of Leda's husband, the Spartan king Tyndareus. Herodotus is swiftly moving us to the outbreak of the Trojan War, for which Helen's abduction was the catalyst since she was married to the Spartan king, Menelaus, at the time of the abduction.

πέμψαντας: although the Greeks first appear in the dative (**τοῖσι Ἕλλησι**) the participle in the accusative also refers to them as part of an accusative and infinitive construction – 'it seemed good to the Greeks [that they] having sent messengers . . .'

δίκας τῆς ἁρπαγῆς: the genitive is more easily translated as 'for' – 'satisfaction for the abduction'.

τοὺς δέ: referring to the Trojans – the use of **δέ** helps to clarify the contrast. Accusative as part of the indirect speech (with **προφέρειν** as the infinitive).

προϊσχομένων ταῦτα: rather than have the participle agree with **σφι** which follows and refers to the Greeks, Herodotus chooses to isolate the participle by having it stand alone as a genitive absolute (with **ταῦτα** as the object) – 'while they put these things forward'.

ὡς . . . βουλοίατό: the string of participles (**δόντες, ἐκδόντες, ἀπαιτεόντων**) can make these final phrases seem confusing. Fundamentally, **ὡς** and **βουλοίατό** are the scaffolding for the sentence as a whole:

- **ὡς . . . βουλοίατό** – 'since they [the Greeks] wished' (**βουλοίατό** is third person plural optative).
- **σφι παρ' ἄλλων δίκας γίνεσθαι** – 'there to be justice for them from others' (**σφι** also refers to the Greeks and stands in place of ἑωυτοῖς, the Ionic equivalent of ἑαυτοῖς).

οὐ δόντες αὐτοὶ δίκας οὐδὲ ἐκδόντες: the participles describe **αὐτοὶ** which refers to the Greeks – 'themselves not paying the penalty nor returning those they had taken'. ἐκδίδωμι refers specifically to the giving up of people (often refugees or abductees).

ἀπαιτεόντων: like **προϊσχομένων** previously, **ἀπαιτεόντων** is a single word genitive absolute (referring to the Trojans) – 'when they asked'.

Chapter 4

1.4.1

μέχρι . . . τούτου: 'as far as this', i.e. 'up to this point'.

ὦν: Ionic form of the Attic οὖν.

εἶναι: with the continued narration of the Persian account, Herodotus carries on using the accusative and infinitive construction to convey the indirect statement – '[they say] that there were only abductions . . .' As in previous chapters, this will be a major feature here.

παρ' ἀλλήλων: 'on each side'.

τὸ δὲ ἀπὸ τούτου: 'but after this' – literally, 'from this'.

ἢ σφέας ἐς τὴν Εὐρώπην: 'than they [began to make expeditions] into Europe' – **σφέας** refers to the Persians. In the blame game, Herodotus suggests that the Persians feel, despite the various abductions, it was the Greeks who first used force. The reference is clearly to the action taken by the Greeks during the Trojan War in an effort to force the return of Helen.

1.4.2

τὸ . . . ἁρπάζειν: the infinitives in this sentence are all paired with the article (articular infinitive) and should be treated as nouns. **τὸ . . . ἁρπάζειν γυναῖκας** – 'abducting women', **τὸ . . . σπουδὴν ποιήσασθαι** – 'making haste', **τὸ . . . μηδεμίαν ὤρην ἔχειν** – 'having no concern'. All are accusatives within the implied indirect statement '[the Persians say] that they think abducting women is . . .', etc.

ἀνδρῶν ἀδίκων: genitive modifying **ἔργον** – 'the work of unjust men'.

ἁρπασθεισέων: aorist passive participle from ἁρπάζω – 'having been snatched'. As the participle is feminine it must be referring to the abductions of women, as previously mentioned, and in the genitive is likely a stand-alone genitive absolute – 'when they [the women] have been carried off'. The same form appears in the following clause and should be treated the same way.

ἀνοήτων: imply **ἔργον** as with **ἀνδρῶν ἀδίκων** earlier – 'is the work of foolish men'. **σωφρόνων** requires the same treatment – 'is the work of wise men'.

δῆλα: treat plural as singular – 'it is clear . . .'

αὐταὶ: i.e. the women who were abducted.

ἐβούλοντο . . . ἡρπάζοντο: because of the recurrent nature of the events being discussed, the imperfect tense is used here. **ἂν** is used to create a supposition – 'if they did not want . . . they would not have . . .' The nature of the comment is uncomfortable to modern readers; however, this argument is not unheard of in the ancient world.

1.4.3

σφέας . . . λέγουσι Πέρσαι: **σφέας** is accusative as part of an indirect statement following **λέγουσι Πέρσαι**, while **τοὺς ἐκ τῆς Ἀσίης** is descriptive – 'The Persians say that they, the people of Asia . . .'

λόγον: although usually speech or story, **λόγον** (particularly paired with **ποιήσασθαι** which follows) has the sense of 'valuing' or 'esteeming'. When taken with **οὐδένα**, perhaps 'think nothing of it' or 'set no store by it' would be useful English renderings.

Ἕλληνας δὲ: the contrast is clear. The Persians ignored abductions of their women, but the Greeks went to war. Accusative as part of the indirect statement with **συναγεῖραι** and **κατελεῖν**.

ἀπὸ τούτου: as above – 'after this'.

1.4.4

ἡγήσασθαι: although usually to lead, Herodotus sometimes uses ἡγέομαι with the sense of believing or considering. This is particularly true of the perfect tense (as with **ἥγηνται** in the next sentence). The implied subject of the indirect statement is still the Persians.

ἔθνεα βάρβαρα: the Persian Empire contained a vast array of different cultures and ethnicities stretching from the Balkans and Egypt in the west to the borders of India in the East. The sentiment expressed here is perhaps most striking in the context of the Greeks living on the Ionian coast (of modern Turkey). The Ionian Revolt (499 BCE) in which a number of these Greek city-states tried to throw off Persian dominance, although a failure, was a major catalyst for the Persian invasions both under Darius and his son Xerxes. Here, the Persians lay their claim to Greeks living in Asia as much as any other people within their empire.

τὸ Ἑλληνικὸν: Herodotus sometimes uses the adjective Ἑλληνικός in the neuter to mean the Greeks collectively or 'the Hellenic people'.

κεχωρίσθαι: the use of the perfect infinitive (from χωρίζω, I separate or divide) shows the ongoing nature of the action – Greece and Europe have been divided from Persia and thus is separate now.

Chapter 5

1.5.1

οὕτω μὲν Πέρσαι: resolves the **Περσέων μέν νυν οἱ λόγιοι** of Chapter 1. Herodotus has now finished telling the Persian account and will provide additional information, alternatives and comment.

εὑρίσκουσι: although εὑρίσκω usually means find in the sense of discover, the nuance here is a little different – something more along the lines of 'find x to be the case', i.e. 'they believe' or 'they think'.

σφίσι: possessive dative – 'they find for them the beginning of hatred . . .', i.e. 'they find that the beginning of their hatred . . .'

ἐοῦσαν: Ionic form of the participle from εἰμί – 'being'. The participle forms an indirect statement after **εὑρίσκουσι** – 'they find the beginning being . . .', i.e. 'they find that the beginning was . . .'

τῆς ἐς τοὺς Ἕλληνας: **τῆς** links **τῆς ἔχθρης** to **ἐς τοὺς Ἕλληνας** – 'their hostility [the one] towards the Greeks' – more simply 'their hostility towards the Greeks'.

1.5.2

περὶ δὲ τῆς Ἰοῦς: Io (as mentioned in Chapter 1) – Herodotus is not a historian in the modern sense but is happy to present multiple accounts of the same event rather than establishing a single, definitive version for his reader. Here he will compare the Persian account of Io's abduction with that of the Phoenicians.

οὐκ ὁμολογέουσι Πέρσῃσι οὕτω Φοίνικες: Herodotus has overdone this phrase slightly as **οὕτω** is not really required – 'The Phoenicians do not agree with the Persians [in this way] . . .'

ἁρπαγῇ . . . χρησαμένους: literally, 'using an abduction'. χράομαι is often used with nouns which imply a verb (e.g. λόγῳ or βοῇ) where we would likely use the verb, in this case, 'by abducting . . .'

ὡς . . . ἐμίσγετο: dependent on **λέγουσι** – 'they do not say that . . . but they say that she . . .' This is the alternative version of events. Io is still the subject.

ἐν τῷ Ἄργει: i.e. while she was still at home and the Phoenicians were visiting.

AS

ἐοῦσα: feminine referring to Io – '[when she learnt] that she was . . .'

αἰδεομένη τοὺς τοκέας: αἰδέομαι is a tricky verb as it has no direct equivalent in English. It is often translated as, 'I am ashamed,' however, it can also take a direct object (as it does here) which does not translate well. Alternative translations often include, 'I am afraid of . . .,' or 'I stand in awe of . . .' Here, it is possibly best to include an additional phrase to encompass the idea that Io fears her parents will discover the secret of which she is ashamed – 'afraid that her parents would find out'. **τοὺς τοκέας**, although masculine, refers to both parents in the plural.

αὐτὴν . . . συνεκπλῶσαι: accusative and infinitive indirect statement. – '[They say] that she [Io] sailed with . . .'

ὡς ἂν μὴ κατάδηλος γένηται: 'so that it [the pregnancy] would not be discovered' – **κατάδηλος**, usually meaning visible, has this particular nuance when used with γίγνομαι.

1.5.3

ταῦτα . . . λέγουσι: this is typically Herodotean – having told both stories, he caps them off with a phrase to bring the narrative to an end.

ἐγὼ δὲ: Herodotus brings the focus to his own role in the narrative, giving us a little insight into his methods.

οὐκ ἔρχομαι ἐρέων: Herodotus sometimes uses **ἔρχομαι** as an auxiliary verb with participles – 'I am not going to say . . .' This is non-standard and peculiar to Herodotus.

ὡς οὕτω ἢ ἄλλως . . . ταῦτα ἐγένετο: 'that these things happened in this way or otherwise', i.e. that either one story or the other is true. In his work, Herodotus persistently fails to give his backing to one version of events where he has multiple available to him.

κως: Ionic form of the Attic πως. Here the meaning is determined by the adverbs **οὕτω** and **ἄλλως** – 'by any means in this way or otherwise'.

τὸν δὲ οἶδα αὐτὸς: 'but I myself know the man who . . .' **τὸν** is the object of **οἶδα** and is then modified by **ὑπάρξαντα** which follows.

τοῦτον σημήνας: **τοῦτον** refers to the same man as **τὸν** in the previous phrase. **σημήνας** is aorist participle referring to Herodotus – 'having pointed him out I . . .'

ἐς τὸ πρόσω τοῦ λόγου: 'further into my work' – **πρόσω** can either be used as an adverb on its own or with the article followed by a noun in the genitive (as here).

ἐπεξιών: from ἐπέξειμι, the verb means to traverse something in a physical sense but can also be used figuratively in literature meaning 'go through in detail'.

1.5.4

τὰ γὰρ τὸ πάλαι μεγάλα ἦν: this is one of the major, recurring themes of Herodotus' narrative – the unpredictability of fortune and the impact of fate on man's existence. King Croesus, whom Herodotus will introduce in the next chapter, is a famous example of this, but there are a number throughout his work. This culminates in the failure of the Persian king Xerxes to conquer the Greek states despite the enormous size of his army and the abundance of wealth at his disposal.

τὰ . . . μεγάλα ἦν: 'Those which were great . . .,' i.e. the cities (**ἄστεα**) mentioned in the previous sentence.

τὸ πάλαι: similar to **τὸ πρόσω**, above, **πάλαι** can appear both with or without an article. The meaning is unchanged.

γέγονε: perfect form of γίγνομαι – 'have become'.

ἐπ' ἐμεῦ: 'in my time' – **ἐπ'** is an elided form of ἐπί which can be used to show time. **ἐμεῦ** is the Ionic form of ἐγώ in the genitive (Attic: ἐμοῦ).

πρότερον ἦν σμικρά: Herodotus completes the circle of fate – places which were once great have diminished and those which are great in my day grew from small beginnings. The theme is one of inconstancy – nothing is permanent.

τὴν ἀνθρωπηίην . . . εὐδαιμονίην: having introduced the theme in the context of great towns and cities, Herodotus edges us closer to his first historical character by broadening the theme to include not just the prosperity of states but that of humans as a whole and, by inference, individual human beings within that.

ἐν τὠυτῷ: crasis for τῷ and αὐτῷ – 'in the same [state of being / situation]'.

ἐπιμνήσομαι: verbs of remembering (μιμνήσκω – 'I remember' is the root of the verb) often take the genitive in Greek. Thus, **ἐπιμνήσομαι ἀμφοτέρων** – 'I shall make mention of both,' or simply, 'I will mention both.'

Chapter 6

1.6.1

Κροῖσος: Croesus was king of the Lydians from 560–546 BCE when Lydia was conquered by the Persians under Cyrus the Great. He is most famous for his wealth, which will become a feature of Herodotus' narrative in later sections, giving rise to the (slightly old-fashioned) English phrase *as rich as Croesus*.

Λυδὸς: the Lydian Empire spanned roughly the western half of modern Turkey with its capital at Sardis (modern Sart in Turkey). The kingdom of Lydia also included Greek settlements along the Ionian coast of Turkey.

γένος: accusative of respect – 'in respect of his race' – consider 'Lydian by birth' or 'of the Lydian race'.

Ἀλυάττεω: Alyattes, Croesus' father, was king of Lydia from 610–560 BCE.

τύραννος: although the origin of the English word 'tyrant', **τύραννος** does not have the same negative associations in Greek. It is perfectly acceptable to translate as 'tyrant' but you may also wish to consider 'sovereign' or 'sole ruler'.

ἐντός Ἅλυος ποταμοῦ: the Halys River (modern Kizilirmak River) flows through central Turkey, past Ankara, and empties into the Black Sea on Turkey's northern coast. The use of **ἐντός** ('on this side') should be taken from a Greek perspective, so means 'to the west' of the Halys.

μεταξὺ Συρίων τε καὶ Παφλαγόνων: both **Συρίων** and **Παφλαγόνων** are in the genitive following **μεταξὺ** and are plural referring to the peoples rather than the lands. The term Syrian was used to refer to the people of Cappadocia (south-eastern Turkey) as well as the people of modern Syria. The Paphlagonians lived on the Black Sea coast of central Turkey.

ἐξιεῖ: when used of rivers, ἐξίημι means the point at which the river 'empties' or 'discharges' into the sea.

πρὸς βορῆν ἄνεμον: literally, 'towards the north-wind' – or just 'to the north'.

τὸν Εὔξεινον καλεόμενον πόντον: 'the sea called Euxine' – although εὔξεινος means hospitable, it is also the name the Greeks used to refer to the Black Sea.

1.6.2

τῶν ἡμεῖς ἴδμεν: **τῶν** is here used like a relative pronoun – 'of whom we know'.

τοὺς . . . Ἑλλήνων: **τοὺς** is a paired construction with **τοὺς δὲ φίλους** which follows – 'some . . . others . . .' **Ἑλλήνων** is a partitive genitive – 'some of the Greeks'.

ἐς φόρου ἀπαγωγήν: 'to the payment of tribute' – ἀπαγωγή is usually used with the sense of 'leading [X] away' but with money Herodotus uses it to mean payment. With **κατεστρέψατο** you may wish to translate as 'subjugated and extracted tribute from them'.

Ἴωνάς τε καὶ Αἰολέας καὶ Δωριέας: the Greeks normally considered themselves to belong to one of four Hellenic tribes: Ionians, Aeolians, Dorians and Achaeans. These tribes were well known and were even considered when making alliances and declaring war. The Ionians referred to here are those living along the west coast of Turkey. Dorian Greeks are said to have arrived in the Peloponnese and replaced the Mycenaean Greek communities of the Bronze Age (although this theory is controversial) but by Herodotus' time, there were also communities of Dorian Greeks in Asia Minor (including Herodotus' home town of Halicarnassus). The Aeolians (said to have been named after the mythical Aeolus, keeper of the winds) were originally from thessaly, a central region of Greece, and are said to have migrated across the Aegean and into Asia Minor during the Dorian Invasion.

τοὺς ἐν τῇ Ἀσίῃ: descriptive 'those in Asia' – referring to the Dorians previously mentioned.

1.6.3

Κιμμερίων στράτευμα: the Cimmerians were a nomadic steppe people from the area around the Black Sea. They were said to have invaded Asia Minor as a result of being driven from their homes by Scythian migrations. Croesus' father, Alyattes, expelled them in 619 BCE.

Κροίσου ἐὸν πρεσβύτερον: literally, 'being older' – in this context meaning that the event happened before Croesus. **Κροίσου** is a genitive of comparison ('than Croesus') while **ἐὸν** is the Ionic form of the participle ὄν from εἰμί.

ἐξ ἐπιδρομῆς ἁρπαγή: 'seizing from a raid', i.e. 'they raided and plundered' – **ἁρπαγή** means stealing of property and not (necessarily) an abduction of women as in earlier chapters.

7: As an introduction to the chapters which follow and the story of Gyges and Candaules, Herodotus describes the lineage of Candaules. Candaules was the last of the Heraclids to rule Sardis (a dynasty which Herodotus tells us lasted 505 years) and would be succeeded by the Mermnadae from which family Croesus was descended.

AS

Chapter 8

1.8.1

οὗτος δὴ ὢν ὁ Κανδαύλης: Candaules (introduced in Chapter 7) was king of Lydia in the early part of the seventh century BCE. He is the last in the line of Heraclid (i.e. descended from Heracles) kings, ruling until around 687 BCE.

ἠράσθη: although ἔραμαι can be translated as 'love' it has a real sense of physical passion – 'lust after' or 'became passionately fond of' are possible translations.

ἑωυτοῦ γυναικός: **ἑωυτοῦ** is the Ionic form of the reflexive pronoun ἑαυτοῦ – 'his own [wife]'.

οἱ . . . γυναῖκα: 'the wife to him' (possessive dative) – 'his wife'.

πασέων: Ionic form of πασῶν. As it is in the feminine, the adjective also stands in for the noun 'of all women'.

ὥστε: although commonly seen introducing result clauses, **ὥστε** can also function as a conjunction meaning 'in as much as' or simply 'since' – 'in as much as he thought this' or just 'since he thought this'. The participle which follows is more easily taken as a main verb.

ἦν γάρ οἱ: 'for there was to him', i.e. 'he had'.

Γύγης ὁ Δασκύλου: 'Gyges the [son] of Dascylus' – the use of the genitive needs expanding in English to include the patronymic.

καὶ τὰ σπουδαιέστερα τῶν πρηγμάτων: when used of people, σπουδαῖος means earnest or serious. When used of business it means 'worthy of serious attention' – 'as well as the most serious of his affairs'. **πρηγμάτων** is Ionic for πραγμάτων.

καὶ δὴ καὶ τὸ εἶδος τῆς γυναικὸς: **καὶ δὴ καὶ** is often translated as 'furthermore' or 'moreover', i.e. Candaules is divulging much more information to Gyges than he should. 'even' would probably function well here. **τὸ εἶδος** is, literally, just 'the shape' but (like Latin *forma*) it also refers to beauty or good looks when talking about people.

1.8.2

χρῆν: from the impersonal verb χρή ('it is necessary') the nuance is slightly stronger here. 'it was fated' probably reflects Herodotus' meaning more effectively.

γενέσθαι κακῶς: γίγνομαι can be used with an adverb to suggest a change of state – literally, 'to become badly'. This is not an expression used in English so you may wish to consider 'to meet a bad end' or 'for things to turn out badly' or similar.

τοιάδε: this is a common way for Herodotus to begin speech – '[he spoke] in the following way . . .'

μοι λέγοντι: dative following **πείθεσθαι** – 'I don't think that you believe me when I talk . . .'

ὦτα γὰρ τυγχάνει ἀνθρώποισι ἐόντα ἀπιστότερα ὀφθαλμῶν: this short maxim adds a philosophical character to the narrative (some believe that Herodotus is imitating the philosopher Heraclitus – fragment 15). These sorts of brief sayings containing life lessons were common in the ancient world. ὀφθαλμῶν is a genitive of comparison 'the ears happen to be less trustworthy . . . than the eyes'.

ποίεε ὅκως ἐκείνην θεήσεαι γυμνήν: the phrasing here does not translate naturally into English. **ποίεε** is the imperative form of ποιέω (uncontracted) and when combined with **ὅκως** means 'do in such a way as . . .' with a sense of 'bring it about that . . .' **θεήσεαι** is aorist subjunctive – 'that you might see'. Thus 'do such that you might see her naked' – more naturally 'make sure you see her naked' or 'you need to see her naked'.

1.8.3

ὁ δὲ: i.e. Gyges.

μέγα ἀμβώσας: contracted form of ἀναβώσας – 'having cried aloud'. **μέγα** should be taken adverbially.

λόγον οὐκ ὑγιέα: λόγος has a wide variety of meanings and can be difficult to pin down. Here 'argument' or 'suggestion' probably work best.

ἅμα δὲ κιθῶνι ἐκδυομένῳ συνεκδύεται καὶ τὴν αἰδῶ γυνή: **ἅμα** and **καὶ** work in parallel here meaning 'no sooner . . . than . . .' – 'no sooner are her clothes taken off than a woman also lays aside her modesty', i.e. 'a woman lays aside her modesty together with her clothes'. **κιθῶνι** is an Ionic form of χιτών and is dative following **ἅμα**.

1.8.4

τὰ καλὰ . . . ἐξεύρηται: 'fine things were invented' – 'fine' in the sense of 'right' to contrast with **ἀνόμων** ('lawless' or 'impious') which follows. You could go so far as to translate **τὰ καλὰ** as 'good rules' or 'moral codes'. καλός and κακός are often used in relation to virtue and vice (virtue being beautiful and vice being ugly) in a way in which we do not associate them in English.

ἐκ τῶν: 'from which' – **τῶν** is functioning as a relative pronoun.

ἐν τοῖσι ἓν τόδε ἐστί: 'among these this is one . . .', – i.e. out of man's moral code, this [the following] is a rule . . .

σκοπέειν τινὰ τὰ ἑωυτοῦ: 'to look to one's own affairs', i.e. keep your nose out of other people's business. Gyges knows that he is crossing a line if he does as Candaules suggests.

καὶ σέο δέομαι μὴ δέεσθαι ἀνόμων: **σέο** is an Ionic form of the pronoun σύ in the genitive. **δέομαι** and **δέεσθαι** are both forms of the verb 'to need', 'require' or 'ask' which (because of its root meaning 'be in need of') is followed by a genitive – 'I need you not to ask unlawful things [of me]'.

Chapter 9

1.9.1

ὁ μὲν δὴ λέγων: i.e. Gyges.

τί . . . κακόν: 'some misfortune'.

ἐξ αὐτῶν: although plural, this is probably best translated in the singular – 'from the matter' or 'from the situation'.

ὁ δ' ἀμείβετο: i.e. Candaules.

μὴ φοβεῦ: present imperative – 'do not fear'.

ὡς: Herodotus has varied the construction after **μὴ φοβεῦ**, first using **ὡς** and later **μή** – here **ὡς** is probably best taken with **μήτε ἐμέ** – 'do not fear that I . . .'

σέο πειρώμενος: **σέο** is genitive after **πειρώμενος** – '[that I say this] testing you'.

λέγω λόγον τόνδε: the use of both **λέγω** and **λόγον** makes for an awkward translation. It is probably best to ignore **λόγον** – 'I say this' or to use a different verb for **λέγω** – 'I make this suggestion.'

μὴ τί τοι ἐξ αὐτῆς γένηται βλάβος: this clause still follows **μὴ φοβεῦ**, above, but varies from the previous construction using **μή** rather than **ὡς** – 'do not fear [me] that I say this . . . nor my wife, that any harm may come to you from her'. **αὐτῆς**, in the feminine, refers specifically to Candaules' wife rather than the situation in general.

ἀρχήν: this should be taken adverbially – 'from the beginning'.

ὥστε μηδέ μαθεῖν μιν ὀφθεῖσαν: as a result clause using the nfinitive, **μιν** in the accusative is the new subject – 'that she will not know that she has been seen . . .' Where a result clause suggests a likely outcome, rather than a definite one, the infinitive (with a subject in the accusative) is used instead of the indicative.

σεῦ: Ionic form of Attic: σου.

ἐγὼ . . . σε . . . στήσω: this sentence looks complicated because the key components are spread out. The basic structure is quite simple: **ἐγὼ . . . σε . . . στήσω** – 'I will stand you . . .' the remaining phrases will then fit neatly around this.

1.9.2

ἐν τῷ κοιμώμεθα: **τῷ** is functioning as a relative pronoun referring to **τὸ οἴκημα** – 'in which we sleep'.

μετὰ δ' ἐμὲ ἐσελθόντα: **ἐμὲ** is accusative following **μετὰ** ('after me') but is complicated by the participle which follows – 'after me having entered'. Although **ἡ γυνὴ**, which follows, is the subject it is more sensible to say 'after I enter, my wife will also arrive . . .'

ἐς κοῖτον: although κοῖτος is the bed itself, with **ἐς** it likely refers to the act of going to sleep.

κεῖται: can be used of both people (meaning 'I lie down') and objects (with the sense of 'be situated') as **θρόνος** is the subject, perhaps – 'a chair is positioned'.

ἐπὶ τοῦτον: i.e. onto the chair.

τῶν ἱματίων κατὰ ἓν ἕκαστον ἐκδύνουσα: 'each of her clothes, one by one, having taken them off' – **κατά** with a number suggests 'at a time', here 'one at a time' or 'one by one'. **τῶν ἱματίων** is partitive following **ἕκαστον** – 'each of her clothes'. **ἐκδύνουσα** in the feminine agrees with Candaules' wife – 'having taken [them] off'.

θήσει: follows **ἐκδύνουσα** in the nominative – 'having taken them off, she will place . . .'

κατ' ἡσυχίην πολλὴν: 'at great leisure', i.e. without needing to hurry.

παρέξει τοι: παρέχω used impersonally means 'it is in one's power' or 'it is possible'. **τοι** is an alternative for the Attic σοι 'for you' – 'it will be possible for you'.

1.9.3

κατὰ νώτου τε αὐτῆς γένῃ: **κατὰ νώτου** as a phrase means 'in the rear' or 'from behind' – 'and has her back to you'.

σοὶ μελέτω: μελέτω is a third person imperative – 'let it be a care to you . . .', i.e. 'make sure that . . .'
τὸ ἐνθεῦτεν: this should be taken adverbially – 'next'
ὅκως: introduces the instruction after **μελέτω** with **ὄψεται** (in the future) – 'that she does not see you . . .'
θυρέων: Ionic form of the Attic: θυρῶν.

Chapter 10

1.10.1

ὃ μὲν: i.e. Gyges.
ὡς: causative – 'since . . .'
ὥρη τῆς κοίτης: literally, 'the time of bed' but 'for bed' is more natural.
Γύγεα: alternative accusative ending (Herodotus himself used **Γύγην** in Chapter 8) – this is common in nouns ending in – ης in Ionic dialect.
μετὰ ταῦτα: i.e. after Candaules led Gyges to the bedchamber.
ἐσελθοῦσαν δὲ καὶ τιθεῖσαν: both feminine agreeing with Candaules' wife – 'Gyges watched [her] come in and put down . . .'

1.10.2

ὡς δὲ κατὰ νώτου ἐγένετο: as in Chapter 9 – 'when she had her back to him . . .'
ἰούσης τῆς γυναικός: all in the genitive modifying the previous phrase. More easily taken as the subject – 'When she had her back to him and the woman went . . .'
ὑπεκδὺς ἐχώρεε ἔξω: ὑπεκδὺς is the aorist participle of ὑπεκδύομαι ('I slip out') in the nominative and masculine agreeing with Gyges. He is also the subject of **ἐχώρεε. ἔξω** is being used adverbially (rather than as a preposition) so just means 'out'.
τὸ ποιηθέν ἐκ τοῦ ἀνδρὸς: literally, 'the thing having been done from her husband', so, more naturally, 'what her husband had done'.
οὔτε ἔδοξε μαθεῖν: 'nor did she seem to have noticed', i.e. she is playing dumb temporarily in order to bide her time.
οὔτε ἀνέβωσε αἰσχυνθεῖσα: αἰσχυνθεῖσα is the aorist passive participle of αἰσχύνω. In the active it means 'I shame [someone else]' but in the passive means 'I feel shame.' Here, the whole phrase is probably best translated as 'she neither cried out in shame'.
τίσεσθαι τὸν Κανδαύλεα: τίσεσθαι is the future middle infinitive of τίνω. As an active verb it means 'I pay the penalty,' whereas in the middle 'I punish' or 'I make [someone else] pay.'

1.10.3

παρὰ γὰρ τοῖσι Λυδοῖσι: Herodotus looks to explain the different approaches to nudity between Greeks and Barbarian peoples and in doing so helps to clarify Candaules' wife's outrage.

AS

σχεδὸν δὲ καὶ παρὰ τοῖσι ἄλλοισι βαρβάροισι: σχεδὸν helps to create a more general statement – 'and *generally* among other barbarians . . .', i.e. not just the Lydians.

καὶ ἄνδρα ὀφθῆναι γυμνόν: 'even for a man to be seen naked . . .' – this phrase functions as the subject. Again, it heightens the understanding of the outrage of Candaules' wife: if it is socially unacceptable that a man be seen naked, it is even more so for a woman. Herodotus may be taking this too far, however, as, although Greek men of his era often performed athletics in the nude (and there are numerous surviving statues of the naked male form), most Greek women were considerably more sheltered and modest and would have considered this situation just as indecent had it happened to one of them.

ἐς αἰσχύνην μεγάλην φέρει: φέρω is being used intransitively with the sense of 'lead to', i.e. the act of being seen naked 'leads to great shame'.

Chapter 11

1.11.1

τότε: i.e. at the moment Candaules' wife realizes what has happened – 'at that time'.

οὕτω: 'in this way' – i.e. 'as I have already mentioned'. Herodotus has already made it clear in Chapter 10 that she kept quiet at the point she realized she had been seen.

δηλώσασα: the feminine participle shows that Candaules' wife is the subject of the sentence.

ἡσυχίην εἶχε: i.e. she did not say anything.

ὡς δὲ ἡμέρη τάχιστα ἐγεγόνεε: **ὡς** with a superlative adjective usually means 'as . . . as possible' however when suggesting speed it can also be translated 'as soon as . . .' – 'as soon as it became day . . .'

τῶν οἰκετέων: partitive genitive – 'of her household, the ones she saw were . . .'

ἑωυτῇ: Ionic form of the Attic ἑαυτῇ – 'to her'.

ἑτοίμους ποιησαμένη: 'having made them ready', i.e. she prepared them (by telling them what had happened).

ἐκάλεε: καλέω can mean both 'I call' and 'I summon' as in a formal situation like this. The imperfect is used to show that the process took some time.

ὁ δὲ οὐδὲν δοκέων αὐτὴν . . . ἐπίστασθαι: δοκέων introduces an accusative and infinitive indirect statement ('he thinking that . . .') with the feminine **αὐτὴν** as the subject of the indirect speech ('he thinking that she . . . [i.e. Candaules' wife]) while **οὐδὲν** is the object of **ἐπίστασθαι** – 'he thinking that she knew nothing . . .'

ἐώθεε: pluperfect form of ἔθω ('I am accustomed') – this verb only appears in the present tense in participle forms using the perfect and pluperfect tenses as the present and imperfect respectively. Here: 'he was accustomed'.

πρόσθε . . . φοιτᾶν: literally, 'to go to and fro before her', i.e. 'to attend to her'.

ὅκως: Ionic form of the Attic ὅπως which, when used with an optative (here: **καλέοι**), can refer to time and should be taken as 'whenever'.

1.11.2

ὡς: temporal – 'when'.
τοί: Ionic for Attic σοι – 'to you'.
δυῶν ὁδῶν παρεουσέων: 'of the two roads present' – this phrase is reliant on **αἵρεσιν** which follows. **παρεουσέων** means present in the sense of 'available'.
αἵρεσιν: the noun form of the verb αἱρέω literally means 'a taking' but can also mean 'a choice' (based on the middle form of the same verb αἱρέομαι).
βούλεαι: Ionic second person singular present – 'you want'.
ἀποκτείνας . . . ἔχε: the aorist participle followed by the imperative expresses the subsequent nature of the actions – 'having killed . . . have . . .' Although the Greek is much more accurate (Gyges cannot take his wife and the kingdom without having first killed Candaules) it is more natural in English to imagine both are imperative (i.e. kill Candaules and take me and the kingship of the Lydians . . .) The reference to having her is shorthand for 'as your wife'.
αὐτόν σε ... ἀποθνήσκειν δεῖ: the impersonal **δεῖ** is often followed by an accusative and infinitive (in the style of an indirect statement) – 'it is necessary that you yourself . . .' **αὐτόν** reinforces the contrast – one of the men must die.
οὕτω: 'in this way' – this is the reason Candaules' wife has readied her attendants. If Gyges does not agree to kill Candaules, he will perish on the spot.
ὡς ἂν . . . ἴδῃς: used here to express a purpose clause – 'so that you might [not] see'.
πάντα: adverbial – 'in every respect' or 'in all things'
τοῦ λοιποῦ: literally, 'the remainder', τό λοιπόν can be used figuratively to mean 'the future'. The genitive shows time within – 'in the future'.
τὰ μή σε δεῖ: **τὰ** is the object of **ἴδῃς** but is also functioning as a relative pronoun – 'so that you might not see *things which* . . .' **μή σε δεῖ** then completes the phrase – '[things which] it is not necessary for you [to see]', i.e. 'so that you do not see things which you shouldn't.'

1.11.3

ἤτοι . . . ἤ: an emphatic form of ἤ . . . ἤ . . . ('either . . . or . . .') – the suffix – τοι is often translated as 'in truth [either . . . or . . .]' but 'indeed' or 'absolutely' would also do the job. The choice is the same as that already laid out, however, Candaules' wife heightens her sense of outrage by including the charges against the two men.
ποιήσαντα οὐ νομιζόμενα: νομίζω, although often taken as 'I think', is also used in the passive to mean 'be customary' (e.g. ὡς νομίζεται – 'as is the custom'). τὰ νομιζόμενα (using the neuter plural of the participle) forms the noun from this – 'customs'. As a phrase, **ποιήσαντα οὐ νομιζόμενα** (literally, 'having done things which are not customary') can be taken as 'having acted against custom'.
μή μιν ἀναγκαίῃ ἐνδεῖν: 'not to bind him by compulsion', i.e. 'not to force him'. **μιν** is reflexive referring to Gyges.
διακρῖναι: with a variety of meanings ('I separate' or 'I distinguish') here most easily taken with **τοιαύτην αἵρεσιν** as 'to make such a choice'. The aorist infinitive follows **ἐνδεῖν** – 'to bind him to make . . .'

1.11.4

οὐκ ὦν δὴ ἔπειθε: **ὦν** (standing in for Attic οὖν) is often inserted by Herodotus between **οὐκ** and a verb. Here it functions as a link to the previous sentence – 'however he failed to persuade her [despite his pleas] . . .'

αἱρέεται αὐτὸς περιεῖναι: this sort of asyndeton (lack of conjunction) after **οὐκ ὤν** can be found throughout Herodotus' work. You may wish to include a conjunction 'and he decided to live' or enjoy the dramatic emphasis which the phrase has in English without one.
δεσπότεα: like **Γύγεα** (Chapter 10), **δεσπότεα** is an alternative accusative form of δεσπότην.
οὐκ ἐθέλοντα: literally, 'not being willing' but an adverbial phrase is probably more natural – 'unwillingly'.
φέρε ἀκούσω: **ἀκούσω** is first person singular aorist subjunctive used in a hortative manner (i.e. providing encouragement). These are much more common in the first person plural ('let us . . .') but can appear in the singular, as here, meaning 'let me . . .' They are sometimes introduced by other words like **φέρε** or ἄγε to give additional force ('come now' or 'well'). The literal meaning of the phrase is 'come now let me hear' but there are various, less literal, ways of phrasing your translation e.g. 'I would like to hear' or 'so tell me'.
τέῳ καὶ τρόπῳ: **τέῳ** is an alternative form of τίνι and agrees with **τρόπῳ** – 'by what means . . .' **καὶ** adds additional emphasis to **τρόπῳ** – 'by what means exactly . . .'

1.11.5

ὑπολαβοῦσα ἔφη: while ὑπολαμβάνω, which has a variety of meanings, is often used in the sense of 'take up' or 'interrupt', when combined with a verb of saying (like **ἔφη**) it means 'say in reply' – literally, 'having taken up [the conversation] she said . . .'
ἐκεῖνος: referring to Candaules.
ἐπεδέξατο γυμνήν: ἐπιδείκνυμι usually means 'I display' or 'I exhibit' but in the middle (as here) involves a sense of personal pleasure in the act – e.g. 'I show off'. This is fitting considering Candaules' insistence that Gyges see his wife naked and the associated pleasure that he seems to have taken from the whole situation.
ὑπνωμένῳ: the passive form of ὑπνόω ('I put [X] to sleep') is easiest taken to mean 'sleeping' or 'while asleep'.

Chapter 12

1.12.1

ὡς: temporal – 'when'.
ἤρτυσαν: Herodotus has chosen this word carefully – it is usually associated with preparations which require cunning or deception. The third plural ending refers to Gyges and Candaules' wife.
οὐ γὰρ ἐμετίετο ὁ Γύγης: Herodotus reinforces Candaules' wife's determination – Gyges cannot escape the arrangement.
οὐδέ οἱ ἦν ἀπαλλαγὴ οὐδεμία: the use of the double negative **οὐδὲ . . . οὐδεμία** places further emphasis on the hopelessness of Gyges' situation. **οἱ** is possessive dative – 'nor was there . . . to him.'
τὸν θάλαμον: we have not encountered this word before (Herodotus instead referring to the οἴκημα in Chapters 9 and 10). While θάλαμος can refer to any internal room, it is often used specifically of women's quarters or the

bedchamber of the lady of the house. This may be reflective of the changing power dynamic.

ἐκείνη ἐγχειρίδιον δοῦσα κατακρύπτει: Candaules' wife takes centre stage in the events (despite remaining nameless throughout) as the instigator and enabler (by providing the dagger), while Gyges is but a tool for her machinations. Herodotus presents other women in this manner in his narrative (most famously Artemisia, queen of Halicarnassus).

ὑπὸ τὴν αὐτὴν θύρην: i.e. the door which Candaules chose to hide Gyges behind when he arranged the original plan. Candaules' own scheme is now being used against him.

1.12.2

ὑπεκδύς τε καὶ ἀποκτείνας: the subject of these participles (and the verb **ἔσχε** which follows) is Gyges who is not named until the end of the phrase.

ἔσχε καὶ τὴν γυναῖκα καὶ τὴν βασιληίην: it was not uncommon in Eastern kingdoms for a usurper to claim the previous monarch's wife as his own. This would not have been considered a cause for suspicion. Although Herodotus' account of Gyges' rise to power is, perhaps, the most well known, he also features in Plato's *Republic* and Cicero's *de Officiis*.

τοῦ καὶ Ἀρχίλοχος ὁ Πάριος . . .: these lines are generally considered spurious and are often bracketed by editors. They interrupt the narrative unnecessarily to give a reference for an individual, Gyges, who was far too well known in Herodotus' time to require one. The term used to describe Archilochus' poetry (**ἐν ἰάμβῳ τριμέτρῳ**) is also thought to be a later expression. Herodotus himself uses different terminology to describe iambic trimeter elsewhere in his work. Archilochus himself was a lyric poet from the island of Paros writing in the early to mid-seventh century BCE. Although only fragments of Archilochus' work survive, his line referring to Gyges can be found in Aristotle's *Rhetoric*.

τοῦ καὶ Ἀρχίλοχος . . . ἐπεμνήσθη: Archilochus is the subject of the sentence ('Archilochus made mention') while **τοῦ** functions as a relative pronoun referring to Gyges (in the genitive to follow **ἐπεμνήσθη**) – 'Archilochus made mention of him . . .'

κατὰ τὸν αὐτὸν χρόνον γενόμενος: when used in time phrases, κατά can signify 'around' or 'about'. i.e Archilochus was alive at about the same time as Gyges.

Chapter 13

1.13.1

ἔσχε δὲ τὴν βασιληίην: referring to Gyges.

ἐκ τοῦ ἐν Δελφοῖσι χρηστηρίου: ἐκ is more easily taken as 'by' in this instance. The oracle at Delphi was the most famous in the Greek world. Greek city-states and monarchs from further afield would regularly seek its advice in times of crisis or on day-to-day political matters. Herodotus' introduction of the oracle prefaces its more detailed role in Croesus' decision to make war against the Persian Empire.

δεινόν ἐποιεῦντο: in addition to its more common meaning of 'make' or 'do', ποιέω has a variety of associated meanings including (in the middle voice) to 'deem' or 'consider'. When combined with an adjective, this means to 'think it [terrible]' and thus to 'take it badly' or to 'take exception' to something.

ἐν ὅπλοισι ἦσαν: to be 'in arms' means to 'take up arms' or to be 'under arms' – i.e. they revolted.

συνέβησαν ἐς τὠυτὸ: the basic meaning of συμβαίνω is to 'come together' but it is often used figuratively to mean 'reach an agreement'. Here this is further reinforced with **ἐς τὠυτὸ** – 'they came together to this . . .', i.e. 'they reached an agreement that . . .'

ἢν: a contracted form of ἐάν – 'if'.

ἀνέλῃ: usually meaning 'take up', ἀναιρέω has a particular nuance when associated with oracles – 'I ordain' or 'I appoint'. It is used in the same way in the sentence which follows.

ἀποδοῦναι ὀπίσω: although **ἀποδοῦναι** already conveys the sense of 'give back', Herodotus has reinforced this with the adverb **ὀπίσω** ('back' or 'backwards'). This is difficult to convey in English and is probably best ignored.

Ἡρακλείδας: the Heracleidae (or Heraclids) are the descendants of the hero Heracles, many of whom became rulers of Greek kingdoms and kingdoms further afield. As mentioned in Chapter 8, Candaules was considered one of the Heracleidae, so it is only natural that, should the Delphic Oracle refuse to support Gyges' kingship, the throne of Lydia should return to his family line.

1.13.2

τοσόνδε μέντοι: the use of **τοσόνδε** here is unusual in that it reinforces the contrast created by **μέντοι** – 'in addition, however . . .' or 'furthermore, however . . .' may be reasonable ways of reflecting this.

ὡς . . . ἥξει: ὡς used to introduce the indirect statement – 'that [vengeance] would come . . .'

Ἡρακλείδῃσι τίσις: the possessive dative (**Ἡρακλείδῃσι**) shows that the Heracleidae would be the beneficiaries of vengeance, not subject to it – 'the Heracleidae would gain vengeance. . .'

ἐς τὸν πέμπτον ἀπόγονον Γύγεω: 'in the fifth generation from Gyges' – **ἀπόγονον**, usually a descendant, is more easily taken as 'generation' here. The genitive **Γύγεω** shows the separation from Gyges. Croesus, to whom this prophecy refers is the fourth Lydian king after Gyges, however, as the Greeks counted inclusively, from Gyges to Croesus becomes five generations.

λόγον οὐδένα ἐποιεῦντο: literally, 'they made no reckoning' – more naturally 'paid no attention'. The genitive **τούτου τοῦ ἔπεος** then follows – 'they paid no attention to this oracular utterance . . .'

ἐπετελέσθη: generally, ἐπιτελέω means 'I complete' or 'I accomplish' but is often used of oracular prophecies meaning 'I fulfil.'

14–18: Gyges, having become king of Sardis, sends offerings to Delphi which Herodotus details. He also briefly informs us of Gyges' military conquests. Gyges is then succeeded by his son, Ardys, who continues the military expansion during his forty-nine-year reign. Ardys is succeeded by his son Sadyattes and, in turn, by his son Alyattes. Under Alyattes, military expansion continues including the continuation of Sadyattes' war against Miletus (near modern Balat on the western coast of Turkey). In total Sadyattes and Alyattes waged war against Miletus for twelve years.

Chapter 19

1.19.1

ληίου ἐμπιπραμένου: genitive absolute – 'while the crops were being burnt'.

συνηνείχθη τι τοιόνδε γενέσθαι πρῆγμα: from συμφέρω, **συνηνείχθη** is impersonal meaning 'it happened'. The remainder of the phrase is accusative and infinitive indirect statement – 'it happened that the following event took place'.

ὡς . . . τάχιστα: as in Chapter 11, this should be taken as 'as soon as' rather than the usual 'as quickly as possible'.

ἀνέμῳ βιώμενον: 'driven by the wind' – i.e. the fire was whipped up by the wind and travelled further than intended. **βιώμενον**, from βιάω, usually means to 'constrain' or 'force' but has a particular usage in the passive and in the context of fire – 'drive on'.

ἅψατο νηοῦ Ἀθηναίης: the crop (**τὸ λήιον**) is the subject of the sentence while **νηοῦ** in the genitive follows the verb – 'caught (and set fire to) the temple of Athena'.

ἐπίκλησιν Ἀσσησίης: the noun ἐπίκλησις usually refers to a name. Here the accusative is used adverbially to mean 'named' or 'known as'. **Ἀσσησίης** is the adjectival form (in the genitive singular – agreeing with **Ἀθηναίης**) of Ἀσσησός (Assesos), a town near Miletus in Ionia – 'called [Athena] of Assesos'.

ἀφθεὶς δὲ ὁ νηὸς κατεκαύθη: the burning down of a temple, even by accident and in times of war, was a major act of sacrilege and usually had consequences. King Xerxes, during his invasion of Greece, burns the Acropolis of Athens an act which, perhaps, contributes to his eventual defeat.

1.19.2

τὸ παραυτίκα: **παραυτίκα** usually functions as an adverb ('presently' or 'immediately'); however, with the article it refers to 'the present'. Here – 'for the present'.

λόγος οὐδεὶς ἐγένετο: as a phrase – 'no account was paid to it'.

μετὰ δὲ: functioning as an adverb (and contrasting with **παραυτίκα**) – 'but afterwards . . .'

ἐς Σάρδις: Sardis (Ionic: Σάρδιες, Attic: Σάρδεις) was the capital of the Lydian Empire and the seat of the Lydian kings. Alyattes is returning home having finished campaigning. **Σάρδις** is accusative plural (following **ἐς**).

ἐνόσησε ὁ Ἀλυάττης: Alyattes' misfortune could easily be construed by Greek readers as a direct consequence of the accidental burning of the temple of Athena.

μακροτέρης δέ οἱ γινομένης τῆς νούσου: 'with his illness becoming longer' – i.e. it went on for longer than expected and there is concern about his recovery. **οἱ** is possessive dative – 'the illness to him', i.e. 'his illness'.

θεοπρόπους: originally an adjective meaning 'prophetic', when used as a substantive it can mean a 'seer' or a 'prophet' but can also be used of the messengers sent to enquire of an oracle. Following **πέμπει**, this is undoubtedly the meaning here.

εἴτε . . . εἴτε: usually seen as a pair, **εἴτε** introduces Herodotus' potential reasons for Alyattes' decision – 'either [because . . .] or [because . . .]'.

τευ: genitive singular, is an Ionic form of τινος. It functions as part of a genitive absolute with **συμβουλεύσαντός** – '[either because] someone advised him to . . .'

πέμψαντα τὸν θεὸν ἐπειρέσθαι: the accusative **πέμψαντα** refers to Alyattes even though he appears in the dative (as **αὐτῷ**) earlier in the sentence. This is the same pattern as previously mentioned in Chapter 3. **τὸν θεὸν** is the object of **ἐπειρέσθαι.**

1.19.3

τοῖσι δὲ ἡ Πυθίη ἀπικομένοισι: While the Pythia (the priestess of Apollo at Delphi) is the subject of the sentence and Alyattes' messengers are in the dative, a more natural flow is achieved by breaking the phrase into two clauses in English – 'When they arrived, the Pythia . . .'

οὐκ ἔφη: while ἔφη usually means 'he / she said', in combination with a negative it can be taken as 'deny' or (as here) 'refuse'.

χρήσειν: future infinitive of χράω. When used of oracles this should usually be taken as 'proclaim' or 'declare'.

πρὶν ἢ: 'before' or 'until' – Attic would normally write πρὶν ἄν (which can also be found in Herodotus' work).

τὸν ἐνέπρησαν: referring to the temple – 'the one they burnt down'.

χώρης τῆς Μιλησίης: the genitive modifies Assesos (which follows) – 'in Assesos of the Milesian land' i.e 'at Assesos in Milesian territory'.

Chapter 20

Δελφῶν οἶδα ἐγὼ οὕτω ἀκούσας γενέσθαι: an intervention from Herodotus – he reveals his sources (although usually only by naming groups of people rather than individuals) relatively frequently, often giving alternative accounts of events and leaving interpretation open to his readers.

οἶδα ἐγὼ οὕτω ... γενέσθαι: indirect statement with an infinitive after a verb of knowing – 'I know that [it] happened thus . . .', i.e. 'I know this is the case . . .'

Δελφῶν . . . ἀκούσας: the genitive **Δελφῶν** follows **ἀκούσας** – 'having heard [it] of the Delphians', i.e. 'having heard it from . . .'

προστιθεῖσι: Ionic third person plural present tense (Attic: προστιθέασι). The Milesians are the subject while the thing added appears in the accusative (**τάδε**) and the thing added to appears in the dative (**τούτοισι**).

Περίανδρον τὸν Κυψέλου: 'Periander, son of Cypselus' – tyrant of Corinth from 625–585 BCE. He is often considered one of the Seven Sages of Greece and is said to have aided his friend Thrasybulus by devising a stratagem which would trick Alyattes and the Lydians into making peace. Periander is in the accusative as part of an indirect statement following **προστιθεῖσι** – 'they add that . . .'

Θρασυβούλῳ τῷ τότε Μιλήτου τυραννεύοντι: 'Thrasybulus who was then tyrant of Miletus' – during Thrasybulu' rule over Miletus, a war was fought against Lydia under the rule of Alyattes. Thrasybulus is said to have convinced a Lydian messenger that Miletus was still well resourced by putting on a false show of extravagance (detailed in Chapter 21). This deception, suggested by Periander (as mentioned above), caused the Lydians to make peace.

ἐς τὰ μάλιστα: 'to the highest degree' – modifying **ξεῖνον.**

πυθόμενον: agreeing with **Περίανδρον** – **Περίανδρον . . . ἐόντα . . . πυθόμενον** ('Periander being . . . and having learnt . . .').

κατειπεῖν: infinitive to resolve the indirect statement – 'The Milesians add that Periander . . . reported [it – the oracle]'.

ὅκως ἄν: introduces the purpose clause – using **ἄν** with the subjunctive (**βουλεύηται**) creates additional vividness (which using the optative in historic sequence would not).

πρὸς τὸ παρεὸν: 'for the present circumstances' – **παρεὸν** is the present participle (in the neuter) of πάρειμι ('being present'). Combined with the article it becomes simply 'the present'.

Chapter 21

1.21.1

Μιλήσιοι μέν νυν οὕτω λέγουσι γενέσθαι: a very similar pattern to that which started Chapter 20. This is the additional information provided by the Milesians.

σπονδὰς ποιήσασθαι: 'to make a treaty' – **σπονδὰς** is plural as it references the drink offerings (**ἡ σπονδή**) which were made after such truces.

χρόνον ὅσον ἂν: 'for as much time as . . .' – ὅσος is often used with ἄν and the subjunctive when there is uncertainty. Alyattes does not know how long the truce needs to be as he does not know how long it will take to rebuild the temple.

ὁ μὲν δὴ ἀπόστολος ἐς τὴν Μίλητον ἦν: while **ἀπόστολος** is a noun ('he [the herald] was an envoy to Miletus') and the meaning is clear, it is much more easily translated by implying a different verb – 'he was sent as an ambassador to Miletus'.

προπεπυσμένος: the perfect participle of προπυνθάνομαι – 'having heard beforehand'. This is a reference to Periander in Chapter 20.

1.21.2

ἑωυτοῦ καὶ ἰδιωτικός: i.e. Thrasybulus opened up his own stores and demanded that private citizens release their stores of food for the execution of the plan.

τοῦτον πάντα: i.e. the food.

σημήνῃ: (in this instance) 'gave the signal'.

πίνειν τε πάντας καὶ κώμῳ χρᾶσθαι: **πάντας** refers to the Milesians and forms an indirect statement following **προεῖπε** – '[he proclaimed] that they all . . .'

κώμῳ χρᾶσθαι ἐς ἀλλήλους: 'engage in revelry with one another' – by looking as if they have sufficient resources to enjoy themselves, even in a time of war, Thrasybulus hopes the envoy will report these circumstances back to Alyattes who will then reconsider his prospects in the campaign. These sorts of deceptions are not uncommon in ancient literature and these reports were definitely felt to have an impact – Xerxes, for instance, is incredulous at the report of the Spartans combing their hair before the battle of Thermopylae (7.209).

Chapter 22

1.22.1

ταῦτα δὲ ἐποίεέ τε καὶ προηγόρευε Θρασύβουλος: Thrasybulus is the subject of these two verbs, despite his position in the phrase. Both verbs refer to the actions stated in the previous chapter. Although the primary meaning of προαγορεύω is to 'declare beforehand', here it should be taken as 'order publicly'.

τῶνδε εἵνεκεν: i.e. the reasons which Herodotus is about to give.

ὅκως ἂν: as in Chapter 20, this is the beginning of a purpose clause.

κεχυμένον: perfect passive participle of χέω ('I pour') which, when referring to solid articles means 'heaped up'.

ἐν εὐπαθείῃσι ἐόντας: literally, 'being in comfort' – here 'enjoying themselves' or 'making merry' may be more suitable (particularly considering Thrasybulus' instruction in the previous chapter).

1.22.2

τὰ δὴ καὶ ἐγένετο: a slight aside – 'this is what happened'.

εἴπας πρὸς Θρασύβουλον: remember, the herald has been sent to discuss a truce with Thrasybulus. **εἴπας** is an Ionic form of the aorist participle εἰπών ('having spoken') – Herodotus uses both.

τοῦ Λυδοῦ: modifies **τὰς ἐντολὰς** which follows – 'the Lydian's commands'.

ἀπῆλθε ἐς τὰς Σάρδις: when used with **ἐς**, ἀπέρχομαι implies both motion away from the current location and motion towards a destination – 'he departed for Sardis'.

ὡς ἐγὼ πυνθάνομαι: an aside 'as I understand it' or 'so I learn'.

δι᾽ οὐδὲν ἄλλο: literally, 'on account of nothing else', i.e. 'for no other reason'. Thrasybulus' ploy has paid off more than anticipated as **διαλλαγή** suggests a more long-term reconciliation than the truce which was previously sought by Alyattes.

1.22.3

σιτοδείην τε εἶναι ἰσχυρὴν: although ἰσχυρός is usually translated as strong, it can mean powerful in a more abstract sense – with a food shortage it should probably be taken as 'severe'.

τετρῦσθαι ἐς τὸ ἔσχατον κακοῦ: 'had descended to the depths of misery' – **τετρῦσθαι** is perfect passive from τρύω ('I wear out') while ἔσχατος when used with the article means 'the extremes'. Literally, 'had been worn down to the extremes of evil'.

τοῦ κήρυκος νοστήσαντος: while νοστέω can mean either 'I come' or 'I go', here it should be taken with its more well-known meaning of 'return' (as in the English *nostalgia*).

τοὺς ἐναντίους λόγους ἢ ὡς αὐτὸς κατεδόκεε: 'an account which was the opposite of what he had assumed' – καταδοκέω is primarily used by Herodotus and contains a nuance which suggests an individual is prejudiced towards a particular mode of thinking. Alyattes expects Miletus to be in dire straits. It is likely, however, that on account of Miletus' position by the sea (even without

Thrasybulus' scheme) would not have been in as bad a position as the Lydians anticipated.

1.22.4

ἐπ᾽ ᾧ: 'on the condition that' – i.e the terms of the reconciliation were that they would be friends and allies. ξεῖνος implies guest-friendship and hospitality during times of peace while σύμμαχος offers a military alliance during times of war. Again, considerably further than either party envisaged.

δύο τε ἀντὶ ἑνὸς νηοὺς: an immense show of piety on Alyattes' behalf for which he is duly rewarded.

οἰκοδόμησε: ᾠκοδόμησα is the aorist form in Attic dialect, however, Herodotus does not augment **οἰ-** when it appears at the beginning of a verb.

κατὰ ... τὸν ... πόλεμον: in the context of events or situations, κατά with the accusative means 'in relation to' or 'concerning'.

ὧδε ἔσχε: with adverbs ἔχω can carry the nuance of 'turn out'. – 'it turned out in this way'.

23–28: Herodotus digresses briefly, discussing Periander's experience with Arion while he was king of Corinth. Arion, a talented lyre-player and inventor of the dithyramb (a form of music dedicated to Dionysus), voyages from Corinth to Italy and Sicily. On his return journey, the crew of the ship on which he is travelling decide to steal his money and kill him. After an impromptu performance, which the sailors are keen to hear, Arion throws himself into the sea. He is then miraculously conveyed back to Corinth by riding a dolphin. On his arrival, Periander is unsure of the story and questions the sailors who have now arrived in the city. When he reveals Arion, the sailors crack and admit their guilt.

Herodotus returns to the narrative of Alyattes, detailing his death, the offerings he made at Delphi and the succession of his son, Croesus. Croesus continues to make war, attacking Ephesus first and then other Ionian and Aeolian cities. Having subdued the Greeks of Asia, Croesus plans to build ships to attack the Greek islanders. On receipt of advice, Croesus abandons his plans and befriends the Greek islanders while continuing to subjugate other races in Asia. Under him, Sardis reaches the height of its prosperity.

Chapter 29

1.29.1

Σάρδις ἀκμαζούσας πλούτῳ: Sardis is feminine agreeing with the participle. The mention of the city's wealth provides context for the tale which follows although some suggest that it is also a reminder of the perceived money-grabbing nature of the sophists (who are mentioned immediately afterwards).

ἄλλοι τε οἱ πάντες . . . σοφισταί . . . καὶ δὴ καὶ Σόλων: the positioning of **ἄλλοι** is interesting as it seems to exclude Solon from association with the Sophists – 'others, all the Sophists . . . and moreover Solon . . .'

σοφισταί: particularly associated with Athens in the mid- to late fifth century, the sophists were philosophers who taught courses related to language, culture and the natural world. These were usually carried out in the form of private tuition in wealthy households in exchange for money resulting in condemnation from other sectors of ancient society.

ἐτύγχανον ἐόντες: 'happened being', i.e. 'who were living [at the time]'.

ὡς ἕκαστος αὐτῶν ἀπικνέοιτο: the optative shows the haphazard nature of their arrival. Some commentators suggest it shows various means of arrival 'in whatever way each might come' others suggest it shows reason 'on whatever grounds each might come' while others suggest it shows the more itinerant nature of a sophist's lifestyle 'on their several errands'. It seems to make most sense to place the emphasis on their arrival in the city – 'each arriving one by one' – as this shows the draw of the city on a number of individuals.

Σόλων ἀνὴρ Ἀθηναῖος: Solon the Athenian was a lawmaker, statesman (and poet) of the early sixth century BCE. He is credited with a series of reforms to the Athenian constitution around 594 BCE (although the precise date is disputed) which paved the way for the emergence of Athenian democracy in 508 BCE. As a result of these changes, Solon is said to have left Athens for a period of ten years (593–583 BCE) in order to ensure that his laws, which required his presence to be

A
Level

amended or removed, stayed in place. As Croesus did not ascend to the throne of Lydia until 560 BCE, it is highly unlikely that the narrative of Herodotus which follows has any basis in historical fact.

Ἀθηναίοισι νόμους κελεύσασι ποιήσας: Solon remains the subject ('who having made laws') while **κελεύσασι** is dative agreeing with the Athenians ('for the Athenians who had ordered it').

κατὰ θεωρίης πρόφασιν: 'with the pretext of seeing the world' – πρόφασις can suggest a true cause or motive; however, the word is often used of a stated motive (whether true or false). In this instance, the given reason is certainly secondary (even if a welcome benefit) to the political considerations at Athens which necessitated Solon's departure. Some translators choose to reflect this by offering the translation 'saying that he wanted to see the world'.

ἵνα δὴ μή τινα τῶν νόμων ἀναγκασθῇ λῦσαι: unlike the aside which provides us with Solon's stated reason, Herodotus gives the actual reason additional prominence within a purpose clause. When referring to laws, λύω carries the technical meaning of 'repeal' or 'annul'.

τῶν ἔθετο: **τῶν** functions as the relative – '[the laws] which he had made'. Like λύω, τίθημι also functions in a technical capacity when referring to the law meaning 'make' or 'pass'.

1.29.2

οὐκ οἷοί τε ἦσαν αὐτὸ ποιῆσαι: i.e. the act of repealing Solon's laws.

ὁρκίοισι γὰρ μεγάλοισι: 'by sacred oaths' – μεγάλοισι is used figuratively reflecting the seriousness of the oaths which were taken.

χρήσεσθαι: when used in relation to external events χράομαι can be taken as 'be subject to'.

τοὺς ἂν σφι Σόλων θῆται: the use of **ἂν** with the subjunctive θῆται creates an indefinite clause – 'whatever [laws] Solon might make for them'.

Chapter 30

1.30.1

αὐτῶν δὴ ὦν τούτων καὶ τῆς θεωρίης: genitive following **εἵνεκεν**. **αὐτῶν . . . τούτων** refers to the inability of the Athenians to repeal Solon's laws in his absence.

ἐς Αἴγυπτον: Solon's trip to Egypt is also noted by Plato (*Timaeus* 23d) and is given as the origin of the story about Atlantis.

παρὰ Ἄμασιν: when used with a person in the accusative, παρά means 'at the house of' – as Amasis is royalty 'at the court of' may be a more suitable translation. Amasis II was pharaoh of Egypt 569–525 BCE and the last pharaoh before the domination of Egypt by the Persians under Cambyses. He had good relations with various Greek communities, opening up Egypt to Greek trade, and with Croesus in Lydia. Herodotus gives further information about him throughout Book 2 of his work but his rise to power is particularly covered in 2.162–169. Amasis' influence on Solon is also further detailed in 2.177.

A Level

καὶ δὴ καὶ ἐς Σάρδις παρὰ Κροῖσον: as previously mentioned, this is unlikely to be true. **παρὰ Κροῖσον** should be treated in the same way as **παρὰ Ἄμασιν** above.

ἐν τοῖσι βασιληίοισι: plural – treat as singular.

ἡμέρῃ τρίτῃ ἢ τετάρτῃ: dative showing time when 'on the third or fourth day' – inclusive counting means this could be rendered as 'two or three days after'.

κελεύσαντος Κροίσου: genitive absolute – **τὸν Σόλωνα**, which follows, is the object of the later **περιῆγον**, not **κελεύσαντος**.

κατὰ τοὺς θησαυρούς: κατά can be used in a very localized sense – 'around the treasure houses'.

πάντα ἐόντα μεγάλα τε καὶ ὄλβια: 'all the things which were great and blessed', i.e. they showed off all of Croesus' riches. **ὄλβια** will become the theme of the remainder of this interaction. Its introduction here, in relation to material things, highlights the coming difference in understanding between Croesus and Solon when it comes to prosperity. For Croesus prosperity is wealth and possessions while for Solon it is a less tangible concept.

1.30.2

θεησάμενον . . . σκεψάμενον: referring to Solon – accusative (showing person asked) following **εἴρετο** which also takes a second accusative in the form of **τάδε**. This may be more easily dealt with by separating into two clauses in English – 'When Solon had seen and examined all these things . . . Croesus asked him the following.'

ὥς οἱ κατὰ καιρὸν ἦν: – 'when it was the appropriate time for him' – i.e. 'when he found an appropriate opportunity'.

περὶ σέο: 'about you' – **σέο** is Ionic for Attic σου.

λόγος ἀπῖκται πολλὸς: 'much word has arrived' – Solon's reputation precedes him. **ἀπῖκται** is perfect tense.

σοφίης εἵνεκεν τῆς σῆς καὶ πλάνης: some commentators suggest the removal of **εἵνεκεν** and that the genitives (**σοφίης** and **πλάνης**) should instead modify **λόγος** ('much word . . . of your wisdom and wanderings'). The impact of leaving it in is negligible ('much word . . . on account of your wisdom and wanderings') and also allows **περὶ σέο** to sit more comfortably in the phrase.

ὡς φιλοσοφέων . . . ἐπελήλυθας: elaborates further on the information which has arrived in Lydia concerning Solon and his travels – 'how being a lover of wisdom, you have visited . . .' **ἐπελήλυθας** is the perfect tense of ἐπέρχομαι.

ἵμερος . . . μοι ἐπῆλθε: 'a longing has come upon me' – the use of ἐπέρχομαι is figurative (some even go so far as to translate this as 'it occurs to me'). An elaborate means of saying, 'I want to . . .'

εἴ τινα ἤδη πάντων εἶδες ὀλβιώτατον: although traditionally the question asked is remembered as 'who is the happiest man of all', Croesus phrases his question in a slightly more complex way. **εἰ εἶδες** introduces an open question ('if you have seen'), the object of which is **τινα** ('anyone [who is . . .]'). The rest of the question then falls into place around this.

1.30.3

ὀλβιώτατον: echoes of **ὄλβια** (1.30.1).

A Level

ὃ μὲν ἐλπίζων: refers to Croesus – although the implication of the question is reasonably clear, Herodotus spells out his intentions to ensure the moral lesson which follows is not lost.

οὐδὲν ὑποθωπεύσας: 'without using flattery at all' – **οὐδὲν** is more easily taken as an adverb here.

τῷ ἐόντι χρησάμενος: χράομαι has a variety of meanings and, while a simple translation of 'using' would probably work, in this instance 'relying on' or 'keeping to' might be more suitable. **τῷ ἐόντι** is dative following and just means 'that which is' so should be interpreted as 'the truth' or 'reality'.

Τέλλον Ἀθηναῖον: Unless you are already familiar with this story, there is no reason you should have ever heard of Tellus the Athenian – this is precisely the point of Solon's story. Croesus hasn't heard of him either.

1.30.4

τὸ λεχθὲν: 'the thing said' – i.e. 'what was said'.

ἐπιστρεφέως: as an adverb usually translated as 'earnestly' or 'vehemently', the latter is probably more appropriate here (Croesus certainly being unhappy with the answer given), but 'bitterly' or 'spitefully' are probably more nuanced. The root of the word is ἐπιστρέφω – Croesus is verbally turning on Solon.

κοίῃ: Ionic form of the Attic ποίᾳ – 'in what way' or 'how'.

τοῦτο μὲν . . . τοῦτο δὲ: 'first of all . . . but also . . .' – a more emphatic form of the usual **μέν . . . δέ . . .** pattern.

τῆς πόλιος εὖ ἡκούσης: 'of a city doing well' – as an idiom εὖ ἥκειν means 'to do well' or 'to prosper'. i.e. 'he came from a prosperous city'.

καλοί τε κἀγαθοί: this is a common pairing which covers both physical and moral attributes. **κἀγαθοί** is crasis for καί and ἀγαθοί.

σφι εἶδε ἅπασι: 'he saw to them all', i.e. 'he saw them all have . . .'

πάντα παραμείναντα: while the literal meaning of παραμένω is 'I stay beside', here it is being used figuratively – 'survive'. Infant mortality was a big issue in the ancient world so for Tellus to see all of his grandchildren survive would have been considered highly unusual.

τοῦ βίου εὖ ἥκοντι: we have already seen the idiom εὖ ἥκειν being used in relation to Tellus' city. Here it is being used directly in relation to him. **τοῦ βίου** is genitive to show in what respect he was prosperous – 'to him leading a prosperous life'. The participle is dative to show dative of possession with **τελευτὴ** which follows – 'to him leading a prosperous life, the end was . . .'

ὡς τὰ παρ' ἡμῖν: 'as things [are] with us' – Tellus' life may not have been prosperous by Croesus' or wider Lydian standards but, for an Athenian, he was pretty comfortable.

1.30.5

πρὸς τοὺς ἀστυγείτονας ἐν Ἐλευσῖνι: although this sounds like the Athenians are fighting the people of Eleusis, the battle was almost certainly against the Megarians as part of an ongoing war over possession of Salamis. The town of Eleusis (most famous for the Eleusinian Mysteries) was a border town between Athenian and Megarian territory approximately 11 miles north-west of Athens. It now forms part of the greater metropolitan area of the modern city of Athens.

A Level

βοηθήσας: 'having gone to help' – although usually not translated, βοηθέω includes a sense of 'coming to aid' not just of simply helping.

τροπὴν ποιήσας τῶν πολεμίων: literally, 'having made a turn of the enemy', the idiom means that he routed them.

δημοσίῃ: Athenians who fell in war were usually buried in an area of the city known as the Kerameikos and their funerals were paid for from the public purse.

αὐτοῦ τῇ περ ἔπεσε: 'there, on the spot where he fell' – this extra special treatment of Tellus adds an additional level of honour to the manner of his death.

ἐτίμησαν μεγάλως: quite in what form the Athenians honoured him is unclear. Solon probably means that he was remembered as a local hero of sorts. It seems unlikely that any great monument or memorial was built to him (if nothing else, this would not suit the character of Solon's story).

Chapter 31

1.31.1

τὰ κατὰ τὸν Τέλλον: 'concerning Tellus' – this phrase should be taken with **εἴπας πολλά τε καὶ ὀλβία** which follows.

εἴπας πολλά τε καὶ ὀλβία: hendiadys – **πολλά** and **ὀλβία** should be taken together ('the many fortunate circumstances').

ἐπειρώτα: there is a change of subject here – Croesus asked Solon rather than the other way around.

τίνα δεύτερον μετ' ἐκεῖνον ἴδοι: Croesus asks his follow-up question in a similar way to that expressed in Chapter 30 (although here expressed as an indirect question) – 'who he had seen second after him', i.e. who was the second most fortunate man after Tellus. Croesus' character is such that he cannot let the matter drop.

γῶν: Ionic contraction of γοῦν (itself a contraction of γε οὖν) – 'at any rate'. The force is often no more than that carried by γε on its own.

Κλέοβίν τε καὶ Βίτωνα: as previously, Solon's chosen individuals are selected not on the basis of power or wealth but on the nature of their lives and achievements. As with Tellus, Croesus is not expected to have heard of Cleobis or Biton (which undoubtedly means Solon's decision stings all the more).

1.31.2

τούτοισι γὰρ ἐοῦσι γένος Ἀργείοισι: possessive dative – 'for to them . . . there was . . .' **γένος** is accusative of respect – 'being Argive in respect of their race'.

βίος τε ἀρκέων ὑπῆν: although **βίος** is usually translated as 'life' its meaning can extend to 'livelihood'. **ἀρκέων** is from the verb ἀρκέω ('I am sufficient'). Thus 'to them was a sufficient living', i.e. 'they made a good living' or 'had enough to live off'.

πρὸς τούτῳ: 'in addition to this'.

ῥώμη σώματος τοιήδε: 'such strength of body' – they were physically fit and healthy.

ἀεθλοφόροι τε ἀμφότεροι ὁμοίως: although **ἀεθλοφόροι** is an adjective 'bearing the prize' this is easier treated as a verb – 'both were equally successful in athletic contests.'

A Level

ἐούσης ὀρτῆς τῇ Ἥρῃ: the festival of Hera celebrated at Argos (Ἡραῖα) was an important event which was celebrated each year. The festival included an enormous sacrifice, a spear throwing competition and a mystery play commemorating Hera's marriage to Zeus. The extent of the celebrations demonstrate how central Hera was to Argive religion.

ἔδεε πάντως τὴν μητέρα: 'it was absolutely necessary for their mother . . .' The mother of Cleobis and Biton, unnamed here but later recorded as Cydippe by Plutarch, was also priestess of Hera meaning that it was especially urgent for her to be present at the festival. It is possible that the priestess played the role of a bridesmaid in the wedding ceremony.

οἱ δέ σφι βόες: 'their oxen' – **σφι** is possessive dative.

ἐν ὥρῃ: 'in time'.

ἐκκληιόμενοι δὲ τῇ ὥρῃ: 'hindered by the time', i.e. from taking any other course of action.

ὑπὸ τὴν ζεύγλην: 'under the yoke' – the sons take the role of the oxen and convey their mother to the festival. Not only is this a show of great physical strength but of enormous piety towards their mother.

σφι ὠχέετο: 'she was conveyed by them'.

σταδίους δὲ πέντε καὶ τεσσεράκοντα: a Greek stadion (stade) was a unit of measurement the length of which is subject to debate. Estimates vary from around 150 to 200 metres or 164 to 218 yards. Even at the more conservative length, the distance which Cleobis and Biton dragged the wagon would be around 6.75 km or 4.5 miles.

1.31.3

σφι ποιήσασι καὶ ὀφθεῖσι: **ποιήσασι** and **ὀφθεῖσι** are both participles in the dative ('for them having done this and having been seen').

τελευτὴ τοῦ βίου ἀρίστη ἐπεγένετο: although Tellus' death forms a part of Solon's previous story, much greater emphasis is placed on the end of life here. In doing so, Solon develops the theme that it is not the present which should be judged but the entire span of a person's life.

ἐν τούτοισι: 'in them', i.e. 'through Cleobis and Biton'.

ὁ θεὸς: Herodotus regularly refers to an unnamed god when referring to divine phenomena. He does not mean Hera as the patron goddess of the festival (if nothing else the gender of the noun would not be appropriate). 'God' is the simplest rendering.

ὡς ἄμεινον εἴη ἀνθρώπῳ τεθνάναι μᾶλλον ἢ ζώειν: this is the fundamental point of Solon's stories. Both Tellus and Cleobis and Biton can only be treated in this way by Solon as they are no longer alive. The difference in tense between the infinitives **τεθνάναι** (perfect) and **ζώειν** (present) needs to be emphasized 'that it is better *to be dead / to have died* rather than to live.' To die while still in a good position means that there is no longer any possibility of life taking a turn for the worse and, thus, good fortune in life is crystalized at the point of death.

Ἀργεῖοι μὲν . . . αἱ δὲ Ἀργεῖαι: 'the Argive men . . . but the Argive women . . .' – different approaches are taken by the two groups allowing for praise of not only Cleobis and Biton but also their mother.

οἵων τέκνων: 'for the sort of children'.

A Level

1.31.4

τῷ τε ἔργῳ καὶ τῇ φήμῃ: 'at the deed and the praise'.
ἀντίον τοῦ ἀγάλματος: i.e. the statue of Hera in the temple.
εὔχετο . . . ἄριστον ἐστί: this phrase is not as complex as it first appears:

- **εὔχετο** – introduces an indirect statement with **τὴν θεὸν** as the subject and **δοῦναι** as the verb ('prayed that the goddess give').
- **Κλεόβι τε καὶ Βίτωνι τοῖσι ἑωυτῆς τέκνοισι** – this whole phrase is in the dative as the indirect object ('to Cleobis and Biton, who were her children').
- **οἵ μιν ἐτίμησαν μεγάλως** – relative clause describing Cleobis and Biton ('who had honoured her greatly'). Some translators take **μιν** as referring to the goddess but it would seem more natural for it to refer to the mother.
- **τὸ ἀνθρώπῳ τυχεῖν ἄριστον ἐστί** – this whole phrase functions as the object of **δοῦναι** ('that which is best for a man').

1.31.5

ὡς ἔθυσάν τε καὶ εὐωχήθησαν: referring to Cleobis and Biton (although presumably with other participants in the festival).
ἐν αὐτῷ τῷ ἱρῷ: not in the temple proper, but in a building within the precinct.
ἀλλ᾽ ἐν τέλεϊ τούτῳ ἔσχοντο: 'but they were held in this end', i.e. the goddess deemed that the most fitting situation was for them to die and retain the good repute they had gained.
σφέων εἰκόνας ποιησάμενοι ἀνέθεσαν ἐς Δελφοὺς: two *kouroi* statues, usually identified as Cleobis and Biton, can still be seen in the museum at Delphi.
ὡς ἀνδρῶν ἀριστῶν γενομένων: genitive agreeing with **σφέων** earlier in the phrase.

Chapter 32

1.32.1

εὐδαιμονίης δευτερεῖα: 'second place of happiness', i.e. 'second place in happiness'.
ἡ δ᾽ ἡμετέρη εὐδαιμονίη: the use of δέ emphasizes the contrast between Croesus' happiness and the other individuals Solon has mentioned. He is clearly irritated.
τοι ἀπέρριπται: τοι standing in for σοι – 'is cast aside by you'.
ἐς τὸ μηδὲν: the use of **μηδὲν** strengthens **ἀπέρριπται** – 'cast aside to nothing' / 'value at nothing'.
ἰδιωτέων ἀνδρῶν: the primary meaning of ἰδιώτης is to distinguish between public figures (i.e. those involved the workings of the state) and private individuals. It can, however, be used more forcefully than this meaning 'common man' or even 'ignoramus'. Croesus is concerned that Solon views him no better than the ordinary man in the street.
ἡμέας: use of the plural to create grandeur – Croesus is talking only about himself.
ἐπιστάμενόν με . . . ἐπειρωτᾷς: Croesus is the subject of this sentence (**ἐπειρωτᾷς** – 'you ask') while Solon (**με** – me) is the object. Solon is then further modified by **ἐπιστάμενόν** ('who has learnt . . .) The word order can make this appear

A Level

complicated. The theme of a jealous and vengeful divine appears regularly in Herodotus, something which Croesus, who has his mind stuck in human affairs, seems to have no understanding of.

ἀνθρωπηίων πρηγμάτων πέρι: **πέρι** governs **ἀνθρωπηίων πρηγμάτων** and should be taken after **ἐπειρωτᾷς** ('you have asked me about . . .').

1.32.2

ἐν γὰρ τῷ μακρῷ χρόνῳ: 'in the long [span of] time' – Solon is referring to the length of a man's life.

ἐστὶ ἰδεῖν: **ἐστὶ** should be taken in the sense 'it is possible [to see]'.

τὰ μή τις ἐθέλει: 'things which someone would not wish to see' – **μή** introduces a hypothetical statement here.

καὶ παθεῖν: the infinitive still follows **ἐστὶ**.

ἐς γὰρ ἑβδομήκοντα ἔτεα: numerals are commonly found with **ἐς** which should be taken as 'at' or 'about'.

τῆς ζόης ἀνθρώπῳ: 'of life for a man', i.e. 'of a man's life'.

1.32.3

ἐνιαυτοὶ ἑβδομήκοντα: having previously used ἔτος to refer to a year, Herodotus' use of ἐνιαυτός (meaning a cycle or anniversary) allows him to focus on the passing of time (especially as he is about to drill down into the units of time which make up a year). In practice, both words are often indistinguishable in meaning.

διηκοσίας καὶ πεντακισχιλίας καὶ δισμυρίας: Greek numbers are often stacked with the smaller number first (here two hundred and five thousand and twenty thousand giving twenty-five thousand two hundred). It is also worth noting ten thousand (μύριοι) used as an extra unit of counting (although it also has a parallel, figurative, meaning of 'countless' similar to the use of 'myriad' in English). By Solon's reckoning, a year contains 360 days.

ἐμβολίμου μηνὸς μὴ γινομένου: 'an intercalary month not happening', i.e. 'without counting intercalary months'. If Solon's year contains 360 days, the calendar will shift out of alignment with the seasons in a relatively short number of years. Different regions of Greece used different calendars but the use of intercalary months (i.e. an extra month inserted to realign the calendar with the seasons when necessary) was common.

εἰ δὲ δὴ ἐθελήσει τοὔτερον . . . γίνεσθαι: **ἐθέλω** can be used of inanimate objects to express a future event. Here, **τοὔτερον** (crasis for τό and ἕτερον) is the subject – 'if one of the two years becomes . . .' Herodotus' reckoning is a little wide of the mark – inserting an intercalary month every two years would mean the average year was about ten days too long to stay aligned with the seasons. His overall calculation results in a 70-year life, each year consisting of 375 days after the inclusion of intercalary months. Herodotus almost certainly knew this was wrong, but the round numbers make for a simpler calculation within the narrative.

αἱ ὧραι: 'the seasons'.

παραγινόμεναι ἐς τὸ δέον: 'appearing as necessary' – **δέον** is a noun from the neuter participle of δεῖ.

παρὰ τὰ ἑβδομήκοντα ἔτεα: 'during the seventy years'.

A Level

ἐκ τῶν μηνῶν τούτων: 'out of these months', i.e. as a result of inserting these additional months.

1.32.4

τουτων τῶν ἁπασέων ἡμερέων: the use of the genitive does not become clear until you reach **ἡ ἑτέρη αὐτέων** later in the sentence ('of all these days . . . each of them . . .').

παράπαν οὐδὲν ὅμοιον: 'alike in absolutely no respect' – **ὅμοιον** agrees with **πρῆγμα** which follows. Although **πρῆγμα** is often translated as 'business' or 'affair', it is more abstract here ('thing' or 'I') and can almost be omitted in English – 'each one is absolutely unlike any other day'.

πᾶν ἐστὶ ἄνθρωπος συμφορή: 'man is entirely chance' – If an individual has no idea what each day will look like, his circumstances could change at any moment.

1.32.5

φαίνεαι: Ionic second person singular indicative (middle-passive) – 'you seem'.

ἐκεῖνο δὲ τὸ εἴρεό με: 'But the thing which you asked me' – **εἴρεό** is Ionic second person singular.

ἐγὼ λέγω: although usually 'speak' or 'say' **λέγω** can also be taken as 'call' – 'I do not yet call you . . .'

οὐ γάρ τι ὁ μέγα πλούσιος μᾶλλον: Solon is talking in general terms again. **ὁ . . . πλούσιος** refers to a hypothetical rich man. **οὐ . . . τι . . . μαλλον** is used to set up the comparison – '[is] not any more . . .

τοῦ ἐπ' ἡμέρην ἔχοντος: the genitive (**τοῦ ἔχοντος**) completes the comparison – 'than the one having'. **ἐπ' ἡμέρην** means 'sufficient for a day', i.e. living a hand to mouth existence.

τύχη ἐπίσποιτο: **ἐπίσποιτο** is aorist optative of ἐφέπομαι which, when taken with **τύχη** means to 'attend'. Unless good luck stays with an individual right up until the end then what came before was meaningless. It may be more easily translated as 'unless fortune allows him to . . .'

πολλοὶ μὲν . . . πολλοὶ δὲ: Solon sets up the parameters of the argument using an antithesis – the contrast of the rich (but unfortunate) man with the man who has little but is lucky.

ζάπλουτοι: 'exceedingly wealthy' – *ζα* is used as an intensifying prefix.

1.32.6

δυοῖσι . . . μοῦνον: 'in only two respects' – **δυοῖσι** is an Ionic form used in place of δυοῖν.

οὗτος δὲ: brings us back to the fortunate man of moderate means. The parallel structure means that much of the previous statement needs to be implied again – 'the fortunate man surpasses (**προέχει**) . . .'

ὃ μὲν . . . δυνατώτερος: referring to the exceedingly wealthy man. Both **ἐκτελέσαι** and **ἐνεῖκαι** (aorist infinitive of φέρω) follow **δυνατώτερος**.

ὁ δὲ τοῖσιδε προέχει ἐκείνου: a typical rounding off of the narrative – 'and in such ways he surpasses him.'

A Level

οὐκ ὁμοίως δυνατὸς: 'he is not equally able . . .' – referring to the lucky man of moderate means. Interestingly, Herodotus only provides him with the single infinitive **ἐνεῖκαι** ('to bear') for both disaster and his desires.

ἡ εὐτυχίη οἱ ἀπερύκει: the logic of Solon's argument falls down a little here. Having just stated that the rich but unlucky man is superior in two ways (that he can satisfy his desires and weather disaster), Solon immediately states that the lucky man's fortune keeps these away from him. As a result, the rich man surpasses the lucky man in no way at all as he, in the course of his life, will have to service no desires and will experience no disasters.

ἄπηρος δὲ ἐστί, ἄνουσος, ἀπαθὴς κακῶν, εὔπαις, εὐειδής: the list of positive attributes with which Solon finishes his comparison exemplifies the difference in approach taken by the two men.

1.32.7

πρὸς τούτοισι: 'in addition to these things'.

οὗτος ἐκεῖνος τὸν σὺ ζητέεις: the use of both **οὗτος** and **ἐκεῖνος** is difficult to reflect in English – 'this man, the one whom you seek, he . . .'

πρὶν δ' ἂν τελευτήσῃ: the point is hammered home again for Croesus' benefit – death is the moment where fortune in life can be truly measured. Until death there is only luck which can change at any moment.

ἐπισχεῖν: infinitive used in place of an imperative – 'resist!'

1.32.8

συλλαβεῖν ἄνθρωπον ἐόντα ἀδύνατον ἐστί: the subject is the impersonal **ἀδύνατον ἐστί** (it is impossible) while the accusative **ἄνθρωπον ἐόντα** (for one who is human) naturally sits with the infinitive **συλλαβεῖν**.

χώρη οὐδεμία καταρκέει: Plato argues'that man's lack of self-sufficiency is the driving force behind the creation of the *polis*. He, too, recognizes its shortcomings.

ἀλλὰ ἄλλο μὲν ἔχει, ἑτέρου δὲ ἐπιδέεται: the contrast is between **ἄλλο** and **ἑτέρου** – 'it has one thing but needs something else.'

ἣ δὲ ἂν τὰ πλεῖστα ἔχῃ, αὕτη ἀρίστη: the use of **τὰ πλεῖστα** is important here – the best city is the one which has *the most* but they all fall short in something.

ὣς: indistinguishable from οὕτω ('in this way').

τὸ μὲν γὰρ ἔχει, ἄλλου δὲ ἐνδεές ἐστι: parallel with the construction above regarding cities – 'it has something, but is lacking in something else.'

1.32.9

ὃς δ' ἂν αὐτῶν . . . διατελέῃ: hypothetical construction – **ὃς δ' ἂν αὐτῶν** is easiest taken as 'whoever' while **διατελέῃ** (while often meaning 'bring to an end') refers to continuing the course of one's life ('whoever goes through life . . .').

παρ' ἐμοὶ: 'in my opinion'.

τὴν τελευτήν κῇ ἀποβήσεται: 'the end how it turns out' – this phrase may need a little care in English as, despite being the culmination of the argument, it does not translate easily. 'how each situation turns out' may be more natural.

προρρίζους ἀνέτρεψε: the final, somewhat pessimistic, conclusion is one which is echoed elsewhere in Herodotus. Artabanus, Xerxes' uncle, talks of god striking only the high buildings and tall trees. Regardless of your good fortune, and in some cases because of it, god can choose to strike you down utterly in a single moment.

Chapter 33

1.33.1

οὔ κως οὔτε: unlike English, the double negative adds additional force – 'did not in any way'.

ἐχαρίζετο . . . ἀποπέμπεται: although not mentioned, Solon is the subject of **ἐχαρίζετο** while Herodotus abruptly changes subject to Croesus for **ἀποπέμπεται.**

οὔτε λόγου μιν ποιησάμενος οὐδενὸς: literally, 'having made him of no account at all' – this is an idiom meaning 'consider him worth nothing' or 'having no regard for him'. The negative **οὔτε** sits only with the participle, not with **ἀποπέμπεται** which follows.

τὰ παρεόντα ἀγαθὰ: 'present good fortune'.

μετεὶς: aorist participle of μετίημι – 'having cast aside' or 'having ignored'.

τὴν τελευτὴν παντὸς χρήματος ὁρᾶν ἐκέλευε: Croesus has clearly understood Solon's words but, as he will later discover, has not taken them on board. Croesus' later fall from grace valida'es Solon's point of view entirely.

Chapter 34

1.34.1

μετὰ δὲ Σόλωνα οἰχόμενον: the participle **οἰχόμενον** is more easily taken as a noun – 'after Solon's departure . . .'

ἔλαβέ ἐκ θεοῦ νέμεσις μεγάλη Κροῖσον: nemesis, often personified as Νέμεσις, the goddess of retribution, was sent by the gods to administer justice. The name is probably linked to the verb νέμω (I distribute) in the sense that it represents a distribution of fortune based on what is due to an individual. In this instance, Croesus' punishment is retribution for his hubris (arrogance against the gods). Solon has s'ated god's capacity to remove his good fortune, Croesus has dismissed this and will, therefore, reap the appropriate reward. Although ἔλαβέ is usually translated as 'took', 'came upon' might be a more suitable rendering. Again, Herodotus does not cite an individual god, referring only to **ἐκ θεοῦ.**

ὡς εἰκάσαι: εἰκάζω is a difficult word to translate accurately ('I describe by comparison' is one of many possible renderings in the LSJ). As a phrase **ὡς εἰκάσαι** functions as an authorial aside and means 'so it seems'.

ὅτι ἐνόμισε: the particle **ὅτι** is causal here – 'since he thought . . .'

αὐτίκα: heightening the dramatic nature of the divine retribution – in reality, the immediate consequence is a dream, not sudden ruin.

ἐπέστη ὄνειρος: 'a dream appeared' – **ἐπέστη** is the aorist from ἐπίστημι ('I stand near'). When used of dreams 'appeared' is the usual rendering.

τῶν μελλόντων γενέσθαι κακῶν: 'of evils being about to become' – i.e. 'of future evils'

A Level

κατὰ τὸν παῖδα: κατά with the accusative can mean 'concerning' or 'in relation to' when discussing people or events.

1.34.2

τῶν οὕτερος: τῶν functions as a relative pronoun ('of whom') while **οὕτερος** is crasis for **ὁ ἕτερος** ('one [of the two]').

διέφθαρτο: the pluperfect of **διαφθείρω.** The sense of the verb is not as one might expect here'(Croesus' son is disabled, not dead). 'ruined' is possibly more representative of 'erodotus' meaning. While an in-depth examination of disability in the ancient world is outside the scope of this commentary, it is worth noting that ancient perceptions of disability and disabled people were quite different from those of our society.

μακρῷ τὰ πάντα πρῶτος: μακρῷ is used adverbially here ('by far') while **τὰ πάντα** is an accusative of respect ('in all things'). Croesus' other son, by his standards, is a fine specimen of youth.

οὔνομα δέ οἱ ἦν Ἄτυς: Croesus' disabled son, meanwhile, remains unnamed (in a similar fashion'to Gyges' wife).

ὡς ἀπολέει: third person future of ἀπόλλυμι – 'how he [Croesus] would lose . . .'

μιν . . . βληθέντα: although βάλλω means 'I throw' or 'hurl', the passive can be used of people hit by objects which have been thrown. Thus, the participle means 'struck' or 'hit' and modifies **μιν.**

1.34.3

ἑωυτῷ λόγον ἔδωκε: 'he gave a reckoning to himself' – as an idiom 'he pondered' or 'he considered to himself'.

ἄγεται μὲν τῷ παιδὶ γυναῖκα: in a similar fashion to the Latin idiom *in matrimonium ducere*, 'to bring in a wife for his son' means to 'arrange a marriage for his son'.

ἐωθότα . . . στρατηγέειν μιν . . . ἐξέπεμπε: Croesus remains the subject while **μιν** refers to Atys and, along with **ἐωθότα** (accustomed), functions as the object – 'he [in no way] sent out his son who was accustomed to be general . . .'

ἐς τοὺς θαλάμους: although θάλαμος often refers to women's chambers, its more basic meaning is an 'inner room'. Here it refers to store-rooms.

τί οἱ κρεμάμενον: τί refers to one of the aforementioned spears or javelins and is modified by **κρεμάμενον** ('one, hung up') while **οἱ** refers to Croesus (so that, for him, one might not fall . . .) but is probably just as well ignored.

Chapter 35

1.35.1

ἔχοντι δέ οἱ ἐν χερσὶ: as a phrase 'having in his hands' means 'to be occupied with' or 'to be engaged with'. Some editions suggest ἔχοντος instead – this would mean that the phrase referred not to Croesus but to his son (who follows in the genitive). The former ('to Croesus while occupied with . . .') seems to flow more naturally.

συμφορῇ ἐχόμενος: 'held by misfortune', i.e. 'in great distress'.

A Level

οὐ καθαρὸς χεῖρας: 'not pure in respect of his hands' – it is more straightforward to apply **καθαρὸς** to the hands rather than the individual ('with impure hands') or to take a step away from the Greek and use a phrase ('defiled with pollution').

Φρὺξ: 'Phrygian' – Phrygia was a region in modern western-central Turkey.

γένεος δὲ τοῦ βασιληίου: of the royal house of Phrygia.

κατὰ νόμους τοὺς ἐπιχωρίους: 'according to the customs of the land', i.e. in accordance with Lydian custom.

καθαρσίου: the Phrygian traveller (whom we will shortly learn is called Adrastus) has committed a crime for which he requires purification. Such rituals could be carried out in both Greece and Asia Minor and, although different pollutions required different rituals, they often involved washing the hands of the polluted person in the blood of a pig with accompanying prayers to Zeus. The associated pollution for their crime was thought to be washed away with the blood. The word has made its way into English as the term *cathartic*.

1.35.2

παραπλησίη ἡ κάθαρσις: 'the same manner of purification' – it is possible that the rituals around purification were introduced to Greece from Asia Minor.

τὰ νομιζόμενα: the neuter plural participle from νομίζω. Although often taken as 'think', the origin of the word is 'use customarily' so, here, 'things being used cu'tomarily' just means 'customs'.

ἐπυνθάνετο: 'asked' or 'inquired' rather than 'learnt'.

1.35.3

ὤνθρωπε: crasis for ὦ and ἄνθρωπε – there is no real equivalent in English (perhaps 'my dear man' in this context).

ἐπίστιός μοι ἐγένεο: ἐγένεο is an Ionic second-person singular of γίγνομαι, while the adjective **ἐπίστιός** is derived from ἐπί and ἑστία ('the fireplace') giving the'meanin' 'at one's fireplace'. It is conventionally used to show supplication – 'you have become a suppliant to me' or 'you have come to me as a suppliant'.

τίνα . . . ἐφόνευσας: Croesus now gets to the point. Until the ritual is over, custom dictates that Croesus cannot ask questions of the individual requesting purification. Having done so, Croesus is free to ask whatever he likes.

Γορδίεω μὲν τοῦ Μίδεω εἰμὶ παῖς: a double patronymic 'I am the son of Gordias, the son of Midas . . .'

Ἄδρηστος: Adrastus' name has significance – the root is διδράσκω ('I run') with a privative alpha to create the negative. The implication is that he is unable to run and is thus 'doomed'. He is not a positive addition to Croesus' household.

φονεύσας . . . ἀέκων: 'having killed unwillingly' – the claim is one of accidental death.

ἐμεωυτοῦ: Ionic form of ἐμαυτοῦ – 'my own'.

ἐξεληλαμένος: perfect passive participle from ἐξελαύνω – 'having been driven out . . .'

1.35.4

ἀνδρῶν τε φίλων: referring to the royal family of Phrygia. In fact, they would also have been subjects of Croesus' empire at this time.

A
Level

τυγχάνεις ἔκγονος ἐὼν: 'you happen being a relative' – τυγχάνω commonly takes a participle in Greek which is usually translated as an infinitive: 'you happen to be'.

φίλων . . . ἐς φίλους: the repetition of φίλος shows the emphasis placed on familial ties and the effort Croesus is making to provide a warm welcome.

ἐν ἡμετέρου: 'in my house' – the phrase is used several times by Homer and is mirrored in English, e.g. 'I'm going to Michael's.'

συμφορήν τε ταύτην ὡς κουφότατα φέρων κερδανέεις πλεῖστον: the object of **φέρων** is **συμφορήν τε ταύτην** ('bearing this misfortune') which is then modified by **ὡς κουφότατα** ('as lightly as possible'), while **κερδανέεις πλεῖστον** completes the phrase – 'you will derive the most' – i.e. you will get most out of your time here if you don't dwell on what happened.

Chapter 36

1.36.1

ὃ μὲν δὴ δίαιταν εἶχε: 'he kept his way of life . . .' – i.e. 'he lived his life . . .' **ὃ** refers to Adrastus.

ἐν Κροίσου: as with **ἐν ἡμετέρου** (Chapter 35), 'house' needs to be implied here.

ἐν τῷ Μυσίῳ Ὀλύμπῳ: not to be confused with Greece's tallest peak, Mount Olympus, which can be found in Thessaly. There were several mountains named Olympus throughout Greece and Turkey. Mysian Olympus, as its name would suggest, can be found in Mysia, a region in the north-west of modern Turkey. It is now known as Uludağ.

ὑὸς χρῆμα . . . μέγα: the use of **χρῆμα** is roughly equivalent to the English 'thing' ('a great thing of a boar'). It is frequently used to convey the monstrous size of an object or being and is often translated as 'a great beast of . . .'

ὁρμώμενος: the basic meaning of ὁρμάω is to 'set in motion'. Here it is used intransitively (in the middle voice) meaning 'setting oneself in motion'. As such 'set off', 'r'sh"or 'dart' are all potential translations.

τὰ τῶν Μυσῶν ἔργα: 'the works of the Mysians' – **ἔργα** likely refers to agricultural work so should be taken as 'fields' or 'lands'.

διαφθείρεσκε: a past iterative (frequentative) form of the verb showing a repeated action ('kept destroying' or 'would destroy'). It is characterized by the inclusion of – σκ before the verb ending. **ποιέεσκον** in the following sentence is of the same type and should also be treated in this way (although the inclusion of **πολλάκις** makes this redundant to an extent).

κακὸν οὐδέν: i.e. to the boar.

1.36.2

προθυμεόμενοι: the participle is concessive – 'although eager . . .' or 'although exerting ourselves . . .'

τὸν παῖδα: i.e. Atys – clearly Croesus will not want to do this based on his response to the dream already. Fate's power to realize dreams and prophecies, regardless of human interference, is characteristic of Herodotus' work and Greek myth more generally.

A Level

λογάδας νεηνίας: '[a group of] picked men' – 'picked' in the sense of specially chosen for this mission and so, presumably, hunters of some experience and skill.

συμπέμψαι ἡμῖν: **ἡμῖν** is in the dative following **συμπέμψαι** – 'to send them with us'.

μιν: referring to the boar.

1.36.3

τοῦ ὀνείρου τὰ ἔπεα: while **ἔπος** is conventionally translated as word, when referring to dreams or visions it refers specifically to 'prophecy'. Although plural here, it is more easily treated as singular in English.

παιδὸς μὲν πέρι τοῦ ἐμοῦ: unusual word order – **πέρι** should be taken with **παιδὸς**.

μὴ μνησθῆτε ἔτι: 'don't mention . . . again' – Croesus will not entertain the request if it includes the participation of his son.

νεόγαμός τε γάρ ἐστι: Atys' marriage, undoubtedly contrived as a distraction to the young man, also serves as a convenient excuse to refuse the request.

λογάδας: supply **νεηνίας** as in 1.36.2.

τὸ κυνηγέσιον πᾶν: **κυνηγέσιον** is a collective noun as it implies a group of huntsmen – 'the whole hunting party' or 'all my huntsmen' are both reasonable renderings when combined with **πᾶν**.

διακελεύσομαι: the force of διακελεύομαι can vary dramatically from 'encourage' to 'exhort' to 'give strict orders'. The latter seems to reflect the tone most appropriately here.

Chapter 37

1.37.1

ἀποχρεωμένων δὲ τούτοισι: 'being content with this' – the literal meaning of ἀποχράομαι is 'I use to the full extent' but it is used idiomatically to show satisfaction. The participle forms a genitive absolute with **Μυσῶν** which follows.

ἐπεσέρχεται ὁ τοῦ Κροίσου παῖς: **ἐπεσέρχεται** shows that Atys was not part of the original conversation but joined it afterwards.

ἀκηκοὼς: perfect participle – 'having heard'.

οὐ φαμένου: the Ionic form of the present participle from φημί (usually φάς, φᾶσα, φάν is used in Attic Greek). Remember that the formula οὐ φημί is used to suggest refusal.

τόν γε παῖδά: the use of γε emphasizes that this is not a refusal of their request in its entirety. Croesus is willing to send other men, just not his son.

1.37.2

πρότερον κοτὲ: 'in times past' or 'previously' – the pairing of both **πρότερον** (before) and **κοτὲ** (once) is uncomfortable in English.

ἔς τε πολέμους καὶ ἐς ἄγρας φοιτέοντας εὐδοκιμέειν: **εὐδοκιμέειν** is an epexegetical (explanatory) infinitive – '[going to war and on the chase] to win glory was . . .'

A Level

ἀποκλῃίσας ἔχεις: as well as a number of other meanings and uses, ἔχω can function as an auxiliary verb with an aorist participle to create a perfect tense (in a similar fashion to 'have' in English or 'avoir' in French) – 'you have shut me off from . . .' **ἀποκλείω** can be followed by the genitive (cf. 'you have shut me out of . . .').

μοι παριδὼν: in Ionic Greek **παροράω** usually means 'I notice' or 'observe' (while in Attic it can also mean 'I overlook'). The thing which one observes is in the accusative as normal but is often accompanied by a dative signalling the one in which a quality is observed – in this case 'having observed in me . . .'

τέοισί . . . ὄμμασι: a phrase highly reminiscent of Greek tragedy – 'with what face [must I] . . .', i.e. 'how can I show my face . . .?'

ἔς τε ἀγορὴν καὶ ἐξ ἀγορῆς: Herodotus adds a touch of the Greek to Lydian life by referring to the *agora* (he similarly Hellenizes matters shortly after by referring to **πολιήτῃσι** ('the citizens'). Both are thoroughly Greek concepts. The omission of the article is similar to our use of 'down town'.

1.37.3

κοῖος μέν τις: 'what sort of man . . .'

τῇ νεογάμῳ γυναικί: while Croesus' intention was to prevent Atys from doing such things by distracting him with his new wife, there is a certain irony that Atys views this as a good reason for playing an active role in affairs. As always, divine will outwits the schemes of men.

λόγῳ ἀνάπεισον ὅκως: literally, 'convince me with argument how . . .' but more naturally, 'explain to me why' – this desire to be persuaded by logical argument feels very Greek in nature (as does much of the encounter). Croesus' court would likely have been run on the basis of his authority alone without such challenge as this (even from his own son).

Chapter 38

1.38.1

ἀμείβεται Κροῖσος τοῖσιδε: having already started the previous chapter with **ἀμείψατο**, Herodotus shifts to the present tense and begins not only this chapter but also Chapters 39 and 40 (and later 42) with exactly the same form of the verb creating a back and forth in the discussion.

οὔτε δειλίην οὔτε ἄλλο οὐδὲν ἄχαρι παριδών τοι: the structure is the same as that used in the previous chapter (using **τοι** – 'in you'). **ἄχαρι** is the neuter form of ἄχαρις and is, therefore, accusative agreeing with **οὐδὲν**.

ὄψις ὀνείρου ἐν τῷ ὕπνῳ: 'the vision of a dream in my sleep' – this is unwieldy in English and can be smoothed either by expansion (e.g. 'a vision in a dream while I slept') or contraction (e.g. 'a vision in my sleep'). As mentioned in Chapter 34 **ἐπιστᾶσα** (from **ἐπίστημι**) is often used of dreams. Perhaps 'having come upon me' would provide an appropriate level of drama.

σε ὀλιγοχρόνιον ἔσεσθαι: i.e. he would die.

ἀπολέεσθαι: future infinitive from ἀπόλλυμι – this is a continuation of the previous accusative and infinitive construction. **σε** needs to be supplied again.

A Level

1.38.2

πρὸς ὧν τὴν ὄψιν ταύτην: when used with the accusative, πρός can show result – 'as a consequence of this dream . . .'

ἐπὶ τὰ παραλαμβανόμενα: as a substantive **παραλαμβανόμενα** means 'undertakings'.

φυλακὴν ἔχων: 'keeping watch' – understand 'over you'.

εἴ κως δυναίμην: 'if somehow I might be able . . .' – i.e. 'so that perhaps I could . . .'

σε ζόης διακλέψαι: the root meaning of διακλέπτω is 'I keep back by stealth' or 'I steal at different times'. Herodotus uses it with a very particular, nuanced meaning – 'I keep alive' or 'I save by stealth'. Presumably the development is based on the idea of snatching someone away from death.

εἷς γάρ μοι μοῦνος τυγχάνεις ἐὼν παῖς: we know this is not true. Croesus will elaborate on his feelings concerning the other son. **τυγχάνεις ἐὼν** – 'you happen being . . .', i.e. 'you happen to be . . .'

τὸν γὰρ δὴ ἕτερον . . . οὐκ εἶναί μοι λογίζομαι: 'I do not reckon the other to exist for me' – a striking example of the differing attitudes towards people with disabilities. Croesus' disabled child does not count.

τὴν ἀκοὴν: accusative of respect ('in respect of his hearing'). Some editors dispute these words as the son has already been described as κωφός (mute) in Chapter 34. The lack of precision, however, does not seem to be unreasonable for a Greek author.

Chapter 39

1.39.1

συγγνώμη . . . τοι: '[there is] forgiveness for you', i.e. 'no one could blame you'.

ἰδόντι: dative agreeing with **τοι** ('you, who saw . . .').

περὶ . . . ἔχειν: 'for keeping . . .'

τὸ δὲ οὐ μανθάνεις: **τὸ** is the object of **μανθάνεις** – 'that which you do not understand . . .'

ἀλλὰ λέληθέ σε τὸ ὄνειρον: literally, 'but the dream has escaped you' – it is worth expanding this slightly (consider 'but *the meaning of* the dream has escaped you'. **λέληθέ** is perfect tense from λανθάνω.

ἐμέ τοί δίκαιον ἐστί φράζειν: this phrase brings the previous two together – 'it is right for me to show to you [that which you do not understand . . .]'.

1.39.2

ὑὸς δὲ κοῖαι μὲν εἰσὶ χεῖρες: 'What sort are the hands of a boar?', i.e. 'What sort of hands does a boar have?' The same construction is repeated immediately after (**κοίη δὲ αἰχμὴ σιδηρέη . . .**)

σὺ φοβέαι: Ionic second person singular ('you fear').

τοι εἶπε: the dream is the implied subject.

ἢ ἄλλου τευ: 'or by something else' – **τευ** is Ionic for the genitive τινος. The genitives are following **ὑπὸ** ('by') on the previous line.

ὅ τι τούτῳ ἔοικε: 'which was suitable for this' – **τούτῳ** refers to the scenario with the boar. If Croesus has seen anything in the dream which related to a boar, Atys would have been convinced.

A Level

χρῆν δή σε ποιέειν: following **εἰ** introducing the protasis, you might have expected the apodosis to resolve with ἄν. It is not normally included with **χρῆν** but should still be implied – 'it would have been necessary / right for you to do . . .'
νῦν δὲ: referring to circumstances rather than time – 'but as it is . . .'
ὑπὸ αἰχμῆς: a fragment which needs expanding – 'the dream said . . .'
οὐ πρὸς ἄνδρας ἡμῖν γίνεται ἡ μάχη: clearly Atys has in mind that spears are used on the battlefield, forgetting (somewhat foolishly) that they are also an integral feature of a hunt. That this argument also persuades Croesus seems equally strange.

Chapter 40

1.40.1
ἔστι τῇ: 'somehow' – Croesus is not entirely convinced but is won over all the same (perhaps other forces are at play here).
τοῦ ἐνυπνίου: 'the dream' – in origin, the thing seen 'in sleep' (variation on ὄνειρον which has been used several times already).

Chapter 41

1.41.1
συμφορῇ πεπληγμένον ἀχάρι: 'struck by unseemly misfortune' – **ἀχάρι** is dative agreeing with **συμφορῇ**.
τήν τοι οὐκ ὀνειδίζω: **τήν** refers back to **συμφορῇ** and is accusative following **ὀνειδίζω** while **τοι** is dative referring to Adrastus – 'for which I do not blame you'.
ὑποδεξάμενος ἔχω: as in Chapter 37, **ἔχω** is here used as an auxiliary verb with the aorist participle. The sense is present perfective as the action is ongoing – 'I have welcomed you [and still do] . . .'
παρέχων πᾶσαν δαπάνην: 'covering all your costs' – δαπάνη refers to upkeep.

1.41.2
ὀφείλεις . . . με ἀμείβεσθαι: like *debeo* in Latin, ὀφείλω can be used with both a noun (*I owe*) or with an infinitive (*I ought*). Here it is used with **ἀμείβεσθαι**, more commonly seen with dialogue meaning 'to reply', but which here means 'give in return'.
ἐμεῦ προποιήσαντος χρηστὰ: genitive absolute – 'since I have done good service'.
φύλακα παιδός σε τοῦ ἐμοῦ χρηίζω γενέσθαι: the interleaving of forms is interesting here. More straightforwardly:

- **χρηίζω σε γενέσθαι φύλακα** – 'I ask you to become a guardian.'
- **παιδός τοῦ ἐμοῦ** – 'of my son'.

ὁρμωμένου: agreeing with **παιδός** – 'my son as he hastens to the hunt.'
μή . . . φανέωσι ὑμῖν: **μή** stands for ἵνα μή 'lest' and follows **φύλακα** ('be a guardian lest . . .') The clause is completed by **φανέωσι** ('lest they appear before you').

A Level

ἐπὶ δηλήσι: the use of the noun is tricky in English ('to your detriment') – a verbal phrase might be more appropriate ('to do you harm').

1.41.3

πρὸς δὲ τούτῳ: 'in addition', 'moreover', 'on top of this'.

σέ τοι χρεόν ἐστι: the use of **τοι** adds emphasis to **σέ** – 'certainly it is necessary that you . . .' **σέ** is accusative following **χρεόν**.

ἔνθα ἀπολαμπρυνέαι: 'where you will be made famous' – **ἀπολαμπρυνέαι** is Ionic second person middle / passive of ἀπολαμπρύνω. Croesus' warm words, encouraging Adrastus, foreshadow the terrible events which are to follow.

πατρώιόν τε γάρ τοι ἐστὶ: a slightly cryptic phrase with much needing to be implied – 'it is [right] for you that your patrimony [be made famous by these deeds]'. Most translators opt for something rather more brief – 'that is right for your father's son'.

προσέτι ῥώμη ὑπάρχει: 'besides, there is sufficient strength' – **τοι** needs to be supplied again and should be taken as possessive ('besides, you have sufficient strength'). Croesus' words will prove to be fatal to his own son as it is against him that Adrastus' strength will be deployed. They also bring to mind the contrast with Croesus' other son of whom little account is taken because of his disability.

Chapter 42

1.42.1

ἔγωγε ἂν οὐκ ἤια: **ἤια** is an Ionic form of the imperfect of εἶμι ('I will go'). When combined with **ἂν** it creates a closed conditional – 'I would not have gone.'

ἐς ἄεθλον τοιόνδε: 'into such an arena' – i.e. on the hunt. Adrastus feels that the shame he has suffered should preclude him from engaging in such prestigious activities with others.

κεχρημένον: perfect participle from **χράομαι** but with the meaning 'experience' or 'suffer' – the force of the perfect is present perfective (i.e. the effect of the past action is still current) 'one who has experienced such misfortune' meaning 'one so unfortunate'.

οἰκός: Ionic participle (Attic: εἰκός) from ἔοικα ('I am fitting'). As a phrase with **ἐστι** – 'it is reasonable' or 'it is suitable'.

ἐς ὁμήλικας . . . ἰέναι: when used with people, εἶμι can carry the sense of 'associate with' or 'consort with'.

εὖ πρήσσοντας: literally, 'faring well', i.e 'prosperous'.

τὸ βούλεσθαι πάρα: here **πάρα** stands for πάρεστι. **τὸ** stands with the infinitive **βούλεσθαι** to form a noun – '[nor] is the desire present', i.e. '[nor] would I want to . . .'

πολλαχῇ: although often of place ('in many places') read as 'for many reasons'.

ἂν ἶσχον ἐμεωυτόν: again, a closed conditional – 'I would have held myself back,' i.e. Adrastus would not have gone on the hunt.

1.42.2

ἐπείτε: causal – 'since'.

A Level

σὺ σπεύδεις: the variety of nuances which σπεύδω can carry can lead to confusion. The sense here is 'urge' or 'encourage'.

δεῖ: imply 'for me' or 'that I'.

ὀφείλω γάρ σε ἀμείβεσθαι χρηστοῖσι: Adrastus echoes Croesus' words signalling his agreement and obligation to him.

παῖδα τε σόν: the object of **προσδόκα** which follows – 'expect your son'.

τὸν διακελεύεαι φυλάσσειν: **τὸν** functions as the relative – 'whom you order [me] to watch over'.

τοῦ φυλάσσοντος εἵνεκεν: while **εἵνεκεν** should usually be taken as 'on account of' the meaning here is more like 'as far as regards' – i.e. 'as far as depends on the one watching over him . . .' Adrastus is suggesting that he will do everything he is capable of to ensure Atys' safety.

Chapter 43

1.43.1

οὗτος: i.e. Adrastus.

μετὰ ταῦτα: adverbial – 'presently' or 'immediately'.

Ὄλυμπον τὸ ὄρος: as mentioned in Chapter 36, Mysian Olympus in modern Turkey.

περιστάντες αὐτὸ κύκλῳ: 'stand around it in a circle', i.e. 'surrounded it' or 'encircled it'.

ἐσηκόντιζον: the use of the imperfect suggests a prolonged attack rather than a single strike.

1.43.2

ὁ ξεῖνος: Herodotus' use of **ξεῖνος** is poignant as it recalls the ties of guest-friendship and obligation to which Croesus referred earlier. Adrastus' actions will betray the welcome which Croesus has offered him.

οὗτος δὴ ὁ καθαρθεὶς τὸν φόνον: Herodotus adds further weight by reminding us of the purification which Adrastus received. **δὴ** emphasizes this all the more 'he indeed who had been cleansed of his blood-guilt . . .'

καλεόμενος δὲ Ἄδρηστος: despite having already introduced his readers to Adrastus by name, Herodotus is compelled to name him again so that there can be no doubt in our minds. His name, as mentioned in Chapter 35, has great significance as, by his actions, Adrastus completes his own doom. The alternative interpretation of his name, *the inescapable*, is also relevant as he is the medium by which Atys meets his fate.

ἀκοντίζων τὸν ὗν τοῦ μὲν ἁμαρτάνει: **τὸν ὗν** is the object of **ἀκοντίζων** while **τοῦ** follows **ἁμαρτάνει** ('he misses it'). It is also worthwhile noting the shift to the present tense as the action unfolds.

τυγχάνει δὲ τοῦ Κροίσου παιδός: some have suggested a link between Croesus' son, Atys, and the cult of Attis (or Atys) a localized deity of Phrygia who introduced the cult of Cybele to Lydia. His affection for the goddess drove Zeus to send a boar to Lydia which killed Attis. Although the link is unlikely, the similarities are nonetheless interesting.

1.43.3

ὁ μὲν δὴ βληθεὶς: referring to Atys.

τὴν φήμην: although often referring to 'fame' or 'repute' φήμη also refers to prophetic utterances of the gods. Here 'prophecy' or 'message' may be appropriate.

ἔθεε δέ τις ἀγγελέων τῷ Κροίσῳ: supply '*to tell* Croesus . . .'

τὸ γεγονός: perfect participle from γίγνομαι – 'what had happened'.

τὴν τε μάχην: i.e. with the boar.

Chapter 44

1.44.1

συντεταραγμένος: συνταράσσω can be used literally (e.g. on the battlefield) as 'throw into confusion' but also figuratively of the mind. Here, the latter is clearly the case – 'disturbed' may be a reasonable translation.

μᾶλλον τι: Herodotus is keen on using **τι** to strengthen **μᾶλλον** – 'all the more'.

ὅτι μιν ἀπέκτεινε τὸν αὐτὸς: 'since he killed him whom he himself . . .' A slightly tricky phrase, it can be broken down as follows:

- Adrastus is the subject of **ἀπέκτεινε**.
- **μιν** refers to Atys.
- **τὸν** functions as a relative and refers again to Arastus.
- **αὐτὸς** refers to Croesus.

The fact that Croesus cleansed Adrastus of his guilt and it is he who goes on to fulfil the prophecy in Croesus' dream is all the more galling for him.

1.44.2

Δία καθάρσιον . . . ἐπίστιόν. . . ἑταιρήιον: among his other roles, Croesus calls upon Zeus in three very specific ways:

- 'the purifier'
- 'at the fireside'
- 'of fellowship'

Zeus' role of purification was an official title at sanctuaries in both Olympia and Athens. All three titles, however, reflect his role as the patron god of hospitality (Ζεὺς ξένιος). Croesus' call to Zeus to witness the events which have befallen his son likely reflect both his anger that Zeus has allowed such things to happen, despite Croesus' efforts to help Adrastus, and his wish that Adrastus be punished for his actions.

μαρτυρόμενος τὰ . . . πεπονθὼς εἴη: 'calling him to witness the things he had suffered' – **πεπονθὼς εἴη** is a periphrastic form of the perfect active optative using the participle and the optative form of **εἰμί** (as an alternative to πεπόνθοι). The optative is used here as the indirect question is in historic sequence following **ἐκάλεε**.

A Level

τὸν αὐτὸν τοῦτον ὀνομάζων θεόν: 'naming this same god' – i.e. all three names apply to Zeus. Croesus is invoking him in a variety of capacities.

ἐλάνθανε βόσκων: although λανθάνω usually refers to undertaking an action without others noticing, here Herodotus uses it to mean that Croesus took the action without realising what he himself was doing. 'he had nourished [his son's murderer] without realizing' or simply 'unaware' are reasonable translations here.

ὡς . . . αὐτὸν εὑρήκοι: the optative can be used when quoting a causal sentence. Rather than following the structure introduced with **διότι** for his previous explanation, Herodotus chooses to introduce the causal structure with **ὡς** and follow with the optative ('since he had found that he was . . .'

πολεμιώτατον: the choice of vocabulary is powerful and reflects Croesus' heightened emotional state. Despite Adrastus' intentions and the role of fate in proceedings, Croesus still labels him 'most hostile' or 'his worst enemy'. Since πολέμιος usually refers to an enemy in war, Croesus leaves no room for chance or accident in his assessment of the situation. The contrast with **φύλακα** (that he sent him 'as a guard') heightens the futility of trying to avoid one's destiny.

Chapter 45

1.45.1

μετὰ τοῦτο: 'soon after' – i.e. after Croesus learnt of his son's death.

ὄπισθε δὲ εἵπετό οἱ ὁ φονεύς: Adrastus keeps himself separate from the group as a reflection of his status as an outcast.

παρεδίδου ἑωυτὸν Κροίσῳ: Adrastus accepts his fate completely. Herodotus heightens this feeling through **προτείνων τὰς χεῖρας** ('stretching out his hands'), an act of total surrender and supplication to Croesus' power.

ἐπικατασφάξαι μιν κελεύων τῷ νεκρῷ: Herodotus shows Adrastus as an honourable man, accepting nothing less than complete recompense through the spilling of his own blood. **μιν** is reflexive, referring to Adrastus, while **τῷ νεκρῷ** is dative governed by the verb **ἐπικατασφάξαι** ('to slay . . . over'). The verb itself is powerful potentially implying a more violent death (σφάζω: 'slay' or 'slaughter') and often refers to the cutting of an animal's throat in sacrificial contexts. Adrastus is offering himself as a ritual sacrifice to appease Croesus and the gods.

λέγων τήν τε προτέρην ἑωυτοῦ συμφορήν: Adrastus clearly feels he is still, and will continue to be, tainted with pollution. As such, he may as well forfeit his life.

ὡς . . . τὸν καθήραντα ἀπολωλεκὼς εἴη: as in 44.2, Herodotus expresses Adrastus' reason using **ὡς** with the optative. Again, as also seen in the previous chapter, the perfect optative is periphrastic using the participle and **εἰμί**. Clearly ἀπόλλυμι means a figurative 'undoing' rather than a literal destruction as its object (**τὸν καθήραντα**) refers to Croesus and not his son, Atys. Certainly, Adrastus feels the same level of guilt about his betrayal of Croesus, given his hospitality towards him, as Croesus feels responsibility and anger for taking in the killer of his son.

ἐπ' ἐκείνῃ: 'on top of that' or 'in addition'.

A Level

οὐδέ οἱ εἴη βιώσιμον: despite no negative in the previous clause, Herodotus links the two with **οὐδέ**. Although **βιώσιμον** is an adjective (βιώσιμος -ον) it carries a sense of necessity or obligation (similar to a Latin gerundive) and should be taken as 'ought to live' or 'right to live'. It is further complicated as the verb (**εἴη**) is impersonal (explaining why **βιώσιμον** is neuter) with possessive dative **οἱ** – 'and for him it was not right to live', i.e. 'he should live no more'.

1.45.2

τούτων ἀκούσας: although usually the accusative is used after things heard while the genitive refers to people, Herodotus uses both interchangeably.

τόν τε Ἄδρηστον κατοικτείρει: Adrastus' willingness to pay the ultimate price induces a sudden change of heart in Croesus.

καίπερ ἐὼν ἐν κακῷ οἰκηίῳ τοσούτῳ: referring to Croesus – despite his own sorrows, Croesus can still be moved to compassion.

ἐπειδὴ σεωυτοῦ καταδικάζεις θάνατον: Croesus is absolutely open about his feelings. Seeing Adrastus accepting responsibility is what has moved Croesus to pity so quickly.

εἶς δὲ οὐ σύ μοι . . . αἴτιος: **εἶς** is an Ionic second person singular form of **εἰμί** – 'you are not to blame . . .' The dative **μοι** ('for me') heightens that this is Croesus' judgement – 'as far as I am concerned . . .').

εἰ μὴ ὅσον: 'except in as much as' – **ὅσον** is used adverbially here.

ἐξεργάσαο: Ionic second person singular aorist (unaugmented) – 'you brought it about'.

κού: 'doubtless'.

τὰ μέλλοντα ἔσεσθαι: 'the things which were going to be' – i.e. 'what would happen' or 'what the future would hold'. Croesus now recognizes the unavoidable nature of fate and, to some extent, the truth of Solon's earlier words: God can bring a man down at any time.

1.45.3

ὡς οἰκὸς ἦν: referring to the style of the burial (i.e. under a funeral mound in a way which was suitable for the son of a king) rather than it being a fitting thing for Croesus to bury him at all.

Ἄδρηστος δὲ ὁ Γορδίεω τοῦ Μίδεω: the restating of Adrastus' lineage (previously given 1.35.3) increases the dramatic tension by lending gravitas to the moment.

ὁ φονεὺς μὲν τοῦ ἑωυτοῦ ἀδελφεοῦ . . . φονεὺς δὲ τοῦ καθήραντος: the charge sheet against Adrastus ('murderer of his own brother . . . murderer of the man who purified him') is severe. Both actions are crimes against the gods as well as man. This reiteration of his crimes also emphasizes how, rather than improving his situation, Adrastus' time in Croesus' household has only made matters worse. As with ἀπόλλυμι in 1.45.1 Adrastus is not the literal murderer (**φονεὺς**) of Croesus, however, the use of the word is a reflection of the destruction Adrastus has brought to Croesus' life.

ἡσυχίη τῶν ἀνθρώπων: while **ἡσυχίη** usually is taken to mean 'quiet' or 'peace' with the genitive which follows (literally, 'quiet of men') it shows the absence of people – 'there was no one . . .'

A Level

ἀνθρώπων εἶναι τῶν αὐτὸς ᾔδεε: **εἶναι** signals a nominative and infinitive following **συγγινωσκόμενος** ('recognizing that he was . . .') while the genitive **ἀνθρώπων** follows and is modified by **τῶν** which is functioning as a relative pronoun (he was of the men whom [he knew] . . .).

ἐπικατασφάζει τῷ τύμβῳ ἑωυτόν: to mirror the request which Adrastus made of Croesus, Herodotus uses the same verb for his sacrificial final act. As before, **τῷ τύμβῳ** is dative following **ἐπικατασφάζει**.

A Level

Vocabulary

An asterisk (*) denotes a word (or its equivalent Attic form) which is in OCR's defined vocabulary list for AS. Some specific forms of verbs which are unique to Herodotus are also noted.

***ἀγαθός -ή -όν**	good, brave, gentle
ἄγαλμα -ατος, τό	statue (of a god)
***ἀγγέλλω**	I announce, I report
***ἄγγελος -ου, ὁ, ἡ**	messenger, envoy
***ἀγορή -ῆς, ἡ**	marketplace, agora
ἄγρη -ης, ἡ	hunting, the chase
ἀγρός -οῦ, ὁ	field, land
ἀγχοῦ (+ gen.)	near
***ἄγω**, aor. **ἤγαγον**	I lead, bring
***ἀδελφεός -οῦ, ὁ**	brother
ἀδίκημα -ατος, τό	wrong, injury
***ἀδικίη -ης, ἡ**	wrongdoing, offence
***ἄδικος -ον**	wrongdoing, unjust
Ἄδρηστος -ου, ὁ	Adrastus (son of the Phrygian king, Gordias)
ἀδύνατος -ον	impossible, unable
ἄεθλος -ου, ὁ	contest, struggle, arena (Attic: ἆθλος)
ἀεθλοφόρος -ον	victorious, bearing the prize
***ἀέκων -ουσα -ον**	unwillingly, involuntarily, accidentally (Attic: ἄκων)
Ἀθηναίη -ης, ἡ	Athena (Attic: Ἀθηνᾶ)
***Ἀθηναῖος -η -ον**	Athenian
ἀθυμίη -ης, ἡ	lack of spirit, faintheartedness
Αἶα -ης, ἡ	Aea
Αἰγύπτιος -α -ον	Egyptian
Αἴγυπτος -ου, ἡ	Egypt
***αἰδέομαι**	I am ashamed, I stand in fear of
αἰδώς -όος, ἡ	shame, modesty
***αἰεί**	always (Attic: ἀεί)
Αἰολέες -ων, οἱ	the Aeolians
αἵρεσις -εως, ἡ	taking, choice
***αἱρέω**, aor. **εἷλον**	I take, I grasp, I capture (in mid.) I prefer, I choose
αἰσχύνη -ης, ἡ	shame, dishonour
***αἰσχύνω**, aor. pass. **ᾐσχύνθην**	I dishonour, I shame, (in pass. I feel shame
***αἰτεω**	I ask for, I demand, I beg
***αἰτίη -ης, ἡ**	cause, reason
***αἴτιος -α -ον**	to blame, responsible
αἰχμή -ῆς, ἡ	spear, point of a spear
αἰχμοφόρος -ον	spearman, bodyguard
αἰών -ῶνος, ὁ	life, lifetime
ἀκλεής -ές	without fame
ἀκμάζω	I flourish, I abound in
ἀκοή -ῆς, ἡ	hearing, sense of hearing
ἀκοντίζω	I throw a javelin at
ἀκόντιον -ου, τό	javelin
***ἀκούω**, perf. **ἀκήκοα**, perf. ppl. **ἀκηκοώς**	I hear
Ἀλέξανδρος -ου, ὁ	Alexander (Greek rendering of Paris)
ἀληθείη -ης, ἡ	truth
ἀληθέως	truly, in reality
Ἁλικαρνησεύς -έος, ὁ	Halicarnassian, of Halicarnassus
***ἀλλά**	but
ἄλλῃ	elsewhere, among other places
***ἀλλήλων**	one another
***ἄλλος -η -ο**	other, another, the rest
ἄλλως	otherwise

Ἀλυάττης -ου, ὁ	Alyattes, father of Croesus
Ἅλυς -υος, ὁ	the River Halys
ἅλωσις -ιος, ἡ	capture, conquest
***ἅμα**	at once, at the same time, (with καί) no sooner . . . than . . .
ἀμαθής -ές	ignorant, stupid, foolish
ἅμαξα -ης, ἡ	wagon, cart
***ἁμαρτάνω**	I fail, I miss (esp. of spears)
Ἄμασις -ιος, ὁ	Amasis (the last ruler of Egypt prior to the Persian invasion)
ἀμείβω, aor. mid. **ἀμειψάμην**	I change, I exchange, I give in exchange, I reply, I answer
ἀμείνων -ον	better (compar. of ἀγαθός)
ἀμηχανάω, fut. **ἀμηχανήσω**	I am at a loss for, I am in want of, I am in need of
***ἀμφότερος -α -ον**	either, both
***ἄν**	would (+ opt.)
ἀναβοάω, aor. **ἀνέβωσα**, aor. ppl. **ἀμβώσας**	I cry out, I cry aloud
***ἀναγκάζω**, aor. pass. **ἠναγκάσθην**	I force, I compel
***ἀναγκαίη -ης, ἡ**	force, compulsion, necessity (Attic: ἀνάγκη)
ἀναιρέω, aor. **ἀνεῖλον**	(of oracles) I appoint, I ordain
ἀναπαύω	I rest, (in mid.) I take rest, I sleep
ἀναπείθω, aor. **ἀνέπεισα**	I persuade, I convince
ἀνατίθημι, aor. **ἀνέθηκα**	I set up, I dedicate
ἀνατρέπω, aor. **ἀνέτρεψα**	I ruin, I overthrow
ἀναφαίνω, aor. pass. **ἀνεφάνην**	I show, (in pass.) I appear openly
ἀνδρέων -ῶνος, ὁ	men's quarters, men's apartment
***ἄνεμος -ου, ὁ**	wind
***ἀνήρ, ἀνδρός, ὁ**	man
ἀνθρωπήϊος -η -ον	human, of man
***ἄνθρωπος -ου, ὁ**	man, human being
ἀνίστημι, aor. **ἀνέστησα** or **ἀνέστην**	I stand up, I wake, I rise, (of sickness) I recover
ἀνόητος -ον	foolish, senseless
ἀνοίγνυμι	I open, (in pass.) be open, stand open
ἀνόλβιος -ον	wretched, luckless, unfortunate
ἄνομος -ον	lawless, impious
ἀνορθόω, aor. **ἀνώρθωσα**	I restore, I rebuild
ἄνουσος -ον	without sickness
***ἀντί** (+ gen.)	instead of
ἀντίον	before, in front of
***ἄξιος -η -ον**	worthy of
ἀπαγινέω	I lead away, carry off, bring
ἀπαγωγή -ῆς, ἡ	leading away, (of money) payment
ἀπαθής -ές	without suffering
ἀπαιτέω	demand back, demand to have returned
ἀπαλλαγή -ῆς, ἡ	[means of] escape, getting away
***ἅπας, ἅπασα, ἅπαν**	all
ἀπερύκω	I keep [acc.] from [dat.]
ἀπέρχομαι, aor. **ἀπῆλθον**	I go away, I go back
ἀπηγέομαι	I lead the way, tell, relate
ἀπήμων -ον	unhurt, unharmed
ἄπηρος -ον	unmaimed, without deformity
***ἀπικνέομαι**, aor. **ἀπικόμην**, perf. **ἀπῖγμαι**	I arrive at, come to, reach (Attic: ἀφικνέομαι)
ἄπιστος -ον	untrustworthy, suspicious
***ἀπό** (+ gen.)	from
ἀποβαίνω, fut. **ἀποβήσομαι,**	(of events) I turn out, I resolve
ἀπόγονος, ον	born from, descendant, generation
ἀποδείκνυμι, aor. pass. **ἀπεδέχθην**	I display, I bring forward, I produce
ἀπόδεξις -εως, ἡ	display, setting forth
ἀποδημέω, aor. **ἀπεδήμησα**	I am abroad, I am on my travels
ἀποδίδωμι, aor. inf. **ἀποδοῦναι**	I give back, I return, I restore
***ἀποθνήσκω**, aor. **ἀπέθανον**	I die, I am killed
ἀποθωμάζω	I marvel greatly at, I am greatly astonished (Attic: ἀποθαυμάζω)
ἀποκλείω, aor. part. **ἀποκληίσας**	I shut off, I exclude from
***ἀποκτείνω**	I kill, I slay
ἀπολαμπρύνω	I make famous, I make bright

***ἀπόλλυμι**, pres. inf. **ἀπολλύναι**, pres. inf. mid./pass. **ἀπόλλυσθαι**, fut. **ἀπολέω**, perf. inf. **ἀπολωλέναι**, perf. ppl. **ἀπολωλεκώς**	I destroy utterly, I kill, I lose, (in mid.) I die, I perish
ἀπομάχομαι	I fight off, I resist, I decline
ἀπονοστέω, fut. inf. **ἀπονοστήσειν**	I return, I come home
ἀποπέμπω	I send off, (in mid.) I send away
ἀποπλέω	I sail away
ἀπορρίπτω, perf. **ἀπέρριφα**	I cast aside, I reject
ἀπόστολος -ου, ὁ	messenger, ambassador, envoy
ἀποφαίνω	I display, I make know, I declare
ἀποφεύγω, aor. **ἀπέφυγον**	I get away, escape
ἀποχράομαι (+ dat.)	I use to the full, I am satisfied with
***ἅπτω**, aor. pass. **ἅφθην**	I fasten, I bind to, (of fire) I kindle, I set aflame
Ἀργεῖος -η -ον	Argive, of Argos
Ἄργος -εος, τό	Argos
ἀρέσκω	I am pleasing, I satisfy
ἄριστος -η -ον	excellent, best (superl. of ἀγαθός)
ἀρκέω	I am sufficient, I am enough
ἁρπαγή -ῆς, ἡ	rape, abduction, seizing
***ἁρπάζω**, aor. **ἥρπαξα**, aor. pass. **ἡρπάσθην**	I snatch, I seize, I carry off
ἀρρωδέω	I dread, I fear
ἀρτύω, aor. **ἤρτυσα**	I arrange, I prepare
***ἀρχή -ῆς, ἡ**	beginning, origin, reign, empire
Ἀρχίλοχος -ου, ὁ	Archilochus (a lyric poet of Paros)
***ἄρχω**, aor. **ἦρξα**	I rule, I begin, I make a beginning of
Ἀσίη -ης, ἡ	Asia
Ἀσσησίος -η -ον	of Assesos
Ἀσσησός -οῦ, ἡ	Assesos (a small town near Miletus)
Ἀσσύριος -α -ον	Assyrian
***ἄστυ -εος, τό**	town, city
ἀστυγείτων -ονος, ὁ	neighbour
ἄτη -ης, ἡ	disaster, ruin
Ἄτυς, Ἄτυος, ὁ	Atys (son of Croesus)
αὐτάρκης -ες	self-sufficient, independent of others
***αὐτίκα**	straight away, at once
***αὐτός, αὐτή, αὐτό**	self, (not nom.) him, her, it, (with art.) the same
ἄχαρις -ιτος (m./f.), **ἄχαρι** (neut.)	without grace, unseemly, disagreeable
***βάλλω**, aor. pass. **ἐβλήθην**	I throw, I hurl, (in pass.) I am hit, I am struck
***βάρβαροι -ων, οἱ**	barbarians, foreigners
***βάρβαρος -ον**	foreign, barbarous
βαρυσύμφορος -ον	weighed down by misfortune
***βασίλεια -ης, ἡ**	queen
***βασιλεύς -έος, ὁ**	king
βασιλεύω, aor. **ἐβασίλευσα**	I am king, I rule, I reign
βασιληίη -ης, ἡ	kingdom, throne
βασιλήιον, τό	palace (Attic: βασίλειον)
βιάω	I constrain, (of fire, in pass.) I am driven
***βίος -ου, ὁ**	life, livelihood
Βίτων -ωνος, ὁ	Biton (An Argive)
βιώσιμος -ον	fit to live
βλάβος -εος, τό	harm, damage
***βοηθέω**, aor. **ἐβοήθησα**	I come to aid, I help, I assist
Βορῆς -έω, ὁ	the north wind, the north
βόσκω	I feed, I nourish, I nurture
***βουλεύω**, aor. **ἐβούλευσα**	I plan, I deliberate, I contrive
***βούλομαι**	I wish, am willing
βοῦς, βοός, ὁ, ἡ	ox, cow
γάμος -ου, ὁ	wedding
***γάρ**	for
***γε**	at least, at any rate
γενεή -ῆς, ἡ	generation, race, family
γενναῖος -ον	noble, high-born
***γένος -εος, τό**	race, stock, kin
***γῆ -ῆς, ἡ**	land, earth
***γίνομαι**, aor. **ἐγενόμην**, perf. **γέγονα**	come into being, happen (Attic: γίγνομαι)
***γνώμη -ης, ἡ**	thought, judgement, opinion
Γορδίης -ίεω, ὁ	Gordias (king of Phrygia, father of Adrastus)
Γύγης -ου, ὁ	Gyges, Candaules' bodyguard
***γυμνός -ή -όν**	naked

***γυνή, γυναικός, ἡ**	woman
***γῶν**	at least (Attic: γοῦν)
δαπάνη -ης, ἡ	cost, expenditure, keep
Δάσκυλος -ου, ὁ	Dascylus, father of Gyges
***δέ**	and, but
***δεῖ**, imperf. **ἔδεε**	it is necessary, one must (impers.)
δειλίη -ης, ἡ	timidity, fear, cowardice
δεινολογέομαι	I complain loudly, I cry out
***δεινός -ή -όν**	terrible, fearful
δέκα	ten
Δελφοί -ῶν, οἱ	Delphi, the Delphians
***δέομαι**	I require, I ask, I beg
δέον -οντος, τό	that which is necessary, that which is right
δέσποινα -ας, ἡ	mistress
***δεσπότης -ου, ὁ** (acc. **δεσπότεα**)	master, lord
δευτερεῖα -ων, τά	second prize
δεύτερος -α -ον	second, next
***δή**	indeed
δήλησις -εως, ἡ	mischief, harm
***δῆλος -η -ον**	plain, visible, manifest
***δηλόω**, aor. **ἐδήλωσα**	I show, I make known, I reveal
δημοσίῃ	at public expense
***διά**	(+ acc.) because of, on account of, (+ gen.) through
διαδείκνυμι, aor. (3rd sing.) **διέδεξε**	I show plainly, I make clear
δίαιτα, -ης ἡ	way of life, mode of living
διακελεύομαι, fut. **διακελεύσομαι**	I encourage, I direct, I order
διακλέπτω, aor. inf. **διακλέψαι**	I steal, I save by stealth
διακομίζω	I carry over, I carry across, I convey
διακρίνω	I separate, I distinguish, I determine, I make (a choice)
διαλλαγή -ῆς, ἡ	reconciliation
διαπράσσω	I bring about, accomplish
διατελέω	I continue, I go through life
διατίθημι	(of cargo) I set out for sale, I dispose of
διαφεύγω	I get away, I escape
***διαφθείρω**, perf. **διέφθαρκα**, pluperf. mid./pass. **διεφθάρμην**	I ruin, I destroy
διαφορά -ῆς, ἡ	dispute, disagreement
***δίδωμι**, fut. **δώσω**, aor. **ἔδωκα**	I give, I grant, I assign
διέρχομαι, aor. **διῆλθον**	(of time) I pass, I elapse
διηκόσιοι -αι -α	two hundred
***δίκαιος -η -ον**	right, lawful
***δίκη -ης, ἡ**	justice, satisfaction, reparation, penalty
***διότι**	because, since
δισμύριοι -αι -α	twenty thousand
***δοκέω**, fut. **δόξω** aor. **ἔδοξα**	I think, I suppose, I seem, (impers.) it seems good (thus: I decide)
δόρυ, δόρατος, τό	spear
***δύναμαι**	I am able, I am strong enough
***δύναμις -ιος, ἡ**	power, might, authority
***δυνατός -ή -όν**	capable, able
δύο	two
δωδέκατος -η -ον	twelfth
Δωριέες -ων, οἱ	the Dorians
ἑβδομήκοντα	seventy
ἔγκυος -ον	pregnant
ἐγχειρίδιον -ου, τό	dagger
***ἐγώ**	I
***ἐγώγε**	I indeed, I for my part (emph. form of ἐγώ)
ἐθελοντήν	voluntarily
***ἐθέλω**, fut. **ἐθελήσω**, aort **ἠθέλησα**	I wish, I want, I am willing
***ἔθνος -εος, τό**	nation, people
ἔθω, perf. (for imperf.) **ἐώθεα**, perf. ppl. **ἐωθώς**	I am used to, I am accustomed to
***εἰ**	if
εἶδος -εος, τό	shape, form, figure, beauty
εἰκάζω, aor. **εἴκασα**	I describe by comparison, (in pass.) I resemble
εἰκών -όνος, ἡ	likeness, statue
εἶμα -ατος, τό	garment, item of clothing
***εἶμι**, pres. inf. **ἰέναι**	I will go
***εἰμί**, pres. inf. **εἶναι**, fut. **ἔσομαι**	I am
***εἵνεκεν**	on account of, for the sake of (Attic: ἕνεκα)
εἷς, μία, ἕν	one

***εἴτε . . . εἴτε . . .**	whether . . . or . . ., either . . . or . . .
***ἐκ, ἐξ** (+ gen.)	from, out of
***ἕκαστος -η -ον**	each
ἐκγίγνομαι (+ dat.)	I am born to
ἔκγονος -ου, ὁ	child, offspring
ἐκδημέω	I am abroad, I am on my travels
ἐκδίδωμι	give up, surrender
ἐκδύω	I take off, I strip off (of clothes / armour, etc.)
***ἐκεῖνος, ἐκείνη, ἐκεῖνο**	that person, that thing
ἐκκληιω	I hinder, I prevent (by a lack of time)
ἐκκομίζω	I carry out, I bring out
ἐκπέμπω	I send out
ἐκπίμπλημι, aor. **ἐξέπλησα**	I fill up, (of prophecies) I fulfil
ἐκπλέω, aor. **ἐκέπλωσα**	I sail out, I sail away
ἐκτελέω, aor. **ἐξετέλεσα**	I accomplish, I achieve, I bring to an end
ἕκτος -η -ον	sixth
Ἑλένη -ης, ἡ	Helen
***ἐλεύθερος -η -ον**	free
Ἐλευσίς -ῖνος, ἡ	Eleusis (a town about 11 miles (17.7 km) north-west of Athens)
***ἕλκω**, imperf. **εἷλκον**	I drag, I draw (a plough, wagon, etc.)
***Ἑλλάς -άδος, ἡ**	Greece
***Ἕλληνες -ων, οἱ**	Greeks
Ἑλλην-ικός -ή -όν	Greek
***ἐλπίζω**	I hope, I expect, I suppose
ἐμβόλιμος -ον	intercalary
ἐμεῦ	of me (Ionic form of ἐμοῦ from ἐγώ)
ἐμεωυτόν	myself (refl., Attic: ἐμαυτόν)
***ἐμός -ή -όν**	my, mine
ἐμπίμπρημι, aor. **ἐνέπρησα**	I burn, I set on fire
ἐμπίπτω, aor. **ἐνέπεσον**	I fall upon
***ἐν** (+ dat.)	in
***ἐναντίος -η -ον**	opposite
ἐνδεής -ές	wanting, lacking, in need of
ἐνδέω	I bind, I entangle (both lit. and fig.)
***ἔνθα**	there, where
***ἐνθεῦτεν**	(of place) hence, thence, (of time) henceforth, thereupon
***ἐνιαυτός -ου, ὁ**	year
ἐνοικέω	I inhabit, I dwell in
ἐντολή -ῆς, ἡ	order, command
ἐντός (+ gen.)	within, inside, on this side
ἐνύπνιον -ου, τό	thing seen in sleep, vision, dream
ἐξαγγέλλω, aor. pass. **ἐξηγγέλθην**	I report, I proclaim
ἐξαιρέω, aor. **ἐξεῖλον**, aor. inf. **ἐξελεῖν**	I get rid of, I drive out, I remove
ἑξακισχίλιοι -αι -α	six thousand
ἐξαρτύω, perf. **ἐξήρτυκα**	I get ready, (in pass.) I am prepared, I am equipped
ἐξεγείρω, aor. pass. **ἐξηγέρθην**	I wake up, I awaken
ἐξελαύνω, perf. **ἐξελήλακα**	I drive out, I banish
ἐξεμπολάω	I sell off
ἐξεργάζομαι, aor. **ἐξηργασάμην**	I accomplish, I achieve, I bring to completion
ἐξέρχομαι, aor. **ἐξῆλθον**	I go out, I withdraw, I march out (against)
ἐξευρίσκω, perf. **ἐξεύρηκα**	I find out, I discover, I invent
ἐξίημι	send out, (of rivers) empty, discharge
ἐξίτηλος -ον	lost to memory, forgotten
ἔξω	(as adverb) out, (as prep. + gen.) outside
ἔοικα (usu. impers.: **ἔοικε**)	I am fitting, I am seemly, I am suitable, I am probable
ἐπεάν	when, whenever
***ἐπεί**	when, since
***ἐπειδή**	since indeed, since in truth
ἐπεῖπον (aor. only)	I said besides, I said in addition
ἐπείρομαι	I ask, I question, I consult, I enquire of a god
ἐπειρωτάω	I ask
ἐπεισέρχομαι	I come in after
***ἔπειτα**	then
ἐπείτε	when, after, ever since, since
ἐπέξειμι	I traverse, (in writing) I go through in detail

ἐπέρχομαι, aor. **ἐπῆλθον**, perf. **ἐπελήλυθα**	I come upon, I go the rounds, I visit, (of ideas) occur
***ἐπί**	(+ acc.) against, onto, on, at, (+ gen.) on, (+ dat.) on condition of
ἐπιβουλή -ῆς, ἡ	plan, scheme
ἐπιγίνομαι, aor. **ἐπεγενόμην**	I come (at the end), I come (as a fulfilment) (Attic: ἐπιγίγνομαι)
ἐπιδείκνυμι, aor. **ἐπέδεξα**	I exhibit, (in mid.) I show off, I display
ἐπιδέω	I need, lack, (in mid.) am in want of (+ gen.)
ἐπιδρομή -ῆς, ἡ	raid, attack
ἐπιθυμίη -ης, ἡ	desire, longing, appetite
ἐπικατασφάζω, aor. inf. **ἐπικατασφάξαι**	I slay [acc.] over [dat.]
ἐπίκλησις -εως, ἡ	name, additional name, (in acc. as adv.) named
ἐπιμιμνήσκομαι (+ gen.), fut. **ἐπιμνήσομαι**, aor. pass. **ἐπεμνήσθην**	I make mention of
* **ἐπίσταμαι**	I know, I am certain
ἐπίστημι, aor. **ἐπέστην**	I stand near, (of dreams) I appear
ἐπίστιος -ον	suppliant, by one's fireside
ἐπιστρεφέως	earnestly, vehemently
ἐπίσχω	I restrain, I hold off
ἐπιτελέω, aor. pass. **ἐπετελέσθην**	I complete, I fulfil
ἐπιτίθημι (in mid. + dat.), aor. **ἐπέθηκᾰ**	I apply oneself to, employ oneself in
ἐπιχειρέω, fut. **ἐπιχειρήσω**	I lay my hands at, I attempt, I attack
ἐπιχείρησις -εως, ἡ	attempt, attack
ἐπιχώριος -ον	of a country, of the land
***ἕπομαι** (+ dat.), imperf. **εἱπόμην**	I follow
ἐποράω	I see, I observe (Attic: ἐφοράω)
ἔπος -εος, τό	word, utterance, (of dreams or oracles) prophecy
ἔραμαι, aor. **ἠράσθην**	I love, I lust after, I am passionately fond of
***ἔργον -ου, τό**	deed, work, action
ἐρέω	I will say, I will speak, I will tell
ἔρομαι, imperf. **εἰρόμην**	I ask
ἐρυθρός -ά -όν	red
***ἔρχομαι**, aor. **ἦλθον**, perf. **ἐλήλυθα**	I go, I come
***ἐς** (+ acc.)	to, into (Attic: εἰς)
ἐσακοντίζω	I throw a javelin at
ἐσαπικνέομαι	I come to, arrive at
***ἐσβάλλω**, aor. **ἐσέβαλον**	I invade, I put on board (a ship) (Attic: εἰσβάλλω)
ἐσέρχομαι, aor. **ἐσῆλθον**	I go in, I enter
ἔσοδος -ου, ἡ	entrance
***ἔσχατος -η -ον**	farthest, uttermost, extreme
ἑταιρήιος -η -ον	of companions, presiding over fellowship
***ἕτερος -η -ον**	one of two, each of two
***ἔτι**	still, yet
***ἑτοῖμος -η -ον**	ready
***ἔτος -εος, τό**	year
***εὖ**	well
εὐδαιμονίη -ης, ἡ	prosperity, good fortune
εὐδοκιμέω	I am highly esteemed, I gain good repute
εὕδω	I sleep
εὐειδής -ές	good looking, handsome, beautiful
εὐνή -ῆς, ἡ	bed
εὔξεινος -ον	hospitable, Euxine (name of the Black Sea)
εὐπαθείη -ης, ἡ	ease, comfort
εὔπαις -παιδος, ὁ, ἡ	blest with fine children
***εὑρίσκω**, aor. **ηὗρον**, perf. **εὕρηκα**	I find, I discover
Εὐρώπη -ης, ἡ	Europa, Europe
***εὐτυχής -ές**	successful, fortunate
εὐτυχίη -ης, ἡ	good luck, success
εὐχάριστος -ον	agreeable, happy
εὐχή -ῆς, ἡ	prayer
***εὔχομαι**	I pray
εὐωχέω, aor. pass. **εὐωχήθην**	I feast, I entertain (in mid. or pass.) I fare sumptuously, I feast
ἐφέπω, aor. **ἐπέσπον**	I apply, I direct towards, (in mid.) I follow, I accompany, I attend
ἔχθρη -ης, ἡ	hatred, enmity
***ἔχω**, imperf. **εἶχον**, aor. **ἔσχον**	I have, I hold, I have the ability
***ἑωυτόν**	himself (refl.) (Attic: ἑαυτόν)
ζάπλουτος -ον	very rich, exceedinly wealthy

ζεύγλη -ης, ἡ yoke (of a plough, wagon, etc.)
ζεῦγος -εος, τό carriage, wagon
***Ζεύς, Διός, ὁ** Zeus
***ζητέω** I seek, I look for
ζόη -ης, ἡ life, living
***ζώω** I live (Attic: ζάω)

***ἤ** or, than
***ἤ . . . ἤ . . .** either . . . or . . .
***ἡγέομαι**, aor. **ἡγησάμην**, perf. **ἥγημαι** I lead, I regard
***ἤδη** already, now, by this time
***ἥκω**, fut. **ἥξω** I have come, I am present, (with εὖ), I am well off
ἧλιξ -ικος, ὁ, ἡ peer, comrade, person of the same age
***ἡμεῖς, ἡμῶν** we
***ἡμέρη -ης, ἡ** day
***ἡμέτερος -η -ον** our
***ἤν** if (contr.: ἐάν)
Ἡρακλεῖδαι -ῶν, οἱ the Heracleidae
Ἥρη -ης, ἡ Hera, wife of Zeus
Ἡρόδοτος -ου, ὁ Herodotus
ἡσυχίη -ης, ἡ rest, quiet, leisure
ἤτοι . . . ἤ . . . in truth either . . . or . . .

θάλαμος -ου, ὁ inner room, bedchamber
***θάλασσα -ης, ἡ** sea
***θάνατος -ου, ὁ** death
***θάπτω**, aor. **ἔθαψα** I bury
***θαρσέω** I am bold, I am of good courage
***θηέομαι**, aor. inf. **θεήσασθαι**, 3rd sing. imperf. **ἐθηεῖτο** I gaze at, I behold, I see (Attic: θεάομαι)
θεῖον -ου, τό divinty, the divine
θεοπρόπος -ου, ὁ messenger (specifically sent to enquire of an oracle)
***θεός -οῦ, ὁ, ἡ** god, divinity
***θεράπων -οντος, ὁ** attendant, servant
θέω, 3rd sing. imperf. **ἔθεε** I run
θεωρίη -ης, ἡ sightseeing, seeing the world
θήρη -ης, ἡ hunt, chase
***θηρίον -ου, τό** beast, wild animal
θησαυρός -οῦ, ὁ treasure house
θνήσκω, perf. **τέθνηκα** I die, I am killed
Θρασύβουλος -ου, ὁ Thrasybulus (tyrant of Miletus)
θρόνος -ου, ὁ chair, seat
***θυγάτηρ -έρος, ἡ** daughter
θυμός -ου, ὁ desire, longing
***θύρη -ης, ἡ** door (Attic: θύρα)
***θύω**, aor. **ἔθυσα** I sacrifice, I offer
θωμαστός -η -ον wonderful, marvellous, admirable

ἴαμβος -ου, ὁ iambus, iambic verse
ἰδιώτης -ου, ὁ private person, individual
ἰδιωτικός -ή -όν private, of a private person
ἱκετεύω I beg, I beseech, I supplicate
Ἴλιος -ου, ἡ Troy, Ilium
ἱμάτια -ων, τά clothes
ἵμερος -ου, ὁ longing, desire, yearning
***ἵνα** so that, in order that (introduces purpose clause)
Ἴναχος -ου, ὁ Inachus
***ἱρόν -οῦ, τό** temple (Attic: ἱερόν)
***ἴσος -η -ον** equal
***ἵστημι**, fut. **στήσω**, aor. **ἔστησα**, aor. ppl. **στάς** I stand, I make stand, I halt
ἱστορίη -ης, ἡ enquiry, knowledge obtained from enquiry
***ἰσχυρός -ή -όν** strong, powerful, severe
ἴσχω, imperf. **ἴσχον** I hold back, I restrain
Ἰώ, Ἰοῦς, ἡ Io
Ἴωνες -ων, οἱ the Ionians
Ἰωνίη -ης, ἡ Ionia
καθαίρω, aor. **ἐκάθηρα**, aor. pass., **ἐκαθάρθην** I cleanse, I purify
καθαρός -ή -όν clean, free from pollution
καθάρσιον -ου, τό cleansing, purification, expiation
κάθαρσις -εως, ἡ cleansing, purification
***καί** and, also, even
***καίπερ** even though, although
***καιρός -οῦ, ὁ** right time, suitable opportunity
***κακός -ή -όν** bad, base, ugly
κάκουργος -ον malicious, doing ill, doing harm
***καλέω**, perf. **κέκλημαι** I call, I summon
***καλός -ή -όν** beautiful, fine

Κανδαύλης -ου, ὁ	Canduales, King of Lydia (7th century)
κάρτα	very, extremely
***κατά** (+ acc.)	by, at, according to
κατάδηλος -ον	visible, (with γίγνομαι) be discovered
καταδικάζω	I pass judgement, I sentence
καταδοκέω	I think, I expect, I assume, I guess
καταιρέω, aor. **κατεῖλον**	I take down, I destroy
κατακαίω, aor. pass. **κατεκαύθην**	I burn down, I burn completely
κατακοιμάω, aor. pass. **κατεκοιμήθην**	I sleep, I lay down to sleep, (in pass.) I lie down to sleep
κατακρύπτω	I hide away, I conceal
καταπλώω	I sail down
καταρκέω	I am fully sufficient
καταρρωδέω	I fear, I dread
καταστρέφω, aor. **κατέστρεψα**	I trample, (in mid.) I subjugate
καταστροφή -ῆς, ἡ	subjugation
κατεῖπον (aor. only)	I tell, I report
κατέχω, imperf. **κατεῖχον**	I hold fast, I restrain, (in pass.) I am bound
κατοικτείρω	I have mercy on, I take pity on
***κεῖμαι**	I lie, (of places) I am situated
***κεῖνος, κείνη, κεῖνο**	that person, that thing (Attic: ἐκεῖνος)
***κελεύω**	I order, I bid, I urge, I drive on
κερδαίνω, fut. **κερδανέω**	I gain, I profit
κῇ	in what way, how
***κῆρυξ, κήρυκος, ὁ**	messenger, herald
κιθών -ῶνος, ὁ	tunic, clothes (Attic: χιτών)
Κιμμέριοι -ων, οἱ	Cimmerians
Κλέοβις -ιδος, ὁ	Cleobis (an Argive)
κλώψ, κλωπός, ὁ	thief, bandit
***κόθεν**	from where, whence (Attic: πόθεν)
κοίῃ	in what way (Attic: ποίᾳ)
κοιμάω	(mid.) I fall asleep, I go to bed
***κοῖος -η -ον**	what sort? (Attic: ποῖος)
κοίτη -ης, ἡ	bed
κοῖτος -ου, ὁ	bed, resting place
Κολχίς -ίδος, ἡ	Colchis
Κόλχος -οῦ, ὁ	Colchian, inhabitant of Colchis
***κομίζω**, aor. passiv.**ἐκομίσθην**	I convey
***κοτε**	once, at some time (Attic: ποτε)
***κού**	somewhere, anywhere, (as particle), I suppose (Attic: πού)
***κου**	I suppose (Attic: που)
κοῦφος -η -ον	light, easy, nimble
κρατύνω	I strengthen, I confirm
κρεμάννυμι	I hang
Κρής, Κρήτος, ὁ	Cretan
***κρίνω**	I judge, I choose
Κροῖσος -ου, ὁ	Croesus, King of Lydia
κτείνω	I kill, I slay
***κύκλος -ου, ὁ**	circle
κυνηγέσιον -ου, τό	hunting party, huntsmen, hounds
κυρέω, aor. **ἐκύρησα**	I obtain, I attain
Κύψελος -ου, ὁ	Cypselus (tyrant of Corinth)
κύων, κυνός, ὁ, ἡ	dog
κω	yet (Attic: πω)
κῶμος -ου, ὁ	revelry, merry-making, celebration
κως	how (Attic: πως)
κωφός -ή -όν	mute
***Λακεδαιμόνιος -η -ον**	Spartan, Lacedaemonian
***λαμβάνω**, aor. **ἔλαβον**	I take, I capture
λαμπρός -ή -όν	bright
***λανθάνω**, perf. **λέληθα**	I escape notice, I unwittingly do [ppl.]
***λέγω**, aor. **εἶπον or ἔλεξα**, aor. ppl. **εἴπας**, aor. pass. **ἐλέχθην**	I say
λεώς, λεώ, ὁ	the people
λήιον -ου, τό	crop
λογάς -άδος, ὁ	chosen (man), picked (man)
λογίζομαι	I count, I reckon, I consider
λόγιος -α -ον	learned, skilled in history
***λόγος, ὁ**	word, story, theory, reckoning
***λοιπόν -οῦ, τό**	the rest, the remainder, (of time) hereafter, the future
λοιπός -ή -όν	rest, remaining, left over
Λυδός -οῦ, ὁ	Lydian

***λύω**, aorist **ἔλυσα**	I release, (of laws) I repeal
μακαρίζω	I bless, I pronounce happy
μακρός -ή -όν	big, long, far
***μάλιστα**	especially, most
***μᾶλλον**	rather, more
***μανθάνω**, aor. **ἔμαθον**	I learn
μαρτύρομαι	I call to witness, (esp. of gods) I invoke
***μάχη -ης, ἡ**	battle, combat
μεγάλως	greatly, very much
***μέγας -άλη -α**	big, great
***μείς, μηνός, ὁ**	month (Attic: μήν)
***μέλλω**	I intend, I am about to
μέλω	I am a concern, I am an object of care
***μέν . . . δέ . . .**	on the one hand . . . on the other
***μέντοι**	however
***μένω**	I stay, I wait, I remain
μεσαμβρίη -ης, ἡ	the south
***μετά**	(+ acc.) after, (+ gen.) with
μεταγιγνώσκω	I change my mind
μεταξύ (+ gen.)	between, inbetween
***μεταπέμπω**	I send for, I summon
μετίημι, 3rd sing. imperf. passive **ἐμετίετο**, aor. ppl. **μετείς**, aor. imperat. **μέτες**	I let go, I release, I cast aside, I ignore (Attic: μεθίημι)
μετρίως	moderately
***μέχρι** (+ gen.)	as far as
***μή**	not
μηδέ	not, and not, neither
Μηδείη -ης, ἡ	Medea
μηδείς, μηδεμία, μηδέν	no one, nothing, no
μήτε . . . μήτε . . .	neither . . . nor . . .
***μήτηρ -έρος, ἡ**	mother
μηχανάομαι, fut. **μηχανήσομαι**	I contrive, I devise, I arrange
μίγνυμι, imperf. **ἐμισγόμην**	I mix, I have intercourse with
Μίδης -εω, ὁ	Midas (king of Phrygia, father of Gordias)
Μιλήσιοι -ων, οἱ	the Milesians
Μιλήσιος -α -ον	Milesian, of the Milesians
Μίλητος -ου, ἡ	Miletus (a city in Ionia)
μιμνήσκω, aor. **ἔμνησα**	I remind, I make mention of

μιν	him, her, it (acc.)
μνημονεύω	I call to mind, I remember, I think of
μόρος -ου, ὁ	fate, destiny, doom, death
***μοῦνος -η -ον**	only, alone (Attic: μόνος)
Μύσιος -η -ον	Mysian (a region in north-west Turkey)
Μυσοί -ῶν, οἱ	the Mysians (people of north-west Turkey)
ναύκληρος -ου, ὁ	captain (of a ship)
ναυτιλίη -ης, ἡ	voyage
***νεηνίης -ίεω, ὁ**	young man, youth (Attic: νεανίας)
***νεκρός -οῦ, ὁ**	corpse, body
νέμεσις -εως, ἡ	retribution, nemesis, wrath
νέμω	I grant, I distribute, I dispense
νεόγαμος -ον	newly married
νηός -οῦ, ὁ	temple, shrine (Attic: ναός)
***νηῦς νεός, ἡ**	ship (Attic: ναῦς)
***νικάω**, perf. **νενίκηκα**	I conquer, I prevail, I win
νομιζόμενα -ων, τά	customs
***νομίζω**, aor. **ἐνόμισα**	I deem, I think, I believe
***νόμος -ου, ὁ**	law, custom
νόος -ου, ὁ	mind
***νοσέω, ἐνόσησα**	I am sick, I fall ill
νοστέω, aor. **νόστησα**	I come, I go, I return
***νοῦσος -ου, ἡ**	sickness, disease (Attic: νόσος)
***νῦν**	now
***νύξ, νυκτός, ἡ**	night
νῶτον -ου τό	back
ξεινίζω	I entertain (as a guest), I host (Attic: ξενίζω)
***ξεῖνος -ου, ὁ**	guest, friend, stranger, foreigner (Attic: ξένος)
ὁ, ἡ, τό	the
***ὅδε, ἥδε, τόδε**	this
***ὁδός -οῦ, ἡ**	road, way, path
ὀδούς -όντος, ὁ	tooth, tusk
***ὅθεν**	from where
οἱ (dat.)	to whom
***οἶδα**, ppl. **εἰδώς**	I know
οἰκέτης -ου, ὁ	household slave, (in plur.) household

***οἰκέω**, aor. **ᾤκησα**	I inhabit, occupy
οἰκήιος -η -ον	of one's own, private, personal
οἰκηϊόω	I claim as my own, I make a kinsman, I appropriate
οἴκημα -ατος, τό	dwelling place, bed chamber
οἰκίον -ου, τό	house, palace (often plural for sing.)
οἰκοδομέω, aor. **οἰκοδόμησα**	I build
οἰκώς -υῖα -ός	fitting, suitable
***οἷος, οἵη, οἷον**	such, of such a sort, (with εἰμί) able
οἴχομαι	I go, depart
***ὁκόθεν**	from where, whence (Attic: ὁπόθεν)
***ὁκότερος -η -ον**	which (of two) (Attic: πότερος)
***ὅκως**	how, as, in this manner (Attic: ὅπως)
ὄλβιος -ον	happy, blessed, prosperous
ὄλβος, ὁ	happiness, bliss
ὀλιγοχρόνιος -ον	short-lived, of short duration
Ὄλυμπος -ου, ὁ	Olympus (mountain in north-west Turkey)
ὁμῆλιξ, ὁμήλικος, ὁ	peer, person of the same age
ὄμμα -ατος, τό	face
***ὁμοῖος -α -ον**	similar, like
***ὁμολογέω**	I agree
ὀνειδίζω	I reproach, I blame
ὄνειρος -ου, ὁ (or ὄνειρον, τό)	dream
ὀνομάζω	I call, I call by name, (in pass.) I am called, I am named
***ὄπισθε(ν)** (+ gen.)	behind, at the back
ὀπίσω	back, back again
***ὅπλα -ων, τά**	weapons, arms
***ὁράω**, fut. **ὄψομαι**, aor. **εἶδον**, aor. pass. **ὤφθην**	I see, I look
ὅρκιον -ου, τό	oath
***ὁρμάω**, aor. **ὥρμησα**	I rush at, set upon, (in mid.) I rush, I hasten
ὁρμή -ῆς, ἡ	attack, assault
***ὄρος -εος, τό**	mountain, hill
***ὁρτή -ῆς, ἡ**	festival, feast (Attic: ἑορτή)
***ὅς, ἥ, ὅ**	who, which, whoever, whichever
***ὅσος -η -ον**	as great as, as much as
***ὅτι**	that
***οὐ, οὐκ, οὐχ**	not
οὐδαμά	in no way, never
οὐδαμῇ	in no way, in no direction
***οὐδέ**	but not, and not
οὐδέ . . . οὐδέ . . .	neither . . . nor . . .
***οὐδείς, οὐδεμία, οὐδέν**	no one, nothing, no
***οὐκέτι**	no more, no longer
***οὔνομα -ματος, τό**	name (Attic: ὄνομα)
οὖρον -ου, τό	limit, boundary
οὖς, ὠτός, τό	ear
***οὔτε . . . οὔτε . . .**	neither . . . nor . . .
***οὗτος, αὕτη, τοῦτο**	this
***οὕτω**	thus, so, in this way
ὀφείλω	I owe, I am obliged, I ought
ὀφθαλμός -οῦ, ὁ	eye
ὀχέω, imperf. **ὤχουν**	I carry, (in mid.) I am conveyed, I am carried
ὄψις -ιος, ἡ	appearance, vision, apparition
πάγχυ	fully, entirely
πάθος -εος, τό	what happens (to a person), experience, misfortune
***παῖς, παιδός, ὁ, ἡ**	child, son
***πάλαι**	long ago (sometimes τό πάλαι)
πανήγυρις -ιος, ἡ	assembled people, assembly
πάντως	in all ways, absolutely
***παρά**	(+ acc.) contrary to, along, to, (+ gen.) from, (+ dat.) beside
παραγίνομαι	I appear, I arrive, I am at hand, I come to
***παραδίδωμι**	I give up, I surrender
παραλαμβανόμενα -ων, τά	undertakings, endeavours
παραμένω, aor. **παρέμεινα**	I stay beside, I survive
παράπαν	absolutely, (with negative) not at all
παραπλήσιος -η -ον	the same, resembling, similar
παραυτίκα	presently, (with τό) the present
***πάρειμι**, future **παρέσομαι**, imperfect **παρῇ**	I am present, I have arrived

παρεόν, τό	the present state of affairs
παρέρχομαι, aorist **παρῆλθον**	I arrive at, I come to
***παρέχω**, fut. **παρέξω**	I provide, I furnish, I supply, (impers.) it is allowed, it is in one's power
Πάριος -α -ον	Parian, of Paros (an island in the Aegean)
παρoράω, aor. **παρεῖδον**	I observe, I notice
***πᾶς, πᾶσα, πᾶν**	all, every
πασέων	of all (Ionic variant of πασῶν)
***πάσχω**, aor. **ἔπαθον**, perf. **πέπονθα**	I suffer, I endure
***πατήρ, πατρός, ὁ**	father
***πατρώιος -η -ον**	of one's father, ancestral (Attic: πατρῷος)
Παφλαγών -όνος, ὁ	Paphlagonian
***πείθω**	I persuade, (in mid.) I am persuaded, I believe, I obey
***πειράομαι**	I try, I attempt
πέμπτος -η -ον	fifth
***πέμπω**, aor. **ἔπεμψα**	I send
πεντακισχίλιοι -αι -α	five thousand
πέντε	five
πεντήκοντα	fifty
πέρ	particle adding force (e.g. from the *very* place)
***περί**	(+ acc.) around, (+ gen.) about
περιάγω	I lead around, I show around
Περίανδρος -ου, ὁ	Periander (tryant of Corinth)
περίειμι	I am around, I am superior, I survive
περιημεκτέω	I am agrieved, I suffer grief
περιίστημι, aor. ppl. **περιστάς**	I stand around
περιχαρής -ές	exceedingly glad
***Πέρσης -ου, ὁ**	Persian
***πίνω**	I drink
***πίπτω**, aor. **ἔπεσον**	I fall, (fig.) I die
***πιστός -ή -όν**	faithful, trustworthy
πλάνη -ης, ἡ	wandering, roaming
πλεῖστος -η -ον	most, greatest (superl. of πολλός)
πλεῦνες -ων (+ art.)	most, the majority
πλήσσω, perf. **πέπληγα**	I strike
***πλούσιος -η -ον**	rich, wealthy
πλουτέω	I am rich, I am wealthy
πλοῦτος -ου, ὁ	wealth, riches
***ποιέω**, aor. **ἐποίησα**, aor. pass. **ἐποιήθην**	I make, I do
***πολεμέω**, aor. **ἐπολέμησα**	I go to war, I make war
***πολέμιος -α -ον**	hostile, enemy
***πόλεμος -ου, ὁ**	war
πολιήτης -οῦ, ὁ	citizen (Attic: πολίτης)
***πόλις -ιος, ἡ**	city
***πολλάκις**	many times, often
πολλαχῇ	for many reasons
***πολλός πολλή πολλόν**	much, many (in plur.) (Attic: πολύς)
πόντος -ου, ὁ	sea
***ποταμός -οῦ, ὁ**	river, stream
πρεσβύτερος -α -ον	older, earlier
***πρῆγμα -ατος, τό**	matter, affair (Attic: πρᾶγμα)
***πρήσσω**, aor. pass. **ἐπρήχθην**	I achieve, I accomplish, I do (Attic: πράσσω)
Πρίαμος -ου, ὁ	Priam (king of Troy)
***πρίν**	before, until
***πρό** (+ gen.)	before (of space or time)
προαγορεύω	I declare beforehand, I order publicly
προβαίνω, fut. **προβήσομαι**	I advance, I proceed
προεῖπον (aor. only)	I proclaim, I declare publicly
προέχω, imperf. **προεῖχον**	surpass, excel
***προθυμέομαι**	I am eager, I am willing, I exert myself
***πρόθυμος -ον**	ready, eager, willing
προίσχω (in mid.)	I put forward, allege, plead
πρόκειμαι	I lie before, I am set before
πρόοιδα, ppl **προειδώς**	I know in advance, I am forewarned
προποιέω	I do before, I do already
προπυνθάνομαι, perf. **προπέπυσμαι**	I hear beforehand
πρόρριζος -ον	root and branch, utterly
***πρός**	(+ acc.) to, towards, (+ dat.) in addition to
προσάγω	I bring forth
προσδέομαι (+ gen.)	I am in need of, I desire, I beg, I ask
προσδοκάω	I expect, I wait for, I look for

προσεπικτάομαι	I gain, I add to
προσέτι	over and above, besides
προσέχω	I put in at, land at (in a ship)
προσημαίνω	I foretell, I announce
***πρόσθε(ν)**	before, in front
προσπίπτω, aor. **προσέπεσον**	I fall upon, I befall
προσποιέω, aor. **προσεποίησα**	I make over, I add, (in mid.) I win over
προστίθημι	I give besides, I add
***πρόσω**	onwards, further
προτείνω	I stretch forth, I hold out
***πρότερος -η -ον** (compar.)	before, earlier, former
προτίθημι	I set before, I fix, I set
προτρέπω, aor. mid. **προετρεψάμην**	I rouse, I provoke
πρόφασις -εως, ἡ	motive, pretext
προφέρω	bring forward (as an objection)
πρύμνη -ης, ἡ	stern (of a ship)
***πρῶτος -η -ον**	first
Πυθίη -ης, ἡ	the Pythia, priestess of Apollo at Delphi
***πυνθάνομαι**, aor. **ἐπυθόμην**	I learn, I ascertain
ῥέω	I flow, I run
ῥώμη -ης, ἡ	strength, might
Σάρδιες -εων, αἱ (acc. plur. **Σάρδις**)	Sardis (capital of the Lydian Empire)
Σαρδιηνός -ή -όν	of Sardis (capital of the Lydian Empire)
σαφέως	clearly
σέο	of you (Attic: σου)
σεῦ	of you (Attic: σου)
***σεωυτοῦ**	of yourself (Attic: σεαυτοῦ)
***σῆμα -ατος, τό**	sign, marker, grave, tomb
***σημαίνω**, aor. **ἐσήμηνα**	I show, I indicate, I point out, I announce
σιδήρεος -η -ον	iron, made of iron
σιτοδείη -ης, ἡ	lack of food, famine
***σῖτος -ου, ὁ**	grain, food
σκέπτομαι, aor. **ἐσκεψάμην**	I look at, I examine
***σκοπέω**	I examine, I consider, I look to (esp. of business)
σμικρός -ά -όν	small
Σόλων -ωνος, ὁ	Solon (Athenian statesman)
***σοφίη -ης, ἡ**	wisdom, cleverness (Attic: σοφία)
σοφιστής -οῦ, ὁ	sophist, wise man
σπέρχω, aor. ppl. **σπερχθείς**	I am vexed, I am angry, I am quick tempered
σπεύδω, aor. **ἔσπευσα**	I hurry, I hasten, I urge
***σπονδαί -ῶν, αἱ**	treaty, truce
σπουδαῖος -α -ον	weighty, worth serious attention
σπουδή -ῆς, ἡ	haste, speed
στάδιον -ου, τό	stade (unit of measurement, approx. 607 feet, 185 metres)
στασιώτης -ου, ὁ	member of a party or faction
στείχω	I walk, I march, I go
στερέω, perf. **ἐστέρηκα**	I deprive of, I rob of
***στόλος -ου, ὁ**	equipment, army, fleet
***στράτευμα -ατος, τό**	expedition, army
***στρατεύω**	I advance with an army, I wage war
στρατηγέω	I am general, I lead
στρατιή -ῆς, ἡ	army
***σύ**	you (sing.)
συγγινώσκω	I recognize, I realize, I acknowledge
συγγνώμη -ης, ἡ	pardon, forgiveness, allowance
συγκομίζω, aor. ppl. **συγκομίσας**	I bring together, I collect
συλλαμβάνω, aor. **συνέλαβον**	I obtain at the same time
συμβαίνω, aor. **συνέβην**	I come together, I come to an agreement, (of time) I tally, I correspond
***συμβουλεύω**, aor. **συνεβούλευσα**	I advise, I counsel
***σύμμαχος -ου, ὁ**	ally
συμπέμπω, fut. **συμπέμψω** aor. **συνέπεμψα**	I send together, I dispatch at the same time
συμφέρω, aor. pass. **συνηνείχθην**	I bring together, (impers. pass.) it happens, it turns out
***συμφορή -ῆς, ἡ**	event, circumstance, chance (Attic: συμφορά)
***σύν** (+ dat.)	with
συναγείρω, aor. **συνήγειρα**	I gather together, I assemble

συνεκδύομαι I take off together, I cast aside at the same time
συνεκπλέω, aor. inf. **συνεκπλῶσαι** I sail away
συνεξαιρέω, aor. inf. **συνεξελεῖν** I take out together, I help remove
συννέω, aor. **συνένησα** I pile up, I heap together
συνοικέω I live with, I live in wedlock with
συνταράσσω, perf. mid./pass. **συντετάραγμαι** I throw into confusion, I disturb
Σύριος -α -ον Syrian
***σφεῖς** (dat. **σφι**) they
***σχεδόν** nearly, almost, generally
***σῶμα -ατος, τό** body
σωρός -οῦ, ὁ heap, mound, quantity
***σώφρων, σῶφρον** of sound mind, wise, sensible

ταραχώδης -ες troubling, disturbing
***ταχύς, ταχεῖα, ταχύ** quick, swift, soon
***τε . . . καί . . .** both . . . and . . .
τέκνον -ου, τό child
***τελευτάω**, aor. **τελεύτησα** I finish, I complete, I die
***τελευτή -ῆς, ἡ** end, completion
Τέλλος -ου, ὁ Tellus (an Athenian Solon proclaims happiest of all men)
***τέλος** finally, in the end, at last
***τέλος -εος, τό** end, (fig.) death
τεσσαράκοντα forty
τέταρτος -η -ον fourth
τευ (gen. sing.) of anyone, of anything, of someone, of something (Attic: τινος)
τέῳ someone, anyone (Attic: τίνι)
τέως for a while, for some time
τῇ (as adv.) here, there
***τίθημι**, fut. **θήσω**, aor. **ἔθηκα** I put, I place, (of laws) I make
***τιμάω**, aor. **ἐτίμησα** I honour
τιμωρέω I seek vengeance, I exact revenge
τίνω, fut. **τίσω** I pay the price, (in mid.) I punish, I make [x] pay
***τίς, τί** (acc. **τίνα**) who? what?
***τις, τι** (acc. **τινα**) a certain, anyone, anything, someone, something
τίσις -εως, ἡ vengeance, retribution
τοι to you (Attic: σοι)
τοιόσδε -ήδε -όνδε such, as follows
***τοιοῦτος -αύτη -οῦτο** such
τοκεύς -εως, ὁ father, (in plur.) parents
τοσόσδε -ήδε -όνδε so much, such great, sufficient
***τοσοῦτος -αύτη -οῦτο** so much, so great
***τότε** at that time, then
***τρέπω**, aor. **ἔτρεψα**, aor. pass. **ἐτράπην** I turn, (in mid.) I turn (myself), I take a course
τριήκοντα thirty
τρίμετρος -ον trimeter, (with ἴαμβος) iambic trimeter
τρίτος -η -ον third
τροπή -ῆς, ἡ turn, turning, (with ποιέω) I make turn, I rout
***τρόπος -ου, ὁ** way, manner
τρύω, perf. pass. **τέτρυμαι** I wear out
***τυγχάνω**, aor. **ἔτυχον** I happen, I befall, I hit
τύμβος -ου, ὁ tomb
τυραννεύω I am ruler of
τύραννος -ου, ὁ, ἡ tyrant, ruler
Τύρος -ου, ἡ Tyre
***τύχη -ης, ἡ** fortune, chance, fate

ὑγιής -ές (acc. **ὑγιέα**) sound, fitting, healthy
***ὑμεῖς, ὑμῶν** you (plur.)
ὑπάρχω (+ gen.), aor. **ὑπῆρξα** I begin, I take the initiative, I exist, I am there
ὕπειμι, imperf. **ὑπῆ** I am available, I exist
ὑπεκδύομαι, aor. ppl. **ὑπεκδύς** I slip out, I escape
ὑπερεπαινέω I praise beyond measure
ὑπερτίθημι (in mid.) I communicate, I consult
***ὕπνος -ου, ὁ** sleep, slumber
ὑπνόω I put to sleep, (in pass. I fall asleep
***ὑπό** (+ gen.) by, (+ acc. or dat.) under
ὑποδείκνυμι, aor. ppl. **ὑποδέξας** I show, I give a glimpse of
ὑποδέχομαι, aor. **ὑπεδεξάμην** I welcome, I receive into my house

ὑποδύομαι, aor **ὑπέδυν**	I go under, I take on my shoulders
ὑποθωπεύω	I flatter, I win by flattery
ὑποκρίνομαι	I reply, answer
ὑπολαμβάνω, aor. **ὑπέλαβον**	I take up, (with v. of saying) I say in reply
ὗς, ὑός, ὁ	boar
***φαίνομαι**	I seem, I appear, I show myself
φαίνω	I show, I bring to light, I reveal
Φᾶσις -ιδος, ὁ	the river Phasis (in Colchis)
***φέρω**, fut. mid. **οἴσομαι**, aor. **ἤνεικα**, aor. inf. **ἐνεῖκαι**	I bring, I carry, I bear
φήμη -ης, ἡ	fame, praise, good repute, prophetic utterance
***φημί**, pres. ppl. **φάμενος**, aor. **ἔφην**	I say, assert, declare
φθονερός -ή -όν	jealous, envious, grudging
***φίλος -οῦ, ὁ**	friend
φιλοσοφέω	I love learning, I pursue knowledge
***φοβέομαι**	I fear, I am afraid
Φοινίκη -ης, ἡ	Phoenicia
Φοῖνιξ -ικος, ὁ, ἡ	Phoenician
φοιτάω (also: **φοιτέω**)	I go to and fro, I frequent, I go off to
φονεύς -έως, ὁ	slayer, murderer
***φονεύω**, aor. **ἐφόνευσα**	I murder, I slay, I kill
φόνος	murder, slaughter, blood crime
φόρος -ου, ὁ	tribute
φορτίον -ου, τό	wares, merchandise (in plur.)
φόρτος -ου, ὁ	load, freight, cargo
φράζω	I point out, I show
Φρυγίη -ης, ἡ	Phrygia
Φρύξ, Φρυγός, ὁ	Phrygian

φυλακή -ῆς, ἡ	guard, watch
***φύλαξ -ακος, ὁ**	guard, guardian
***φυλάσσω**	I keep watch, I guard
χαρίζομαι	I please, I gratify, I make myself agreeable
***χείρ, χειρός, ἡ**	hand
χέω, perf. mid./pass. **κέχυμαι**	I pour, (in pass.) I am heaped up
χίλιοι -αι -α	thousand
***χράομαι** (+ dat.), fut. **χρήσομαι**, aor. **ἐχρησάμην**, perfect **κέχρησμαι**	I use, I enjoy, I take part in, I experience, I suffer, I am furnished with
χράω, fut. **χρήσω**	(of gods and oracles) I proclaim, I declare
χρεόν (indeclinable)	right, necessary
***χρή**	(impers.) it is necessary
χρηΐζω	I ask, I desire
***χρῆμα -ατος, τό**	matter, affair
χρηστά -ῶν, τά	benefits, kindnesses
***χρηστήριον -ου, τό**	oracle
***χρόνος -ου, ὁ**	time
***χωρέω**	I go, I come
***χώρη -ης, ἡ**	country, land territory (Attic: χώρα)
χωρίζω, perf. pass. **κεχώρισμαι**	I separate, I distinguish, I divide
***χωρίον -ου, τό**	place, spot
χῶρος -ου, ὁ	land, country
ὦ	O! (exclamation)
***ὧδε**	thus, in this way
***ὦν**	and so, therefore, certainly, indeed (Attic: οὖν)
ὠνέομαι (+ gen.)	I bargain for
***ὥρη -ης, ἡ**	hour, time (Attic: ὥρα)
ὤρη -ης, ἡ	care, concern, heed
***ὡς**	as, when, that, because, how, (+ superl.) as . . . as possible
***ὥσπερ**	just like, just as
***ὥστε**	in as much as, since, that, so that (to show result)

Plato, *Republic*

Introduction, Commentary Notes and Vocabulary by Stuart R.Thomson

AS: Book 1, 327a–332b

A Level: Book 1, 336b–337a7, 338a4–342

Introduction

What is justice? What does it mean to be good, and is it worthwhile trying? Although these seem like fairly fundamental questions, they are explicitly explored for the first time (at least in the West) in the *Republic*. It is Plato's best-known and most read work; it is quite possibly the most influential work of philosophy ever written, and certainly ranks amongst the most significant works of what became Western culture. A great part of its appeal lies not only in its lively and engaging style – particularly visible in the selection found in this volume – but in its richness and depth: for all its accepted significance, there is very little consensus as to the *Republic*'s ultimate meaning. In the words of Julia Annas, one of the work's most significant twentieth-century interpreters, it has been variously used by different readers to paint Plato 'as a revolutionary, a conservative; a fascist, a communist; a fiercely practical reformer and an ineffective dreamer' (1981: 1).

There is some warrant in the text for all of these (some more than others, of course!), and it is no surprise that so many conflicting interpretations arise out of one and the same text: it is written not as a textbook laying out the philosopher's reasoned conclusions, but as a combination of dialogue between semi-fictionalized historical characters, constructed myth, tongue-in-cheek polemic and deliberately unrealistic utopian thought-experiment. A reader can never be sure whose opinion is really being expressed – Socrates'? Plato's? Neither? And, after all, the very purpose of Socrates' teaching and Plato's writing, as expressed in many different ways throughout the Socratic corpus, is not to give easy answers, but to give readers the impetus for questioning themselves and their worlds: to become philosophers.

Socrates: his life and times

At the centre of the *Republic* stands the character of Socrates, Plato's teacher and the star of his dialogues. Undoubtedly charismatic, he repelled and attracted in equal measure, but as a philosopher left no writings of his own: teasing out the historical Socrates from the character presented by Plato (and others) is a challenge, but there is a great deal of which we are certain. He was born in Athens in 470/69 BCE. The city had recently led a collection of allied city-states against the Persian invasion of Xerxes I in 480–479, and remained a dominant Greek power as the leader of the Delian League, an association of city-states which aimed to maintain Greek unity and maintain a war chest against any future invasion attempts.

As Athens pushed itself from pre-eminence (as just one leading city amongst many other independent cities) to dominance – effectively an imperial power – tensions rose between it and a loose alliance which looked to Sparta as their protector, eventually leading to the Peloponnesian War of 432–404 BCE. Plato records that Socrates was notable in this conflict as a soldier – both in the Battle of Potidaea (432 BCE), saving the great statesman and general Alcibiades' life (*Symposium* 219e–221b), and at the Athenian defeat at Delium 424, where he showed great courage in retreat. Not just his bravery, but his endurance of the hardships of the military life – hunger, cold, and discomfort – were remarkable.

It is obviously not as a soldier but as a philosopher that Socrates is remembered, however. As a young man, he had been attracted by the kind of speculation that seems to characterize what we now refer to as pre-Socratic philosophy, which to modern perceptions seems often to have had a scientific bent – concerned with, for instance, the basic elements of which matter consists and the movements of heavenly bodies. (These concerns continued to be seen as part of the purview of philosophy in the ancient world – and indeed even up until the nineteenth century, the sciences were still sometimes referred to as 'natural philosophy'.) Socrates, however (according to the account given to us by Plato in the *Phaedo* 96 ff.), wanted to go deeper than what he saw as a mere description, to the ultimate causes of the phenomena of nature.

His subsequent enquiries were not generally positive in nature: that is, rather than establishing a theory of the underlying causes of the world and then expounding or defending it, his approach was to question, critically and carefully, the ideas held by others (and himself) to attempt to establish rigorously notions that were demonstrably and defensibly true. This is his famous elenchic method: critical questioning and dialogue (*elenchus*), often leading not to a definite conclusion, but to *aporia* (an argumentative dead-end, where a position has been definitely refuted, but no positive answer is given). This method goes hand in hand with the famous story of the response of the oracle at Delphi to Socrates' friend Chaerophon: asked if there were anyone wiser than Socrates, the priestess replied that there was not (Plato, *Apology* 21a; a roughly similar version of the story is given by Xenophon, *Apology* 14). Socrates is initially puzzled by the claim, but by questioning those reputed to be wise (politicians, poets, craftsmen) he discovers that the oracle is true insofar as he (unlike those he questions) knows that he knows nothing: only in his consciousness of his ignorance is he wiser than all (echoing neatly the inscription above the entrance to the oracle, γνῶθι σεαυτόν 'know thyself').

Socrates' challenging method, though infuriating to some (perhaps *because* infuriating to some) was extremely popular with others, and in particular, he drew around him a circle of younger men mostly from the aristocratic classes of Athens. By the end of the fifth century, he was a well-known Athenian figure, famed for his dishevelled appearance and idiosyncratic teaching methods. As far back as the 420s, he had been paraded and parodied on the Athenian stage as a character in Aristophanes' comedy, *The Clouds*: in Socrates' defence speech at his trial (as reported by Plato), this misleading comic representation is partly blamed for his reputation.

Accounts of Socrates' development into a philosopher come from dialogues written about the final days of his life. Despite avoiding direct engagement in politics, he was condemned to death at the age of seventy by the Athenian assembly in 399, charged with introducing new gods and corrupting the youth. His trial was part of the political and social upheaval in the aftermath of the Peloponnesian War. After Athens' defeat in 404, a new, oligarchic constitution was forced on the city by Sparta – the so-called Tyranny of the Thirty. Their rule was extremely brief (democracy was restored the following year), but extremely bloody. Socrates had taught a number of the Thirty; he remained in the city during their rule when many leading democrats fled, but refused to collaborate with the regime – disobeying an order to participate in the extrajudicial execution of a democratic general, Leon of Salamis. Despite this, he was tainted by association, and his long history of goading and questioning had left him with a great many enemies, and the prosecution against him was brought. In 399, Socrates held his last philosophical conversation and, in accordance with the death penalty imposed by an Athenian democratic court, drank the hemlock that would end his life.

It was probably after Socrates' death (possibly a little before) that Plato started writing his fictionalized accounts of Socrates' conversations, his dialogues. The youngest of four children, Plato (428/7–347 BCE) was born to an aristocratic family in Athens, a much younger contemporary of Socrates. Both his brothers, Adeimantus and Glaucon, appear as characters in the *Republic* (there was also a sister). By birth and by friendship, he was linked to many of the most influential politicians of his time, and like many of them, joined the circle gathered round the mesmerizing figure of Socrates.

Plato could have followed a similar path to become an influential Athenian statesman; instead, he founded a philosophical school, the Academy, and devoted himself to teaching and writing. For someone obviously so concerned with politics, why did he not get involved himself? Partly it was his experience of on-the-ground politics: it left him disillusioned with the possibilities and scope of what was achievable, and disappointed with the realities of democracy and what he saw as courting the favour of the masses. But it was also the encounter with Socrates which made a deep and lasting impression on Plato: beyond the awareness that the reality of politics was grubby, Socrates' teaching had shown him that there were more important realities.

Socrates and the sophists

Plato's Socratic dialogues are all set in the late fifth century, their dramatic date several decades prior to their actual period of composition, and to some degree they reflect the concerns and debates of that earlier time (although often overlaid or interlacing with Plato's own, later, concerns). It was a time of intellectual questioning and tension, where old established norms of behaviour and hierarchy were increasingly irrelevant in the democratic system, a time of a 'weakening of social and moral continuity and consensus' (Annas 1981: 7). This questioning of the old ways was particularly the stock-in-trade of a group of teachers known as the 'sophists'; Aristophanes' misrepresentation of Socrates in the *Clouds* was to lump him in as one of these sophists, even to paint him as the paradigmatic sophist.

These sophists were not so much philosophers as teachers of rhetoric (amongst whom was probably counted Thrasymachus, a key character in the *Republic*). They taught aspiring politicians, generally from elite backgrounds, the art of persuasion and public speaking – always for pay (although it is left out of the A Level specification, this occurs as part of the characterization of Thrasymachus at *Republic* 368d). Hailing from all over the Greek world, their appearance in Athens was due to its burgeoning democratic culture, in which public success depended on one's ability to sway public opinion by artful rhetoric; but they were also drawn to Athens because of its wealth and status.

Core to the concerns of the sophists was the distinction between *nomos* and *physis*, or (roughly speaking) 'custom' and 'nature'. What was intrinsic to the world or to human beings, and what was contingent to specific times and places – and therefore changeable – was an important dividing line for a radical democracy, in which the political power to change laws could be so easily exercised by a persuasive speaker. Institutions, patterns of behaviour, relationships between men and women, divisions of nationality and status, and even morality itself: which were part of the unchangeable order of the cosmos, and which were established by chance, or luck, or arbitrary imposition? The maxim of one of the sophists, Protagoras, stands as one end of the sophistic spectrum on these questions: 'man is the measure of all things'. That is, there are no absolute morals or values, only human constructions.

This thinking lent itself to a relativism which suggested that there can be no right and wrong, only more or less successful persuasion: hence the profitable line of work in teaching the arts of speech-making and debating. This in turn led to degrees of cynicism and scepticism, as well as fear and reactionary conservatism. There was undoubtedly a degree of the latter in the prosecution of Socrates, and the former is amply illustrated by the character of Thrasymachus in the prescribed section of the *Republic*.

Socrates, by contrast, saw himself, and was seen by his supporters as something quite different (though whether the ordinary Athenian would have been convinced by the distinction is another matter . . .). He refused to take payment for his teaching; more importantly, rather than teaching the art of persuasion, he was suspicious of the privileging of convincing speech over the search for true knowledge. He was more concerned with demonstrating the falsity of the notions that others set up as wisdom or truth.

However, even if only in the responsive sense of arguments showing that the sophists' notions were unfounded or false, Socrates' philosophy dealt in the same questions that interested the sophists. The *Republic* in general treads a difficult line, rejecting the relativism redolent of the sophists, but also critiquing the unthinking acceptance of tradition as sufficient for securing a basis for an absolute concept of justice or morality.

Socrates and Plato in conversation

The choice of form for Plato's philosophical works – the dialogue – may seem strange: rather than published lecture notes, or systematic treatises, we have the dramatized accounts of Socrates' conversations. In some ways it is surprising that Plato writes at all: a suspicion of the written word, as opposed to the interactive relationships possible in dialogue, permeates Platonic and Socratic thought. This is most famously expressed in the *Phaedrus* (274b–277a), and echoed in the *Seventh Epistle*, which criticizes a treatise on metaphysics on the basis that it is impossible to write on such a topic. (There is some debate as to whether this is really by Plato – even if not, it is almost certainly near-contemporary and built on a plausible understanding of Plato's work.) There is also evidence in Aristotle (who started as a member of Plato's Academy) that there were some doctrines, firmly held by Plato, which he never committed to writing; and there is, of course, Socrates' own decision not to write any works of his own.

There are two important points which flow from this observation. First, part of the criticism raised in the *Phaedrus* is that learning happens in dialogue, rather than in the immutability of text: text is passive where speech can be responsive. The written word can act as a reminder or sign of what is already known, but cannot answer back, respond to objections and challenge the individual circumstances of the reader: real philosophy can only be embarked upon by active and critical discussion. In Plato's view, therefore, the written word is not a format designed to give definitive answers to problems, but rather to stimulate the reader to examination and discussion. When we find Plato's dialogues confronting and provoking, it is because their role is to open the floor to questions and criticisms, not to foreclose them. It is important to recognize that the dialogues are written as the opening of a conversation with the reader, not as an intended conclusion.

Secondly, although you may encounter in modern works loosely phrased claims that 'Socrates said . . .' and 'the Socratic view is . . .', the figure of Socrates and what he may have taught is more elusive than many imagine. He himself wrote nothing, and what he said and did is therefore mediated by those who knew him, usually writing after his death. Their views and experiences – and their understanding of his life and death – deeply colour their presentation of him. Plato is the most influential source for our knowledge of Socrates, but the writer Xenophon also wrote Socratic dialogues (some of these survive), as did Aeschines of Sphettus (though these have not survived); these present quite a different Socrates. When reading the *Republic*, we must keep in mind that we are not reading Socrates' own words: we are reading Plato's Socrates.

How much of what we read, then, is a reflection of what the historical Socrates thought and said, and how much is Plato's own developed thought? We have no evidence, apart from reading the texts themselves and using the internal evidence to guide us, of when the dialogues were written or in what order. In one sense, however, it doesn't matter: when we are grappling with the text as a literary creation, looking at the arrangement and choice of words and arguments, and the presentation of characters, we are definitely dealing with Plato's creative genius. When we are dealing purely with the philosophical arguments, then the authorship is irrelevant: ideas and arguments ought to stand or fall by their own merits, not by virtue of the authority of the speaker.

That said, scholars generally agree that we can trace a development of Plato's thought and practice through his dialogues, which move from more accurate representation of the historical Socrates to a more developed Platonic philosophy where the dialogues, including 'Socrates', are a vehicle for Plato's thought. This movement can be seen in both the form and the content of the dialogues. The early dialogues (e.g. *Crito*, *Ion*, *Laches* and *Euthyphro*) are shorter, with Socrates almost exclusively a questioner of others, and they tend to be dramatic and vivid in their scene-setting. Socrates presents no theories of his own, but merely picks holes in his interlocutors' arguments, showing their self-contradictions and lack of secure grounding, and these dialogues end in *aporia* – no definite conclusion to the problem in question, and no clear way of getting there. These also echo the description of Socrates given by Aristotle: that his philosophy was solely concerned with ethical questions, but that he often pursued questions of definitions without claiming an answer himself (see *Metaphysics* 987b1, *Sophistical Refutations* 183b7).

In contrast, through the so-called 'middle period' and into the 'late period', the dialogues generally become more dogmatic and didactic: stylistically, the dialogue becomes more vestigial, simply a device to break up what becomes explanation of positive theories delivered as a monologue, and they become much longer as Plato expands on key theories, such as the immortality of the soul and the existence of the Forms. The *Phaedo* is often said to be the first dialogue in which Plato moves beyond the thought of his teacher, and these developments can be traced through the 'middle' works (e.g. *Cratylus* and *Symposium*) and into the 'late' works such as *Timaeus*, *Critias* and the *Laws*. The starkness of the contrast can be seen in the question of the soul's immortality: in the earlier *Apology*, Socrates quite explicitly says what happens after death is a mystery which no one knows; in the middle and later dialogues, the eternity of the soul is a key tenet.

The *Republic* seems to sit somewhere in the middle of this shift: Book 1 has clear affinities with the early dialogues; it is dramatic and lively in form, with clearly drawn and vivid characters, especially in Cephalus and Thrasymachus; Socrates' role is as a questioner, not advancing any positive definition himself, merely leading his interlocutors to *aporia*: an image of how the historical Socrates may have pursued a definition of justice. The rest of the dialogue, however (another nine books), has much more in common with the middle dialogues: although Socrates is still nominally the speaker, and Glaucon and Admeimantus feature as interlocutors, it is clearly an expansive setting out of a positive Platonic definition of justice.

Some have hypothesized on the basis of this division between Book 1 and the rest of the *Republic* that the first book was originally an independent composition, on which the later, more developed philosophical argument was later attached as Plato's thought developed; others suggest a deliberate compositional ploy to pay homage to Socrates whilst also demonstrating the limits of a purely negative approach, showing how a new, positive, Platonic approach might lead to greater insight, dramatizing the former Socratic method leading naturally into the latter.

Platonic politics

Philosophy, as a way of life necessarily separate from everyday concerns (and in some ways necessarily opposed to them), and politics, the common life of the city as the proper concern of philosophy, is the double helix that constitutes the DNA of Plato's writing. The need for introspection, challenge, and necessary separation from society in order to both examine oneself and the world as it really is, is balanced by the competing claim that philosophy, done properly, necessarily makes both individuals and societies better. In Annas' words: 'he wants to combine the values of intellectual perfection, which demand that one's life be devoted to study, and the values of practical activity, which demand that one improve the political world which is in such a mess. Plato sees the force of both claims and does not want to admit that they are irreconcilable' (1981: 7).

In the *Gorgias*, the theoretical way of life of the philosopher is defended against the sophistic claim that such a pursuit is merely juvenile self-indulgence, and that the mature man thrusts such idle speculation aside to make a real difference amongst the ambiguous and compromising realities of life. The *Republic*, on the other hand, represents the other strand of the double helix with its model of a state geared towards producing philosophers, whose proper role and duty is government of the state (the so-called 'philosopher-king', who is educated to rule the ideal city). Whether or not it is serious about proposing that model – and an ancient audience would have been shocked by aspects of it, just as a modern one is – it is certainly serious about the claim that philosophy is not merely an individual, abstract, pursuit, but has something to offer to real political life. Several of Plato's students from the Academy went from education to involvement in politics, including in some cases quite revolutionary politics (Critias, for example, who became one of the Thirty Tyrants): we do not know whether at his prompting, or even with his blessing, but certainly unsurprisingly.

The combination of the two forces, the theoretical and the political, is dramatized most clearly in the famous allegory of the cave, which occurs later on in the *Republic* (Book 7, 514a–521d). The work of the philosopher in seeking the truth necessarily puts him at odds with his fellow citizens; and yet he returns to the cave to help his fellow citizens, the other prisoners. The outlook, from the allegory, is rather bleak for the politically engaged philosopher: persecution and death (with the knowledge that Socrates' own death is prefigured); and yet it takes place in the broader context of a philosophical argument which connects the philosopher intimately to the life of the city.

There is a long tradition of interpreting this bleak view of the futility but necessity of political engagment biographically: Plato's ideas about politics are a result of his life experiences. Interpreters in this vein see Plato's disillusionment with Athenian democracy reflected in his philosophy – the fickle mind of the democratic crowd, easily swayed by demagoguery, was, after all, the cause of Socrates' death. The behaviour of Athens as a major Greek power in the fifth century further showed that democracy was no guarantee of morality or success. The debacle of the trial of the generals after the battle of Arginusae in 406 highlighted the flaws of Athenian democracy: an inexperienced Athenian fleet, having won a surprising victory against the Spartans, was afterwards struck by a terrible storm which prevented the rescue of sailors whose ships had been wrecked or damaged in the battle, and a large number drowned. In a bitter debate in the assembly, presided over by chance by Socrates (this was an office assigned by lot), the generals were condemned to death and executed, despite aspects of the prosecution being clearly unconstitutional. Athens came to regret its hasty decision, and to many – Plato included – it became apparent how blurred the line between popular democracy and violent mob rule could be. The Athenian defeat in the Peloponnesian War further put paid to the argument that democracy was the engine for military and political success more broadly. Yet the Tyranny of the Thirty (amongst whom were counted one of Plato's cousins and an uncle) was such a dire, brutal failure, that other practical alternatives seem no better.

There may have been later forays into practical politics (depending on whether we believe the *Seventh Epistle* to be genuine or not): Plato made three journeys to Sicily, in 387, 367 and 362. Some of these may have been part of an attempt to turn the theory of the *Republic* into reality under the rule of Dionysius II of Syracuse, a man with the potential to become Plato's philosopher-king. The attempt ended in failure: Dionysius eventually spurned Plato's advice, and Plato's strongest Sicilian supporter, Dion, was assassinated. Whether or not we can draw so direct a connection with Plato's experience and his philosophical speculation, the fortunes of the polities with which Plato was familiar certainly give significant context to the issues that he writes about.

The dramatic setting of the dialogue

Just as the date of the composition of the *Republic* is uncertain, the dramatic date of the dialogue – that is, exactly when this discussion is supposed to have taken place – is a matter of uncertainty. Jowett, the influential nineteenth-century translator of Plato, saw Plato as principally a writer of fiction for whom historical detail was entirely irrelevant; others, although recognizing that a precise historical date is both impossible to establish and not itself hugely important, nonetheless point out the importance of the setting to Plato's contemporary audience: an understanding of the historicity of the characters (especially Cephalus and his family) and knowledge of their subsequent fates contributes implicitly to the force of Plato's arguments.

Although the dramatic setting is the first celebration of the festival of the goddess Bendis at the Piraeus (Athens' port), there is no record elsewhere of when this might have been. What does give us a clue is the characters: these are all historical, and well attested elsewhere, particularly the family of Cephalus. One of his sons, Lysias (who appears in the dialogue), went on to become an extremely successful Athenian orator, who detailed his family's fortunes in the speech *Against Eratosthenes*.

In this speech, Lysias relates how his father, Cephalus, migrated to Athens from Syracuse, the city of his birth, at the invitation of Pericles, sometime in the later 450s. He remained there as a *metic* (resident foreigner) for thirty years, building up a successful business, a shield factory employing 120 slaves, which became the source of his family's wealth and influence. Cephalus participated actively in Athenian civic life, undertaking on a number of occasions the 'liturgies', public benefactions expected of the wealthy.

His involvement in the city did not protect his children from the ravages of the Tyranny of the Thirty in 404–403: orders were issued for the arrest of his two sons, perhaps as non-citizens being seen as easy targets by the new regime. Although Lysias managed to bribe his way to safety, Polemarchus was put to death by being forced to drink hemlock; all their property was confiscated. *Against Eratosthenes* was Lysias' successful prosecution of one of the Thirty for the murder of his brother; given the prominence of the family, the original audience of the *Republic* would have had the tragic after-story of Cephalus' sons in their minds as they read Book 1.

Cephalus is introduced in the dialogue as an old man; this would put its dramatic date in the late 420s, but there are other indications which militate against this: there is a reference at *Rep.* 368a3 to Plato's brothers' success in a battle at Megara. There are two battles this could be a reference to, in 424 and 409 – but given Plato was born around 429, the earlier battle seems unrealistic as Plato's brothers would have been too young to fight. The inclusion of Thrasymachus gives further support to a later date: he seems to have been active in the late fifth century, with one speech reasonably certainly dated to 407. There are a few other pieces of evidence which muddy the waters: a passing comment about an athlete, Polydamas, who did not win his first Olympic victory until 408, and a reference to an incident involving Ismenias of Thebes, which probably did not take place until after Socrates' death.

This leaves us with a dialogue that is clearly ahistorical, though working with well-known historical characters and facts: either Cephalus has been brought back to life sometime around 411, or Plato's brothers and Thrasymachus have been shifted back more than a decade to engage in a dialogue in the 420s. Of course, Plato was not intending to write a history: here (as in other dialogues) he has brought together historically impossible or improbable combinations of characters and references for his own purposes. The resonances of Cephalus and his wealthy complacency, or Thrasymachus and his bullish sophistry, are implicitly part of the argument being made, rather than markers of chronology.

The arguments of *Republic* 1

The *Republic* as a whole is clearly an exploration of justice, *dikaiosunē*, although this key term is more elusive than it seems at first. Justice is probably too narrow a definition for it (although even in those translations where the translator makes a point of eschewing the simple equivalence, it tends to be used regardless). Aristotle notes the ambiguity of the term – *Topics* 106b29, and at the start of Book 5 of the *Nicomachean Ethics* – and it might better be understood as 'righteousness' or 'morality'. The character of Socrates himself seems to broaden the scope of *dikaiosunē* considerably at 352e, when he defines the search for it as looking simply for 'the right way to live'. As discussed above, the discussion is set against the backdrop of debates over the relationship between traditional norms of behaviour, the challenge of relativism and the search for a defensible grounding of morality.

Thrasymachus, the bullish sophist in Book 1, sets the grounds for the entirety of the work by his definition of justice as simply whatever is to the advantage of the stronger. In a way, the subsequent nine books are a refutation of this position, and an attempt to demonstrate that justice has an absolute value. It is too simplistic, however, to suggest that the work is a conservative affirmation of morality against the moral scepticism of the sophists. There is too much irony in the character of Socrates – famous for his puncturing of simple acceptance of traditional notions – bearing the standard for a repressive crackdown on novel theories of any kind. Moreover, the first object of critique – gentle though that critique may be – is not Thrasymachus, but the genial aristocrat Cephalus and his son Polemarchus.

In fact, the structure of Book 1 circles around three key discussions, a tripartite division, where each interlocutor in turn is shown to be wanting by Socrates' incisive questioning: first Cephalus, then Polemarchus, and then Thrasymachus. In this, Book 1 is distinctively different from the rest of the work, and Book 2 takes as its starting point Adeimantus and Glaucon following up on Thrasymachus' line of attack: although Thrasymachus himself has admitted defeat, Plato's brothers are not sure his argument has really been vanquished. The threefold division is very similar to earlier works of Plato, particularly the *Gorgias*, but with significant differences. Dramatically, rather than simply an *elenchus*, each character in Book 1 is given a distinctive style of conversation with Socrates: the discourse both echoes the distinctive character Plato is presenting, but also characterizes the kind of argument itself.

Thus, the kindly Cephalus has more of a social chat than an argument with Socrates, presenting the genteel face of traditional, and somewhat unreflective or complacent, aristocratic notions of virtue. Polemarchus – younger, and more intellectually demanding – has a more traditional Socratic *elenchus* with the philosopher; and lastly, Thrasymachus, the sophistic brawler, charges in with a much more confrontational style of speaking. This takes in an explicit and direct challenge to Socrates' style of discussion, and a large part of the argument is not *elenchus*, but debate over whether the *elenchus* is an appropriate or fair style of argumentation at all (e.g. 336b7 ff.), or whether expository speeches instead are a better format. Although Socrates and his *elenchus* wins the day, the core of Thrasymachus' argument in his expository speech (343b1–344c9) is what is taken up in the continuation of the debate by Glaucon and Adeimantus in Book 2. This takes yet another form: paired epideictic speeches, speaking in praise of a particular position. So, all three – character, style of presentation, and argument – work together throughout Book 1, and set the ground for the new style of philosophizing on display in the rest of the *Republic*.

The discussion with Cephalus

The *Republic* does not start with an abstract philosophical question – the definition of justice – but rather raises it obliquely, as part of the chit-chat accompanying a social occasion, an unexpected visit from an old friend. The literary frame of Socrates being comically waylaid by old friends to stay with them for dinner, courtesy of Cephalus, leads to polite conversation between philosopher and host. The discussion quickly gets deeper – from a relatively polite starting point of asking how Cephalus finds old age, Socrates goes on to probe him about his wealth being a significant factor in his enjoyment of his life, rather than his character; quite possibly (as it would be now) a touchy subject, especially perhaps for a wealthy metic. The discussion takes us from there to a discussion about how wealth allows one to approach death peaceably, and this in turn leads to a consideration of what it means to have led a just life.

It is only at this point that the heart of the philosophical issue of the *Republic* comes out: what does Cephalus mean by justice? Rather than being drawn into a Socratic *elenchus*, Cephalus excuses himself to attend to the sacrifice. His departure (331d) either underscores his attachment to conventional religion and morality, or possibly (according to Annas) is meant to undermine his credibility – the sacrifice is already over, and this is a patently false excuse, introduced to avoid thinking too much about difficult matters.

Cephalus represents the stable, traditional Greek view of morality, linked to inherited ritual (hence the bookending of his appearance with references to sacrifice), bolstered by deference to the authority of canonical poetry, and comfortably cossetted by wealth. Although there is agreement that Cephalus' view of morality is presented as both flawed and limited, scholars are sharply divided on whether the presentation of Cephalus is generous and sympathetic, or carefully and deliberately malicious. Is the audience's knowledge of the fate of his family an ironic knife-twist: Plato showing the futility of an easy morality which rests on wealth and complacency? Or is it a sympathetically poignant and nostalgic view of an unreflective morality rooted in a stable social order which – though perhaps well-meaning – was clearly not robust enough to survive political change?

Cephalus' polite welcome to Socrates, expressing his delight in *logoi*, is clearly presented as almost comically understating the depth and critique of what it means to hold a discussion with Socrates – he is clearly anticipating light conversation or 'a little gentle sententious moralising' (Emlyn-Jones 2006: 14), rather than any serious reflection that might actually affect his life. More critically, he claims his appetite for discussion increases as his capacity for bodily pleasure diminishes – perhaps a sly criticism of philosophy as unimportant or second-best, a reasonable pastime once one is beyond anything else, clearly antithetical to the Socratic view that the unexamined life is not worth living.

Socrates' probing of his enjoyment of his old age, questioning whether it is just because he is wealthy that he is content, leads to perhaps Cephalus' most useful argument, that character (*tropos*) is more important than wealth for being just, although wealth helps. The issue of money is important on several levels. Attitude to money is used to characterize several interlocutors: Socrates' pursuit of philosophy kept him poor, in particular in contrast with Thrasymachus, whose avarice is made a point of when Glaucon offers to pay him on Socrates' behalf (337d; this small segment is skipped in the specified text), and reiterated again at 338b7–8. By the end of the *Republic*, it is clear that Plato holds a life dedicated to making money in contempt, but the knowledge that Cephalus' fortune does not survive long in his heirs' hands, under the Tyranny of the Thirty, already implicitly makes the point of the fickleness of wealth. Money also underlies much of the transactional language that is used later in Book 1 to try to define justice, giving back what is owed.

It is in this connection that Cephalus first raises the question of justice: the greatest value of wealth, he says, is to enable one to approach death peaceably, able to make sure no debts – to man or god – are left unpaid. This is expressed in somewhat selfish terms: the paying off of debts and the avoidance of injustice is not so much good in itself, or for others, in Cephalus' presentation, but valuable in warding off any fear about the afterlife. What, though, is justice, Socrates wants to know – and it is at this point that Polemarchus takes over in a more elenchic conversation with Socrates.

It is clear that Cephalus' unformed views and unreflective attitude towards philosophy are presented by Plato as shallow, and unable to withstand even cursory examination: nevertheless, there might be grounds for evaluating some of his lines of thinking more positively than Plato's dialogue would suggest at first glance. The idea that morality is a matter of character and internal qualities – *tropos* – rather than duties in a relationship (which is where Socrates moves the discussion with Polemarchus) has much to be said for it, and this is idea is later developed into something more sophisticated by Aristotle (384–322) and his follower Theophrastus (370–285).

The *elenchus* with Polemarchus

Whereas Cephalus presents an image of unreflective traditional morality, Polemarchus represents a more serious attempt to defend and justify this position. The traditional, conservative nature of his morality is underscored by his use of the lyric poet Simonides (*c.* 556–468) as his starting point, just as Cephalus had quoted Pindar earlier in the dialogue as an authority. Although Simonides had been a great innovator in his day, the mindset being presented by Polemarchus is clearly that what has been handed down is authoritative – rather than Socrates' more iconoclastic attitude to traditional poetry (which is explored in much greater depth later in the *Republic*).

Simonides is brought out to give a definition – *horos* – of justice which can answer Socrates' objection to Cephalus' characterization of the virtue. The search for a definition of a particular key term is often indicative of Socrates' style of *elenchus* in Plato's dialogues, particularly the early ones: in the *Meno* it is virtue, in the *Laches*, courage, and in *Euthyphro*, piety. The discussion proceeds by an attempt at a definition, which is then tested by Socrates through examples which undermine the proposed answer. Here, Polemarchus' definition is brought in as a response to just such an objection to Cephalus' implied definition of justice (although it is actually unclear whether Cephalus meant to provide such an absolute and universal definition of justice, rather than a general indication).

To give back what is owed (331e3): this is Polemarchus' starting point for a description of justice. This is met by Socrates' example of returning a weapon to a friend who has gone mad. But what is owed to a friend (explains Polemarchus) is to do him good, and what is owed to enemies is to do them harm: hence it is clear to see how this example would not really be giving back 'what is owed' to a friend.

Socrates goes on to challenge Polemarchus' definition by grounding his argument in the idea of justice as a *technē*. This term is crucial to Socrates' *elenchus*: it is generally rendered 'skill', but 'art' and 'craft' are possible translations as well. It is a term used frequently and with great significance by Plato – for instance, at *Gorgias* 462–465, where it is contrasted with 'mere practice' (ἐμπειρία καὶ τριβή): the *technē* of medicine is contrasted to the practice of cookery. The former understands the body and what is really good for it; the latter only aims at superficial appeal, without any deep theoretical understanding of the body. Annas (1981: 12) thus defines *technē* as 'an organized body of knowledge of the ways to achieve a certain end'. Socrates uses an analogy between justice and other skills in his four chief arguments against Polemarchus' definition:

1 331c5–333e3: Socrates points out that many *technai* can be defined by rendering what is due or appropriate to particular people for a particular purpose: e.g. the *technē* of medicine renders appropriate medicine to the body for its health.

Accepting this analogy, however, justice ends up being rather useless – Polemarchus is pressed to explain under what circumstances justice is a useful *technē* for helping friends and harming enemies. At sea, the skill of a navigator is more useful; in matters of health, that of a doctor and so on. In any given circumstance, there is a professional body of knowledge which is more effective than justice in achieving the stated aims of justice. Justice itself is reduced to being useful only when one doesn't need to do something or use something; its usefulness solely in looking after something when it is not in use.

2 333e3–334b9: Still following the analogy of justice as a *technē*, Socrates notes that the practitioners of other skills are equally able to help and harm by their skill. A doctor is the best at curing with medicine, but also the best at poisoning undetected; a skilful military strategist is equally good at establishing a defensive position and finding the weak points in an enemy's deployment. So, a skilful guard of what is not being used will also be a skilful thief: thus justice (concludes Socrates) is basically the skill of theft, as long as it is used to the benefit of friends and the harm of enemies. This argument both trivializes justice (as above, only useful in guarding what is not being used), and paradoxically presents it as a vice.

3 334c1–335b1: Socrates points out that we are often mistaken as to who our friends and our enemies really are. Given a knowledge deficit, it will sometimes be the case that a person exercising justice will inadvertently help enemies and harm friends. So, who really are our friends and our enemies? Socrates argues that those who are really good are our true friends, and our true enemies are those who are in reality bad. Thus, the definition is shifted, quite drastically, from what Polemarchus' initial statement at face value seemed to suggest: justice is not really about helping friends and harming enemies, but helping the good and harming the bad.

4 335b2–335e1: Socrates questions the idea that harming anyone is part of justice: returning to the *technē* analogy, it is pointed out that no other skill has the effect of making the object of its intentions worse off in respect of that skill. So, a musician, by exercising his skill, cannot make anyone else less musical. But by Polemarchus' definition, by harming an enemy, a just man makes him more unjust (or so Socrates argues). Just as it cannot be the function of heat to make things cool, it cannot be the function of justice to make anyone unjust.

This last argument is the least easy to follow in translation (or logically), relying as it does on the slippage in meaning in not one, but two Greek terms: *blaptein* (to harm or to make worse), and *aretē* (excellence or virtue) – keeping in mind that the end to which a *technē* is directed is its excellence (*aretē*). Thus, the argument runs: when a just man 'harms' an enemy, this can be interpreted in Greek as 'making him worse'. Worse in what respect? In respect of human excellence (*aretē*), of course (as opposed to the excellence of dogs or horses); is justice a human virtue (*aretē*)? Of course (responds Polemarchus). If this is so, we must either admit that justice makes people unjust, or that the definition is wrong. Polemarchus concedes the latter, and so ends his part in the discussion.

Of course, this line of reasoning is rather strained: it is a leap to say that being harmed makes one more unjust. This is partly the confusion between two senses of the word *blapto*, but also the odd jump in analogy from animals to humans: harming a dog makes it worse in respect of the excellence of being a dog, in 'doginess' (so to speak). But to say that harming human beings makes them worse in respect of being humans and that justice effectively equals 'humanity' is a stretch, especially when the preceding arguments have identified the fact that justice is actually a fairly insignificant skill. Moreover, even if we accept the analogy, there are numerous skills the exercise of which make others worse at the end to which those skills are directed – any directly competitive skill in a zero-sum game, for instance. Being excellent at chess or boxing or warfare is directed towards the goal of making one's opponent less able to move their pieces to good advantage, box, or defend themselves.

Looking at all four arguments together, what ties them together is the assumption that justice is a *technē*. Although Plato often makes this analogy, and Polemarchus does not question the assumption, it is nonetheless a rather contestable parallel (and even Plato in different dialogues gives varying levels of support to it). Justice might not be best described as a skill, mutually exclusive of other skills, with its own particular *aretē*, but as a personal quality (much like Cephalus perhaps points to). Alternatively, it could be argued that moral rules are not a skill directed to a particular goal, but apply regardless of what end they result in. Alternatively, admitting the analogy, one could argue that justice is an overarching skill that directs where and how other skills ought to be utilized. Just as the skill of medicine is made up of many individual skills (anatomy, pharmacology, etc.), and the overarching skill is the knowledge of when and how to utilize more specific skills or refer a patient to a specialist, towards the goal of the body's health, so justice might be seen as a skill that directs all other skills towards the overarching aim of the soul's happiness.

Polemarchus, however, fails to raise any objections to these arguments: although he does not like the corner Socrates is boxing him into, he is unable to see a way out: the *elenchus* is doomed to *aporia*; Polemarchus rejects the straightforward meaning of Simonides' saying, but no positive definition of justice is advanced.

What are we meant to make of the state of play at the end of the *elenchus*? Older commentators tended to assume that Plato did not see the flaws in the arguments he was presenting, or that modern readers are not sophisticated enough to see the subtlety behind what seem like clear weaknesses. More recently, Annas has argued that Socrates' arguments are deliberately weak in order to highlight just how superficial and indefensible a traditionalist account of morality is: if Cephalus' and Polemarchus' account of justice collapses under the assault of even weak arguments, it simply highlights how unreflective and ineffective this approach is. An extension of this is to see these arguments in Book 1 as proleptic: that is, they point forward to the ground explored in the rest of the *Republic* – this discussion is simply clearing the ground of popular views of morality. In particular, the fourth argument, which sets out the idea that justice never countenances harming anyone, hints towards the absolute concept of justice and the theory of Forms at 479a.

In both of these latter interpretations, it is assumed that the audience recognizes the vapidity of Polemarchus' argument, but also the weakness of Socrates' attacks. As a reader, are we meant to be frustrated with the shortcomings of elenchic argumentation? It is good enough to confound Polemarchus, and to win an argument, but not satisfying for a reader who might want more than this. Two facts seem to militate in favour of this interpretation. First, variants of the *technē* analogy are used in similar ways in other (generally considered) earlier dialogues in more sophisticated ways, with reservations which may have helped a more fruitful line of discussion here: e.g. in *Laches* or *Euthydemus* 288b ff. the idea of a *technē* which sits above and governs other skills is introduced, which could have countered Socrates effectively. Secondly, Socrates seems almost obviously to steer the discussion away from conclusions that might take the definition in a more positive direction: particularly at the end, where the idea that a just person oughtn't harm anyone is simply presented as a contradiction of Polemarchus' definition, rather than as a positive step towards defining what justice really is. So, it may well be that part of the purpose of Book 1 is to dramatize the weaknesses of Socratic *elenchus* in preparation for the introduction of quite a different style of Platonic philosophizing in the rest of the work – this of course fits neatly into the periodization of Plato's work into early, middle and late dialogues, and makes the *Republic*'s nature as a transitional dialogue central to a reading of Book 1.

The battle with Thrasymachus

Thrasymachus is presented as an argumentative bruiser: coarse, aggressive, and blustering. His opening salvo is not a substantive argument about the definition of justice, but an attack on the method of philosophical discussion that Socrates uses. Despite the negative characterization by Plato, some of this criticism has force. Thrasymachus both calls out Socrates' pretended ignorance as a sham, and accuses him of avoiding the real work of philosophy by only asking questions and never seeking really to answer them. Again, the hand of Plato setting the stage for quite a different kind of discussion in the subsequent books of the *Republic* might be detected here.

The substantive argument with Thrasymachus, however, sets out the proposition which establishes the ground for the rest of the *Republic*: that justice is simply the advantage of the stronger (338c2–3). Socrates' initial response teases out what Thrasymachus means by 'the stronger' – obviously not physical strength, but those who wield political power, who rule and have the ability to make laws. These rule to their own advantage: the laws they pass define what justice is, and it is just for the ruled to obey them.

A second clarification is sought, similar to argument (3) with Polemarchus: rulers are apt to be fallible, and mistake their advantage; is it any law that a ruler passes which is just, or only those decisions which are in fact to the ruler's advantage? Thrasymachus' response is that strictly speaking, a ruler is only a ruler when they are acting infallibly for their own interest – and here Thrasymachus himself reintroduces the craft analogy (although not using the term *technē*) by pointing out that when doctors make mistakes, it is not in the capacity of doctor (which they have temporarily failed to be in reality) but in the capacity of human being. Thus, when rulers introduce laws that are not to their own advantage, they are not really being rulers at that point.

This seems like an odd distinction to make; it traps the discussion in an unreal world, talking about doctors who are always infallible and rulers with perfect knowledge – and indeed, the onlookers to the argument, before Thrasymachus replies, suggest that he must mean laws passed even mistakenly to the detriment of the ruler. Thrasymachus seemed to be making a bold, iconoclastic definition initially: that justice was a sham, simply invented by rulers for their own convenience, and therefore entirely relative. The introduction of the idea of an infallible ruler seems to make his argument needlessly complex. It allows Socrates, in an *elenchus* with Thrasymachus, to fall back on a variant of argument (4) with Polemarchus: that no *technē* is concerned with the advantage of the craftsman him- or herself, but with the proper end of the skill. This, in the case of a ruler, will be the good of his city and his subjects. *(This is the point at which the A Level set text concludes in the Greek, at the end of 342, though up to 347d must be read in English.)*

Thrasymachus does not take Socrates' bait, but (breaking from *elenchus* into a long speech) instead makes the argument that in reality, rulers are concerned with their own welfare, not that of their subjects, just like a shepherd is only concerned for his flock not for its own sake but for how it can be used as an object for its owners. Justice, he concludes, is simply serving someone else's ends. By contrast, the unjust serve their own ends and their own happiness, who benefits at the expense of the just. Justice is therefore the advantage of the stronger; and injustice is profitable to oneself (344c).

There are again four arguments which Socrates deploys against this; the first two of them are again predicated on the craft analogy, with the same flaws and difficulties if a reader does not accept the analogy:

1 345b8–347e2: returning to Thrasymachus' shepherding analogy, Socrates argues that as a *technē* in the most accurate sense, ruling has only the good of the ruled as its end, not personal advantage: profit-making is a separate skill to ruling with its own end, and just as when a ruler makes a mistake he is not *really* a ruler, so when a ruler makes decisions for his own benefit, he is not *really* a ruler, but a profit-maker.

The division of profit-making or wage-earning into a separate skill is open to two obvious objections: first, it undermines the assertion that the exercise of a *technē* never seeks to benefit the practitioner. More importantly, it muddies the distinctions that Socrates is intent on keeping clear between *technai* and their ends: wage-earning as a skill can only function by the effective exercise of other *technai*, not by any recognizable excellence in itself. A doctor can only effectively exercise the skill of being a wage-earner by effectively exercising the skill of being a doctor, for instance. This does not mean that the best doctor will earn the most money; but it does undermine the proposition that one cannot both be a ruler and a money-earner at the same time.

2 347e2–350c11: Socrates attacks Thrasymachus' assertion that injustice is wisdom, and justice a form of stupidity; by comparing justice/injustice with other *technai* and what is considered wisdom in their spheres of influence, Socrates contends that it is justice which fits the definition of being wise and excellent, rather than injustice. The argument relies on the idea that wisdom and excellence in other crafts does not attempt to surpass other instances of excellence in that craft: a musician does not attempt to retune a musical instrument when it has been tuned properly. An unjust person always tries to get the better of another, whether unjust or not, whereas a just person can recognize when justice is served, and does not try to – and cannot – surpass it. Therefore, justice must be excellence and wisdom, and injustice the opposite. This is as odd an argument as it seems, and it is worth looking over the notes in the commentaries recommended in the further reading to try to make sense of it!

3 350e11–352d2: Not only is justice wiser than injustice, it is more powerful, since justice promotes co-operation, whereas injustice creates division. It is only, in fact, by being at least a little just – at least enough to co-operate with others – that the unjust achieve anything at all.

4 352d2–354a9: Socrates now turns to the question of who has a better and happier life: the just or the unjust? This is Socrates' most ambitious positive argument in Book 1, which defines the goal of human life as justice, the excellence or virtue which defines a successful human life.

Thrasymachus more or less grudgingly accedes to each of these objections, but as noted earlier, Socrates has not done enough work, or Thrasymachus has not propounded his arguments carefully enough, to convince the spectators to the argument that his claims really have been defeated by Socrates. Although Thrasymachus' definitions seem to shift a little inconsistently through the argument, there is a thread of principle running through all he says: trying to do what is right all the time, to be just, leads to being exploited and used by those who have no such moral qualms. The unjust will get the better of the just in terms of wealth, power and status, at every turn. This is the thread that Glaucon and Adeimantus take up at the outset of Book 2.

Plato's language and style

The standard version of Classical Greek found in textbooks and grammars is that of Athens in the fifth and fourth century BCE, so Plato's grammar and morphology wil seem regular and familiar – though there will be a few Attic forms that might seem odd: e.g. ἅττα for ἅτινά at 329a, and ἑ for the reflexive pronoun, 'him', at 327b, but these are few and far between and are noted in the commentary.

Plato is a careful stylist, however; even at a quick scan it is easy to note his familiarity with elite Greek literature, and his dialogues often features writers and poets, so it is worthwhile paying careful attention to his language. The first thing you will note about the layout of the work is the effect of the dialogic form: it is almost like a film script, with a little authorial/directorial input from the first-person narrator, Socrates. Beware the lack of quotation marks to introduce and close speech, and note that most of the text is direct speech. The paragraphing and punctuation will guide you as to changes in speaker, but the real work is done by particles and verbs of speaking to flag these changes – ancient readers would not have had the same advantages of punctuation and layout that modern editions lend us. The use of particles in Plato is often quite important, especially when shifting between speakers, marking levels of agreement, tone and nuance in response: see, for instance, the note on ἀλλὰ at at 327b. Sometimes these particles are quite a challenge to translate, as English is far less prone to particles than Greek – hence the value of being able to read the original!

Plato is also careful in his use of register: more and less formal styles of language to give vividness to the personalities and relationships in the dialogue. See, for example, the note on πῶς γὰρ οὔ; at 327c, contrasted with Cephalus' more formal style of speaking later on. Where there is more authorial intervention and description around the direct speech – for instance, when Thasymachus interrupts at 336b – it is often full of literary style and dramatic characterization.

Further reading

The focus of the commentary in this edition is to help students understand and translate the Greek text; stylistic and philosophical commentary is necessarily at a minimum. For the longer essay (20 mark), and commentary (15 mark) questions tested in the examination, this introduction will be useful, but wider reading will certainly give candidates an edge. I have deliberately kept this list extremely short, although there is, of course, a wealth of academic work on the *Republic*. Those who wish to delve more deeply will find the 'Further Reading' section in Chris Emlyn-Jones' (2006) edition a good starting place.

Allan, D. J. (1998), *Plato: Republic 1*, London: Bristol Classical Press.

First published in 1940 as a student edition, this contains an introduction, Greek text and commentary. Although brief and at points dated, an extremely useful work for elucidation both of the context and of the Greek. The commentary is useful (referred to several times in this volume), as is the introduction.

Annas, J. (1981), *An Introduction to Plato's* Republic, Oxford: Clarendon Press.

The author is one of the most influential interpreters of Plato in the twentieth century; the introduction is particularly useful, and the book, though not a commentary, does go through the *Republic* in chronological order, so the chapters on Book 1 are particularly relevant to this text.

Emlyn-Jones, C. (2006), *Plato: Republic 1–2.368c*, Liverpool: Liverpool University Press.

This edition includes both the Greek text and a very useful English translation on the facing page, as well as a commentary and introduction. Both of the latter are particularly concerned with philosophical interpretation.

Kraut, R., ed. (1992), *The Cambridge Companion to Plato*, Cambridge: Cambridge University Press.

In this collection of essays by various scholars, the most useful for students will be Kraut's own introduction, and T. H. Irwin's 'Plato: The Intellectual Background', to give broader contextual understanding.

Santas, G., ed. (2006), *The Blackwell Guide to Plato's Republic*, Malden, MA, and Oxford: Blackwell.

The chapter by Christopher Rowe on 'The Literary and Philosophical Style of the Republic' gives an excellent overview of some key introductory issues, and Rachel Barney's chapter, 'Socrates' Refutation of Thrasymachus', and Santas' own chapter, 'Methods of Reasoning about Justice in Plato's Republic', are particualrly relevant for the text here.

Steadman, G. (2012), *Plato's Republic 1*. Available online: https://geoffreysteadman.com/files-republic-i/ (accessed 11 June 2022).

The author has produced a range of Classical texts with commentary, available as free PDF downloads, that are extremely useful for the student: his editions come with a list of the most frequently used words in the text to memorize, and then a running vocabulary on the facing page to the Greek text, along with translational notes.

A note on the text

The text used is the Oxford Classical Text, *Plato: Respublica* by Simon Slings (Oxford: Oxford University Press, 2003). Plato's works are referenced rather differently to most other Classical texts; rather than the work and paragraph numbers, the entirety of the Platonic corpus fits into an overall sequence of what are called 'Stephanus pages', so called because these are the page numbers of one of the first printed editions of Plato by Henri Estienne (Latinized to Henricus Stephanus), in Geneva in 1578. Hence, *Republic* 1 does not start at chapter 1, but at 327a.

Text

[327a] Σωκράτης· κατέβην χθὲς εἰς Πειραιᾶ μετὰ Γλαύκωνος τοῦ Ἀρίστωνος προσευξόμενός τε τῇ θεῷ καὶ ἅμα τὴν ἑορτὴν βουλόμενος θεάσασθαι τίνα τρόπον ποιήσουσιν ἅτε νῦν πρῶτον ἄγοντες. καλὴ μὲν οὖν μοι καὶ ἡ τῶν ἐπιχωρίων πομπὴ ἔδοξεν εἶναι, οὐ μέντοι ἧττον ἐφαίνετο πρέπειν ἣν οἱ Θρᾷκες
[327b] ἔπεμπον. προσευξάμενοι δὲ καὶ θεωρήσαντες ἀπῇμεν πρὸς τὸ ἄστυ. κατιδὼν οὖν πόρρωθεν ἡμᾶς οἴκαδε ὡρμημένους Πολέμαρχος ὁ Κεφάλου ἐκέλευσε δραμόντα τὸν παῖδα περιμεῖναί ἑ κελεῦσαι. καί μου ὄπισθεν ὁ παῖς λαβόμενος τοῦ ἱματίου, Κελεύει ὑμᾶς, ἔφη, Πολέμαρχος περιμεῖναι. καὶ ἐγὼ μετεστράφην τε καὶ ἠρόμην ὅπου αὐτὸς εἴη. Οὗτος, ἔφη, ὄπισθεν προσέρχεται· ἀλλὰ περιμένετε. ἀλλὰ περιμενοῦμεν, ἦ δ᾽ ὃς ὁ Γλαύκων.

[327c] καὶ ὀλίγῳ ὕστερον ὅ τε Πολέμαρχος ἧκε καὶ Ἀδείμαντος ὁ τοῦ Γλαύκωνος ἀδελφὸς καὶ Νικήρατος ὁ Νικίου καὶ ἄλλοι τινὲς ὡς ἀπὸ τῆς πομπῆς.

ὁ οὖν Πολέμαρχος ἔφη· ὦ Σώκρατες, δοκεῖτέ μοι πρὸς ἄστυ ὡρμῆσθαι ὡς ἀπιόντες.

οὐ γὰρ κακῶς δοξάζεις, ἦν δ᾽ ἐγώ.

ὁρᾷς οὖν ἡμᾶς, ἔφη, ὅσοι ἐσμέν;

πῶς γὰρ οὔ;

ἢ τοίνυν τούτων, ἔφη, κρείττους γένεσθε ἢ μένετ᾽ αὐτοῦ.

οὐκοῦν, ἦν δ᾽ ἐγώ, ἔτι ἐλλείπεται τὸ ἢν πείσωμεν ὑμᾶς ὡς χρὴ ἡμᾶς ἀφεῖναι;

ἦ καὶ δύναισθ᾽ ἄν, ἦ δ᾽ ὅς, πεῖσαι μὴ ἀκούοντας;

οὐδαμῶς, ἔφη ὁ Γλαύκων.

ὡς τοίνυν μὴ ἀκουσομένων, οὕτω διανοεῖσθε.

[328a] καὶ ὁ Ἀδείμαντος, ἆρά γε, ἦ δ᾽ ὅς, οὐδ᾽ ἴστε ὅτι λαμπὰς ἔσται πρὸς ἑσπέραν ἀφ᾽ ἵππων τῇ θεῷ;

ἀφ᾽ ἵππων; ἦν δ᾽ ἐγώ· καινόν γε τοῦτο. λαμπάδια ἔχοντες διαδώσουσιν ἀλλήλοις ἁμιλλώμενοι τοῖς ἵπποις; ἢ πῶς λέγεις;

οὕτως, ἔφη ὁ Πολέμαρχος. καὶ πρός γε παννυχίδα ποιήσουσιν, ἣν ἄξιον θεάσασθαι· ἐξαναστησόμεθα γὰρ μετὰ τὸ δεῖπνον καὶ τὴν παννυχίδα θεασόμεθα. καὶ συνεσόμεθά τε πολλοῖς τῶν νέων αὐτόθι καὶ διαλεξόμεθα. ἀλλὰ μένετε καὶ μὴ ἄλλως ποιεῖτε. [328b]

καὶ ὁ Γλαύκων, ἔοικεν, ἔφη, μενετέον εἶναι.

ἀλλ᾽ εἰ δοκεῖ, ἦν δ᾽ ἐγώ, οὕτω χρὴ ποιεῖν.

ἦιμεν οὖν οἴκαδε εἰς τοῦ Πολεμάρχου, καὶ Λυσίαν τε αὐτόθι κατελάβομεν καὶ Εὐθύδημον, τοὺς τοῦ Πολεμάρχου ἀδελφούς, καὶ δὴ καὶ Θρασύμαχον τὸν Καλχηδόνιον καὶ Χαρμαντίδην τὸν Παιανιᾶ καὶ Κλειτοφῶντα τὸν Ἀριστωνύμου. ἦν δ᾽ ἔνδον καὶ ὁ πατὴρ ὁ τοῦ Πολεμάρχου Κέφαλος καὶ μάλα πρεσβύτης μοι ἔδοξεν εἶναι· διὰ χρόνου γὰρ καὶ ἑωράκη αὐτόν. καθῆστο δὲ [328c]
ἐστεφανωμένος ἐπί τινος προσκεφαλαίου τε καὶ δίφρου· τεθυκὼς γὰρ ἐτύγχανεν ἐν τῇ αὐλῇ. ἐκαθεζόμεθα οὖν παρ᾽ αὐτόν· ἔκειντο γὰρ δίφροι τινὲς αὐτόθι κύκλῳ.

εὐθὺς οὖν με ἰδὼν ὁ Κέφαλος ἠσπάζετό τε καὶ εἶπεν· ὦ Σώκρατες, οὐδὲ θαμίζεις ἡμῖν καταβαίνων εἰς τὸν Πειραιᾶ. χρῆν μέντοι. εἰ μὲν γὰρ ἐγὼ ἔτι ἐν δυνάμει ἦ τοῦ ῥᾳδίως πορεύεσθαι πρὸς τὸ ἄστυ, οὐδὲν ἂν σὲ ἔδει δεῦρο ἰέναι, ἀλλ᾽ ἡμεῖς [328d]
ἂν παρὰ σὲ ᾖμεν· νῦν δέ σε χρὴ πυκνότερον δεῦρο ἰέναι. ὡς εὖ ἴσθι ὅτι ἔμοιγε ὅσον αἱ ἄλλαι αἱ κατὰ τὸ σῶμα ἡδοναὶ ἀπομαραίνονται, τοσοῦτον αὔξονται αἱ περὶ τοὺς λόγους ἐπιθυμίαι τε καὶ ἡδοναί. μὴ οὖν ἄλλως ποίει, ἀλλὰ τοῖσδέ τε τοῖς νεανίσκοις σύνισθι καὶ δεῦρο παρ᾽ ἡμᾶς φοίτα ὡς παρὰ φίλους τε καὶ πάνυ οἰκείους.

καὶ μήν, ἦν δ᾽ ἐγώ, ὦ Κέφαλε, χαίρω γε διαλεγόμενος τοῖς σφόδρα πρεσβύταις· δοκεῖ γάρ μοι χρῆναι παρ᾽ αὐτῶν πυνθάνεσθαι, ὥσπερ τινὰ ὁδὸν [328e]
προεληλυθότων ἣν καὶ ἡμᾶς ἴσως δεήσει πορεύεσθαι, ποία τίς ἐστιν, τραχεῖα καὶ χαλεπή, ἢ ῥᾳδία καὶ εὔπορος. καὶ δὴ καὶ σοῦ ἡδέως ἂν πυθοίμην ὅτι σοι φαίνεται τοῦτο, ἐπειδὴ ἐνταῦθα ἤδη εἶ τῆς ἡλικίας ὃ δὴ ἐπὶ γήραος οὐδῷ φασιν εἶναι οἱ ποιηταί, πότερον χαλεπὸν τοῦ βίου, ἢ πῶς σὺ αὐτὸ ἐξαγγέλλεις.

ἐγώ σοι, ἔφη, νὴ τὸν Δία ἐρῶ, ὦ Σώκρατες, οἷόν γέ μοι φαίνεται. πολλάκις γὰρ [329a]
συνερχόμεθά τινες εἰς ταὐτὸν παραπλησίαν ἡλικίαν ἔχοντες, διασῴζοντες τὴν παλαιὰν παροιμίαν· οἱ οὖν πλεῖστοι ἡμῶν ὀλοφύρονται συνιόντες, τὰς ἐν τῇ νεότητι ἡδονὰς ποθοῦντες καὶ ἀναμιμνῃσκόμενοι περί τε τἀφροδίσια καὶ περὶ πότους τε καὶ εὐωχίας καὶ ἄλλ᾽ ἄττα ἃ τῶν τοιούτων ἔχεται, καὶ

ἀγανακτοῦσιν ὡς μεγάλων τινῶν ἀπεστερημένοι καὶ τότε μὲν εὖ ζῶντες, νῦν
[329b] δὲ οὐδὲ ζῶντες. ἔνιοι δὲ καὶ τὰς τῶν οἰκείων προπηλακίσεις τοῦ γήρως
ὀδύρονται, καὶ ἐπὶ τούτῳ δὴ τὸ γῆρας ὑμνοῦσιν ὅσων κακῶν σφίσιν αἴτιον.
ἐμοὶ δὲ δοκοῦσιν, ὦ Σώκρατες, οὗτοι οὐ τὸ αἴτιον αἰτιᾶσθαι. εἰ γὰρ ἦν τοῦτ᾽
αἴτιον, κἂν ἐγὼ τὰ αὐτὰ ταῦτα ἐπεπόνθη, ἕνεκά γε γήρως, καὶ οἱ ἄλλοι πάντες
ὅσοι ἐνταῦθα ἦλθον ἡλικίας. νῦν δ᾽ ἔγωγε ἤδη ἐντετύχηκα οὐχ οὕτως ἔχουσιν
καὶ ἄλλοις, καὶ δὴ καὶ Σοφοκλεῖ ποτε τῷ ποιητῇ παρεγενόμην ἐρωτωμένῳ ὑπό
[329c] τινος· "πῶς," ἔφη, "ὦ Σοφόκλεις, ἔχεις πρὸς τἀφροδίσια; ἔτι οἷός τε εἶ γυναικὶ
συγγίγνεσθαι"; καὶ ὅς, "εὐφήμει," ἔφη, "ὦ ἄνθρωπε· ἁσμενέστατα μέντοι
αὐτὸ ἀπέφυγον, ὥσπερ λυττῶντά τινα καὶ ἄγριον δεσπότην ἀποφυγών." εὖ
οὖν μοι καὶ τότε ἔδοξεν ἐκεῖνος εἰπεῖν, καὶ νῦν οὐχ ἧττον. παντάπασι γὰρ τῶν
γε τοιούτων ἐν τῷ γήρᾳ πολλὴ εἰρήνη γίγνεται καὶ ἐλευθερία· ἐπειδὰν αἱ
ἐπιθυμίαι παύσωνται κατατείνουσαι καὶ χαλάσωσιν, παντάπασιν τὸ τοῦ
[329d] Σοφοκλέους γίγνεται, δεσποτῶν πάνυ πολλῶν ἐστι καὶ μαινομένων
ἀπηλλάχθαι. ἀλλὰ καὶ τούτων πέρι καὶ τῶν γε πρὸς τοὺς οἰκείους μία τις αἰτία
ἐστίν, οὐ τὸ γῆρας, ὦ Σώκρατες, ἀλλ᾽ ὁ τρόπος τῶν ἀνθρώπων. ἂν μὲν γὰρ
κόσμιοι καὶ εὔκολοι ὦσιν, καὶ τὸ γῆρας μετρίως ἐστὶν ἐπίπονον· εἰ δὲ μή, καὶ
γῆρας, ὦ Σώκρατες, καὶ νεότης χαλεπὴ τῷ τοιούτῳ συμβαίνει.

καὶ ἐγὼ ἀγασθεὶς αὐτοῦ εἰπόντος ταῦτα, βουλόμενος ἔτι λέγειν αὐτὸν ἐκίνουν
[329e] καὶ εἶπον· ὦ Κέφαλε, οἶμαί σου τοὺς πολλούς, ὅταν ταῦτα λέγῃς, οὐκ
ἀποδέχεσθαι ἀλλ᾽ ἡγεῖσθαί σε ῥᾳδίως τὸ γῆρας φέρειν οὐ διὰ τὸν τρόπον ἀλλὰ
διὰ τὸ πολλὴν οὐσίαν κεκτῆσθαι· τοῖς γὰρ πλουσίοις πολλὰ παραμύθιά φασιν
εἶναι.

ἀληθῆ, ἔφη, λέγεις· οὐ γὰρ ἀποδέχονται. καὶ λέγουσι μέν τι, οὐ μέντοι γε ὅσον
οἴονται· ἀλλὰ τὸ τοῦ Θεμιστοκλέους εὖ ἔχει, ὃς τῷ Σεριφίῳ λοιδορουμένῳ καὶ
[330a] λέγοντι ὅτι οὐ δι᾽ αὑτὸν ἀλλὰ διὰ τὴν πόλιν εὐδοκιμοῖ, ἀπεκρίνατο ὅτι οὔτ᾽ ἂν
αὐτὸς Σερίφιος ὢν ὀνομαστὸς ἐγένετο οὔτ᾽ ἐκεῖνος Ἀθηναῖος. καὶ τοῖς δὴ μὴ
πλουσίοις, χαλεπῶς δὲ τὸ γῆρας φέρουσιν, εὖ ἔχει ὁ αὐτὸς λόγος, ὅτι οὔτ᾽ ἂν ὁ
ἐπιεικὴς πάνυ τι ῥᾳδίως γῆρας μετὰ πενίας ἐνέγκοι οὔθ᾽ ὁ μὴ ἐπιεικὴς
πλουτήσας εὔκολός ποτ᾽ ἂν ἑαυτῷ γένοιτο.

πότερον δέ, ἦν δ᾽ ἐγώ, ὦ Κέφαλε, ὧν κέκτησαι τὰ πλείω παρέλαβες ἢ ἐπεκτήσω;

[330b] ποῖ᾽ ἐπεκτησάμην, ἔφη, ὦ Σώκρατες; μέσος τις γέγονα χρηματιστὴς τοῦ τε
πάππου καὶ τοῦ πατρός. ὁ μὲν γὰρ πάππος τε καὶ ὁμώνυμος ἐμοὶ σχεδόν τι
ὅσην ἐγὼ νῦν οὐσίαν κέκτημαι παραλαβὼν πολλάκις τοσαύτην ἐποίησεν,
Λυσανίας δὲ ὁ πατὴρ ἔτι ἐλάττω αὐτὴν ἐποίησε τῆς νῦν οὔσης. ἐγὼ δὲ ἀγαπῶ
ἐὰν μὴ ἐλάττω καταλίπω τούτοισιν, ἀλλὰ βραχεῖ γέ τινι πλείω ἢ παρέλαβον.

οὗ τοι ἕνεκα ἠρόμην, ἦν δ᾽ ἐγώ, ὅτι μοι ἔδοξας οὐ σφόδρα ἀγαπᾶν τὰ χρήματα, [330c]
τοῦτο δὲ ποιοῦσιν ὡς τὸ πολὺ οἳ ἂν μὴ αὐτοὶ κτήσωνται· οἱ δὲ κτησάμενοι
διπλῇ ἢ οἱ ἄλλοι ἀσπάζονται αὐτά. ὥσπερ γὰρ οἱ ποιηταὶ τὰ αὑτῶν ποιήματα
καὶ οἱ πατέρες τοὺς παῖδας ἀγαπῶσιν, ταύτῃ τε δὴ καὶ οἱ χρηματισάμενοι περὶ
τὰ χρήματα σπουδάζουσιν ὡς ἔργον ἑαυτῶν, καὶ κατὰ τὴν χρείαν ᾗπερ οἱ
ἄλλοι. χαλεποὶ οὖν καὶ συγγενέσθαι εἰσίν, οὐδὲν ἐθέλοντες ἐπαινεῖν ἀλλ᾽ ἢ
τὸν πλοῦτον.

ἀληθῆ, ἔφη, λέγεις.

πάνυ μὲν οὖν, ἦν δ᾽ ἐγώ. ἀλλά μοι ἔτι τοσόνδε εἰπέ· τί μέγιστον οἴει ἀγαθὸν [330d]
ἀπολελαυκέναι τοῦ πολλὴν οὐσίαν κεκτῆσθαι;

ὅ, ἦ δ᾽ ὅς, ἴσως οὐκ ἂν πολλοὺς πείσαιμι λέγων. εὖ γὰρ ἴσθι, ἔφη, ὦ Σώκρατες,
ὅτι, ἐπειδάν τις ἐγγὺς ᾖ τοῦ οἴεσθαι τελευτήσειν, εἰσέρχεται αὐτῷ δέος καὶ
φροντὶς περὶ ὧν ἔμπροσθεν οὐκ εἰσῄει. οἵ τε γὰρ λεγόμενοι μῦθοι περὶ τῶν ἐν
Ἅιδου, ὡς τὸν ἐνθάδε ἀδικήσαντα δεῖ ἐκεῖ διδόναι δίκην, καταγελώμενοι τέως,
τότε δὴ στρέφουσιν αὐτοῦ τὴν ψυχὴν μὴ ἀληθεῖς ὦσιν· καὶ αὐτός, ἤτοι ὑπὸ τῆς [330e]
τοῦ γήρως ἀσθενείας ἢ καὶ ὥσπερ ἤδη ἐγγυτέρω ὢν τῶν ἐκεῖ μᾶλλόν τι καθορᾷ
αὐτά, ὑποψίας δ᾽ οὖν καὶ δείματος μεστὸς γίγνεται καὶ ἀναλογίζεται ἤδη καὶ
σκοπεῖ εἴ τινά τι ἠδίκησεν. ὁ μὲν οὖν εὑρίσκων ἑαυτοῦ ἐν τῷ βίῳ πολλὰ
ἀδικήματα καὶ ἐκ τῶν ὕπνων, ὥσπερ οἱ παῖδες, θαμὰ ἐγειρόμενος δειμαίνει καὶ
ζῇ μετὰ κακῆς ἐλπίδος· τῷ δὲ μηδὲν ἑαυτῷ ἄδικον συνειδότι ἡδεῖα ἐλπὶς ἀεὶ [331a]
πάρεστι καὶ ἀγαθὴ γηροτρόφος, ὡς καὶ Πίνδαρος λέγει. χαριέντως γάρ τοι, ὦ
Σώκρατες, τοῦτ᾽ ἐκεῖνος εἶπεν, ὅτι ὃς ἂν δικαίως καὶ ὁσίως τὸν βίον διαγάγῃ,

γλυκεῖά οἱ καρδίαν
ἀτάλλοισα γηροτρόφος συναορεῖ
ἐλπίς, ἃ μάλιστα θνατῶν
πολύστροφον γνώμαν κυβερνᾷ.

εὖ οὖν λέγει θαυμαστῶς ὡς σφόδρα. πρὸς δὴ τοῦτ᾽ ἔγωγε τίθημι τὴν τῶν
χρημάτων κτῆσιν πλείστου ἀξίαν εἶναι, οὔ τι παντὶ ἀνδρὶ ἀλλὰ τῷ ἐπιεικεῖ. [331b]
τὸ γὰρ μηδὲ ἄκοντά τινα ἐξαπατῆσαι ἢ ψεύσασθαι, μηδ᾽ αὖ ὀφείλοντα ἢ θεῷ
θυσίας τινὰς ἢ ἀνθρώπῳ χρήματα ἔπειτα ἐκεῖσε ἀπιέναι δεδιότα, μέγα μέρος
εἰς τοῦτο ἡ τῶν χρημάτων κτῆσις συμβάλλεται. ἔχει δὲ καὶ ἄλλας χρείας
πολλάς, ἀλλὰ γε ἓν ἀνθ᾽ ἑνὸς οὐκ ἐλάχιστον ἔγωγε θείην ἂν εἰς τοῦτο ἀνδρὶ
νοῦν ἔχοντι, ὦ Σώκρατες, πλοῦτον χρησιμώτατον εἶναι.

παγκάλως, ἦν δ᾽ ἐγώ, λέγεις, ὦ Κέφαλε. τοῦτο δ᾽ αὐτό, τὴν δικαιοσύνην, [331c]
πότερα τὴν ἀλήθειαν αὐτὸ φήσομεν εἶναι ἁπλῶς οὕτως καὶ τὸ ἀποδιδόναι ἄν
τίς τι παρά του λάβῃ, ἢ καὶ αὐτὰ ταῦτα ἔστιν ἐνίοτε μὲν δικαίως, ἐνίοτε δὲ

ἀδίκως ποιεῖν; οἷον τοιόνδε λέγω· πᾶς ἄν που εἴποι, εἴ τις λάβοι παρὰ φίλου ἀνδρὸς σωφρονοῦντος ὅπλα, εἰ μανεὶς ἀπαιτοῖ, ὅτι οὔτε χρὴ τὰ τοιαῦτα ἀποδιδόναι, οὔτε δίκαιος ἂν εἴη ὁ ἀποδιδούς, οὐδ᾽ αὖ πρὸς τὸν οὕτως ἔχοντα πάντα ἐθέλων τἀληθῆ λέγειν.

[331d] ὀρθῶς, ἔφη, λέγεις.

οὐκ ἄρα οὗτος ὅρος ἐστὶν δικαιοσύνης, ἀληθῆ τε λέγειν καὶ ἃ ἂν λάβῃ τις ἀποδιδόναι.

πάνυ μὲν οὖν, ἔφη, ὦ Σώκρατες, ὑπολαβὼν ὁ Πολέμαρχος, εἴπερ γέ τι χρὴ Σιμωνίδῃ πείθεσθαι.

καὶ μέντοι, ἔφη ὁ Κέφαλος, καὶ παραδίδωμι ὑμῖν τὸν λόγον· δεῖ γάρ με ἤδη τῶν ἱερῶν ἐπιμεληθῆναι.

οὐκοῦν, ἔφη, ἐγώ, ὁ Πολέμαρχος, τῶν γε σῶν κληρονόμος;

πάνυ γε, ἦ δ᾽ ὃς γελάσας, καὶ ἅμα ᾔει πρὸς τὰ ἱερά.

[331e] λέγε δή, εἶπον ἐγώ, σὺ ὁ τοῦ λόγου κληρονόμος, τί φῂς τὸν Σιμωνίδην λέγοντα ὀρθῶς λέγειν περὶ δικαιοσύνης;

ὅτι, ἦ δ᾽ ὅς, τὸ τὰ ὀφειλόμενα ἑκάστῳ ἀποδιδόναι δίκαιόν ἐστι· τοῦτο λέγων δοκεῖ ἔμοιγε καλῶς λέγειν.

ἀλλὰ μέντοι, ἦν δ᾽ ἐγώ, Σιμωνίδῃ γε οὐ ῥᾴδιον ἀπιστεῖν, σοφὸς γὰρ καὶ θεῖος ἀνήρ· τοῦτο μέντοι ὅτι ποτὲ λέγει, σὺ μέν, ὦ Πολέμαρχε, ἴσως γιγνώσκεις, ἐγὼ δὲ ἀγνοῶ. δῆλον γὰρ ὅτι οὐ τοῦτο λέγει, ὅπερ ἄρτι ἐλέγομεν, τό τινος
[332a] παρακαταθεμένου τι ὁτῳοῦν μὴ σωφρόνως ἀπαιτοῦντι ἀποδιδόναι. καίτοι γε ὀφειλόμενόν πού ἐστιν τοῦτο ὃ παρακατέθετο. ἦ γάρ;

ναί.

ἀποδοτέον δέ γε οὐδ᾽ ὁπωστιοῦν τότε ὁπότε τις μὴ σωφρόνως ἀπαιτοῖ;

ἀληθῆ, ἦ δ᾽ ὅς.

ἄλλο δή τι ἢ τὸ τοιοῦτον, ὡς ἔοικεν, λέγει Σιμωνίδης τὸ τὰ ὀφειλόμενα δίκαιον εἶναι ἀποδιδόναι.

ἄλλο μέντοι νὴ Δί᾽, ἔφη· τοῖς γὰρ φίλοις οἴεται ὀφείλειν τοὺς φίλους ἀγαθὸν μέν τι δρᾶν, κακὸν δὲ μηδέν.

μανθάνω, ἦν δ᾽ ἐγώ, ὅτι οὐ τὰ ὀφειλόμενα ἀποδίδωσιν ὃς ἄν τῳ χρυσίον ἀποδῷ παρακαταθεμένῳ, ἐάνπερ ἡ ἀπόδοσις καὶ ἡ λῆψις βλαβερὰ γίγνηται, φίλοι [332b]
δὲ ὦσιν ὅ τε ἀπολαμβάνων καὶ ὁ ἀποδιδούς· οὐχ οὕτω λέγειν φῂς τὸν Σιμωνίδην;

πάνυ μὲν οὖν.

τί δέ; τοῖς ἐχθροῖς ἀποδοτέον ὅτι ἂν τύχῃ ὀφειλόμενον; [5]

παντάπασι μὲν οὖν, ἔφη, ὅ γε ὀφείλεται αὐτοῖς· ὀφείλεται δέ γε, οἶμαι, παρά γε τοῦ ἐχθροῦ τῷ ἐχθρῷ ὅπερ καὶ προσήκει, κακόν τι.

ᾐνίξατο ἄρα, ἦν δ᾽ ἐγώ, ὡς ἔοικεν, ὁ Σιμωνίδης ποιητικῶς τὸ δίκαιον ὃ εἴη.

332c–336a: Socrates, through elaboration of the craft analogy, convinces Polemarchus that it is never just to harm anyone.

[336b] καὶ ὁ Θρασύμαχος πολλάκις μὲν καὶ διαλεγομένων ἡμῶν μεταξὺ ὥρμα ἀντιλαμβάνεσθαι τοῦ λόγου, ἔπειτα ὑπὸ τῶν παρακαθημένων διεκωλύετο βουλομένων διακοῦσαι τὸν λόγον· ὡς δὲ διεπαυσάμεθα καὶ ἐγὼ ταῦτ᾽ εἶπον, οὐκέτι ἡσυχίαν ἦγεν, ἀλλὰ συστρέψας ἑαυτὸν ὥσπερ θηρίον ἧκεν ἐφ᾽ ἡμᾶς ὡς διαρπασόμενος.

καὶ ἐγώ τε καὶ ὁ Πολέμαρχος δείσαντες διεπτοήθημεν· ὁ δ᾽ εἰς τὸ μέσον
[336c] φθεγξάμενος, τίς, ἔφη, ὑμᾶς πάλαι φλυαρία ἔχει, ὦ Σώκρατες; καὶ τί εὐηθίζεσθε πρὸς ἀλλήλους ὑποκατακλινόμενοι ὑμῖν αὐτοῖς; ἀλλ᾽ εἴπερ ὡς ἀληθῶς βούλει εἰδέναι τὸ δίκαιον ὅτι ἔστι, μὴ μόνον ἐρώτα μηδὲ φιλοτιμοῦ ἐλέγχων ἐπειδάν τίς τι ἀποκρίνηται, ἐγνωκὼς τοῦτο, ὅτι ῥᾷον ἐρωτᾶν ἢ ἀποκρίνεσθαι, ἀλλὰ καὶ αὐτὸς ἀπόκριναι καὶ εἰπὲ τί φῂς εἶναι τὸ δίκαιον.
[336d] καὶ ὅπως μοι μὴ ἐρεῖς ὅτι τὸ δέον ἐστὶν μηδ᾽ ὅτι τὸ ὠφέλιμον μηδ᾽ ὅτι τὸ λυσιτελοῦν μηδ᾽ ὅτι τὸ κερδαλέον μηδ᾽ ὅτι τὸ συμφέρον, ἀλλὰ σαφῶς μοι καὶ ἀκριβῶς λέγε ὅτι ἂν λέγῃς· ὡς ἐγὼ οὐκ ἀποδέξομαι ἐὰν ὕθλους τοιούτους λέγῃς.

καὶ ἐγὼ ἀκούσας ἐξεπλάγην καὶ προσβλέπων αὐτὸν ἐφοβούμην, καί μοι δοκῶ, εἰ μὴ πρότερος ἑωράκη αὐτὸν ἢ ᾽κεῖνος ἐμέ, ἄφωνος ἂν γενέσθαι. νῦν δὲ ἡνίκα ὑπὸ τοῦ λόγου ἤρχετο ἐξαγριαίνεσθαι, προσέβλεψα αὐτὸν πρότερος, ὥστε
[336e] αὐτῷ οἷός τ᾽ ἐγενόμην ἀποκρίνασθαι, καὶ εἶπον ὑποτρέμων· ὦ Θρασύμαχε, μὴ χαλεπὸς ἡμῖν ἴσθι· εἰ γάρ τι ἐξαμαρτάνομεν ἐν τῇ τῶν λόγων σκέψει ἐγώ τε καὶ ὅδε, εὖ ἴσθι ὅτι ἄκοντες ἁμαρτάνομεν. μὴ γὰρ δὴ οἴου, εἰ μὲν χρυσίον ἐζητοῦμεν, οὐκ ἄν ποτε ἡμᾶς ἑκόντας εἶναι ὑποκατακλίνεσθαι ἀλλήλοις ἐν τῇ ζητήσει καὶ διαφθείρειν τὴν εὕρεσιν αὐτοῦ, δικαιοσύνην δὲ ζητοῦντας, πρᾶγμα πολλῶν χρυσίων τιμιώτερον, ἔπειθ᾽ οὕτως ἀνοήτως ὑπείκειν ἀλλήλοις καὶ οὐ σπουδάζειν ὅτι μάλιστα φανῆναι αὐτό. οἴου γε σύ, ὦ φίλε. ἀλλ᾽, οἶμαι, οὐ
[337a] δυνάμεθα· ἐλεεῖσθαι οὖν ἡμᾶς πολὺ μᾶλλον εἰκός ἐστίν που ὑπὸ ὑμῶν τῶν δεινῶν ἢ χαλεπαίνεσθαι.

καὶ ὃς ἀκούσας ἀνεκάγχασέ τε μάλα σαρδάνιον καὶ εἶπεν· ὦ Ἡράκλεις, ἔφη, αὕτη "κείνη ἡ εἰωθυῖα εἰρωνεία Σωκράτους, καὶ ταῦτ" ἐγὼ ᾔδη τε καὶ τούτοις προύλεγον, ὅτι σὺ ἀποκρίνασθαι μὲν οὐκ ἐθελήσοις, εἰρωνεύσοιο δὲ καὶ πάντα μᾶλλον ποιήσοις ἢ ἀποκρινοῖο, εἴ τίς τί σε ἐρωτᾷ.

337a7–338a4: Thrasymachus claims he can give an answer as to what justice really is.

[338a5] εἰπόντος δέ μου ταῦτα ὅ τε Γλαύκων καὶ οἱ ἄλλοι ἐδέοντο αὐτοῦ μὴ ἄλλως ποιεῖν. καὶ ὁ Θρασύμαχος φανερὸς μὲν ἦν ἐπιθυμῶν εἰπεῖν ἵν᾽

A Level

εὐδοκιμήσειεν, ἡγούμενος ἔχειν ἀπόκρισιν παγκάλην· προσεποιεῖτο δὲ
φιλονικεῖν πρὸς τὸ ἐμὲ εἶναι τὸν ἀποκρινόμενον. τελευτῶν δὲ συνεχώρησεν, [338b]
κἄπειτα, αὕτη δή, ἔφη, ἡ Σωκράτους σοφία· αὐτὸν μὲν μὴ ἐθέλειν
διδάσκειν, παρὰ δὲ τῶν ἄλλων περιιόντα μανθάνειν καὶ τούτων μηδὲ χάριν
ἀποδιδόναι.

ὅτι μέν, ἦν δ᾽ ἐγώ, μανθάνω παρὰ τῶν ἄλλων, ἀληθῆ εἶπες, ὦ Θρασύμαχε, ὅτι [5]
δὲ οὔ με φῄς χάριν ἐκτίνειν, ψεύδη· ἐκτίνω γὰρ ὅσην δύναμαι. δύναμαι δὲ
ἐπαινεῖν μόνον· χρήματα γὰρ οὐκ ἔχω. ὡς δὲ προθύμως τοῦτο δρῶ, ἐάν τίς μοι
δοκῇ εὖ λέγειν, εὖ εἴσῃ αὐτίκα δὴ μάλα, ἐπειδὰν ἀποκρίνῃ· οἶμαι γάρ σε εὖ
ἐρεῖν.

ἄκουε δή, ἦ δ᾽ ὅς. φημὶ γὰρ ἐγὼ εἶναι τὸ δίκαιον οὐκ ἄλλο τι ἢ τὸ τοῦ κρείττονος [338c]
συμφέρον. ἀλλὰ τί οὐκ ἐπαινεῖς; ἀλλ᾽ οὐκ ἐθελήσεις.

ἐὰν μάθω γε πρῶτον, ἔφην, τί λέγεις· νῦν γὰρ οὔπω οἶδα. τὸ τοῦ κρείττονος
φῄς συμφέρον δίκαιον εἶναι. καὶ τοῦτο, ὦ Θρασύμαχε, τί ποτε λέγεις; οὐ γάρ
που τό γε τοιόνδε φῄς· εἰ Πουλυδάμας ἡμῶν κρείττων ὁ παγκρατιαστὴς καὶ [5]
αὐτῷ συμφέρει τὰ βόεια κρέα πρὸς τὸ σῶμα, τοῦτο τὸ σιτίον εἶναι καὶ ἡμῖν τοῖς
ἥττοσιν ἐκείνου συμφέρον ἅμα καὶ δίκαιον. [338d]

βδελυρὸς γὰρ εἶ, ἔφη, ὦ Σώκρατες, καὶ ταύτῃ ὑπολαμβάνεις ᾗ ἂν κακουργήσαις μάλιστα τὸν λόγον.

οὐδαμῶς, ὦ ἄριστε, ἦν δ᾽ ἐγώ· ἀλλὰ σαφέστερον εἰπὲ τί λέγεις.

εἶτ᾽ οὐκ οἶσθ᾽, ἔφη, ὅτι τῶν πόλεων αἱ μὲν τυραννοῦνται, αἱ δὲ δημοκρατοῦνται, [5]
αἱ δὲ ἀριστοκρατοῦνται;

πῶς γὰρ οὔ;

οὐκοῦν τοῦτο κρατεῖ ἐν ἑκάστῃ πόλει, τὸ ἄρχον;

πάνυ γε.

τίθεται δέ γε τοὺς νόμους ἑκάστη ἡ ἀρχὴ πρὸς τὸ αὑτῇ συμφέρον, δημοκρατία [338e]
μὲν δημοκρατικούς, τυραννὶς δὲ τυραννικούς, καὶ αἱ ἄλλαι οὕτως· θέμεναι δὲ
ἀπέφηναν τοῦτο δίκαιον τοῖς ἀρχομένοις εἶναι, τὸ σφίσι συμφέρον, καὶ τὸν
τούτου ἐκβαίνοντα κολάζουσιν ὡς παρανομοῦντά τε καὶ ἀδικοῦντα. τοῦτ᾽ οὖν
ἔστιν, ὦ βέλτιστε, ὃ λέγω ἐν ἁπάσαις ταῖς πόλεσιν ταὐτὸν εἶναι δίκαιον, τὸ [339a]
τῆς καθεστηκυίας ἀρχῆς συμφέρον· αὕτη δέ που κρατεῖ, ὥστε συμβαίνει τῷ
ὀρθῶς λογιζομένῳ πανταχοῦ εἶναι τὸ αὐτὸ δίκαιον, τὸ τοῦ κρείττονος
συμφέρον.

νῦν, ἦν δ᾽ ἐγώ, ἔμαθον ὃ λέγεις· εἰ δὲ ἀληθὲς ἢ μή, πειράσομαι μαθεῖν. τὸ [5]
συμφέρον μὲν οὖν, ὦ Θρασύμαχε, καὶ σὺ ἀπεκρίνω δίκαιον εἶναι, καίτοι ἔμοιγε

A Level

[339b] ἀπηγόρευες ὅπως μὴ τοῦτο ἀποκρινοίμην· πρόσεστιν δὲ δὴ αὐτόθι τὸ "τοῦ κρείττονος."

σμικρά γε ἴσως, ἔφη, προσθήκη.

οὔπω δῆλον οὐδ᾽ εἰ μεγάλη· ἀλλ᾽ ὅτι μὲν τοῦτο σκεπτέον εἰ ἀληθῆ λέγεις, δῆλον. ἐπειδὴ γὰρ συμφέρον γέ τι εἶναι καὶ ἐγὼ ὁμολογῶ τὸ δίκαιον, σὺ δὲ προστίθης καὶ αὐτὸ φῂς εἶναι τὸ τοῦ κρείττονος, ἐγὼ δὲ ἀγνοῶ, σκεπτέον δή.

σκόπει, ἔφη.

ταῦτ᾽ ἔσται, ἦν δ᾽ ἐγώ. καί μοι εἰπέ· οὐ καὶ πείθεσθαι μέντοι τοῖς ἄρχουσιν δίκαιον φῂς εἶναι;

ἔγωγε.

[339c] πότερον δὲ ἀναμάρτητοί εἰσιν οἱ ἄρχοντες ἐν ταῖς πόλεσιν ἑκάσταις ἤ οἷοί τι καὶ ἁμαρτεῖν;

πάντως που, ἔφη, οἷοί τι καὶ ἁμαρτεῖν.

οὐκοῦν ἐπιχειροῦντες νόμους τιθέναι τοὺς μὲν ὀρθῶς τιθέασιν, τοὺς δέ τινας οὐκ ὀρθῶς;

οἶμαι ἔγωγε.

τὸ δὲ ὀρθῶς ἄρα τὸ τὰ συμφέροντά ἐστι τίθεσθαι ἑαυτοῖς, τὸ δὲ μὴ ὀρθῶς ἀσύμφορα; ἢ πῶς λέγεις;

οὕτως.

ἃ δ᾽ ἂν θῶνται ποιητέον τοῖς ἀρχομένοις, καὶ τοῦτό ἐστι τὸ δίκαιον;

πῶς γὰρ οὔ;

[339d] οὐ μόνον ἄρα δίκαιόν ἐστιν κατὰ τὸν σὸν λόγον τὸ τοῦ κρείττονος συμφέρον ποιεῖν ἀλλὰ καὶ τοὐναντίον, τὸ μὴ συμφέρον.

τί λέγεις σύ; ἔφη.

ἃ σὺ λέγεις, ἔμοιγε δοκῶ· σκοπῶμεν δὲ βέλτιον. οὐχ ὡμολόγηται τοὺς ἄρχοντας τοῖς ἀρχομένοις προστάττοντας ποιεῖν ἄττα ἐνίοτε διαμαρτάνειν τοῦ ἑαυτοῖς βελτίστου, ἃ δ᾽ ἂν προστάττωσιν οἱ ἄρχοντες δίκαιον εἶναι τοῖς ἀρχομένοις ποιεῖν; ταῦτ᾽ οὐχ ὡμολόγηται;

οἶμαι ἔγωγε, ἔφη.

[339e] οἴου τοίνυν, ἦν δ᾽ ἐγώ, καὶ τὸ ἀσύμφορα ποιεῖν τοῖς ἄρχουσί τε καὶ κρείττοσι δίκαιον εἶναι ὡμολογῆσθαί σοι· ὅταν οἱ μὲν ἄρχοντες ἄκοντες κακὰ αὑτοῖς προστάττωσιν, τοῖς δὲ δίκαιον εἶναι φῇς ταῦτα ποιεῖν ἃ ἐκεῖνοι προσέταξαν,

ἆρα τότε, ὦ σοφώτατε Θρασύμαχε, οὐκ ἀναγκαῖον συμβαίνειν αὐτὸ ούτωσί, δίκαιον εἶναι ποιεῖν τοὐναντίον ἢ ὃ σὺ λέγεις; τὸ γὰρ τοῦ κρείττονος ἀσύμφορον δήπου προστάττεται τοῖς ἥττοσιν ποιεῖν.

ναὶ μὰ Δί᾽, ἔφη, ὦ Σώκρατες, ὁ Πολέμαρχος, σαφέστατά γε. [340a]

ἐὰν σύ γ᾽, ἔφη, αὐτῷ μαρτυρήσῃς, ὁ Κλειτοφῶν ὑπολαβών.

καὶ τί, ἔφη, δεῖται μάρτυρος; αὐτὸς γὰρ Θρασύμαχος ὁμολογεῖ τοὺς μὲν ἄρχοντας ἐνίοτε ἑαυτοῖς κακὰ προστάττειν, τοῖς δὲ δίκαιον εἶναι ταῦτα ποιεῖν.

τὸ γὰρ τὰ κελευόμενα ποιεῖν, ὦ Πολέμαρχε, ὑπὸ τῶν ἀρχόντων δίκαιον εἶναι ἔθετο Θρασύμαχος.

καὶ γὰρ τὸ τοῦ κρείττονος, ὦ Κλειτοφῶν, συμφέρον δίκαιον εἶναι ἔθετο. ταῦτα δὲ ἀμφότερα θέμενος ὡμολόγησεν αὖ ἐνίοτε τοὺς κρείττους τὰ αὑτοῖς [340b] ἀσύμφορα κελεύειν τοὺς ἥττους τε καὶ ἀρχομένους ποιεῖν. ἐκ δὲ τούτων τῶν ὁμολογιῶν οὐδὲν μᾶλλον τὸ τοῦ κρείττονος συμφέρον δίκαιον ἂν εἴη ἢ τὸ μὴ συμφέρον.

ἀλλ᾽, ἔφη ὁ Κλειτοφῶν, τὸ τοῦ κρείττονος συμφέρον ἔλεγεν ὃ ἡγοῖτο ὁ κρείττων αὑτῷ συμφέρειν· τοῦτο ποιητέον εἶναι τῷ ἥττονι, καὶ τὸ δίκαιον τοῦτο ἐτίθετο.

ἀλλ᾽ οὐχ οὕτως, ἦ δ᾽ ὃς ὁ Πολέμαρχος, ἐλέγετο.

οὐδέν, ἦν δ᾽ ἐγώ, ὦ Πολέμαρχε, διαφέρει, ἀλλ᾽ εἰ νῦν οὕτω λέγει Θρασύμαχος, [340c] οὕτως αὐτοῦ ἀποδεχώμεθα. καί μοι εἰπέ, ὦ Θρασύμαχε· τοῦτο ἦν ὃ ἐβούλου λέγειν τὸ δίκαιον, τὸ τοῦ κρείττονος συμφέρον δοκοῦν εἶναι τῷ κρείττονι, ἐάντε συμφέρῃ ἐάντε μή; οὕτω σε φῶμεν λέγειν;

ἥκιστά γε, ἔφη· ἀλλὰ κρείττω με οἴει καλεῖν τὸν ἐξαμαρτάνοντα ὅταν ἐξαμαρτάνῃ;

ἔγωγε, εἶπον, ᾤμην σε τοῦτο λέγειν ὅτε τοὺς ἄρχοντας ὡμολόγεις οὐκ ἀναμαρτήτους εἶναι ἀλλά τι καὶ ἐξαμαρτάνειν.

συκοφάντης γὰρ εἶ, ἔφη, ὦ Σώκρατες, ἐν τοῖς λόγοις· ἐπεὶ αὐτίκα ἰατρὸν καλεῖς [340d] σὺ τὸν ἐξαμαρτάνοντα περὶ τοὺς κάμνοντας κατ᾽ αὐτὸ τοῦτο ὃ ἐξαμαρτάνει; ἢ λογιστικόν, ὃς ἂν ἐν λογισμῷ ἁμαρτάνῃ, τότε ὅταν ἁμαρτάνῃ, κατὰ ταύτην τὴν ἁμαρτίαν; ἀλλ᾽ οἶμαι λέγομεν τῷ ῥήματι οὕτως, ὅτι ὁ ἰατρὸς ἐξήμαρτεν καὶ ὁ λογιστὴς ἐξήμαρτεν καὶ ὁ γραμματιστής· τὸ δ᾽ οἶμαι ἕκαστος τούτων, καθ᾽ ὅσον τοῦτ᾽ ἔστιν ὃ προσαγορεύομεν αὐτόν, οὐδέποτε ἁμαρτάνει· ὥστε [340e] κατὰ τὸν ἀκριβῆ λόγον, ἐπειδὴ καὶ σὺ ἀκριβολογῇ, οὐδεὶς τῶν δημιουργῶν ἁμαρτάνει. ἐπιλειπούσης γὰρ ἐπιστήμης ὁ ἁμαρτάνων ἁμαρτάνει, ἐν ᾧ οὐκ ἔστι δημιουργός· ὥστε δημιουργὸς ἢ σοφὸς ἢ ἄρχων οὐδεὶς ἁμαρτάνει τότε

ὅταν ἄρχων ᾖ, ἀλλὰ πᾶς γ᾽ ἂν εἴποι ὅτι ὁ ἰατρὸς ἥμαρτεν καὶ ὁ ἄρχων ἥμαρτεν. τοιοῦτον οὖν δή σοι καὶ ἐμὲ ὑπόλαβε νυνδὴ ἀποκρίνεσθαι· τὸ δὲ ἀκριβέστατον
[341a] ἐκεῖνο τυγχάνει ὄν, τὸν ἄρχοντα, καθ᾽ ὅσον ἄρχων ἐστίν, μὴ ἁμαρτάνειν, μὴ ἁμαρτάνοντα δὲ τὸ αὑτῷ βέλτιστον τίθεσθαι, τοῦτο δὲ τῷ ἀρχομένῳ ποιητέον. ὥστε, ὅπερ ἐξ ἀρχῆς ἔλεγον, δίκαιον λέγω τὸ τοῦ κρείττονος ποιεῖν συμφέρον.

εἶεν, ἦν δ᾽ ἐγώ, ὦ Θρασύμαχε· δοκῶ σοι συκοφαντεῖν;

πάνυ μὲν οὖν, ἔφη.

οἴει γάρ με ἐξ ἐπιβουλῆς ἐν τοῖς λόγοις κακουργοῦντά σε ἐρέσθαι ὡς ἠρόμην;

[341b] εὖ μὲν οὖν οἶδα, ἔφη. καὶ οὐδέν γέ σοι πλέον ἔσται· οὔτε γὰρ ἄν με λάθοις κακουργῶν, οὔτε μὴ λαθὼν βιάσασθαι τῷ λόγῳ δύναιο.

οὐδέ γ᾽ ἂν ἐπιχειρήσαιμι, ἦν δ᾽ ἐγώ, ὦ μακάριε. ἀλλ᾽ ἵνα μὴ αὖθις ἡμῖν τοιοῦτον ἐγγένηται, διόρισαι ποτέρως λέγεις τὸν ἄρχοντά τε καὶ τὸν κρείττονα, τὸν ὡς ἔπος εἰπεῖν ἢ τὸν ἀκριβεῖ λόγῳ, ὃ νυνδὴ ἔλεγες, οὗ τὸ συμφέρον κρείττονος ὄντος δίκαιον ἔσται τῷ ἥττονι ποιεῖν.

τὸν τῷ ἀκριβεστάτῳ, ἔφη, λόγῳ ἄρχοντα ὄντα. πρὸς ταῦτα κακούργει καὶ
[341c] συκοφάντει, εἴ τι δύνασαι· οὐδέν σου παρίεμαι. ἀλλ᾽ οὐ μὴ οἷός τ᾽ ᾖς.

οἴει γὰρ ἄν με, εἶπον, οὕτω μανῆναι ὥστε ξυρεῖν ἐπιχειρεῖν λέοντα καὶ συκοφαντεῖν Θρασύμαχον;

νῦν γοῦν, ἔφη, ἐπεχείρησας, οὐδὲν ὢν καὶ ταῦτα.

ἅδην, ἦν δ᾽ ἐγώ, τῶν τοιούτων. ἀλλ᾽ εἰπέ μοι· ὁ τῷ ἀκριβεῖ λόγῳ ἰατρός, ὃν ἄρτι ἔλεγες, πότερον χρηματιστής ἐστιν ἢ τῶν καμνόντων θεραπευτής; καὶ λέγε τὸν τῷ ὄντι ἰατρὸν ὄντα.

τῶν καμνόντων, ἔφη, θεραπευτής.

τί δὲ κυβερνήτης; ὁ ὀρθῶς κυβερνήτης ναυτῶν ἄρχων ἐστὶν ἢ ναύτης;

[341d] ναυτῶν ἄρχων.

οὐδὲν οἶμαι τοῦτο ὑπολογιστέον, ὅτι πλεῖ ἐν τῇ νηί, οὐδ᾽ ἐστὶν κλητέος ναύτης· οὐ γὰρ κατὰ τὸ πλεῖν κυβερνήτης καλεῖται, ἀλλὰ κατὰ τὴν τέχνην καὶ τὴν τῶν ναυτῶν ἀρχήν.

ἀληθῆ, ἔφη.

οὐκοῦν ἑκάστῳ τούτων ἔστιν τι συμφέρον;

πάνυ γε.

οὐ καὶ ἡ τέχνη, ἦν δ᾽ ἐγώ, ἐπὶ τούτῳ πέφυκεν, ἐπὶ τῷ τὸ συμφέρον ἑκάστῳ ζητεῖν τε καὶ ἐκπορίζειν;

ἐπὶ τούτῳ, ἔφη.

ἆρ᾽ οὖν καὶ ἑκάστῃ τῶν τεχνῶν ἔστιν τι συμφέρον ἄλλο ἢ ὅτι μάλιστα τελέαν εἶναι;

πῶς τοῦτο ἐρωτᾷς; [341e]

ὥσπερ, ἔφην ἐγώ, εἴ με ἔροιο εἰ ἐξαρκεῖ σώματι εἶναι σώματι ἢ προσδεῖταί τινος, εἴποιμ᾽ ἂν ὅτι "παντάπασι μὲν οὖν προσδεῖται. διὰ ταῦτα καὶ ἡ τέχνη ἐστὶν ἡ ἰατρικὴ νῦν ηὑρημένη, ὅτι σῶμά ἐστιν πονηρὸν καὶ οὐκ ἐξαρκεῖ αὐτῷ τοιούτῳ εἶναι. τούτῳ οὖν ὅπως ἐκπορίζῃ τὰ συμφέροντα, ἐπὶ τοῦτο παρεσκευάσθη ἡ τέχνη." ἢ ὀρθῶς σοι δοκῶ, ἔφην, ἂν εἰπεῖν οὕτω λέγων, ἢ οὔ;

ὀρθῶς, ἔφη.

[342a] τί δὲ δή; αὐτὴ ἡ ἰατρική ἐστιν πονηρά, ἢ ἄλλη τις τέχνη ἔσθ᾽ ὅτι προσδεῖταί τινος ἀρετῆς, ὥσπερ ὀφθαλμοὶ ὄψεως καὶ ὦτα ἀκοῆς καὶ διὰ ταῦτα ἐπ᾽ αὐτοῖς δεῖ τινος τέχνης τῆς τὸ συμφέρον εἰς ταῦτα σκεψομένης τε καὶ ἐκποριούσης, ἆρα καὶ ἐν αὐτῇ τῇ τέχνῃ ἔνι τις πονηρία, καὶ δεῖ ἑκάστῃ τέχνῃ ἄλλης τέχνης ἥτις αὐτῇ τὸ συμφέρον σκέψεται, καὶ τῇ σκοπουμένῃ ἑτέρας αὖ τοιαύτης, καὶ τοῦτ᾽ ἔστιν ἀπέραντον; [342b] ἢ αὐτὴ αὑτῇ τὸ συμφέρον σκέψεται; ἢ οὔτε αὑτῆς οὔτε ἄλλης προσδεῖται ἐπὶ τὴν αὑτῆς πονηρίαν τὸ συμφέρον σκοπεῖν· οὔτε γὰρ πονηρία οὔτε ἁμαρτία οὐδεμία οὐδεμιᾷ τέχνῃ πάρεστιν, οὐδὲ προσήκει τέχνῃ ἄλλῳ τὸ συμφέρον ζητεῖν ἢ ᾽κείνῳ οὗ τέχνη ἐστίν, αὐτὴ δὲ ἀβλαβὴς καὶ ἀκέραιός ἐστιν ὀρθὴ οὖσα, ἕωσπερ ἂν ᾖ ἑκάστη ἀκριβὴς ὅλη ἥπερ ἐστίν; καὶ σκόπει ἐκείνῳ τῷ ἀκριβεῖ λόγῳ· οὕτως ἢ ἄλλως ἔχει;

οὕτως, ἔφη, φαίνεται.

οὐκ ἄρα, ἦν δ᾽ ἐγώ, ἰατρικὴ ἰατρικῇ τὸ συμφέρον σκοπεῖ ἀλλὰ σώματι. [342c]

ναί, ἔφη.

οὐδὲ ἱππικὴ ἱππικῇ ἀλλ᾽ ἵπποις· οὐδὲ ἄλλη τέχνη οὐδεμία ἑαυτῇ, οὐδὲ γὰρ προσδεῖται, ἀλλ᾽ ἐκείνῳ οὗ τέχνη ἐστίν.

φαίνεται, ἔφη, οὕτως.

ἀλλὰ μήν, ὦ Θρασύμαχε, ἄρχουσί γε αἱ τέχναι καὶ κρατοῦσιν ἐκείνου οὗπέρ εἰσιν τέχναι.

συνεχώρησεν ἐνταῦθα καὶ μάλα μόγις.

οὐκ ἄρα ἐπιστήμη γε οὐδεμία τὸ τοῦ κρείττονος συμφέρον σκοπεῖ οὐδ᾽
[342d] ἐπιτάττει, ἀλλὰ τὸ τοῦ ἥττονός τε καὶ ἀρχομένου ὑπὸ ἑαυτῆς.

συνωμολόγησε μὲν καὶ ταῦτα τελευτῶν, ἐπεχείρει δὲ περὶ αὐτὰ μάχεσθαι· ἐπειδὴ δὲ ὡμολόγησεν, ἄλλο τι οὖν, ἦν δ᾽ ἐγώ, οὐδὲ ἰατρὸς οὐδείς, καθ᾽ ὅσον ἰατρός, τὸ τῷ ἰατρῷ συμφέρον σκοπεῖ οὐδ᾽ ἐπιτάττει, ἀλλὰ τὸ τῷ κάμνοντι; ὡμολόγηται γὰρ ὁ ἀκριβὴς ἰατρὸς σωμάτων εἶναι ἄρχων ἀλλ᾽ οὐ χρηματιστής. ἢ οὐχ ὡμολόγηται;

συνέφη.

[342e] οὐκοῦν καὶ ὁ κυβερνήτης ὁ ἀκριβὴς ναυτῶν εἶναι ἄρχων ἀλλ᾽ οὐ ναύτης;

ὡμολόγηται.

οὐκ ἄρα ὅ γε τοιοῦτος κυβερνήτης τε καὶ ἄρχων τὸ τῷ κυβερνήτῃ συμφέρον σκέψεταί τε καὶ προστάξει, ἀλλὰ τὸ τῷ ναύτῃ τε καὶ ἀρχομένῳ.

συνέφησε μόγις.

οὐκοῦν, ἦν δ᾽ ἐγώ, ὦ Θρασύμαχε, οὐδὲ ἄλλος οὐδεὶς ἐν οὐδεμιᾷ ἀρχῇ, καθ᾽ ὅσον ἄρχων ἐστίν, τὸ αὑτῷ συμφέρον σκοπεῖ οὐδ᾽ ἐπιτάττει, ἀλλὰ τὸ τῷ ἀρχομένῳ καὶ ᾧ ἂν αὐτὸς δημιουργῇ, καὶ πρὸς ἐκεῖνο βλέπων καὶ τὸ ἐκείνῳ συμφέρον καὶ πρέπον, καὶ λέγει ἃ λέγει καὶ ποιεῖ ἃ ποιεῖ ἅπαντα.

Commentary Notes

327a

Σωκράτης: The text begins by identifying the speaker as Socrates (as if in a dramatic script).

κατέβην: (strong – sometimes also called second or root) aorist of καταβαίνω. This opening is a deceptively conversational and casual opening to a work of powerful philosophy, and was much admired (and imitated) in the ancient world: Dionysius of Halicarnassus (first century BCE) recounts the anecdote that after Plato's death, a tablet was discovered with numerous different arrangements of this first sentence, as an illustration of Plato's attention to stylistic detail. Some later commentators on Plato (both ancient, like Proclus in the fifth century CE, and modern, like Myles Burnyeat) have read a great deal into this word, seeing in it a foreshadowing of the allegory of the cave (into which the philosopher 'goes down') in Book 7 of the *Republic*.

Πειραιᾶ: the Piraeus is the port of Athens, about 5 miles (8 km) distant from the city itself (though nominally still part of it): thematically, Plato takes us into the home of a non-citizen, in the multinational melting pot of the port, outside the city proper, precisely to discuss what makes an ideal city.

τοῦ Ἀρίστωνος: a patronymic, 'son of Ariston'; the article refers back to Glaucon, as can be seen by the parallel construction **Πολέμαρχος ὁ Κεφάλου** (327b) and **Νικήρατος ὁ Νικίου** (327c).

προσευξόμενός: the future participle here is used to denote purpose.

τῇ θεῷbnotice the gender – goddess, rather than god; later (354a) it is made clear this is Bendis. Bendis was a Thracian goddess, sometimes identified with Artemis, a cult probably introduced to Attica sometime in the mid-fifth century. Despite the Athenians making 'introducing new gods' one of the charges against Socrates, the introduction of new gods was not uncommon: Asclepius (to whom Socrates famously owed the sacrifice of a cockerel – his last words) was only introduced to Athens from Epidaurus with a formal ceremony in 420 BCE.

τὴν ἑορτὴν . . . τίνα τρόπον ποιήσουσιν: **ἑορτὴν** precedes the indirect question, but is best translated as part of it, as the object of **ποιήσουσιν** rather than **θεάσασθαι**. Note that the verb in the indirect question is kept in the indicative, even though it is in secondary (historic) sequence: this is the more vivid form than the use of the optative.

ἅτε . . . ἄγοντες: **ἅτε** + participle is used to give a cause from the writer's or speaker's point of view, whereas *ὡς* + participle gives an alleged cause.

πρῶτον: adverbial accusative, 'for the first time'.
ἧττον: another adverbial accusative, modifying **πρέπειν** – 'to be less fitting'.
ἣν οἱ Θρᾷκες ἔπεμπον: the implied antecedent of **ἣν** is **πομπὴ**; this whole phrase (translate as something like 'the one which the Thracians sent') is the subject of **ἐφαίνετο**. The Thracians are either the community of resident foreigners, or possibly a special delegation sent from Thrace for the festival.

327b
πρὸς τὸ ἄστυ: that is, back to Athens itself from Piraeus.
ἀπῇμεν: imperfect of *ἀπέρχομαι*.
τὸν παῖδα: not child, but (as commonly), slave.
δραμόντα: aorist participle of τρέχω; as usual, Greek prefers participle and verb, as opposed to two verbs in coordination (i.e. 'running, to order', rather than the more natural English 'to run and order').
περιμεῖναί: dependent on **κελεῦσαι** as an indirect command; *ἡμᾶς* needs to be supplied as the subject of **περιμεῖναί**.
ἑ: reflexive pronoun, 'him' (i.e. Polemarchus), the object of **περιμεῖναί**. This is not commonly encountered in later Attic literature outside Plato, and might be indicative of more colloquial speech.
μου . . . τοῦ ἱματίου: partitive genitive: translate as 'by my cloak', or 'catching me by my cloak'.
ὅπου αὐτὸς εἴη: indirect question, with the indirect form of the interrogative **ὅπου**, and the optative **εἴη** as it is in secondary sequence. **αὐτὸς** is intensifying, but needn't be translated as 'he himself' – 'where he was' is the most natural rendering in English. It is often used to refer to any kind of superior – here, the slave's master; again, it is probably a marker of colloquial speech, like **Οὗτος** directly after – 'here he is', a deictic use (i.e. it is effectively pointing him out as he arrives).
ἀλλὰ περιμένετε: **ἀλλὰ** is often attached to an imperative to 'remonstrate, encourage, persuade' (so LSJ, s.v. *ἀλλά* 2.2, which picks this reference as an exemplar of *ἀλλά* echoed in response. The use of the present imperative here suggests a continuous action; colloquially this could be construed 'Come on, stick around', or more formally 'Do wait.'
περιμενοῦμεν: future tense.

327c
ὀλίγῳ: dative of degree of difference, with **ὕστερον** (another adverbial accusative), 'later by a little' or more smoothly, 'a little later'.
ὡς ἀπὸ τῆς πομπῆς: **ὡς** here has the force 'as if'; Emlyn-Jones translates effectively 'apparently from the procession'. The dialogue following is deliberately conversational and humorous in tone.
ὡρμῆσθαι: perfect middle infinitive of *ὁρμάω*.
δοκεῖτέ: the Greek prefers a personal construction where English would find the impersonal more natural ('you seem to be . . .' rather than 'it seems like you are . . .').
ὡς ἀπιόντες: again with the force 'as if', used with a participle, but just as easily translated by a finite verb in English 'as if leaving' or 'as if you were leaving'.

οὐ γὰρ κακῶς: The litotes (making a statement by negating its opposite) is here ironic and comic in force; like the English 'you're not wrong' to mean 'you're exactly right'.

ὁρᾷς . . . ἐσμέν: Though the tone and diction are light, there is a contrast between force (jokingly suggested by Polemarchus) and persuasion (on Socrates' part, **πείσωμεν ὑμᾶς**); this foreshadows Socrates' verbal sparring with Thrasymachus, but also possibly subtly hints at the difficulties of the one persuading the many: see the introduction on the relationship between Socrates, Plato and democracy.

πῶς γὰρ οὔ; literally, 'For how not?', the ellipsis of a verb continues to give a colloquial, comic tone to the dialogue: 'How could I not?' gets the sense of it across without adding too much to the Greek.

τούτων: genitive of comparison ('than') depending on **κρείττους**.

γένεσθε: aorist imperative of *γίγνομαι*; the aorist mood gives the sense of a one-off action (especially contrasted with present **μένετ'** as the alternative) ; *γίγνομαι* often simply carries the sense of just 'be' rather than become, but the English imperative 'be!' cannot carry this punctiliar aorist force: 'prove yourselves' (Emlyn-Jones) conveys the sense accurately.

αὐτοῦ: not a pronoun, but the adverb 'here'.

τὸ . . . ἀφεῖναι: the whole phrase is the subject of **ἐλλείπεται**; the article is attached to the whole clause so that it is treated as a noun. (Other editions of the text have **ἓν λείπεται**; this doesn't really change the meaning: 'one [option] is left, namely, that . . .')

ἢν: a contracted form of *ἐάν*, a protasis of a future more vivid construction with the aorist subjunctive *πείσωμεν*.

δύναισθ' ἄν: present potential optative: 'could you'.

μὴ ἀκούοντας: the force of the participle here is conditional (hence the use of **μὴ**) modifying an implied 'us' – 'even if we weren't listening'.

ὡς . . . ἀκουσομένων: again, supply 'us'; the phrase is a genitive absolute. *ὡς* + future participle is used to indicate alleged cause.

328a

ἴστε: second person plural of *οἶδα*.

λαμπὰς: a relay-race in which a burning torch was passed from one runner to another (much like the baton in a modern relay-race) while keeping it alight. Herodotus mentions a similar race in honour of Hephaestus (8.98). Neither the dinner which Polemarchus promises nor the race are mentioned again in the *Republic*.

πρὸς ἑσπέραν: *πρὸς* + accusative with a time suggests near, at, or about a certain time – 'in the evening'.

ἀφ' ἵππων: literally, 'from horses', i.e. 'on horseback'.

πῶς λέγεις: literally, 'how do you say', but more naturally, 'what do you mean'.

καινόν γε τοῦτο: supply *ἐστίν*.

καὶ πρός γε: adverbial; 'and in addition'.

ἄξιον: again, *ἐστίν* must be understood.

συνεσόμεθά: future of *σύνειμι*, which takes a dative case.

328b

μενετέον: the adjectival form of the verb ending in -*τεος* is the gerundive, suggesting obligation, and takes a dative case for the agent (although absent, *ἡμῖν* is implied here): 'necessary to remain' or (with **εἶναι**) 'we must remain'.

ἤιμεν: imperfect of *ἔρχομαι*.

οἴκαδε εἰς τοῦ Πολεμάρχου: 'to the house of Polemarchus'.

τὸν Παιανιᾶ: 'of the deme of Paeania'; Athens was divided into 'demes', both political and geographical divisions of the city (something like a local council area, with its own officials, but subsidiary to the larger state).

τὸν Ἀριστωνύμου: 'the [son] of Aristonymus'; this form of patronymic is very common in Greek.

328c

διὰ χρόνου: literally, 'over a [long] time': more natural English would prefer putting the sentence in the negative, i.e. 'I had not seen him for a long time'. **ἑωράκη** is the pluperfect of *ὁράω*.

καθῆστο ... δίφρου: The wreath is part of formal ritual wear for the sacrifice, though there is no special significance to the cushioned chair – perhaps part of Plato's characterization of Cephalus as a comfortable old man.

τεθυκὼς: perfect participle of *θύω*; *τυγχάνω* + participle = happen to be doing. The sacrifice is unconnected to the religious festival of Bendis, but is rather a more quotidian domestic sacrifice to Zeus 'Protector of the Household'.

ἠσπάζετό: The force of the imperfect here is that 'he began to welcome'.

οὐδὲ: is difficult to understand in context, and is amended by many editors. If our text is correct, it must mean, 'You do not come often *either* [i.e. in addition to other lapses which are not mentioned].' Other conjectures have been *οὐ δὲ,* and οὔ τι – the latter would make this a quotation of Homer, *Od.* V.87: given Cephalus' other quotations from literature, perhaps very fitting for his cultured, traditional characterization.

328d

εἰ ... ἦ ... ἂν ... ἔδει: A present counterfactual or unfulfilled conditional – **ἦ** is imperfect indicative (of *εἰμί*), with **εἰ**, forming the protasis, followed by **ἂν** + imperfect indicative (of the impersonal *δεῖ*) as the apodosis. 'If I were . . . it would be necessary. . .'

ἰέναι: infinitive of *εἶμι (ibo)*, 'to come'; likewise **ᾖμεν**, imperfect indicative of the same verb (continuing the counterfactual – 'we would come').

πυκνότερον: comparative adverb.

ἴσθι: imperative singular of *οἶδα*.

ἔμοιγε: simply an emphatic form of **ἔμοι,** 'for my part' or 'as far as I'm concerned'.

ὅσον ... τοσοῦτον: correlatives – 'as much. . .so much'. English would more naturally use the idiom 'the more . . . the more . . .' Some commentators have read here an implicit denigration of philosophy from Cephalus – something that 'is fine as long you have nothing better to do' (Annas 19); in contrast, Emlyn-Jones *ad loc.* suggests that it represents 'a characteristically Platonic contrast between the ephemeral pleasures of the body and the enduring delights of the mind'.

μὴ . . . ποίει: negative imperative (the form looks indicative as *ποιέω* is an epsilon-contract verb).

νεανίσκοις: a variant of νεανίας; although many of those present are clearly adults, at least in their late twenties, but from Cephalus' perspective clearly 'youths': the theme of old age versus youth is being established here.

σύνισθι: imperative of *σύνειμι* (be with, spend time with, associate with), rather than σύνοιδα (know about a person), though in form it could be either.

καὶ μήν . . . γε: 'and truly'; surrounding **χαίρω** with the particles lays greater stress on it: a very positive affirmative response.

χαίρω γε διαλεγόμενος τοῖς σφόδρα πρεσβύταις: a claim not necessarily borne out by the Platonic corpus: Socrates' interlocuters are almost invariably young men, rather than old ones, including in the rest of the *Republic*. Plato, however, is drawing out the key theme of youth, old age, and the afterlife.

328e

προεληλυθότων: genitive plural perfect active participle of *προέρχομαι*; **τινὰ ὁδὸν** is not the object of the verb, but an accusative of extent: 'over' or 'along a certain road'.

δεήσει: future of *δεῖ*.

ποία τίς: an indirect question, 'whatever sort', dependent on **πυνθάνεσθαι**, expressed in more vivid form (rather than *ὁποία*); the elided noun they are modifying is *ὁδός*, assumed from the previous clause.

καὶ δὴ καὶ: in particular, moreover.

εὔπορος: notice what looks like a masculine ending, despite being feminine – all compound adjectives in Greek are two-termination (i.e. they use the masculine form for both masculine and feminine).

ἂν πυθοίμην: potential optative, 'I would learn.'

ἐνταῦθα: 'at that point', with the partitive genitive **τῆς ἡλικίας; ὃ** is the neuter of the relative pronoun, taking this whole phrase as its antecedent.

ἐπὶ γήραος οὐδῷ: a proverbial phrase, attested as early as Homer (*Iliad* 22.60 and *Odyssey* 15.246). The metaphor has been variously interpreted: either the image of life as a house, with old age being the threshold on the way out to death; or old age itself is the house, into which Cephalus is just entering – or possibly leaving. In Homer, the phrase seems clearly to refer to extreme old age.

χαλεπὸν τοῦ βίου: a partitive genitive; 'a difficult part of life'.

329a

νὴ τὸν Δία: A common exclamation, for which the accusative is used: 'by Zeus'.

ταὐτὸν: crasis of *τὸ αὐτὸν*, 'the same [sc. place]'.

τὴν παλαιὰν παροιμίαν: what this is not exactly known, but presumably something along the lines of 'birds of a feather'; *Phaedrus* 240c mentions a similar proverb ('like age delights in like'), and the scholiast (early commentator) on this passage suggests 'jackdaw sits next to jackdaw'.

συνιόντες: participle of *σύνέρχομαι*.

τὰς . . . ἡδονὰς ποθοῦντες: complaining about the difficulties of age and longing for youth are commonplace ideas in lyric and elegiac poetry: e.g. Mimnermus fr. 1, Simonides fr. 520; and cf. also Sophocles *Oedipus at Colonus* 1235 ff.

ἄλλ᾽ ἄττα: an Attic form of *ἄλλα ἅτινά*, 'some other things'.

ἔχεται: 'pertain to', which takes a genitive case; note the verb is singular as the subject is neuter plural. A clear translation would be 'which go along with these'.

ὡς with a participle, as here, introduces an alleged cause: 'as if'.

ζῶντες . . . ζῶντες: the first of these present participles represents an imperfect, and the second a present: '[as if] we used to live . . . but now we live'.

329b

τῶν οἰκείων . . . τοῦ γήρως: the two genitives are used in different senses, one subjective (**τῶν οἰκείων,** best translated by 'at the hands of . . .'), the other objective (**τοῦ γήρως** – old age is the object of the abuse). **γήρως** is the contracted *γήρα-ος*.

προπηλακίσεις: the word has strong connotations of physical violence (literally, to cover with mud). Respect for elders was an important Greek and Athenian value, and legal penalties for maltreatment of one's parents had long been established; conflict between generations, however, forms part of the intellectual backdrop to the *Republic* as well as other fifth-century literature, most notably comedy (e.g. Aristophanes' *Wasps* and *Clouds*).

ἐπὶ τούτῳ δὴ: 'especially on this account'.

τὸ γῆρας ὑμνοῦσιν ὅσων: the construction is very common in Greek, but unwieldy in English; **ὑμνοῦσιν** has a direct object in **τὸ γῆρας,** and an indirect question as its object; the phenomenon is called prolepsis (grammatical anticipation, here of the indirect question with a direct object). The difficulty in translation is solved by moving **τὸ γῆρας** into the indirect question and treating it as if it is nominative. Older translations of the Bible still carry the Greek construction literally: 'I know thee who thou art' (Mk. 1:24).

σφίσιν = *αὐτοῖς* (alternative form).

κἂν: crasis of *καὶ ἄν*.

ἐπεπόνθη: pluperfect indicative of *πάσχω*, in a counterfactual conditional (with *ἄν*) – 'I would have suffered . . .'

οὕτως ἔχουσιν: *ἔχω* + adverb is idiomatic for being in a particular state, or equivalent to 'to be + adjective' (rather archaically, often explained as 'to fare . . .'). **ἔχουσιν** is not the present indicative, but the dative plural present active participle, agreeing with **ἄλλοις** and depending on **ἐντετύχηκα** which takes the dative. **καὶ** here is adverbial, 'as well'.

Σοφοκλεῖ: Sophocles, the famous Athenian playwright, would have been an elderly man at the dramatic date of the *Republic*; the anecdote here chimes with the picture of him as a genial and easy-going man that we also see in Aristophanes' *Frogs* 82.

329c

πῶς . . . ἔχεις: *ἔχω* + adverb as above in 329b.

τἀφροδίσια: another crasis: *τὰ ἀφροδίσια*.

καὶ ὅς: 'and he'; the relative is used here as a demonstrative.

εὐφήμει: imperative (of an epsilon contract verb). Literally, 'speak auspiciously', it both means 'hush', but also suggests Sophocles warding off an ill omen.

λυττῶντά τινα καὶ ἄγριον δεσπότην: the sentiment of sexual desire as a burden is a commonplace in Greek lyric poetry; see, e.g., Ibycus fr. 287, Anacreon fr. 358.
ἀποδράς: aorist participle of ἀποδιδράσκω.
καὶ τότε: adverbial **καὶ**, 'even at the time'.
τῶν γε τοιούτων: genitive of separation ('from such things'), dependent on **εἰρήνη . . . καὶ ἐλευθερία**.
τὸ τοῦ Σοφοκλέους: i.e. 'the [saying] of Sophocles'; the following clause is explanatory of this.

329d
ἐστι . . . ἀπηλλάχθαι: the subject is unexpressed; it might be 'one is . . .' or 'old age is . . .'; **ἀπηλλάχθαι** is the perfect passive infinitive of *ἀπαλλάσσω*, and with **ἐστι** here means 'one is delivered from' or (avoiding the lack of subject), 'there is deliverance from . . .'
πολλῶν . . . καὶ μαινομένων: Greek will often join adjectives with a conjunction where it seems odd in English; **καὶ** is simply best left out in translation.
τούτων πέρι καὶ τῶν γε πρὸς τοὺς οἰκείους: **πέρι** governs **τούτων** (this is evident from the anastrophe of the accent – i.e. normally the accent falls on the second syllable, but when it follows the word it governs, it moves forward in the word). It also governs **τῶν πρὸς τοὺς οἰκείους**, literally 'the things in relation to relatives', i.e. the insults mentioned earlier; Emlyn-Jones has 'their relationship with their families'.
ὦσιν: third person plural subjunctive of *εἰμί*, with **ἂν**, a contracted *ἐάν*, a future open conditional.
καὶ τὸ γῆρας: another adverbial **καὶ**, 'even old age' or 'old age, too'.
τῷ τοιούτῳ: 'for such a person'.
ἀγασθεὶς: note that *ἄγαμαι* takes a genitive. Plato often has Socrates react with favourable amazement to another's opinion, only to follow up with a critical and devastating elenchus: e.g. *Protagoras* 328d, *Symposium* 198a. Is this meant to be ironic or complimentary here? It depends on whether one sees the overall the portrayal of Cephalus as critical or sympathetic (see the Introduction, 'The discussion with Cephalus').

329e
οἶμαί: syncopated (i.e. shortened) form of *οἴομαι*.
σου: genitive of source: 'from you'.
ἡγεῖσθαί σε . . . κεκτῆσθαι: *ἡγέομαι* here means 'believe' or 'think', hence is followed by an accusative + infinitive construction for indirect speech. **κεκτῆσθαι** is the perfect middle infinitive of *κτάομαι*.
διὰ τὸ πολλὴν οὐσίαν κεκτῆσθαι: an articular infinitive (i.e. a verbal noun) depending on the preposition; a translation might be 'on account of the possession of . . .' Socrates is often critical of great wealth: e.g. *Apology* 29d, 41e and following, though here he politely attributes criticism to unnamed **τοὺς πολλούς**.
τοῖς . . . πλουσίοις: dative of possession (with **εἶναι**).
ἀληθῆ: neuter plural, 'true things', but simply 'the truth' is better in English.
λέγουσι . . . τι: literally, 'they say something'; idiomatic for 'to talk sense' or 'to be right' – cf. the English idiom 'there is something in what they say'.

τὸ τοῦ Θεμιστοκλέους: literally, 'the [thing] of Themistocles', i.e. 'Themistocles' saying', which follows. Herodotus also gives a version of this anecdote (8.125), with slightly different details. The critic was Timodemus of Aphidnae (an Athenian deme), who attributed Themistocles' Spartan honours to his Athenian birth. Themistocles responded, 'If I were from Belbina [a small island to the south of Sunium], I wouldn't have been famous, but you wouldn't have been famous, had you been from Athens.'

εὖ ἔχει: the same idiom as in 329b (i.e. *ἔχω* + adverb); it is most simply translated here as 'is good'.

τῷ Σεριφίῳ: Seriphus is a small island (the modern Greek Serifos) in the western Cyclades, apparently notable for the muteness of its frogs: its significance here is of course its poverty and insignificance (also referenced by Aristophanes, in *Acharnians* 542); for this reason it became a place of exile in Roman times.

330a

δι᾽ αὑτὸν: literally, 'through himself' (= διὰ ἑαυτόν); more smoothly 'on his own account'.

ἂν . . . ἐγένετο: ἂν + indicative shows this is a past nfulfilled condition 'would have been'. The subject is Themistocles.

ὢν: the force of the participle here is conditional, and provides the protasis: 'if he were . . .'

οὔτ᾽ ἐκεῖνος Ἀθηναῖος: referring to the speaker (the Seriphian); the phrase is very condensed, and provides a contrast to the whole of the preceding conditional, from which we have to supply the parallel clauses: 'nor would that man [have been famous, if he were] an Athenian'.

φέρουσιν: dative plural present active participle, rather than the present indicative; the meaning is metaphorical here, 'put up with/bear'.

εὖ ἔχει: as just above, 'is good'; Emlyn-Jones translates effectively as 'nicely fits'.

ὁ αὐτὸς λόγος: note the position of **αὐτὸς** here between article and noun; hence meaning 'same'.

ὅτι: explanatory of **ὁ αὐτὸς λόγος**, i.e. 'namely, that . . .'

ὁ ἐπιεικὴς: 'the reasonable man', contrasted with 'the unreasonable man' (**ὁ μὴ ἐπιεικὴς**). The choice of word is both vague, and important for Cephalus' claim; it has something of the same force as 'any reasonable person' or 'any decent human being' might have in the mouth of a contemporary speaker. Plato uses the term in the *Apology* to refer to thoughtful or sensible people 22a), and the superlative form is used later in the *Republic* to describe the Guardians.

ἂν . . . ἐνέγκοι: potential optative, from *φέρω*.

ποτ᾽= ποτε (indefinite – note the lack of accent), 'ever'.

ἑαυτῷ: 'with himself' (depending on **εὔκολός**).

πότερον: introduces a disjunctive (either/or) question; English does not mark the first alternative with an interrogative, so there is no need to translate this word.

ὧν: condensed form of τούτων ἅ, with the relative 'attracted' into the case of the (elided!) antecedent.

τὰ πλείω = *τὰ πλείο(ν)α* (with the ν dropping out and a contraction of *α*+ο) – i.e. the neuter plural comparative.

ἐπεκτήσω: although this might look like a first person, it is in fact the second person singular aorist middle indicative of *ἐπικτάομαι* (another contraction of α+ο), not a form regularly encountered.

330b

ποῖ' ἐπεκτησάμην: the repetition of the question with the interrogative **ποῖα** (neuter plural) has been variously interpreted – it might suggest surprise, or be comic in tone, or even suggest some deafness on Cephalus' part! Allen suggests it 'is a mannerism of old age'. It has the effect of something like 'How much did I make, eh?!'

τε καὶ ὁμώνυμος ἐμοὶ: 'who also had the same name as me'.

σχεδόν τι: 'somewhat almost', i.e. 'just about'.

πολλάκις: not 'often', but its original sense of 'many times', with **τοσαύτην**: 'many times as great'.

ἐλάττω: like **τὰ πλείω** above, a contracted form of the neuter plural comparative (also just below as well, both **ἐλάττω** and **πλείω**).

τῆς νῦν οὔσης: comparative (following **ἐλάττω**) 'than it is now'.

ἀγαπῶ: here, simply, 'I am satisfied.'

τούτοισιν: dative plural (of interest); the longer ending **-οισιν** is archaic, but not infrequently used by Plato. Here, however, it might have special significance – as an old form, to reflect Cephalus' age; or maybe (as a foreigner) to reflect his old-fashioned provincialism; or, in context, as a playful form 'for these lads' (Allan).

βραχεῖ . . . τινι: dative of degree of difference, with **πλείω**, 'a little bit more'.

330c

οὗ: neuter genitive of a connecting relative pronoun, dependent on **ἕνεκα**, and then explained by **ὅτι**; 'On account of this, namely that . . .'

ὡς τὸ πολὺ: 'for the most part', 'generally'.

οἱ δὲ κτησάμενοι διπλῇ ἢ οἱ ἄλλοι ἀσπάζονται αὐτά: διπλῇ ἤ: 'twice as much as . . .'; **οἱ ἄλλοι** is the comparison; the subject of **ἀσπάζονται** is **οἱ . . . κτησάμενοι. αὐτά** is neuter plural, referring back to **τὰ χρήματα** in the previous sentence.

ὥσπερ γὰρ οἱ ποιηταὶ: The same comparison reoccurs in Aristotle, *Nichomachean Ethics* 4.1.20, 1120b14.

ταύτῃ . . . καί: to be understood together, with **καί** adverbial, 'even in this [way]'.

ὡς ἔργον ἑαυτῶν: 'as if it were their own creation'.

κατὰ τὴν χρείαν: the preposition means here 'according to', but could be simply translated as 'for' or 'because of'.

ᾗπερ οἱ ἄλλοι: 'in the same way that others [are serious about money]'. **ᾗπερ** echoes **ταύτῃ** above, 'in the way which . . .', and **σπουδάζουσιν** is implied as a a parallel.

συγγενέσθαι: an explanatory infinitive following **χαλεποὶ**.

οὐδὲν . . . ἀλλ' ἤ: elision of *ἀλλο*; 'nothing other than. . .'

ἀληθῆ . . . λέγεις: the same construction as at 329e above.

330d

τοσόνδε: best translated here as simply 'this'.

τί μέγιστον οἴει ἀγαθὸν ἀπολελαυκέναι: rendering into English is a little tricky: 'what do you think is the greatest good that you have enjoyed . . .' **οἴει** is the second person present indicative of *οἴομαι*.

τοῦ πολλὴν οὐσίαν κεκτῆσθαι: articular infinitive 'sandwiching' its object; the genitive is dependent on **ἀπολελαυκέναι**.

ὅ is the object of **λέγων**; a connecting relative – treat as if it is demonstrative. The force of the participle is conditional, with **ἂν . . . πείσαιμι** as the apodosis with a potential optative: 'if I said . . . I would'.

ἴσθι: imperative singular of οἶδα.

ἐγγὺς . . . τοῦ οἴεσθαι: articular infinitive in the genitive, governed by **ἐγγὺς**: 'close to thinking'.

ᾖ: present subjunctive of *εἰμί*; subjunctive as it is an indefinite clause in primary sequence (after **ἐπειδάν**).

εἰσῄει: imperfect of *εἴσ-ειμι (εἰσ-έρχομαι)*.

οἵ . . . λεγόμενοι μῦθοι: the myths referenced are probably of two kinds: ancient myths describing torments of the wicked in the underworld (like Tantalus, etc.; e.g. in Homer, *Odyssey* 11.576–600); and secondly, myths of judgement at the point of death, which were common in the mystery cults (like the Athenian mysteries of Eleusis; e.g. Pindar, fr. 121). This kind of myth-making is taken up by Plato himself in the *Gorgias, Phaedo,* and most famously in the 'myth of Er' later in the *Republic.*

περὶ τῶν ἐν Ἅιδου: 'concerning affairs in Hades' [house]'; Hades in Greek is not a designation of the underworld, but the name of the God of the underworld, but the change in meaning came about because of this circumlocution.

ὡς: explanatory of the myths – 'namely, how . . .'

330e

μὴ . . . ὦσιν: fearing clause, 'lest they are. . .' **ὦσιν** is the present subjunctive of *εἰμί*.

καὶ αὐτός: 'he himself', referring back to **αὐτοῦ** above.

ἤτοι . . . αὐτά: treat all of this as effectively a parenthesis, and **αὐτός** as the subject of **γίγνεται**.

ὥσπερ ἤδη ἐγγυτέρω ὢν τῶν ἐκεῖ μᾶλλόν τι καθορᾷ αὐτά: *ὡς* + participle gives an alleged cause; the **-περ** in **ὥσπερ** is simply an intensifying suffix; 'as if being'. **ἐγγυτέρω** (the comparative adverbial form of *ἐγγύς*) takes the genitive **τῶν ἐκεῖ** to mean 'nearer to the [things] there', i.e. in Hades. **τι** is adverbial, so **μᾶλλόν τι** is 'somewhat better', and **αὐτά** refers back to **τῶν ἐκεῖ**.

δ' οὖν: 'at any rate'.

τινά τι ἠδίκησεν: the verb takes a double accusative: to wrong someone (accusative), by doing something (an internal accusative). Translate as 'wrong someone in some way'.

καὶ ἐκ τῶν ὕπνων: adverbial **καὶ**, 'even'.

ἐλπίδος: note that this can be used in a negative as well as a positive sense in Greek – expectation or foreboding, rather than hope.

331a

συνειδότι: participle from *σύν-οιδα*. The force of the participle is again conditional; 'if he is conscious, sweet hope is present [for him]'.

γηροτρόφος: feminine (as a two-termination compound adjective), agreeing with **ἐλπὶς**.
ὅτι: explanatory, giving the content of what Pindar says.
ὃς ἂν . . . διαγάγῃ: an indefinite clause, taking **ἂν** + subjunctive, 'whoever . . .'
γλυκεῖά . . . κυβερνᾷ: an otherwise unknown fragment of Pindar, in a style and form of Greek quite different to Plato's own. **οἱ**: dative of possession; a form equivalent to *αὐτῷ*. **ἐλπὶς** is the subject, modified by both **γλυκεῖά** and **γηροτρόφος**, and the participle **ἀτάλλοισα**, a dialect form equivalent to *ἀτάλλουσα*, of which **καρδίαν** is the object. Other forms in the fragment which differ from Attic are as follows: **ἁ** = *ἣ*; **θνατῶν** = *θνητῶν*; **γνώμαν** = *γνώμην*. **πολύστροφον** is feminine (another two-termination compound adjective) and hence modifies **γνώμαν**.
ὡς σφόδρα: intensifying **θαυμαστῶς**, 'so exceedingly wonderfully'.
ἔγωγε: emphatic form of 'I'; also in the next section.
πλείστου: genitive dependent on **ἀξίαν**, 'worthy of . . .' It is easiest to translate the whole phrase as 'most worthwhile'.

331b
οὔ τι παντὶ ἀνδρὶ: the **τι** is adverbial, 'not at all for every man'.
τῷ ἐπιεικεῖ: see note on **ὁ ἐπιεικὴς** at 330a above.
τὸ . . . ἐξαπατῆσαι ἢ ψεύσασθαι: articular (aorist) infinitives; they are accusative in apposition to **εἰς τοῦτο**.
μηδὲ ἄκοντά τινα: these are not in agreement! Rather, **ἄκοντά** is accusative as the subject of the infinitive, and **τινα** as its object. Translate as 'not to have cheated anyone, even against one's will'. Likewise, **ὀφείλοντα** and **δεδιότα** are the subject of **ἀπιέναι**.
ἐκεῖσε: 'to that place', i.e. Hades.
ἓν ἀνθ' ἑνὸς: '[setting] one thing against another', or '[taking] one thing with another'.
οὐκ ἐλάχιστον . . . εἰς τοῦτο: 'for this [purpose] not the least'.
θείην ἂν: potential optative of *τίθημι*, 'I would claim.'
ἀνδρὶ νοῦν ἔχοντι: 'for a man with good sense'; as is often the case, *ἔχων* is used simply to mean 'with'.

331c
παγκάλως . . . λέγεις, ὦ Κέφαλε: as earlier, an enthusiastically positive affirmation is often used by Socrates in Plato's dialogues as the starting point for a critical examination, not without a suggestion of irony.
τοῦτο δ' αὐτό, τὴν δικαιοσύνην: accusative of respect, 'as for the thing itself, justice' (as usual, Greek uses the definite article for an abstract quality).
πότερα . . . ἢ . . .: this presents two options; English does not mark the first option in a direct either/or question, so **πότερα** can be left untranslated.
τὴν ἀλήθειαν αὐτὸ . . . εἶναι: **αὐτὸ** is the subject of the infinitive (referring back to **τὴν δικαιοσύνην**) and **τὴν ἀλήθειαν** its complement; i.e. 'that it is truthfulness'.
ἁπλῶς οὕτως: Allan: 'in this absolute way'; more colloquially, 'just simply'.

αὐτὰ ταῦτα: neuter plural object of **ποιεῖν**, referring to the actions just mentioned (i.e. telling the truth and returning things taken).

ἄν τίς τι παρά του λάβῃ: **ἄν** = *ἐάν*; **παρά** = 'at the hands of' or just 'from'; **του** = τινὸς.

ἔστιν: 'it is possible', rather than simply 'it is' (the accentuation makes the difference clear).

οἷον τοιόνδε: 'the following kind of thing'; **λέγω** here (as often) is better translated 'I mean' than 'I say.'

παρὰ φίλου ἀνδρὸς: here, 'from a friend'.

σωφρονοῦντος: 'while he was in his right mind'.

οὕτως ἔχοντα: 'thus disposed' or 'in this frame of mind'; the same idiom of *ἔχω* + adverb seen first in this text at 329b.

τἀληθῆ = τα *ἀληθῆ*.

331d

ἄρα: often used to connote the drawing of a conclusion, with a suggestion of surprise or heightened emotion; 'so then . . .' might be a reasonable translation.

ὅρος: literally, 'limit/boundary', but usually translated here as 'definition'. The idea is that it is the demarcation of the boundary between justice and other ideas.

πάνυ μὲν οὖν: in contradiction to Socrates' negation; **μὲν οὖν** is used to express a correction: 'But that's precisely what it is!'. It is a rather sudden and surprising introduction to Polemarchus taking up (**ὑπολαβὼν**) the discourse from his father.

εἴπερ γέ τι χρὴ Σιμωνίδῃ πείθεσθαι: the saying in question is otherwise unknown; up until this point, poets have been quoted uncontroversially, but here Polemarchus is relying on poetic authority to make a contentious argument. Similarly in the *Protagoras*, a poem of Simonides is analysed as part of the dialogue (339a ff.).

τὸν λόγον: here, 'the argument' or 'the discussion'.

τῶν ἱερῶν: literally, 'the holy things', i.e. the sacrifice; the genitive is dependent on the verb **ἐπιμεληθῆναι**. Likewise, **πρὸς τὰ ἱερά** at the end of this passage.

οὐκοῦν: indicates a question seeking an affirmative response; here, 'Aren't I . . .?'

ἔφη, ἐγώ, ὁ Πολέμαρχος: the word order here is puzzling; either it is an instance of hyperbaton, and we are to understand **ἔφη ὁ Πολέμαρχος** as part of the narration, 'Polemarchus said' (thus Allan); but this seems strained. The other interpretation is to make this part of Polemarchus' speech: 'I, Polemarchus – am I not . . .' Emlyn-Jones says this rather artificial self-reference 'well reflects [Polemarchus'] dramatic and assertive character'.

τῶν σῶν κληρονόμος: Polemarchus is playing with the fact that he, as eldest son, is his father's heir, but also that he is inheriting the argument from his father. **τῶν σῶν** leaves an ambiguity open – without a noun expressed, it could either be 'your possessions' or 'your argument'.

πάνυ γε: a positive affirmation; 'quite so'.

ἅμα is adverbial here, 'at the same time'.

ᾔει: imperfect of *εἶμι* (*ἔρχομαι*). Cicero (*Ad Atticum* 4.16.3) remarks on this passage: 'I believe that Plato thought that it would be hardly natural if he had kept a man of that age any longer in such a long conversation.'

331e

ὅτι: introducing indirect speech following either **τί φῄς** (although this would normally take an accusative + infinitive construction rather than **ὅτι**) or **ὀρθῶς λέγειν περὶ δικαιοσύνης**; i.e. either '[I say] that . . .', or '[Simonides says] that . . .'

τὸ . . . ἀποδιδόναι: articular infinitive; 'giving back'.

δίκαιόν ἐστι: despite the mention of a definition of justice, the lack of a definite article here suggests that this is being adduced as an instance of justice, not a definition – i.e. 'it is just . . .', rather than 'justice is . . .'

ἔμοιγε: emphatic form 'to me'; Emlyn-Jones renders it 'to me, at least'.

οὐ ῥᾴδιον ἀπιστεῖν: supply *ἐστιν*; **ῥᾴδιον** means 'rather easy', or more smoothly in English, 'it is not particularly easy to distrust . . .'

σοφὸς γὰρ καὶ θεῖος ἀνήρ: there may be a hint of irony here; Plato's Socrates often uses 'inspired' critically, to suggest a lack of accuracy or clarity in such poetic wisdom. The *Ion* explores more generally Plato's critical attitude to the divine inspiration of poetry.

τοῦτο . . . ὅτι: 'this, which he . . .'

δῆλον γὰρ ὅτι: supply *ἐστιν*.

τό . . . ἀποδιδόναι is again an articular infinitive, governing everything in between.

τινος παρακαταθεμένουs genitive absolute.

ὁτῳοῦν: dative of *ὁστισοῦν*, anyone whatsoever.

332a

καίτοι γε: 'and yet'; the γε stresses **καίτοι**.

ὃ παρακατέθετο: 'what is lent' is the subject, with **ὀφειλόμενόν** the predicate.

ἦ γάρ; 'is this not so?'

ἀποδοτέον . . . ἀπαιτοῖ: the gerundive (with **-τέον** suffix; cf. 328b) is difficult to translate when there is neither a subject expressed, nor an agent (in this construction, with a dative)! The closest would be 'must one return'. **ὁπωστιοῦν:** 'under any circumstances'. There are two possible explanations of the optative **ἀπαιτοῖ** here; either an optative of indefinite frequency (with **ὁπότε τις**): effectively, 'whenever anyone asked'. Alternatively, the whole sentence is effectively in indirect discourse in historic sequence, '[we admitted that . . .]'; Allan prefers the latter interpretation.

ἄλλο δή τι ἢ τὸ τοιοῦτον: the object of **λέγει Σιμωνίδης**, again with the force 'means'. **τοιοῦτον** frequently refers back to what has already been mentioned; **τὸ . . . ἀποδιδόναι** thus is explanatory of **ἄλλο**; we might say in English 'means something else by "giving back what is owed is just"'.

μέντοι: often indicative of eager assent; 'of course,' or 'certainly'.

νὴ Δί': a variant of **νὴ τὸν Δία**, 'by Zeus!' (cf. 329a).

τοῖς γὰρ φίλοις: take with **ὀφείλειν**. The subject of **οἴεται** is Simonides, followed by an accusative (**τοὺς φίλους**) and infinitive (**δρᾶν**) construction.

μανθάνω: (here) 'I understand.'

ὅτι: might introduce indirect speech, dependent on **λέγειν** much further down (in 332b); though the punctuation of our text favours another interpretation, taking **ὅτι** to mean 'because': 'because whoever returns gold to someone who had deposited it is not returning what is owed, if . . .' Emlyn-Jones (punctuating as in the current text) in his translation inserts 'you mean that . . .' and assumes it is indirect speech. Note as in my translation here **τῳ** = τινι (though it could be understood as an article with the participle, **τῳ . . . παρακαταθεμένῳ**).

ἀποδίδωσιν: third person present singular of *ἀπο-δίδωμι*.

ὃς ἄν . . . ἀποδῷ: the verb is **ἀποδῷ,** the aorist subjunctive of the same verb as above, *ἀπο-δίδωμι,* in an indefinite clause.

332b

ἐάνπερ: 'if' with an intensifying suffix, followed by subjunctives **γίγνηται** and **ὦσιν** (from *εἰμί*).

τί δέ; is an expression of surprise, introducing a further question.

ἀποδοτέον: gerundive, as in 332a.

ὅτι ἂν τύχῃ ὀφειλόμενον: *ὅ τι*, 'whatever'; *τυγχάνω* (here, subjunctive in an indefinite clause) takes a participle (**ὀφειλόμενον**) 'happens [to be owed]'.

γε . . . γε . . . γε: note the repetition, as if Polemarchus is trying desperately to make his point.

παρά . . . τοῦ ἐχθροῦ: 'from an enemy'.

κακόν τι is explanatory of, or stands in apposition to, **ὅπερ** (an emphatic form of the neuter nominative relative pronoun) **. . . προσήκει. καὶ** is adverbial here, 'even'.

ἠινίξατο: aorist of *αἰνίσσομαι*. It is taking both an internal accusative **τὸ δίκαιον,** which anticipates the indirect question **ὃ εἴη** (prolepsis); to translate into sensible English, take **τὸ δίκαιον** inside the indirect question, 'what the just is'; cf. the note on **τὸ γῆρας ὑμνοῦσιν ὅσων** above at 329b.

ποιητικῶς: again, Socrates' attitude towards poetic inspiration has a touch of irony to it.

AS

332c–336a: Socrates goes on to develop his craft analogies in his elenchus with Polemarchus, which gradually backs Polemarchus into a corner, forcing him to admit that by his interpretation of Simonides, justice is useless as a skill. He then challenges Polemarchus' definition of justice as including 'harming enemies', and the elenchus concludes with Polemarchus affirming, with Socrates, that it is never just to harm anyone. For a summary of the arguments in this section, see the section 'The elenchus with Polemarchus' in the Introduction.

336b

The description of Thrasymachus' interjection is an interlude in the argument, and is deliberately comically over the top and unflattering to the sophist, who comes across as rude and boorish.

διαλεγομένων ἡμῶν: genitive absolute. Notice the repetition of the prefix *δια-* in this sentence (**διεκωλύετο . . . διακοῦσαι**) highlighting the sudden interjection of Thrasymachus.

ὥρμα: conative imperfect of *ὁρμάω*, 'tried to push forward'; to be taken with **ἀντιλαμβάνεσθαι**, as a complementary infinitive, or expressing purpose.

διακοῦσαι: from *δι-ακούω*.

ἡσυχίαν ἦγεν: kept quiet.

ὥσπερ θηρίον: Plato is playing humorously with Homeric-style similes, painting Thrasymachus as a pound-shop Achilles or Hector; cf. *Iliad* 16.352 ff. with some notable verbal echoes. The unbridled animal passions of Thrasymachus perhaps foreshadow the later discussion of the soul in the *Republic*, representative of a tripartite soul dominated by the *θυμός* element – see Book IV 434d ff.

ἧκεν ἐφ' ἡμᾶς: not from *ἥκω* (as in the English 'he came at us'), but rather the aorist of *ἵημι*, 'he threw himself at us'.

ὡς διαρπασόμενος: not equivalent to a purpose clause (as *ὡς* + future participle often is), but 'as if about to . . .'

δείσαντες διεπτοήθημεν: 'we were panic-stricken in fear'; both pleonastic and alliterative to heighten the melodrama.

τίς agrees with **φλυαρία** as the subject of **ἔχει**; the present tense is used to convey continuous past action that is still ongoing: 'what nonsense has had a hold . . .'

336c

τί: 'why', rather than 'what'.

εὐηθίζεσθε: Thrasymachus despises naivete more than any other trait; cf. 343c, 348c.

ὑποκατακλινόμενοι: the language is metaphorical, either referring to taking a lower place at the table in deference to someone else, or possibly, from the world of wrestling, allowing oneself to be beaten.

ὡς ἀληθῶς: 'truly'.

εἰδέναι: infinitive of *οἶδα*.

τὸ δίκαιον ὅτι ἔστι: another circumstance of prolepsis (cf. the note on **τὸ γῆρας ὑμνοῦσιν ὅσων** above at 329b).

μὴ μόνον . . . ἀλλὰ καὶ: 'not only . . . but also . . .'

ἐρώτα . . . φιλοτιμοῦ: both present imperative.

ἐλέγχων: 'by criticizing.'

ἐπειδάν τίς τι ἀποκρίνηται: subjunctive in an indefinite clause.

A
Level

ἐγνωκὼς: perfect participle of *γιγνώσκω*.
τοῦτο, ὅτι: 'this, namely that . . .'
αὐτὸς: here, 'you yourself'.
ἀπόκριναι καὶ εἰπὲ: both aorist imperatives.

336d
ὅπως . . . μὴ ἐρεῖς: *ὅπως* + future indicative is an idiomatic form of an imperative; here it comes across as abrupt and rude.
ὅτι τὸ: (repeatedly), 'that it is what is necessary, useful, etc.' or 'that it is the fitting, the useful, etc.'
ὡς: with causal force here, 'since'.
ἀκούσας ἐξεπλάγην καὶ προσβλέπων αὐτὸν ἐφοβούμην: the extent of Socrates' fear is comically overexaggerated.
πρότερος . . . ἢ: 'earlier . . . than'; although grammatically an adjective, functionally it is adverbial. **'κεῖνος** = *ἐκεῖνος* (an example of prodelision, where a contraction occurs by removal of a vowel at the start of a word instead of the end).
ἄφωνος ἂν γενέσθαι: 'I would have become dumb'; counterfactual conditional, with an infinitive, representing an aorist indicative, dependent on **μοι δοκῶ** (note that the Greek uses a personal construction where the English would more naturally use the impersonal 'it seems to me . . .'). Apparently, it was believed that meeting a wolf could strike someone speechless if the wolf saw them first; cf. Vergil, *Eclogue* 9.53.
ὑπὸ τοῦ λόγου: agent of the passive **ἐξαγριαίνεσθαι.**

336e
οἷός τ᾽ ἐγενόμην: a variant on *οἷός τ᾽ εἰμί*, 'I was able.'
μὴ χαλεπὸς ἡμῖν ἴσθι: imperative of *εἰμί*, with a dative of advantage (**ἡμῖν**). The language here is formal and elevated.
εὖ ἴσθι: imperative of *οἶδα*.
οἴου: imperative of *οἴομαι*; it is balanced further down in Socrates' speech with **οἴου γε σύ**.
εἰ μὲν χρυσίον ἐζητοῦμεν: an *a fortiori* argument – i.e. if gold is valuable, and we would exert ourselves in the search for it; how much more ought we to exert ourselves to discover justice, since it is even more valuable. Gold as a metaphor for justice is ancient, appearing in Heraclitus, as well as with a slightly different emphasis in Psalm 19:10.
πολλῶν χρυσίων τιμιώτερον: comparative with genitive of comparison.
ὅτι μάλιστα: 'as much as possible'.
φανῆναι αὐτό: 'that it appear'.
οἴου γε σύ: 'believe me'.
οὐ δυνάμεθα: 'we are not able', hence, 'we lack the ability'.

337a
ὑπὸ ὑμῶν τῶν δεινῶν: to be read with a measure of irony, 'by you clever chaps'.
χαλεπαίνεσθαι: the use of a verb that generally takes a dative ('to be angry with . . .) in the passive is a little irregular; translate as 'to be victims of your anger' (Allan).
ἀνεκάγχασέ: note the onomatapoea of this word, combining with the assonance of **ἀκούσας**, to create a striking aural effect.

A Level

σαρδάνιον: whence the English 'sardonic'; it probably derives from 'to grin' so is apposite here with Thrasymachus' laugh.
'κείνη = ἐκείνῃ; see above on prodelision
εἰωθυῖα: feminine nominative perfect participle of *ἔθω*.
εἰρωνεία Σωκράτους: the basic meaning of *εἰρωνεία* is feigned ignorance or inferiority, rather than what is meant by the English 'irony'.
ᾔδη: pluperfect of *οἶδα*.
προὔλεγον = *προ-έλεγον*.
ὅτι: referring back to **τούτοις**, 'namely, that . . .'

337a7–338a4: The verbal sparring between Socrates and Thrasymachus continues from 337a–338a, with Socrates claiming ignorance. Thrasymachus bullishly claims that he can give an answer as to what justice is; Socrates claims to be delighted to have the opportunity to learn from him.

338a5
εἰπόντος δέ μου ταῦτα: genitive absolute; what Socrates has just said is: 'So don't hesitate, but gratify me by answering, and don't begrudge your teaching to Glaucon here and the others' (Emlyn-Jones *ad loc.*).
ἐδέοντο: here, 'were begging'; note it takes the genitive **αὐτοῦ**, and the indirect command **μὴ ἄλλως ποιεῖν**.
φανερὸς: although an adjective modifying **ὁ Θρασύμαχος**, clearly an adverb in force.
ἦν ἐπιθυμῶν: 'was keen', a periphrasis for *ἐπεθύμει*, possibly to draw extra attention to the participle and suggest Thrasymachus' inability to control his passions. See the note on **ὥσπερ θηρίον** above at 336b.
ἵν᾽ εὐδοκιμήσειεν: *ἵνα* + aorist optative for a purpose clause in secondary sequence.
ἡγούμενος ἔχειν: a condensed accusative + infinitive, 'thinking [that he] had'.
ἀπόκρισιν παγκάλην: the prefix *παν-* on the adjective is deliberately over the top, highlighting with irony Thrasymachus' arrogance.
πρὸς τὸ ἐμὲ εἶναι: 'with regard to me being . . .'

338b
τελευτῶν: literally, a present participle agreeing with the subject (i.e. Thrasymachus), 'ending', but again adverbial: 'finally'.
κἄπειτα: crasis of *καὶ ἔπειτα*.
αὕτη δή: supply *ἐστιν*: 'this is precisely . . .'
αὐτὸν . . . μὴ ἐθέλειν: the accusative + infinitive construction (continued with **διδάσκειν, μανθάνειν** and **ἀποδιδόναι**) is explanatory of **αὕτη** in the preceding sentence; 'This is Socrates' wisdom: namely, that he . . .'
παρὰ . . . τῶν ἄλλων: 'at the hands of other' or simply 'from'.
περιιόντα: participle from *περί-ειμι* (*περιέρχομαι*).
τούτων . . . χάριν ἀποδιδόναι: 'render thanks for these things' or 'show gratitude'. At 337d, Thrasymachus demanded that Socrates pay him for his discourse on justice; the implication here is that Socrates does not pay for his sophistic tuition, brought out explicitly by Socrates below. See the remarks on attitudes towards money in the *Republic* in the Introduction, 'The discussion with Cephalus.'

ὅτι . . . μανθάνω: indirect speech dependent on **ἀληθῆ εἶπες**.
ὅτι δὲ οὔ με φῂς χάριν ἐκτίνειν, ψεύδῃ: there is indirect speech (**ὅτι . . . οὔ . . . φῂς**) dependent on **ψεύδῃ**, best rendered into English as 'you speak falsely when you deny'; and mixed in with the **ὅτι** clause, there is also an accusative + infinitive dependent on **φῂς**: **με . . . χάριν ἐκτίνειν**.
ὅσην δύναμαι: supply *χάριν*.
ὡς δὲ προθύμως τοῦτο δρῶ: an indirect question, 'and how eagerly I do this', dependent on **εὖ εἴσῃ** (second person future indicative of *οἶδα*).
ἐρεῖν: irregular future infinitive of *λέγω* (ἐρέω, 'I will say' is an entirely separate defective verb – i.e. with no tenses other than the future; the same thing has occurred in English with 'go' and 'went', originally two entirely separate verbs).

338c
ἄκουε δή: a phrase often used to mark an important statement (e.g. *Protagoras* 353c, *Apology* 20d, and later in the *Republic* 595c).
οὐκ ἄλλο τι ἢ εἶναι τὸ δίκαιον: the word is deliberately emphatic, deliberately delaying Thrasymachus' bold definition by placing the unnecessary **οὐκ ἄλλο τι ἢ** first, then the verb, and keeping the definition to the end.
τὸ . . . συμφέρον: neuter participle of the verb *συμφέρω* used substantively with the article: 'the advantage' or 'what is advantageous'
ἀλλὰ τί οὐκ ἐπαινεῖς; ἀλλ᾽ οὐκ ἐθελήσεις; τί here = 'why'; the two short emphatic questions are deliberately confrontational from Thrasymachus, and comic for the reader: the repetition of **ἀλλὰ** expresses Thrasymachus' sarcastic surprise.
ἐὰν μάθω: first person aorist subjunctive, in a future more vivid conditional; the apodosis is inferred from **ἐθελήσεις** in Thrasymachus' question: i.e. 'I will praise you, if . . .'
τί λέγεις: as in several earlier instances, best translated as 'what do you mean'; an indirect question dependent on **μάθω**.
τοῦτο . . . τί ποτε λέγεις: 'whatever do you mean by this', or 'what in the world'.
οὐ . . . φῄς: an effective English translation would be 'You're not suggesting . . .'
τό γε τοιόνδε: points forward to the hypothetical Socrates is about to pose, 'the following'; **γε** has the sense 'at any rate'.
Πουλυδάμας . . . παγκρατιαστὴς: Polydamus was a famous athlete born in Thessaly and a victor at the Olympic games of 408 BCE. The pankration was an all-in physical contest which combined wrestling and boxing.
ἡμῶν is a genitive of comparison (with **κρείττων**).
συμφέρει: takes a dative case; its subject here is the neuter plural **τὰ βόεια κρέα**.
πρὸς τὸ σῶμα: (here) 'as regards the body'.
καὶ ἡμῖν τοῖς ἥττοσιν ἐκείνου: 'for us, too, who are weaker than him [sc. Polydamus]'.
τοῦτο τὸ σιτίον εἶναι: the apodosis is accusative + infinitive as indirect discourse following **φῄς** in the previous sentence.

338d
γὰρ: the particle suggests a reason for the preceding sentence; here, it carries the force 'you would only suggest that because . . .'

A Level

ταύτῃ . . . ᾗ: 'in the way which'.

ὑπολαμβάνεις: literally, 'take up', but with the metaphorical sense here 'understand' or 'interpret'.

ἂν κακουργήσαις μάλιστα τὸν λόγον: 'you would do the most mischief to the argument'. Thrasymachus' criticism is well-founded: Socrates frequently reduces an interlocutor's argument to nonsense by suggesting extreme or unlikely circumstances as hypotheticals; e.g. *Gorgias* 490d.

τῶν πόλεων: the genitive is partitive, and not easy to keep in a smooth English translation; 'of cities, some are . . .' More natural (but losing the literal sense of the partitive) would be 'some cities are . . . others are . . .' The verb *εἰσίν* is understood after **ὅτι**. Plato himself elsewhere does not accept this simple tripartite division of forms of government, however: see *Statesman* 302–303.

πῶς γὰρ οὔ; 'How could I not?', an idiomatic response expressing surprise and the obviousness of the answer.

οὐκοῦν: introduces a question presupposing an affirmative answer; could be translated 'Then . . . not . . .'

τοῦτο . . . τὸ ἄρχον: 'the [element] . . . that is the ruling [element]?' The latter is the neuter singular present participle, in apposition to **τοῦτο**.

338e

ἡ ἀρχὴ: a change in grammatical form from **τὸ ἄρχον**, but referring to exactly the same thing, 'the ruling faction'.

πρὸς τὸ αὑτῇ συμφέρον: 'with a view to its own advantage'. The view of legislation put forward here by Thrasymachus is not unique, and is reflected in the contemporary text, *The Constitution of the Athenians* (falsely attributed to another of Socrates' pupils, Xenophon). A similar argument is expressed in Plato's *Laws* 4.714b–d.

δημοκρατικούς . . . τυραννικούς: scilicet *νόμους*.

θέμεναι: aorist participle of *τίθημι*, echoing **τίθεται**; feminine plural, assuming *ἀρχαί* as a subject; 'in making [laws], they . . .'

τοῖς ἀρχομένοις: passive paticiple, 'for the ruled'.

τὸ σφίσι συμφέρον: in apposition to **τοῦτο**: 'this is just: their own advantage'. **σφίσι** = *αὐταῖς*, 'for them'.

τὸν τούτου ἐκβαίνοντα: 'the one deviating from this'; **τούτου** refers to **τὸ συμφέρον**.

ὡς παρανομοῦντά τε καὶ ἀδικοῦντα: *ὡς* + participle for alleged cause; the manner of expression underscores Thrasymachus' point, that illegal and unjust are simply terms made up and invested with meaning by those in control.

τοῦτ᾽ οὖν ἐστιν . . . ὃ λέγω: 'this is what I mean [by saying that] . . .'

ταὐτὸν εἶναι δίκαιον: 'justice is the same'; **ταὐτὸν** is a crasis of *τὸ αὐτόν*, equivalent to *τὸ αὐτό*.

ὦ βέλτιστε: clearly ironic!

339a

καθεστηκυίας: 'established' (feminine genitive singular perfect active participle of καθίστημι), describing **ἀρχῆς**.

αὕτη: scilicet *ἀρχή*.

A Level

ὥστε συμβαίνει: a result clause; 'so that the result is that . . .' followed by an accusative (**δίκαιον**) + infinitive (**εἶναι**) dependent on **συμβαίνει**; 'justice is the same thing everywhere', or 'the same justice exists everywhere'.
τὸ τοῦ κρείττονος συμφέρον: stands in apposition to **τὸ αὐτό**.
τῷ ὀρθῶς λογιζομένῳ: 'to anyone using their reason correctly' – again, the arrogance of Thrasymachus is being emphasized.
εἰ δὲ ἀληθὲς ἢ μή: an indirect question dependent on **μαθεῖν**.
τὸ συμφέρον... δίκαιον εἶναι: accusative + infinitive, following **ἀπεκρίνω** (second person singular aorist of *ἀποκρίνομαι*).
ἀπεκρίνω: second person singular aorist of *ἀποκρίνομαι*.

339b

ἀπηγόρευες ὅπως μὴ τοῦτο ἀποκρινοίμην: 'you forbade me from . . .', with an optative in secondary sequence.
πρόσεστιν δὲ δὴ αὐτόθι: 'there is just in addition to it', with the implication, 'you just added . . .'
σμικρά γε ἴσως . . . προσθήκη: 'A trivial addition, I suppose!' (thus Emlyn-Jones); the comment is sarcastic – Thrasymachus clearly believes in its significance.
οὔπω . . . οὐδ': Greek has no problem with double negatives; unlike in English, their function is to intensify, rather than cancel one another out.
δῆλον: is the predicate – supply *ἐστίν*.
μεγάλη: feminine, referring back to **προσθήκη**; again, *ἐστίν* must be supplied.
ὅτι: indirect discourse dependent on the following **δῆλον**; supply *ἐστίν*.
σκεπτέον: gerundive; 'must be examined', with another implied *ἐστίν*. It introduces the following indirect question, **εἰ ἀληθῆ λέγεις**.
συμφέρον γέ τι εἶναι ... τὸ δίκαιον: accusative + infinitive dependent on **ὁμολογῶ**; 'that justice is some kind of advantage'.
καὶ ἐγὼ: 'I, too' (adverbial *καί*).
σκόπει: preson singular imperative of an epsilon contract verb, rather than a third person form (which would have a circumflex accent on the final syllable).
ἔσται: future tense of *εἰμί*, singular with the neuter plural subject **ταῦτα**.
οὐ: expects an affirmative answer to the question.
τοῖς ἄρχουσιν: dative substantival participle (i.e. used as a noun = 'those who rule'), object of **πείθεσθαι**.
ἔγωγε: 'I do indeed.' Emphatic, brusque affirmation.

339c

πότερον . . . ἤ: disjunctive direct question; as with the previous examples earlier in the text, **πότερον** does not need to be translated.
ἐν ταῖς πόλεσιν ἑκάσταις: 'in their various cities'.
οἷοί: treat as if it is part of the fuller expression *οἷοί τ' εἰσίν*.
τι καὶ ἁμαρτεῖν: **τι** is an internal accusative to the verb, 'are they able to make any kind of mistake'; the adverbial **καὶ** is probably best rendered 'in fact'. For an examination of the arguments being made here, see the Introduction, 'The Battle with Thrasymachus'.
οὐκοῦν: expecting an affirmative response.

A Level

τοὺς μὲν . . . τοὺς δέ τινας: 'some . . . others . . .', object of **τιθέασιν**, which is understood to be repeated in the second clause.

τὸ δὲ ὀρθῶς ἄρα τὸ τὰ συμφέροντά ἐστι τίθεσθαι ἑαυτοῖς: the word order makes this slightly harder to follow, and **τίθεσθαι** must be understood twice, with *νόμους* implied in the first instance: **τὸ . . . ὀρθῶς** [νόμους τίθεσθαι] is the subject, followed by **ἐστι** and the complement is **τὸ . . . τίθεσθαι**; the object of the articular infinitive is **τὰ συμφέροντά**, 'advantages' with the dative of advantage **ἑαυτοῖς**, 'for themselves'. **τὸ δὲ μὴ ὀρθῶς ἀσύμφορα** has to be understood in parallel to this, i.e. in full: *τὸ δὲ μὴ ὀρθῶς νόμους τίθεσθαι ἐστι τὸ τὰ συμφέροντά ἑαυτοῖς τίθεσθαι.*

ἃ δ᾽ ἂν θῶνται: 'whatever they put in place'.

ποιητέον τοῖς ἀρχομένοις: understand *ἐστι*; gerundive with a dative of the agent.

πῶς γὰρ οὔ; see above at 327c and 338d.

339d

οὐ μόνον . . . ἀλλὰ καὶ: 'not only . . . but also'.

κατὰ τὸν σὸν λόγον: 'according to'.

τοὐναντίον: crasis of *το ἐναντίον,* 'the opposite'.

τὸ μὴ συμφέρον: 'what is not to their advantage'; the object of an implied **ποιεῖν** repeated in parallel.

ἃ σὺ λέγεις: 'what you yourself mean' (the **σὺ** is emphatic) answering **λέγεις** in Thrasymachus' question.

ἔμοιγε δοκῶ: English would prefer the impersonal 'as it seems to me, at least'.

σκοπῶμεν: hortatory subjunctive: 'let us'.

βέλτιον: comparative adverb, 'better'; the force is 'more carefully'.

οὐχ ὡμολόγηται: 'has it not been agreed' (perfect passive); the verb governs two accusative + infinitive clauses: (1) **τοὺς ἄρχοντας . . . διαμαρτάνειν**, (2) **δίκαιον εἶναι.** The repetition of the question just below is Socrates' laying on his Socratic irony rather thickly.

τοῖς ἀρχομένοις προστάττοντας ποιεῖν ἄττα: **τοῖς ἀρχομένοις** is the dative object of **προστάττοντας**, also followed by the infinitive with its object **ἄττα** = *τινα*, object of **ποιεῖν**: 'enjoining those they rule to do something'.

διαμαρτάνειν: takes a genitive, **τοῦ ἑαυτοῖς βελτίστου:** 'make mistakes in respect of what is best for them'.

ἃ δ᾽ ἂν προστάττωσιν οἱ ἄρχοντες: a relative clause acting as the object of **ποιεῖν** at the end of the sentence.

339e

οἴου: imperative of *οἴομαι*, with a force of 'you must recognize', followed by **ὡμολογῆσθαί σοι**, 'that it has been agreed by you' (passive infinitive with a dative of the agent)

τὸ ἀσύμφορα ποιεῖν τοῖς ἄρχουσί τε καὶ κρείττοσι δίκαιον εἶναι: all of this constitutes what has been agreed; take **δίκαιον εἶναι** first, followed by **τὸ ἀσύμφορα ποιεῖν**. The datives **τοῖς ἄρχουσί τε καὶ κρείττοσι** are probably to be taken equally as datives of disadvantage dependent on **ἀσύμφορα**, and with **δίκαιον**. An English translation can encapsulate both: 'it is just for both rulers and the more powerful to do what is disadvantageous for them'.

A Level

κακὰ αὑτοῖς: 'things that are bad for themselves'.
τοῖς δὲ: 'but for others', i.e. the ruled.
δίκαιον εἶναι: accusative + infinitive following **φῇς**, and then expounded by the further infinitive **ταῦτα ποιεῖν**.
ἃ ἐκεῖνοι προσέταξαν: 'that they [i.e. the rulers] ordered'. *ἐκεῖνος* generally refers to 'the former', and *οὗτος*, 'the latter'.
ὦ σοφώτατε Θρασύμαχε: the superlative is clearly cuttingly ironic; *σοφός* can have pejorative undertones in Greek (e.g. Euripides *Bacchae* 395), suggesting glibness and haughtiness: this barbed language comes as Socrates comes to the conclusion of this part of elenchus showing the contradictions in Thrasymachus' argument.
οὐκ ἀναγκαῖον συμβαίνειν αὐτὸ οὑτωσί: supply *ἐστι*; 'is it not necessary this should be our conclusion, thus', with the explanatory accusative + infinitive **δίκαιον εἶναι** following. The extra iota on the end of **οὑτωσί** is deictic, pointedly demonstrating the conclusion of the argument.
τοὐναντίον: *το ἐναντίον*, 'the opposite' (as at 339d).
τὸ γὰρ τοῦ κρείττονος ἀσύμφορον is the subject of **προστάττεται**, with **τοῖς ἥττοσιν** in the dative as those being ordered. This is, however, tricky to render into English: taking **τοῖς ἥττοσιν** as the subject makes it clearer: 'Those who are weaker are ordered to do what is disadvantageous to the stronger.'

340a
ναὶ μὰ Δί': By Zeus.
ἔφη . . . ὁ Πολέμαρχος: Polemarchus acts as a focalizer for what Plato is intending his readers to think, surprise at the acumen of Socrates' devastating line of argument against Thrasymachus. The short dialogue between Cleitophon and Polemarchus serves to summarize the key points made.
ἐὰν . . . αὐτῷ μαρτυρήσῃς: 'if you are his witness'.
τί . . . δεῖται: 'why is there need'.
αὐτὸς γὰρ Θρασύμαχος: 'Thrasymachus himself.'
τὸ γὰρ . . .: The use of the conjunction *γάρ* is illustrated particularly well here, and with **καὶ γὰρ** just below. In English we tend to use 'yes' and imply the connection; 'Yes, [because] Thrasymachus set out'; in Greek, the opposite occurs: explicit affirmation is implied, and the conjunction is expressed.
ἔθετο: aorist of *τίθημι* 'he set forth', i.e. established as his argument. **τὸ . . . ποιεῖν** is explanatory of the accusative + infinitive **δίκαιον εἶναι**, 'that it is just to do . . .'
ὑπὸ τῶν ἀρχόντων: agents of the passive participle **τὰ κελευόμενα**, 'the things ordered by the rulers'.

340b
ταῦτα δὲ ἀμφότερα: 'both these propositions', object of **θέμενος** (aorist middle participle of *τίθημι*).
τοὺς κρείττους . . . κελεύειν: accusative + infinitive after **ὡμολόγησεν**; **τοὺς ἥττους τε καὶ ἀρχομένους ποιεῖν** follow **κελεύειν** as an indirect command.
τὰ αὑτοῖς ἀσύμφορα: 'things disadvantageous to themselves'.

A Level

τὸ τοῦ κρείττονος συμφέρον is the subject of the sentence, with the predicate **οὐδὲν μᾶλλον ... δίκαιον ἂν εἴη**, 'would be no more just', followed by the comparative **ἢ τὸ μὴ συμφέρον**.

ἔλεγεν: 'he meant'; the imperfect perhaps suggests a lack of completion, contrasted with **ἐλέγετο** just below.

ὃ ἡγοῖτο ὁ κρείττων: 'that which the stronger believes . . .'; the optative is due to **ἔλεγεν** (as it is in secondary sequence), and might stand either for the present indicative or the present subjunctive with *ἄν* (i.e. indefinite) – it makes little difference to the meaning. The whole clause is explanatory of **τὸ . . . συμφέρον**; i.e. 'by the advantage of . . . he meant . . .'

αὑτῷ: dative dependent on **συμφέρειν**, 'advantages himself' (i.e. **ὁ κρείττων**).

ἐτίθετο: governs both **τοῦτο ποιητέον εἶναι τῷ ἥττονι** and **τὸ δίκαιον** [*εἶναι*] **τοῦτο; τῷ ἥττονι** is dative of the agent after the gerundive. **τοῦτο** is ambiguous, but in both cases probably refers back to the sentence before, i.e. what the stronger believes is to his advantage.

ἐλέγετο: passive; to contrast the suggestion of **ἔλεγεν**: 'he meant' earlier on.

340c

οὐδέν . . . διαφέρει: adverbial **οὐδέν**; 'it doesn't make a difference'.

ἀποδεχώμεθα: hortatory subjunctive; **αὐτοῦ** 'from him', genitive of source.

τοῦτο: i.e. Cleitophon's interpretation

ὃ ἐβούλου λέγειν τὸ δίκαιον: **ὃ** is the neuter relative pronoun, and **ἐβούλου** the seecond person middle imperfect of *βούλομαι*. Supply *εἶναι* to form the accusative + infinitive with **τὸ δίκαιον**.

δοκοῦν: infinitive of *δοκέω*, to appear.

ἐάντε . . . ἐάντε: strong constrastive forms, 'whether . . . or'.

φῶμεν: deliberative subjunctive of *φημί*. The accusative infinitive **οὕτω σε . . . λέγειν** should be translated 'that this is what you meant'.

ἥκιστά γε: literally, adverbial 'very little'; i.e. 'by no means' or 'not in the least'.

ἀλλὰ: expresses strong contrast.

οἴει: from *οἴομαι*, 'do you think', followed by accusative **με** + infinitive **καλεῖν**. **κρείττω** is masculine accusative singular, agreeing with **τὸν ἐξαμαρτάνοντα**, and is used predicatively, i.e. 'that I call the one erring stronger'.

ὅταν ἐξαμαρτάνῃ: indefinite temporal clause with the subjunctive; it has the force 'at the moment when'.

ᾤμην: first person imperfect indicative of *οἴομαι*.

340d

συκοφάντης: not at all what one might expect from the English word sycophant; a **συκοφάντης** was a malicious informer in the Athenian court system who attempted to extort money from defendants. The etymology and original meaning of the term is unclear, but is possibly related obscurely to the export of figs. The term carried connotations both of underhandedness and viciousness.

ἐπεὶ αὐτίκα: 'since to begin with'.

ἰατρὸν καλεῖς σὺ τὸν ἐξαμαρτάνοντα: 'do you call a man who errs a doctor . . .'

κατ᾽ αὐτὸ τοῦτο ὃ ἐξαμαρτάνει: 'by reason of the very thing in which he errs'.

A Level

ἢ λογιστικόν: *καλεῖς* must be supplied from the parallel.
τότε ὅταν ἁμαρτάνῃ: 'at the point at which he errs'.
οἶμαι: parenthetical.
λέγομεν τῷ ῥήματι οὕτως: i.e. 'we express it thus in speech', followed by **ὅτι** with indirect discourse.
τὸ δ': 'whereas in fact', a common idiom in Plato.

340e

καθ' ὅσον τοῦτ' ἔστιν ὅ: 'insofar as this is what . . .'
ἁμαρτάνει: the subject of this verb is **ἕκαστος τούτων**, i.e. the doctor, mathematician, etc.
ὥστε: The whole sentence is expressed as a result clause – i.e. the conclusion of the foregoing explanation. Translate 'as a result' or 'consequently'.
κατὰ τὸν ἀκριβῆ λόγον: 'strictly speaking' or 'in accurate language'.
ἐπιλειπούσης γὰρ ἐπιστήμης: genitive absolute.
ἐν ᾧ: neuter relative pronoun, referring to the circumstances just mentioned: 'in which', or more naturally 'and under these circumstances'.
ὥστε: Again, 'consequently'.
τότε ὅταν . . . ᾖ: the same construction as in 340d; **ᾖ** is the subjunctive of *εἶναι*. Translate 'whenever he is'.
πᾶς γ' ἂν εἴποι: potential optative, aorist in aspect rather than tense: 'everyone might say'; the force of it is iterative, suggesting this is kind of thing that people often actually do say.
τοιοῦτον: internal accusative of **ἀποκρίνεσθαι**, which also goes with **σοι**. Allan suggests taking the infinitive as representing a conative imperfect: 'this is the kind of answer I was trying to give to you'.
ὑπόλαβε: imperative, in the sense of 'understand', followed by accusative (**ἐμὲ**) and infinitive construction.

341a

τυγχάνει ὄν: 'happens to be'; best understood as having as its subject is **ἐκεῖνο**, with **τὸ δὲ ἀκριβέστατον** the complement, both neuter, and standing in apposition to the following accusative infinitive statement: 'That happens to be the most accurate, that . . .'
καθ' ὅσον: 'insofar as'; literally, 'according to how much'.
τὸ αὑτῷ βέλτιστον τίθεσθαι: 'he establishes what is best for himself'.
τοῦτο δὲ τῷ ἀρχομένῳ ποιητέον: supply *ἐστίν*; the dative is of the agent with the gerundive of obligation.
ὅπερ: 'exactly as'; emphatic form of the neuter accusative relative pronoun.
ἐξ ἀρχῆς: 'from the beginning'.
τὸ τοῦ κρείττονος ποιεῖν συμφέρον: the article forms an articular infinitive with **ποιεῖν**, the object of which is **τοῦ κρείττονος . . . συμφέρον**; as a whole: 'the doing of what is to the advantage of the stronger'.
εἶεν: not from *εἰμί*, but the particle, 'well then!'
οἴει γάρ: See the note on *γάρ* at 340a. **οἴει** is the second person single of *οἴομαι*, followed by accusative + infinitive.

A
Level

με ἐξ ἐπιβουλῆς ἐν τοῖς λόγοις κακουργοῦντά σε ἐρέσθαι: the participle modifies **με**, and (especially with **ἐξ ἐπιβουλῆς**) has a suggestion of purpose; **σε** is the object, probably to be understood with **ἐρέσθαι** as well: 'I questioned you deliberately to do you harm.'

ὥς ἠρόμην: 'as I asked', to be taken with **ἐρέσθαι**, i.e. 'I questioned you as I did.'

341b

καὶ οὐδέν γέ σοι πλέον ἔσται: Emlyn-Jones (*ad loc.*) translates rather loosely: 'And you won't get the upper hand.' Literally, 'And there will be nothing more for you', in the sense 'You won't get any further.'

οὔτε γὰρ ἄν με λάθοις: potential optative (second person aorist; **δύναιο** is in parallel, second person present middle optative, and the **ἄν** must be understood as repeated): 'you couldn't escape my notice'; *λανθάνω* takes a participle, 'to do something secretly': here, **κακουργῶν**.

μὴ λαθὼν: participle with conditional force, 'if not escaping my notice', or more smoothly: 'failing to do it secretly'. The dichotomy between stealth and force is a commonplace of Greek literature. Here, the emphasis is on the idea of conflict and opposition as inherent to the nature of the argument, unlike Socrates' framing of the debate, which is to engage in a mutual effort of uncovering the truth by discussion.

τῷ λόγῳ: instrumental dative, 'with your argument'.

ἂν ἐπιχειρήσαιμι: another potential optative.

ὦ μακάριε: another example of Socrates' overt and ironic politeness; Emlyn-Jones renders it rather charmingly, 'My dear fellow.'

ἵνα μὴ . . . ἐγγένηται: purpose clause; the subject is **τοιοῦτον**, 'so that such a situation doesn't arise'; *ἐγγίγνομαι* takes a dative, 'to spring up among', hence **ἡμῖν**.

διόρισαι: aorist middle imperative.

λέγεις: 'do you mean'.

τὸν ὡς ἔπος εἰπεῖν ἢ τὸν ἀκριβεῖ λόγῳ: the two clauses function as adjectives describing **τὸν ἄρχοντά τε καὶ τὸν κρείττονα** (hence the article), and are the two options which **ποτέρως** flags. **ὡς ἔπος εἰπεῖν** usually means 'so to speak' (literally, 'to speak a word'), so here, 'in ordinary speech', as opposed to the other option, **ἀκριβεῖ λόγῳ**, 'in the strict sense'; i.e. as Thrasymachus was saying above, we speak of a doctor or ruler erring, even though, he claims, in a strict sense, insofar as they err, they are not really a doctor or a ruler. Plato makes specific reference to this by **ὃ νυνδὴ ἔλεγες**. **ὃ** is the neuter accusative relative pronoun, with no antecedent, 'that which' – but is most clearly translated: 'as you were saying just now'.

οὗ τὸ συμφέρον: **οὗ** is the genitive masculine singular of the relative pronoun, 'whose advantage'; **κρείττονος ὄντος** modifies it, and is best understood in a causal sense, 'as he is the stronger'. **τὸ συμφέρον** is accusative, as the object of **ποιεῖν** – but the whole phrase is in apposition to **δίκαιον** and the subject **ἔσται**; i.e. if it were not a relative clause: 'it is just to do what is to the advantage of the stronger'.

τὸν . . . ἄρχοντα ὄντα: The answer to Socrates' question, expressed in the same grammatical form as it was asked, with the correlating *λέγω* assumed. **ὄντα** here emphasizes 'the one who is *really* a ruler'.

τῷ ἀκριβεστάτῳ λόγῳ: 'in the strictest sense'.
πρὸς ταῦτα: 'against this' or 'on this', i.e. the definition Thrasymachus has just affirmed (Greek prefers 'these things' where English naturally uses 'this').

341c
παρίεμαι: first person present middle of *παρ-ίημι*. **οὐδέν** is adverbial, 'I don't at all ask for your leniency.'
οὐ μὴ οἷός τ' ᾖς: *οὐ μή* + present subjunctive is used for strong denials: 'You won't be able.'
οἴει γάρ: See the note on *γάρ* at 340a; here, rather than answering a question, it poses one that is rhetorical and incredulous, but connected as explanatory to the preceding statement, something like: '[Are you really saying this] because you think . . .' **οἴει** is the second person singular of *οἴομαι*, followed by accusative + infinitive.
ἄν με . . . οὕτω μανῆναι: indirect discourse representing a potential optative, 'that I would be so mad'. **οὕτω** precedes the result clause **ὥστε . . . ἐπιχειρεῖν**; note the infinitive as expressing not an actual result, but as one which tends to result: 'that I would try'.
ξυρεῖν . . . λέοντα: this must be a Greek proverb; the scholiast interprets as 'to dare the impossible', like the English 'beard the lion'.
οὐδὲν ὢν καὶ ταῦτα: the participle is describing Socrates (as the subject of **ἐπεχείρησας** is second person), with concessive force: 'though being worthless in respect even of these things'; i.e. Socrates' earlier attempts to 'shave the lion' were a failure.
ἅδην, ἦν δ' ἐγώ, τῶν τοιούτων: flags the return of the dialogue back to the actual discussion about justice.
ὃν ἄρτι ἔλεγες: 'whom you were talking about just now'.
πότερον: as noted earlier (e.g. 330a), does not need to be translated.
καὶ λέγε τὸν τῷ ὄντι ἰατρὸν ὄντα: **λέγε** here: 'speak about' (imperative). The emphasis of the request is in **τῷ ὄντι . . . ὄντα**, i.e. 'the one who is really a doctor in reality'.
τί δὲ . . .: 'what about . . .?'
ὁ ὀρθῶς κυβερνήτης: 'the ship's captain, rightly understood' or 'properly speaking'.

341d
οὐδὲν οἶμαι τοῦτο ὑπολογιστέον: supply *εἶναι*, accusative + infinitive after **οἶμαι** with the gerundive; **οὐδὲν** is adverbial.
κατὰ τὸ πλεῖν: 'as regards sailing'.
ἑκάστῳ τούτων: i.e. each of the skilled craftsmen that Socrates has mentioned. The dative is possessive with **ἔστιν**, and could be translated as 'each of these has . . .'
ἐπὶ τούτῳ πέφυκεν: 'has been naturally formed for this' (which the subsequent clause goes on to specify). *ἐπί* + dative can be used to express an or purpose. **πέφυκεν**: perfect of φύω; in the aorist and perfect tenses, this is intransitive and as well as the meaning 'grow', often means 'to be by nature'.
ἑκάστῳ: again, referring to each of the skilled professionals.
ἐπὶ τούτῳ: repetition of the key phrase in affirmation.
ἑκάστῃ τῶν τεχνῶν: dative of possession with **ἔστιν**.

A
Level

τι: indefinite here rather than interrogative (as can be seen from the lack of acute accent). 'Is there some advantage to each . . .' or 'Does each have some advantage . . .'

ἄλλο ἢ ὅτι μάλιστα τελέαν εἶναι: 'other than to be perfect as far as possible'. **τελέαν** is feminine accusative, referring to each *τέχνη*. The question is asking whether a skill has any goal (expressed here in terms of advantage) beyond the perfection of its own art; it is laying the groundwork for the argument that a ruler, in Thrasymachus' strict sense, is never looking for personal advantage, but only the perfect exercise of the art of ruling, just as a doctor (in the strict sense) is uninterested in making a profit, but only in the health of his patients.

341e

πῶς τοῦτο ἐρωτᾷς; 'What do you mean by that question?'

ἔροιο: second person optative of *ἔρομαι* in a counterfactual conditional: 'if you were to ask'.

εἰ ἐξαρκεῖ σώματι εἶναι σώματι: 'whether it is sufficient for the body to be the body', i.e. 'whether the body is self-sufficient'.

προσδεῖταί τινος: *προσδέομαι* takes a genitive of what is lacking; either it is impersonal ('is there a lack of something'), or *σῶμα* needs to be understood ('is it lacking something'): both are possible, and the meaning is the same either way; the same applies to **προσδεῖται** just below.

εἴποιμ᾽ ἂν: aorist optative of *λέγω*, 'I would say'; the apodosis of the conditional posed by **εἴ με ἔροιο**.

διὰ ταῦτα: 'for this reason'.

ἐστὶν . . . ηὑρημένη: 'has been invented'; periphrastic construction for the perfect passive The hyperbaton draws attention to **νῦν**, i.e. 'in our advanced stage of civilization' (Emlyn-Jones commentary *ad loc.*).

ὅτι: because.

πονηρὸν: 'defective' or 'faulty' here.

οὐκ ἐξαρκεῖ αὐτῷ τοιούτῳ εἶναι: the same construction as **ἐξαρκεῖ σώματι εἶναι σώματι** above: literally, 'it is not sufficient for it to be of such a kind'; **τοιούτῳ** either echoes **εἶναι σώματι** above, i.e. 'it is not self-sufficient' (so Emlyn-Jones), or refers more specifically to **πονηρὸν** (thus Allan).

τούτῳ: dative of advantage following **τὰ συμφέροντα**.

ὅπως ἐκπορίζῃ: purpose clause, explanatory of **ἐπὶ τοῦτο** in the following clause: 'for this purpose, so that . . .' The subjunctive is a more vivid choice; as it is in secondary sequence, it could be optative.

παρεσκευάσθη: aorist passive of *παρασκευάζω*.

ὀρθῶς σοι . . . ἂν εἰπεῖν: as noted above (336d, 339d), **δοκῶ** is better rendered impersonally in English; the **ἂν** shows that **εἰπεῖν** represents a potential optative, still following from the condition **εἴ . . . ἔροιο** above: 'Does it seem to you that I would be speaking correctly?'

οὕτω λέγων: participle with conditional force, 'if I were to speak thus'.

ὀρθῶς: repetition of the key phrase to express assent.

342a

τί δὲ δή; 'But what about this?'

A Level

αὐτὴ ἡ ἰατρική: 'skill of medicine itself'.

ἔσθ' ὅτι = *ἔστιν*; supply **πονηρά** parallel to the previous clause. The **ὅτι** clause is explanatory; i.e. 'or is any other art [deficient], in that needs in addition . . .'

ὥσπερ ὀφθαλμοὶ ὄψεως καὶ ὦτα ἀκοῆς: *προσδεῖταί* is the implied verb for both.

διὰ ταῦτα: 'for this reason'

ἐπ' αὐτοῖς: 'over these things' (i.e. the eyes and ears).

δεῖ τινος τέχνης: a variant for *προσδεῖταί*, still with the genitive: 'there is a need of'.

τῆς τὸ συμφέρον . . . σκεψομένης τε καὶ ἐκποριούσης: as is often the case, the future participle expresses purpose.

εἰς ταῦτα: 'for these things themselves', i.e. seeing and hearing.

ἔνι = *ἔν-εστι*, 'is in'.

δεῖ: again, 'there is a need of', with the genitive **ἄλλης τέχνης**.

ἥτις: simply 'which'.

αὑτῇ τὸ συμφέρον: 'its own advantage' or 'what is advantageous to itself'.

καὶ τῇ σκοπουμένῃ ἑτέρας αὖ τοιαύτης: supply *τῇ τέχνῃ δεῖ*. That is, if a skill lacks competence to look to its own advantage (as the body lacks self-sufficiency), another skill needs to be posited; that skill in turn ('the skill doing the looking'), another is needed, **καὶ τοῦτ' ἔστιν ἀπέραντον** ('and this is endless').

342b

ἢ αὐτὴ: supply *τέχνη*.

ἄλλης: again, supply *τέχνης*.

ἐπὶ τὴν αὑτῆς πονηρίαν: 'in the case of its own deficiency' (ἐπὶ + accusative for the end or purpose).

οὔτε . . . οὔτε . . . οὐδεμία οὐδεμιᾷ: The preponderance of negatives is striking: Socrates is making his point rhetorically emphatic; having painted one option as ridiculous (an endless chain of defective skills), here he emphasizes in the strongest terms the self-sufficiency of each of them.

οὐδεμιᾷ τέχνῃ πάρεστιν: dative with the verb: 'is there prsent in any art'.

προσήκει: 'is it fitting', with the dative **τέχνῃ**.

ἄλλῳ τὸ συμφέρον . . . ἢ 'κείνῳ: *ἄλλῳ* though dative is not feminine and does not agree with **τέχνῃ**; it is rather neuter, of advantage, with **τὸ συμφέρον**, and is paralleled by (ἐ)**κείνῳ**: 'what is beneficial to anything other than that . . .'

οὗ τέχνη ἐστίν: **οὗ** is the neuter genitive singular relative pronoun, with antecedent **κείνῳ**: 'of which it is the skill'; as he goes on to explain, medicine is the skill of the body, etc.

αὐτὴ δὲ: 'but the skill itself'.

ὀρθὴ οὖσα: participle of *εἰμί*, either with conditional force, as Emyln-Jones' translation suggests with 'when it is correct' or causal, 'by being correct' (Allan).

ἕωσπερ ἂν ᾖ ἑκάστη ἀκριβὴς ὅλη ἥπερ ἐστίν: this clause clarifies what **ὀρθὴ οὖσα** means 'as long as each [art] is precisely and wholly what it is'; **ἀκριβὴς** reiterates Thrasymachus' insistence on each skilled practitioner be defined κατὰ τὸν ἀκριβῆ λόγον (340e). Hence, **ἐκείνῳ τῷ ἀκριβεῖ λόγῳ**: 'in that precise sense of yours'.

A
Level

σκόπει: again imperative, as at 339b (with note).

οὕτως ἢ ἄλλως ἔχει: The same idiom of *ἔχω* + adverb seen several times above (see, e.g., note on 329b), used impersonally: 'Is this the case, or it is otherwise?'

οὕτως, ἔφη, φαίνεται: another positive affirmation, but given this time guardedly by Thrasymachus by specifying only that it appears (**φαίνεται**) to be the case.

342c

ναί: The assent from Thrasymachus is now clearly only grudgingly given, even more so with **φαίνεται, ἔφη, οὕτως** below, as if he is suspicious about where Socrates' argument is leading.

οὐδὲ ἱππικὴ ἱππικῇ ἀλλ' ἵπποις: supply *τὸ συμφέρον σκοπεῖ*; likewise the next sentence.

ἐκείνῳ οὗ τέχνη ἐστίνb i.e. to its field of expertise, 'the thing of which it is the art'.

ἀλλὰ μήν: signals a transition in the argument. The force of the new departure is in **ἄρχουσί γε . . . καὶ κρατοῦσιν** (flagged by *γε*, which always emphasizes the preceding word): that is, as well as looking to the advantage of the object of their skill, arts also have power over them.

ἐκείνου: both *ἄρχω* and *κρατέω* take a genitive of what is ruled.

οὗπέρ εἰσιν τέχναι: like **οὗ τέχνη ἐστίν** above, with the same meaning.

συνεχώρησεν . . . μόγις: rather than dialogue, Thrasymachus grudging acquiescence to Socrates' argument is now simply narrated; by reducing Thrasymachus' ability to respond, Plato dramatizes the cogency of Socrates' argument. (Keep in mind, though, that all the characters are under the creative control of Plato's pen.)

ἄρα: inferential, setting up the logical conclusion at which Socrates has been aiming.

ἐπιστήμη: seems here to be used interchangeably with **τέχνη**; Emlyn-Jones translates as 'body of knowledge'.

342d

ὑπὸ ἑαυτῆς: agent of the participle **ἀρχομένου** (i.e. 'ruled by it'), referring back to **ἐπιστήμη**.

συνωμολόγησε μὲν καὶ ταῦτα τελευτῶν: the participle is adverbial, 'finally'. On the tone of this, see the note on **συνεχώρησεν . . . μόγις** (above, 342c).

μάχεσθαι: the character of Thrasymachus as an argumentative bruiser is re-emphasized here; see the Introduction, 'The Battle with Thrasymachus'. Plato paints a picture of objections being (rudely, forcefully) raised, none of which are worthy of recording.

ἄλλο τι οὖν: 'Is it not the case, therefore'; the words are entirely redundant, serving merely to underscore the obviousness of the claim being made – perhaps like the phrase 'am I right?' added to claims in US English.

καθ' ὅσον ἰατρός: 'insofar as he is a doctor'.

ὁ ἀκριβὴς ἰατρὸς: 'the doctor in the strict sense'; cf. the note on **ἀκριβὴς** at 342b. The doctor is the subject of **ὡμολόγηται** where English would make the sentence impersonal: 'It has been agreed that the doctor . . .'

συνέφη: again, Thrasymachus is reduced to being narrated, rather than speaking.

A Level

342e

οὐκοῦν: expecting a positive answer.

οὐκ ἄρα: again,as in 432c, inferential, flagging the conclusion of a line of reasoning.

συνέφησε: cf. **συνέφη** (342d) – aorist here, rather than the imperfect above, perhaps signalling here his assent just to the preceding question, as opposed to a longer chain of reasoning: though the difference is in all likelihood minimal at most.

οὐκοῦν: here, not as part of a question assuming a positive answer, but flagging up the obvious inference.

οὐδὲ ἄλλος οὐδεὶς καθ' ὅσον ἄρχων ἐστίν: 'nobody at all, insofar as they are in a position of authority'.

τῷ ἀρχομένῳ καὶ ᾧ ἂν αὐτὸς δημιουργῇ: datives, dependent on **συμφέρον**. **ᾧ** is the relative pronoun; it could be masculine (equally **τῷ ἀρχομένῳ**, 'the person being ruled'; this is how Emlyn-Jones takes them), but given **ἐκεῖνο** in the following sentence, this is unlikely. Both are more likely neuter, referring to the skill's sphere of operation. The whole relative clause means 'for which he practises his craft', an alternative phrase meaning the same thing as **ἐκείνῳ οὗ τέχνη ἐστίν** (at 342b and c above).

πρὸς ἐκεῖνο βλέπων: 'looking to that', referring to **τῷ ἀρχομένῳ**.

καὶ λέγει ἃ λέγει καὶ ποιεῖ ἃ ποιεῖ ἅπαντα: the two relative clauses make this look odd at first glance, but the translation is reasonably straightforward: 'he both says everything he says, and does everything he does'.

A
Level

Vocabulary

An asterisk * denotes a word in the OCR's Defined Vocabulary List for AS.

ἀβλαβής, -ές	without harm; unharmed; harmless
*ἀγαθος, -η, -ον (superl. ἄριστος)	good
ἄγαμαι	wonder, be amazed at
ἀγαπάω	love, be fond of, be content
*ἀγνοέω	not to perceive or recognize
ἄγω	lead, guide, bring
ἄδην + gen.	to one's fill, enough
*ἀδικέω	do wrong to, injure, harm
*ἄδικος	unjust
αἰνίσσομαι	speak in riddles
ἀκέραιός, -όν	pure, unmixed
ἀκοή, -ῆς, ἡ	hearing
*ἀκούω	hear, listen to
ἀκριβής, -ές	accurate, precise
ἀκριβολογέομαι	be precise in language
*ἄκων, ἄκουσα, ἄκον	unwilling, involuntary
ἀλήθεια, -ης, ἡ	truthfulness
*ἀληθής, -ές	true
*ἀλλὰ	but, however
*ἀλλήλους, -ας, -α	each other
*ἄλλος, -η, -ον	other, another
*ἅμα	at the same time; together with
*ἁμαρτάνω	make a mistake, miss, fail
ἁμαρτία, -ας, ἡ	failure, fault
*ἀμφότερος, -η, -ον	both
*ἄν	would, could (indef.)
ἀναγκαῖος, -α, -ον	necessary
*ἀνακαγχάζω	force, compel
ἀναμάρτητος, -ον	unerring, unfailing
*ἀνήρ, ἀνδρός, ὁ	man, husband
*ἄνθρωπος, -ου, ὁ	man, person
ἀνόητος, -ον	not understanding, not thought of
*ἀντί + gen.	instead of, over against
ἀντιλαμβάνω	lay hold of
*ἄξιος, ἀξία, ἄξιον	worthy, deserving
ἀπαγορεύω	forbid
ἀπαιτέω	demand back
ἀπαλλάσσω	set free, release, deliver
*ἅπας, -ασα, -αν	all, every
ἀπέραντος, -ον	boundless, endless
ἀπέρχομαι	go away, depart
ἀπιστέω	disbelieve, distrust
ἁπλῶς	simply, singly
ἀποδέχομαι	accept, receive
ἀποδίδωμι	give back
ἀπόδοσις, -εως, ἡ	giving back, return
*ἀποκρίνομαι	answer
ἀπόκρισις, -εως, ἡ	answer, response
ἀπολαμβάνω	receive, recover, regain
ἀπολαύω + gen.	enjoy, have enjoyment of
ἀποφαίνω	show forth, display
*ἄρα	. . . then . . .
*ἆρα	(marks out a question)
*ἀρετή, -ῆς, ἡ	excellence, virtue
ἀριστοκρατέομαι	live under an aristocracy
*ἄρτι	recently
*ἀρχή, ῆς, ἡ	beginning, rule, power
*ἄρχω + gen.	rule
ἀσύμφορος, -ον	inconvenient, prejudicial
ἀτάλλω	rear, foster
ἄττα = Attic for ἅτινα; see ὅστις	
*αὖ/αὖθις	again
*αὐτίκα	at once
*αὐτός, -ή, -ό	him/her/it(self)
ἄφωνος, -ον	voiceless, dumb
βδελυρός, -ά, -όν	disgusting, loathsome
βελτίων and βέλτιστος	Compar. and superl. of ἀγαθός
βιάζω	constrain; (mid.) do violence to, force
βλαβερός, -ά, -όν	harmful

***βλέπω**	look
βόειος, -α, -ον	of an ox
***βούλομαι**	want, wish, be willing
***γάρ**	for
***γε**	at any rate, even
***γελάω**	laugh
***γίγνομαι**	become, be, happen, occur
***γιγνώσκω**	(get to) know, realize, understand
***γοῦν**	at any rate, at least
γραμματιστής, -οῦ, ὁ	schoolmaster
***δέ**	but, and
δείδω, aor. **ἔδεισα**; perf. ppl. **δεδιώς**	fear
***δεῖ**	it is necessary
***δεινός, -ή, -όν**	terrible, clever, strange
***δέω**	lack, be in want of, beg from (+ gen.)
***δή**	(emphasizes preceding word)
***δῆλος, -η, -ον**	clear, certain
δημιουργέω	practise a craft, fashion, create
δημιουργός, -οῦ, ὁ	craftsman, creator
δημοκρατέομαι	have a democratic constitution
δημοκρατία, -ας, ἡ	democracy
δημοκρατικός, -ή, όν	democratic
***δήπου**	of course
***διά**	(+acc.) on account of; (+ gen.) through
διακούω	hear out
διακωλύω	hinder, prevent
***διαλέγομαι**	converse
διαμαρτάνω	miss entirely; be quite wrong
διαπαύω	bring to an end, conclude
διαπτοέω	scare away; (pass.) be panic-stricken
διαρπάζω	tear in pieces
διαφέρω	differ, make a difference
***διαφθείρω**	destroy, corrupt
***διδάσκω**	teach, tell
***δίκαιος, -α, -ον**	just, upright, fair
***δικαιοσύνη, -ης, ἡ**	justice
διορίζω	distinguish, delimit, determine
***δοκεῖ**	it seems (good)
***δοκέω**	seem, think
***δράω**	do
***δύναμαι**	be able, can
***ἐάν**	if
ἐάνπερ	strengthened form of **ἐάν**
ἐάντε . . . ἐάντε	whether . . . or, if . . . or if
***ἑαυτόν, -ήν, -ό**	him/her/itself
ἐγγίγνομαι	spring up, intervene
***ἐγώ**	I
***ἐθέλω**	wish, be willing
ἔθω, perf. ppl. **εἰωθώς**	be accustomed to
***εἰ**	if
εἶεν	well then
***εἰκός, -ότος, τό**	probability, likelihood
***εἶμι**	I shall go (fut. of ἔρχομαι)
***εἰμί**	I am
εἰρωνεία, -ας, ἡ	dissimulation, pretence
εἰρωνεύομαι	feign ignorance
***εἰς** + acc.	to, into
εἷς, μία, ἕν	one
εἶτα	then, next
***ἐκ, ἐξ** + gen.	out of, from
***ἕκαστος, -η, -ον**	each
ἐκβαίνω	go out, depart from
***ἐκεῖνος, -η, -ο**	that
***ἐκεῖσε**	thither, to there
ἐκπλήσσω	strike out of, amaze, astound
ἐκπορίζω	invent, contrive, provide
ἐκτίνω	pay off, pay back
***ἑκών, -οῦσα, -όν**	willing
ἐλάχιστος, -η, -ον (superl. of **ἐλαχύς**)	least, smallest
ἔλεγχος, -ου, ὁ	argument, cross-examining
ἐλεέω	have pity on
ἐλλείπω	be wanting, lack
***ἐν**	in (+ dat.)
ἐναντίος, α, ον	opposite
ἔνειμι	be in, among
ἐνίοτε	at times, sometimes
***ἐνταῦθα**	then, here, there
ἐξαγριαίνω	make savage
ἐξαμαρτάνω	miss the mark, err, do wrong
***ἐξαπατάω**	deceive
ἐξαρκέω	be quite enough, suffice; to be satisfied
ἔοικα	be like, look like, seem
***ἐπαινέω**	praise
***ἐπεί/ ἐπειδή/ ἐπειδάν**	when, since

ἐπί	(+ acc.) against, onto, on, at; (+ gen.) on; (+ dat.) on condition of
ἐπιβουλή, -ῆς, ἡ	plan, plot; ἐξ ἐπιβουλῆς: deliberately, designedly
ἐπιεικής, ές	fitting, suitable
ἐπιθυμέω	long for, desire
ἐπιλείπω	leave behind, fail
ἐπιμελέομαι	to take care of, see to (+ gen.)
ἐπιστήμη, -ης, ἡ	understanding, skill, knowledge
ἐπιτάττω	enjoin, impose commands
ἐπιχειρέω	put one's hand to, attempt
ἔπος, -εος, τό	word, utterance, speech
ἐρέω fut. of λέγω	
*ἐρωτάω	ask
*ἕτερος, -α, -ον	one, the other, different
*εὖ	well
εὐδοκιμέω	be esteemed, popular
εὐηθίζομαι	play the fool
εὕρεσις, -εως, ἡ	discovery, invention
*εὑρίσκω	find
*ἐχθρός, -ά, -όν	hostile
*ἔχω	have, hold; (+ adv.) be in a particular state
*ἕως	while, until
*ζητέω	seek
ζήτησις , εως, ἡ	inquiry, investigation, search for
*ἡγέομαι	lead; think, believe
*ἤδη	now, already
*ἥκιστος , -η, -ον	least
*ἥκω	I have come
ἡνίκα	at the time when
ἠρόμην strong aor. of ἐρωτάωἡσυχία, -ας, ἡ	peace, rest, quiet
ἥττων, ἧττον	less, inferior, weaker
θαυμαστός, -ή, -όν	wonderful, marvellous
θεῖος, -α, -ον	divine
θεραπευτής, -οῦ, ὁ	attendant, carer
*θεός, -οῦ, ὁ	god
*θηρίον, -ου, τό	wild beast
θυσία, -ας, ἡ	sacrifice
ἰατρικος, -ή, -όν	of a doctor, medical
*ἰατρός, -οῦ, ὁ	doctor
*ἱερός, -ά, -όν	holy
*ἵνα	so that, in order to
ἱππικός, -ή, -όν	of horses, of horsemanship

*ἵππος, -ου, ὁ	horse
*ἴσως	perhaps
*καθίστημι	set up, establish
*καὶ	and, also, too
*καίτοι	and yet
*κακός, -ή, -όν	bad, cowardly, wicked
κακουργέω	do evil
*καλέω	call, summon
*καλός, -ή, -όν	good, fine, beautiful
*κάμνω	toil, be weary of
*κατά	(+ acc.) down, according to, by
*κελεύω	order
κερδαλέος, -α, -ον	profitable, to one's advantage
κληρονόμος, -ου, ὁ	heir
*κολάζω	punish
κόσμιος, -α, -ον	well-ordered, regular, moderate
*κρατέω	control, conquer
κρέας, κρέως, τό	meat
κρείττων, -ον (gen. -ονος)	stronger, better
κτάομαι	get for oneself, acquire; (perf.) possess
κτῆσις, -εως, ἡ	acquisition, possession, property
κυβερνήτης, -ου, ὁ	pilot, navigator
*λαμβάνω	take
*λανθάνω	escape the notice of; do something secretly + ppl.
*λέγω	say, speak, tell
λέων, -οντος, ὁ	lion
λῆψις, -εως, ἡ	taking hold, seizing
λογίζομαι	count, reckon
λογισμός, -οῦ, ὁ	counting, calculation
λογιστής, -οῦ, ὁ	mathematician, teacher of arithmetic
λογιστικός, -ή, -όν	skilled in calculating; (as a subst.) mathematician
*λόγος, -ου, ὁ	word, account, speech, reason
λυσιτελέω	pay what is due, avail
λυσιτελής, -ές	profitable, advantageous
μά	in the phrase ναὶ μὰ followed by a god (in the acc.), an affirm. oath – 'By . . .!'
μαίνομαι	be mad, rave
μακάριος, -α, -ον	blessed, happy
*μάλα	very

***μάλιστα**	very much, especially
***μᾶλλον**	more, rather
***μανθάνω**	learn, understand
μαρτυρέω	bear witness
μάρτυρος	witness
***μάχομαι**	fight
***μέγας, μεγάλη, μέγα**	great, big
***. . . μέν . . . δέ**	on the one hand . . . on the other
***μέντοι**	however, certainly
***μέρος, -εος, τό**	part, share
***μέσος, -η, -ον**	middle
μεταξύ	in the midst
***μή** (and comp.)	see under οὐ
μήν	truly
μόγις	hardly, scarcely
***μόνον**	only
***μόνος, -η, -ον**	alone, solitary
***ναί**	yes; see also μά *supra*
***ναῦς, νεώς, ἡ**	ship
***ναύτης, -ου, ὁ**	sailor
νή	part. of strong affirm.
***νόμος, -ου, ὁ**	law, custom
***νόος (νοῦς), νόου, ὁ**	mind
***νῦν**	now
νυνδή	strengthened form of **νῦν**
ξυρέω	shave
***ὅδε , ἥδε, τόδε**	this
***οἶδα, εἰδέναι**	know
οἴομαι	think, suppose
***οἷος, -η, -ον**	such (as)
***οἷος τ' εἰμι**	be able, can
ὅλος, -η, -ον	whole, entire
***ὁμολογέω**	agree, admit
***ὅπλα, -ων, τά**	arms, weapons, armour
ὁπότε	when (adv. correlative to **πότε**)
***ὅπως**	how, so that
ὁπωστιοῦν	in any way whatever, in some way or other
***ὁράω**	see
***ὀρθός, -ή, -όν**	straight, correct
***ὁρμάω**	set in motion, rush into; (mid.) set out
ὅρος, -ου, ὁ	boundary, definition
***ὅς , ἥ, ὅ**	who, which
***ὅσος, -η, -ον**	as much as, (plur.) as many as
ὅσπερ, ἥπερ, ὅπερ	the very person who/thing which
ὅστις, ἥτις, ὅ τι	whoever
ὁστισοῦν, ὁτιοῦν	anyone whatsoever
***ὅτε / ὅταν**	when, whenever
***ὅτι**	because, that
***οὐ**	not
***οὐδαμῶς**	in no way
***οὐδὲ**	neither, nor
***οὐδείς, οὐδεμία, οὐδέν**	no one, nothing
***οὐδέποτε**	never
***οὐκέτι**	no longer
***οὐκοῦν**	therefore, then
***οὖν**	and so, therefore
οὔπω	not yet, not at all
οὖς, ὠτός, τό	ear
***οὔτε**	neither, and not
***οὗτος, αὕτη, τοῦτο**	this
***οὕτω / οὕτως**	thus, so
ὀφείλω	owe
***ὀφθαλμός, -οῦ, ὁ**	eye
ὄψις, ὄψεως, ἡ	aspect, appearance
πάγκαλος, -η, -ον	all beautiful, very good
παγκρατιαστής, -οῦ, ὁ	pancratist, all-in wrestler
***πάλαι**	formerly, in the past
παντάπασι	wholly; (in affirm. answers) by all means
πανταχοῦ	everywhere
πάντως	in all ways, especially, at any rate
πάνυ	altogether, very
***παρά**	(+ acc.) contrary to, along, to; (+ gen.) from (a person); (+dat.) beside
***παραδίδωμι**	I hand over, surrender
παρακάθημαι	be seated beside or near
παρακατατίθεμαι	deposit one's property with another, entrust it to someone's keeping
παρανομέω	act unlawfully
***παρασκευάζω**	get ready, prepare
***πάρειμι**	be present
***πάρεστιν**	it is possible
παρίεμαι (mid. of **παρίημι**)	beg to be excused; ask quarter
***πᾶς, πᾶσα, πᾶν**	every, all

***πείθω**	persuade; (pass. and mid.) obey, believe, trust
***πειράομαι**	try
***περί**	(+ acc.) around; (+ gen.) about
περίειμι (ppl. **περιιών**)	go around, go about
πλεῖστος, -η, -ον	most, greatest
πλέον neut. compar. of **πολύς**	
***πλέω**	sail
πλοῦτος, -ου, ὁ	wealth, riches
***ποιέω**	make, do
ποιητικῶς	poetically, like a poet
***πόλις, πόλεως, ἡ**	city
***πολλάκις**	often; many times
***πολύς, πολλή, πολύ**	much, many
πονηρία, άς, ἡ	wickedness, baseness
πονηρός, -ά, -όν	toilsome, grievous, base
***ποτέ**	at some time, once
***πότερον . . . ἤ . . .**	whether . . . or . . .
ποτέρως	in which of two ways
***που**	anywhere, somewhere; I suppose, doubtless
***πρᾶγμα, -ατος, τό**	thing, affair, matter
πρέπω	be seemly, be proper
***προθύμως**	eagerly
προλέγω	foretell, announce beforehand
***πρός**	(+ acc.) towards, upon, against, in addition to, in respect of
προσαγορεύω	address, greet
προσβλέπω	look at
προσδέομαι	lack (+ gen.)
πρόσειμι	be added to, be present as well
προσήκω	be at hand, belong to; (impers.) it concerns, it is fitting
προσθήκη, -ης, ἡ	addition, assistance
προσποιέομαι	pretend
προστάσσω	command, enjoin
προστίθημι	make additions
πρότερος, -η, -ον	before, former
πρῶτος, -η, -ον	first
***πῶς**	how
***ῥᾴδιος, -η, -ον**	easy
ῥῆμα, -ατος, τό	word, that which is said
σαρδάνιος, -η, -ον	bitter, scornful
***σαφής, -ές**	clear, plain
σιτίον, -ου, τό	grain, food
σκέπτομαι	look about, view, examine
***σκοπέω**	behold, contemplate
σμικρός, -ά, -όν (variant of ***μικρός**)	small
***σός, -ή, -όν,**	your, yours
***σοφία, -ας, ἡ**	wisdom
***σοφός, -ή, -όν,**	wise, clever
σπουδάζω	be serious, be eager, hasten
***σύ**	you
συγγίγνομαι	engage with, associate with
συγχωρέω	yield, accede, acquiesce in
συκοφαντέω	be or act as a συκοφάντης
συκοφάντης	informer, swindler, con-man
συμβαίνω	tally, correspond with, come to pass, happen
συμβάλλομαι	contribute
συμφέρω	be useful
σύμφημι	assent, concede, agree to
συναορέω	accompany
σύνειμι	be with, associate with
σύνοιδα	be conscious of
συνομολογέω	agree with, concede
συστρέφω	gather [oneself] together, clench
σφόδρα	very much, exceedingly
***σῶμα, -ατος, τό**	body
σωφρονέω	be of sound mind, come to one's senses
***σώφρων**	of sound mind
***τε**	both, and
τέλεος, -α, -ον	perfect
τελευτῶν, ῶσα, ῶν used with v. as an adv.	to finish with, at the end, at last
***τέχνη, -ης, ἡ**	art, skill, craft
***τίθημι**	put, place
τίμιος, -η, -ον	valued, worthy, costly
***τις**	a certain, a
***τίς**	who
τοίνυν	therefore, accordingly
τοιόσδε, -άδε, -όνδε	such, so
***τοιοῦτος, -αύτη, -οῦτο**	such
τοσόσδε, -ήδε, -όνδε,	so much
***τότε**	then, at that time
***τυγχάνει** + ppl.	happen to . . . (expressing co-incidence)
τυραννεύω	to be a monarch, rule (as a tyrant)
τυραννικός, ή, όν,	befitting a ruler, despotic
τυραννίς , -ίδος, ἡ	monarchy, tyranny

***τύχη, -ης, ἡ**	chance, fortune, fate
ὕθλος, -ου, ὁ	idle talk, nonsense
ὑπείκω	give way, yield
ὑπό	(+ acc./dat.) under; (+ gen.) by
ὑποκατακλίνομαι	give place to, give in
ὑπολαμβάνω	take up, assume, understand
ὑπολογιστέον	one must take into account
ὑποτρέμω	tremble a little
***φαίνω**	bring to light, make known; (pass.) come to light, appear, seem
φανερός, -ά, -όν,	visible, manifest, clear
***φέρω**	bring, bear, endure
***φημί**	say, speak
φθέγγομαι	utter a sound, speak loudly
***φίλος, -η, -ον**	dear, beloved; (as n.) friend
φιλονεικέω	be fond of strife, engage in rivalry
φιλοτιμέομαι	strive eagerly
φλυαρία, ᾱς, ἡ	nonsense
***φοβέομαι**	be afraid of
φύω	(in the perf.) be (by nature), exist
χαλεπαίνομεν	be judged/treated harshly
***χαλεπός, -ή, -όν**	difficult
***χάριν ἀποδιδόναι** or **ἐκτίνειν**	thank, give thanks (lit., to give thanks back, pay thanks in full)
χρεία, -ας, ἡ	need, want
***χρή**	it is necessary
***χρήματα, -ων, τά**	money, wealth
χρηματιστής, οῦ, ὁ	money-maker
***χρήσιμος, -η, -ον**	useful, advantageous
χρυσίον, -ου, τό	gold
***ψεύδομαι**	lie, speak falsely
***ὡς**	as, when, that, because, how
***ὥσπερ**	as if
***ὥστε**	so that
ὦτα	See **οὖς**
ὠφέλιμος, ον	helping, useful

Plutarch, *Antony*

Introduction, Commentary Notes and Vocabulary by Sam Baddeley

A Level: 76–86

Introduction

Plutarch

Plutarch was born in Chaeronea (a town in Boeotia, in Greece) in *c.* 45/46 CE. He enjoyed something of an international career: he studied in Athens under the philosopher Ammonius, travelled widely (including trips to Italy, Egypt and Asia), and became a Roman citizen. However, he seems to have lived most of his life in the city in which he had been born and raised, as a Greek under Roman rule. He died sometime between 119 and 125 CE.

Plutarch wrote extensively; amongst his surviving works are 22 *Parallel Lives* (on which see below) and the *Moralia*, a series of essays and speeches that range across a number of topics, including education, the love of wealth, systems of government, oracles and the ethics of meat-eating, and some of which are now believed to have been written by others. He also held various public offices in Chaeronea, and for the last thirty years of his life he was one of the two priests of Apollo at Delphi.

The Greek East under the Roman Empire

Plutarch lived through a fascinating and (at times) turbulent period of Roman history, encompassing the end of the Julio-Claudian period, the chaos which resulted after the death of Nero (the so-called 'Year of the Four Emperors'), the reigns of the Flavians (Vespasian, Titus and Domitian) and those of Nerva, Trajan and Hadrian. He lived in the Greek East, an area which was of great importance to the Roman elite in political and cultural terms during the Imperial Period (a period which is generally defined as running from 27 BCE – the start of the reign of Augustus – to sometime in the fourth or fifth centuries CE). The various city-states which made up 'Hellas' (the area later known to Romans as 'Greece') had been gradually conquered by the Romans in the second century BCE, and no one could doubt the reality of Roman rule in Greece after the Battle of Actium (see below). Graeco-Roman connections were many and varied: Roman aristocrats often travelled to Greece to study philosophy as the final stage of their education; Greek aristocrats were able to enter the imperial service; and several emperors – the so-called 'philhellenes' – openly declared their love of Greece and Greek culture. Indeed, Plutarch lived under two such rulers: Nero, who visited the country in 66 CE, participated in the Olympic Games, and subsequently proclaimed the freedom of Greece in 67 CE; and Hadrian, who completed the building of the Temple of Zeus in Athens, and in whose honour the Athenians built the Arch of Hadrian (otherwise known as Hadrian's Gate) in the style of a Roman triumphal arch. An attentive reader will notice parallels between the life/career of Nero and that of Antony. Plutarch seems keen to emphasize these: indeed, his life ends with an account of Antony's descendants, of which Nero was one (see Pelling, *Commentary*, pp. 9–10), and it is worth asking whether or not he may have exaggerated the parallels for literary effect.

The relationship between Greece and Rome in the Imperial Period was complex, not least due to the profound tension which lay at its core, that between military strength versus cultural achievement. The most memorable and frank acknowledgement of the effects of Greek civilization on Rome and the Romans from the perspective of an educated Roman of the first century BCE comes to us from the Roman poet Horace: *Graecia capta ferum victorem cepit et artes/ intulit agresti Latio*: 'captive Greece took her savage conqueror captive and brought the arts to rustic Latium' (*Odes* 1.37). Horace is writing earlier than Plutarch, and is perhaps more concerned with being witty than with being historically accurate; nevertheless, many historians have agreed with his assessment of Greek cultural superiority. Although Plutarch could read Latin and made use of Latin sources for this *Life* and others, it is clear that he was influenced in literary terms primarily by Greek writing. This is perhaps unsurprising: he lived through a period (known as the 'Second Sophistic' and dating from the first to the early part of the third centuries CE) in which there was renewed interest in literature and oratory (speech-writing) from Classical Athens, an interest which led to much new writing in Greek. Plutarch was therefore living in a world of dual cultural and political loyalties. The scholar Simon Swain has noted that the *Antony* is more complicated still: 'Antony moves within three differing cultural systems – Roman, Hellenic and Egyptian' and concludes that 'the major axis is Egyptian–Roman' (*Cultural Interchange*, pp. 151–2).

Rome's interest in Egypt was not new at the time of Mark Antony's arrival there in the mid-first century BCE: Egypt had long been of great importance to a city which relied heavily on imported grain to feed its ever-growing population, and Roman politicians had been interfering in Egyptian politics for many decades, attracted by the opportunities it afforded for both financial and political gain. The question of who should (or could) take control of Egypt was a very live one. One reading of Plutarch's Antony is that of a man who chooses Egypt/the East over Rome and Roman values – temporarily, but with significant consequences. Swain argues that 'the success of the *Antony* depends in large part upon this oscillation from the one culture to the other' (*Cultural Interchange*, p. 152), citing the contrast between Antony's earlier rejection of Roman customs and his final words, in which he declares with pride that he has been conquered οὐκ ἀγεννῶς Ῥωμαῖος ὑπὸ Ῥωμαίου 'not ignobly, a Roman by a Roman' (77.4).

Plutarch's *Life of Antony* is therefore of equal interest to historians of Roman provincial rule and to students of Greek literature of the Roman Imperial Period. It also has much to offer scholars of Shakespeare: Shakespeare used Sir Thomas North's translation of Plutarch's *Lives* as a major source for his Roman plays, most importantly (for our purposes) his *Antony and Cleopatra* (see below).

Genre, literary influences and Plutarch's sources

Plutarch is often used as a source by historians of antiquity; however, despite the fact that there were many Greek historiographical models available for him to follow (not least the works of Herodotus and Thucydides), 'history' is not his chosen genre. The *Life of Antony* is a biography, written as part of Plutarch's series of *Parallel Lives*, of which 22 survive: each contains biographies of a well-known Greek and a well-known Roman, and concludes with a comparison between the two. (An exception is the double-pairing of *Agis/Cleomenes* with *Tiberius/Gaius Gracchus*.) He touches on that which is of interest to him in the context of the life of his subject, focusing on those events which might provide a positive or negative moral example; indeed, he does not shy away from the latter, as he himself indicates in his introduction to the *Demetrius* biography which forms a pair with the *Life of Antony*:

> The most consummate arts, self-control, justice, and wisdom, involve judgements not only of what is good, just and useful, but also of what is harmful, disgraceful and wrong . . . Perhaps, then, it is no bad thing to include in our examples of Lives one or two pairs of those who have behaved recklessly or have become conspicuous for evil in positions of power or in great affairs.
>
> *Life of Demetrius*, 1.3–4 (trans. Pelling, p. 11)

He was writing approximately 150 years after the latest events in the *Antony*. He was therefore reliant on both written sources and collective historical memory, a memory which had from a very early stage become a vehicle for Augustan propaganda and the pseudo-myth of Augustus' role as the saviour of the Republic from a great eastern threat.

It is not entirely clear which sources Plutarch consulted in his writing of this work. Below is a brief summary of those generally agreed to be the likeliest contenders as identified by B. X. de Wet (see *Contemporary Sources in Plutarch's* Life of Antony) and Pelling (pp. 26–31):

- Cicero's *Philippics* (particularly *Philippics* 2), a series of speeches, delivered after the death of Julius Caesar, in which Cicero attacked Antony; these speeches led to the declaration of Antony as an enemy of the state (and, ultimately, to Antony's revenge in the form of Cicero's proscription). Needless to say, their picture of Antony is very negative. (NB: it is also possible that Plutarch knew Antony's replies to Cicero.)
- *The Memoirs of Augustus* (Augustus' biography, now lost), which again provides a negative depiction.
- A (now lost) history of the Civil Wars written by the Roman soldier, politician, contemporary and sometime supporter of Antony, C. Asinius Pollio.
- A history of Antony's campaign in Parthia by Quintus Dellius, a Roman military commander and politician of the second half of the first century BCE who was a friend of Antony but betrayed him and went over to Octavian just before the Battle of Actium.

- Eyewitness narrative accounts/descriptions of certain events/places, such as the Parthian campaign and the court of Cleopatra.
- Miscellaneous oral sources: Pelling (p. 29) suggests that Plutarch used these in particular for the later portions of Antony's life.

It seems probable that Plutarch obtained some of the information found in these earlier sources indirectly, through his reading of the works of later historians. But history is just one of many different genres which influenced him, and elements of epic, oratory, drama, philosophy and the ancient novel can all be discerned (see Swain, *Novel and Pantomime* and Duff, *Plato, Tragedy, the Ideal Reader*). At the heart of the work lies his interest in character. Indeed, all of the *Lives* are driven to some degree by a desire to show what a good life and good leadership could/should (and could/should not) look like (on leadership see Jacobs, *Pragmatic Biographies*, pp. 325–66 on *Demetrius–Antony*). We should not be surprised if they contain harsh judgements, inconsistencies, pathos and admiration: these are the luxuries of the ancient biographer, and Plutarch exploits them to the full. In the *Antony*, the presentation of title character as a tragic hero is very prominent and it seems highly likely that Plutarch will have exaggerated aspects of his characterization and/or omitted certain details in order to serve his vision of the *Life of Antony* as a cautionary tale and a work of literature to rival that of the great tragedies of the fifth century BCE.

The life of Antony and *The Life of Antony*

Plutarch's *Life* deals with the fortunes, trials and tribulations of Mark Antony (83–30 BCE). Antony is best known as the Roman general and statesman who, after the death of Julius Caesar, formed one third of a political alliance known as the Second Triumvirate. His co-triumvirs were Octavian, Caesar's great-nephew and adopted son and heir, later styled 'Augustus', and Marcus Aemilius Lepidus, another general, statesman and supporter of Caesar. Their initial aim was to avenge Caesar's death: this was achieved at the Battle of Philippi in 42 BCE, when Brutus and Cassius (Caesar's assassins) were defeated, and the triumvirs subsequently divided Rome's government and territories between them. Antony was assigned to the East and Octavian to the West; Lepidus was essentially sidelined. A bitter rivalry developed between Octavian and Antony, with each hoping to manoeuvre the other out of power.

As part of his tour of Rome's eastern provinces, in 41 BCE Antony asked Cleopatra, Queen of Egypt, to meet him at Tarsus, and they soon became lovers. This was not her first love affair with a Roman politician: she and Caesar had been romantically involved, and she had given birth to a son, Caesarion – whom she later declared to have been Caesar's child – in 47 BCE. (Caesarion is mentioned in the later chapters of the *Antony*.) Our assessment of the historical Cleopatra has been much altered by myths and legends in which gender stereotyping, objectification and misogyny abound. Indeed, the French philosopher Blaise Pascal, who was obsessed with Cleopatra's beauty, famously stated that had her nose been shorter, 'the whole face of the earth would have changed' (*Pensées*, 162).

Antony's love of the East and relationship with Cleopatra became major weapons in the propaganda war which Octavian was waging against him back in Italy, and tensions rose to a pitch. The final showdown came at the Battle of Actium in 31 BCE: Octavian's army won out against the combined forces of Antony and Cleopatra, and they committed suicide the following year in Alexandria; it is with their final days that the Greek portion of the A-level prescription is concerned. Actium undoubtedly represents a watershed moment in Roman history, but we must not underestimate the extent to which our perception of it has been influenced by the Augustan poets who, with all the sycophantic hyperbole characteristic of those seeking patronage under a new regime, instantly reframed it as a battle between the forces of civilization and those of barbarism, between good and evil.

It is clear that Roman politics were a major determining factor in the life of Mark Antony: he contributed to shifts in the political landscape, and political life provided him with many of the opportunities which came his way, and the limitations which he encountered. But Plutarch only deals with major political events as and when they touch on the life of his subject, and Actium is a perfect example: this *Life* is far more interested in Antony's character and in the personal relations which – to Plutarch's mind – played such a big role in his downfall. He shows much interest in Cleopatra, and contrary to the practice of many classical authors, this interest extends beyond her involvement with, and perceived effect on, the male subject of the work. There is undoubtedly some of that, but Plutarch also shows much admiration and sympathy for her; it is striking that he devotes a comparatively large chunk of his text – indeed, a chunk which comes after the death of his subject – to the narration of her suicide. It is tempting to think that we are being given two *Lives* for the price of one. (See Pelling, p. 16 for more on this, and pp.14–16 for Plutarch's interest in the psychological and moral aspects of the story.)

Plutarch pairs his biography of Antony with that of Demetrius of Macedon (336–283 BCE); Demetrius was the son of Antigonus, one of the twelve men who inherited part of the empire of Alexander the Great after the latter's death. The overlapping traits and themes of military success, generosity, extravagance, and the reversal of fortune are highlighted near the opening of the work (*Life of Demetrius*, 1.8); to this has been added a susceptibility to flattery (Pelling, p. 19). The motif of the theatre, particularly (but not exclusively) in the context of Greek tragedy (see Pelling, pp. 21–2, and Duff, *Plato, Tragedy, The Ideal Reader*) and pantomime (Swain, *Novel and Pantomime*), also unites the two *Lives*. Plutarch ends where he began, namely with a passage in which he compares the two men (a *synkresis*) and lays out what he sees to be the core differences between them. Plutarch's *synkresis* does not necessarily highlight the things which jump out from the narrative, and you may prefer to read both biographies carefully yourself in order to tease out the similarities and differences.

Synopsis and structure

The prescribed A-level passages are sections 56–75 and 87 in English translation and 76–86 in Greek. This takes us from the Battle of Actium through to the suicides of Antony and, a little later, Cleopatra. Do consider reading the whole of the *Antony* in translation if this is possible: it will undoubtedly give you a clearer understanding of the key events of the period and of how Plutarch develops his portrait of each character, not least in terms of the narrative techniques he uses. (For more details, see below p. 184.) Here follows a brief synopsis of the main events in the A-level selection.

Chapters 1–55 deal with Antony's childhood, education, early military successes and interactions with Julius Caesar, and the aftermath of Caesar's death, including his uneasy relationship with Octavian and the whole events of the Second Triumvirate. Plutarch dwells on Antony's infamous meeting with Cleopatra at Tarsus. The key military campaigns in Mutina and Parthia are also detailed, an understanding of which is needed for a full appreciation of the ways in which Plutarch uses them to support his assessment of Antony's character.

The Battle of Mutina was a battle between Antony and Octavian (supported by the Senate) which took place in 43 BCE, i.e. just after the death of Julius Caesar. Mark Antony had been the senior political figure in Rome since Caesar's death; unsurprisingly, tensions had arisen between him and Octavian. The Senate decided to join forces with Octavian in order to try to break Antony's hold on power. After an earlier clash at the Battle of Forum Gallorum, Octavian and his troops attacked Antony's camp at Mutina in Cisalpine Gaul. The outcome was initially unclear, but Antony's decision to withdraw from the site meant that Octavian and the Senate emerged as victorious. This battle was decisive but not condemnatory with respect to Antony and his political future: Octavian's relationship with the Ciceronian faction in the Senate subsequently broke down, and the Second Triumvirate was established the following autumn.

The Parthian Campaign was a large military expedition into Parthia led by Antony in 36 BCE. The Parthians had used the disruption generated by conflict after the death of Caesar to gain control of some Roman territory in the East; they were forced out from here, but Antony wanted to go further, not least because a successful campaign would win him money and prestige and help him to regain some of the authority amongst the Roman political elite that he had lost. The campaign was risky and large scale: it involved joining forces with several client kingdoms, and Cleopatra had to provide much of the money that he needed to undertake it. Overall, it was a disaster, and many men were lost on the retreat.

In Chapters 52–55, i.e. those immediately prior to the first English translation portion of the A-level selection, Antony snubs his wife Octavia (the sister of Octavian), who has sailed out East to meet him, and she returns home to Rome. Antony then sets up two thrones in Alexandria, one for himself and one for Cleopatra. He declares her Queen of Egypt, Cyprus, Libya and Coele Syria: she will rule jointly with Caesarion, whom he declares to be the true son of Julius Caesar (a very provocative claim). He proclaims his sons by Cleopatra 'Kings of Kings', and shares out parts of the East amongst them. This event, which occurred in 34 BCE, is known as the Donations of Alexandria, and added much fuel to the fire of the propaganda war between Octavian and Antony. Indeed, its significance cannot be overstated: Antony had publicly (and ostentatiously) demonstrated his loyalty to Cleopatra/Egypt over Octavian/Rome. Moreover, he had challenged Octavian's authority as the rightful heir of Julius Caesar by acknowledging Caesar's paternity of Caesarion.

Chapters 56–69 deal with events leading up to the Battle Actium, the battle itself and its immediate aftermath. The betrayal of Antony by his men, many of whom defect before/during/after the battle, is a constant theme; however, such is Antony's ability to inspire devotion that some remain loyal, at least at this stage.

Pelling notes that Actium is clearly a turning point for Antony: 'This is the third great reverse of Antony's life, following Mutina and Parthia: the points of similarity with the Parthian campaign are especially close' (p. 254). The link with the narrative arc of a Greek tragedy is strong (see below on Chapter 67).

Beginning of the English prescription

Numbers in square brackets indicate chapter numbers.

- The preparations for war are lavish [56]: the theme of excess continues.
- Antony divorces Octavia [57].
- The battle continues to be delayed, something which Plutarch sees as a major cause of its failure.
- Octavian obtains Antony's will, and reads it in the Senate. The generosity and loyalty towards Cleopatra evidenced by the will anger the senators, and charges are brought against Antony [58].
- Antony's friends try – unsuccessfully – to intervene in order to save him/the situation [59].
- Octavian wages war on Cleopatra (rather than Antony). By doing this, he hopes to avoid civil war (in name, at least): the upcoming conflict will be between Rome and a foreign power (Egypt) [60].
- Various omens prophesy Antony's defeat [60].
- Catalogue of forces on each side, reminiscent of the catalogues found in the *Iliad*, *Aeneid* and the writings of various Greek historians (including Herodotus and Thucydides). Antony's fleet is showy; Octavian's is well equipped and well governed [61].
- Antony submits to Cleopatra's wish to fight at sea, even though he knows that his army is better by land [62].
- Octavian calls Antony out, and Antony challenges him to single combat [62].
- Antony's positive qualities are detailed. Several kings go over to Octavian. Antony turns to his land forces, but Cleopatra remains firm in her desire to fight by sea. Antony acquiesces [62].
- Antony burns some ships, but leaves Cleopatra's 60 ships untouched [64].
- Battle of Actium: there is another delay, then the line-up is described.
- The battle has begun. Antony's forces are drawn out, but things are still equal. Nevertheless, Cleopatra makes preparations to sail and her ships start passing through the enemy lines. Antony follows her [65–66].
- Antony sits on the prow of the ship and holds his head in his hands. The loneliness he experiences feels very much like that of a Greek tragic hero at

the moment of *anagnorisis* (or 'recognition'): Antony's *peripeteia* ('reversal of fortune') is complete, and he knows it. Nevertheless, he offers gifts to his friends and treats them with kindness [67].

- The focus shifts back to Actium. Plutarch praises the bravery of Antony's soldiers, but they eventually go over to Octavian [68].
- Antony tries to kill himself, but is prevented from doing so by his friends [69].
- He comes back to Alexandria. He finds Cleopatra trying to escape by dragging her ships over land to the Red Sea (i.e. what is now the site of the Suez Canal); she stops [69].
- Antony builds a dwelling at Pharos and imitates the life of Timon of Athens (a famous 'misanthrope', or 'despiser of men'). Timon is described [69–70].
- There are further defections over to Octavian. Antony and Cleopatra enjoy feasts and distribute gifts. Cleopatra collects and tries out poisons; she then does the same with dangerous animals. The effect of the asp is described [71].
- Antony and Cleopatra send an embassy to Octavian, who is now in Asia [72].
- Octavian replies to Cleopatra, rather than to Antony, stating that she must either kill Antony or cast him out. Agrippa informs Octavian that he is needed back in Rome [73].
- The war is suspended for the winter months. When spring arrives, Octavian marches his forces through Syria, and his generals march through Libya. This 'pincer movement' is aimed to give Antony and Cleopatra no chance of escape. Cleopatra's tomb near the temple of the goddess Isis is described, as is a small battle [74].
- Antony challenges Octavian to single combat; this is refused. Antony then decides to attack by land and sea. A big feast is held, and Bacchic revelry is seen as an omen of what is to come [75].

Beginning of the Greek prescription:

- Octavian's forces have arrived; there is a further battle. Antony watches as his crews desert him. His cavalry follow suit. Fearing the strength of his reaction, Cleopatra flees to the tomb she has built for herself. She manages to get word to Antony that she has died. Antony asks his slave Eros to kill him, but Eros commits suicide instead. Antony stabs himself, but the wound is not (yet) fatal. Cleopatra sends her secretary Diomedes with instructions to bring Antony to her tomb [76].
- Antony is carried to Cleopatra's tomb. She refuses to let him in through the doors, so he is winched up through a window; the scene is one of great pathos. Once he has arrived, Cleopatra mourns excessively over him. Antony

advises her to look to her own safety, and out of all of Octavian's companions to trust (only) Proculeius. Antony dies [77].

- The focus shifts to Octavian. One of Antony's bodyguards had taken a sign (the bloodied sword) to Octavian to say that Antony had died. Octavian weeps, then reads aloud the letters they exchanged. He sends Proculeius to Cleopatra, as he wants to capture her alive (in order to lead her in a triumph) and is worried about the treasures in her funeral pyre. Proculeius tries to manipulate Cleopatra into trusting Octavian, but she refuses to let him in: they converse through a door [78].
- Proculeius takes the dimensions of Cleopatra's tomb back to Octavian; he then returns with an associate (Gallus) and manages to get in whilst Gallus is keeping Cleopatra busy with conversation. Cleopatra tries to kill herself; Proculeius prevents her from doing so and lies about Octavian's intentions. She is put under strict guard [79].
- Octavian drives into Alexandria, conversing with Areius the philosopher. He makes a magnanimous speech in which he acquits the people as a whole of all blame, and pardons many individuals [80].
- The fates of the children of Antony and Cleopatra are described: Antony's son Antyllus is betrayed, and we learn that Caesarion is to be put to death later, i.e. after Cleopatra's suicide. However, the rest of Cleopatra's children are spared and treated well [81–82].
- Octavian permits Cleopatra to bury Antony's body. She mourns intensely and falls ill. She welcomes this and stops eating, hoping that she will die. She tells her physician, Olympus, that she intends to commit suicide. Octavian threatens her children, so she gives in and eats [82].
- Octavian comes to speak with Cleopatra. She manipulates him into believing that she wishes to live [83].
- As associate of Octavian with a soft spot for Cleopatra, Cornelius Dolabella, lets her know that Octavian is planning to march through Syria and send both her and her children away. Cleopatra asks Octavian to allow her to pour libations over Antony; the request is granted, and she addresses her dead lover's ashes [84].
- Cleopatra orders a bath to be prepared. She then prepares a sumptuous meal. A man arrives with a basket of figs and is admitted by the guards. Cleopatra takes out a tablet addressed to Caesar, and orders it to be sent to him; she also sends out everyone except her two trusted servants. The focus then shifts to Octavian, who sends messengers to Cleopatra with great urgency. They find her dead, and her two servants near death.
- The focus now shifts back to the basket of figs: it had contained the asp with which Cleopatra committed suicide. Plutarch details an alternative version of the tale in which the asp had been contained in a water jar. Octavian admires Cleopatra's spirit and allows her to be buried with Antony and in a royal manner [86].

Final chapter of the English prescription (and of the *Life*)

- A list of Antony's descendants, ending with the last Julio-Claudian emperor, Nero [87].

Key characters and themes

Here follows an overview of Plutarch's presentations of Antony, Cleopatra and Octavian, including themes and motifs.

Antony

Plutarch's narrative is full of admiration and sympathy for Antony, but does not shy away from detailing his problematic character traits and the consequences of his mistakes.

Antony is a very able soldier and general, and he inspires great loyalty in his men. However, a repeated pattern of delay in military conflicts leads to a series of reverses (Mutina, Parthia, and of course Actium), the consequences of which are increasingly serious: the question of whether or not he really is a good leader deserves some attention (see below).

Antony's philhellenism and willingness to adopt himself to the customs of the East (e.g. wearing Egyptian dress) is another key characteristic. This runs in direct opposition to his loyalty to Rome and adherence to Roman moral and cultural norms (see above p. 176), and in the end he is forced to make a choice. He chooses Egypt, and whilst the movement away from Rome is a gradual one, there are several clear turning points, not least the divorce of his Roman wife Octavia, the Donations of Alexandria (including the favour shown to Cleopatra/acknowledgement of Julius Caesar's paternity of Caesarion), and the revelation of the pro-Egyptian contents of his will. He turns back to Rome in his final moments.

Excess in all things is a trait which Plutarch's Antony shares with his Cleopatra; this often spills over into depravity, as we see in the feasting and drinking which takes place in Alexandria and elsewhere (and often at seemingly wholly inappropriate times, e.g. after the Battle of Actium). Excess links with the hubris (overwhelming pride/arrogance) he shows in believing that he could shift the whole balance of power in the Roman world. Antony's self-identification with deities is another aspect of this hubris; indeed, his identification with the god of wine (Dionysus) is very suggestive of hedonistic excess (see Mossman, *Tragedy and Epic*, p. 97).

Excess and hubris are traits which contribute to Antony's status as a (pseudo-) tragic hero. Loneliness is another: although popular amongst his men, Antony refuses the entreaties of his friends when they intervene to help him, and the image of a once successful military commander sat in isolation on the prow of the ship after abandoning his fleet at Actium is perhaps the culmination of this theme.

Antony is very easily swayed by Cleopatra. She dominates him and he submits, seemingly willingly. There are several clear examples in and around the Actium story: his acquiescence to her desire to fight by sea despite his own concerns (and stronger abilities by land) is one, as is his decision to flee from the battlefield as soon as she does so. His willingness to give in to Cleopatra's wishes on matters of military strategy despite his own concerns combines with his lack of self-control and his propensity to delay to complicate the picture of his leadership.

There are many ways of reading Plutarch's Antony, and much of the above outlines how a Roman audience might have received this portrayal. However, later interpretations have not always deviated significantly from it. Indeed, several of its elements – such as the admiration of his virtues even when they sit alongside significant vices, and the tragic nature of the lovers' story – were taken up by Shakespeare, and he has (arguably) had even more influence than Plutarch on our interpretation of Cleopatra in particular.

Cleopatra

Cleopatra in the popular imagination

Scholars have identified several fundamental difficulties with the received view of Cleopatra in the West, or perhaps with the view which has made its way into general circulation.

First of all, we should not underestimate the strength of prejudice within the patriarchal (and, to a greater extent than is often suggested, insular) society that was the late Republican/early Imperial Roman world. As a female from the East, Cleopatra represented 'the other' in two respects, and Roman stereotypes (about women and about non-Romans), motivated to some degree by fear, appear in all of the Graeco-Roman presentations of her. Indeed, these sources often exclude and ignore the positive qualities which scholars such as Okasha El Daly have discovered in medieval Arabic sources, e.g. her abilities as a scholar, philosopher, scientist and administrator.

The received presentation of Cleopatra has to a large extent been shaped by Augustan propaganda. Octavian needed to consolidate his grip on power in the 30s BCE. A military victory of some sort would provide him with credibility amongst the Roman military and political elite, and a victory against Antony would neutralize the specific threat posed by the latter's popularity and influence. Waging war against Antony would therefore have seemed the obvious solution, but he was keen to avoid being associated with another civil war. His solution was to wage war against Cleopatra rather than Antony; he and his propagandists therefore exploited all of the above-mentioned Roman male prejudices to present her as a dangerous threat from the East. The consequences have been lasting.

History is written by the winners. Octavian emerged victorious at Actium, and his subsequent successes and careful management of his own self-image meant that he almost immediately became a highly mythologized figure; Roman historical memory down the centuries did nothing to challenge this. Unsurprisingly, Graeco-Roman sources of the Imperial Period generally provide us with a positive assessment of

Octavian and a negative one of Antony and Cleopatra. There are, of course, exceptions, and they come in the form of subtle hints/an underlying ironic or subversive tone, rather than outright denunciation: the so-called 'private voice' of Virgil's *Aeneid* (as detailed by scholars such as Adam Parry and David West) is such an example.

Our knowledge of Cleopatra comes from many sources, and both Shakespeare's *Antony and Cleopatra* and post-Shakespearean retellings of this story in fiction and film have done much to popularize an image of Cleopatra as a seductive and charming queen who destroyed Mark Antony and threatened Roman order and civilization. We may encounter this image before coming to the Graeco-Roman texts, be unwittingly influenced by it as we read and thus be unable to see the more nuanced portraits which exist in *some* of the sources.

Finally, we must remember that Shakespeare's work owes much to his own socio-political context. The early seventeenth century was an age which was just emerging from – and in many ways still experiencing – a large degree of political and religious turmoil. It would be surprising if this had not impacted on his presentation of the key themes of honour, betrayal, manipulation/deception, gender relations, power and love, and if these presentations did not influence our interpretation of the historical figures on which the play's central characters are based.

As we can see, Graeco-Roman prejudices and Shakespeare's *Antony and Cleopatra* (and its afterlife) have had a very lasting impact on the way in which the contemporary Western world has come to think about Antony and Cleopatra, and we will want to be aware of this as we read.

Plutarch's Cleopatra

Plutarch's Cleopatra is complex. His work seems to overcome some of the difficulties outlined above with respect to the Graeco-Roman sources, but by no means all of them. The prejudice and stereotyping discussed above loom large in certain sections of the narrative, and we have no way of really knowing how much of her characterization is based on historical fact.

Plutarch's Cleopatra is beautiful, charming and intelligent. She speaks several languages and is a smooth political operator who forms alliances with two of the most important Roman politicians of the day. She is a highly able leader: she is in command of one of the wealthiest and most desirable areas of the Eastern world. She is brave and daring: she risks everything at Actium. As often in Roman literature and thought, suicide in the face of total defeat wins her a certain dignity, and there is something admirable about her ability to plan for all eventualities. She acts as a foil to Antony: she has the intelligence, decisiveness and boldness which he sometimes lacks.

She is at times hard to read: she is clearly devoted to her children, and does all she can to secure their good treatment after (and before) the Battle of Actium, but it is unclear how much of this is concern for the dynasty rather than the individuals themselves. She also shares some character traits with Antony: she is excessive in her drinking/feasting and is hubristic, as evidenced by both her excessive military and political ambition and her highly theatrical self-presentation (which includes identifications with the goddesses Venus and Isis). There is implied cowardice in her flight at Actium and her subsequent attempt to flee with her ships overland to the Red Sea. Moreover, these actions betray self-interest and a lack of genuine concern for Mark Antony: his total devotion to her contrasts with her desperation to save herself and willingness to subordinate his needs to her own. She is also highly manipulative and deceptive: she sends a message to Antony saying that she is dead when she is not (see Chapter 76), then mourns excessively over his still-living body.

Octavian/Augustus

Octavian has a much smaller part to play in the *Antony* than would have been the case in a narrative history of this period written by a present-day historian. One way of accounting for this is the fact that Plutarch had already written a biography of him in the *Lives of the Caesars*; it is a shame that this biography has not survived, as a comparative analysis of his presentation in both works would make for an interesting exercise.

It also seems likely that Octavian appears less than expected in this piece because of Plutarch's own interests, not least his chosen genre and subject, and his desire to present the tale as the tragedy of two lovers. We should bear this in mind as we think about Octavian: it is not in Plutarch's interest to present Octavian in a positive light.

Plutarch's Octavian provides a great contrast to his Antony, and in some ways, he is more similar to his Cleopatra. We hear of no excess, but we also get none of the warmth which is characteristic of Antony's human relationships. He is organized: his fleet at Actium is orderly, and is contrasted directly with the ostentatious fleet of Antony. He is very concerned with how people perceive him – perhaps suggestive of an insecurity, not least because of Antony's popularity in the East – and his ride into Alexandria after Actium is presented as a calculated attempt to *appear* magnanimous and win people over. He is cruel and determined to get what he wants: he threatens Cleopatra's children when his ambitions are at risk. Moreover, he is self-serving, manipulative and deceptive. We see this, for example, in his reading of Antony's will in the Senate (something which breaks several moral codes), in the way in which he uses Proculeius and Gallus to get into Cleopatra's tomb, and indeed in the whole way in which he deals with her after Actium (which is designed – despite what he says to her – to keep her alive so that he can celebrate a military triumph with her as part of the procession). He is also greedy: one of his fears is that Cleopatra's suicide might deprive him not only of a perfect triumph, but also of the treasures which she has hidden in her funeral pyre.

Literary/linguistic features

Plutarch's Greek is very accessible to those with a training in the Attic dialect (the Greek spoken in and around Athens) of the fifth century BCE, and he employs the standard literary features of Greek prose of that period. A selection of such features with Plutarchan examples is provided below:

Imagery (literal and figurative), e.g. 82.1 οἷς ἐκείνη καθάπερ μηχανήμασιν ὑπηρείπετο: 'by which she was laid low as if they were siege engines'. In this image, Cleopatra = a besieged city.

Choice of vocabulary (to add drama/create a vivid scene, etc.), e.g. 77.2 πεφυρμένος γὰρ αἵματι καὶ δυσθανατῶν: 'for, drenched/stained with blood and struggling against death'. The language used (in particular the participles πεφυρμένος and δυσθανατῶν) generates a very dramatic image of Antony's final moments.

Overuse *or omission of conjunctions (polysyndeton/asyndeton)*, e.g. 77.3: δεσπότην ἐκάλει καὶ ἄνδρα καὶ αὐτοκράτορα: 'she called him master and husband and general'. The polysyndeton here adds emotion to Cleopatra's listing of titles over the (nearly dead) body of Antony. This is also a tricolon (see below).

Tricolon (a rhetorical device often used in classical literature, consisting of three parallel words, phrases or clauses), e.g. 78.2 ἀπεδάκρυσεν ἄνδρα **κηδεστὴν** γενόμενον καὶ **συνάρχοντα** καὶ **πολλῶν ἀγώνων καὶ πραγμάτων κοινωνόν**: 'he wept for a man who had been his brother-in-law and co-ruler and partner in many conflicts and deeds': the use of a tricolon with polysyndeton perhaps emphasizes the close relationship which had existed between Octavian and Antony. The third branch of the tricolon is longer than the other two; this gives it added weight.

Contrast/antithesis, e.g. 78.2: ἀνεγίνωσκεν ὡς εὐγνώμονα γράφοντος αὐτοῦ καὶ δίκαια φορτικὸς ἦν καὶ ὑπερήφανος ἀεὶ περὶ τὰς ἀποκρίσεις ἐκεῖνος: 'he read aloud how, when he [Octavian] wrote reasonable and just things, he [ἐκεῖνος: Antony] was always vulgar and arrogant with regard to his answers'. The contrast is between the sorts of things written in letters by Octavian and those written by Antony. Contrasts are often, but (as we see here) not always, represented in Greek by the use of the particles μέν/δέ, and/or by the juxtaposition (see below) of contrasting words or phrases (δίκαια φορτικός: just/vulgar).

Juxtaposition (the placing together of two [sometimes contrasting] ideas/words), e.g. 76.3 ἀλλ᾽ ὅτι <u>γυναικὸς ὁ τηλικοῦτος αὐτοκράτωρ</u> εὐψυχίᾳ πεφώραμαι λειπόμενος: 'but (I am grieved that) I, such a great general, have been discovered to be inferior in courage to a woman'; the juxtaposition of γυναικός and ὁ τηλικοῦτος αὐτοκράτωρ serves to draw out the irony for Antony.

Repetition of a word or an idea for emphasis/redundancy (NB: this includes tautology and pleonasm), e.g. 77.3 τὰ στέρνα **τυπτομένη** καὶ **σπαράττουσα** ταῖς χερσί: 'beating and tearing her breasts with her hands'. Cleopatra's action of assaulting her breasts is emphasized by the use of two participles with subtly different meanings. If there were more, we could term it a lexical (or semantic) field/cluster' (i.e. linguistic field/cluster revolving around a shared meaning [or topic]).

Likewise, note 82.1: ἐκ δὲ **λύπης** ἅμα τοσαύτης καὶ **ὀδύνης**: 'as a result of so much grief and pain at once'. The redundancy/tautology of λύπης . . . ὀδύνης indicates the extent of Cleopatra's pain.

Polyptoton (the repetition of the same word but with different inflections, i.e. different endings), e.g. 83.5 **ἐξηπατηκέναι** μὲν οἰόμενος, **ἐξηπατημένος** δὲ μᾶλλον: 'thinking that he [Octavian] had deceived [her], but rather having been deceived'; the polyptoton here emphasizes the irony, and Cleopatra's skill.

Pun (a play on words, either on the various different meanings of a single word, or on two words with different meanings which sound the same/similar), e.g. 81.2 οὐκ ἀγαθὸν πολυκαισαρίη: 'a plurality of Caesars is not a good thing'. The noun πολυκαισαρίη is a pun on πολυκοιρανίη (= the rule of many), which appears in *Iliad* 2.204–205: οὐκ ἀγαθὸν πολυκοιρανίη· εἷς κοίρανος ἔστω,/ εἷς βασιλεύς: 'a plurality of rulers is not a good thing; let there be one lord, one king'.

Hyperbaton (disruption of conventional word order in order to promote, delay or otherwise emphasize key words), e.g. 76.3 **τὴν μόνην** ἡ τύχη **καὶ λοιπὴν** ἀφῄρηκε τοῦ φιλοψυχεῖν **πρόφασιν**: 'the only remaining reason'; the hyperbaton emphasizes μόνην. See also 77.2 **οὐδὲν** ἐκείνου λέγουσιν **οἰκτρότερον** γενέσθαι οἱ παραγενόμενοι **θέαμα**: [literally] 'those who were beside him say that no sight was more pitiable than that (one)'. The hyperbaton draws attention to the misery of Antony's state, thereby generating pathos.

The flexibility of word order in prose allows Plutarch to promote verbs to the start of a clause, and delay their subjects, if he so wishes; he does this regularly.

Litotes (an understatement in which something is stressed by the negation of its opposite), e.g. 84.1 οὗτος εἶχε πρὸς τὴν Κλεοπάτραν οὐκ ἀηδῶς: (literally) 'he was not unpleasant towards Cleopatra', i.e. 'he felt warm towards Cleopatra'.

Analysis of purpose, structure and form

Students of classical literature sometimes find it hard to write meaningfully about prose, particularly Greek prose. It is important to be attentive to genre and form, and it is true that it is not always possible to say the same sorts of things about, e.g. a (prose) biography and love poetry. However, there is much to be enjoyed and explored.

Analysis of structure (in particular narrative structure, or narratology) and of form the type of writing, which, in this case, means a narrative biography – see above pp. 174–5 are useful ways of looking at prose texts, in particular when attention is paid to the purpose of the writing (see pp. 174–5). Readers will want in particular to think about the following questions/ideas:

- Plutarch's presentation of characters: does he tell us what he thinks of Antony/Cleopatra (i.e. provide interpretation), or leave us to make our own judgements? How are anecdotes used, and how (if at all) does Plutarch balance the reporting of an anecdote with his interpretation of it?
- The structure/sequencing of events: is the narrative chronological or non-linear? Does it delay any crucial pieces of information in order to reveal them

at a later point? Are certain events/actions missed out, and if so, why? How and why are digressions used? The story contains several climaxes, e.g. the Battle of Actium, and the suicides: where is the point of greatest tension/suspense, or is there more than one?

- How events are presented:
  - When and why does Plutarch use direct rather than indirect speech? (NB: with the direct speech, it is worth asking ourselves how he knows what was said, and if he really does . . .).
  - Why does he spend a disproportionate amount of time on certain events/aspects of Antony's life and so little on others? Consider, e.g., the use of one chapter (22) for the Battle of Philippi vs chapter after chapter on Actium.
  - How are the deaths described? Think about the language used and the amount of space devoted to each one.
- The importance of place/setting: how does setting contribute to characterization? How, when and why does Plutarch move between different locations?
- The perspective through which each section of the narrative is 'focalized' (e.g. Antony, Cleopatra or someone else).
- Tone: is the work's tone consistent or does it shift? How is a certain tone achieved? How and when is pathos generated?
- Closure: is closure achieved at the end of the life, or at the end of individual sections? If so, how is it achieved?

  [*Closure* is a literary term used to describe the process whereby a narrative or other literary work achieves the sense of an ending.]

As with the literary and linguistic techniques examined above, it is better (at least initially) to look at the technique/feature/significant moment that you have identified, and its effect, on its own merits. At a later stage, you may decide that there is indeed a single overarching motive behind, or effect achieved by, the use of, e.g., digressions, but you can only make this judgement once you have enough evidence. Sometimes the same technique is used again and again, but the effect achieved is different each time.

Further reading

For an excellent, detailed and very accessible introduction and commentary, consult the following:

Pelling, C. B. R. (2005), *Plutarch: Life of Antony*, Cambridge: Cambridge University Press.

For a readable and accurate translation, see:

Perrin, B., trans. (1914), *Plutarch: Lives, Volume 9: Demetrius and Antony; Pyrrhus and Caius Marius*, Cambridge, MA: Harvard University Press, Loeb Classical Library.

On genre in Plutarch:

Duff, T. E. (2004), 'Plato, Tragedy, the Ideal Reader and Plutarch's "Demetrios and Antony"', *Hermes*, 132 (3): 271–91.

Swain, S. (1992), 'Novel and Pantomime in Plutarch's "Antony"', *Hermes*, 120 (1): 76–82.

On the characterization of Antony:

Jacobs, S. G. (2017), *Plutarch's Pragmatic Biographies: Lessons for Statesmen and Generals in* The Parallel Lives, Columbia Studies in the Classical Tradition, vol. 43, Leiden: Brill.

Mossman, J. M. (1995), 'Tragedy and Epic in Plutarch's Alexander', in B. Scardigli, *Essays on Plutarch's Lives*, pp. 209–28, Oxford: Clarendon Press. (Although this essay is about Alexander, Antony is mentioned at various points.)

On sources for the *Life of Antony*, see Pelling, pp. 26–31 and:

Wet, B. X. de (1990), 'Contemporary Sources in Plutarch's Life of Antony', *Hermes*, 118 (1): 80–90.

On the blend of Greek, Roman and Egyptian identities and influences in the *Life of Antony*:

Swain, S. (1990), 'Cultural Interchange in Plutarch's "Antony"', *Quaderni Urbinati Di Cultura Classica: Nesw Series*, 34 (1): 151–7.

Okasha El Daly's research into Cleopatra is summarized here:

(2005), 'The Virtuous Scholar: Cleopatra Seduced through Intellectual Prowess not Physical Beauty, Says New Book', *UCL News*, University College London, 23 February. Available online: https://www.ucl.ac.uk/news/2005/feb/virtuous-scholar-cleopatra-seduced-through-intellectual-prowess-not-physical-beauty-says (accessed 4 May 2022).

For a general overview of Plutarch, see the following:

Roskam, G. (2021), *Plutarch*, Greece & Rome, New Surveys in the Classics, no. 47, Cambridge: Cambridge University Press.

Text

76

Ἅμα δὲ ἡμέρᾳ τὸν πεζὸν αὐτὸς ἐπὶ τῶν πρὸ τῆς πόλεως λόφων ἱδρύσας ἐθεᾶτο τὰς ναῦς ἀνηγμένας καὶ ταῖς τῶν πολεμίων προσφερομένας· καὶ περιμένων ἔργον τι παρ᾽ ἐκείνων ἰδεῖν ἡσύχαζεν. οἱ δὲ ὡς ἐγγὺς ἐγένοντο, ταῖς κώπαις ἠσπάσαντο τοὺς Καίσαρος, ἐκείνων τε ἀντασπασαμένων μετεβάλοντο, καὶ πάσαις ἅμα ταῖς ναυσὶν ὁ στόλος εἷς γενόμενος ἐπέπλει πρὸς τὴν πόλιν ἀντίπρῳρος. [2] τοῦτο Ἀντώνιος ἰδὼν ἀπελείφθη μὲν εὐθὺς ὑπὸ τῶν ἱππέων μεταβαλομένων, ἡττηθεὶς δὲ τοῖς πεζοῖς ἀνεχώρησεν εἰς τὴν πόλιν, ὑπὸ Κλεοπάτρας προδεδόσθαι βοῶν οἷς δι᾽ ἐκείνην ἐπολέμησεν. ἡ δὲ τὴν ὀργὴν αὐτοῦ φοβηθεῖσα καὶ τὴν ἀπόνοιαν εἰς τὸν τάφον κατέφυγε καὶ τοὺς καταρράκτας ἀφῆκε κλείθροις καὶ μοχλοῖς καρτεροὺς ὄντας· πρὸς δὲ Ἀντώνιον ἔπεμψε τοὺς ἀπαγγελοῦντας ὅτι τέθνηκε. [3] πιστεύσας δὲ ἐκεῖνος καὶ εἰπὼν πρὸς αὐτόν, "Τί ἔτι μέλλεις, Ἀντώνιε; τὴν μόνην ἡ τύχη καὶ λοιπὴν ἀφῄρηκε τοῦ φιλοψυχεῖν πρόφασιν," εἰσῆλθεν εἰς τὸ δωμάτιον, καὶ τὸν θώρακα παραλυων καὶ διαστέλλων, "Ὦ Κλεοπάτρα," εἶπεν, "οὐκ ἄχθομαί σου στερούμενος· αὐτίκα γὰρ εἰς ταὐτὸν ἀφίξομαι· ἀλλ᾽ ὅτι γυναικὸς ὁ τηλικοῦτος αὐτοκράτωρ εὐψυχίᾳ πεφώραμαι λειπόμενος."

[4] Ἦν δέ τις οἰκέτης αὐτοῦ πιστὸς Ἔρως ὄνομα. τοῦτον ἐκ πολλοῦ παρακεκληκώς, εἰ δεήσειεν, ἀνελεῖν αὐτόν, ἀπῄτει τὴν ὑπόσχεσιν. ὁ δὲ σπασάμενος τὸ ξίφος ἀνέσχε μὲν ὡς παίσων ἐκεῖνον, ἀποστρέψας δὲ τὸ πρόσωπον ἑαυτὸν ἀπέκτεινε. πεσόντος δὲ αὐτοῦ πρὸς τοὺς πόδας ὁ Ἀντώνιος "Εὖγε," εἶπεν, "ὦ Ἔρως, ὅτι μὴ δυνηθεὶς αὐτὸς ἐμὲ ποιεῖν ὃ δεῖ διδάσκεις·" καὶ παίσας διὰ τῆς κοιλίας ἑαυτὸν ἀφῆκεν εἰς τὸ κλινίδιον. [5] ἦν δὲ οὐκ εὐθυθάνατος ἡ πληγή. διὸ καὶ τῆς φορᾶς τοῦ αἵματος, ἐπεὶ κατεκλίθη, παυσαμένης, ἀναλαβὼν ἐδεῖτο τῶν παρόντων ἐπισφάττειν αὐτόν. οἱ δὲ ἔφευγον ἐκ τοῦ δωματίου βοῶντος καὶ σφαδάζοντος, ἄχρι οὗ παρὰ Κλεοπάτρας ἧκε Διομήδης ὁ γραμματεύς, κομίζειν αὐτὸν ὡς ἐκείνην εἰς τὸν τάφον κελευσθείς.

77

Γνοὺς οὖν ὅτι ζῇ, προθύμως ἐκέλευσεν ἄρασθαι τοῖς ὑπηρέταις τὸ σῶμα, καὶ διὰ χειρῶν προσεκομίσθη ταῖς θύραις τοῦ οἰκήματος. ἡ δὲ Κλεοπάτρα τὰς μὲν θύρας οὐκ ἀνέῳξεν, ἐκ δὲ θυρίδων τινῶν φανεῖσα σειρὰς καὶ καλῴδια καθίει. καὶ τούτοις ἐναψάντων τὸν Ἀντώνιον ἀνεῖλκεν αὐτὴ καὶ δύο γυναῖκες, ἃς μόνας ἐδέξατο μεθ᾽ αὑτῆς εἰς τὸν τάφον. [2] οὐδὲν ἐκείνου λέγουσιν οἰκτρότερον γενέσθαι οἱ παραγενόμενοι θέαμα. πεφυρμένος γὰρ αἵματι καὶ δυσθανατῶν εἵλκετο, τὰς χεῖρας ὀρέγων εἰς ἐκείνην καὶ παραιωρούμενος. οὐ γὰρ ἦν γυναιξὶ ῥᾴδιον τὸ ἔργον, ἀλλὰ μόλις ἡ Κλεοπάτρα ταῖν χεροῖν ἐμπεφυκυῖα καὶ κατατεινομένη τῷ προσώπῳ τὸν δεσμὸν ἀνελάμβανεν, ἐπικελευομένων τῶν κάτωθεν αὐτῇ καὶ συναγωνιώντων. [3] δεξαμένη δὲ αὐτὸν οὕτως καὶ κατακλίνασα περιερρήξατο τε τοὺς πέπλους ἐπ᾽ αὐτῷ, καὶ τὰ στέρνα τυπτομένη καὶ σπαράττουσα ταῖς χερσί, καὶ τῷ προσώπῳ τοῦ αἵματος ἀναματτομένη, δεσπότην ἐκάλει καὶ ἄνδρα καὶ αὐτοκράτορα· καὶ μικροῦ δεῖν ἐπιλέληστο τῶν αὑτῆς κακῶν οἴκτῳ τῶν ἐκείνου. καταπαύσας δὲ τὸν θρῆνον αὐτῆς Ἀντώνιος ᾔτησε πιεῖν οἶνον, εἴτε διψῶν, εἴτε συντομώτερον ἐλπίζων ἀπολυθήσεσθαι. [4] πιὼν δὲ παρῄνεσεν αὐτῇ τὰ μὲν ἑαυτῆς, ἂν ᾖ μὴ μετ᾽ αἰσχύνης, σωτήρια τίθεσθαι, μάλιστα τῶν Καίσαρος ἑταίρων Προκληΐῳ πιστεύουσαν, αὐτὸν δὲ μὴ θρηνεῖν ἐπὶ ταῖς ὑστάταις μεταβολαῖς, ἀλλὰ μακαρίζειν ὧν ἔτυχε καλῶν, ἐπιφανέστατος ἀνθρώπων γενόμενος καὶ πλεῖστον ἰσχύσας καὶ νῦν οὐκ ἀγεννῶς Ῥωμαῖος ὑπὸ Ῥωμαίου κρατηθείς.

78

Ὅσον δὲ ἀπολιπόντος αὐτοῦ Προκλήϊος ἧκε παρὰ Καίσαρος. ἐπεὶ γὰρ ἑαυτὸν πατάξας ὁ Ἀντώνιος ᾤχετο πρὸς Κλεοπάτραν κομιζόμενος, Δερκεταῖός τις τῶν δορυφόρων λαβὼν τὸ ἐγχειρίδιον αὐτοῦ καὶ ἀποκρύψας ὑπεξῆλθε, καὶ δραμὼν πρὸς Καίσαρα πρῶτος ἤγγειλε τὴν Ἀντωνίου τελευτήν, καὶ τὸ ξίφος ἔδειξεν ᾑμαγμένον. [2] ὁ δὲ ὡς ἤκουσεν, ἐνδοτέρω τῆς σκηνῆς ἀποστὰς ἀπεδάκρυσεν ἄνδρα κηδεστὴν γενόμενον καὶ συνάρχοντα καὶ πολλῶν ἀγώνων καὶ πραγμάτων κοινωνόν. εἶτα τὰς ἐπιστολὰς λαβὼν καὶ τοὺς φίλους καλέσας ἀνεγίνωσκεν ὡς εὐγνώμονα γράφοντος αὐτοῦ καὶ δίκαια φορτικὸς ἦν καὶ ὑπερήφανος ἀεὶ περὶ τὰς ἀποκρίσεις ἐκεῖνος. [3] ἐκ δὲ τούτου τὸν Προκλήϊον ἔπεμψε κελεύσας, ἢν δύνηται, μάλιστα τῆς Κλεοπάτρας ζώσης κρατῆσαι· καὶ γὰρ ἐφοβεῖτο περὶ τῶν χρημάτων, καὶ μέγα πρὸς δόξαν ἡγεῖτο τοῦ θριάμβου καταγαγεῖν ἐκείνην. εἰς μὲν οὖν χεῖρας τῷ Προκληΐῳ συνελθεῖν οὐκ ἠθέλησεν· [4] ἐγίνοντο δὲ λόγοι τῷ οἰκήματι προσελθόντος ἔξωθεν αὐτοῦ κατὰ θύρας ἐπιπέδους, ἀποκεκλειμένας μὲν ὀχυρῶς, φωνῇ δὲ διέξοδον ἐχούσας. καὶ διελέχθησαν ἡ μὲν αἰτουμένη τοῖς παισὶ τὴν βασιλείαν, ὁ δὲ θαρρεῖν καὶ πάντα πιστεύειν Καίσαρι κελεύων.

79

Ὡς δὲ κατιδὼν τὸν τόπον ἀπήγγειλε Καίσαρι, Γάλλος μὲν ἐπέμφθη πάλιν ἐντευξόμενος αὐτῇ· καὶ πρὸς τὰς θύρας ἐλθὼν ἐπίτηδες ἐμήκυνε τὸν λόγον. ἐν τούτῳ δὲ Προκλήϊος κλίμακος προστεθείσης διὰ τῆς θυρίδος εἰσῆλθεν ᾗ τὸν Ἀντώνιον αἱ γυναῖκες ἐδέξαντο. καὶ πρὸς τὰς θύρας αὐτὰς εὐθύς, αἷς ἡ Κλεοπάτρα παρειστήκει προσέχουσα τῷ Γάλλῳ, κατέβαινεν ὑπηρέτας ἔχων δύο μεθ᾽ αὑτοῦ. [2] τῶν δὲ συγκαθειργμένων τῇ Κλεοπάτρᾳ γυναικῶν τῆς ἑτέρας ἀνακραγούσης, "Τάλαινα Κλεοπάτρα, ζωγρεῖ," μεταστραφεῖσα καὶ θεασαμένη τὸν Προκλήϊον ὥρμησε μὲν αὑτὴν πατάξαι· παρεζωσμένη γὰρ ἐτύγχανέ τι τῶν λῃστρικῶν ξιφιδίων· προσδραμὼν δὲ ταχὺ καὶ περισχὼν αὐτὴν ταῖς χερσὶν ἀμφοτέραις ὁ Προκλήϊος, "Ἀδικεῖς," εἶπεν, "ὦ Κλεοπάτρα, καὶ σεαυτὴν καὶ Καίσαρα, μεγάλην ἀφαιρουμένη χρηστότητος ἐπίδειξιν αὐτοῦ, καὶ διαβάλλουσα τὸν πρᾳότατον ἡγεμόνων ὡς ἄπιστον καὶ ἀδιάλλακτον." [3] ἅμα δὲ καὶ τὸ ξίφος αὐτῆς παρείλετο, καὶ τὴν ἐσθῆτα, μὴ κρύπτοι τι φάρμακον, ἐξέσεισεν. ἐπέμφθη δὲ καὶ παρὰ Καίσαρος τῶν ἀπελευθέρων Ἐπαφρόδιτος, ᾧ προσετέτακτο ζῶσαν αὐτὴν φυλάττειν ἰσχυρῶς ἐπιμελόμενον, τἆλλα δὲ πρὸς τὸ ῥᾷστον ἐνδιδόναι καὶ ἥδιστον.

80

Αὐτὸς δὲ Καῖσαρ εἰσήλαυνεν εἰς τὴν πόλιν, Ἀρείῳ τῷ φιλοσόφῳ προσδιαλεγόμενος καὶ τὴν δεξιὰν ἐνδεδωκώς, ἵνα εὐθὺς ἐν τοῖς πολίταις περίβλεπτος εἴη καὶ θαυμάζοιτο τιμώμενος ὑπ᾽ αὐτοῦ διαπρεπῶς. εἰς δὲ τὸ γυμνάσιον εἰσελθὼν καὶ ἀναβὰς ἐπὶ βῆμά τι πεποιημένον, ἐκπεπληγμένων ὑπὸ δέους τῶν ἀνθρώπων καὶ προσπιπτόντων, ἀναστῆναι κελεύσας ἔφη πάσης αἰτίας τὸν δῆμον ἀφιέναι, πρῶτον μὲν διὰ τὸν κτίστην Ἀλέξανδρον· δεύτερον δὲ τῆς πόλεως θαυμάζων τὸ κάλλος καὶ τὸ μέγεθος· τρίτον δὲ Ἀρείῳ τῷ ἑταίρῳ χαριζόμενος. [2] ταύτης δὴ τῆς τιμῆς ἔτυχε παρὰ Καίσαρος Ἄρειος, καὶ τῶν ἄλλων ἐξῃτήσατο συχνούς· ὧν ἦν καὶ Φιλόστρατος, ἀνὴρ εἰπεῖν μὲν ἐξ ἐπιδρομῆς τῶν πώποτε σοφιστῶν ἱκανώτατος, εἰσποιῶν δὲ μὴ προσηκόντως ἑαυτὸν τῇ Ἀκαδημείᾳ. διὸ καὶ Καῖσαρ αὐτοῦ βδελυττόμενος τὸν τρόπον οὐ προσίετο τὰς δεήσεις. [3] ὁ δὲ πώγωνα πολιὸν καθεὶς καὶ φαιὸν ἱμάτιον περιβαλόμενος ἐξόπισθεν Ἀρείῳ παρηκολούθει, τοῦτον ἀεὶ τὸν στίχον ἀναφθεγγόμενος·

> σοφοὶ σοφοὺς σῴζουσιν, ἂν ὦσιν σοφοί.

πυθόμενος δὲ Καῖσαρ, καὶ τοῦ φθόνου μᾶλλον Ἄρειον ἢ τοῦ δέους Φιλόστρατον ἀπαλλάξαι βουλόμενος, διῆκε.

81

Τῶν δὲ Ἀντωνίου παίδων ὁ μὲν ἐκ Φουλβίας Ἄντυλλος ὑπὸ Θεοδώρου τοῦ παιδαγωγοῦ παραδοθεὶς ἀπέθανε· καὶ τὴν κεφαλὴν αὐτοῦ τῶν στρατιωτῶν ἀποτεμόντων, ὁ παιδαγωγὸς ἀφελὼν ὃν ἐφόρει περὶ τῷ τραχήλῳ πολυτιμότατον λίθον εἰς τὴν ζώνην κατέρραψεν· ἀρνησάμενος δὲ καὶ φωραθεὶς ἀνεσταυρώθη. [2] τὰ δὲ Κλεοπάτρας παιδία φρουρούμενα μετὰ τῶν τρεφόντων ἐλευθέριον εἶχε δίαιταν. Καισαρίωνα δὲ τὸν ἐκ Καίσαρος γεγονέναι λεγόμενον ἡ μὲν μήτηρ ἐξέπεμψε μετὰ χρημάτων πολλῶν εἰς τὴν Ἰνδικὴν δι᾽ Αἰθιοπίας, ἕτερος δὲ παιδαγωγὸς ὅμοιος Θεοδώρῳ Ῥόδων ἀνέπεισεν ἐπανελθεῖν, ὡς Καίσαρος αὐτὸν ἐπὶ βασιλείαν καλοῦντος. βουλευομένου δὲ Καίσαρος Ἄρειον εἰπεῖν λέγουσιν· οὐκ ἀγαθὸν πολυκαισαρίη.

82

Τοῦτον μὲν οὖν ὕστερον ἀπέκτεινε μετὰ τὴν Κλεοπάτρας τελευτήν. Ἀντώνιον δὲ πολλῶν αἰτουμένων θάψαι καὶ βασιλέων καὶ στρατηγῶν, οὐκ ἀφείλετο Κλεοπάτρας τὸ σῶμα Καῖσαρ, ἀλλὰ ἐθάπτετο ταῖς ἐκείνης χερσὶ πολυτελῶς καὶ βασιλικῶς, πᾶσιν ὡς ἐβούλετο χρῆσθαι λαβούσης. ἐκ δὲ λύπης ἅμα τοσαύτης καὶ ὀδύνης (ἀνεφλέγμηνε γὰρ αὐτῆς τὰ στέρνα τυπτομένης καὶ ἥλκωτο) πυρετῶν ἐπιλαβόντων ἠγάπησε τὴν πρόφασιν, ὡς ἀφεξομένη τροφῆς διὰ τοῦτο καὶ παραλύσουσα τοῦ ζῆν ἀκωλύτως ἑαυτήν. [2] ἦν δὲ ἰατρὸς αὐτῇ συνήθης Ὄλυμπος, ᾧ φράσασα τἀληθὲς ἐχρῆτο συμβούλῳ καὶ συνεργῷ τῆς καθαιρέσεως, ὡς αὐτὸς ὁ Ὄλυμπος εἴρηκεν ἱστορίαν τινὰ τῶν πραγμάτων τούτων ἐκδεδωκώς. ὑπονοήσας δὲ Καῖσαρ ἀπειλὰς μέν τινας αὐτῇ καὶ φόβους περὶ τῶν τέκνων προσέβαλλεν, οἷς ἐκείνη καθάπερ μηχανήμασιν ὑπηρείπετο καὶ παρεδίδου τὸ σῶμα θεραπεύειν καὶ τρέφειν τοῖς χρῄζουσιν.

83

Ἧκε δὲ καὶ αὐτὸς ἡμέρας ὀλίγας διαλιπὼν ἐντευξόμενος αὐτῇ καὶ παρηγορήσων. ἡ δὲ ἔτυχε μὲν ἐν στιβάδι κατακειμένη ταπεινῶς, εἰσιόντι δ᾽ αὐτῷ μονοχίτων ἀναπηδήσασα προσπίπτει, δεινῶς μὲν ἐξηγριωμένη κεφαλὴν καὶ πρόσωπον, ὑπότρομος δὲ τῇ φωνῇ καὶ συντετηκυῖα ταῖς ὄψεσιν. ἦν δὲ πολλὰ καὶ τῆς περὶ τὸ στέρνον αἰκίας καταφανῆ· καὶ ὅλως οὐθὲν ἐδόκει τὸ σῶμα τῆς ψυχῆς ἔχειν βέλτιον. [2] ἡ μέντοι χάρις ἐκείνη καὶ τὸ τῆς ὥρας ἰταμὸν οὐ κατέσβεστο παντάπασιν, ἀλλὰ καίπερ οὕτως διακειμένης ἔνδοθέν ποθεν ἐξέλαμπε καὶ συνεπεφαίνετο τοῖς κινήμασι τοῦ προσώπου. κελεύσαντος δὲ τοῦ Καίσαρος αὐτὴν κατακλιθῆναι καὶ πλησίον αὐτοῦ καθίσαντος, ἥψατο μέν τινος δικαιολογίας εἰς ἀνάγκην καὶ φόβον Ἀντωνίου τὰ πεπραγμένα τρεπούσης, ἐνισταμένου δὲ πρὸς ἕκαστον αὐτῇ τοῦ Καίσαρος ἐξελεγχομένη ταχὺ πρὸς οἶκτον μεθηρμόσατο καὶ δέησιν, ὡς δή τις ἂν μάλιστα τοῦ ζῆν περιεχομένη. [3] τέλος δὲ τοῦ πλήθους τῶν χρημάτων ἀναγραφὴν ἔχουσα προσέδωκεν αὐτῷ· Σελεύκου δέ τινος τῶν ἐπιτρόπων ἐλέγχοντος ὡς ἔνια κρύπτουσαν καὶ διακλέπτουσαν, ἀναπηδήσασα καὶ τῶν τριχῶν αὐτοῦ λαβομένη πολλὰς ἐνεφόρει τῷ προσώπῳ πληγάς. [4] τοῦ δὲ Καίσαρος μειδιῶντος καὶ καταπαύοντος αὐτήν, "Ἀλλ᾽ οὐ δεινόν," εἶπεν, "ὦ Καῖσαρ, εἰ σὺ μὲν ἠξίωσας ἀφικέσθαι πρὸς ἐμὲ καὶ προσειπεῖν οὕτω πράττουσαν, οἱ δὲ δοῦλοί μου κατηγοροῦσιν εἴ τι τῶν γυναικείων ἀπεθέμην, οὐκ ἐμαυτῇ δήπουθεν, ἡ τάλαινα, κόσμον, ἀλλ᾽ ὅπως Ὀκταουίᾳ καὶ Λιβίᾳ τῇ σῇ μικρὰ δοῦσα δι᾽ ἐκείνων ἵλεώ σου τύχοιμι καὶ πραοτέρου;" [5] τούτοις ὁ Καῖσαρ ἥδετο, παντάπασιν αὐτὴν φιλοψυχεῖν οἰόμενος. εἰπὼν οὖν ὅτι καὶ ταῦτα ἐπιτρέπει καὶ τἆλλα πάσης ἐλπίδος αὐτῇ χρήσεται λαμπρότερον, ᾤχετο ἀπιών, ἐξηπατηκέναι μὲν οἰόμενος, ἐξηπατημένος δὲ μᾶλλον.

84

Ἦν δὲ Κορνήλιος Δολοβέλλας ἐπιφανὴς νεανίσκος ἐν τοῖς Καίσαρος ἑταίροις. οὗτος εἶχε πρὸς τὴν Κλεοπάτραν οὐκ ἀηδῶς· καὶ τότε χαριζόμενος αὐτῇ δεηθείσῃ κρύφα πέμψας ἐξήγγειλεν ὡς αὐτὸς μὲν ὁ Καῖσαρ ἀναζεύγνυσι πεζῇ διὰ Συρίας, ἐκείνην δὲ μετὰ τῶν τέκνων ἀποστέλλειν εἰς τρίτην ἡμέραν ἔγνωκεν. [2] ἡ δὲ ἀκούσασα ταῦτα πρῶτον μὲν ἐδεήθη Καίσαρος ὅπως αὐτὴν ἐάσῃ χοὰς ἐπενεγκεῖν Ἀντωνίῳ· καὶ συγχωρήσαντος ἐπὶ τὸν τάφον κομισθεῖσα καὶ περιπεσοῦσα τῇ σορῷ μετὰ τῶν συνήθων γυναικῶν, "Ὦ φίλε Ἀντώνιε," εἶπεν, "ἔθαπτον μέν σε πρώην ἔτι χερσὶν ἐλευθέραις, σπένδω δὲ νῦν αἰχμάλωτος οὖσα, καὶ φρουρουμένη μήτε κοπετοῖς μήτε θρήνοις αἰκίσασθαι τὸ δοῦλον τοῦτο σῶμα καὶ τηρούμενον ἐπὶ τοὺς κατὰ σοῦ θριάμβους. [3] ἄλλας δὲ μὴ προσδέχου τιμὰς ἢ χοάς· ἀλλ᾽ αὗταί σοι τελευταῖαι Κλεοπάτρας ἀγομένης. ζῶντας μὲν γὰρ ἡμᾶς οὐθὲν ἀλλήλων διέστησε, κινδυνεύομεν δὲ τῷ θανάτῳ διαμείψασθαι τοὺς τόπους· σὺ μὲν ὁ Ῥωμαῖος ἐνταῦθα κείμενος, ἐγὼ δ᾽ ἡ δύστηνος ἐν Ἰταλίᾳ, τοσοῦτο τῆς σῆς μεταλαβοῦσα χώρας μόνον. [4] ἀλλ᾽ εἰ δή τις τῶν ἐκεῖ θεῶν ἀλκὴ καὶ δύναμις (οἱ γὰρ ἐνταῦθα προὔδωκαν ἡμᾶς), μὴ πρόῃ ζῶσαν τὴν σεαυτοῦ γυναῖκα, μηδ᾽ ἐν ἐμοὶ περιΐδῃς θριαμβευόμενον σεαυτόν, ἀλλ᾽ ἐνταῦθά με κρύψον μετὰ σεαυτοῦ καὶ σύνθαψον, ὡς ἐμοὶ μυρίων κακῶν ὄντων οὐδὲν οὕτω μέγα καὶ δεινόν ἐστιν ὡς ὁ βραχὺς οὗτος χρόνος ὃν σοῦ χωρὶς ἔζηκα."

85

Τοιαῦτα ὀλοφυραμένη καὶ στέψασα καὶ κατασπασαμένη τὴν σορὸν ἐκέλευσεν αὐτῇ λουτρὸν γενέσθαι. λουσαμένη δὲ καὶ κατακλιθεῖσα λαμπρὸν ἄριστον ἠρίστα. καί τις ἧκεν ἀπ᾽ ἀγροῦ κίστην τινὰ κομίζων· τῶν δὲ φυλάκων ὅ τι φέροι πυνθανομένων ἀνοίξας καὶ ἀφελὼν τὰ θρῖα σύκων ἐπίπλεων τὸ ἀγγεῖον ἔδειξε. [2] θαυμασάντων δὲ τὸ κάλλος καὶ τὸ μέγεθος μειδιάσας παρεκάλει λαβεῖν· οἱ δὲ πιστεύσαντες ἐκέλευον εἰσενεγκεῖν. μετὰ δὲ τὸ ἄριστον ἡ Κλεοπάτρα δέλτον ἔχουσα γεγραμμένην καὶ κατασεσημασμένην ἀπέστειλε πρὸς Καίσαρα, καὶ τοὺς ἄλλους ἐκποδὼν ποιησαμένη πλὴν τῶν δυεῖν ἐκείνων γυναικῶν τὰς θύρας ἔκλεισε.

[3] Καῖσαρ δὲ λύσας τὴν δέλτον, ὡς ἐνέτυχε λιταῖς καὶ ὀλοφυρμοῖς δεομένης αὐτὴν σὺν Ἀντωνίῳ θάψαι, ταχὺ συνῆκε τὸ πεπραγμένον. καὶ πρῶτον μὲν αὐτὸς ὥρμησε βοηθεῖν, ἔπειτα τοὺς σκεψομένους κατὰ τάχος ἔπεμψεν. ἐγεγόνει δ᾽ ὀξὺ τὸ πάθος. δρόμῳ γὰρ ἐλθόντες καὶ τοὺς μὲν φυλάττοντας οὐδὲν ᾐσθημένους καταλαβόντες, τὰς δὲ θύρας ἀνοίξαντες, εὗρον αὐτὴν τεθνηκυῖαν ἐν χρυσῇ κατακειμένην κλίνῃ, κεκοσμημένην βασιλικῶς. [4] τῶν δὲ γυναικῶν ἡ μὲν Εἰρὰς λεγομένη πρὸς τοῖς ποσὶν ἀπέθνησκεν, ἡ δὲ Χάρμιον ἤδη σφαλλομένη καὶ καρηβαροῦσα κατεκόσμει τὸ διάδημα τὸ περὶ τὴν κεφαλὴν αὐτῆς. εἰπόντος δέ τινος ὀργῇ· "Καλὰ ταῦτα, Χάρμιον." "Κάλλιστα μὲν οὖν," ἔφη, "καὶ πρέποντα τῇ τοσούτων ἀπογόνῳ βασιλέων." πλέον δὲ οὐδὲν εἶπεν, ἀλλ᾽ αὐτοῦ παρὰ τὴν κλίνην ἔπεσε.

86

Λέγεται δὲ τὴν ἀσπίδα κομισθῆναι σὺν τοῖς σύκοις ἐκείνοις καὶ τοῖς θρίοις ἄνωθεν ἐπικαλυφθεῖσαν, οὕτω γὰρ τὴν Κλεοπάτραν κελεῦσαι, μηδὲ αὐτῆς ἐπισταμένης τῷ σώματι προσπεσεῖν τὸ θηρίον· ὡς δὲ ἀφαιροῦσα τῶν σύκων εἶδεν, εἰπεῖν· "Ἐνταῦθα ἦν ἄρα τοῦτο·" καὶ τὸν βραχίονα παρασχεῖν τῷ δήγματι γυμνώσασαν. [2] οἱ δὲ τηρεῖσθαι μὲν ἐν ὑδρίᾳ τὴν ἀσπίδα καθειργμένην φάσκουσιν, ἠλακάτῃ δέ τινι χρυσῇ τῆς Κλεοπάτρας ἐκκαλουμένης αὐτὴν καὶ διαγριαινούσης ὁρμήσασαν ἐμφῦναι τῷ βραχίονι. τὸ δὲ ἀληθὲς οὐδεὶς οἶδεν· ἐπεὶ καὶ φάρμακον αὐτὴν ἐλέχθη φορεῖν ἐν κνηστίδι κοίλῃ, τὴν δὲ κνηστίδα κρύπτειν τῇ κόμῃ· πλὴν οὔτε κηλὶς ἐξήνθησε τοῦ σώματος οὔτε ἄλλο φαρμάκου σημεῖον. [3] οὐ μὴν οὐδὲ τὸ θηρίον ἐντὸς ὤφθη, συρμοὺς δέ τινας αὐτοῦ παρὰ θάλασσαν, ᾗ τὸ δωμάτιον ἀφεώρα καὶ θυρίδες ἦσαν, ἰδεῖν ἔφασκον. ἔνιοι δὲ καὶ τὸν βραχίονα τῆς Κλεοπάτρας ὀφθῆναι δύο νυγμὰς ἔχοντα λεπτὰς καὶ ἀμυδράς· οἷς ἔοικε πιστεῦσαι καὶ ὁ Καῖσαρ. ἐν γὰρ τῷ θριάμβῳ τῆς Κλεοπάτρας αὐτῆς εἴδωλον ἐκομίζετο καὶ τῆς ἀσπίδος ἐμπεφυκυίας. ταῦτα μὲν οὖν οὕτω λέγεται γενέσθαι.

[4] Καῖσαρ δέ, καίπερ ἀχθεσθεὶς ἐπὶ τῇ τελευτῇ τῆς γυναικός, ἐθαύμασε τὴν εὐγένειαν αὐτῆς·

καὶ ταφῆναι τὸ σῶμα σὺν Ἀντωνίῳ λαμπρῶς καὶ βασιλικῶς ἐκέλευσεν. ἐντίμου δὲ καὶ τὰ γύναια κηδείας ἔτυχεν αὐτοῦ προστάξαντος. ἐτελεύτησε δὲ Κλεοπάτρα μὲν ἑνὸς δέοντα τεσσαράκοντα ἔτη βιώσασα, καὶ τούτων δύο καὶ εἴκοσι βασιλεύσασα, συνάρξασα δὲ Ἀντωνίῳ πλείω τῶν δεκατεσσάρων. [5] Ἀντώνιον δὲ οἱ μὲν ἕξ, οἱ δὲ τρισὶ τὰ πεντήκοντα ὑπερβαλεῖν φασιν. αἱ μὲν οὖν Ἀντωνίου καθῃρέθησαν εἰκόνες, αἱ δὲ Κλεοπάτρας κατὰ χώραν ἔμειναν, Ἀρχιβίου τινὸς τῶν φίλων αὐτῆς δισχίλια τάλαντα Καίσαρι δόντος, ἵνα μὴ τὸ αὐτὸ ταῖς Ἀντωνίου πάθωσιν.

Commentary Notes

Chapter divisions and numbering in the Text and Commentary follow the Loeb edition of Bernadotte Perrin. I have benefitted greatly from consulting his translation, though I have not always chosen to follow it.

I have frequently sought clarification on linguistic and other matters from the excellent commentary by Chris Pelling. References to specific page numbers in Pelling's commentary are given in brackets after any direct quotation.

76.1

Ἅμα δὲ ἡμέρᾳ: the date is 1 August 30 BCE. As often, **ἡμέρα** here means 'dawn/daybreak'.

ἐπὶ τῶν πρὸ τῆς πόλεως λόφων: 'on the hills in front of the city' (Alexandria). Pelling notes that such hills do not exist, but that this is 'imaginative reconstruction', i.e. 'a hill would give Antony . . . a fine view of his naval catastrophe' (p. 305).

ἐθεᾶτο τὰς ναῦς ἀνηγμένας καὶ ταῖς τῶν πολεμίων προσφερομένας: 'watched his ships which had put out to sea and were attacking those of the enemy' (supply ναυσι with **ταῖς**).

ἀνηγμένας: perfect participle middle (accusative feminine plural) from ἀνάγομαι = I put out to sea. Note that perfect participles retain the reduplication which is characteristic of this tense (here in the form of a lengthened vowel: η); by contrast, aorist participles do not retain their augment.

ἰδεῖν: aorist infinitive of ὁράω, here used aspectually (i.e. to indicate a single or fleeting action).

ἡσύχαζεν: 'he remained silent', i.e. he does not prepare his infantry for an immediate encounter.

οἱ δέ: i.e. his naval crews.

ὡς ἐγγὺς ἐγένοντο: 'when they were near'.

ἠσπάσαντο: third plural (weak) aorist of ἀσπάζομαι (= I greet), taken with **ταῖς κώπαις** = 'saluted with oars'.

τοὺς Καίσαρος: 'Caesar's crews', contrasting with **οἱ δέ** above. 'Caesar' refers to Octavian, who as the heir and adopted son of Julius Caesar, took the latter's name after his death. I have adopted Plutarch's use of 'Caesar' when translating from the Greek, but used the name 'Octavian' elsewhere.

ἐκείνων τε ἀντασπασαμένων: 'and when they [Octavian's crews] had greeted them in turn' (genitive absolute).

μετεβάλοντο: third plural (strong) aorist of μεταβάλλομαι = I change sides.

πάσαις ἅμα ταῖς ναυσὶν ὁ στόλος εἷς γενόμενος ἐπέπλει: 'the expedition/fleet, having become one, together with all the ships sailed . . .' The language (πάσαις, ἅμα, εἷς γενόμενος) emphasizes the unity of this new fleet.

ἐπέπλει: ἐπιπλέω = I sail against/upon/attack by sea, so **ἐπέπλει πρὸς τὴν πόλιν** = 'sailed towards/upon the city'. Hostile intent is implied not only by the 'ἐπι-' prefix of the verb, but also by the accompanying adjective **ἀντίπρῳρος** (= 'with the prow forwards', i.e. 'ready for action'; the prow is the front of the ship, also known as the bow).

76.2

The themes of the rapid desertion (**εὐθύς**) of Antony's supporters (leading to further isolation) and the hopelessness of his situation continue. His navy has just defected to Octavian; his cavalry follow suit (note the repetition of the verb used in 76.1: **μεταβαλομένων**) and his infantry are overcome (**ἡττηθεὶς τοῖς πεζοῖς**: 'having been defeated with his infantry'; **ἡττηθείς** = nominative masculine singular aorist participle passive from **ἡσσάομαι** = I am defeated). Antony's military defeat is complete.

ὑπὸ Κλεοπάτρας προδεδόσθαι βοῶν οἷς δι' ἐκείνην ἐπολέμησεν: 'shouting that he had been betrayed by Cleopatra to those against whom he had waged war on her account'. Translate **βοῶν** first; it introduces an indirect statement (infinitive construction). **προδεδόσθαι**: perfect passive infinitive of προδίδωμι = I betray. The subject of the infinitive is not expressed, as it is the same as the subject of the introductory participle. As often in Greek, the antecedent of the relative pronoun **οἷς** has been omitted.

ἡ δὲ τὴν ὀργὴν αὐτοῦ φοβηθεῖσα καὶ τὴν ἀπόνοιαν εἰς τὸν τάφον κατέφυγε: 'she, fearing his anger and his madness, fled into her tomb'. The themes of Cleopatra's self-interest and cowardice (prominent in the Actium narrative and its immediate aftermath, e.g. chapters 66 and 69) return: she flees (**κατέφυγε**) in fear (**φοβηθεῖσα**) into the tomb (**εἰς τὸν τάφον**) which she had constructed near the temple of Isis (see Chapter 74).

καὶ τοὺς καταρράκτας ἀφῆκε κλείθροις καὶ μοχλοῖς καρτεροὺς ὄντας: 'and she let down the portcullis, which was strong with bars and bolts'. As Pelling notes, **τοὺς καταρράκτας** refers to defences in front of the door (p. 305). **ἀφῆκε** is third singular aorist of ἀφίημι (= I let fall). There is a degree of redundancy in **κλείθροις καὶ μοχλοῖς**: Cleopatra is taking no chances.

πρὸς δὲ Ἀντώνιον ἔπεμψε τοὺς ἀπαγγελοῦντας ὅτι τέθνηκε: 'she sent messengers to Antony to report that she had died'. **τοὺς ἀπαγγελοῦντας** = literally, 'those who will report'; the future participle here has the force of a purpose clause. Of course, she has not yet died, and her exact motivation is unclear. She appears to fear that Antony might harm her; Cassius Dio, another historian of the period, suggested (51.10.6) that she was trying to force his suicide.

76.3

Τί ἔτι μέλλεις, Ἀντώνιε: 'Why do you still delay, Antony?' Plutarch employs direct speech at significant moments in his narrative; here it is coupled with the use of a high rhetorical style (use of a short question and third person self-reference) to add to the drama and emotion of the occasion. The next section provides a brief delay as we build to the mini-climax of Antony's suicide.

τὴν μόνην ... καὶ λοιπὴν ... πρόφασιν: 'the only remaining reason'. The hyperbaton (emphasising **μόνην**) is striking.

ἀφῄρηκε: third singular perfect indicative active of ἀφαιρέω (= I take away from).

τοῦ φιλοψυχεῖν: 'of loving life' (φιλοψυχέω = I love my life). This is an example of an articular infinitive (the use of the infinitive with the article to create a noun, the equivalent of the gerund in Latin; note that the article declines, but the infinitive does not).

τὸν θώρακα παραλυων καὶ διαστέλλων: 'loosening and laying aside his breastplate'. This serves a practical as well as a symbolic purpose: 'the soldier needs his armour no more' (Pelling, p. 306).

Ὦ Κλεοπάτρα: Antony now turns from a self-address to an apostrophe of Cleopatra, adding further to the high emotion of the scene. Apostrophe = an address to someone who is absent, or an inanimate object/abstract concept, etc.

αὐτίκα γὰρ εἰς ταὐτὸν ἀφίξομαι: literally, 'for I shall straight away arrive into the same [state]', i.e. 'for I shall immediately join you in death'. **ταὐτόν** = τὸ αὐτόν (= τὸ αὐτό), i.e. death. The process whereby a word ending in a vowel and word beginning with a vowel become fused is called 'crasis'.

ἀλλ' ὅτι γυναικὸς ὁ τηλικοῦτος αὐτοκράτωρ εὐψυχίᾳ πεφώραμαι λειπόμενος: 'but (I am grieved that: resupply ἄχθομαί) I, such a great general, have been discovered to be inferior in courage to a woman', i.e. because she committed suicide first (so he currently believes). The juxtaposition of **γυναικός** and **ὁ τηλικοῦτος αὐτοκράτωρ** serves to draw out the irony.

λειπόμαι in the passive means 'I am left without (+ genitive)/I am left behind' and therefore comes to mean 'I am inferior to' (+ genitive). **πεφώραμαι** ('I have been discovered') is first singular perfect passive of φωράω.

76.4

Drama and a high emotional style continue in the description of Eros' death.

Ἔρως: this may indeed have been the slave's real name; either way, it certainly seems appropriate for the man charged with killing Antony, given the fact that – to Plutarch's mind – it is Antony's love for Cleopatra which has caused his downfall.

τοῦτον ἐκ πολλοῦ παρακεκληκώς, εἰ δεήσειεν, ἀνελεῖν αὐτόν, ἀπῄτει τὴν ὑπόσχεσιν: 'having encouraged him [Eros] a while ago (**ἐκ πολλοῦ**) to kill him [Antony] if he should need it, he [Antony] demanded (the fulfilment of) his promise'.

παρακεκληκώς = masculine nominative singular perfect participle active of παρακαλέω (= 'I call, summon'; Pelling [p. 306] notes that it should be translated here as 'encourage'); it introduces an indirect command, which in Greek is simply an infinitive. **ἀνελεῖν** = strong aorist infinitive of ἀναιρέω (here = 'I kill'). **δεήσειεν** = third singular aorist optative from (the impersonal) δεῖ. The optative is used because this is a subordinate clause within an indirect command in historic sequence. **ἀπῄτει** = third singular imperfect indicative active of ἀπαιτέω (= 'I demand in payment').

ὡς παίσων ἐκεῖνον: 'as if about to strike him', also with the force of a purpose clause (ὡς + future participle).

ἑαυτὸν ἀπέκτεινε: 'he killed himself'. Rather than undermining the force of the adjective previously used to describe him (**πιστός** = 'faithful'), this action rather reinforces it: 'he cannot bear to kill his master' (Pelling, p. 306).

Εὖγε: 'well done'.

ὅτι μὴ δυνηθεὶς αὐτὸς ἐμὲ ποιεῖν ὃ δεῖ διδάσκεις: literally, 'because, (although) not having been able yourself, you are teaching me what it is necessary to do'.

παίσας διὰ τῆς κοιλίας ἑαυτον: literally, 'having struck himself through the belly', i.e. 'having cut through his belly'. **ἑαυτον** should be taken with both this phrase and the one following.

ἑαυτόν ἀφῆκεν εἰς τὸ κλινίδιον: 'he fell onto the couch' (literally, 'he let himself fall onto the couch').

76.5

ἦν δὲ οὐκ εὐθυθάνατος ἡ πληγή: 'the wound was not mortal'; it is tempting to add 'straightaway' as a qualification, for it will indeed be the one which eventually causes his death.

τῆς φορᾶς τοῦ αἵματος, ἐπεὶ κατεκλίθη, παυσαμένης: 'the rush of blood having ceased [genitive absolute] when he reclined'; lying on the couch prolongs his life further.

ἀναλαβών: 'having recovered'; translate the verb intransitively.

ἐδεῖτο: third singular imperfect from **δέομαι** (= [here] I beg X [genitive] to do Y [infinitive]).

ἐπισφάττειν αὐτόν: 'to finish him off' (**ἐπισφάττειν** = 'to strike the death blow').

βοῶντος καὶ σφαδάζοντος: '(while he was) shouting and struggling' – genitive absolute; the subject is Antony (not supplied in Greek).

ἄχρι οὗ παρὰ Κλεοπάτρας ἧκε Διομήδης ὁ γραμματεύς: 'until Diomedes the secretary came from Cleopatra'. **ἧκε** = third singular imperfect from ἥκω (= [in the present] 'I have come').

77.1

Γνούς . . . ὅτι: indirect statement; here γιγνώσκω is followed by **ὅτι** rather than the participle construction. This regularly happens when the verb of knowing or perceiving is itself a participle (and indeed, interchange between these two types of indirect statement is very common in general in Greek).

προθύμως ἐκέλευσεν ἄρασθαι τοῖς ὑπηρέταις τὸ σῶμα: 'he [Antony] eagerly ordered his servants to raise his body'. κέλευω can, as here, be followed by a dative of the person being commanded (**τοῖς ὑπηρέταις**). The adverb (**προθύμως**) suggests that Cleopatra's hold over Antony is as strong as ever. **ἄρασθαι** = aorist infinitive middle from αἴρω, which has the same meaning in the middle and active ('I raise, lift').

καὶ διὰ χειρῶν προσεκομίσθη ταῖς θύραις τοῦ οἰκήματος: 'and he was brought in their arms to the doors of the tomb'.

ἐκ δὲ θυρίδων τινῶν φανεῖσα: 'appearing (literally, having appeared) at some windows'.

καθίει: 'she let down/dropped' – third singular imperfect from καθίημι.

τούτοις ἐναψάντων τὸν Ἀντώνιον: 'when they had bound Antony to these [the ropes/cords]'. Cassius Dio (51.10.9) tells us that the ropes and cords were part of the building equipment which was still in place, as the monument was unfinished.

ἐναψάντων = masculine genitive plural aorist participle of **ἐνάπτω** ('I bind/fit X on to Y'). This is a genitive absolute. The subject (omitted in Greek) = the people who were with Antony (see 76.5).

ἀνεῖλκεν αὐτὴ καὶ δύο γυναῖκες: **ἀνεῖλκεν** is singular (third singular imperfect of ἀνέλκω), so a translation such as 'she dragged him up herself, with two women' would be appropriate.

ἃς μόνας ἐδέξατο: 'the only ones she had welcomed/accepted'.

77.2

οὐδὲν ἐκείνου λέγουσιν οἰκτρότερον γενέσθαι οἱ παραγενόμενοι θέαμα: literally, 'those who were present say that no sight was more pitiable than that (one)'. **ἐκείνου** is a genitive of comparison. The hyperbaton in **οὐδέν . . . οἰκτρότερον . . . θέαμα** draws attention to the misery of Antony's state, thereby generating pathos.

On **λέγουσιν**, Pelling states: 'the present tense marks a quotation from a source' (p. 307). Note also that it is here followed by the infinitive construction (rather than the expected ὅτι).

πεφυρμένος γὰρ αἵματι καὶ δυσθανατῶν: 'for, drenched/stained with blood and struggling against death' – a very dramatic image. **πεφυρμένος** = masculine nominative singular perfect participle passive from φύρω (here = 'I mix X with Y', 'I stain/defile'). **δυσθανατῶν** = masculine nominative singular present participle active from δυσθανατέω ('I struggle against death'), a verb which suggests vigorous movement.

τὰς χεῖρας ὀρέγων εἰς ἐκείνην καὶ παραιωρούμενος: 'stretching out his hands towards her even as he hung there' – a scene of great pathos. The **καί** is adverbial.

ταῖν χεροῖν ἐμπεφυκυῖα καὶ κατατεινομένη τῷ προσώπῳ: 'clasping with her hands and with a strained face' (literally, 'strained with/in/by her face': **κατατεινομένη** is either middle or passive). **ταῖν χεροῖν** is dual. **ἐμπεφυκυῖα** is the perfect participle from ἐμφύω; the passive ('I cling closely to') makes use of the perfect active form ἐμπέφυκα.

ἐπικελευομένων τῶν κάτωθεν αὐτῇ καὶ συναγωνιώντων: 'while those down below cheered her on and shared the struggle' (genitive absolute). **ἐπικελευομένων** is middle; in terms of strict grammar, **αὐτῇ** follows **ἐπικελευομένων**, but its sense extends to **συναγωνιώντων**.

77.3

περιερρήξατο τε τοὺς πέπλους ἐπ᾽ αὐτῷ: 'she ripped her garments over him'. This is the start of a series of mourning rituals which Cleopatra performs over the (still-living) body of Antony. It is emphasized by polysyndeton (repetition of conjunctions) and a list of participles.

τὰ στέρνα τυπτομένη καὶ σπαράττουσα ταῖς χερσί: 'beating and tearing her breasts with her hands'; **τυπτομένη** is a middle participle which takes a direct object.

καὶ τῷ προσώπῳ τοῦ αἵματος ἀναματτομένη: 'and wiping (some of) his blood on her face'. **τοῦ αἵματος** is a partitive genitive, with the part ('some of') omitted.

δεσπότην ἐκάλει καὶ ἄνδρα καὶ αὐτοκράτορα: 'she called him master and husband and general'. The tricolon of titles with polysyndeton suggests high emotion, as do the word choices: **δεσπότην** is usually used of a master of enslaved persons, and thus suggests her own submission to him, a reversal of the presentation of their relationship so far; **ἄνδρα** suggests her regard for his masculinity and perhaps in particular his role as a lover; **αὐτοκράτορα** refers not to their relationship but her recognition of the respect he has gained as a military commander.

καὶ μικροῦ δεῖν ἐπιλέληστο τῶν αὑτῆς κακῶν οἴκτῳ τῶν ἐκείνου: 'and she had almost forgotten her own suffering through pity for his'. Note the adverbial phrase **μικροῦ δεῖν** ('almost'): Plutarch does not grant her a single moment of complete selflessness.

ἐπιλέληστο is third singular pluperfect of ἐπιλανθάνομαι (+ genitive = 'I forget'). **αὑτῆς** is a contracted form of the reflexive pronoun, feminine genitive singular (= **ἑαυτῆς**); resupply **κακῶν** with **τῶν ἐκείνου**.

εἴτε διψῶν, εἴτε συντομώτερον ἐλπίζων ἀπολυθήσεσθαι: 'either because he was thirsty or because he was hoping to be released [from life] more quickly'. **εἴτε . . . εἴτε . . .** (introducing alternatives) is followed by two participles (**διψῶν** and **ἐλπίζων**). **συντομώτερον** is a comparative adverb (from **συντόμως** = 'quickly, immediately'). **ἀπολυθήσεσθαι** is the future passive infinitive of ἀπολύω (= 'I release').

77.4

On this section, Pelling notes: 'Antony's dying words are doubtless imaginary, and Plutarch credits him with admirable sentiments' (p. 307).

παρῄνεσεν αὐτῇ τὰ μὲν ἑαυτῆς . . . σωτήρια τίθεσθαι: 'he advised her to see to her own safety'.

παρῄνεσεν introduces an indirect command followed by three infinitives (**τίθεσθαι**, **θρηνεῖν** and **μακαρίζειν**). **τά . . . σωτήρια** is an example of the definite article + neuter plural adjective being used substantively: 'safety'. **τίθεσθαι** = present infinitive middle/passive of τίθημι; here it means 'to prepare/see to'.

ἂν ᾖ μὴ μετ᾽ αἰσχύνης: 'if it were possible [to see to her safety] without shame/honourably'. **ἄν** = ἐάν = if. **ᾖ** = third singular present subjunctive of εἰμί ('I am'); the indicative ἐστι is sometimes used as a shorthand for the impersonal ἔξεστι (= 'it is possible'), and we see this here in the subjunctive **ᾖ**.

μάλιστα τῶν Καίσαρος ἑταίρων Προκληΐῳ πιστεύουσαν: 'trusting most of all, from the companions of Caesar, in Proculeius'. The irony of this statement becomes clear in Chapter 79: Proculeius was a close friend of Octavian.

αὐτὸν δὲ μὴ θρηνεῖν ἐπὶ ταῖς ὑστάταις μεταβολαῖς: 'not to lament him for his last misfortunes'.

ἀλλὰ μακαρίζειν ὧν ἔτυχε καλῶν: 'but to think him happy for the good things he had got (i.e. enjoyed)'. **μακαρίζειν** = to deem X (accusative: resupply **αὐτόν**) to be happy on account of Y (genitive)'. **ὧν . . . καλῶν**: literally, 'for which good things [he had got]'. **ὧν** is the genitive of the relative pronoun'. There follows a polysyndetic tricolon (each branch signalled by a participle) of things which Antony has enjoyed.

πλεῖστον ἰσχύσας: 'having won the most power'. **πλεῖστον** is adverbial.

νῦν οὐκ ἀγεννῶς Ῥωμαῖος ὑπὸ Ῥωμαίου κρατηθείς: 'having now been conquered, a Roman by a Roman, not ignobly'. The polyptoton (repetition of the same word but with different inflections, i.e. endings) emphasizes Antony's pride in his status as a Roman and in the manner of his demise: being conquered by a fellow Roman (with all that implies in terms of status and military ability) is to some degree far more honourable than being conquered by a foreign enemy. Moreover, it perhaps signals a (partial) return to the values he rejected when he chose Cleopatra over his Roman wife, Octavia (see Pelling, p. 14: 'finally, he asserts those values which in his life he has regretfully abandoned').

78.1

Ὅσον δὲ ἀπολιπόντος αὐτοῦ Προκλήϊος ἧκε παρὰ Καίσαρος: 'when he had only just died, Proculeius came from Caesar'. The adverb **ὅσον** (= 'only just') indicates the speed of Proculeius' arrival.

ἐπεὶ γὰρ ἑαυτὸν πατάξας ὁ Ἀντώνιος ᾤχετο πρὸς Κλεοπάτραν κομιζόμενος: literally, 'For when Antony, having struck himself, was being carried (literally, 'was off, being carried') to Cleopatra.' **ᾤχετο** = third singular imperfect indicative active of οἴχομαι ('I have departed, I am off/gone'). Note that the narrative has shifted back to the moment of Antony's self-stabbing. As we see in the work of other writers of Greek prose (not least Thucydides), Plutarch sometimes delays a revelation or otherwise disrupts the expected chronological narrative. There are many possible reasons for this, not least the need to make a 'scene change' between two key locations, or the desire to group together related events, to highlight thematic links between events, to create effective juxtapositions and/or to enhance the dramatic impact of an event by choosing a significant moment for its revelation (see Introduction pp. 186–7).

Δερκεταῖός τις τῶν δορυφόρων λαβὼν τὸ ἐγχειρίδιον αὐτοῦ καὶ ἀποκρύψας ὑπεξῆλθε: 'Dercetaeus, one of his bodyguard, having taken his dagger and having hidden it, withdrew secretly.' We return to the theme of the betrayal/defection of Antony's men (even those very close to him: **τις τῶν δορυφόρων**). Note that ὑπεξέρχομαι has a sense of 'withdraw in secret'.

τὸ ξίφος . . . ᾑμαγμένον: 'the sword stained with blood'. **ᾑμαγμένον** is a neuter accusative singular perfect participle passive from αἱμάσσω (= 'I stain with blood').

78.2

ἐνδοτέρω τῆς σκηνῆς ἀποστάς: 'having withdrawn further into his tent'. **ἀποστάς** = aorist participle of ἀφίσταμαι (= 'I withdraw'). **ἐνδοτέρω** is a comparative adverb (but one which governs a genitive).

ἀπεδάκρυσεν ἄνδρα κηδεστὴν γενόμενον καὶ συνάρχοντα καὶ πολλῶν ἀγώνων καὶ πραγμάτων κοινωνόν: 'he wept for a man who had been his brother-in-law and co-ruler and partner in many conflicts and deeds': a tricolon with polysyndeton, emphasizing the close relationship (blood and political) which had existed between Octavian and Antony; the third branch is longer, which perhaps gives it added emphasis. Are we to understand this as said with genuine feeling, or do his subsequent actions (see below) suggest that he is manipulating those around him?

τὰς ἐπιστολὰς λαβών: the following statement indicates that this refers to letters written by both Antony and Octavian.

ἀνεγίνωσκεν ὡς εὐγνώμονα γράφοντος αὐτοῦ καὶ δίκαια φορτικὸς ἦν καὶ ὑπερήφανος ἀεὶ περὶ τὰς ἀποκρίσεις ἐκεῖνος: 'he read aloud how, when he [Octavian] wrote reasonable and just things, he [**ἐκεῖνος**: Antony] was always vulgar and arrogant with regard to his answers'. The juxtaposition of **δίκαια φορτικός** perhaps serves to bring out the contrast between the two men.

78.3

ἐκ δὲ τούτου: 'after this', a very common prepositional phrase.

ἢν δύνηται: 'if he was able' (ἢν = ἐάν).

μάλιστα τῆς Κλεοπάτρας ζώσης κρατῆσαι: 'particularly to get Cleopatra into his control alive'; the reasons for this given by Plutarch are all rather mercenary/ self-interested. κρατέω + genitive = 'I conquer, prevail over, am master over.'

τῶν χρημάτων: this refers to the goods/treasures she has with her in her tomb.

μέγα πρὸς δόξαν ἡγεῖτο τοῦ θριάμβου καταγαγεῖν ἐκείνην: 'he believed (that it would add) greatly to the glory of his triumph to lead her [in it]'. **μέγα** is an adverb (= 'much, exceedingly, greatly'). A triumph was a Roman military procession voted to those generals who had achieved a notable victory. It involved a procession through the city of the spoils captured on the campaign; it was considered a real coup if this procession included the commander of the enemy forces. κατάγω has a sense of 'bring home' as well as 'lead'.

εἰς μὲν οὖν χεῖρας τῷ Προκληΐῳ συνελθεῖν οὐκ ἠθέλησεν: 'therefore she did not want to come into the hands of Proculeius' (literally, 'to meet with Proculeius, into his hands'); the subject of **ἠθέλησεν** is Cleopatra. She is shrewder than Antony (who had advised complete Trust in Proculeius, 77.4), as suggested by **οὖν**.

78.4

ἐγίνοντο δὲ λόγοι τῷ οἰκήματι προσελθόντος ἔξωθεν αὐτοῦ κατὰ θύρας ἐπιπέδους: 'they conversed (**ἐγίνοντο λόγοι**) when he had come to the tomb (**τῷ οἰκήματι προσελθόντος αὐτοῦ**) from outside (**ἔξωθεν**) by a door on the ground (**κατὰ θύρας ἐπιπέδους**)'. **θύρας** probably refers to a set of double doors. The context demands a translation of **κατά** as 'by'; this is an extension of 'in the region of' (a common meaning).

ἀποκεκλειμένας μὲν ὀχυρῶς, φωνῇ δὲ διέξοδον ἐχούσας: 'which was strongly fastened but had (or 'allowed') a passage for the voice'. **ἀποκεκλειμένας** is the perfect participle passive (feminine accusative plural) from ἀποκλείω (= 'I shut up, close').

ἡ μὲν αἰτουμένη τοῖς παισὶ τὴν βασιλείαν, ὁ δὲ θαρρεῖν καὶ πάντα πιστεύειν Καίσαρι κελεύων: 'Cleopatra asking for the kingdom for her children [i.e. 'that her kingdom might be given to her children'], and Proculeius instructing her to be of good courage and to trust Caesar in everything'. **αἰτουμένη**: the middle has the same meaning as the active ('ask for'). **πάντα** is an accusative of respect ('with respect to all things').

79.1

Ὡς δὲ κατιδὼν τὸν τόπον ἀπήγγειλε Καίσαρι: 'when, having observed the place, he reported back to Caesar'. The report presumably contained information about the size, defences, entry points, etc. of the tomb: 'the real purpose of Proculeius' first visit' (Pelling, p. 309).

Γάλλος μὲν ἐπέμφθη πάλιν ἐντευξόμενος αὐτῇ: 'Gallus was sent to converse with her again'. **ἐντευξόμενος** is the future participle from ἐντυγχάνω (here = I interview/converse with); the future participle has the force of a purpose clause. Gallus refers to Gaius Cornelius Gallus, a Latin love poet (of whose work only fragments survive), orator and politician who was later made prefect of Egypt.

ἐπίτηδες: this adverb means both 'on purpose' and 'deceitfully'.

ἐν τούτῳ δὲ Προκλήϊος κλίμακος προστεθείσης διὰ τῆς θυρίδος εἰσῆλθεν ᾗ τὸν Ἀντώνιον αἱ γυναῖκες ἐδέξαντο: 'meanwhile, Proculeius, having set up a ladder, went in through the window by which the women had received Antony'. **προστεθείσης** is aorist participle passive (feminine genitive singular) from προστίθημι ('I apply, hold close, put to'), agreeing (as part of a genitive absolute) with **κλίμακος**.

καὶ πρὸς τὰς θύρας αὐτὰς εὐθύς, αἷς ἡ Κλεοπάτρα παρειστήκει προσέχουσα τῷ Γάλλῳ, κατέβαινεν: 'and he went down immediately to the very door beside which Cleopatra was standing as she listened to Gallus'. **παρειστήκει** is a pluperfect (third singular pluperfect indicative from παρίσταμαι), but translated (as is standard with the pluperfect of ἵστημι and its compounds) as an imperfect: the idea is that she 'had stood herself beside', therefore she 'was standing beside' the door. **προσέχουσα τῷ Γάλλῳ** literally means 'paying attention to Gallus'.

79.2

τῶν δὲ συγκαθειργμένων τῇ Κλεοπάτρᾳ γυναικῶν τῆς ἑτέρας ἀνακραγούσης: 'when one of the women shut up with Cleopatra cried out'; **τῆς ἑτέρας ἀνακραγούσης** is a genitive absolute (**ἀνακραγούσης** is the aorist participle active [feminine genitive singular] of ἀνακράζω = 'I cry out'). **συγκαθειργμένων** is the perfect participle passive (feminine genitive plural) of συγκαθείργω (= 'I shut X up [with + dative]').

Τάλαινα Κλεοπάτρα, ζωγρεῖ: 'wretched Cleopatra, you are being taken captive!' ζωγρεῖ is second singular present passive indicative from ζωγρέω ('I take alive/take captive'). Again, direct speech is used for dramatic effect (see on 76.3).

μεταστραφεῖσα καὶ θεασαμένη τὸν Προκλήϊον: 'turning herself around and beholding Proculeius'. The subject of these aorist participles (and of the main verb **ὥρμησε** ['she hastened/rushed']) is Cleopatra.

παρεζωσμένη γὰρ ἐτύγχανέ τι τῶν λῃστρικῶν ξιφιδίων: 'for (**γάρ**) she happened to have hanging at her girdle (**παρεζωσμένη ἐτύγχανέ**) one (**τι**) of those daggers (**τῶν . . . ξιφιδίων**) which thieves have (**λῃστρικῶν**)'.

τυγχάνω + nominative participle = I happen to be X-ing, I am X-ing. **παρεζωσμένη** = perfect participle middle (feminine nominative singular) from παραζώννυμι which in the middle means 'I wear at the girdle' (girdle = a long strip of cloth tied around the waist).

Ἀδικεῖς . . . ὦ Κλεοπάτρα, καὶ σεαυτὴν καὶ Καίσαρα, μεγάλην ἀφαιρουμένη χρηστότητος ἐπίδειξιν αὐτοῦ, καὶ διαβάλλουσα τὸν πρᾳότατον ἡγεμόνων ὡς ἄπιστον καὶ ἀδιάλλακτον: 'Cleopatra, you are wronging both yourself and Caesar by taking away a great show of kindness/goodness from him, and by slandering the gentlest of leaders as untrustworthy and not open to reconciliation.' The 'show of kindness/goodness' (**χρηστότητος ἐπίδειξιν**) implied by Proculeius is Octavian's sparing of and reconciliation with her. Of course, we have been told that what he really wants to do is put her in his triumphal procession (78.3). The implied slander is emphasized by the use of two alpha-private adjectives (**ἄπιστον/ἀδιάλλακτον**) and the alliteration/assonance generated.

ἀφαιρέομαι = I take X (accusative) away from Y (genitive); the middle implies that it is for one's own purposes/gain. **πρᾳότατον** is the superlative form of πρᾶος ('gentle').

79.3

ἅμα δὲ καὶ τὸ ξίφος αὐτῆς παρείλετο, καὶ τὴν ἐσθῆτα, μὴ κρύπτοι τι φάρμακον, ἐξέσεισεν: 'at the same time he both took away her sword and shook out her clothing in case she was hiding some poison [within it]'. **ἐξέσεισεν** is third singular aorist indicative active of ἐκσείω (= 'I shake out'). **μή** + optative (**κρύπτοι**) is the construction used after a verb of fearing (here omitted) when the fear relates to the future but the main verb is an historic tense.

ἐπέμφθη δὲ καὶ παρὰ Καίσαρος τῶν ἀπελευθέρων Ἐπαφρόδιτος: 'And also sent from Caesar was one of his freedmen, Epaphroditus' (literally, 'Epaphroditus out of his freedmen').

ἀπελεύθερος is the Greek term for a formerly enslaved person (*libertus* in Latin).

ᾧ προσετέτακτο ζῶσαν αὐτὴν φυλάττειν ἰσχυρῶς ἐπιμελόμενον: literally, 'to whom it had been ordered (**ᾧ προσετέτακτο**) to keep her alive (**ζῶσαν αὐτὴν φυλάττειν**), taking care [of her] vigorously (**ἰσχυρῶς ἐπιμελόμενον**)', i.e. 'who had been ordered to keep her alive by guarding her strictly'. **προσετέτακτο** = third singular pluperfect passive indicative of προστάσσω (= 'I order, command' + dative). We would expect the present middle participle **ἐπιμελόμενον** to be dative (agreeing with ᾧ and likewise referring to Epaphroditus) but it has shifted into the accusative (as though preceded by ὅν ἐκέλευσε rather than ᾧ προσετέτακτο).

τἆλλα δὲ πρὸς τὸ ῥᾷστον ἐνδιδόναι καὶ ἥδιστον: 'but otherwise (**τἆλλα**) to concede with respect to (**πρός**) the easiest and sweetest (course of action)'. **τἆλλα** = τὰ ἄλλα by crasis (see on 76.3); it literally means '[with respect to] the other things' and thus comes to mean 'otherwise'. **ἐνδιδόναι** is the present infinitive active of ἐνδίδωμι. A noun or noun-phrase such as 'course of action' needs to be supplied with the definite article + adjective combination **τὸ ῥᾷστον καὶ ἥδιστον**.

80.1

The narrative now shifts focus and tone: we move from Cleopatra's tomb to the arrival of Octavian in Alexandria. 'After the climaxes of 76–79 a less intense sequence is welcome, and Plutarch again develops Octavian as a foil to the warm-hearted lovers' (Pelling, p. 310). We get further insight into Octavian the politician: he is generous to the Alexandrians, but, as at 78.2, we sense that it might be for show.

Ἀρείῳ τῷ φιλοσόφῳ: a Stoic and friend/teacher of Octavian.

ἵνα εὐθὺς ἐν τοῖς πολίταις περίβλεπτος εἴη καὶ θαυμάζοιτο τιμώμενος ὑπ᾽ αὐτοῦ διαπρεπῶς: 'so that he [Areius] might at once be looked at from all sides among the citizens and admired, (on account of his) being magnificently honoured by him [Octavian]'. **ἵνα** introduces a purpose clause with two optative verbs (**εἴη/**

θαυμάζοιτο: **εἴη** is third singular optative of εἰμί [I am]). The participle **τιμώμενος** has a causal sense.

τὸ γυμνάσιον: the gymnasium in Classical and Hellenistic Greece had served as a space for athletic training, medical practice and education.

ἀναβὰς ἐπὶ βῆμά τι πεποιημένον: 'having gone up onto a platform which had been made/set up'. **πεποιημένον** is the perfect participle passive (neuter accusative singular) of ποιέω.

ἐκπεπληγμένων ὑπὸ δέους τῶν ἀνθρώπων καὶ προσπιπτόντων: 'the people, panicked by fear and falling down before him' (genitive absolute). **ἐκπεπληγμένων** is the perfect participle passive (masculine genitive plural) of ἐκπλήσσω.

ἀναστῆναι κελεύσας: 'having ordered them to get up'. **ἀναστῆναι** is the root aorist infinitive ('to get up/rise') of ἀνίσταμαι ('I get up, rise').

ἔφη πάσης αἰτίας τὸν δῆμον ἀφιέναι: 'he said that he acquitted the people of all blame' – an ostentatiously magnanimous gesture, characteristic of a conquering hero entering a city. Note that there is no accusative subject in this indirect statement (infinitive construction), as the subject of the infinitive (**ἀφιέναι**) is the same as that of the main verb (**ἔφη**), so it is either put into the nominative or – more often – left out (as here: see also 76.2). **ἀφιέναι** is present infinitive active of ἀφίημι, which here has a legal meaning ('I acquit X [accusative] of Y [genitive]').

διὰ τὸν κτίστην Ἀλέξανδρον: 'on account of their founder Alexander', a reference to Alexander the Great.

On this and the following lines, Pelling states: 'praises of a city's founder, its beauty, and its inhabitants were regular *topoi* of a rhetorical *epibaterion* (a speech made on arrival)' (p. 310); and later: 'Alexander was always a potent model for Roman generals' (p. 311). Octavian's interest in Alexander is documented in the writings of Suetonius (*Life of Augustus*, 18). Julius Caesar admired him, too (Plutarch, *Life of Julius Caesar*, 11.3), and it seems possible that Octavian's keenness to identify himself as Caesar's heir may also be a motivating factor for some of his actions here.

80.2

καὶ τῶν ἄλλων ἐξῃτήσατο συχνούς: 'and he gained/secured pardon for many of the others'; the subject of **ἐξῃτήσατο** is Arieus (who was the subject of the last main verb: **ἔτυχε**). **τῶν ἄλλων** is a partitive genitive.

ὧν ἦν καὶ Φιλόστρατος: 'among them was Philostratus'. **ὧν** is a connecting relative. **καί** is here used adverbially (= 'indeed/also'), but may be left untranslated in English.

ἀνὴρ εἰπεῖν μὲν ἐξ ἐπιδρομῆς τῶν πώποτε σοφιστῶν ἱκανώτατος: 'a man most able (**ἀνήρ ... ἱκανώτατος**) of all sophists hitherto (literally, 'of the sophists ever yet': **τῶν πώποτε σοφιστῶν**) to speak (**εἰπεῖν**) off the cuff/on the spur of the moment (**ἐξ ἐπιδρομῆς**)'. **ἀνήρ ... ἱκανώτατος** is in apposition with **Φιλόστρατος**. Sophists were paid teachers who gave lessons in rhetoric and philosophy.

εἰσποιῶν δὲ μὴ προσηκόντως ἑαυτὸν τῇ Ἀκαδημείᾳ: literally, 'adding (**εἰσποιῶν**) himself (**ἑαυτόν**) improperly (**μὴ προσηκόντως**) to the Academy (**τῇ Ἀκαδημείᾳ**)', i.e. 'falsely representing himself as a member of the Academy'.

As Pelling notes, we are to assume this means the Athenian Academy (Plato's philosophical school).

διὸ καὶ Καῖσαρ αὐτοῦ βδελυττόμενος τὸν τρόπον οὐ προσίετο τὰς δεήσεις: 'therefore (**διὸ καί**) Caesar, feeling disgust at (**βδελυττόμενος**) his way/manner (**αὐτοῦ . . . τὸν τρόπον**), did not allow/listen to (**οὐ προσίετο**) his entreaties (**τὰς δεήσεις**)'.

προσίετο is third singular imperfect indicative middle of προσίημι (which is found more frequently in the middle as προσίεμαι, meaning 'I admit X/allow X to approach').

80.3

ὁ δέ: refers to Philostratus. The reason for the following digression (Philostratus' annoying protest) is unclear; Pelling suggests a comic purpose (p. 311), and this is perhaps welcome given the tone and subject matter of the next section (see note on 81.1).

πώγωνα πολιὸν καθεὶς καὶ φαιὸν ἱμάτιον περιβαλόμενος: literally, 'having let his white beard grow and having put on a grey cloak', i.e. 'letting his white beard grow long and wearing a grey cloak'. These are the traditional attributes of a philosopher. **καθείς** is the aorist participle active (masculine nominative singular) of καθίημι (= I let fall); here it has the very specific meaning of 'having let his beard grow long'. **περιβαλόμενος** is the aorist participle middle of περιβάλλω (= 'I throw round'; in the middle = 'I put on [clothes]').

ἐξόπισθεν Ἀρείῳ παρηκολούθει: 'used to follow Areius from behind'. παρακολουθέω takes a dative; **ἐξόπισθεν** is an adverb.

τοῦτον ἀεὶ τὸν στίχον ἀναφθεγγόμενος: 'always/repeatedly calling out this verse'.

σοφοὶ σοφοὺς σῴζουσιν, ἂν ὦσιν σοφοί: 'wise men save wise men, if they [the former] are wise'. **ἄν** = ἐάν; **ὦσιν** is third plural present subjunctive of **εἰμί** (I am). Pelling labels this 'an unattractive line from an unknown tragedy' (p. 312), on the basis of the (inelegant) wordplay (**σοφοί/σοφούς/σοφοί**), sibilance and excessive alliteration.

καὶ τοῦ φθόνου μᾶλλον Ἄρειον ἢ τοῦ δέους Φιλόστρατον ἀπαλλάξαι βουλόμενος: 'and wanting to free Areius from hatred more than (to free) Philostratus from fear'. **ἀπαλλάξαι** is aorist infinitive active of ἀπαλλάσσω (= 'I set free').

διῆκε: 'he let him go'; third singular aorist indicative active of διίημι (= 'I let go, dismiss, pardon').

81.1

The focus shifts again, this time onto the differing fates of some of Antony's and Cleopatra's children. The theme of betrayal returns, as does the pathetic tone of earlier sections.

The brief description of the violent deaths of both the child Antyllus and of the tutor who betrayed him take the reader by surprise: we are shocked into remembering the brutality and violence with which Octavian sealed his grip on power.

ὁ μὲν ἐκ Φουλβίας Ἄντυλλος: 'Antyllus, his son by Fulvia'. Fulvia was a woman of aristocratic origin who was involved in Roman political life, in part through her marriages to Publius Clodius Pulcher, Gaius Scribonius Curio and finally Mark Antony.

παραδοθείς: 'having been handed over/betrayed'; aorist participle passive (masculine nominative singular) of παραδίδωμι.

καὶ τὴν κεφαλὴν αὐτοῦ τῶν στρατιωτῶν ἀποτεμόντων: 'and, when the soldiers had cut off his head' (genitive absolute).

ἀφελών: 'having taken away'; aorist participle active (masculine nominative singular) of ἀφαιρέω.

ὃν ἐφόρει περὶ τῷ τραχήλῳ πολυτιμότατον λίθον: 'the very expensive stone which he used to wear around his neck'; the antecedent (**πολυτιμότατον λίθον**) of the relative pronoun (**ὅν**) has been delayed until after the relative clause. **ἐφόρει** is third singular imperfect indicative active of φορέω (= 'I wear constantly'; it is the frequentative of φέρω, with the frequentative sense further enhanced by the use of the imperfect).

εἰς τὴν ζώνην κατέρραψεν: 'he stitched it onto his belt'. The betrayal grows worse with each sentence.

ἀρνησάμενος δὲ καὶ φωραθεὶς ἀνεσταυρώθη: 'although he denied it, he was indeed discovered/convicted and crucified'.

The aorist participle **ἀρνησάμενος** (masculine nominative singular, from ἀρνέομαι) has a concessive force. **φωραθείς** is aorist participle passive (masculine nominative singular) from **φωράω** (= 'I detect, discover/convict'). ἀνασταυρόω = 'I crucify' (aorist passive ἀνεσταυρώθην).

81.2

Note the contrast between the treatment of Antyllus and that of Cleopatra's children (except Caesarion; see below).

φρουρούμενα μετὰ τῶν τρεφόντων: 'being guarded along with their attendants' (literally, 'being guarded with those nourishing/raising them'); this seems to have been their only hardship (see below), and it is tempting to translate **φρουρούμενα** with a concessive force ('although guarded . . .').

ἐλευθέριον εἶχε δίαιταν: 'enjoyed a free-spirited way of life'. The subject of **εἶχε** is **τὰ δὲ Κλεοπάτρας παιδία** (in Greek, neuter plural subjects take a singular verb).

Καισαρίωνα δὲ τὸν ἐκ Καίσαρος γεγονέναι **λεγόμενον ἡ μὲν μήτηρ ἐξέπεμψε μετὰ χρημάτων πολλῶν εἰς τὴν Ἰνδικὴν δι᾽ Αἰθιοπίας**: 'but as for Caesarion, the son said (**τόν . . . λεγόμενον**) to have been begotten (**γεγονέναι**) of Caesar (**ἐκ Καίσαρος**), his mother sent him away with much money through Ethiopia into India'. **γεγονέναι** is the perfect infinitive of **γίγνομαι**. With **τὴν Ἰνδικήν** supply χώραν.

Καισαρίων (Ptolemy XV Caesar; 'Caesarion', or 'little Caesar', was his nickname) was Cleopatra's eldest son. He ruled jointly with his mother until his death at the age of seventeen. As noted in the Introduction (p. 175), Cleopatra claimed that he was Julius Caesar's son, and Mark Antony asserted this in 34 BCE at the Donations of Alexandria. Plutarch has chosen not to express an opinion on this issue (**τόν . . . λεγόμενον**).

ἕτερος δὲ παιδαγωγὸς ὅμοιος Θεοδώρῳ Ῥόδων: 'Rhodon, another tutor like Theodorus'.

ὡς Καίσαρος αὐτὸν ἐπὶ βασιλείαν καλοῦντος: 'on the grounds that Caesar was calling him to take the kingdom'. Note that **ὡς** + (present) participle = 'on the grounds that', i.e. it indicates an alleged reason (thereby suggesting yet further treachery). It does not start a new main clause and therefore is here followed by a genitive absolute. The preposition **ἐπί** + accusative = 'to', but its meaning needs to be extended here.

βουλευομένου δὲ Καίσαρος Ἄρειον εἰπεῖν λέγουσιν: 'they say that, while Caesar was deliberating, Areius said . . .' **λέγουσιν** indicates hearsay; note that here it introduces an indirect statement with the infinitive construction (accusative subject **Ἄρειον**), rather than (the expected) ὅτι; as we have already seen, indirect statement in actual Greek usage is more flexible than the rules found in grammar books would suggest.

οὐκ ἀγαθὸν πολυκαισαρίη: 'a plurality of Caesars is not a good thing'. The noun **πολυκαισαρίη** has been coined by Plutarch; it is a witty adaptation of/pun on πολυκοιρανίη (= 'the rule of many'), which appears in *Iliad* 2.204–205:

> οὐκ ἀγαθὸν πολυκοιρανίη· εἷς κοίρανος ἔστω,/ εἷς βασιλεύς: 'a plurality of rulers is not a good thing; let there be one lord, one king'.

82.1

Τοῦτον μὲν οὖν ὕστερον ἀπέκτεινε μετὰ τὴν Κλεοπάτρας τελευτήν: 'And so he [Octavian, who is the subject of **ἀπέκτεινε**] later killed him [Caesarion: **τοῦτον**] after the death of Cleopatra'.

Ἀντώνιον δὲ πολλῶν αἰτουμένων θάψαι καὶ βασιλέων καὶ στρατηγῶν: 'although many kings and generals were asking to bury Antony'; the focus shifts again, to Antony's body. **αἰτουμένων** is another example of a participle with a concessive force; as noted at 78.4, the middle αἰτέομαι has essentially the same meaning as the active αἰτέω.

οὐκ ἀφείλετο Κλεοπάτρας τὸ σῶμα Καῖσαρ: 'Caesar did not take the body away from Cleopatra'; another ostentatiously magnanimous gesture (see note on 80.1). **ἀφείλετο** is third singular aorist indicative middle of ἀφαιρέω (= I take X [accusative] away from Y [genitive]).

ἀλλὰ ἐθάπτετο ταῖς ἐκείνης χερσὶ πολυτελῶς καὶ βασιλικῶς: 'but it was buried by her [Cleopatra's] hands in an extravagant and royal manner'.

πᾶσιν ὡς ἐβούλετο χρῆσθαι λαβούσης: 'having got/obtained (**λαβούσης**) everything (**πᾶσιν**) to use (**χρῆσθαι**) as she wished (**ὡς ἐβούλετο**)'. **λαβούσης** agrees with **ἐκείνης** and refers to Cleopatra. As Pelling (p. 313) notes, **πᾶσιν** (as the object of **λαβούσης**) should be accusative plural but it has been attracted into the dative case due to the presence of **χρῆσθαι** (the present infinitive of χράομαι, which takes a dative). Such attraction is common in Greek, and is seen most commonly with the relative pronoun.

ἐκ δὲ λύπης ἅμα τοσαύτης καὶ ὀδύνης: 'as a result of so much grief and pain at once'; **ἅμα** is an adverb here. Both **λύπης** and **ὀδύνης** can refer to physical pain and mental/emotional distress; the seeming redundancy/tautology is perhaps emphasizing that she experienced both.

ἀνεφλέγμηνε γὰρ αὐτῆς τὰ στέρνα τυπτομένης καὶ ἥλκωτο: 'for her breasts became inflamed/swollen and covered in sores/wounded as she beat herself' (literally, 'for the breasts of her beating herself became inflamed and had become wounded'). Are we to see her desire to bury Antony, and such intense mourning, as signs of genuine affection, or as an attempt to manipulate her audience? (There are parallels with the behaviour of Octavian: see on 78.2.)

ἀνεφλέγμηνε is third singular aorist indicative active of ἀναφλεγμαίνω (= 'I become inflamed/I swell up [intransitive]'). **ἥλκωτο** is third singular pluperfect indicative passive of **ἑλκόω** (= 'I wound, ulcerate, lacerate'). The neuter plural **τὰ στέρνα** is the subject of both (singular) verbs (see on 81.2). Pelling (p. 312) notes that both of verbs are medical terms. **τυπτομένης** is a middle participle.

πυρετῶν ἐπιλαβόντων: 'when fevers had seized her' (genitive absolute).

ἠγάπησε τὴν πρόφασιν ὡς ἀφεξομένη τροφῆς διὰ τοῦτο καὶ παραλύσουσα τοῦ ζῆν ἀκωλύτως ἑαυτήν: 'she welcomed the excuse for abstaining from food on account of this and for releasing herself from living in an unhindered manner': as Pelling notes, this is 'hardly an easy mode of suicide' (p. 313). A partial explanation comes in the form of the adverb **ἀκωλύτως**: she is afraid of being stopped by others if she were to try to commit suicide using a method which would perhaps be swift but likely to be noticed by those around her. **ὡς** is used here with a sense of purpose (it is followed by two future participles – **ἀφεξομένη** and **παραλύσουσα**).

ἀφεξομένη = future participle middle (feminine nominative singular) from ἀπέχω (+ genitive = 'I refrain/abstain from'). **παραλύσουσα** is a future active participle (feminine nominative singular) from παραλύω, which (here) = 'I release from' (+ accusative of the person, genitive of the thing). **τοῦ ζῆν** is an articular infinitive (= 'the act of living'); see on 76.3.

82.2

ἦν δὲ ἰατρὸς αὐτῇ συνήθης: 'there was a doctor in her company/dwelling with her'. The adjective **συνήθης** suggests intimacy; this is developed in the relative clause.

ᾧ φράσασα τἀληθὲς ἐχρῆτο συμβούλῳ καὶ συνεργῷ τῆς καθαιρέσεως: 'to whom she told the truth and whom she used as an adviser and assistant in her death' (literally, 'of her reduction [of body]' – another medical term). The dative relative pronoun ᾧ is the indirect object of the aorist participle **φράσασα** and must be resupplied as the dative object of **ἐχρῆτο**, with **συμβούλῳ** and **συνεργῷ** in apposition with it. **τἀληθές** = τὸ ἀληθές ('the truth'), another example of crasis (see note on 76.3).

εἴρηκεν: 'has said'; third singular perfect indicative active of λέγω.

ἱστορίαν τινὰ τῶν πραγμάτων τούτων ἐκδεδωκώς: 'having published an account of these events'. **ἐκδεδωκώς** is the perfect participle active (masculine nominative singular) from **ἐκδίδωμι** (= 'I publish'). The perfect tenses in **εἴρηκεν** and **ἐκδεδωκώς** indicate past actions whose effects are ongoing; this suggests that Plutarch may have used Olympus' work as a source (as noted by Pelling, p. 313).

ἱστορία (the word used by Herodotus – albeit in the Ionic dialect [ἱστορίη] – to describe his work) has a broad range of meanings: 'inquiry', 'investigation', 'examination', and (by extension) 'history' and 'written account'.

ὑπονοήσας δὲ Καῖσαρ ἀπειλάς μέν τινας αὐτῇ καὶ φόβους περὶ τῶν τέκνων προσέβαλλεν: literally, 'Caesar, having grown suspicious, threw certain threats and fears concerning her children at her,' i.e. 'Caesar, having grown suspicious, attacked her with certain threats and fears concerning her children.' The imperfect tense of **προσέβαλλεν** (προσβάλλω = 'I throw X [accusative] at Y [dative]') suggests a repeated action, perhaps 'kept on throwing'.

οἷς ἐκείνη καθάπερ μηχανήμασιν ὑπηρείπετο: 'by which she was laid low as if they were siege engines'; the antecedent of **οἷς** (dative, hence the dative in **μηχανήμασιν**) is both the threats (**ἀπειλάς**) and the fears (**φόβους**). **ὑπηρείπετο** is third singular imperfect indicative passive of ὑπερείπω, which means 'I undermine/subvert', and in the passive therefore comes to mean 'I am unable to stand.' The image of Cleopatra as a city being besieged is striking, and indicates both her care for her children and Octavian's cruelty.

παρεδίδου τὸ σῶμα θεραπεύειν καὶ τρέφειν τοῖς χρῄζουσιν: 'she surrendered/handed over her body to those desiring to care for and nourish it'; **παρεδίδου** is third singular imperfect indicative active of παραδίδωμι. **τοῖς χρῄζουσιν** = present participle (masculine dative plural) of χρῄζω (= 'I want/crave/desire'). Definite article + participle = a relative clause.

83.1

Ἧκε δὲ καὶ αὐτὸς ἡμέρας ὀλίγας διαλιπών: 'indeed, he himself [Octavian] came after a few days (literally, 'having left a few days')'; **διαλιπών** is the aorist participle of διαλείπω (= 'I leave an interval of time'). ἥκω (in the present) = 'I have come.'

ἐντευξόμενος αὐτῇ καὶ παρηγορήσων: 'in order to meet with her and provide comfort'; two future participles of purpose (note that ἐντυγχάνω takes the dative [here **αὐτῇ**]).

ἡ δὲ ἔτυχε μὲν ἐν στιβάδι κατακειμένη ταπεινῶς: 'she was lying on a bed in a downcast state'. τυγχάνω + participle = 'I happen to be X-ing, I am [actually] X-ing'.

εἰσιόντι δ' αὐτῷ μονοχίτων ἀναπηδήσασα προσπίπτει: 'wearing only a tunic, she sprang up and fell down before him as he entered' (προσπίπτω + dative = 'I fall down before, prostrate myself in front of'). Meekness and humility are emphasized, qualities which Plutarch did not emphasize in his earlier portrayal of Cleopatra.

δεινῶς μὲν ἐξηγριωμένη κεφαλὴν καὶ πρόσωπον: literally, 'having made herself terribly wild with respect to her head and face', i.e. 'with terribly wild hair and (a terribly wild) face'. **ἐξηγριωμένη** is perfect participle middle (feminine nominative singular) from ἐξαγριόω (= 'I make wild'). **κεφαλήν** and **πρόσωπον** are accusatives of respect (otherwise known as 'retained accusatives').

ὑπότρομος δὲ τῇ φωνῇ: 'trembling in her voice'. **ὑπότρομος** is feminine nominative singular; it is two-termination adjective (masculine and feminine ending = -ος, neuter ending = -ον), as is the case with all compound adjectives.

συντετηκυῖα ταῖς ὄψεσιν: literally, 'having melted/dissolved/wasted away with her eyes', i.e. 'her eyes were sunken'; **συντετηκυῖα** is perfect participle active (feminine nominative singular) from συντήκω (= 'I cause to waste/melt away'; its perfect is used intransitively to mean 'I am melted/consumed'). ὄψις = 'aspect/appearance' (singular), 'eyes' (plural).

ἦν δὲ πολλὰ καὶ τῆς περὶ τὸ στέρνον αἰκίας καταφανῆ: 'there were also many clear signs of suffering around her chest'. Take **πολλά . . . καταφανῆ** as a noun phrase (literally, 'many manifest things', i.e. 'many clear signs'). **καί** is adverbial, and is emphasizing that these marks were in addition to the signs of suffering as seen in her face/hair/eyes. **αἰκίας** (= 'suffering', 'assault', or 'torture') suggests physical blows.

καὶ ὅλως οὐθὲν ἐδόκει τὸ σῶμα τῆς ψυχῆς ἔχειν βέλτιον: 'and her body seemed to be not at all (in a) better (state) than her spirit'. **βέλτιον** is a comparative adverb (from ἀγαθός). ἔχω + adverb = 'I am X' (equivalent to εἰμί + adjective; this is a very common idiom). **τῆς ψυχῆς** is a genitive of comparison after **βέλτιον**. **οὐθέν** = οὐδέν; here is it used adverbially to reinforce **ὅλως**, with the overall meaning 'not at all'.

83.2

ἡ μέντοι χάρις ἐκείνη καὶ τὸ τῆς ὥρας ἰταμόν: 'however, that charm [of hers] and the vigour of her beauty'; **ὥρα** means 'fitting time' or 'season' and thus comes to mean 'prime of life', i.e. 'beauty'.

οὐ κατέσβεστο: 'had not been extinguished'; third singular pluperfect indicative passive of κατασβέννυμι (= 'I put out, quench'). The subject of the verb is both **ἡ χάρις** and **τὸ ἰταμόν**, but it has been attracted into the number of the latter (hence it is singular).

ἀλλὰ καίπερ οὕτως διακειμένης: 'but despite being in such a [bad] state'; διάκειμαι + adverb (here **οὕτως**) = 'I am in X state of mind/body.'

ἔνδοθέν ποθεν ἐξέλαμπε καὶ συνεπεφαίνετο τοῖς κινήμασι τοῦ προσώπου: 'they shone forth from somewhere within (literally, 'from within from somewhere') and appeared/were visible in the movements/emotions of her face'; the verbs are singular but refer to both Cleopatra's charm and her beauty (see above). **συνεπεφαίνετο** is third singular middle imperfect of συνεπιφαίνω and means 'I appear/am visible'. **τοῖς κινήμασι** could mean 'movements' or 'emotions': either works.

κατακλιθῆναι: aorist passive infinitive of κατακλίνω (= 'I make to lie down'; in the passive: 'I lie down').

καὶ πλησίον αὐτοῦ καθίσαντος: 'and having himself sat near [her]'; **πλησίον** is an adverb and **αὐτοῦ** is the subject of the participle **καθίσαντος** (which is being used intransitively, i.e. 'having sat down' rather than 'having made X sit down').

Are we to see Octavian's request that she should lie down whilst he sits as indicative of his admiration and/or compassion for Cleopatra? Or are we seeing a parallel between (Plutarch's perception of) her effect on Antony and on Octavian?

ἥψατο τινος δικαιολογίας εἰς ἀνάγκην καὶ φόβον Ἀντωνίου τὰ πεπραγμένα τρεπούσης: 'she began/undertook a sort of justification attributing events to necessity and fear of Antony'; **ἥψατο** = third singular aorist indicative middle of ἅπτομαι. ἅπτομαι + genitive generally means 'I lay hold of', but can sometimes (as here) mean 'I begin/undertake'. **τρεπούσης** (literally, 'turning/directing') agrees with **δικαιολογίας** ('justification'). **τὰ πεπραγμένα** = 'the events' (literally, 'the things having been done').

ἐνισταμένου δὲ πρὸς ἕκαστον αὐτῇ τοῦ Καίσαρος: 'when Caesar resisted her with regard to each [justification/point]'. ἐνίσταμαι + dative = 'I stand in the way, resist, block.'

ἐξελεγχομένη ταχὺ πρὸς οἶκτον μεθηρμόσατο καὶ δέησιν: 'being refuted/convicted, she quickly adapted herself, aiming for pity and using entreaties' (literally, 'towards pity and with entreaties'). **μεθηρμόσατο** = third singular aorist indicative middle of μεθαρμόζω which in the middle = 'I adopt new habits, adapt myself.' Pelling (p. 314) states that the language 'suggests a careful theatricality'.

ὡς δή τις ἂν μάλιστα τοῦ ζῆν περιεχομένη: 'as indeed anyone would [cling] if they were very much clinging to life'. περιέχομαι + genitive = 'I hold fast to, cling to'; **τοῦ ζῆν** is another example of the articular infinitive (see note on 76.3).

This is a future remote condition, but with a lot missed out: supply an optative verb (περιέχοιτο) after **ἄν**. (The full sentence would in fact be: περιεχομένη τοῦ ζῆν, ὡς δή τις περιέχοιτο ἄν, εἰ περιέχοιτο μάλιστα: 'clinging to life, as indeed anyone would cling, if one were to cling very much'). The use of a remote condition indicates that her desire to cling on to life is not genuine (in Plutarch's opinion, at least).

83.3

τέλος δὲ τοῦ πλήθους τῶν χρημάτων ἀναγραφὴν ἔχουσα προσέδωκεν αὐτῷ: literally, 'and finally, having a list/register of the size of her wealth, she gave it to him', i.e. 'and finally she gave him a list she had of the size of her wealth/treasures'.

ἐλέγχοντος ὡς ἔνια κρύπτουσαν καὶ διακλέπτουσαν: '(when Seleucus . . .) proved that she was hiding and stealing some of it away'. ἐλέγχω has a wide range of meanings, include 'refute', 'test' and 'prove'. It is here followed by **ὡς** + participle (literally, 'proving/convicting her *as* hiding . . .'). **ἔνια** is neuter plural; we need to supply τῶν χρημάτων (or similar) as a partitive genitive.

τῶν τριχῶν αὐτοῦ λαβομένη: 'grabbing him [Seleucus] by the hair'. λαμβάνομαι + genitive = I touch, grasp hold of; a literal translation would be 'grabbing his hair'. Pelling suggests that interpretation of this whole scene, particularly the Seleucus bit, is not straightforward: 'Possibly she is stage-managing the whole episode, *including Seleucus' intervention*, to fool Octavian into believing that she wishes to live . . . But neither Plutarch nor Shakespeare really makes the matter clear. We are simply left with a vague impression of skilful deception' (p. 314).

83.4

εἰ σὺ μὲν ἠξίωσας ἀφικέσθαι πρὸς ἐμὲ καὶ προσειπεῖν οὕτω πράττουσαν: 'when you have thought it right to come to me and to address me when I am in this state' (literally, 'faring thus'; πράσσω can mean 'I fare' + adverb). **ἠξίωσας** is second singular aorist indicative active of ἀξιόω (= 'I think/think it right'). Note this idiomatic translation of **εἰ** as 'when'.

οἱ δὲ δοῦλοί μου κατηγοροῦσιν εἴ τι τῶν γυναικείων ἀπεθέμην: 'my slaves accuse me of keeping back for myself (literally, 'if I kept back for myself') some of my women's things'. **εἴ** (literally, 'if') does not usually have an accent, but one has been thrown onto it by the enclitic **τι**. **ἀπεθέμην** is first singular aorist indicative middle of ἀποτίθημι = (in the middle) 'I put away from myself'. γυναικεῖος, -α, -ον = 'of a woman, womanly, feminine'; **τὰ γυνακεῖα** (here) = 'women's garments/items': further detail is not given.

οὐκ ἐμαυτῇ δήπουθεν, ἡ τάλαινα, κόσμον: 'not of course as an adornment for myself, wretched as I am'. **δήπουθεν** = δήπου = 'of course'.

ἀλλ' ὅπως Ὀκταουίᾳ καὶ Λιβίᾳ τῇ σῇ μικρὰ δοῦσα δι' ἐκείνων ἵλεώ σου τύχοιμι καὶ πρᾳοτέρου; 'but so that, having given some small gifts to Octavia and to your (wife) Livia, through them I might find you to be gentle and more mild?'. **ὅπως** introduces a purpose clause (+ optative **τύχοιμι**). **δοῦσα** is the aorist participle (feminine nominative singular) of δίδωμι (= I give). With **μικρά** supply a noun (items/gifts, etc). τυγχάνω + genitive = 'I get, obtain, meet with'; **ἵλεω** and **πρᾳοτέρου** are adjectives (the second a comparative); both are genitive, agreeing with **σου** (ἵλεως in the masculine/feminine declines as follows: ἵλεων [accusative], ἵλεω [genitive], ἵλεῳ [dative]).

Note the punctuation: this closes the question begun at the beginning of her direct speech (**"ἀλλ' οὐ δεινόν"** = 'but is it not terrible . . .?').

83.5

τούτοις ὁ Καῖσαρ ἥδετο: 'Caesar rejoiced at these words'; **ἥδετο** is third singular imperfect indicative active of ἥδομαι (+ dative = 'I enjoy, am pleased with').

παντάπασιν αὐτὴν φιλοψυχεῖν οἰόμενος: 'thinking her to be completely desirous of living'; indirect statement (infinitive construction).

εἰπὼν οὖν ὅτι καὶ ταῦτα ἐπιτρέπει καὶ τἆλλα πάσης ἐλπίδος αὐτῇ χρήσεται λαμπρότερον: 'and so, having said that he both entrusted these things to her and in all other matters he would treat her more splendidly than anything she could expect (literally, 'than all expectation')'. **χρήσεται** is third singular future indicative of χράομαι, which can mean 'I treat someone (+ dative; here = **αὐτῇ**) in a particular way'; it is here qualified by the comparative adverb **λαμπρότερον**.

τἆλλα = **τὰ ἄλλα** (by crasis; see on 76.3) = (literally) 'the other things', i.e. 'all else'. **τἆλλα** is very commonly used as an accusative of respect/adverbially: 'with respect to everything else'; also at 79.3.

ᾤχετο ἀπιών: literally, 'going away, he went away', so 'he left and went away'; **ἀπιών** is the present participle (masculine nominative singular) of ἄπειμι (= I shall go); **ᾤχετο** = third singular imperfect indicative active of οἴχομαι (= 'I have gone/departed/I go').

ἐξηπατηκέναι μὲν οἰόμενος, ἐξηπατημένος δὲ μᾶλλον: 'thinking that he had deceived [her], but rather having been deceived'. Note the polyptoton (on which device see note on 77.3) – **ἐξηπατηκέναι** (perfect infinitive active), and **ἐξηπατημένος** (perfect participle passive), both from ἐξαπατάω ('I deceive'): it emphasizes the irony of the situation, and Cleopatra's skill.

84.1

ἐπιφανὴς νεανίσκος: 'a young man of distinguished rank'. Cornelius Dolabella was a member of an important Roman patrician (aristocratic) family; little is known of him other than this episode.

οὗτος εἶχε πρὸς τὴν Κλεοπάτραν οὐκ ἀηδῶς: literally, 'he was not unpleasant towards Cleopatra', i.e. 'he felt warm towards Cleopatra' (the implication is certainly one of romantic sensibilities). On ἔχω + adverb = 'I am X,' see note on 83.1. **οὐκ ἀηδῶς** is an example of litotes (= an understatement in which something is stressed by negating the opposite: 'he was not unpleasant' = 'he felt positive about').

καὶ τότε χαριζόμενος αὐτῇ δεηθείσῃ κρύφα πέμψας ἐξήγγειλεν ὡς αὐτὸς μὲν ὁ Καῖσαρ ἀναζεύγνυσι πεζῇ διὰ Συρίας: literally, 'and at that time, showing kindness to her, having begged, (and he) having secretly sent (information), he reported that Caesar himself was preparing to march on foot through Syria', i.e. 'and at that time when she begged (for information), showing her kindness, he secretly sent news that Caesar himself was preparing to march on foot through Syria'. ἀναζεύγνυμι literally = 'I yoke/harness again', i.e. 'prepare to march/move off'. **δεηθείσῃ** (agreeing with **αὐτῇ**) is the aorist participle passive (feminine dative singular) from δέομαι (= 'I ask for, beg'); like many other middle verbs, this one has an aorist which is passive in form.

ἔγνωκεν: third singular perfect indicative active of γιγνώσκω, which can mean 'I form a judgement/decide/resolve. Remember that this is still within the indirect statement introduced by **ἐξήγγειλεν ὡς**, so the tense needs to be shifted back: 'he had resolved . . .'

ἐκείνην . . . μετὰ τῶν τέκνων ἀποστέλλειν εἰς τρίτην ἡμέραν: 'to send her away with her children on the third day'. Pelling clarifies that this means 'to Rome, for the triumph' (p. 316).

84.2

ἐδεήθη Καίσαρος ὅπως αὐτὴν ἐάσῃ χοὰς ἐπενεγκεῖν Ἀντωνίῳ: 'she begged Caesar to allow her to pour libations for Antony'. δέομαι is here followed by genitive of person begged and an indirect command. The indirect command uses the construction **ὅπως** + subjunctive. Over time, this started to replace the infinitive in indirect commands; we see it, for example, in the Greek of the New Testament. **ἐάσῃ** is third singular aorist subjunctive active of ἐάω. **ἐπενεγκεῖν** is the aorist infinitive active of ἐπιφέρω which literally = 'I throw/lay upon'.

Libations were ritual offerings made to a god, generally of a liquid (oil or unmixed wine). They were often used as part of Roman funerals and subsequent rituals aimed at soothing the spirits of the dead.

συγχωρήσαντος: 'when he had agreed'; genitive absolute (aorist participle active, masculine genitive singular from συγχωρέω = 'I agree, assent to'); supply αὐτοῦ.

περιπεσοῦσα τῇ σορῷ μετὰ τῶν συνήθων γυναικῶν: 'having embraced his coffin along with the women usually with her'. **περιπεσοῦσα** is the aorist participle active (feminine nominative singular) from περιπίπτω, which means 'I fall around', therefore 'I embrace' (+ dative).

ἔτι χερσὶν ἐλευθέραις: 'with hands which were still free'.

αἰχμάλωτος οὖσα: 'being a prisoner'.

φρουρουμένη μήτε κοπετοῖς μήτε θρήνοις αἰκίσασθαι τὸ δοῦλον τοῦτο σῶμα: 'and being kept under watch to prevent me from disfiguring this enslaved body either by lamentations or by tears'. **αἰκίσασθαι** is the aorist infinitive from αἰκίζομαι (= 'I injure, disfigure, maltreat'); the construction here is infinitive after a verb of hindering or preventing. **δοῦλον** is an adjective agreeing with **σῶμα. κοπετοῖς** indicates noises of lamentation, and thus the implication is of physical blows accompanied by sound.

καὶ τηρούμενον ἐπὶ τοὺς κατὰ σοῦ θριάμβους: 'and being guarded for the triumph over you'; **θριάμβους** is probably a poetic plural; on the triumph, see note on 78.3. **κατά** + genitive really means 'against'.

84.3

ἄλλας δὲ μὴ προσδέχου τιμὰς ἢ χοάς: 'do not expect other honours or libations'. **προσδέχου** is second singular present imperative from προσδέχομαι.

ἀλλ᾽ αὗταί σοι τελευταῖαι Κλεοπάτρας ἀγομένης: 'but these are the last for you from Cleopatra the captive' (literally, 'with Cleopatra being carried off'; **Κλεοπάτρας ἀγομένης** is a genitive absolute). **σοι** is an ethic dative (dative of interest). The third-person self-reference raises the register and emotional temperature, and adds to the theatricality of the scene.

ζῶντας μὲν γὰρ ἡμᾶς οὐθὲν ἀλλήλων διέστησε: 'for nothing separated us from each other while we were alive'; **οὐθέν** = οὐδέν (see on 83.1). **ἀλλήλων** is a genitive (of separation) after the verb **διέστησε** (third singular aorist indicative active of διίστημι = 'I set apart, separate X [accusative] from Y [genitive]').

κινδυνεύομεν δὲ τῷ θανάτῳ διαμείψασθαι τοὺς τόπους: 'but in death we are likely to change places', a common meaning of κινδυνεύω + infinitive. **διαμείψασθαι** = aorist infinitive middle of διαμείβω = I change, exchange (same meaning in active and middle).

σὺ μὲν ὁ Ῥωμαῖος ἐνταῦθα κείμενος, ἐγὼ δ᾽ ἡ δύστηνος ἐν Ἰταλίᾳ, τοσοῦτο τῆς σῆς μεταλαβοῦσα χώρας μόνον: 'you, a Roman, lying here, but I, the wretched one, (lying) in Italy, having gained only so much of your country in exchange'. The μετα- prefix on **μεταλαβοῦσα** (aorist participle from μεταλαμβάνω) generates a meaning of 'take something instead, gain something in exchange'.

84.4

ἀλλ᾽ εἰ δή τις τῶν ἐκεῖ θεῶν ἀλκὴ καὶ δύναμις: 'but if indeed there is any strength or power in the gods of Rome/Italy'. **τῶν ἐκεῖ θεῶν** literally = 'of the gods there' (possessive genitive).

οἱ γὰρ ἐνταῦθα προὔδωκαν ἡμᾶς: 'for the gods in Egypt have betrayed us'. **προὔδωκαν** is an aorist, but a translation as a perfect works better in English in the context. Note the idiomatic translation of **οἱ ἐνταῦθα** (which literally means 'those here').

μὴ πρόῃ ζῶσαν τὴν σεαυτοῦ γυναῖκα: 'do not abandon/betray your own wife while she is alive'. **πρόῃ** is second singular aorist subjunctive middle from προίημι (= 'I give up, deliver, betray, abandon'). **μή** + aorist subjunctive is used for a specific prohibition. Pelling notes that the use of **γυναῖκα** is striking: 'now a wife indeed . . . and it is death which makes her so' (p. 318).

μηδ᾽ ἐν ἐμοὶ περιΐδῃς θριαμβευόμενον σεαυτόν: 'and do not allow yourself to be triumphed over by means of me'. **ἐν** + dative [here] = 'by means of'. **περιΐδῃς** = second singular present subjunctive active of **περιοράω** (= 'I overlook, allow'). The two dots over the second iota indicates that this vowel is to be pronounced as a separate sound (i.e. the two iotas do not make a diphthong); this symbol is called a diaeresis. **θριαμβευόμενον** = present participle passive from θριαμβεύω (= 'I lead a triumph, triumph over').

κρύψον ... καὶ σύνθαψον: 'hide ... and bury together'; these are both aorist imperatives active (second singular).

μετὰ σεαυτοῦ: 'with you(rself)'; an emphatic form of μετὰ σοῦ.

ὡς ἐμοὶ μυρίων κακῶν ὄντων οὐδὲν οὕτω μέγα καὶ δεινόν ἐστιν ὡς ὁ βραχὺς οὗτος χρόνος ὃν σοῦ χωρὶς ἔζηκα: 'since of my countless evils, none is as great and terrible as this brief time which I have lived apart from you'. The first **ὡς** = 'since/because'; the second picks up **οὕτω**: 'as great and terrible as . . .' **ἔζηκα** = perfect indicative active (first singular) of ζάω.

85.1

The final two chapters deal with Cleopatra's death. As Pelling has noted, scholars ancient and modern have debated the method of Cleopatra's suicide, i.e. snakebite or poison (see Pelling, pp. 318–320 for a summary of the arguments): Plutarch gives us both versions in Chapter 86. Aside from the question of practicalities (i.e. poison would be easier), it seems almost too appropriate that Cleopatra should use the very creature with which Egyptian royalty was associated (all Egyptian royals wore snakes as part of their headdress), and which seems to link so clearly with her self-identification with the goddess Isis (with whom the snake is associated).

However, Pelling concludes that the snake-bite seems more plausible than any other method: 'Poison was less dignified and could be associated with Oriental witchcraft: that version might better have suited Octavian's propaganda, and if he spread the story of the asps, it may well be because it was essentially true' (pp. 319–20).

στέψασα καὶ κατασπασαμένη τὴν σορόν: 'having garlanded and embraced his coffin'. The first participle (aorist active from στέφω) suggests wreathing with flowers, the second (aorist participle middle from κατασπάζομαι) a human embrace.

ἐκέλευσεν αὑτῇ λουτρὸν γενέσθαι: 'she ordered a bath to be prepared for herself'. **αὑτῇ** = **ἑαυτῇ** (reflexive pronoun, feminine dative singular). In English, we need to expand on the basic meaning of **γενέσθαι** (hence 'to be prepared'). On this section, Pelling states: 'The bathing and robing of the body preceded real funerals, and sometimes in tragedy the motifs are applied to doomed living mortals: here, paradoxically, they seem appropriate rather than chilling' (p. 320).

κατακλιθεῖσα: 'having reclined'; aorist participle passive from κατακλίνω (which in the passive = 'I lie down/recline').

λαμπρὸν ἄριστον ἠρίστα: 'she ate a sumptuous meal'. **ἠρίστα** = third singular imperfect indicative active from ἀριστάω (= 'I eat a meal' [the ἄριστον, which means a midday meal in Greek of this period]).

τῶν δὲ φυλάκων ὅ τι φέροι πυνθανομένων: 'when the guards asked him what he was carrying': genitive absolute introducing an indirect question (with the indirect interrogative **ὅ τι** and an optative verb).

ἀνοίξας καὶ ἀφελὼν τὰ θρῖα σύκων ἐπίπλεων τὸ ἀγγεῖον ἔδειξε: 'having opened it (**ἀνοίξας**) and having removed (**ἀφελών**) the (fig)leaves (**τὰ θρῖα**), he showed (**ἔδειξε**) that the vessel/dish (**τὸ ἀγγεῖον**) was full (**ἐπίπλεων**) of figs (**σύκων**)'. **ἀνοίξας** = aorist participle (masculine nominative singular) from ἀνοίγνυμι (= 'I open'). **ἀφελών** = aorist participle active (masculine nominative singular) from ἀφαιρέω (= 'I take away from, remove'). **ἔδειξε** introduces either an indirect statement (for which a verb would need to be supplied in English) or a direct object ('he showed a vessel full of figs').

85.2

θαυμασάντων δὲ τὸ κάλλος καὶ τὸ μέγεθος: 'when they [the guards] had admired the beauty and size [of the figs]': genitive absolute.

μειδιάσας παρεκάλει: 'having smiled, he asked/encouraged . . .' – the man from the country is the subject of both the participle (**μειδιάσας**) and the main verb (**παρεκάλει**).

οἱ δὲ πιστεύσαντες ἐκέλευον εἰσενεγκεῖν: 'they, trusting him (literally, 'having trusted'), ordered him to bring them [i.e. the figs] in'. **εἰσενεγκεῖν** is the aorist infinitive active of εἰσφέρω.

δέλτον ἔχουσα γεγραμμένην καὶ κατασεσημασμένην: 'taking a (writing) tablet which had been written on and sealed up'. δέλτος is a second declension feminine noun. 'Taking' is a necessarily idiomatic translation of **ἔχουσα. γεγραμμένην** and **κατασεσημασμένην** are both perfect passive participles, the first from γράφω and the second from κατασημαίνω (= 'I seal up').

τοὺς ἄλλους ἐκποδὼν ποιησαμένη: 'sending away the rest' (literally, 'making the rest out of the way'). **ποιησαμένη** is an aorist participle middle (feminine nominative singular) of ποιέω.

πλὴν τῶν δυεῖν ἐκείνων γυναικῶν: 'except those two women'; **δυεῖν** is a dual form: it is used for two things/pairs. It appears more frequently in the Greek of certain periods and genres than others, and in general Greek prose will use the plural instead.

85.3

λύσας: [here] 'having opened'

ὡς ἐνέτυχε λιταῖς καὶ ὀλοφυρμοῖς δεομένης αὐτὴν σὺν Ἀντωνίῳ θάψαι: 'when he found entreaties and lamentations [i.e. of Cleopatra – understand αὐτῆς] begging (him) to bury her with Antony'.

συνῆκε τὸ πεπραγμένον: 'he perceived/understood what had happened'; third singular aorist indicative active of συνίημι. For **τὸ πεπραγμένον** see on 83.2.

τοὺς σκεψομένους κατὰ τάχος ἔπεμψεν: 'he sent men who would have a look at/investigate the situation with haste'. **τοὺς σκεψομένους** = definite article + future participle (which in effect creates a purpose clause). **κατὰ τάχος** = ταχύ = 'quickly, with haste'.

ἐγεγόνει δ᾽ ὀξὺ τὸ πάθος: 'but the suffering had been quick'. **ἐγεγόνει** = third singular pluperfect indicative active of γίγνομαι.

δρόμῳ γὰρ ἐλθόντες καὶ τοὺς μὲν φυλάττοντας οὐδὲν ᾐσθημένους καταλαβόντες, τὰς δὲ θύρας ἀνοίξαντες: 'for, having gone at a run and having found those guarding (Cleopatra) perceiving nothing, having opened the doors . . .' **ᾐσθημένους** is a perfect participle middle (masculine accusative plural) from αἰσθάνομαι: 'having perceived'.

The subject of the participles **ἐλθόντες, καταλαβόντες** and **ἀνοίξαντες** is the messengers sent by Octavian to investigate the situation (see above: **τοὺς σκεψομένους κατὰ τάχος ἔπεμψεν**).

εὗρον αὐτὴν τεθνηκυῖαν: 'they found her dead'. **τεθνηκυῖαν** = perfect participle active (feminine accusative singular) from (ἀπο)θνῄσκω.

ἐν χρυσῇ κατακειμένην κλίνῃ, κεκοσμημένην βασιλικῶς: 'lying on a golden couch, adorned/dressed in a royal manner': a noble and splendid sight. **κεκοσμημένην** is perfect participle passive (feminine accusative singular) from κοσμέω (= I adorn, embellish, dress).

85.4

πρὸς τοῖς ποσίν: 'at her feet'. **πρός** + dative = 'at, on, near'.

ἤδη σφαλλομένη καὶ καρηβαροῦσα: 'by now/already staggering and drowsy'. σφάλλω = 'I make to fall, overthrow, trip up'. The present participle passive **σφαλλόμενος** can have the meaning 'reeling, staggering', as of someone drunk or ill.

κατεκόσμει τὸ διάδημα τὸ περὶ τὴν κεφαλὴν αὐτῆς: 'was trying to arrange the crown around her [Cleopatra's] head'. **κατεκόσμει** is third singular imperfect indicative active of **κατακοσμέω**; the imperfect tense can be used, as here, in a conative sense ('trying to . . .').

On these two loyal companions, Iras and Charmion, Pelling notes: 'only now are they named, when their role is most moving' (p. 320).

Καλὰ ταῦτα, Χάρμιον: 'A fine deed, this, Charmion!' (Perrin). Pelling notes that the language is colloquial; moreover, the statement is ironic (p. 321).

Κάλλιστα μὲν οὖν: 'indeed, it is *very* fine'. **μὲν οὖν** corrects **καλά** and replaces it with the superlative **κάλλιστα** (Pelling, p. 321).

πρέποντα τῇ τοσούτων ἀπογόνῳ βασιλέων: 'befitting/appropriate for the descendant of so many kings'. **πρέποντα** is the present participle (nominative neuter plural, referring back to ταῦτα) of πρέπει (+ dative = 'it befits').

πλέον: 'more' (neuter accusative singular from πλέων, which is the comparative of πολύς).

αὐτοῦ: here an adverb meaning 'just there'.

86.1

Λέγεται δὲ τὴν ἀσπίδα κομισθῆναι σὺν τοῖς σύκοις ἐκείνοις καὶ τοῖς θρίοις ἄνωθεν ἐπικαλυφθεῖσαν: 'it is said that the asp was brought in/conveyed with those figs and the leaves, covered up beneath them'. **Λέγεται** introduces an indirect statement (but here with the infinitive construction rather than the expected ὅτι – this is standard after the impersonal use of the passive). The passive indicates a degree of uncertainty regarding the manner of Cleopatra's death, an uncertainty shared by our other main source (Cassius Dio), and reflected in differences between Plutarch/Dio and earlier sources (Virgil, Horace and Propertius). **τὴν ἀσπίδα** here means 'asp/Egyptian cobra'. **ἄνωθεν** = 'on high/above/from above'. **ἄνωθεν ἐπικαλυφθεῖσαν** = 'covered from above', which can be translated as 'hidden beneath'. **ἐπικαλυφθεῖσαν** is aorist participle passive (feminine accusative singular) from **ἐπικαλύπτω** (= 'I cover over').

οὕτω γὰρ τὴν Κλεοπάτραν κελεῦσαι, μηδὲ αὐτῆς ἐπισταμένης τῷ σώματι προσπεσεῖν τὸ θηρίον: 'for thus Cleopatra had ordered [refers to the previous clause], and (it is said that) the creature had attached itself to her body with her being unaware (**μηδὲ αὐτῆς ἐπισταμένης**: genitive absolute)'. Note that the indirect statement (infinitive construction) continues (**τὴν Κλεοπάτραν κελεῦσαι** and **προσπεσεῖν τὸ θηρίον**). **προσπίπτω** + dative = (here) 'I fasten myself to'.

Ἐνταῦθα ἦν ἄρα τοῦτο: 'So here it was all along' (Pelling), or 'There it is, you see' (Perrin). **τοῦτο** refers to the snake; **ἄρα** is a particle often translated as 'then', or 'so, then, in that case'.

καὶ τὸν βραχίονα παρασχεῖν τῷ δήγματι γυμνώσασαν: 'and (it is said that) exposing/laying bare her arm, she held it out for the bite'. **τὴν Κλεοπάτραν** is the accusative subject of this continuing indirect statement.

86.2

οἱ δὲ τηρεῖσθαι μὲν ἐν ὑδρίᾳ τὴν ἀσπίδα καθειργμένην φάσκουσιν: 'others allege/say that the snake was guarded carefully, shut up in a water jar'. **φάσκουσιν** again introduces an indirect statement (infinitive construction). τηρέω (of which **τηρεῖσθαι** is the present passive infinitive) has a sense of 'I watch over with care, guard carefully.'

ἠλακάτῃ δέ τινι χρυσῇ τῆς Κλεοπάτρας ἐκκαλουμένης αὐτὴν καὶ διαγριαινούσης ὁρμήσασαν ἐμφῦναι τῷ βραχίονι: 'and that while Cleopatra was provoking and making it [**αὐτήν**] angry with a golden distaff [genitive absolute;], having jumped up, it bit her arm' . A distaff is a stick/tool used in spinning (wool is wound onto it). ἐκκαλέω in the middle can mean 'I provoke'. διαγριαίνω is a strengthened form of ἀγριαίνω = 'I make angry, provoke'. **ἐμφῦναι** is aorist infinitive active from ἐμφύω which in the middle means 'I bite/clasp/cling fast to'; note that this middle has some (intransitive) active forms (perfect: ἐμπέφυκα; aorist: ἐνέφυν; root aorist infinitive: ἐμφῦναι)

ἐπεὶ καὶ . . . ἐλέχθη: 'for/since it was also said', with the (aorist) passive **ἐλέχθη** again introducing a series of indirect statements with the infinitive construction. **καί** is adverbial.

πλὴν οὔτε κηλὶς ἐξήνθησε τοῦ σώματος οὔτε ἄλλο φαρμάκου σημεῖον: 'except neither a spot/stain nor another sign of poison broke out/blistered on her body'. **πλήν** is in this instance an adverb rather than a preposition. The genitive **τοῦ σώματος** is governed by the prefix in **ἐξήνθησε**, which is third singular aorist indicative active from ἐξανθέω (= 'I put out flowers'; therefore, metaphorically, 'I burst forth/break out').

86.3

οὐ μὴν οὐδὲ τὸ θηρίον ἐντὸς ὤφθη: 'moreover, the creature was never seen within [her chamber]'. **οὐ μὴν οὐδέ** = 'certainly not either' (but I have translated it as 'moreover . . . never'); **μήν** is a particle used to strengthen statements.

συρμοὺς δέ τινας αὐτοῦ παρὰ θάλασσαν . . . ἰδεῖν ἔφασκον: 'but people said they saw some traces of it near the sea'.

ᾗ τὸ δωμάτιον ἀφεώρα καὶ θυρίδες ἦσαν: 'where her chamber looked out upon it [the sea] and there were windows'. **ᾗ** is the dative feminine singular of the relative pronoun, used here (as often) as an adverb to mean 'where/which way'. **ἀφεώρα** is third singular imperfect indicative active from **ἀφοράω** (= 'I look out over, look towards').

ἔνιοι δὲ καί: 'and some also say': supply φάσκουσι (introducing another indirect statement with infinitive).

τὸν βραχίονα τῆς Κλεοπάτρας ὀφθῆναι δύο νυγμὰς ἔχοντα λεπτὰς καὶ ἀμυδράς: 'that Cleopatra's arm was seen to have two small/slight and faint dots/marks' **ὀφθῆναι** introduces an indirect statement with participle.

οἷς ἔοικε πιστεῦσαι καὶ ὁ Καῖσαρ: 'which Caesar seems also to have believed'. **οἷς** is a connecting relative, dative (after **πιστεῦσαι**) neuter plural, meaning 'which things'. **ἔοικε** is usually used impersonally ('it seems'), but here is used with a personal subject (**ὁ Καῖσαρ**).

τῆς Κλεοπάτρας αὐτῆς εἴδωλον . . . καὶ τῆς ἀσπίδος ἐμπεφυκυίας: 'an image of Cleopatra herself and the snake clinging [to her]'.

86.4

καίπερ ἀχθεσθεὶς ἐπί: 'despite grieving at/with respect to': **ἀχθεσθείς** is the aorist participle of ἄχθομαι (= 'I am vexed, grieved'; literally = 'I am burdened').

ἐντίμου δὲ καὶ τὰ γύναια κηδείας ἔτυχεν αὐτοῦ προστάξαντος: 'her women also obtained an honourable funeral (**ἐντίμου . . . κηδείας**) by his orders (**αὐτοῦ προστάξαντος**)'. ἔντιμος (= 'honoured/honourable') is a two-termination adjective (see on 83.1). τὸ γύναιον, -ου is a diminutive form of γυνή. [NTS: please ensure that hyphen with a space *before* it is on the same line as the word it is attached to, e.g. here: -ου]

ἐτελεύτησε δὲ Κλεοπάτρα μὲν ἑνὸς δέοντα τεσσαράκοντα ἔτη βιώσασα: literally, 'Cleopatra died having lived forty years [accusative of duration of time] lacking one', i.e. 'Cleopatra died at the age of thirty-nine.' δέων, -ον + genitive = 'lacking' (it is an adjective formed from the verb δέω [+ genitive] = 'I lack').

συνάρξασα δὲ Ἀντωνίῳ πλείω τῶν δεκατεσσάρων: 'having ruled jointly with Antony for more than fourteen'.

86.5

Ἀντώνιον δὲ οἱ μὲν ἕξ, οἱ δὲ τρισὶ τὰ πεντήκοντα ὑπερβαλεῖν φασιν: 'some say Antony was [literally, 'had crossed/gone beyond'] fifty-six years old, others that he was fifty-three'. Supply ἐτή with **τὰ πεντήκοντα.**

καθηρέθησαν: 'were demolished'; third plural aorist passive from καθαιρέω (= 'I take down, raze to the ground, demolish').

κατὰ χώραν: 'throughout the country'.

δόντος: aorist participle (genitive masculine singular) from δίδωμι, agreeing with **Ἀρχιβίου.**

δισχίλια τάλαντα: 'two thousand talents'.

ἵνα μὴ τὸ αὐτὸ ταῖς Ἀντωνίου πάθωσιν: 'in order that they might not suffer the same as those of Antony'. **ταῖς** refers to the statues (supply εἰκόσιν); when **αὐτός** = 'the same as' it is followed by the dative. **πάθωσιν** is third plural aorist subjunctive active of πάσχω.

Vocabulary

While there is no Defined Vocabulary List for A Level, words in the OCR Defined Vocabulary List for AS are marked with * so that students can quickly see the vocabulary with which they should be particularly familiar.

***ἀγαθός, -ή, -όν** (compar. **βελτίων, -ον**)	good
ἀγαπάω	I greet with affection, welcome
ἀγγεῖον, -ου, neut.	vessel, dish
***ἀγγέλλω** (aor. **ἤγγειλα**)	I announce
ἀγεννῶς	sordidly, ignobly
***ἀγρός, -οῦ**, m.	field, countryside
***ἄγω**	I lead, bring, carry, carry off
***ἀγών, -ῶνος**, m.	contest, trial
ἀδιάλλακτος, -ον	irreconcilable
***ἀδικέω**	I wrong, injure (someone)
***ἀεί**	always
ἀηδῶς	unpleasantly
Αἰθιοπία, -ας, f.	Ethiopia
αἰκία, -ας, f.	torture, torments, assault, suffering
αἰκίζομαι (aor. inf. mid. **αἰκίσασθαι**)	I disfigure, maltreat, injure
***αἷμα, -ατος**, neut.	blood
αἱμάσσω (perf. pass. ppl. **ᾑμαγμένος**)	I make bloody, stain with blood
***αἴρω** (aor. inf. mid. **ἄρασθαι**)	I raise, lift (same meaning in the mid.)
***αἰτέω**	I ask for (same meaning in the mid.)
***αἰτία, -ας**, f.	cause, charge, blame
***αἰχμάλωτος, -ου**, m./f.	prisoner, prisoner of war
Ἀκαδήμεια, -ας, f.	the Academy (school of philosophy)
***ἀκούω** + gen.	I hear, listen
ἀκώλυτος, -ον	unhindered
Ἀλέξανδρος, -ου, m.	Alexander (the Great)
***ἀληθής, -ές**	true (**τὸ ἀληθές** = the truth)
ἀλκή, -ῆς, f.	strength
***ἀλλά**	but
***ἀλλήλους**	each other
***ἄλλος, -η, -ον**	other, another
***ἅμα**	(prep. + dat.) at the same time as, together with; (adv.) at the same time, at once
ἀμυδρός, -ά, -όν	faint, weak
***ἀμφότερος, -α, -ον**	both
***ἄν** (= **ἐάν**)	if
ἀναβαίνω (aor. ppl. **ἀναβάς**)	I mount, go up, ascend
***ἀναγιγνώσκω** (imperf. **ἀνεγίνωσκον**)	I read aloud
ἀνακράζω (aor. ppl. **ἀναγκραγών**)	I cry out, shout
***ἀνάγκη, -ης**, f.	necessity
***ἀνάγομαι**	I put to sea
ἀναγραφή, -ῆς, f.	list, register
ἀναζεύγνυμι	I yoke/harness again, i.e. I prepare to march/move off
ἀναιρέω (aor. inf. **ἀνελεῖν**)	I kill
ἀναλαμβάνω	I take/pull up; recover, regain
ἀναμάττω	I rub/wipe
ἀναπείθω (aor. **ἀνέπεισα**)	I persuade, convince
ἀναπηδάω	I spring up, leap up
ἀνασταυρόω (aor. pass. **ἀνεσταυρώθην**)	I crucify
ἀναφθέγγομαι	I call out aloud

ἀναφλεγμαίνω (ἀνεφλέγμηνε = 3rd sing. aor.)	I become inflamed (intrans.)
***ἀναχωρέω**	I retreat, withdraw
ἄνωθεν	from above, on high
ἀνέλκω (imperf. **ἀνεῖλκον**)	I draw up, drag up
ἀνέχω	I hold up, lift up
***ἀνήρ, ἀνδρός**, m.	man, husband
***ἄνθρωπος, -ου**, m.	person, man
ἀνίσταμαι (root aor. inf. **ἀναστῆναι**)	I get up, rise (root aor. inf. = 'to get up/get oneself up')
ἀνοίγνυμι (aor. **ἀνέῳξα**)	I open
ἀντασπάζομαι	I greet in turn
ἀντίπρῳρος, -ον	ready for action, 'with the prow forwards'
Ἄντυλλος, -ου, m.	Antyllus (Antony's son)
Ἀντώνιος, -ου, m.	Mark Antony
***ἀξιόω**	I think, think fit, demand
ἀπαλλάσσω (aor. inf. **ἀπαλλάξαι**)	I set free
ἀπαγγέλλω (fut. **ἀπαγγελῶ**)	I report, report back to
ἀπαιτέω	I demand (in payment)
ἀπειλή, -ῆς, f.	threat
ἄπειμι	I will go away, depart (**ἀπιών** = 'going away' [pres. ppl.])
ἀπελεύθερος, -ου, m.	freedman
***ἀπέχω** (fut. ppl. mid. **ἀφεξομένος**)	I am distant; I refrain/abstain from (+ gen.)
ἄπιστος, -ον	faithless, untrustworthy
***ἀπό** + gen.	from
ἀπόγονος, -ον	born, descended from; as a n.: descendant
***ἀποθνῄσκω** (aor. **ἀπέθανον;** perf. **τέθνηκα**)	I die; I am killed/put to death
ἀποδακρύω	I lament loudly, weep much for
ἀπολείπω	I leave, quit
ἀποκλείω (perf. pass. ppl. **ἀποκεκλειμένος**)	I shut off/up/close
ἀπόκρισις, -εως, f.	answer
ἀποκρύπτω	I hide, conceal
***ἀποκτείνω** (aor. **ἀπέκτεινα**)	I kill
ἀπολύω	I release
ἀπόνοια, -ας, f.	madness, desperation
ἀποστέλλω	I send off/away, dispatch
ἀποστρέφω	I turn away
ἀποτίθημι (aor. mid. **ἀπεθέμην**)	I stow away, put away; mid.: I put away for myself
ἀποτέμνω (aor. **ἀπέτεμον**)	I cut off, sever
***ἅπτομαι** + gen.	I begin, undertake (lit. 'I touch')
***ἄρα**	. . . then . . . (part.)
Ἄρειος, -ου, m.	Areius (a Stoic and friend of Octavian)
ἀριστάω	I eat a meal (the **ἄριστον**)
ἄριστον, -ου, neut.	a meal (taken at midday)
ἀρνέομαι (aor. **ἠρνησάμην**)	I deny
Ἀρχιβίος, -ου, m.	Archibius (friend of Cleopatra)
ἀσπάζομαι	I greet, salute
***ἀσπίς -ίδος**, f.	asp, Egyptian cobra
***αὐτίκα**	at once
***αὐτός, -ή, -ό**	himself; same; (acc.: him, her, it, them, etc.)
αὐτοκράτωρ, -ορος, m.	ruler, general
αὐτοῦ	just there (adv.)
ἀφαιρέω (aor. **ἄφειλον;** perf. **ἀφῄρηκα)**	I take away from; mid.: take away for oneself (both + acc. of thing, gen. of person)
ἀφίημι (pres. inf. **ἀφιέναι;** aor. **ἀφῆκα**)	I let fall; I acquit X (acc.) of Y (gen.)
***ἀφικνέομαι** (fut. **ἀφίξομαι;** aor. **ἀφικόμην**)	I arrive
***ἀφίσταμαι** (aor. ppl. **ἀποστάς**)	I withdraw
ἀφοράω	I look out over, look towards
ἄχθομαι (aor. ppl. **ἀχθεσθείς**)	I am grieved, vexed
ἄχρι οὗ	until (temporal conj.)
***βασιλεύς, -έως**, m.	king
βασιλεία, -ας, f.	kingdom
βασιλεύω	I rule, reign
βασιλικῶς	in a royal manner
βδελύττομαι	I feel a loathing at

βελτίων, -ον (gen. **-ονος**) better (compar. of **ἀγαθός**)
βῆμα, -ατος, neut. tribunal, platform
βιόω (aor. **ἐβίωσα**) I live
***βοηθέω** + dat. I help, came to help
***βουλεύω/βουλεύομαι** I discuss, plan, consider, deliberate
***βούλομαι** I wish
βραχίων, -ονος, m. arm
βραχύς, -εῖα, -ύ short, brief

Γάλλος, -ου, m. Gallus
***γάρ** for
***γίγνομαι** (aor. **ἐγένομην**; perf. inf. **γεγονέναι**) I become, happen, occur
***γιγνώσκω** (aor. **ἔγνων**) I (get to) know, realize, understand; resolve, determine
γραμματεύς, -έως, m. secretary
***γράφω** (perf. ppl. pass. **γεγραμμένος**) I write, draw
γυμνάσιον, -ου, m. gymnasium
γυμνόω I expose, lay bare
γύναιον, -ου, neut. woman (dim. of **γυνή**)
γυνακεῖα, -ῶν, neut. plur. women's items/garments
***γυνή, γυναικός**, f. woman, wife

***δέ** and, but
δέησις, -εως, f. entreaty
***δεῖ** + acc. it is necessary
***δείκνυμι** (aor. **ἔδειξα**) I show, present
***δεινός, -ή, -όν** terrible, clever, strange
δεκατέσσαρες, -α fourteen
δέλτος, -ου, f. tablet, writing tablet
***δεξιά, -ᾶς**, f. right hand
***δέομαι** (aor. **ἐδεήθην**) I lack, need (+ gen.)/I beg for X (gen.) from Y (gen.), ask for, want
δέων, -ον + gen. lacking (adj. formed from the verb **δέω** = I lack + gen.)
δέος, -ους, neut. fear, alarm
Δερκεταῖος, -ου, m. Dercetaeus (one of Antony's bodyguards)
***δεσμός, -οῦ**, m. bond, chain, fetter
***δεσπότης, -ου**, m. master
δεύτερος, -α, -ον second
***δέχομαι** (aor. **ἐδέξαμην**) I receive, welcome
***δή** indeed [emphasizes preceding word]
δῆγμα, -ατος, neut. bite, sting
***δήπου** of course
δήπουθεν = δήπου of course
***δῆμος, -ου**, m. people, community
***διά** + acc. on account of, because of
***διά** + gen. through
διαβάλλω I slander
διαγριαίνω I make angry, provoke
διάδημα, -ατος, neut. crown, diadem
διάκειμαι I am in X state of mind/body (+ adv.)
διακλέπτω I hide/steal away (trans.)
***διαλέγομαι** (aor. **διελέχθην**) I converse
διαλείπω I leave an interval of time
διαμείβω change, exchange (same meaning in mid.)
δίδωμι (aor. ppl. **δούς, δοῦσα, δόν**) I give
διαπρεπῶς magnificently
διαστέλλω I separate, set apart
δίαιτα, -ας, f. way of life
διέξοδος, -ου, f. passage, outlet
διίημι (aor. **διῆκα**) I let X go, pardon, dismiss
διίστημι (aor. **διέστησα**) I set apart, separate X (acc.) from Y (gen.)
δικαιολογία, -ας, f. plea, justification
***δίκαιος, -α, -ον** upright, just, fair
διό/διὸ καί wherefore, on which account, therefore
Διομήδης, -εος, m. Diomedes
δισχίλιοι, -αι, -α two thousand
διψάω I am thirsty
***δοκέω** I seem, think (**δοκεῖ** = it seems)
δορυφόρος, -ου, m. bodyguard (sing.)
***δόξα, -ης**, f. glory, opinion
δοῦλος, -η, -ον slavish, servile, enslaved
***δρόμος, -ου**, m. flight, run
***δύναμαι** (aor. pass. **ἐδυνήθην**) I can
***δύναμις, -εως**, f. power, capacity
δύο two
δυσθανατέω I struggle against death
δύστηνος, -ον wretched, unhappy, unfortunate

δωμάτιον, -ου, neut.	chamber, bedchamber
***ἑαυτόν/αὑτόν** (acc.: **ἑαυτήν/αὑτήν**, etc.)	himself (herself)
***ἐάω**	I allow
***ἐγγύς**	near (adv. or prep. + gen.)
ἐγτυχάνω (ἐνέτυχον)	I light upon, find (+ dat.)
ἐγχειρίδιον, -ου, neut.	dagger
***ἐγώ/ἔγωγε** (acc.: **με/ἐμέ**; gen.: **μου/ἐμοῦ**; dat.: **μοι/ἐμοί**)	I
***ἐθέλω**	I am willing, wish
***εἰ**	if
εἴδωλον, -ου, neut.	image
εἴκοσι	twenty
εἰκών, -όνος, f.	statue, image
***εἰμί**	I am
Εἰράς, [-άδος,] f.	Iras (attendant of Cleopatra)
***εἰς** + acc.	into, to
εἷς, μία, ἕν	one
εἰσελαύνω	I drive in
εἰσέρχομαι (aor. **εἰσῆλθον**)	I go/come in, enter
εἰσποιέω	I put in, add
εἰσφέρω (aor. inf. act. **εἰσενεγκεῖν**)	I bring in
εἶτα	then, afterwards
***εἴτε . . . εἴτε . . .**	whether . . . or . . .
***ἐκ/ἐξ** + gen.	out of, from; as a result of
ἐκδίδωμι (perf. ppl. act. **ἐκδεδωκώς**)	I publish
***ἐκεῖ**	there
***ἐκεῖνος, -η, -ο**	that; he, she, it
ἐκκαλέομαι	I call out to myself; I provoke
ἐκλάμπω	I shine
ἐκπέμπω	I send away
ἐκπλήσσω (perf. ppl. pass. **ἐκπεπληγμένος**)	I drive out of one's senses, amaze, shock
ἐκποδών	out of the way, away (adv.)
ἐκσείω (aor. **ἐξέσεισα**)	I shake out
ἐλέγχω	I refute; I prove, bring convincing proof
ἐλευθέριος, -α, -ον	free-spirited
***ἐλεύθερος, -α, -ον**	free
ἑλκόω (**ἥλκωτο** = 3rd sing. pluperf. indic. mid.)	I wound, lacerate, ulcerate
***ἕλκω** (imperf. **εἷλκον**)	I drag
ἐλπίς, -ίδος, f.	hope, expectation
ἐμαυτόν/ήν (gen. **-οῦ/ῆς**; dat.: **-ῷ/ῇ**)	myself
ἐμφορέω	I inflict X (acc.) on Y (dat.)
ἐμφύομαι (perf. ppl. **ἐμπεφυκώς, -υῖα, -ός**; aor. inf. **ἐμφῦναι**)	I cling closely (the form of this v. in Greek varies: mid. in pres.; intrans. act. in perf. and aor.)
***ἐν** + dat.	in, on; among; by means of
ἐνάπτω	I bind/fit on
ἐνδίδωμι (perf. ppl. **ἐνδεδωκώς**)	I allow/concede, give way to; give
ἔνδοθεν	from within
ἐνδοτέρω (adv.) + gen.	further into
***ἔνιοι, -αι, -α**	some
ἐνίσταμαι + dat.	I stand in the way, resist, block
***ἐνταῦθα**	here/there/then
ἔντιμος, -ον	honoured, honourable
ἐντός	within, inside (adv. or prep. + gen.)
***ἐντυγχάνω** + dat. (fut. ppl. **ἐντευξόμενος**)	I meet with/converse with, interview
ἕξ	six
ἐξ ἐπιδρομῆς	on the spur of the moment, off the cuff, *extempore*
ἐξαγγέλλω	I proclaim, announce
ἐξαγριόω	I make wild (pass.: I am made wild)
ἐξαιτέομαι	I gain/seek pardon for
ἐξανθέω	I burst forth, break out
***ἐξαπατάω** (perf. inf. act. **ἐξηπατηκέναι;** perf. ppl. pass. **ἐξηπατημένος**)	I deceive
ἐξελέγχω	I refute, confute, convict
***ἔξεστι** (sometimes **ἔστι**) + dat.	it is allowed, is possible
ἐξόπισθεν	from behind
ἔξωθεν	from outside (adv.)
ἔοικε(ν)	he/she/it seems (here with a pers. subj.; it is generally used impers.)
***ἐπανέρχομαι** (aor. **ἐπανῆλθον**)	I return
Ἐπαφρόδιτος, -ου, m.	Epaphroditus

***ἐπεί**	since, when
***ἔπειτα, εἶτα**	then, afterwards
***ἐπί** + acc.	on; onto, to, towards, against; for, in quest of
***ἐπί** + gen.	on
***ἐπί** + dat.	over; for; at; with respect to
ἐπίδειξις, -εως, f.	demonstration, exhibition, display
ἐπικαλύπτω	I cover over
ἐπικελεύομαι	(mid.) I cheer, exhort, encourage
ἐπιλαμβάνω	I lay hold of, seize
***ἐπιλανθάνομαι** (pluperf. **ἐπελελήσμην**) + gen.	I forget
ἐπιμελέομαι	I have charge of, take care of
ἐπίπεδος, -ον	on the ground/ground floor
ἐπιπλέω	I sail against/upon, attack by sea
ἐπίπλεος, -ον	(quite) full of
***ἐπιστολή, -ῆς**, f.	letter
ἐπισφάζω (inf. **ἐπισφάττειν**)	I strike the death blow
ἐπίτηδες	(adv.) on purpose; cunningly, deceitfully
***ἐπιτρέπω**	I entrust, commit, refer something to someone
ἐπίτροπος, -ου, m.	steward, administrator
ἐπιφανής, -ές	conspicuous, distinguished/ coming to light, in full view
ἐπιφέρω (aor. inf. act. **ἐπενεγκεῖν**)	I throw/lay upon, impose
***ἔργον, -ου**, neut.	work, deed, task, action
***ἔρχομαι** (aor. **ἦλθον**)	I go, come
ἐσθής, -ῆτος, f.	clothes, clothing
***ἑταῖρος, -ου**, m.	companion
***ἕτερος, -α, -ον**	one of two, the other
***ἔτι**	still, yet
***ἔτος, -ους**, neut.	year
εὐγένεια, -ας, f.	nobility
εὐγνώμων, -ον (gen. **-ονος**)	reasonable, sensible
εὐθυθάνατος, -ον	quick-killing, mortal
***εὐθύς**	at once, immediately
***εὑρίσκω** (aor. **εὗρον**)	I find
εὐψυχία, -ας, f.	(good) courage
***ἔχω**	I have, hold; + adv. = be
***ζάω** (pres. inf. **ζῆν**; perf. **ἔζηκα**)	I live
ζωγρέω	I take alive, take captive
ζώνη, -ης, f.	belt
***ἤ / ἤ . . . ἤ . . .**	than; or/either . . . or . . .
ᾗ	where (adv.)
***ἡγεμών, -όνος**, m.	leader, guide
***ἡγέομαι**	I think, believe
***ἤδη**	(by) now, already
***ἥδομαι**	I enjoy, am glad, am pleased with (+ dat.)
***ἡδύς, -εῖα, -ύ** (superl. **ἥδιστος**)	pleasant, sweet
***ἥκω** (imperf. **ἧκον**)	I have come
ἠλακάτη, -ης, f.	distaff
***ἡμεῖς** (acc.: **ἡμᾶς**, etc.)	we
***ἡμέρα, -ας**, f.	day, daybreak
***ἅμ' ἡμέρᾳ**	at daybreak
ἤν (= **ἐάν**)	if
ἡσσάομαι (aor. **ἡττήθην**)	I am defeated
***ἡσυχάζω**	I am calm, am quiet
***θάλασσα, -ης**, f.	sea
***θάνατος, -ου**, m.	death
***θάπτω** (aor. pass. inf. **ταφῆναι**)	I bury
***θαρρέω**	I have confidence/ trust, I am of good courage
***θαυμάζω**	I am amazed, admire
***θεάομαι** (aor. ppl. **θεασάμενος**)	I look at, behold
θέαμα, -ατος, neut.	sight, spectacle
Θεοδώρος, -ου, m.	Theodorus (tutor to Antyllus, Antony's son)
***θεραπεύω**	I care for
***θηρίον, -ου**, neut.	wild beast, creature
θρῆνος, -ου, m.	dirge, lament, complaint
θρηνέω	I bewail, lament
θριαμβεύω	I lead in triumph, triumph over

θρίαμβος, -ου, m.	triumph
θρῖον, -ου, neut.	fig leaf
θρίξ, τριχός, f.	hair
***θύρα, -ας**, f.	door
θυρίς, -ίδος, f.	window
***θώραξ, -ακος**, m.	breastplate
***ἰατρός, -οῦ**, m.	doctor
ἱδρύω	I establish, settle, encamp (an army)
***ἱκανός, -ή, -όν**	sufficient; capable
ἵλεως, ἵλεων	gracious, kindly, gentle
ἱμάτιον, -ου, neut.	cloak
***ἵνα**	so that, in order to (+ subjunc./opt.)
Ἰνδικός, -ή, -όν	Indian
***ἱππεύς, -έως**, m.	cavalryman, (plur.) the cavalry
ἱστορία, -ας, f.	written account, history, inquiry
***ἰσχυρός, -ά, -όν**	strong
ἰσχύω	I am strong, I am powerful/prevail
ἰταμόν, -οῦ, neut.	vigour
καθαιρέσις, -εως, f.	reduction (of body), i.e. killing, death
καθαιρέω (aor. pass. **καθῃρέθην**)	I take down, raze to the ground, demolish
καθάπερ	just as, just like, as if (adv.)
***καθίζω**	trans.: I make to sit down; intrans.: I sit down
καθίημι (imperf. **καθίην**; aor. ppl. act. **καθείς**)	I send down/let fall; I let a beard grow long
καθοράω (aor. **καθεῖδον**)	I behold, observe, survey
***καί**	and, even, also, actually
καί . . . καί . . .	both . . . and . . .
***καίπερ**	although, despite
Καῖσαρ, -αρος, m.	Caesar (in this text = Octavian)
Καισαρίων, -ωνος, m.	Caesarion (son of Julius Caesar and Cleopatra)
***κακός, -ή, -όν**	bad, cowardly, wicked
***καλέω**	I call, summon
κάλλος, -ους, neut.	beauty
***καλός, -ή, -όν**	fine, beautiful, handsome
καλώδιον, -ου, neut.	small cord
καρηβαρέω	I am heavy in the head, drowsy
καρτερός, -ά, -όν	strong
***κατά** + acc.	in the region of/by; throughout
κατά + gen.	against, over
καταβαίνω	I go down
κατάγω	I lead, bring home
κατάκειμαι	I lie down
κατακλίνω (aor. pass. **κατεκλίθην**)	I lay down (i.e. I make X lie down); pass.: I lie down
κατακοσμέω	I set in order, arrange
καταλαμβάνω	I seize; seize with the mind, comprehend
καταπαύω	I put an end to, stop
καταρράκτης, -ου, m.	trap-door, defence in front of a door; here = portcullis
καταρράπτω	I sew/stich on/over
κατασβέννυμι	I put out, quench
κατασημαίνω (perf. ppl. pass. **κατασεσημασμένος**)	I seal up
κατασπάζομαι (aor. **κατεσπάσαμην**)	I embrace, kiss
κατατείνω	I stretch out, strain
καταφανής, -ές	clearly seen, manifest, evident
καταφεύγω	I flee for refuge
κατείργω (perf. ppl. pass. **καθειργμένος**)	I shut up in, shut into
***κατηγορέω** + gen.	I accuse, denounce
***κεῖμαι**	I lie; I am situated
***κελεύω** (aor. pass. **ἐκελεύσθην**)	I order
***κεφαλή, -ῆς**, f.	head
κηδεία, -ας, f.	funeral, care for the dead
κηδεστής, -οῦ, m.	relation by marriage (e.g. at 78.2, brother-in-law)
κηλίς, -ῖδος, f.	stain, spot, blemish
***κινδυνεύω**	I risk; I am likely to
κίνημα, -ατος, neut.	movement; (in plur.) emotions
κίστη, -ης, f.	basket, hamper
κλεῖθρον, -ου, neut.	bar
κλείω (aor. **ἔκλεισα**)	I close
Κλεοπάτρη, -ας, f.	Cleopatra
κλῖμαξ, -ακος, f.	ladder
κλίνη, -ης, f.	couch
κλινίδιον, -ου, neut.	couch
κνηστίς, -ίδος, f.	hairpin

κοιλία, -ας, f.	belly
κοίλος, -η, -ον	hollow
κοινωνός, -οῦ, m.	companion, partner
κόμη, -ης, f.	hair
***κομίζω** (aor. pass. inf. **κομισθῆναι**)	I bring, carry, convey
κοπετός, -οῦ, m.	(noise of) lamentation
Κορνήλιος (-ου) Δολοβέλλας (-αδος), m.	Cornelius Dolabella (companion of Octavian)
κοσμέω (perf. ppl. pass. **κεκοσμημένος**)	I adorn, embellish, dress
κόσμος, -ου, m.	adornment
***κρατέω**	I conquer, control; + gen. = I prevail over/am master over
***κρύπτω**	I hide (something: trans.)
κρύφα	secretly
κτίστης, -ου, m.	founder
κώπη, -ης, f.	oar
***λαμβάνω**	I take, capture; mid. + gen.: I touch, seize, lay hold of
λαμπρός, -ά, -όν	bright, splendid, brilliant
***λέγω** (aor. **εἶπον**; aor. pass. **ἐλέχθην**)	I say, tell, speak
***λείπω**	I leave (behind); pass.: I am inferior to (+ gen.)
λεπτός, -ή, -όν	small, fine, narrow, slight
ληστρικός, -ή, -όν	of/belonging to pirates/robbers
***λίθος, -ου**, m.	stone
λιτή, -ῆς, f.	prayer, entreaty
***λόγος, -ου**, m.	word, conversation
***λοιπός, -ή, -όν**	remaining
λουτρόν, -οῦ, neut.	bath, bathing place
λούομαι	I bathe (intrans.)
λόφος, -ου, m.	crest of a hill, ridge
***λύπη, -ης**, f.	pain, distress, grief
***λύω**	I loose, untie, set free
μακαρίζω	I deem X (acc.) to be happy on account of/for Y (gen.)
***μάλιστα**	very much, especially
***μᾶλλον**	more, rather
***μέγας, μέγαλη, μέγα**	great, big
μέγα	greatly, much, exceedingly (adv.)
μέγεθος, -ους, neut.	greatness, magnitude, size
μεθαρμόζω	I correct; (in mid.): I adopt new habits, adapt myself
μειδιάω	I smile, laugh, grin
***μέλλω**	I hesitate, delay/ intend, am going to
***. . . μέν . . . δέ**	on the one hand . . . on the other . . . [marks a contrast]
***μέντοι**	however; certainly
***μένω** (aor. **ἔμεινα**)	I remain, await
***μετά** + acc.	after
***μετά** + gen.	with
μεταβάλλομαι	I change sides
μεταβολή, -ῆς, f.	change (plur. changes, vicissitudes)
μεταλαμβάνω	I get a share of (+ gen.); gain in exchange, take instead (+ acc.)
μεταστρέφομαι (ppl. **μεταστραφείς**)	I turn myself about/ around
***μή** (and comp.)	see under **οὐ** (and comp.)
μηκύνω	I lengthen, prolong, spin out (a speech)
μήν	certainly, truly (part. used to strengthen statements)
***μήτηρ, μητρός**, f.	mother
μηχάνημα, -ατος, neut.	siege-engine, engine of war
***μικρός, -ά, -όν**	small, little
μικροῦ δεῖν	almost (adv.)
***μόλις**	scarcely, with difficulty
***μόνον**	only
***μόνος, -η, -ον**	alone, only
μονοχίτων, -ωνος	wearing only a tunic
μοχλός, -οῦ, m.	bolt, bar
μυρίος, -α, -ον	numberless, countless, infinite
***ναῦς, νέως**, f.	ship
νεανίσκος, -ου, m.	young man
νυγμή, -ῆς, f.	dot, mark, puncture
***νῦν**	now
ξιφίδιον, -ου, neut.	dagger
***ξίφος, -οῦς**, neut.	sword
ὀδύνη, -ης, f.	pain
***οἶδα**	I know

οἰκέτης, -ου, m.	household slave
οἴκημα, -ατος, m.	chamber, room
οἰκτρός, -ά, -όν	pitiable
οἶκτος, -ου, m.	pity, compassion
***οἶνος, -ου**, m.	wine
οἴομαι	I think, suppose, believe
οἴχομαι	I have come/gone/departed (with a perf. sense)
ὀλοφυρμός, -οῦ, m.	lamentation
ὀλοφύρομαι	I lament, wail, moan
Ὄλυμπος, -ου, m.	Olympus (Cleopatra's doctor)
ὅλως	wholly, completely
***ὅμοιος, -α, -ον**	similar, like (+ dat.)
***ὄνομα, -ατος**, neut.	name
***ὀξύς, -εῖα, -ύ**	sharp, bitter; quick, hasty
***ὁράω** (aor. **εἶδον;** aor. pass. **ὤφθην**, inf. **ὀφθῆναι**)	I see
ὀρέγω	I reach out, stretch out
***ὀργή, -ῆς**, f.	anger
ὁρμάω (aor. **ὥρμησα**)	I hasten, rush, start, jump up
***ὅς, ἥ, ὅ**	who, which
ὅσον	only just (adv.)
***ὅτι**	because, that
***οὐ/οὐκ/οὐχ/οὐχί/μή**	not
***οὐδέ/μηδέ**	and not, nor, not even
***οὐδείς, -μία, -έν/μηδείς**, etc.	no one, nothing
***οὖν**	and so, therefore
***οὔτε . . . οὔτε/μήτε . . . μήτε**	neither . . . nor
***οὗτος, αὕτη, τοῦτο**	this
***οὕτω(ς)**	thus, so
ὀχυρός, -ά, -όν	firm, strong
ὄψις, -εως, f.	aspect, appearance; (in plur.) eyes
πάθος, -ους, neut.	suffering
παιδαγωγός, -οῦ, m.	tutor
παιδίον, -ου, neut.	child (diminutive of **παῖς**)
***παῖς, παιδός**, m./f.	boy, girl, child, son, daughter
παντάπασι(ν)	all in all, wholly, altogether
παίω	I strike, smite
***πάλιν**	back, again
***παρά** + acc.	along, beside
***παρά** + gen.	from (a person)
παραγίγνομαι	I am present
***παραδίδωμι** (aor. pass. ppl. **παραδοθείς**)	I hand over, betray, surrender (+ acc.)
παραιρέω (aor. **παρεῖλον**)	I take away from, remove
παραζώννυμι (perf. mid. ppl. **παρεζωσμένος**)	I hang at the girdle; mid.: I wear at the girdle
***παραινέω** + dat.	I advise
παραιωρέω	I hang up beside
παρακαλέω	I send for, summon, call in; encourage, invite
παρακολουθέω + dat.	I follow
παραλύω	I unfasten, detach; release from (+ acc. of the person, gen. of the thing)
***πάρειμι**	I am present
***παρέχω**	I provide, cause, produce; hold in readiness, hold out
παρηγορέω	I comfort, console
παρίσταμαι (pluperf. **παρειστήκειν**)	I stand beside/near (lit. 'I make myself stand beside/near')
***πᾶς, -ᾶσα, -ᾶν**	every, all
***πάσχω** (aor. **ἔπαθον**)	I suffer, experience
πατάσσω (aor. **ἐπάταξα**)	I strike, hit
***παύομαι**	I cease (from doing something)
***πεζῇ**	on foot (adv.)
***πεζοί, -ῶν**, m. plur.	infantry
πεζός, οῦ, m.	infantry (collect. sing.)
***πέμπω**	I send, escort
πεντήκοντα	fifty
πέπλος, -ου, m.	garment
***περί** + acc.	with regard to; around
περί + dat.	in, on; around
***περί** + gen.	about
περιβάλλω	I throw round; mid.: I throw round myself, put on [clothes]
περίβλεπτος, -ον	admired by all, looked at from all sides
περιέχω (aor. ppl. **περισχών**)	I embrace; mid. + gen.: hold fast to, cling to
περιμένω	I wait for, expect
περιρρήγνυμι (aor. **περιερρηξάμην**)	I tear off (e.g. garments)
περιοράω	I overlook, allow

περιπίπτω	I fall around, I embrace (+ dat.)
***πίνω** (aor. **ἔπιον**)	I drink
***πίπτω** (aor. **ἔπεσον**)	I fall
***πιστεύω** + dat.	I believe, trust
***πιστός, -ή, -όν**	reliable, faithful
πλεῖστος, -η, -ον	most, greatest, largest (superl. of **πολύς**)
πλέων, πλέον	more (compar. of **πολύς**)
πληγή, -ῆς, f.	blow
***πλῆθος, -ους**, neut.	crowd, large number
***πλήν**	except (+ gen., as preposition; also as adv.: except, besides)
πλησίον + gen.	near
***ποιέω** (perf. ppl. pass. **πεποιημένος**)	I make, do
***πολεμέω**	I fight a war; (+ dat.) I make war upon
***πολέμιος, -ου**, m.	enemy
πολιός, -ά, -όν	grey, grey-white
***πόλις, -εως**, f.	city-state, city
***πολίτης, -ου**, m.	citizen
πολυκαισαρίη, -ης, f.	a plurality of Caesars
***πολύς, πολλή, πολύ** (superl. **πλεῖστος**)	much (plur. many)
πολυτελῶς	lavishly, extravagantly
πολύτιμος, -ον	much-revered, very expensive
***πόθεν**	whence? from where?
ποθεν	from somewhere
***πούς, - ποδός**, m.	foot
***πρᾶγμα, -ατος**, neut.	thing, matter, situation, event
πρᾶος (compar. **πραότερος**, superl. **πραότατος**)	mild, gentle
***πράσσω** (perf. pass. ppl. **πεπραγμένος**)	I do, fare, manage
πρέπει (ppl. **πρέπων, -ον** [gen. = **-οντος**])	it is befitting + dat. (ppl.: 'befitting' + dat.)
***πρό** + gen.	in front of, before
***προδίδωμι** (perf. pass. inf. **προδεδόσθαι**)	I betray
προθύμως	eagerly
προίημι	I give up, deliver, betray, abandon
Προκληΐος, -ου, m.	Proculeius (a friend of Octavian)
***πρός**	(+ acc.) to, towards, against; with regard to; (+ dat.) at, on, near
***προσβάλλω**	I throw X (acc.) at Y (dat.)
προσδέχομαι	I expect, await
προσδιαλέγομαι	I converse with (+ dat.)
προσδίδωμι (aor. **προὔδωκα**)	I give, hand X (acc.) to Y (dat.), betray
προσειπεῖν	to address, speak to
προσέρχομαι	I go to, approach (+ dat.)
προσέχω	I pay attention to (+ dat.)
προσηκόντως	suitably/as is fitting
προσίεμαι (pres. mid. of **προσίημι**)	I admit X/allow X to approach
προσκομίζω	I carry, convey (to a place)
προσπίπτω	I fall down before, prostrate (myself) in front of (+ dat.); I fasten/attach myself to (+ dat.)
προστάσσω (aor. **προσέταξα**; pluperf. pass. 3rd sing. **προσετέτακτο**)	I order, command (+ dat. of person)
προστίθημι (aor. pass. ppl. **προστεθείς**)	I put to, hold close, apply
προστρέχω (aor. **προσέδραμον**)	I run towards
προσφέρομαι + dat.	I attack, assault
πρόσωπον, -ου, neut.	face
πρόφασις, -εως, f.	motive, reason; excuse, pretence
πρώην	lately, just now
πρῶτον	at first, first (adv.)
πρῶτος, -η, -ον	first
***πυνθάνομαι**	I ascertain, learn, ask
πυρετός, -οῦ, m.	fever, burning heat
πώγων, -ωνος, m.	beard
πώποτε	ever yet
***ῥᾴδιος, -α, -ον** (superl. **ῥᾷστος**)	easy
Ῥόδων, m.	Rhodon (a tutor)
Ῥωμαῖος, -ου, m.	Roman
σεαυτόν/ήν	yourself (acc.; gen. = **σεαυτοῦ**, etc.)
σειρά, -άς, f.	cord, rope
σημεῖον, -ου, neut.	sign

σκέπτομαι I examine, consider, investigate have a look
***σκηνή, -ῆς**, f. tent, hut
σορός, -οῦ, f. coffin; funerary urn
***σός, -ή, -όν** your
σοφιστής, -οῦ, m. sophist
***σοφός, -ή, -όν** clever, wise
σπάομαι I draw (a sword)
σπαράττω I tear, rip
σπένδω I pour a libation, make a drink offering
στερέω I deprive X (acc.) of Y (gen.)
στέρνον, -ου, neut. breast, chest
στέφω (aor. **ἐστέψα**) I crown, encircle, wreathe
στιβάς, -άδος, f. bed, mattress
στίχος, -ου, m. line of poetry, verse
***στόλος, -ου**, m. expedition, fleet, army
***στρατηγός, -οῦ**, m. general, commander
***στρατιώτης, -ου**, m. soldier
***συ** (acc.: **σε;** gen.: **σου;** dat.: **σοι**) you (sing.)
συγκαθείργω (perf. ppl. pass. **συγκαθειργμένος**) I shut X up (with others = + dat.)
σῦκον, -ου, neut. fig
***συγχωρέω** I agree, assent to
συμβούλος, -ου, m. adviser, counsellor
***σύν** + dat. with
συναγωνιάω I share in anxiety, share the struggle
συνάρχω I rule jointly with
συνάρχων, -οντος, m. colleague in office, co-ruler
συνεπιφαίνω I show forth, display; pass: I appear, am visible/manifest
συνεργός, -οῦ, m. colleague, assistant
συνέρχομαι come together, meet
συνήθης, -ες dwelling with, in the same company as (+ dat.); habitual, customary, usual
συνθάπτω I bury together
συνίημι (aor. **συνῆκα**) I perceive, understand
συντήκω I melt down, cause to waste away; the perf. is intrans.: I am melted/ consumed
συντόμως (**συντομώτερον** = compar.) quickly, immediately
συρμός, -οῦ, m. trail, trace
συχνός, -ή, -όν long; (in plur.) many
σφαδάζω I struggle
σφάλλω I make to fall, overthrow, trip up
***σῴζω** I save
σωτήρια, -ων, neut. plur. safety, deliverance
***σῶμα, -ατος**, neut. body
τάλαντον, -ου, neut. talent (a certain weight of metal/ sum of money corresponding to this weight)
τάλας, τάλαινα, τάλαν wretched
ταπεινῶς in a lowly/downcast/ dejected state
***τάφος, -ου**, m. tomb
τάχος, -ους, neut. speed
ταχύ quickly (adv.)
***τε / τε . . . τε** and / both . . . and . . .
τέκνον, -ου, neut. child
τελευταῖος, -α, -ον last
***τελευτάω** I end; I die
***τελευτή, -ῆς**, f. end, death
***τέλος** (adv.) in the end, at last, finally
τεσσαράκοντα forty
τηλικοῦτος, -αύτη -οῦτο so great, such a great
τηρέω I watch over, take care of, guard
***τίθημι** I place; make; mid.: see to, prepare
***τιμάω** I honour, respect
***τιμή, -ῆς**, f. honour
***τίς; τί;** who? what? (interrog.)
τί; why?
***τις, τι** a, a certain; plur.: some
***τοιοῦτος, -αύτη, -οῦτο** such
***τόπος, -ου**, m. place
***τοσοῦτος, -αύτη, -οῦτο** so great; plur.: so many
***τότε** at that time, then
τράχηλος, -ου, m. throat, neck
τρεῖς, τρία three
***τρέπω** I turn, direct
τρέφω I raise, bring up
***τρέχω** (aor. **ἔδραμον**) I run

τρίτος, -η, -ον	third
τριχῶν	see **θρίξ**
***τρόπος, -ου**, m.	way, manner, custom
τροφή, -ῆς, f.	food, nourishment
***τυγχάνω**	I happen to be/am actually X-ing (+ ppl.); I get, obtain, meet with (+ gen.)
***τύπτω**	I strike; mid.: beat/strike oneself
***τύχη, -ης**, f.	chance, luck, fortune (good or bad)
ὑδρία, -ας, f.	water jar, wine jar
***ὑμεῖς** (acc: **ὑμᾶς**, etc.)	you (plur.)
ὑπεξέρχομαι (aor. **ὑπεξῆλθον**)	I withdraw, retire, go out secretly
ὑπερβάλλω	I cross over, go beyond, exceed
ὑπερέτης, -ου, m.	servant, attendant
ὑπερήφανος, -ον	arrogant, proud
***ὑπό**	(+ gen.) by
ὑπονοέω	I suspect
ὑπόσχεσις, -εως, f.	promise
ὑπότρομος, -ον	quivering, shaking; afraid
ὕστατος, -η, -ον	last
***ὕστερον**	later
***φαίνομαι** (aor. ppl. **φανείς, -εῖσα, -έν**)	I appear, seem
φαιός, -ά, -όν	grey
φάρμακον, -ου, neut.	drug, poison
φάσκω	I say, affirm, assert, allege
***φέρω**	I carry, bear, endure
***φεύγω**	I flee, run away
***φημί** (imperf. **ἔφην**)	I say
***φθόνος, -ου**, m.	grudge, envy/hatred
φίλος, -η, -ον	loved, beloved, dear
***φίλος, -ου**, m.	friend
φιλόσοφος, -ου, m.	philosopher
Φιλόστρατος, -ου, m.	Philostratus (a rhetorician/sophist)
φιλοψυχέω	I love my life
***φοβέομαι** (aor. **ἐφοβήθην**)	I fear
***φόβος, -ου**, m.	fear
φορά, -ᾶς, f.	rush, rapid motion
φορέω	I carry, bear, wear (constantly)
φορτικός, -ή, -όν	common, vulgar, coarse
Φουλβία, -ας, f.	Fulvia (former wife of Antony)
φράζω (aor. **ἔφρασα**)	I tell, declare
φρουρέω	I keep watch over, guard
***φύλαξ, -ακος**, m.	guard
***φυλάττω**	I guard
φύρω (perf. pass. **πέφυρμαι**)	I stain, spoil
***φωνή, -ῆς**, f.	voice
φωράω (aor. ppl. pass. **φωραθείς**; perf. pass. **πεφώραμαι**)	I detect, discover, convict
χαρίζομαι	I gratify, show favour to (+ dat.)
χάρις, -ιτος, f.	grace, charm
Χάρμιον, f.	Charmion (attendant of Cleopatra)
***χείρ, χειρός**, f.	hand
χοή, -ῆς, f.	drink-offering; in plur.: libations
***χράομαι** (pres. inf. **χρῆσθαι**)	I use (+ dat.); I treat someone (dat.) in a certain way;
χρῄζω	I desire, crave, want
***χρῆμα, -ατος**, neut.	thing; (in plur.) goods, property, money
χρηστότης, -ητος, f.	honesty, goodness, uprightness
***χρυσοῦς, -ῆ, -οῦν** (contr. from **χρύσεος**)	golden
***χώρα, -ας**, f.	land, place, country
χωρίς + gen.	apart from
ψυχή, -ῆς, f.	spirit, soul
ὦ	O (+ voc.)
***ὥρα, -ας**, f.	beauty
***ὡς**	as, when, that, how
ὡς + acc.	to/towards (a person)
ὡς + ppl.	on the grounds that [an alleged reason]

Homer, *Iliad*

Introduction, Commentary Notes and Vocabulary by Chris Tudor

AS: Book 16: 20–47, 644–867

A Level: Book 24: 349–595

Introduction

Homer's *Iliad* is one of the earliest surviving works of ancient Greek literature, and must be ranked as one of its greatest. Emerging from an oral tradition that can be dated back to the early second millennium BCE, the poem centres on the tragic figure of Achilles, his wrath, and its terrible consequences for those around him. Along the way, the poem engages with some of most fundamental questions of human existence: not simply what it means to be a 'hero', but the relationship between man and the gods, man's purpose on earth and the meaning of human suffering. It is undeniably a poetic masterpiece.

The influence of the *Iliad* on Greek culture was colossal, determining much of later literature, thought and art. The tragedian Aeschylus described his own plays as 'mere slices from the great banquet of Homer', while Aristotle studied it in detail in his *Poetics*. Plato quoted the poem extensively in his *Republic*, while Alexander the Great was said to carry a copy of the poem with him wherever he went. In the history of Western literature, few works have enjoyed a similar status and influence.

The following sections are aimed at providing students with a simple and concise introduction to Homer's *Iliad*. We start with the story of the *Iliad*, before moving on to consider the origin, date and authorship of the poem, the metre of epic poetry, the use of formulae, type scenes and story patterns, and the language and style of Homeric verse.

The mythic background of the *Iliad*

The *Iliad* describes a single episode in the tenth year of the Trojan War: the wrath of Achilles, his withdrawal from the fighting, and its impact on those around him. The story was a traditional one, and the poet could rely on his audience to be familiar both with its major characters – on the Greek side, Achilles, Agamemnon, Odysseus, Diomedes, etc. and for the Trojans, Hector, Paris, Priam and a range of female characters – as well as with the events of the Trojan War itself. For the benefit of the modern reader, however, who may be less familiar with this material, there follows a detailed introduction to the mythic background to the Trojan War, up to the point where the *Iliad* starts.

For the ancient Greeks, the origins of the Trojan War could be traced back to the wedding of the goddess Thetis to the mortal Peleus. Invitations to the wedding had been extended to everyone except for the goddess Eris ('Strife'), a well-known mischief-maker who had been told to stay at home. Angered by the snub, Eris had come to the wedding anyway, leaving a golden apple in the middle of the wedding feast which she had labelled καλλίστῃ ('for the most beautiful woman'). This apple was claimed by three goddesses: Hera, Athena, and Aphrodite. Unable to decide between themselves which of them was κάλλιστη ('the most beautiful'), they asked Zeus to make the decision for them, who swiftly refused and delegated the decision to the Trojan prince, Paris. With Hermes as their guide, the three goddesses met on Mount Ida for what came to be known as the **Judgement of Paris**.

On the day of the Judgement, each of the goddesses offered Paris a gift related to her personal sphere of influence: Hera offered him kingship, Athena wisdom and success in war, and Aphrodite the world's most beautiful woman, Helen of Sparta. After some consideration, Paris rejected Hera and Athena in favour of Aphrodite and Helen. Shortly afterwards, he made a trip to Sparta where he 'seduced' Helen and smuggled her back to Troy. Helen's husband, **Menelaus**, furious at the theft of his wife, appealed to his brother, **Agamemnon**, to defend his honour and recover Helen. An army was mustered at Aulis and, after a short delay, the Greek forces set sail for Troy – and so began the Trojan War.

The first nine years of the war were inconclusive. Some of the key events in this period included the initial arrival of the Greeks at Troy, the loss of several Greek heroes (e.g. Protesilaus, Philoctetes, etc.), the attempt by Odysseus and Menelaus to settle the matter by negotiation, and the Greek raids on towns in the surrounding area. While most of these events have little impact on the narrative of the *Iliad*, two incidents are of particular importance: first, the raid on Lyrnessus, in which Achilles captures the girl Briseïs; second, the raid on Thebe, in which Achilles captures the girl Chryseïs. It is shortly after the raid on Thebe and the capture of Chryseïs that the action of the *Iliad* begins.

The setting of the *Iliad*

There are three basic settings for the human action in the *Iliad*: the Greek encampment, the city of Troy, and the plain in between the two. All of these are located in a region known as the Troad. Important geographical landmarks include Mount Ida, located about twenty miles south-east of the city of Troy, as well as two major rivers, the Scamander and the Simoeis.

The Trojans are based in the city of Troy, otherwise known as Ilium (whence the name 'Iliad' = 'the song of Ilium'). The city is distinguished by its huge walls, said to have been built by Apollo and Poseidon, and the monumental Scaean gate, which provides the major entrance to the city. Other landmarks include the grand palace of Priam (the king of Troy) and the temple of Athena, which forms the highest point of the city.

The Greeks (always referred to as **Argives**, **Achaeans** or **Danaans**) are based in a military encampment on the coast, made up of several hundred Greek ships dragged up onto the beach. In Book 7, the Greeks construct a large rampart and a ditch to further protect their ships. The Greek army is comprised of forces from every part of Greece, and each contingent occupies a different part of the camp. Agamemnon, as commander-in-chief of the whole expedition, is located in the middle, while Achilles and Ajax, the two strongest warriors, are located at either end.

In between the Greek camp and the city of Ilium lies the **plain of Troy**, where (almost) all the fighting in the poem takes place.

The other key location in the poem is Olympus, the divine realm which provides the residence for most of the gods in the poem. It is in this realm that the gods can discuss how they might intervene in the affairs below, where they can receive and dispatch messengers, tend to any injuries they have sustained in the fighting, or generally eat, drink and be merry.

A handful of gods do not live on Olympus. Hades is thought of as living in the Underworld with his consort Persephone, while Poseidon lives under the sea. The most important of the non-Olympian gods, however, is Achilles' mother Thetis, who lives in a submarine grotto with her father, Nereus, and with her several dozen sisters, known collectively as the Nereïds.

Humans and gods

The *Iliad*, like the *Odyssey*, is a world of both gods and mortals, and the dynamic between the two provides much of the ethical interest of the poem. The gods, for their part, live lives that are, with one or two notable exceptions, entirely free of care: they are physically invulnerable, and, while many of the gods will prefer one side or the other (Poseidon, Hera and Athena are pro-Greek, Apollo and Aphrodite are pro-Trojan), their emotional investment in the human action is ultimately limited.

The humans, by contrast, live lives that are almost defined by suffering. This is the lesson of the great meeting with Achilles and Priam in Book 24, where each man weeps for the tragedy of the human condition, as well as for the final 200 or so lines of the book (and the poem as a whole), in which the three women of Troy (Hecuba, Andromache and Helen) mourn over the dead Hector. It is instructive that the very last line of a poem whose subject is ostensibly the wrath of Achilles is not when this wrath finally dissipates, but when his final victim, Hector, is given a proper funeral.

The contrast between the lives of men and gods is summed up succinctly by Achilles in Book 24, who says:

> ὡς γὰρ ἐπεκλώσαντο θεοὶ δειλοῖσι βροτοῖσι
> ζώειν ἀχνυμένοις: αὐτοὶ δέ τ᾽ ἀκηδέες εἰσί.
>
> This is the fate the gods have spun for poor mortal men, that we should live in misery, but they themselves have no sorrows.
>
> (24.525–526)

The word ἀκηδής here means 'free from care', though the same word also has an important passive meaning, 'uncared for', and I think the two meanings intertwine when it comes to thinking about the gods in the *Iliad*. In short, it is precisely because the gods lead lives that are 'free from care' that they are also 'uncared for' by the reader, who finds them ethically unserious.

The humans in the Iliad, by contrast, lead lives that are full of 'cares', i.e. great sorrow and suffering, and for this they are rewarded with the 'cares', i.e. attention, of the reader. It is the actions of the human characters in the poem, and their attempts to negotiate a world in which suffering and violence are absolutely guaranteed, that pose the most serious ethical questions in the poem. The gods, for everything they bring in spectacle and splendour, do not.

Fate

To take just one nexus of examples, we are told time and time again in the poem that Achilles is fated to die at Troy, and the prophecies relating to his death become more frequent and more detailed as his death approaches. By the time Hector is killed in Book 22, it is clear that Achilles' death is imminent, though the poem ends before it actually happens.

Among some of the most dramatic moments in the poem are those when a character *almost* achieves something that has been forbidden by fate. In Book 16, for example, as Patroclus is rampaging on the battlefield, there is a sense that he might single-handedly sack the city. Only the timely intervention of Apollo prevents this from happening, who addresses Patroclus in the following terms:

> χάζεο διογενὲς Πατρόκλεες: οὔ νύ τοι αἶσα
> σῷ ὑπὸ δουρὶ πόλιν πέρθαι Τρώων ἀγερώχων,
> οὐδ᾽ ὑπ᾽ Ἀχιλλῆος, ὅς περ σέο πολλὸν ἀμείνων.
>
> Back, lord Patroclus! It is not fate for the proud Trojans' city to be sacked by your spear, not even by Achilles, a far greater man that you.
>
> (16.707–709)

Humans in the *Iliad* generally do not know their fates, with two exceptions. First, Achilles knows *some* aspects of his fate thanks to his divine mother, who seems to be able to see the future. In Book 18, for example, she tells him that if he returns to battle, she will 'lose [him] to an early death [. . .] since directly after Hector dies your own doom is certain' (18.95–96). Second, characters on the brink of death are occasionally granted the opportunity to see what lies in store for the person who has killed them. Patroclus is granted this power at the end of Book 16, when he tells Hector:

> ἄλλο δέ τοι ἐρέω, σὺ δ᾽ ἐνὶ φρεσὶ βάλλεο σῇσιν:
> οὔ θην οὐδ᾽ αὐτὸς δηρὸν βέῃ, ἀλλά τοι ἤδη
> ἄγχι παρέστηκεν θάνατος καὶ μοῖρα κραταιὴ
> χερσὶ δαμέντ᾽ Ἀχιλῆος ἀμύμονος Αἰακίδαο.
>
> I tell you another thing, and you mark it well in your mind. You yourself, you too will not live long, but already now death and strong fate are standing close beside you, to bring you down at the hands of Achilles, great son of Aeacus' stock.
>
> (16.851–854)

For the most part, however, humans do not know their fate, which allows for moments of great pathos and dramatic irony. One such moment come at the beginning of Book 16, where Patroclus ends his appeal to Achilles by asking 'if there is some prophecy known in your heart which prevents you [from sending me into battle in your armour]'. The poet intervenes at this point with a prophecy that Patroclus *will* in fact be killed ('So he spoke in entreaty, the poor fool – what he was begging would be a wretched death for himself and his own destruction'), before Achilles can respond by saying that he is *not* aware of any prophecy ('I am not influenced by any prophecy known to me, and there is no word from Zeus told me by my honoured mother').

One other episode in Book 16 is worth mentioning, if only in brief. This is the curious moment before the (fated) death of Sarpedon, where Zeus ponders whether he should simply save Sarpedon from his fate. This is what Zeus says:

> Alas, that it is fate for Sarpedon, dearest of men to me, to be brought down by Patroclus son of Menoetius. As I think on it, there are two ways my heart pulls – should I snatch him out of the ruinous fighting and set him alive in the rich land of Lycia, or should I bring him down now at the hands of the son of Menoetius? (16.433–438).

Hera responds to Zeus' question with horror ('Dread son of Cronus, what is this you are saying?'), going on to explain why saving Sarpedon from his fate would be a bad idea. What she also makes clear, however, is the fact that Zeus *could* do this if he really wanted ('Do it then – but we the other gods will not at all approve you').

There is more to be said about fate in the *Iliad*, some of which can be found below. Before we get onto that, however, it is worth going through what actually happens in the poem.

The story of the *Iliad*

The *Iliad* begins as all ancient epics do – by announcing its subject ('the wrath of Achilles', 1.1) and giving a brief overview of what will happen in the poem ('which brought uncounted anguish on the Greeks', 1.2). This traditional opening is known as the proem, and it is here that we are told that the wrath of Achilles will cause of deaths of 'countless heroes', whose bodies will 'provide a feast for the dogs and birds' (1.3–5).

After the proem, the narrative proper begins by describing a plague in the Greek camp. This has been sent by the god Apollo in revenge for the Greeks' treatment of his priest, Chryses. Chryses' daughter, Chryseïs, had recently been captured by the Greeks and her father had offered a ransom to the Greeks to get her back. When this request is refused by Agamemnon, Chryses prays to Apollo to punish Agamemnon's insolence.

After almost two weeks of plague, Achilles decides to call an assembly of the Greek leaders to discuss a solution to the problem, during which it is suggested that Agamemnon return Chryseïs to her father. Agamemnon reluctantly agrees to this, but demands another girl to replace the one he is losing. Achilles suggests waiting until a later raid, but Agamemnon instead demands that Achilles hand over *his* concubine, Briseïs. An argument breaks out, during which Achilles must be physically restrained from killing Agamemnon by the goddess Athena. After levelling vicious insults at the king, Achilles agrees to let Briseïs go, but announces his intention to withdraw from the fighting with immediate effect on the grounds that his honour has been slighted. Furthermore, he prays to his mother, Thetis, to ask Zeus to bring death and destruction to the Greeks in order that Agamemnon should recognize his mistake in insulting him so gravely. Zeus agrees to this with a solemn nod that shakes Mount Olympus to its very core (Book 1).

The poem continues with Agamemnon rallying the troops, followed by a long list of the various contingents fighting on the Greek or Trojan side known as the Catalogue of Ships (Book 2). The sides approach one another, but before general fighting begins, a duel is arranged between Menelaus and Paris, with both sides swearing a 'great oath' that the duel will settle the war. The duel begins, which Menelaus dominates. When Menelaus is on the brink of killing Paris, however, the goddess Aphrodite spirits Paris away to the city of Troy, leaving Menelaus grasping at thin air. While Menelaus is trying to figure out what has happened, the Trojan archer Pandarus aims at him with his bow, hitting Menelaus and drawing blood. The Greeks are appalled that the Trojans have broken their 'great oath' and general hostilities begin (Books 3–5).

The champion warrior on the Trojan side is Paris' brother, Hector, who decides to find out where his brother has gone and goes to look for him in the city of Troy. While in Troy, he speaks with his wife, Andromache, who tries to persuade him not to go back out to fight, which he refuses. Hector finds Paris and the two return to the battlefield (Book 6). Another duel is arranged, this time between Hector and the Greek hero, Ajax, which ends in a draw and a handshake. Night falls, and the Greeks decide to reinforce their camp, building a wall and digging a ditch (Book 7). At sunrise, hostilities are resumed and the Trojans begin to gain the upper hand, pushing the Greek forces back towards their ships. Night falls again, and the Trojans decide to camp out in the plain, rather than returning to the city (Book 8).

The Greeks assemble to discuss how they can turn the tide of battle against the Trojans and agree to send an appeal to Achilles, who is still refusing to fight. Agamemnon in particular offers grand reparations to Achilles if he will return to the fighting and save the Greeks from the Trojan onslaught. The appeal is made by a delegation of three men – Odysseus, Phoenix and Ajax – each of whom try to persuade Achilles to return to battle. Achilles refuses, although his position does change from leaving immediately in the morning to waiting and seeing what will happen, and then to agreeing to fight if and when Hector reaches his ships (Book 9). There follows a short night-time mission, in which Odysseus and Diomedes capture and execute a Trojan spy (Book 10), before morning comes and fighting resumes again (Book 11).

Over the course of the next five books – and thanks in part to Zeus' continued support of the Trojans – the Trojans gain the upper hand, injuring several Greek heroes, smashing through the gates into the Greek encampment and setting fire to one of their ships (Books 11–15).

At this point, Achilles' second-in-command, Patroclus, begs Achilles to be allowed into battle in order to push the Trojans back from the Greek ships. Achilles reluctantly agrees, lending Patroclus his weapons and armour for the job, but ordering him only to push the Trojans out of the Greek camp, and not to fight on beyond that. He prays to Zeus to protect his companion in battle, a prayer that Zeus refuses. Patroclus storms into battle and almost single-handedly pushes the Trojans into a mass retreat, killing the Lycian hero Sarpedon in the process. However, he ignores Achilles' advice and pushes on as far as the walls of Troy, where he is killed by Hector, who strips him of his (i.e. Achilles') armour (Book 16). There is furious fighting over Patroclus' body, and the Greeks are once again pushed back towards their camp (Book 17).

Achilles observes the retreat of the Greeks and fears that something terrible has happened to Patroclus. Almost immediately after this, the Greek hero Antilochus arrives to announce that Patroclus has been killed by Hector, sending Achilles into the depths of grief, despair and rage. Achilles announces to his mother, Thetis, that he will return to battle to kill Hector, even if this means that his own death must follow. Thetis reluctantly agrees to this, but Achilles cannot return to battle until he has a new suit of armour, which Thetis agrees to arrange for him. In the meantime, Achilles stands on the ramparts of the Greek camp and lets out an almighty war-cry, pushing the Trojans back, and allowing the Greeks to recover Patroclus' body. Night falls, bringing hostilities to an end. Meanwhile, Thetis visits the blacksmith god Hephaestus to ask him to construct a new set of armour for Achilles. The full set of armour, and especially the shield, is described in great detail (Book 18).

After a few formalities, including an apology from Agamemnon to Achilles and the delivery of the gifts that had been promised earlier (Book 19), Achilles returns to battle and devastates the Trojan forces (Books 20–21). With the Trojans in complete disarray, Hector decides to take a stand against Achilles outside the Scaean gate. In full view of the whole city, including his wife and parents, Hector is pursued three times round the city of Troy, before he is finally killed by Achilles. In his rage, Achilles ties Hector's body to the back of his chariot, dragging it in the dust back to the Greek camp (Book 22).

After a ceremonial funeral for Patroclus, which includes a whole programme of athletic events (Book 23), we are treated to the climactic moment of the poem: Priam's visit to Achilles in the middle of the night to ask for the body of his son back. After an extraordinary meeting between the two men, where they weep for those they have lost and reflect on the meaning of human suffering, Achilles releases Hector's body, which is brought back to the city of Troy. The three women in Hector's life lament for him, and the last lines of the poem describe the funeral of Hector (Book 24).

Book 16

Book 16 of the *Iliad* begins with the Greek forces in dire straits. Many of the Greek heroes have been wounded in the preceding five books, and the Trojans, led by Hector, have broken into the Greek camp itself. In Book 11, Nestor had advised Patroclus to try and persuade Achilles to return to the fighting and, if not, to allow him (Patroclus) to enter the fighting wearing his (Achilles') armour. This is what Patroclus now does.

Patroclus has been a relatively marginal figure up until this point in the poem. In Book 9, when Odysseus, Phoenix and Ajax come to Achilles' hut in Book 9 to persuade him to return to the fighting, Patroclus is seen sitting in silence as Achilles plays the lyre. His only other action in this book is to help prepare the food, after which he disappears. In Book 16, however, Patroclus is the central focus, so much so that the Alexandrians who first divided the *Iliad* into twenty-four books named this one *Patrocleia*, 'Patroclus' Book'.

The book begins with one of the most touching similes in the *Iliad*, in which Patroclus' visit to Achilles is compared to 'a little girl running up to her mother and demanding to be carried, pulling at her dress and holding her back as she tries to hurry on, and looking up at her tearfully until she picks her up' (16.7–10). What is extraordinary about this simile is not simply the image of Achilles and Patroclus as mother and daughter (*not* father and son), but the fact that it is spoken by Achilles himself. Similes in the *Iliad* are mostly spoken by the poet. We might also note that this is the second time that Achilles has imagined himself as a mother. In Book 9, he compared his exertions on behalf of the Greek forces to a bird collecting food for its chicks. In the simile, Achilles thought of himself as having many children. Here, however, he has just one, and the grief he experiences when that child is lost will be immense. Since Achilles does not know what will happen, however, he agrees to Patroclus' request.

The scene shifts, and we are taken to events on the battlefield, where Hector is threatening to set fire to the Greek ships. Indeed, we might say that Book 16 is one of the most cinematic of the poem, with a pleasing alternation between the 'wide angle' shot of the battle as a whole and the 'narrow angle' focus on Patroclus himself. On top of this, the human action alternates with events on Olympus, as Zeus decides who should live and who should die.

Back at Achilles' hut, Patroclus begins to arm himself in Achilles' armour. This is a fairly typical arming scene, though there is a crucial moment near the end when Patroclus is emphatically *un*able to wield Achilles' spear ('Only the spear of the excellent Achilles did he not take', 16.140). The symbolism of this moment hardly needs spelling out: Patroclus may *look* like Achilles, but he will fall tragically short of matching him on the battlefield.

The return of Patroclus to the fighting is a momentous moment, and the poet 'slows down' the pace of the narrative accordingly. Characters, including Achilles' horses, are given fuller backstories, there are two long similes comparing the Myrmidons first to wolves and then to wasps, and Achilles spends some time making a sacrifice to Zeus and praying for Patroclus' safe return. Prayers of this kind are common in the *Iliad*, though Zeus' response to this one is unique: 'The father [Zeus] granted one half of the prayer but refused the other. He granted that Patroclus should push the battle back from the ships, but refused his safe return from the fighting' (16.251–252).

Much of the rest of Book 16 is taken up with general scenes of fighting, though there are two moments that deserve our attention before we move on. Near the end of the book, Patroclus hurls a rock at Hector which hits Hector's charioteer (Cebriones) right between the eyes and sends him tumbling to the ground. Here is Patroclus' reaction:

ὢ πόποι ἦ μάλ᾽ ἐλαφρὸς ἀνήρ, ὡς ῥεῖα κυβιστᾷ.
εἰ δή που καὶ πόντῳ ἐν ἰχθυόεντι γένοιτο,
πολλοὺς ἂν κορέσειεν ἀνὴρ ὅδε τήθεα διφῶν
νηὸς ἀποθρῴσκων, εἰ καὶ δυσπέμφελος εἴη,

ὡς νῦν ἐν πεδίῳ ἐξ ἵππων ῥεῖα κυβιστᾷ.
ἦ ῥα καὶ ἐν Τρώεσσι κυβιστητῆρες ἔασιν.

Oh, this is a really agile man, a ready acrobat! I should think he would be good too if he was out on the fish-filled sea – this man could feed a large number with the oysters he could find, diving off a ship, even in rough weather, to judge by his easy tumble to the plain from his chariot. Oh yes, the Trojans have their acrobats, too!

(16.745–750)

Hector's words to Patroclus after he has struck him down are no less jarring, both for their boastfulness ('I am renowned for my spear among all the war-loving Trojans,' 16.834–835) and for the threat that Patroclus' body will be left unburied ('but you, the vultures will eat you here', 16.836). It is worth keeping in mind that one definition of what counts as 'heroic' in the *Iliad* is simply what its heroes do and say, which may not chime at all with our definition of heroism.

Book 24

Book 24 begins after Patroclus' funeral games that filled the entirety of the previous book. Achilles is still grief-stricken, however, and in his rage and sorrow continues to abuse Hector's corpse, tying it to his chariot and dragging it round and round Patroclus' funeral mound. This goes on for twelve days before Apollo complains about what Achilles is doing and asks Zeus to do something about it. Zeus agrees and dispatches two messengers to arrange the release of Hector's body: Achilles' mother, Thetis, is sent to Achilles, and the messenger goddess, Iris, is sent to Priam.

Achilles, for his part, agrees to release the body: 'So be it. The man who brings the ransom can take the body, if the Olympian himself in all earnest wishes it.' (24.139–140). In Troy, meanwhile, Iris finds a Priam in deepest mourning presiding over a house in grief. She tells him that he should go to Achilles with precious gifts in order to ransom Hector's body, ensuring him that he will be safe: '[Achilles] is not foolish or blind or godless, but will show a suppliant all kindness and spare him.' (24.186–187).

When Hecuba is told of Priam's plans, she thinks her husband has lost his mind ('Oh, where have your wits gone now, that wisdom for which you used to be famous among men from other lands as well as your own?,' 24.202–203), though she is ultimately powerless to stop him. The modern reader may be surprised by just how visceral Hecuba's hatred for Achilles is: 'I wish I could sink my hands in that man's very liver and eat it!' (24.212–213).

After some final preparations, including a prayer from Hecuba and scene in which Priam rails against his surviving sons, the old man sets out on his journey, which takes us to the start of the set text. We will be discussing that in more detail below, but a few points are worth mentioning here. First, despite Iris' assurances that Priam will not be harmed on his journey to the Greek camp, the atmosphere is tense throughout. Iris has told Priam that Hermes will accompany him across the battlefield, but when a figure emerges from the darkness, Priam is terrified:

ὣς φάτο, σὺν δὲ γέροντι νόος χύτο, δείδιε δ᾽ αἰνῶς,
ὀρθαὶ δὲ τρίχες ἔσταν ἐνὶ γναμπτοῖσι μέλεσσι,
στῆ δὲ ταφών.

So [Idaeus] spoke, and the old man's mind was confounded, and he felt terrible fear: the hairs stood up along the flex of his body, and he stood their dazed.

(24.358–360)

The atmosphere of death is palpable here. It is the middle of the night and the two men have stopped next to a tomb, the figure that emerges from the darkness is Hermes, who was the god who guided the souls of the dead to the Underworld, while even the very language is funerary, the word ταφών ('dazed') in line 360 evoking the word τάφος ('funeral-rites').

The meeting between Achilles and Priam provides the ethical core of the entire poem, more details of which can be found in the line-by-line commentary. For now, however, it is worth highlighting the absolutely extraordinary simile that is used when Priam goes up to Achilles for the first time:

τοὺς δ᾽ ἔλαθ᾽ εἰσελθὼν Πρίαμος μέγας, ἄγχι δ᾽ ἄρα στὰς
χερσὶν Ἀχιλλῆος λάβε γούνατα καὶ κύσε χεῖρας
δεινὰς ἀνδροφόνους, αἵ οἱ πολέας κτάνον υἷας.
ὡς δ᾽ ὅτ᾽ ἂν ἄνδρ᾽ ἄτη πυκινὴ λάβῃ, ὅς τ᾽ ἐνὶ πάτρῃ
φῶτα κατακτείνας ἄλλων ἐξίκετο δῆμον
ἀνδρὸς ἐς ἀφνειοῦ, θάμβος δ᾽ ἔχει εἰσορόωντας.
ὣς Ἀχιλεὺς θάμβησεν ἰδὼν Πρίαμον θεοειδέα:

Huge Priam came in unseen, and moving close to him took Achilles' knees in his arms and kissed his hands, those terrible, murderous hands, which had killed many of his sons. As when a man is held fast by blind folly – he kills a man in his own country, and then comes to another land, to a rich man's house, and amazement takes those who see his entry. So Achilles was amazed when he saw godlike Priam:

(24.477–483)

The comparison between a man whose son has been murdered to a murderer asking for forgiveness makes this one of the most arresting similes in the whole poem. Indeed, similes which present an exact reversal of the situation in the main narrative are always so. Compare the simile in the *Odyssey* where Odysseus weeps upon listening to a bard singing about the sack of Troy:

He wept as a woman weeps when she throws her arms round the body of her beloved husband, fallen in battle in defence of his city and his comrades, fighting to save his city and children from the evil day.

(*Od.* 8.523–524)

After Achilles and Priam have agreed to the release of Hector's body, Hermes appears once again to conduct Priam back across the battlefield. The final three speeches in the poem are laments from the three most important women in Troy:

Hector's mother, Hecuba; his wife, Andromache; and Helen, after which Hector is buried with full honours.

Two final points about Book 24. First, we notice that once Hermes returns to Olympus after conducting Priam and Idaeus back across the battlefield, the gods play no further part in events. Nor are the gods involved in the long meeting between Priam and Achilles, where each man reflects on the meaning of suffering and the tragedy of the human condition. These are uniquely human concerns to which the gods can contribute nothing at all.

Finally, it is vitally important to the meaning of the poem that it ends not with the death of Hector in Book 22, not even with the dissipation of Achilles' anger in Book 24, but with the proper burial of Hector. The poem's first word tells us that its central concern will be Achilles wrath. Its final line shows us that what the *Iliad* is actually about is human suffering.

The structure of the *Iliad*

The above outline has gone through the various books of the *Iliad*, with a more detailed discussion of the books from which your set texts have been taken – 16 and 24. It is important to note, however, that unlike poems such as Virgil's *Aeneid* and Ovid's *Metamorphoses*, which were designed by their authors as 12- and 15-book poems, respectively, the division of the *Iliad* into 24 books only took place in the third century BCE, several centuries after its composition, with the number 24 being chosen for specific, contingent reasons, including the maximum capacity of the papyrus scroll (about 1,000 lines) and the fact that the Greek alphabet had 24 letters.

While the division of the *Iliad* into 24 books was not part of the poem's original conception, many scholars (e.g. Sheppard; Wade-Gery; Taplin) have pointed out that the poem does seem to fall quite naturally into three parts, roughly equivalent to Books 1–9, 11–18 and 19–24. According to Taplin (*Homeric Soundings*), each of these 'movements' corresponds to a day's worth of recitation, with the nightfall in the poem at the end of Books 9 and 18 coinciding with the actual nightfall for the audience after a full day's recitation.

A more recent discussion of the structure of the poem is Bruce Heiden's *Homer's Cosmic Fabrication*, which also conceives of the poem as dividing naturally into three 'movements'. In Heiden's case, however, the tripartite structure of the *Iliad* is not simply about rendering it performable at a three-day festival, as Taplin had argued, but about highlighting the conflict between human agency and the attempts by the gods to control events. If it is a battle, it is one that humanity wins: every time that Zeus articulates 'the plan of Zeus' (Books 8 and 15), Achilles makes an unexpected decision that changes the course of events (Books 9 and 16). By the end of the poem, the gods have disappeared altogether.

The origin, date and authorship of the *Iliad*

Ever since antiquity, there has been a debate about the origin, date and authorship of the *Iliad*. In this section, we trace some of the prevailing views about the composition of the poem, from the ancients' view that the *Iliad* was the work of a single, outstanding poet, through the ideas of the **Analysts** in the nineteenth and twentieth centuries, to the **theory of orality** developed by Milman Parry and Albert Lord in the 1930s.

Homer

In antiquity, the *Iliad* was attributed to a single poet known as Homer. The earliest known reference to Homer is by the seventh-century poet Callinus, who claimed that Homer was the author of an epic poem known as the *Thebaid*. Just over a century later, Homer was already being written about as a poet of exceptional status and influence: the sixth-century poet Xenophanes (born *c.* 570 BCE) wrote that 'everyone has learned in accordance with Homer', while for the philosopher Heraclitus (lived *c.* 500 BCE) Homer was 'the wisest of the Greeks'.

Despite his status, the ancients seemed to have known very little about the basic facts of Homer's life, and opinions on when and where he lived, his parentage, his real name, the manner of his death, etc. varied widely. The most popular traditions described Homer as a native of the Ionian part of Asia Minor, either from the town of Smyrna or the island of Chios, though other traditions associated him with Rhodes, Athens, Argos, Salamis, Egypt and even Rome. Suggestions for *when* he lived were similarly diverse, with dates ranging from the fall of Troy itself (which the Greeks believed happened in *c.* 1200 BCE) to the second half of the ninth century BCE.

Nor could the ancients agree on Homer's poetic output. The fifth-century historian Herodotus, for example, records the tradition that Homer was the author not only of the *Iliad* and the *Odyssey*, but also of the epic poems known as the *Epigoni* and the *Cypria*. A set of thirty-three hymns known as the Homeric Hymns were also ascribed to Homer, as were a number of less serious poems, including a poem called the *Margites*, which is mentioned by Aristotle in his *Politics*. As time went on, however, it seems that fewer and fewer of these works were considered genuinely Homeric. By the late Roman and early Byzantine periods (*c.* 300–400 CE), a consensus had arisen that the only genuine works of Homer were the *Iliad* and the *Odyssey*, a view that was to persist for the next fourteen hundred years.

Analysts and Unitarians

By the seventeenth and eighteenth centuries, new doubts began to be raised over the authorship of the Homeric poems. In 1664, the French playwright and literary critic Abbé d'Aubignac declared that there was no such person as Homer, and that the Homeric poems were cobbled together from earlier oral poems. In 1713, the English scholar Richard Bentley construed a similar picture, suggesting that Homer was an oral poet who lived in the eleventh or tenth centuries BCE whose songs were 'collected together in the form of an epic poem' some five hundred years later. By far the most influential book to be published, however, was that of Friedrich August Wolf, whose *Prolegomena ad Homerum* (1795) argued that the Homeric poems were composed orally in the tenth century BCE in the form of short separate songs, but not written down and joined together until four hundred years later.

Wolf's work began a trend in Homeric scholarship that involved identifying which parts of the poem were older than others. The scholars who engaged in this kind of work came to be known as **Analysts**, and the two basic models that emerged were known as the **lay theory** and the **nucleus theory**. The **lay theory** assumed that the *Iliad* was the result of a combination of several originally separate and independent short poems, while the **nucleus theory** claimed that the *Iliad* consisted of an original 'core' to which material had progressively been added. Certain assumptions, however, commanded broad agreement: first, the Homeric poems had been created over a period of several centuries; and second, they had been created from several smaller poems.

In contrast to the **Analysts** stood a group of scholars known as the **Unitarians**, who argued that the artistic unity of the poems proved that they were the work of a single creative mind, and not the result of the addition of material round an original core or the stitching together of several independent poems. The debate between the Analysts and Unitarians came to be known as the **Homeric Question**, and provided one of the key focuses for Homeric scholarship throughout the nineteenth and twentieth centuries.

The theory of orality

In the 1930s, a new theory came to light, based on the fieldwork of two young American scholars, Milman Parry and Albert Lord. Working with oral poets (or *guslari*) in what was then Yugoslavia, Parry and Lord noticed several similarities between the kind of poetry produced by the *guslari* and that of Homer, particularly in its use of repeated phrases and expressions. Parry and Lord concluded that the *Iliad* must have begun life as an **extemporaneously composed oral poem** like the poems they were hearing in Yugoslavia, with oral poets drawing on set phrases and expressions, typical scenes and story patterns (known as **formulae**) to help them compose in performance.

While the **theory of orality** has proved compelling to many scholars, it is worth keeping in mind that Parry and Lord's fieldwork was designed to explain a single element in the Homeric poems – its repeated phrases and expressions. Indeed, it is important to note what while Parry and Lord's theory came to be known as the **theory of orality,** it did *not* introduce the idea that the Homeric poems were orally composed and transmitted (which had already been suggested by the Abbé d'Aubignac in 1664), but merely the idea that oral composition was responsible for the poem's otherwise inexplicable repetitiveness.

The debate over the origins of the *Iliad* – its authorship, the circumstances of its composition, etc. – is far from settled. One question that remains is whether the *Iliad* is an **oral poem** or merely an **orally derived** one? For the *Iliad* to be a genuinely oral poem, it would have to represent a word-for-word transcription of an oral performance. Many scholars think that this is not the case. Rather, it is argued, the *Iliad* is a poem that has made extensive use of the repeated phrases and expressions that are characteristic of oral poetry, but has actually been composed with the aid of writing. It is, in other words, a poem **formed in the oral tradition**, an **orally derived poem,** but not itself an oral poem.

Neoanalysis

One of the more recent strands in Homeric scholarship is **neoanalysis**. This considers the relationship between the *Iliad* and the other poems of the so-called **epic cycle**, which told of other episodes within the Trojan War. Poems within the epic cycle included the *Cypria*, which dealt with the origins of the war, as well as the *Aethiopis*, *Little Iliad* and *Sack of Ilium*, all of which dealt with events after the *Iliad*. While none of these poems survive in full, we do have brief summaries of their contents as well as a handful of fragments where lines from the poem have been quoted by authors whose works *do* survive.

One relationship that has been of particular interest to the Neoanalysts has been that between the *Iliad* and the lost epic known as the *Aethiopis*, the plots of which appear to have been extremely similar. In both epics, Achilles withdraws from battle based on a prophecy from his mother, but returns when a friend (Patroclus in the *Iliad*, Antilochus in the *Aethiopis*) is killed by a Trojan or Ethiopian champion (Hector in the *Iliad*, Memnon in the *Aethiopis*). Achilles manages to kill the person responsible for his friend's death, but knows that his own death must follow shortly afterwards. The *Iliad* ends with Achilles still alive, although his death has been repeatedly prophesied, while the *Aethiopis* depicts his death at the hands of Apollo and Paris, as well as his funeral.

It has been suggested that the poet of the *Iliad* transposed scenes from the *Aethiopis* into his own poem, putting them into contexts for which they were not primarily intended. We know, for example, that the *Aethiopis* contained a scene where Thetis and the Nereids mourned over the body of Achilles. In the *Iliad*, this becomes the strange scene in Book 18 where Thetis and the Nereids mourn over Achilles while he is still alive. Stranger still is the scene in Book 23 of the *Iliad* where the Greeks cannot get the funeral pyre of Patroclus to light because the winds are refusing to blow, but no explanation is given of why this might be the case. In the *Aethiopis*, however, the refusal of the winds to blow is explained by the fact that the wind gods are mourning the death of their brother, Memnon, whom Achilles has just killed. Both scenes – the appearance of Thetis and the Nereids in Book 18 and the winds' refusal to blow in Book 23 – appear to fit much more comfortably into the narrative of the *Aethiopis* than the *Iliad*.

Performance context

The Homeric poems were created to be performed, but how much do we know about the context of these performances? This depends on the period we are talking about. Before the sixth century BCE, the evidence for the performance context of epic poetry comes from the poems themselves, especially the *Odyssey*, which features two separate performing poets – Phemius in Ithaca and Demodocus in the land of the Phaeacians. In both cases, the poetic performance serves as a kind of post-dinner entertainment for the assembled guests.

There were no doubt other contexts for the performance of epic poetry, too. In another early poem, Hesiod's *Works and Days* (*c.* 700 BCE), we read about the performance of poetry at a funeral games, while in Book 9 of the *Iliad*, Achilles sings about 'the glorious deeds of gods and men' while sitting outside his tent.

Historical evidence for the performance of poetry begins to emerge in the sixth century BCE, at which point religious festivals serve as the context for the performance of poetry. Two important festivals here are the Panionia, which were celebrated among the Greeks of Asia Minor, as well as the Panathenaea, which was celebrated in Athens, both of which were said to feature the performance of at least parts of the *Iliad* and *Odyssey*.

The performance of epic poetry at these festivals may have resulted in the production of a more definitive version of the text, and there is some evidence that an 'authorized' version of both the *Iliad* and *Odyssey* was created in Athens in the sixth century BCE, known as the Peisistratid Recension after the Athenian tyrant, Peisistratus. That said, the evidence for this really is quite slight, and in any case the state of the text of both the *Iliad* and *Odyssey* when the Alexandrians came to edit it in the third century BCE suggests that any 'authorized' versions of the poems did not gain anything like universal acceptance.

The rhythm of epic poetry: Dactylic hexameter

Prosody

Unlike the poetry of English, which is based on patterns of stressed and unstressed syllables, Greek metre is based on patterns of heavy and light syllables. We use a '—' to indicate a heavy syllable, '∪' to indicate a light syllable, and '⊻' or '×' to indicate a syllable that may be heavy or light.

In order to scan Greek verse, it is necessary to know which syllables are heavy and which are light. In brief, a light syllable is one where a single short vowel (ε, ο, and short α, ι and υ) is followed by no more than one consonant; a heavy syllable is one containing either a long vowel (η, ω, and long α, ι and υ;), or a diphthong (e.g. ου, οι, αι, etc.), or where a short vowel is followed by two or more consonants, where ζ [zd], ξ [ks] and ψ [ps] count as double consonants. The scanning of a naturally short vowel as long if it is followed by two consonants is known as **lengthening by position**.

There are a handful of exceptions to these basic rules of scansion.

First, a short vowel followed by two consonants should be scanned short if the consonants in question are a **mute** (e.g. π, β, φ, κ, γ, χ, τ, δ and θ) followed by a **liquid** (λ, μ, ν and ϱ). Thus, the combinations πϱ, τϱ, πλ, etc. do not lengthen the preceding syllable. But there is an exception to the exception: the heaviest combinations of mutes and liquids (e.g. βλ, γλ, γν, γμ, δν, δμ) act like regular double consonants, i.e. they do lengthen the preceding syllable.

Second, a short vowel is sometimes lengthened even before a single consonant (usually δ, λ, μ, ν, or σ), where the word was *originally* spelt with two consonants. This is almost always the case when a word *used* to be spelt with a digamma (ϝ). This was a letter that represented a 'w' sound, but which fell out of use before the Homeric poems could be written down. It nevertheless retained an impact on the scansion of certain words and expressions. The first syllable of καλά, for example, is heavy because the word originally contained a digamma after the λ, i.e. καλϝός.

Elision, hiatus, correption and synizesis

In *most* cases, short open vowels (i.e. not followed by a consonant) at the end of words will be **elided** if the following word begins with a vowel. At 16.26, for example (οὔτασται δ᾽ Ὀδυσεὺς δουρικλυτὸς ἠδ᾽ Ἀγαμέμνων), δέ is elided by Ὀδυσεὺς, leaving δ᾽ Ὀδυσεὺς. The same happens later in the line with ἠδέ and Ἀγαμέμνων.

Note that, unlike in Latin, Greek verse does *not* include elided letters when written out. If Greek conventions applied to Latin verse, the third line of the *Aeneid* would read *litora mult'ill'et terris iactatus et alto*. Instead, we get *litora, multum ille et terris iactatus et alto*.

Sometimes, elision does not happen when we expect it to, a phenomenon known as **hiatus**. Hiatus can occur when the short open vowel at the end of a word immediately precedes one of the main **caesurae** (see below) in the line, or when the word that follows it begins with a vowel, but used to be spelt with a digamma. In the line πάντες, ἐπεὶ βασιλῆα ἴδον βεβλαμμένον ἦτορ (16.660), for example, the reason βασιλῆα does not elide with ἴδον is because ἴδον used to be spelt with a digamma, i.e. ϝίδον.

A long vowel or diphthong followed by a word beginning with a vowel may be scanned as light. This is known as **epic correption**, and is relatively common. In the line ἐξαῦτις Τρῶάς τε καὶ Ἕκτορα χαλκοκορυστὴν (16.654), for example, the word καὶ would be scanned light.

Finally, two vowels together within a word or in successive words may be treated as combining into a single, heavy syllable. This is known as **synizesis**, and is relatively rare. In the line κάππεσ᾽ ἀπ᾽ εὐεργέος δίφρου, λίπε δ᾽ ὀστέα θυμός (16.743), for example, the word εὐεργέος would be scanned heavy light light, with γέος being treated as a single syllable.

Metre

As we have already mentioned, the metre used in epic poetry is known as **dactylic hexameter**. This is a line made of six feet (or **metra**), each of which will either be a **dactyl** (heavy–light–light) or a **spondee** (heavy–heavy). The exception is the sixth foot, which is always made up of two syllables, the second of which may be either heavy or light. Thus, the line can be represented schematically as follows:

– UU | – UU | – UU | – UU | – UU | – ×

To demonstrate the variety of rhythms allowed by the dactylic hexameter line, here is the scansion of lines 16.20–23 which shows three different ways the hexameter line could scan (the second and third lines have the same rhythm):

– U U| – U U| – U U| – –| – UU| – –
τὸν δὲ βαρὺ στενάχων προσέφης Πατρόκλεες ἱππεῦ:

– U U| – –| –U U|– U U| – U U| – –
ὦ Ἀχιλεῦ Πηλῆος υἱὲ μέγα φέρτατ᾽ Ἀχαιῶν

– ∪ ∪| – –| – ∪ ∪| – ∪ ∪|–∪ ∪| – –
μὴ νεμέσα: τοῖον γὰρ ἄχος βεβίηκεν Ἀχαιούς.

– – | – – | – ∪ ∪| – ∪ ∪ |– ∪ ∪| – –
οἳ μὲν γὰρ δὴ πάντες, ὅσοι πάρος ἦσαν ἄριστοι,

We note in passing that line 16.21 is a highly unusual line, metrically speaking, requiring υἱὲ to be scanned light heavy.

Caesurae

Beyond this basic metrical framework, almost every line in Homer has a word break (or **caesura**) near the middle of the line, usually after the first heavy syllable of the third foot (**strong caesura**), or after the first light syllable of the third foot (**weak caesura**), which divides the line into two unequal halves. Here are the same lines as above (16.20–23) with the feet (|) and caesurae (‖) marked:

τὸν δὲ βα | ρὺ στενά | χων ‖ προσέ | φης Πατ | ρόκλεες | ἱππεῦ:
"ὦ Ἀχι | λεῦ Πη | λῆος υἱ | ὲ ‖ μέγα | φέρτατ᾽ | Ἀχαιῶν
μὴ νεμέ | σα: τοῖ | ον ‖ γὰρ ἄχ | ος βεβί | ηκεν Ἀ | χαιούς.
οἳ μὲν | γὰρ δὴ | πάντες, ‖ ὅ | σοι πάρος | ἦσαν ἄ | ριστοι

The presence of a caesura after υἱὲ shows us why the final ὲ is scanned long.

Formulae

The tendency for the hexameter line to accept only certain metrical patterns in certain positions made it relatively difficult for the oral poet to compose verse extemporaneously. In order to help him do so, he memorized a vast number of metrically useful phrases and expressions that he could use as and when required. These stock phrases and expressions are referred to as **formulae** (singular: **formula**), and could be anything from a single word to a whole line, or even several lines.

Repeated verses and formular expressions

One type of formula is the **repeated verse**. These were stock lines that the poet could deploy whenever a particular situation arose. To take a simple example, there are three occasions in the *Iliad* where a hero is deciding between two courses of action. Rather than coming up with a new way to describe this action each time, the poet makes use of exactly the same line on all three occasions: ὧδε δέ οἱ φρονέοντι δοάσσατο κέρδιον εἶναι ('and this seemed the best plan to his thinking', 16.652 = 13.458, 14.23). Similarly, there are four occasions in the *Iliad* where a character attacks something three times in a row, only for something different to happen on the fourth occasion. On each occasion, exactly the same line is used: ἀλλ᾽ ὅτε δὴ τὸ τέταρτον ἐπέσσυτο δαίμονι ἶσος ('but when for the fourth time he flung himself on like a god', 16.705 = 5.438, 16.786, 20.447).

Another type of formula is the **formular expression**. These had exactly the same function as repeated verses, but were shorter in length. Some of the most easily recognizable formular expressions are the **noun–epithet combinations** that are used to describe almost all the major characters in the poem, e.g. 'swift-footed Achilles', 'Agamemnon, lord of men', etc. While the use of epithets throughout the poem can seem gratuitous, they are actually performing an important metrical function in extending the description of characters from the three or four syllables of their name (e.g. Ἀγαμέμνων, 'Agamemnon') to a much more useable length – five, six or seven syllables if the poet wanted to fill the final quarter of the line (e.g. κρείων Ἀγαμέμνων, 'lord Agamemnon'), or eight or nine syllables if he wanted to fill the whole second half of the line (e.g. ἄναξ ἀνδρῶν Ἀγαμέμνων, 'Agamemnon, lord of men').

Noun–epithet combinations can be found throughout the poem, and not just for characters' names. Spears are 'long-shadowed' (δολιχόσκιον ἔγχος), ships are 'hollow' (νῆας . . . γλαφυράς), destruction is 'sheer' (αἰπὺν ὄλεθρον), fate is 'black' (κῆρα μέλαιναν) and so on. In all of these cases, it is important to note that the role of the epithet is primarily metrical, not poetic: when the poet describes spears as 'long-shadowed' or the ships as 'hollow', for example, these descriptors appear only because the poet needed an expression to fit a particular metrical pattern.

Formular expressions exist for a whole range of different parts of speech, not just the noun–epithet combinations we have seen above. Thus, we find formular expressions combining adverbs and verbs, conjunctions and verbs and so on. By far the most common formulae in the poem are those used to describe characters speaking to one another, though the oral poet seems to have memorized stock phrases and expressions for almost every commonly occurring action or situation in the poem, e.g. putting on armour, throwing a spear, falling on the ground, agonizing over what to do, weeping, preparing a meal, drinking wine, offering a sacrifice and so on.

The use of formulae is so embedded in the way this poem is created that they can sometimes appear in inappropriate contexts. The example that exercised the ancient scholars was the reference to Achilles in Book 18 as 'swift-footed' despite the fact that he is sitting on the ground and not doing much. But there are more egregious examples. Near the end of Book 16, for example, Patroclus casts a huge rock at Hector that ends up killing his charioteer, Cebriones. Is it really appropriate in this context to describe the chariot as εὐεργέος ('well-built', 16.743)?

Type scenes

In addition to repeated actions and situations, the *Iliad* also contains entire scenes that recur several times throughout the poem. These are known as **type scenes** and include things like the arrival and reception of a guest, the performance of a sacrifice, the preparation of a meal, the arming of a warrior and so on. The first person to study type scenes in detail was the German scholar Walter Arend, who noted that type scenes tended to be made up of a sequence of events which occurred in the same order every single time. In the case of a warrior arming himself, for example – something that happens four times in the *Iliad* – Arend noticed that the scene always began with a line or two of introduction, before describing (in order) the greaves and the breastplate, the sword, the shield, the helmet and the spear.

The use of type scenes dominates the narrative of the *Iliad*. The scholar Mark Edwards has even gone so far as to say that the narrative of the *Iliad* 'is carried forward almost entirely by a succession of type scenes, with only occasional use of short passages of description, similes, or apostrophes by the poet'. Indeed, one could analyse the beginning of Book 18 in terms of a succession of type scenes: the arrival of a messenger (1–34), a scene of mourning (35–64), a divine visit (65–147), a battle scene (148–64), a divine visit (165–202) and so on.

While type scenes provide the scaffolding for certain scenes in the poem, however, it is not the case that they are all absolutely identical. While the order of elements tended to remain constant, the poet could expand or contract any individual element however he liked, depending on its importance in the context. The type scene of two warriors meeting on the battlefield, for example, could fill anything from a single line to several hundred lines, as in the case of the meeting of Achilles and Aeneas in Book 20.

The poet could also negate elements altogether. In Book 6, for example, the poet follows Hector as he goes to meet his wife, Andromache. Ordinarily, the type scene that involves the arrival of a guest ends with the visitor meeting his host. In this case, however, Hector comes to his family home to find that no one is there, a striking negation of what the audience expected to hear next. In Book 16, similarly, we follow Patroclus as he puts on the armour of Achilles. It is the third such scene in the poem, all of which end with the warrior picking up either a single spear or pair of spears. In this case, however, immediately after Patroclus picks up a pair of spears, the poet adds the detail that there was one spear that he was *not* able to pick up – 'the spear of the excellent Achilles . . . the huge, heavy, massive spear which no other Achaean could wield, but Achilles alone had the skill to handle' (16.140–143). The expectation that the warrior will complete his arming when he picks up his spear is emphatically denied in the case of Patroclus, and the implication is clear: Patroclus is not quite the warrior that Achilles wants him to be.

Story patterns

In the previous section, we thought about the use of type scenes, recurring scenes in the poem such as the arrival and reception of a guest, where a sequence of elements tend to appear in the same order. In this section, we move on to **story patterns**, broader plot structures that underlie whole episodes in the poem.

One of the most fundamental story patterns in the *Iliad* is that which has been described by scholars as **withdrawal, devastation and return**. This is a pattern that involves the withdrawal of the hero from society, the subsequent catastrophic effects for that society and/or for the hero himself, and a final return to society by the hero that restores peace, order and harmony. In some cases, the focus is not on the devastation of the society abandoned by the hero, but on the experience of the hero himself during his withdrawal, which often involves some kind of test, sometimes a symbolic death, and a triumphant return to the society he has left behind.

In any case, it is clear to see how the pattern of withdrawal, devastation and return underpins the main storyline in the poem: Achilles withdraws from battle, the Greek army suffers catastrophic losses in his absence, before Achilles returns to battle and restores order by defeating Hector. At the same time, however, it is interesting to see just how often this basic story pattern recurs, either in part or in full, elsewhere in the poem.

In Book 9, for example, Phoenix attempts to convince Achilles to return to battle by telling him the myth of Meleager (9.524–605). In his story, Phoenix describes how Meleager and the Aetolians were defending their city against the Couretes, when Meleager decided to withdraw from the battle in wrath (550–572), just as Achilles had done (and was continuing to do) at Troy. The story continues with the detail that Meleager had rejected the Aetolians' offer of gifts to return to battle, and had ultimately been forced to return to battle only when his own house was under attack, at which point the gifts were no longer on offer (573–594). While Phoenix has clearly emphasized the similarities between Meleager's situation and Achilles' own for rhetorical effect, it nevertheless remains a repeat of the basic pattern of withdrawal, devastation, return.

We get glimpses of other withdrawals elsewhere in the poem, too. The removal of Paris from the battlefield by Aphrodite in Book 3 leads to a kind of withdrawal on his part for the next three books: he only returns to battle when Hector physically goes to get him in Book 6. Another withdrawal – more fleeting still – is that of Aeneas, who is seen skulking at the back of the fighting in Book 13. The reason for his withdrawal, the poet explains, is on the grounds of his anger at Priam, who has not shown him sufficient honour (13.459–461). No more details are provided, and Aeneas almost immediately returns to battle after some encouragement from Deiphobus, but it is a glimpse of another withdrawal, devastation, return story, nonetheless.

While the withdrawal, devastation, return story pattern provides the narrative superstructure for the poem as a whole, the poet appears to make use of a number of other story patterns in individual episodes. Another story pattern that occurs frequently in the poem is that of the **revenge killing**. Within the main storyline, Patroclus kills Sarpedon, which leads Hector to kill Patroclus, which leads Achilles to kill Hector. But the same basic pattern can be seen in miniature throughout the poem (e.g. in Book 11, Agamemnon kills Iphidamas, which leads Coön to stab Agamemnon, which leads Agamemnon to kill Coön, etc.) while similar chains of revenge killings could be found in other episodes from the Trojan War, too (e.g. in the *Aethiopis*, Memnon kills Antilochus, which leads Achilles to kill Memnon, which leads Apollo and Paris to kill Achilles, etc.).

Story patterns are similar to type scenes in that they provide a poet with a superstructure within which he can build his story. Whereas the type scene only provides the superstructure for a particular action, however, the story pattern can provide the structure for the whole poem. Like type scenes, story patterns can appear in a range of sizes: just as duels between warriors can be anything from 2 to 200 lines, so, too, do we see story patterns recur in both highly condensed and highly expanded forms – from the 10-line withdrawal and return of Aeneas, to the 15,000-line withdrawal and return of Achilles.

Creativity and innovation in oral poetry

The reliance on formulae, type scenes and story patterns throughout the *Iliad* may seem to preclude any kind of creativity or innovation on the part of the poet. Is the *Iliad* anything more than a poetic 'paint-by-numbers', where the poet slots prefabricated blocks of poetry (**formulae**) into predetermined arrangements (**type scenes, story patterns**)?

One argument that has been made in favour of the 'paint-by-numbers' model of poetic composition is the presence of epithets in 'inappropriate' contexts. One of the most egregious examples in this comes in the Odyssey, where Nausicaa's dirty laundry is described as 'radiant' (*Od.* 6.74), though we might also think of the description of Cebriones' chariot as 'well-built' (16.743) at precisely the moment its owner is flung from this very chariot to his death, or the fact that Achilles is constantly described as 'swift-footed' despite the fact that he spends most the poem sitting in his tent.

There is another way of thinking about 'inappropriate' epithets, however, which conceives of the *Iliad* as a poem that attempts to assert its *difference* from the traditional material from which it emerged. On this reading, the reason the epithet 'swift-footed' exists at all is because previous incarnations of the character of Achilles actually demonstrated this characteristic. By having 'swift-footed' Achilles do things that are emphatically not running, the poet of the Iliad is highlighting just how new and radical his telling of the story is.

Indeed, there are moments in the poem where the poet demonstrates a supreme ability to manipulate traditional material to suit the context. When Priam meets Achilles in Book 24, for example, one of the things he does is kiss Achilles' 'terrible, man-slaying hands' (χεῖρας δεινὰς ἀνδροφόνους, 24.477–478). The phrase χεῖρας . . . ἀνδροφόνους was previously used in Book 18 to describe the action of Achilles' placing his hands on the breast of the dead Patroclus, though the epithet ἀνδροφόνος is otherwise used almost exclusively of Hector (11x in the poem, including at line 509). By transferring the epithet to Achilles' hands once again, what we get is a kind of palimpsest in which the figures of deaths of Patroclus and Hector are superimposed on one another, highlighting what Achilles and Priam have in common. The effect is so subtle, so effective, that it cannot possibly have been an accident.

When it comes to **type scenes**, too, we have already seen how the poet could negate individual aspects to add particular emphasis in specific contexts, e.g. Patroclus' emphatic *failure* to pick up Achilles' spear at the end of his arming scene in Book 16, Achilles' emphatic *abstention* from food after the preparation of the meal in Book 19, etc. These, too, represent creative and innovative departures from the traditional material.

Finally, the story of the *Iliad* may well have represented a radical departure from traditional stories about the Trojan War. It has been suggested, for example, that Homer was the first to introduce the tragic deaths of previously immortal heroes such as Heracles and the Dioscuri, that his presentation of Achilles in particular was markedly different from traditional stories in which he was simply an unstoppable killing machine, and that his sympathetic presentation of Troy and the Trojans was untraditional, if not unprecedented.

The manipulation of traditional material was one of the key ways in which oral poets demonstrated their creativity and ingenuity, and the *Iliad* is brimming with it. What is unclear, however, is whether the creativity we observe within the traditional material is the result of a particularly talented oral poet, or a sign of the more expansive creative possibilities afforded by the technology of writing.

If the poem as we have it resembles the kind of compositions that were created by oral poets in the centuries preceding the invention of writing, the innovative manipulation of formulae and type scenes that we find throughout may well indicate an oral poet of particular talent or expertise.

Translating Homer

Those coming to Homer for the first time may find translation difficult, not least because of the epic dialect. While most grammars provide an exhaustive list of *all* the differences between Attic and Homeric Greek, which can be overwhelming, this section outlines the differences that appear most often, and which it might be preferable to learn first of all.

Nouns

When it comes to nouns, Homer makes use of alternative endings across all declensions and cases. Many of these are fairly similar to their Attic equivalent, e.g. -αων or -εων instead of -ῶν in the genitive plural, though one should take particular notice of alternative endings for the **genitive singular**, which are quite different. These include -αο or -εω as alternatives to -ου in the first declension (e.g. Ἀτρεΐδαο and Ἀτρεΐδεω, instead of Ἀτρεΐδου, 'son of Atreus') and -οιο as an alternative to -ου for nouns of the second declension (e.g. πεδίοιο instead of πεδίου, 'the plain').

In addition to this, Homer alternates freely between -σ- and -σσ-, depending on what is required by the metre. ποσί and ποσσί (dative plural of πούς, 'foot') are equivalent, for example. The same doubling of the sigma can be found in adjectives, too, e.g. τόσσος and τόσος, μέσσος and μέσος.

Pronouns

Pronouns have a tendency to look quite different from their Attic equivalents, too. This includes the **genitive singular**, where potential endings include: -εῖο, -εο, -εῦ and -εθεν, e.g. ἐμεῖο, ἐμέο, etc. ('me'), σεῖο, σέο, etc. ('you'), as well as the Ionic forms of common pronouns, e.g. ἄμμες, ἄμμε and ἄμμι, which are alternatives to ἡμεῖς, ἦμας and ἡμῖν ('we', 'us').

It is important to note that what looks like the definite article in Attic Greek (ὁ, ἡ, τό) is (almost always) used not as a definite article, but as a **third-person personal pronoun** ('him, her, it') or **third-person relative pronoun** ('who, whose, to whom'). In the lines ἑτέρηφι δὲ λάζετο πέτρον / μάρμαρον ὀκριόεντα τόν οἱ περὶ χεὶρ ἐκάλυψεν (16.734–735), for example, the word τόν is a relative pronoun referring to πέτρον ('he picked up a stone, which . . .').

In the line ταῦτ᾽ ἄρα οἱ φρονέοντι παρίστατο Φοῖβος Ἀπόλλων (16.715), οἱ means '(to) him' and is governed by the verb παρίστατο ('to come up to, approach'): 'As he was thinking about this, Phoebus Apollo came up *to him*.'

Verbs

When it comes to the **verb**, there are two things to look for. The first is that the aorist and imperfect tenses will often drop their augment: βάλον can appear instead of ἔβαλον, for example, or ἔμβαλε instead of ἐνέβαλε. The second is that verbs can be left uncontracted, i.e. one might find ἐρέω instead of ἐρῶ and so on.

Finally, it is worth noting that the **infinitive** can end in -εμεν, -μεναι, or -ναι, which can make it look like a present participle, e.g. δόμεναι = δοῦναι, ἀκουέμεναι = ἀκούειν. In addition to this, ἔμεν, ἔμμεν and ἔμμεναι are all used as an alternative to the Attic εἶναι ('to be').

The dual

In Attic Greek, nouns, adjectives and verbs are usually one of two numbers: singular or plural: βαίνει ('he/she/it goes') indicates the movement of a single person, while βαίνουσι(ν) indicates the movement of several people and so on.

In Homer, however, there is a third number known as the 'dual', which can be used when the verb has exactly two people or things for its subject, or if a noun or adjective denotes two people or things. Thus, τὼ . . . δηρινθήτην (16.756) = 'the *two* men fought', ὄσσε φαεινώ, (16.645) = 'his (two) eyes', τὼ . . . μνησαμένω (24.509) = 'they *both* remembered', etc.

The dual appears quite rarely in your set texts (but cf. 16.758, which has three of them), though for the sake of completion, the key endings to learn and recognize are: (1) the third-person endings for verbs in the past tense, which are **-την** (active) and **-σθην** (middle/passive); (2) the third-person pronouns, which are **τώ** (nominative and accusative) and **τοῖν** (genitive and dative) across all genders; and (3) the endings for nouns and adjectives in the second declension, which are **-ω** (nominative/accusative) and **-οιν** (genitive/dative).

The structure of Homeric verse

One of the aspects of Homeric verse that makes it slightly easier to translate than other poetry is the relative simplicity of Homeric syntax. Because oral composition is greatly facilitated by lines that are self-contained units of thought, almost three-quarters of the lines in Homer are grammatically complete by the end of the line. This way of structuring the poem gave the poet the freedom to elaborate or qualify a particular thought if he wanted to, or to move on to the next sentence if he did not. An example of this can be seen in the first six lines of the poem quoted below. These have been translated literally to retain the line structure of the original Greek:

μῆνιν ἄειδε, θεὰ, Πηληϊάδεω Ἀχιλῆος
οὐλομένην, ἣ μυρί' Ἀχαιοῖς ἄλγε' ἔθηκε,
πολλὰς δ' ἰφθίμους ψυχὰς Ἄϊδι προΐαψεν
ἡρώων, αὐτοὺς δὲ ἑλώρια τεῦχε κύνεσσιν
οἰωνοῖσί τε πᾶσι, Διὸς δ' ἐτελείετο βουλή,
ἐξ οὗ δὴ τὰ πρῶτα διαστήτην ἐρίσαντε
Ἀτρεΐδης τε ἄναξ ἀνδρῶν καὶ δῖος Ἀχιλλεύς.

Sing, goddess, of the anger of Achilles, son of Peleus
the accursed anger, which brought uncounted anguish on the Achaeans
and hurled down to Hades many mighty souls
of heroes, and which made their bodies the prey to dogs
and to all the birds, and the plan of Zeus was fulfilled,
from the time when the two men quarrelled and stood apart,
Atreus' son, the lord of men, and godlike Achilles.

(1.1–6)

As we can see, the sentence could end at the end of any of the six lines: the first line is a complete sentence, as are the first two lines, as are the first three lines and so on. Despite the difficulties of the epic dialect, the structure of Homeric verse is more straightforward than much of later Greek (and Latin) literature. Translation can be tackled line by line, rather than the more diffuse, difficult syntax of writers like Thucydides and Cicero.

Language and style

Another important aspect of Homeric Greek is the language and style of the poem. In this section, we will discuss the Homeric dialect, before looking at several stylistic elements found within the poem: (1) hapax legomena; (2) similes; (3) ring composition; (4) end-stopping and enjambment; and (5) rhetorical devices.

The epic dialect

Ancient Greek had several literary dialects, which could differ from one another as much as Italian from Spanish. The three major dialects were Ionic, Aeolic and Doric, although there were subdialects of each of these. Attic Greek, the dialect with which students will likely be most familiar, was a subdialect of the Ionic dialect, for example.

Most literature was written in a single dialect: choral lyric tended to be written in Doric, while philosophy, oratory and history tended to be written in Attic. When we come to the language of Homer, however, we find that it is a combination of several dialects: it is primarily Ionic, but also features a great deal of Aeolic and some Attic.

The rationale for using such a mixed language was to provide the poet the widest range of material for composition in performance. Having a larger number of options for filling particular material gaps was more important than maintaining dialectical purity. Thus, the epic dialect allowed for both the Ionic and Aeolic words for 'we'

(Ionic: ἡμεῖς, Aeolic: ἄμμες), which mean the same thing but are scanned differently. Other examples of where words from other dialects gave the poet the same words but in a different rhythm include the use of both προτί (Aeolic) and πρός (Ionic), κεν (Aeolic) and ἄν (Ionic), and of all three of μέν (Ionic), μάν (Aeolic) and μήν (Attic).

Sometimes, the Aeolic word was metrically identical to its Ionic equivalent, but allowed for rhythmic manipulation elsewhere in the line. Examples of this include the use of the Aeolic πτόλις and πτόλεμος alongside the Ionic πόλις and πόλεμος, where the double-consonant at the beginning of the Aeolic form ensured that the syllable that came before it would be scanned long.

The desire for metrical flexibility also manifests itself in nouns and verbs. The poet has no fewer than three options for the nominative plural of υἱός ('son') – υἱέες, υἱεῖς and υἷες – all of which scan differently, while we have already seen the range of grammatically equivalent but metrically different case endings available to the oral poet, such as the use of both -οιο and -ου in the genitive singular. The admission of both uncontracted verbs and artificially lengthened verbs (e.g. the additional ό in εἰσορόωντας, 24.481, a phenomenon known as **diectasis**) also serves the same purpose.

Another aspect of facilitating composition in dactylic hexameter was the preservation of certain words and expressions even where they were already several centuries old. The phrase κλέος ἄφθιτον ('undying glory'), for example, is exactly equivalent to the Sanskrit *srávas ákṣitam* and has thus been dated to the second millennium BCE. The phrase 'two-handled cup' (δέπας ἀμφικύπελλον) must date back to a similar period because two-handled cups seem to have been a product of the Mycenaean period (*c.* 1600–1100 BCE) but not later. In some cases, the metrical usefulness of a word or expression resulted in its preservation even when the meaning of the word itself was lost. The word ἐριούνιος is often used in the *Iliad* as an epithet for Hermes (e.g. Ἑρμείας ἐριούνιος, 24.457), for example, although its meaning was unknown even to the Greeks.

Finally, many of the grammatical oddities of Homeric verse also appear to be of great antiquity, and we should assume that these, too, were preserved in the oral tradition in order to facilitate composition in dactylic hexameter. The separation of prepositional pre-verbs from their verbs (e.g. **ἐν** δ' ἄρα νῶτον **ἔθηκ**' at 9.207 = Attic **ἐνέθηκε**), for example, was archaic even by the Mycenaean period, as was the omission of the augment in past tense verbs, but both gave the poet more flexibility when it came to composing his line.

In general, the epic dialect should be seen as being optimized for composition in performance in dactylic hexameter. Anything that could be done to facilitate this process, e.g. the use of words and expressions from different dialects and periods, the ability to add vowels in the middle of words (**diectasis**) or remove augments or pre-verbs was preserved in the oral tradition, and helps to explain why the epic dialect has the characteristics that it does.

Hapax Legomena

Given the reliance of the oral poet on formulaic lines and phrases, special attention must be paid to words that appear only once in the poem. These words are known by the Greek term *hapax legomenon* (plural: *hapax legomena* or *hapaxes*). According to the most recent count of *hapaxes* in Homer, there are 1,142 such words in the *Iliad*, or 1 every 13.7 verses.

Hapaxes are strongly linked to non-formulaic contexts, where the poet is describing something that does not happen often in the poem. Battle scenes feature very few *hapaxes*, for example, because they happen frequently throughout the poem, and the poet will rarely throw in a completely new word when describing the same kind of event. A warrior will not suddenly produce a totally new kind of weapon, for example, or engage in a totally different set of actions. Consequently, the books with the fewest *hapaxes* are also those which are the most battle-heavy – Books 7, 8 and 17.

Where the poet moves into more 'unusual' subject-matter, however, *hapaxes* are far more common. The seduction of Zeus by Hera in Book 14, for example, takes the poet into relatively uncharted territory and includes a large number of *hapaxes* related to love and seduction, e.g. **παρήπαφεν** εὐνηθῆναι ('she *beguiled* him into sleeping with her', 14.360), θυμὸν ἐνὶ στήθεσσι **περιπροχυθεὶς** ('having *melted* the heart in my breast', 14.316), etc.

The same is true of the description of the Shield of Achilles in Book 18, where the poet describes the images that Hephaestus has depicted on its surface: various planets and stars, a domestic scene featuring a quarrel in a village square, various scenes of agriculture, viticulture and animal husbandry and so on. Almost none of this appears elsewhere in the poem, which is why we get so many *hapaxes* here, too, e.g. κεραμεύς ('potter', 18.601), φορῆες ('grape-bearers', 18.566), παρθένοι **ἀλφεσίβοιαι** ('young girls *sought for their beauty*', 18.593).

The character who uses *hapaxes* more than any other in the *Iliad* is Achilles, who uses a total of 80 (1 every 12.2. lines). Of these words, 18 are never used again in the entirety of Greek literature. His use of *hapaxes* have been seen as a sign of his eloquence, as well as of a character with a uniquely broad philosophical and emotional range. While almost every hero in the poem is concerned with honour, for example, it is only Achilles who uses the adjective ληϊστοὶ ('stealable') to describe the fact that material goods (including enslaved women) can be taken away as well as given. Indeed, it is hard to imagine any other character in the poem describing themselves as παῖδα **παναώριον** ('a child *doomed to die all-untimely*', 24.540), even if they had the foreknowledge that Achilles had.

Some of the *hapaxes* that appear in your set text include: αἰναρέτη ('a man whose valour is fatal to his friends', 16.31), τήθεα ('oysters' or 'sea-squirts', 16.747), διφῶν ('searching after something deeply hidden'), μιαρός ('defiled', 24.420), παιδοφόνοιο ('child-killing', 24.506) and βούβρωστις ('hunger', 24.532).

Similes

A general rule in Homeric verse is that the more important something is, the more time the poet will spend on it. Earlier, we looked at the first six lines of the poem and saw how the structure of Homeric verse allowed for the poet to constantly expand his thoughts, line after line, by the use of qualifying adjectives, conjunctions or subordinate clauses. Before that, we discussed the use of type scenes, which could also be greatly expanded if the poet wanted to pause on a moment of particular significance.

Another way that the poet can slow down the narrative, however, is through the use of similes. In Book 17, for example, the poet adds to the gravity of Menelaus' decision to leave the battlefield by including a simile: he retreats from the battle, we are told, 'like a great bearded lion driven from a farmstead by dogs' (17.109–110). If the poet wants to add great emphasis to the importance of a particular moment, he can use several similes in a row. In Book 2, for example, as the Greeks march into battle, the poet produces no fewer than five similes back-to-back: the Greeks' bronze armour gleams 'like annihilating fire', the various contingents of the Greek forces are 'like great flocks of flying birds' or 'great crowds of swarming flies', their leaders are like herdsman herding cattle, while Agamemnon himself is 'like the foremost of all the cattle'.

Similes can be very short, such as the description of Achilles leaping out of his chair 'like a lion' (λέων ὣς, 24.572), but they can also be very long, expanding over several lines to describe a whole scene, and potentially having several points of contact with the narrative proper. The latter form of similes are generally referred to as 'extended similes'.

Extended similes are far more common in the *Iliad* (about 200 examples in about 16,000 lines) than the *Odyssey* (about 40 in 12,000 lines), but they are not distributed evenly throughout the poem. Book 1 has no extended similes, for example, while Books 6, 9 and 24 have only 2 each. On the other hand, the battle scenes of Books 16–17 contain over extended 40 similes.

Two more points about similes. First, they tend to draw their imagery from the world that is pointedly *not* the world of warfare. The subjects for similes include weather and other natural phenomena (e.g. storms, floods, fires, etc.), hunting, herding and other animals (e.g. lions, boars, birds, etc.) and human technology (e.g. carpentry, weaving, etc.). One of the effects of this is to heighten the emotional impact of a scene by virtue of the contrast between the world of the simile and the world of the narrative. To take one example, consider the description of Gorgythion in Book 8, whose head droops down 'like a poppy in a garden, bent by the weight of its seed and the showers of spring' (8.306–308). The delicacy of the image of the poppy contrasts strongly with the brutality of Gorgythion's death, enhancing its emotional impact.

Second, it is important to note that similes can be used by both the narrator and his characters – although they are much less common in direct speech. As we might expect, the character who uses similes the most is Achilles (8 in total, 4 extended and 4 short), and his doing so is just another sign of his emotional range and self-awareness. Of particular interest are those moments where Achilles uses similes to analyse his own situation, such as the beginning of 16, in which he compares Patroclus' coming up to him in tears as being 'like a little girl running along by her mother and demanding to be carried, pulling at her dress and holding her back as she tries to hurry on, and looking up at her tearfully until she picks her up' (16.7–10).

End-stopping and enjambment

One of the most commonly used stylistic features in Homeric verse is the use of word position to lend special emphasis to a particular word or phrase. Two things that students should look out for are **end-stopping** (where the end of the line marks the end of a clause) and **enjambment** (where the clause runs over to the next line). There is clearly a kind of inevitability to this – lines will either be end-stopped or not end-stopped – so students should look for the **repetition of enjambment or end-stopping**, or for words placed in what is known as the **emphatic runover position**, which is where the enjambment consists of a single word, followed immediately by a pause. In general, frequent end-stopping represents slowly spoken, calm, measured speech, whereas frequent emphatic runover words indicate high emotion, anger, bitterness, vehemence and so on.

One example of the impact of repeated enjambment can be seen in the following lines, which describes Priam's arrival at Achilles' hut in Book 24:

Πρίαμος δ᾽ ἐξ ἵππων ἆλτο χαμᾶζε,
Ἰδαῖον δὲ κατ᾽ αὖθι λίπεν: ὃ δὲ μίμνεν ἐρύκων
ἵππους ἡμιόνους τε: γέρων δ᾽ ἰθὺς κίεν οἴκου,
τῇ ῥ᾽ Ἀχιλεὺς ἵζεσκε Διῒ φίλος: ἐν δέ μιν αὐτὸν
εὗρ᾽, ἕταροι δ᾽ ἀπάνευθε καθήατο: τὼ δὲ δύ᾽ οἴω
ἥρως Αὐτομέδων τε καὶ Ἄλκιμος ὄζος Ἄρηος
ποίπνυον παρεόντε: νέον δ᾽ ἀπέληγεν ἐδωδῆς
ἔσθων καὶ πίνων: ἔτι καὶ παρέκειτο τράπεζα.

Priam jumped down to the ground from his chariot,
and left Idaeus there where he was. He stayed there holding
the horses and mules, and the old man went straight for the house,
where Achilles loved of Zeus was sitting. Inside he found
that man, and his companions sitting apart from him – two only,
the hero Automedon and Alcimus, branch of Ares,
were busy close by him – he had just ceased from his desire
for eating and drinking: the table was still there beside him.
(24.469–476, lightly adapted from Hammond)

Rhetorical devices

The poet of the *Iliad* was highly attuned to the impact of rhetorical devices, and they are deployed carefully and knowingly throughout the poem. Rather than simply *identifying* different rhetorical devices, students should think about how they enact meaning. What is their impact? If a character uses a rhetorical device, what might this say about that character? How might we read the sentence differently if it had *not* included that particular rhetorical device?

Anaphora is the repetition of words at the beginning of two or more consecutive clauses. The repetition might be used for emphasis, with each clause building on the last, or it might invite comparison, in which case the anaphora may be accompanied by the particles μέν and δὲ. In Book 16, for example, we read the following lines:

πολλὰ δὲ **Κεβριόνην ἀμφ᾽** ὀξέα δοῦρα πεπήγει
ἰοί τε πτερόεντες ἀπὸ νευρῆφι θορόντες,
πολλὰ δὲ χερμάδια μεγάλ᾽ ἀσπίδας ἐστυφέλιξαν
μαρναμένων **ἀμφ᾽ αὐτόν**.

> **Many** (πολλὰ) sharp spears had driven in **around Cebriones** (Κεβριόνην ἀμφ'), and feathered arrows leaping from the string, and **many** (πολλὰ) great stones battered their shields as they fought on **over him** (**ἀμφ' αὐτόν**).
>
> (16.772–775)

Here, the use of anaphora (πολλὰ ... πολλὰ, 16.772, 775) emphasizes just how fierce the fighting is over the corpse of Cebriones, an effect that is heightened by the sheer range of the kinds of missile that are indicated ('spears', 'arrows', 'stones'). We might also note the framing of the description with terms meaning 'over Cebriones'/'his body' (Κεβριόνην ἀμφ' ... ἀμφ' αὐτόν, 16.772, 775), and the half rhyme of πτερόεντες ('feathered') and θορόντες (leaping).

Asyndeton is the omission of one or more conjunctions, a technique that can indicate the anxiety or fear of a speaker (when found in direct speech) or the rapid succession of events (when found in the main narrative). A good example of the impact of asyndeton comes in Book 24, when Idaeus and Priam, who are halfway between Troy and the Greek camp in the middle of the night, suddenly spot a man emerging from the darkness. Idaeus speaks:

> φράζεο Δαρδανίδη: φραδέος νόου ἔργα τέτυκται.
> ἄνδρ' ὁρόω, τάχα δ' ἄμμε διαρραίσεσθαι ὀΐω.
>
> 'Take care, stock of Dardanus! Here is something that needs thought and care. I can see a man, and I think that we shall soon be torn apart.'
>
> (24.354–355)

Idaeus is clearly anxious ('I think that we shall soon be torn apart'), an emotional state that is highlighted by the use of three very short sentences, all of which lack a conjunction.

Asyndeton is not only used by anxious characters, however. In Book 16, Hector and Patroclus' struggle over the body of Cebriones is compared to a fight between two lions:

> ὥ τ' ὄρεος κορυφῇσι περὶ κταμένης ἐλάφοιο
> ἄμφω πεινάοντε μέγα φρονέοντε μάχεσθον:
>
> Then these two fought over Cebriones like two lions, who are both hungry and fight in high fury on the peak of a mountain over a deer that is killed.
>
> (16.757–758)

The phrases ἄμφω πεινάοντε ('being hungry') and μέγα φρονέοντε ('with great energy') should have a conjunction between them. The fact that they do not perhaps evokes the intensity of the battle.

Appendix: Homeric Greek

The Homeric dialect has numerous differences from the Attic Greek that students will be most familiar with. The following section, while not exhaustive, lists some of the main features of the Homeric dialect. More extensive notes are provided where necessary in the line-by-line commentary.

Nouns

First declension

- For ᾱ, we always find η, regardless of where it appears in the word, e.g. χώρη = Attic χώρα, θύρη = Attic θύρα, νεηνίης = Attic νεανίας.
- The nominative singular of some masculines in -ης is shortened to ᾰ, e.g. ἱππότα = Attic ἱππότης, νεφεληγερέτα = Attic νεφεληγερέτης.
- The genitive singular of masculines ends in -αω or -εω, e.g. Ἀτρείδαο, Ἀτρείδεω = Attic Ἀτρείδου.
- The genitive plural of masculines ends in -άων or -έων, e.g. θεάων = Attic θεῶν, νυμφάων = Attic νυμφῶν.
- The dative plural almost always ends in -ῃσι(ν) or -ῃς, e.g. πύλῃσιν = Attic πύλαις, but θεαῖς.

Second declension

- The genitive singular ends in -οιο as well as -ου, e.g. πεδίοιο and πεδίου.
- The dative plural ends in -οισι as well as -οις, e.g. φύλλοισι and φύλλοις.
- The genitive and dative dual end in -οιϊν, so ἵπποιϊν, not ἵπποιν.

Third declension

- The accusative singular ends in -ιν as well as -ιδα, e.g. γλαυκῶπιν and γλαυκώπιδα.
- Endings in -ηα correspond to -εα, e.g. βασιλῆα = Attic βασιλέα.
- Genitive singular endings in -ηος and -ιος correspond to -εως, e.g. βασιλῆος = Attic βασιλέως, πόλιος = Attic πόλεως.
- Accusastive plural endings in -ηας correspond to -εας, e.g. βασιλῆας = Attic βασιλέας.
- Genitive plural endings in -ηων correspond to -εων, e.g. βασιλήων = Attic βασιλέων.
- The dative plural ends in -εσσι and -σι, e.g. πόδεσσι = Attic ποσί, ἔπεσσι = Attic ἔπεσι.
- The genitive and dative dual end in -οιιν, e.g. ποδοῖιν.

Pronouns

ἐγώ, σύ, 'I', 'you'

- Genitive singular: ἐμεῖο, ἐμέο, ἐμεῦ, μευ, ἐμέθεν; so with σύ – σεῖο, σέο, etc.

ἕ, 'him'

- Genitive singular: εἷο, ἕο, εὗ, ἕθεν = Attic: αὐτοῦ
- Dative singular: ἑοῖ, οἱ = Attic: αὐτῷ

ἡμεῖς, ὑμεῖς, 'we', 'you'

- Accusative plural: ἡμέας, ἄμμε
- Genitive plural: ἡμείων, ἡμέων
- Dative plural: ἄμμιν; so with ὑμεῖς

σφεῖς, 'they'

- Accuative plual: σφε, σφέας, σφας
- Genitive plural: σφείων, σφέων
- Dative plural: σφι, σφισί

τίς, 'who, what, which'

- Nominative singular: τίς
- Accusative singular: τίνα
- Genitive singular: τέο, τεῦ
- Genitive plural: τέων
- Dative singular: τέῳ

ὁ, ἡ, τό, 'he, she, it'

- In Homer, ὁ, ἡ, τό for the most part denotes a third personal pronoun ('he, she, it'), though there are (rare) occasions where translating as a definite article, as in Attic prose, is appropriate.
- Nominative plural: οἱ, αἱ, or τοί, ταί
- Dative plural: τοῖς, τοῖσι, τῇς, τῇσι as well as ταῖς

Verbs

Future

- Generally uncontracted, e.g. ἐρέω = Attic ἐρῶ, τελέω = Attic τελέσω.

Present/Imperfect

- The endings -σκον and -σκόμην may be used to express repetition of the action, e.g. φύγεσκον = 'they kept on running away'.

Aorist/Imperfect

- The augment may be omitted in both the aorist and imperfect tense, e.g. βάλον = Attic ἔβαλον, ἔμβαλε = Attic ἐνέβαλε.

- third person plural of aorist passive may end in -εν instead of -ησαν, e.g. φόβηθεν = Attic ἐφοβήθησαν, ἔμιχθεν = Attic ἐμίχθησαν.

Moods

Subjunctive

- Appears with a short vowel, e.g. ἴομεν = Attic ἴωμεν.
- second person singular active can end in -σθα, e.g. ἐθέλησθα = Attic ἐθέλῃς.
- second person singular middle ends in -ηαι or -εαι, e.g. εὔξεαι = Attic εὔξῃ.
- third person singular active ends in -σι, e.g. φορεῇσι = φορῇ.
- Occasionally used in place of the future tense.

Infinitive

- Appears with the endings -μεν, -μεναι and -ναι for -ειν and -ναι, e.g. δόμεναι = Attic δοῦναι, ἴμεν = Attic ἰέναι, ἀκουέμεν(αι) = Attic ἀκούειν.
- ἔμεν, ἔμμεν and ἔμμεναι = Attic εἶναι.

Contracted verbs

- Verbs in – άω can appear contracted, uncontracted, or even expanded with the addition of a like-sounding, short vowel either side of the long vowel, e.g. ὁρόωντες = Attic ὁρῶντες.
- Verbs in – έω are generally uncontracted, but sometimes form ει from εε or εει, η from εε, or ευ from εο or εου.
- Verbs in – όω are generally contracted.

Particles

- ἄρα (also ἄρ, ῥά) = 'so, next'
- δή = 'indeed'
- ἦ = 'surely'
- περ = 'just, even'
- τε = 'and', or to show a general remark
- τοι = 'I tell you', but may also = σοι ('to you, for you')

Further reading

All quotations in this Introduction have been taken from Martin Hammond's prose translation of the *Iliad*, first published by Penguin in 1987, unless otherwise indicated. Where necessary, the names of characters have been changed to their more familiar

Latin forms, e.g. 'Achilles' instead of 'Achilleus', 'Achaeans' instead of 'Achaians' and so on.

Short introductions

Barker, E. and J. Christensen (2013), *Homer: A Beginner's Guide*, London: Oneworld Publications.
Graziosi, B. (2016), *Homer*, Oxford: Oxford University Press.
Silk, M. (1987), *Homer: The Iliad*, Cambridge: Cambridge University Press.

Texts and commentaries

Brügger, C. (2018), *Homer's Iliad: The Basel Commentary: Book* 16, trans. by Benjamin W. Millis and Sara Strack and ed. by S. Douglas Olson, Berlin and Boston, MA: De Gruyter.
Brügger, C. (2018), *Homer's Iliad: The Basel Commentary: Book 24*, trans. by Benjamin W. Millis and Sara Strack and ed. by S. Douglas Olson, Berlin and Boston, MA: De Gruyter.
Edwards, M. (1991), *The Iliad: A Commentary, Volume 5: Books 17–20*, Cambridge: Cambridge University Press.
Griffin, J. (1995), *Homer Iliad 9*, Oxford: Clarendon Press.
Hainsworth, J. B. (1993), *The Iliad: A Commentary, Volume 3: Books 9–12*, Cambridge: Cambridge University Press.
Janko, R. (1992), *The Iliad: A Commentary, Volume 4: Books 13–16*, Cambridge: Cambridge University Press.
Jones, P. (2003), *Homer's Iliad: A Commentary on Three Translations*, Bristol: Bristol Classical Press.
Kirk, G. S. (1985), *The Iliad: A Commentary, Volume 1: Books 1–4*, Cambridge: Cambridge University Press.
Kirk, G. S. (1990), *The Iliad: A Commentary, Volume 2: Books 5–8*, Cambridge: Cambridge University Press.
Richardson, (1993), *The Iliad: A Commentary, Volume 6: Books 21–24*, Cambridge: Cambridge University Press.
Willcock, M. M. ed. (1984), *Homer, Iliad 1–12*, Bristol: Bristol Classical Press.
Willcock M. M., ed. (1984), *Homer, Iliad 13–24*, Bristol: Bristol Classical Press.

Dictionaries

Autenrieth, G., ed. and trans. R. P. Keep (1958), *A Homeric Dictionary for Schools and Colleges*, Norman, OK: University of Oklahoma Press.

English translations of *The Iliad*

Green, P. (2015), The Iliad*: A New Translation by Peter Green*, Oakland, CA: University of California Press.
Hammond, M. (1987), *Homer,* The Iliad: *A New Prose Translation*, Harmondsworth: Penguin.
Lattimore, R. (1951), The Iliad *of Homer*, Chicago, IL: University of Chicago Press.

General studies

Cairns, D. L., ed. (2001), *Oxford Readings in Homer's Iliad*, Oxford: Oxford University Press.

Fowler, R., ed. (2004), *The Cambridge Companion to Homer*, Cambridge: Cambridge University Press.
Griffin, J. (1980), *Homer on Life and Death*, Oxford: Oxford University Press.
Morris, I. and B. Powell, eds (1997), *A New Companion to Homer*, Leiden: Brill.
Pache, C. O. (2020), *The Cambridge Guide to* Homer, Cambridge: Cambridge University Press.
Taplin, O. (1992), *Homeric Soundings*, Oxford: Clarendon Press.

Oral poetry and composition in performance

Bakker, E. (2005), *Pointing at the Past: From Formula to Performance in Homeric Poetics*, Cambridge, MA: Harvard University Press.
Lord, B. (1960), *The Singer of Tales*, Cambridge, MA: Harvard University Press.
Parry, M. (1972), *The Making of Homeric Verse: The Collected Papers of Milman Parry*, Oxford: Oxford University Press.

Type scenes

Arend, W. (1993), *Die typischen Scenen bei Homer*, Berlin: Georg Olms Verlag.
Edwards, M. (1980), 'Convention and Individuality in *Iliad* 1', *Harvard Studies in Classical Philology*, 84 (1980): 1–28.

Neoanalysis

West, M. L. (1997), *The East Face of Helicon: West Asiatic Elements in Greek Poetry and Myth*, Oxford: Clarendon Press.

Story patterns

Nagler, M. N. (1974), *Spontaneity and Tradition: A Study in the Oral Art of Homer*, Berkeley and Los Angeles, CA, and London: University of California Press.
Propp, V. (1968), *Morphology of the Folktale*, Austin, TX: University of Texas Press.

Heroes and heroism

Cairns, D. (1993), *Aidōs: The Psychology and Ethics of Honour and Shame in Ancient Greek Literature*, Oxford: Clarendon Press.
Nagy, G. (1999), *The Best of the Achaeans: Concepts of the Hero in Archaic Greek Poetry*, 2nd edn, Baltimore, MD: Johns Hopkins University Press.
Schein, S. L. (1984), *The Mortal Hero: An Introduction to Homer's Iliad*, Berkeley and Los Angeles, CA, and London: University of California Press.

The structure of the *Iliad*

The first two of these items are for reference only.

Heiden, B. A. (2008), *Homer's Cosmic Fabrication: Choice and Design in the Iliad*, Oxford: Oxford University Press.
Sheppard, J. T. (1922), *Pattern of the Iliad*, London: Methuen.
Taplin, O. (1992), *Homeric Soundings*, Oxford: Oxford University Press.
Wade-Gery, H. T. (1952), *Poet of the Iliad*, Cambridge: Cambridge University Press.

Text

Iliad, Book 16

τὸν δὲ βαρὺ στενάχων προσέφης Πατρόκλεες ἱππεῦ:
"ὦ Ἀχιλεῦ Πηλῆος υἱὲ μέγα φέρτατ᾽ Ἀχαιῶν
μὴ νεμέσα: τοῖον γὰρ ἄχος βεβίηκεν Ἀχαιούς.
οἳ μὲν γὰρ δὴ πάντες, ὅσοι πάρος ἦσαν ἄριστοι,
ἐν νηυσὶν κέαται βεβλημένοι οὐτάμενοί τε.
βέβληται μὲν ὁ Τυδεΐδης κρατερὸς Διομήδης,
οὔτασται δ᾽ Ὀδυσεὺς δουρικλυτὸς ἠδ᾽ Ἀγαμέμνων,
βέβληται δὲ καὶ Εὐρύπυλος κατὰ μηρὸν ὀϊστῷ.
τοὺς μέν τ᾽ ἰητροὶ πολυφάρμακοι ἀμφιπένονται
ἕλκε᾽ ἀκειόμενοι: σὺ δ᾽ ἀμήχανος ἔπλευ Ἀχιλλεῦ.
μὴ ἐμέ γ᾽ οὖν οὗτός γε λάβοι χόλος, ὃν σὺ φυλάσσεις
αἰναρέτη: τί σευ ἄλλος ὀνήσεται ὀψίγονός περ
αἴ κε μὴ Ἀργείοισιν ἀεικέα λοιγὸν ἀμύνῃς;
νηλεές, οὐκ ἄρα σοί γε πατὴρ ἦν ἱππότα Πηλεύς,
οὐδὲ Θέτις μήτηρ: γλαυκὴ δέ σε τίκτε θάλασσα
πέτραι τ᾽ ἠλίβατοι, ὅτι τοι νόος ἐστὶν ἀπηνής.
εἰ δέ τινα φρεσὶ σῇσι θεοπροπίην ἀλεείνεις
καί τινά τοι πὰρ Ζηνὸς ἐπέφραδε πότνια μήτηρ,
ἀλλ᾽ ἐμέ περ πρόες ὦχ᾽, ἅμα δ᾽ ἄλλον λαὸν ὄπασσον
Μυρμιδόνων, ἤν πού τι φόως Δαναοῖσι γένωμαι.
δὸς δέ μοι ὤμοιιν τὰ σὰ τεύχεα θωρηχθῆναι,
αἴ κ᾽ ἐμὲ σοὶ ἴσκοντες ἀπόσχωνται πολέμοιο
Τρῶες, ἀναπνεύσωσι δ᾽ Ἀρήϊοι υἷες Ἀχαιῶν
τειρόμενοι: ὀλίγη δέ τ᾽ ἀνάπνευσις πολέμοιο.
ῥεῖα δέ κ᾽ ἀκμῆτες κεκμηότας ἄνδρας ἀϋτῇ
ὤσαιμεν προτὶ ἄστυ νεῶν ἄπο καὶ κλισιάων.
ὣς φάτο λισσόμενος μέγα νήπιος: ἦ γὰρ ἔμελλεν
οἷ αὐτῷ θάνατόν τε κακὸν καὶ κῆρα λιτέσθαι.

48–643: Patroclus arms himself; fighting ensues. *See summary of Book 16, pp. 239–41.*

ὣς ἄρα τοὶ περὶ νεκρὸν ὁμίλεον, οὐδέ ποτε Ζεὺς
τρέψεν ἀπὸ κρατερῆς ὑσμίνης ὄσσε φαεινώ,
ἀλλὰ κατ᾽ αὐτοὺς αἰὲν ὅρα καὶ φράζετο θυμῷ,
πολλὰ μάλ᾽ ἀμφὶ φόνῳ Πατρόκλου μερμηρίζων,
ἢ ἤδη καὶ κεῖνον ἐνὶ κρατερῇ ὑσμίνῃ
αὐτοῦ ἐπ᾽ ἀντιθέῳ Σαρπηδόνι φαίδιμος Ἕκτωρ
χαλκῷ δῃώσῃ, ἀπό τ᾽ ὤμων τεύχε᾽ ἕληται,
ἦ ἔτι καὶ πλεόνεσσιν ὀφέλλειεν πόνον αἰπύν.
ὧδε δέ οἱ φρονέοντι δοάσσατο κέρδιον εἶναι
ὄφρ᾽ ἠῢς θεράπων Πηληϊάδεω Ἀχιλῆος
ἐξαῦτις Τρῶάς τε καὶ Ἕκτορα χαλκοκορυστὴν
ὤσαιτο προτὶ ἄστυ, πολέων δ᾽ ἀπὸ θυμὸν ἕλοιτο.
Ἕκτορι δὲ πρωτίστῳ ἀνάλκιδα θυμὸν ἐνῆκεν:
ἐς δίφρον δ᾽ ἀναβὰς φύγαδ᾽ ἔτραπε, κέκλετο δ᾽ ἄλλους
Τρῶας φευγέμεναι: γνῶ γὰρ Διὸς ἱρὰ τάλαντα.
ἔνθ᾽ οὐδ᾽ ἴφθιμοι Λύκιοι μένον, ἀλλὰ φόβηθεν
πάντες, ἐπεὶ βασιλῆα ἴδον βεβλαμμένον ἦτορ
κείμενον ἐν νεκύων ἀγύρει: πολέες γὰρ ἐπ᾽ αὐτῷ
κάππεσον, εὖτ᾽ ἔριδα κρατερὴν ἐτάνυσσε Κρονίων.
οἳ δ᾽ ἄρ᾽ ἀπ᾽ ὤμοιιν Σαρπηδόνος ἔντε᾽ ἕλοντο
χάλκεα μαρμαίροντα, τὰ μὲν κοίλας ἐπὶ νῆας
δῶκε φέρειν ἑτάροισι Μενοιτίου ἄλκιμος υἱός.
καὶ τότ᾽ Ἀπόλλωνα προσέφη νεφεληγερέτα Ζεύς:
"εἰ δ᾽ ἄγε νῦν φίλε Φοῖβε, κελαινεφὲς αἷμα κάθηρον
ἐλθὼν ἐκ βελέων Σαρπηδόνα, καί μιν ἔπειτα
πολλὸν ἀπὸπρὸ φέρων λοῦσον ποταμοῖο ῥοῇσι
χρῖσόν τ᾽ ἀμβροσίῃ, περὶ δ᾽ ἄμβροτα εἵματα ἕσσον:
πέμπε δέ μιν πομποῖσιν ἅμα κραιπνοῖσι φέρεσθαι
ὕπνῳ καὶ θανάτῳ διδυμάοσιν, οἵ ῥά μιν ὦκα
θήσουσ᾽ ἐν Λυκίης εὐρείης πίονι δήμῳ,
ἔνθά ἑ ταρχύσουσι κασίγνητοί τε ἔται τε
τύμβῳ τε στήλῃ τε: τὸ γὰρ γέρας ἐστὶ θανόντων.

ὣς ἔφατ᾽, οὐδ᾽ ἄρα πατρὸς ἀνηκούστησεν Ἀπόλλων.
βῆ δὲ κατ᾽ Ἰδαίων ὀρέων ἐς φύλοπιν αἰνήν,
αὐτίκα δ᾽ ἐκ βελέων Σαρπηδόνα δῖον ἀείρας
πολλὸν ἀπὸπρὸ φέρων λοῦσεν ποταμοῖο ῥοῇσι
χρῖσέν τ᾽ ἀμβροσίῃ, περὶ δ᾽ ἄμβροτα εἵματα ἕσσε:
πέμπε δέ μιν πομποῖσιν ἅμα κραιπνοῖσι φέρεσθαι,
ὕπνῳ καὶ θανάτῳ διδυμάοσιν, οἵ ῥά μιν ὦκα
κάτθεσαν ἐν Λυκίης εὐρείης πίονι δήμῳ.
Πάτροκλος δ᾽ ἵπποισι καὶ Αὐτομέδοντι κελεύσας
Τρῶας καὶ Λυκίους μετεκίαθε, καὶ μέγ᾽ ἀάσθη
νήπιος: εἰ δὲ ἔπος Πηληϊάδαο φύλαξεν
ἦ τ᾽ ἂν ὑπέκφυγε κῆρα κακὴν μέλανος θανάτοιο.
ἀλλ᾽ αἰεί τε Διὸς κρείσσων νόος ἠέ περ ἀνδρῶν:
ὅς τε καὶ ἄλκιμον ἄνδρα φοβεῖ καὶ ἀφείλετο νίκην

ῥηϊδίως, ὅτε δ᾽ αὐτὸς ἐποτρύνῃσι μάχεσθαι:
ὅς οἱ καὶ τότε θυμὸν ἐνὶ στήθεσσιν ἀνῆκεν.
ἔνθα τίνα πρῶτον τίνα δ᾽ ὕστατον ἐξενάριξας
Πατρόκλεις, ὅτε δή σε θεοὶ θάνατον δὲ κάλεσσαν;
Ἄδρηστον μὲν πρῶτα καὶ Αὐτόνοον καὶ Ἔχεκλον
καὶ Πέριμον Μεγάδην καὶ Ἐπίστορα καὶ Μελάνιππον,
αὐτὰρ ἔπειτ᾽ Ἔλασον καὶ Μούλιον ἠδὲ Πυλάρτην:
τοὺς ἕλεν: οἳ δ᾽ ἄλλοι φύγαδε μνώοντο ἕκαστος.
ἔνθά κεν ὑψίπυλον Τροίην ἕλον υἷες Ἀχαιῶν
Πατρόκλου ὑπὸ χερσί, περιπρὸ γὰρ ἔγχεϊ θῦεν,
εἰ μὴ Ἀπόλλων Φοῖβος ἐϋδμήτου ἐπὶ πύργου
ἔστη τῷ ὀλοὰ φρονέων, Τρώεσσι δ᾽ ἀρήγων.
τρὶς μὲν ἐπ᾽ ἀγκῶνος βῆ τείχεος ὑψηλοῖο
Πάτροκλος, τρὶς δ᾽ αὐτὸν ἀπεστυφέλιξεν Ἀπόλλων
χείρεσσ᾽ ἀθανάτῃσι φαεινὴν ἀσπίδα νύσσων.
ἀλλ᾽ ὅτε δὴ τὸ τέταρτον ἐπέσσυτο δαίμονι ἶσος,
δεινὰ δ᾽ ὁμοκλήσας ἔπεα πτερόεντα προσηύδα:
"χάζεο διογενὲς Πατρόκλεες: οὔ νύ τοι αἶσα
σῷ ὑπὸ δουρὶ πόλιν πέρθαι Τρώων ἀγερώχων,
οὐδ᾽ ὑπ᾽ Ἀχιλλῆος, ὅς περ σέο πολλὸν ἀμείνων.

ὣς φάτο, Πάτροκλος δ᾽ ἀνεχάζετο πολλὸν ὀπίσσω
μῆνιν ἀλευάμενος ἑκατηβόλου Ἀπόλλωνος.
Ἕκτωρ δ᾽ ἐν Σκαιῇσι πύλῃς ἔχε μώνυχας ἵππους:
δίζε γὰρ ἠὲ μάχοιτο κατὰ κλόνον αὖτις ἐλάσσας,
ἦ λαοὺς ἐς τεῖχος ὁμοκλήσειεν ἀλῆναι.
ταῦτ᾽ ἄρα οἱ φρονέοντι παρίστατο Φοῖβος Ἀπόλλων
ἀνέρι εἰσάμενος αἰζηῷ τε κρατερῷ τε
Ἀσίῳ, ὃς μήτρως ἦν Ἕκτορος ἱπποδάμοιο
αὐτοκασίγνητος Ἑκάβης, υἱὸς δὲ Δύμαντος,
ὃς Φρυγίῃ ναίεσκε ῥοῇς ἔπι Σαγγαρίοιο:
τῷ μιν ἐεισάμενος προσέφη Διὸς υἱὸς Ἀπόλλων:
"Ἕκτορ τίπτε μάχης ἀποπαύεαι; οὐδέ τί σε χρή.
αἴθ᾽ ὅσον ἥσσων εἰμί, τόσον σέο φέρτερος εἴην:
τώ κε τάχα στυγερῶς πολέμου ἀπερωήσειας.
ἀλλ᾽ ἄγε Πατρόκλῳ ἔφεπε κρατερώνυχας ἵππους,
αἴ κέν πώς μιν ἕλῃς, δώῃ δέ τοι εὖχος Ἀπόλλων.

ὣς εἰπὼν ὃ μὲν αὖτις ἔβη θεὸς ἂμ πόνον ἀνδρῶν,
Κεβριόνῃ δ᾽ ἐκέλευσε δαΐφρονι φαίδιμος Ἕκτωρ
ἵππους ἐς πόλεμον πεπληγέμεν. αὐτὰρ Ἀπόλλων
δύσεθ᾽ ὅμιλον ἰών, ἐν δὲ κλόνον Ἀργείοισιν
ἧκε κακόν, Τρωσὶν δὲ καὶ Ἕκτορι κῦδος ὄπαζεν.
Ἕκτωρ δ᾽ ἄλλους μὲν Δαναοὺς ἔα οὐδ᾽ ἐνάριζεν:
αὐτὰρ ὃ Πατρόκλῳ ἔφεπε κρατερώνυχας ἵππους.
Πάτροκλος δ᾽ ἑτέρωθεν ἀφ᾽ ἵππων ἆλτο χαμᾶζε
σκαιῇ ἔγχος ἔχων: ἑτέρηφι δὲ λάζετο πέτρον

μάρμαρον ὀκριόεντα τόν οἱ περὶ χεὶρ ἐκάλυψεν,
ἧκε δ᾽ ἐρεισάμενος, οὐδὲ δὴν χάζετο φωτός,
οὐδ᾽ ἁλίωσε βέλος, βάλε δ᾽ Ἕκτορος ἡνιοχῆα
Κεβριόνην νόθον υἱὸν ἀγακλῆος Πριάμοιο
ἵππων ἡνί᾽ ἔχοντα μετώπιον ὀξέϊ λᾶϊ.
ἀμφοτέρας δ᾽ ὀφρῦς σύνελεν λίθος, οὐδέ οἱ ἔσχεν
ὀστέον, ὀφθαλμοὶ δὲ χαμαὶ πέσον ἐν κονίῃσιν
αὐτοῦ πρόσθε ποδῶν: ὃ δ᾽ ἄρ᾽ ἀρνευτῆρι ἐοικὼς
κάππεσ᾽ ἀπ᾽ εὐεργέος δίφρου, λίπε δ᾽ ὀστέα θυμός.
τὸν δ᾽ ἐπικερτομέων προσέφης Πατρόκλεες ἱππεῦ:
ὢ πόποι ἦ μάλ᾽ ἐλαφρὸς ἀνήρ, ὡς ῥεῖα κυβιστᾷ.
εἰ δή που καὶ πόντῳ ἐν ἰχθυόεντι γένοιτο,
πολλοὺς ἂν κορέσειεν ἀνὴρ ὅδε τήθεα διφῶν
νηὸς ἀποθρῴσκων, εἰ καὶ δυσπέμφελος εἴη,
ὡς νῦν ἐν πεδίῳ ἐξ ἵππων ῥεῖα κυβιστᾷ.
ἦ ῥα καὶ ἐν Τρώεσσι κυβιστητῆρες ἔασιν.

ὣς εἰπὼν ἐπὶ Κεβριόνῃ ἥρωϊ βεβήκει
οἶμα λέοντος ἔχων, ὅς τε σταθμοὺς κεραΐζων
ἔβλητο πρὸς στῆθος, ἑή τέ μιν ὤλεσεν ἀλκή:
ὣς ἐπὶ Κεβριόνῃ Πατρόκλεες ἆλσο μεμαώς.
Ἕκτωρ δ᾽ αὖθ᾽ ἑτέρωθεν ἀφ᾽ ἵππων ἆλτο χαμᾶζε.
τὼ περὶ Κεβριόναο λέονθ᾽ ὣς δηρινθήτην,
ὥ τ᾽ ὄρεος κορυφῇσι περὶ κταμένης ἐλάφοιο
ἄμφω πεινάοντε μέγα φρονέοντε μάχεσθον:
ὣς περὶ Κεβριόναο δύω μήστωρες ἀϋτῆς
Πάτροκλός τε Μενοιτιάδης καὶ φαίδιμος Ἕκτωρ
ἵεντ᾽ ἀλλήλων ταμέειν χρόα νηλέϊ χαλκῷ.
Ἕκτωρ μὲν κεφαλῆφιν ἐπεὶ λάβεν οὐχὶ μεθίει:
Πάτροκλος δ᾽ ἑτέρωθεν ἔχεν ποδός: οἳ δὲ δὴ ἄλλοι
Τρῶες καὶ Δαναοὶ σύναγον κρατερὴν ὑσμίνην.

ὡς δ᾽ Εὖρός τε Νότος τ᾽ ἐριδαίνετον ἀλλήλοιιν
οὔρεος ἐν βήσσῃς βαθέην πελεμιζέμεν ὕλην
φηγόν τε μελίην τε τανύφλοιόν τε κράνειαν,
αἵ τε πρὸς ἀλλήλας ἔβαλον τανυήκεας ὄζους
ἠχῇ θεσπεσίῃ, πάταγος δέ τε ἀγνυμενάων,
ὣς Τρῶες καὶ Ἀχαιοὶ ἐπ᾽ ἀλλήλοισι θορόντες
δῄουν, οὐδ᾽ ἕτεροι μνώοντ᾽ ὀλοοῖο φόβοιο.
πολλὰ δὲ Κεβριόνην ἀμφ᾽ ὀξέα δοῦρα πεπήγει
ἰοί τε πτερόεντες ἀπὸ νευρῆφι θορόντες,
πολλὰ δὲ χερμάδια μεγάλ᾽ ἀσπίδας ἐστυφέλιξαν
μαρναμένων ἀμφ᾽ αὐτόν: ὃ δ᾽ ἐν στροφάλιγγι κονίης
κεῖτο μέγας μεγαλωστί, λελασμένος ἱπποσυνάων.
ὄφρα μὲν Ἠέλιος μέσον οὐρανὸν ἀμφιβεβήκει,
τόφρα μάλ᾽ ἀμφοτέρων βέλε᾽ ἥπτετο, πῖπτε δὲ λαός:
ἦμος δ᾽ Ἠέλιος μετενίσετο βουλυτὸν δέ,

καὶ τότε δή ῥ᾽ ὑπὲρ αἶσαν Ἀχαιοὶ φέρτεροι ἦσαν.
ἐκ μὲν Κεβριόνην βελέων ἥρωα ἔρυσσαν
Τρώων ἐξ ἐνοπῆς, καὶ ἀπ᾽ ὤμων τεύχε᾽ ἕλοντο,
Πάτροκλος δὲ Τρωσὶ κακὰ φρονέων ἐνόρουσε.
τρὶς μὲν ἔπειτ᾽ ἐπόρουσε θοῷ ἀτάλαντος Ἄρηϊ
σμερδαλέα ἰάχων, τρὶς δ᾽ ἐννέα φῶτας ἔπεφνεν.
ἀλλ᾽ ὅτε δὴ τὸ τέταρτον ἐπέσσυτο δαίμονι ἶσος,
ἔνθ᾽ ἄρα τοι Πάτροκλε φάνη βιότοιο τελευτή:
ἤντετο γάρ τοι Φοῖβος ἐνὶ κρατερῇ ὑσμίνῃ
δεινός: ὃ μὲν τὸν ἰόντα κατὰ κλόνον οὐκ ἐνόησεν,
ἠέρι γὰρ πολλῇ κεκαλυμμένος ἀντεβόλησε:
στῆ δ᾽ ὄπιθεν, πλῆξεν δὲ μετάφρενον εὐρέε τ᾽ ὤμω
χειρὶ καταπρηνεῖ, στρεφεδίνηθεν δέ οἱ ὄσσε.
τοῦ δ᾽ ἀπὸ μὲν κρατὸς κυνέην βάλε Φοῖβος Ἀπόλλων:
ἣ δὲ κυλινδομένη καναχὴν ἔχε ποσσὶν ὑφ᾽ ἵππων
αὐλῶπις τρυφάλεια, μιάνθησαν δὲ ἔθειραι
αἵματι καὶ κονίῃσι: πάρος γε μὲν οὐ θέμις ἦεν
ἱππόκομον πήληκα μιαίνεσθαι κονίῃσιν,
ἀλλ᾽ ἀνδρὸς θείοιο κάρη χαρίεν τε μέτωπον
ῥύετ᾽ Ἀχιλλῆος: τότε δὲ Ζεὺς Ἕκτορι δῶκεν
ᾗ κεφαλῇ φορέειν, σχεδόθεν δέ οἱ ἦεν ὄλεθρος.
πᾶν δέ οἱ ἐν χείρεσσιν ἄγη δολιχόσκιον ἔγχος
βριθὺ μέγα στιβαρὸν κεκορυθμένον: αὐτὰρ ἀπ᾽ ὤμων
ἀσπὶς σὺν τελαμῶνι χαμαὶ πέσε τερμιόεσσα.
λῦσε δέ οἱ θώρηκα ἄναξ Διὸς υἱὸς Ἀπόλλων.
τὸν δ᾽ ἄτη φρένας εἷλε, λύθεν δ᾽ ὑπὸ φαίδιμα γυῖα,
στῆ δὲ ταφών: ὄπιθεν δὲ μετάφρενον ὀξέϊ δουρὶ
ὤμων μεσσηγὺς σχεδόθεν βάλε Δάρδανος ἀνὴρ
Πανθοΐδης Εὔφορβος, ὃς ἡλικίην ἐκέκαστο
ἔγχεΐ θ᾽ ἱπποσύνῃ τε πόδεσσί τε καρπαλίμοισι:
καὶ γὰρ δὴ τότε φῶτας ἐείκοσι βῆσεν ἀφ᾽ ἵππων
πρῶτ᾽ ἐλθὼν σὺν ὄχεσφι διδασκόμενος πολέμοιο:
ὅς τοι πρῶτος ἐφῆκε βέλος Πατρόκλεες ἱππεῦ
οὐδὲ δάμασσ᾽: ὃ μὲν αὖτις ἀνέδραμε, μίκτο δ᾽ ὁμίλῳ,
ἐκ χροὸς ἁρπάξας δόρυ μείλινον, οὐδ᾽ ὑπέμεινε
Πάτροκλον γυμνόν περ ἐόντ᾽ ἐν δηϊοτῆτι.
Πάτροκλος δὲ θεοῦ πληγῇ καὶ δουρὶ δαμασθεὶς
ἂψ ἑτάρων εἰς ἔθνος ἐχάζετο κῆρ᾽ ἀλεείνων.

Ἕκτωρ δ᾽ ὡς εἶδεν Πατροκλῆα μεγάθυμον
ἂψ ἀναχαζόμενον βεβλημένον ὀξέϊ χαλκῷ,
ἀγχίμολόν ῥά οἱ ἦλθε κατὰ στίχας, οὖτα δὲ δουρὶ
νείατον ἐς κενεῶνα, διάπρο δὲ χαλκὸν ἔλασσε:
δούπησεν δὲ πεσών, μέγα δ᾽ ἤκαχε λαὸν Ἀχαιῶν:
ὡς δ᾽ ὅτε σῦν ἀκάμαντα λέων ἐβιήσατο χάρμῃ,
ὥ τ᾽ ὄρεος κορυφῆσι μέγα φρονέοντε μάχεσθον
πίδακος ἀμφ᾽ ὀλίγης: ἐθέλουσι δὲ πιέμεν ἄμφω:

πολλὰ δέ τ᾽ ἀσθμαίνοντα λέων ἐδάμασσε βίηφιν:
ὣς πολέας πεφνόντα Μενοιτίου ἄλκιμον υἱὸν
Ἕκτωρ Πριαμίδης σχεδὸν ἔγχεϊ θυμὸν ἀπηύρα,
καί οἱ ἐπευχόμενος ἔπεα πτερόεντα προσηύδα:
Πάτροκλ᾽ ἦ που ἔφησθα πόλιν κεραϊξέμεν ἁμήν,
Τρωϊάδας δὲ γυναῖκας ἐλεύθερον ἦμαρ ἀπούρας
ἄξειν ἐν νήεσσι φίλην ἐς πατρίδα γαῖαν
νήπιε: τάων δὲ πρόσθ᾽ Ἕκτορος ὠκέες ἵπποι
ποσσὶν ὀρωρέχαται πολεμίζειν: ἔγχεϊ δ᾽ αὐτὸς
Τρωσὶ φιλοπτολέμοισι μεταπρέπω, ὅ σφιν ἀμύνω
ἦμαρ ἀναγκαῖον: σὲ δέ τ᾽ ἐνθάδε γῦπες ἔδονται.
ἆ δείλ᾽, οὐδέ τοι ἐσθλὸς ἐὼν χραίσμησεν Ἀχιλλεύς,
ὅς πού τοι μάλα πολλὰ μένων ἐπετέλλετ᾽ ἰόντι:
μή μοι πρὶν ἰέναι Πατρόκλεες ἱπποκέλευθε
νῆας ἔπι γλαφυρὰς πρὶν Ἕκτορος ἀνδροφόνοιο
αἱματόεντα χιτῶνα περὶ στήθεσσι δαΐξαι.
ὥς πού σε προσέφη, σοὶ δὲ φρένας ἄφρονι πεῖθε.

τὸν δ᾽ ὀλιγοδρανέων προσέφης Πατρόκλεες ἱππεῦ:
"ἤδη νῦν Ἕκτορ μεγάλ᾽ εὔχεο: σοὶ γὰρ ἔδωκε
νίκην Ζεὺς Κρονίδης καὶ Ἀπόλλων, οἵ με δάμασσαν
ῥηιδίως: αὐτοὶ γὰρ ἀπ᾽ ὤμων τεύχε᾽ ἕλοντο.
τοιοῦτοι δ᾽ εἴ πέρ μοι ἐείκοσιν ἀντεβόλησαν,
πάντές κ᾽ αὐτόθ᾽ ὄλοντο ἐμῷ ὑπὸ δουρὶ δαμέντες.
ἀλλά με μοῖρ᾽ ὀλοὴ καὶ Λητοῦς ἔκτανεν υἱός,
ἀνδρῶν δ᾽ Εὔφορβος: σὺ δέ με τρίτος ἐξεναρίζεις.
ἄλλο δέ τοι ἐρέω, σὺ δ᾽ ἐνὶ φρεσὶ βάλλεο σῇσιν:
οὔ θην οὐδ᾽ αὐτὸς δηρὸν βέῃ, ἀλλά τοι ἤδη
ἄγχι παρέστηκεν θάνατος καὶ μοῖρα κραταιὴ
χερσὶ δαμέντ᾽ Ἀχιλῆος ἀμύμονος Αἰακίδαο.

ὣς ἄρα μιν εἰπόντα τέλος θανάτοιο κάλυψε:
ψυχὴ δ᾽ ἐκ ῥεθέων πταμένη Ἄϊδόσδε βεβήκει
ὃν πότμον γοόωσα λιποῦσ᾽ ἀνδροτῆτα καὶ ἥβην.
τὸν καὶ τεθνηῶτα προσηύδα φαίδιμος Ἕκτωρ:
"Πατρόκλεις τί νύ μοι μαντεύεαι αἰπὺν ὄλεθρον;
τίς δ᾽ οἶδ᾽ εἴ κ᾽ Ἀχιλεὺς Θέτιδος πάϊς ἠϋκόμοιο
φθήῃ ἐμῷ ὑπὸ δουρὶ τυπεὶς ἀπὸ θυμὸν ὀλέσσαι;

ὣς ἄρα φωνήσας δόρυ χάλκεον ἐξ ὠτειλῆς
εἴρυσε λὰξ προσβάς, τὸν δ᾽ ὕπτιον ὦσ᾽ ἀπὸ δουρός.
αὐτίκα δὲ ξὺν δουρὶ μετ᾽ Αὐτομέδοντα βεβήκει
ἀντίθεον θεράποντα ποδώκεος Αἰακίδαο:
ἵετο γὰρ βαλέειν: τὸν δ᾽ ἔκφερον ὠκέες ἵπποι
ἄμβροτοι, οὓς Πηλῆϊ θεοὶ δόσαν ἀγλαὰ δῶρα.

Commentary Notes

Iliad, Book 16

20–47

The Trojans, led by Hector, have broken into the Greek camp and are on the brink of total victory. Achilles' lieutenant, Patroclus, has spent the last few books walking round the Greek camp and surveying the desperate situation. He now returns to Achilles to ask him if he, Patroclus, can lead the Myrmidons into battle in order to push Hector and the Trojans back and save the Greeks.

20

τὸν: 'him', i.e. Achilles. In Homer, ὁ, ἡ, τό, is almost always used as a third-person pronoun, not the definite article as in Attic Greek.

20

προσέφης: 'you spoke': one of eight occasions in Book 16 that the poet addresses Patroclus 'directly' in the second person. The use of the second person has traditionally been interpreted as indicating an especially close relationship between Patroclus and the poet, who rarely speaks in their 'own voice'.

20

Πατρόκλεες ἱππεῦ: vocative case, following the use of the second person **προσέφης** earlier in the line.

20

ἱππεῦ: 'charioteer': chariots in Homer are only ever used to transport individuals to and from the battlefield, with warriors stepping down from their chariots to engage in hand-to-hand combat. This is not how chariots were used in historical times.

21–45

Patroclus' speech represents the third attempt to persuade Achilles to return to battle. None are, strictly speaking, successful, although Achilles' attitude does shift following each appeal. Patroclus' speech can be split into three sections: (1) the dire situation faced by the Greeks (lines 21–29); (2) criticism of Achilles' attitude (lines 29–35); and (3) Patroclus' suggested solution (lines 35–45).

21
ὦ: it is unclear whether the use of the interjection ὦ signifies a particularly emotional appeal.

21
μέγα φέρτατ᾽ Ἀχαιῶν: 'by far the greatest of the Achaeans'. A desire to 'be the best' is the fundamental impulse of the Homeric hero. The phrase is used several times in the poem, but has a special rhetorical impact here: the situation facing the Greeks is so dire that only the 'best of the Achaeans' will be able to save them now.

21
μέγα: adverbial, 'by far'.

21
Ἀχαιῶν: Homer uses the terms Achaeans, Argives, and Danaans interchangeably to refer to the Greeks.

22
μὴ νεμέσα: νεμεσάω derives from νέμεσις, which refers to anger that is justified. Strictly speaking, Patroclus is asking Achilles not to be angry at him, though the appeal obviously has a wider resonance in a poem which is all about Achilles' anger.

22
τοῖον γὰρ . . . Ἀχαιούς: Since the beginning of Book 11, the situation has looked increasingly desperate for the Greeks. The Trojans, led by a divinely rejuvenated Hector, have broken through the walls of the Greek camp and now threaten to burn the ships. The Greek army is on the brink of destruction.

22
ἄχος: 'pain, distress'. Note the echo of **ἄχος** in **Ἀχιλεῦ**, **Ἀχαιῶν** and **Ἀχαιούς**.

22
βεβίηκεν: 'has overwhelmed': perfect of βιάω.

23
μὲν: correlates with **δέ** in 29. The list of injured heroes in 25–27 is felt to interrupt the sequence, which necessitates another **μέν** in 28. The contrast is between the desperate plight of the Greek heroes on the one hand, and the situation of Achilles on the other.

23
πάντες, ὅσοι . . . ἄριστοι: 'all who were before the most capable in battle'. Patroclus exaggerates the situation for rhetorical effect. Several Greek heroes have been

injured, but many more are still in the fray, notably Ajax and Menelaus, the heroes that will later recover Patroclus' body.

23
ὅσοι: literally, 'all the number who . . .'

23
ἄριστοι: 'most capable in battle'. In general, ἄριστος means 'best' or 'greatest', though its meaning is often specified more closely by its particular context.

24
ἐν νηυσὶν: 'among the ships'. When the Greeks first arrived at Troy, they dragged their ships out of the water and set up their tents in their midst. The fighting in the Greek camp can thus be described as taking place 'among the ships'.

24
κέαται = Attic κεῖνται, 'are dead': κεῖμαι literally means 'to lie (down)', although it is very often used metaphorically to mean 'to be dead', as here.

24
βεβλημένοι οὐτάμενοί τε: βάλλω (here) means 'to strike with a missile', whereas οὐτάω means 'to strike with a stabbing or slashing weapon'. Both verbs are perfect passive participles, i.e. 'having been struck or stabbed'.

25–27
βέβληται . . . οὔτασται . . . βέβληται: the repetition of the perfect tense verbs for wounding emphasizes the relentlessness of the injuries to the Greek forces.

25
Τυδείδης κρατερὸς Διομήδης: Diomedes, supported by Athena, dominates the Trojan forces in Book 5, and only falls back when he comes up against Apollo. Patroclus will encounter Apollo later in this book, with much more tragic results.

26
ἠδ = ἠδέ, 'and'.

28
τ(ε): epic τε, used in generalizing statements.

28
ἰητροὶ: usually 'doctors', but given the context we might prefer something like 'combat medics'.

28
πολυφάρμακοι ἀμφιπένονται: the adjectival prefix πολυ and the verbal prefix ἀμφι contribute to the sense that the doctors have a great many patients to look after, emphasizing the plight of the Greek forces. They are tending to people 'all

around' drawing on their knowledge of 'many' kinds of cures. The word πολυφάρμακος is found only here in Homer.

29

ἕλκε᾽ ἀκειόμενοι . . . Ἀχιλλεῦ: We might contrast the willingness of the physically wounded to return to battle with the emotionally wounded Achilles' refusal to do so.

29

ἀκειόμενοι: conative, 'trying to heal'.

29

σὺ δ᾽: 'but you': Patroclus contrasts the situation he has just described, i.e. the wounded Greeks, the busy doctors, with Achilles' situation.

29

ἀμήχανος: this word derives from μηχανή, which is a method or means by which someone can do something. The word ἀμήχανος suggests that Achilles is impervious to μηχαναί. We might say there's 'no getting through to him' or that he's 'impossible to deal with'. Elsewhere in the poem, the word is used of 'inscrutable' dreams.

29

ἔπλευ = ἔπλεο, second person singular aorist of πέλομαι, 'to prove to be, be'.

30

μὴ . . . λάβοι: optative for a wish.

30

οὗτος: 'such'; the word can contain a pejorative undertone.

30

ὃν σὺ φυλάσσεις: 'which you persist in' or even 'which you cherish'.

31

αἰναρέτη: 'man whose valour is fatal to his friends': a *hapax legomenon* that combines two contradictory concepts – αἰνός ('dreadful, dire') and ἀρετή ('excellence'). Achilles' idiosyncratic behaviour necessitates the creation of brand new words to describe it.

31

τί . . . ὀνήσεται: 'what will he gain from you?'

31

ὀψίγονός περ: περ has been read as intensifying ('*especially* one who will be live in the future') as concessive ('*although* he may not be alive yet').

32
αἴ κε = **ἐάν**.

32
ἀεικέα: while this word is usually translated in moral terms, e.g. 'shameful, degrading', there is an important physical resonance too, e.g. 'ugly, disfiguring'. The physical ugliness of death is just as important as the moral disgrace attached to it.

32
ἀμύνῃς: the verb ἀμύνω governs the accusative case (= the person or thing being warded off) and the dative case (= the person or thing being protected).

33
νηλεές: 'pitiless, merciless': Achilles is the only character in the poem described in these terms.

33
οὐκ ἄρα . . . ἦν: 'it is now apparent that he was not', a common Greek idiom, used when one realizes that one has been under a misapprehension.

33–35
Πηλεύς . . . Θέτις . . . θάλασσα . . . πέτραι: Chiasmus, since Peleus was associated with a mountain (Pelion), while Thetis was goddess of the sea. Thus, we have mountain . . . sea . . . sea . . . mountain.

33
ἱππότα: nominative singular.

34
γλαυκὴ: either 'greyish-blue' or 'gleaming'; the meaning is disputed.

34
τίκτε: imperfect, though best translated as if it were an aorist, i.e. 'gave birth to'; the augment can be omitted in Homeric Greek for metrical reasons.

35
ὅτι: 'I say this because . . .'

35
τοι = **σοι**

35
νόος = **νοῦς**: words can be left uncontracted in Homeric Greek for metrical reasons.

36–45
Nestor told Patroclus to make this argument to Achilles in Book 11, and the next ten lines are repeated more or less verbatim from that speech (11.794–803). Patroclus tactfully does not mention this to Achilles.

36
σῇσι = σαῖς.

36
θεοπροπίην: Achilles is the subject of a series of prophecies in the poem, all of which concern the briefness of his life and the idea that he will die shortly after killing Hector. These become increasingly frequent and precise as we move through the poem.

37
τινά . . . ἐπέφραδε πότνια μήτηρ: 'and if your honoured mother has announced some (prophecy)'; the word θεοπροπίην must be understood from the previous line to complete the meaning.

37
πὰρ = πάρα; prepositions show a greater diversity of forms in Homer than in Attic Greek.

37
Ζηνὸς = genitive of Ζεύς.

37
ἐπέφραδε: reduplicated root aorist of φράζω, 'to show, point out, announce'.

38
ἀλλ(ὰ) . . . περ: 'but at least'.

38
πρόες: aorist imperative of προίημι. The sense of 'into battle' must be understood from the context.

38
ὦχ = ὦκα.

38
ὄπασσον: literally, 'cause [the Myrmidons] to follow', i.e. 'ensure that [the Myrmidons] to follow'. ὄπασσον is the aorist imperative of ὀπάζω, which is causative of ἕπομαι, hence 'make someone or something (accusative) follow'. The onus is on Achilles, as leader of the Myrmidons, to ensure that they accept Patroclus as their (temporary) new leader.

39
Δαναοῖσι: Danaans is another term for Greeks. See note on 21 **Ἀχαιῶν** above.

39
φόως: 'deliverance, rescue'; φόως is not the uncontracted form of φῶς (which would be φάος); rather, this is an example of diectasis, the 'artificial lengthening' of a word via the insertion of a short vowel in the middle.

40
ὤμοιιν: 'on my shoulders', locative dative dual of ὦμος, 'shoulder'.

40
τὰ σὰ τεύχεα θωρηχθῆναι: 'so that I may arm myself in your armour'; the verb θωρήσσω takes the accusative case of the item(s) put on, as with all verbs of putting on clothing.

41
ἐμὲ σοὶ ἴσκοντες: literally, 'equating me to you', i.e. 'mistaking me for you'; Patroclus' point is that since he will be wearing Achilles' armour, the Trojans may mistake him for Achilles; ἴσκω is a factitive verb and thus implies a sense of causation, 'to cause someone to compare, equate, etc.'

41
ἀπόσχωνται πολέμοιο: literally, 'they would quit the fight'; the aspect of this verb – aorist rather than present – emphasizes the immediacy of the Trojans' retreat from battle; it would happen in an instant rather than over a period of time.

42
Τρῶες . . . Ἀχαιῶν: the antithesis between Trojans and Greeks is emphasized by the placement of the words at either end of the line.

42–43
ἀναπνεύσωσι . . . τειρόμενοι: 'so that they might take a deep breath after being hard-pressed'. Verbs of stopping or pausing are often constructed with the participle of the action being ceased. The placement of **τειρόμενοι** in the emphatic runover position is very effective.

43
ὀλίγη δέ . . . πολέμοιο: a proverbial phrase, meaning something like 'respite in war need not be long', i.e. even a short amount of rest can make a big difference. Patroclus knows that the ruse of wearing Achilles' armour will only offer temporary relief to the Greek forces – but that's all that may be required.

44
ῥεῖα = ῥᾳδίως, 'easily'.

44
ἀκμῆτες κεκμηότας: both words share the same stem, κάμνω ('to work hard, be exhausted'), further emphasizing the contrast between the 'tired' Trojans and the 'untired' Greeks.

44
ἀϋτῇ: causal dative, governed by κεκμηότας, literally 'having been tired out because of the battle cry', i.e. 'exhausted from the fighting'.

45
νεῶν ἄπο: 'away from the ships'; the position of the accent on ἄπο shows that this is a postposition, governing the word that comes immediately before it.

45
ὤσαιμεν: this is the main verb in the sentence; the optative might suggest ability (i.e. 'we would be capable of pushing them back') or likelihood (i.e. 'we would probably push them back').

46–47
The imminence of Patroclus' death is referred to several times in the poem, creating a strong sense of dramatic irony.

46
φάτο: third person singular imperfect of φημί. On the omission of the augment, see 34 **τίκτε** above.

46
μέγα νήπιος: 'the great fool!': Patroclus has no idea what is he is letting himself in for.

46
ἦ γὰρ: 'truly, indeed'.

46
ἔμελλεν: 'he was going to'.

47
οἷ αὐτῷ = ἑαυτῷ, 'his own', the dramatic irony is intensified by the use of a strong reflexive pronoun. Patroclus aims to cause death and destruction – but not his own.

47
θάνατόν τε κακὸν καὶ κῆρα: 'evil death and doom'; the harsh alliteration of κακὸν καὶ κῆρα is appropriate for its meaning.

47
λιτέσθαι: a resultative aorist, 'to beg, plead for something', taking an accusative of the thing asked for. The verb recalls **λισσόμενος** on the previous line.

48–643: Patroclus arms himself; fighting ensues. See summary of Book 16, pp. 239–41.

644–655

Following the death of Sarpedon, Zeus ponders whether Patroclus should die immediately or later. He decides on the latter.

644
ὣς ἄρα τοὶ: the poet has just compared the crowd of people around the body of Sarpedon to the way flies buzz around a bucket of milk. These three words return us to the action, 'in this way . . .'

644
νεκρὸν: Patroclus has just slain Sarpedon, the leader of the Lycians.

645
ὄσσε φαεινώ: accusative dual.

646
κατ' αὐτοὺς ... ὅρα: 'looked down upon them'; **αὐτοὺς** are the Greeks and Trojans fighting on the battlefield.

647
πολλὰ μάλ ... μερμηρίζων: 'thinking very deeply. . .', πολλὰ is an adverbial adjective governed by μερμηρίζων.

647
ἀμφὶ: 'about' in a metaphorical rather than a literal sense, i.e. 'on the subject of'.

648–561
ἢ . . . ἤ: 'whether . . . or whether'.

648–650
Note how artfully the description of Patroclus' (imagined) death has been put together here. Patroclus appears in the accusative (κεῖνον, 'that man') in the middle of line 648, but we aren't given a subject, i.e. the identity of the person who is going to kill him, until the end of line 649. In the interim, we are told where the killing will take place in three different ways (ἐνὶ κρατερῇ ὑσμίνῃ, 'in the fierce conflict'; αὐτοῦ, 'on the spot'; ἐπ' ἀντιθέῳ Σαρπηδόνι, 'over the body of Sarpedon'). Only then is the identity of Patroclus' killer revealed (φαίδιμος ipἝκτωρ, 'shining Hector'), and even then we have to wait until the next line before we get the actual act of killing (χαλκῷ δῃώσῃ, 'he will slay him with his sword').

649
αὐτοῦ: 'there, on the spot', i.e. over Sarpedon's body.

651
ὀφέλλειεν: the subject is Zeus.

AS

652
δοάσσατο = ἔδοξε, 'it seemed'.

653
ὄφρ(α) : 'that'.

655
ἀπὸ . . . ἕλοιτο: in Homeric Greek, it is possible for prepositions to become detached from the main verb, a phenomenon known as 'tmesis' ('cutting'). In these cases, students should translate as if the preposition and the verb formed a single word, i.e. ἀφέλοιτο.

656–683

The Trojans flee. Meanwhile, Zeus instructs Apollo to make arrangements for Sarpedon's funeral.

657
κέκλετο: reduplicated aorist of κέλομαι, 'to call on, urge'.

658
φευγέμεναι: present infinitive, governed by **κέκλετο** in the previous line.

658
γνῶ = ἔγνω. The poet does not explain how Hector 'recognized' Zeus' decision, though heroes in the *Iliad* are often granted the ability to simply sense when the tide of battle has turned against them.

658
Διὸς . . . τάλαντα: the 'scales of Zeus' are an image of Zeus' control of human events. While here Zeus' scales are used in an abstract, metaphorical sense, elsewhere in the poem we see him literally weighing the souls of heroes against one another to decide who should triumph and who should perish. The fact that the poet can mention the 'scales of Zeus' without any further information suggests that the image was a traditional one.

658
ἱρὰ = ἱερά.

659
Λύκιοι: the Lycians are singled out since Sarpedon, whose body is currently being fought over, was a Lycian. But even they do not stay.

659
φόβηθεν = ἐφοβήθησαν, 'they fled'.

660

βεβλαμμένον ἦτορ: literally, 'damaged with respect to his heart', i.e. 'dead'; **ἦτορ** is an accusative of 'respect'.

661

ἐν νεκύων ἀγύρει: 'in the accumulation of bodies', a bold and vivid image that emphasizes the fierceness of the fighting.

661–662

πολέες γὰρ . . . Κρονίων: this is one of very few passages in the poem where warriors die without even being named. The fact that the dead here are not accorded even the minimum level of recognition shows just how fierce the fighting has become at this point.

662

κάππεσον = κατέπεσον, 'they fell'.

663

οἳ: 'they', i.e. Patroclus and his men.

663

ὤμοιιν: genitive dual.

663

ἔντε᾽ ἕλοντο: The stripping of armour from the dead hero's corpse is a traditional element in a duel between two heroes. Sarpedon's body does not fall into Greek hands, but is rescued by the god Apollo, as we shall see at lines 666 ff.

664

χάλκεα μαρμαίροντα: 'bronze, gleaming', the use of asyndeton emphasizes the quality of Sarpedon's armour.

664

τὰ μὲν: 'and this/these', i.e. Sarpedon's armour, which has just been stripped from his corpse; the reader must understand an **αὐτὸν δέ** to go with **τὰ μὲν**, the distinction being between Sarpedon's armour, which the Greeks do capture, and Sarpedon's corpse, which they do not.

665

ἑτάροισι = ἑταίροις, dative indirect object of δῶκε.

667

εἰ δ᾽ ἄγε νῦν: 'come now!'

667

κάθηρον: aorist imperative of καθαίρω; the verb governs two accusatives, 'to cleanse someone (accusative) of something (accusative), to wash something (accusative) off someone (accusative)'. Washing the corpse was an integral part of ancient Greek burial ritual.

668
ἐλθὼν: the movement implied by ἐλθὼν should be read with ἐκ βελέων ('wash him after you've gone out of range with him').

668
ἐκ βελέων: 'out of range of arrows'.

669
πολλὸν: adverbial accusative with ἄποπρο, 'very far away'.

669
ἀπὸ . . . φέρων: tmesis.

669
πρὸ: adverbial.

670
ἀμβροσίῃ: the gods use ambrosia to anoint corpses as well as for nourishment; later in the poem, Thetis will use ambrosia for the same purpose on Patroclus' corpse.

670
περὶ . . . ἕσσον: tmesis. ἕσσον is the aorist imperative of ἕννυμι, 'to clothe'.

671
πέμπε . . . μιν πομποῖσιν . . . φέρεσθαι: 'send two escorts to carry him off'; **φέρεσθαι** is a transitive middle ('take with, carry home') and governs **μιν** ('him', i.e. Sarpedon).

672
ῥά = ἄρα.

672
ὦκα: adverb, 'swiftly'.

676
οὐδ᾽ . . . ἀνηκούστησεν: 'nor did he fail to obey', i.e. 'he willingly obeyed'; the two negatives combine to form a strong positive, a rhetorical technique known as 'litotes'.

678–683
These lines are almost identical to lines 668–673.

684–867

Patroclus advances to the walls of Troy, where he is killed by Apollo, Euphorbus and Hector.

684–711

Patroclus advances the walls of Troy. Apollo first 'nudges' Patroclus back physically, before addressing him directly to tell him to fall back. Patroclus does so, thus avoiding the wrath of Apollo.

684
ἵπποισι καὶ Αὐτομέδοντι κελεύσας: 'urging Automedon and his horses on'; κελεύω with the dative means 'to urge on'.

685
μετεκίαθε: 'he followed from behind'; it is unclear whether Patroclus is on foot or with Automedon on the chariot at this point.

685
καὶ μέγ' ἀάσθη: 'he was greatly deluded'; μέγ(α) is adverbial, 'greatly'.

686
νήπιος: occupies the emphatic runover position, 'he was greatly deluded – the fool!'

686
δὲ: explanatory, almost equivalent to γαρ. 'The fool – *because . . .*'

686
ἔπος: refers to the 'instructions' Achilles gave to Patroclus earlier in the book, viz. to return once he had driven the Trojans back from the ships and not to push on towards the city of Troy itself.

686
φύλαξεν: 'was concerned about, observed'; for the lack of augment, see note on 34 **τίκτε**.

687
ἦ τ(ε): 'most certainly'.

687
κῆρα κακὴν: 'evil doom', an echo of the phrase **θάνατόν τε κακὸν καὶ κῆρα** at line 47, reminding us that this is exactly what Patroclus had wished for.

688
Διὸς . . . νόος: 'will of Zeus'.

689
ὅς: i.e. Zeus.

688
ἠέ περ: 'than', **περ** simply intensifies the sense of **ἠέ**.

689
καὶ: concessive, '*even* a brave man'.

689
ἀφείλετο: gnomic aorist, common in statements of universal truths such as this.

690
ῥηϊδίως = ῥᾳδίως: the actions of the gods are often described as being 'easy' or 'effortless'. The word occupies the emphatic runover position, 'Zeus frightens even the brave man and takes away his triumph – with great ease.'

690
ὅτε δ(ὲ): 'but on other occasions'; ὅτε is adverbial.

690
ἐποτρύνῃσι: 'he urges him on'; the subjunctive seems out of place here, and several manuscripts have ἐποτρύνει instead.

691
οἱ = αὐτῷ.

691
ἐνὶ = ἐν.

691
ἀνῆκεν: third person aorist of ἀνίημι, which here means 'to fire up'.

693
Πατρόκλεις: vocative; Patroclus is one again addressed directly by the poet.

694–6
Ἄδρηστον . . . Πυλάρτην: long lists of people or items, conventionally referred to as 'catalogues', are common in Homer, and can range from a few lines to several hundred. The longest catalogue in the poem is that enumerating all the different contingents of the Greek and Trojan forces, which continues for some 265 lines at the end of Book 2.

The effect of any given catalogue will depend to some extent on the context, though in every case there is an emphasis on size or multitude, e.g. the walls of the Greek camp are so big that they will need *so many* rivers to wash them away (12.20–22), Achilles is so great that he will have *so many* goddesses mourning his death (18.39–49), etc.

The kind of catalogue that we find here, i.e. an enumeration of a hero's slaughtered foes, is known in Greek as an *androktasia*, and serves both to highlight Patroclus' status as an elite warrior and to generate pathos for his victims, each of whom is deemed morally significant enough to warrant being individually named.
For another *androktasia* featuring Patroclus, cf. 16.415–17.

697
τοὺς = τούτους; this is one of the shortest sentences in the poem.

697
μνώοντο: third person singular imperfect of μιμνήσκομαι ('to turn one's mind to', 'to remember'); for the 'diectasis', i.e. the addition of a short vowel in the middle of the word, see note on 39 **φόως** above.

699
Πατρόκλου ὑπὸ χερσί: 'underneath the hands of Patroclus', i.e. under his guidance, led by him

699
περιπρὸ: 'all around before them'.

700
ἐϋδμήτου: 'well-built'; a generic epithet for structures and settlements, though particularly resonant at this point in the poem, i.e. when Patroclus is about the assault the city walls.

701
ἔστη: literally, 'he placed himself', i.e. he stood.

701
τῷ = αὐτῷ, i.e. Patroclus.

701
ὀλοὰ φρονέων: literally, 'considering destructive things', i.e. 'to be hostile towards someone or something'. Apollo is the character who most frequently reminds humans how puny they are in relation to the gods, the fullest expression of which comes in Book 5, when he tells Diomedes to 'never think [himself] gods' equal – since there can be no likeness ever between the make of immortal gods and of men who walk on the ground'.

701
Τρώεσσι δ᾽ ἀρήγων: Apollo is one of the chief supporters of the Trojan forces throughout the poem.

702
τρὶς μὲν . . . τρὶς δ(ὲ) . . . ἀλλ᾽ ὅτε δὴ τὸ τέταρτον: 'three times . . . three times . . . but on the fourth time'. The construction is used several times in the poem, most

often at key turning points in the poem. The impact is to increase the tension and the drama. As one critic puts it: 'We hold our breath when Apollo thrice thrusts Patroclus back, expecting a fatal blow the fourth time.' The same construction appears again at 784 ff.

702

ἀγκῶνος . . . τείχεος: literally, 'the bend of the wall'. There has been some discussion as to what part of the wall is actually meant here. One scholar has suggested that the 'bend' is the right-angle between the wall and the projecting tower on which Apollo has placed himself at 700–701 – although it is difficult to see how Patroclus being at the base of the wall represents much of a threat to the city, nor why Apollo would bother pushing him back from this position.

A more convincing explanation relies on the archaeology of the historic Troy, whose walls had a sloping bottom half and vertical upper half, and might therefore be described as having a 'bend' in the middle. Thus, we find Patroclus climbing up the sloped lower half of the wall and reaching the 'bend' in the middle (where the wall turns vertical), an inherently more threatening action in which the description of the wall as 'lofty' (**ὑψηλοῖο**) has more contextual relevance.

704

Patroclus' dangerous proximity to Apollo is reflected in the text by the juxtaposition of **χείρεσσ' ἀθανάτῃσι** ('immortal hands') and **φαεινὴν ἀσπίδα** ('shining shield').

704

νύσσων: 'nudging'; the verb usually refers to 'pricking' with something sharp, though Apollo is apparently unarmed at this point. The lightness of Apollo's touch, a mere 'nudge', emphasizes the enormous difference in power between men and gods. Apollo will make this point explicitly to Hector at 722.

705

ἐπέσσυτο: aorist of ἐπισεύομαι, 'to charge at, fall upon'.

705

δαίμονι ἶσος: 'equal to a god'; highly ironic given the ease with which Apollo has just swatted Patroclus aside.

706

δεινὰ: adverb 'terribly', in the sense of 'inducing fear'.

706

ὁμοκλήσας: though technically a participle, **ὁμοκλήσας** here acts also as an adverb, specifying the intent of Apollo's speech to Patroclus, 'threateningly', 'scoldingly'.

707

οὔ νύ τοι αἶσα: 'in no way is it determined by fate that . . .'; ἐστίν is to be supplied.

708
πέρθαι: middle infinitive of πέρθω with passive meaning, 'to be sacked'.

709
οὐδ' ὑπ' Ἀχιλλῆος: we are told several times throughout the poem that Achilles will die before the fall of Troy. This is an *argument a fortiori* – 'If even Achilles is not allowed to capture Troy, you certainly won't be!'

709
οὐδ(έ): 'not even'.

709
ὅς περ: 'who indeed'.

709
πολλὸν: adverb 'by far'.

710
ὣς = οὕτως.

710
φάτο = third person singular imperfect of φημί.

710
ἀνεχάζετο: echoes Apollo's **χάζεο** ('fall back!') on line 707. Patroclus does exactly what he is told.

710
πολλὸν: adverb 'by far'; Patroclus falls back further than other heroes when given the same instructions. (When Apollo tells Diomedes to fall back in Book 5, for example, we are told he only falls back 'a little'). This detail may serve to characterize Patroclus as especially willing to do what he is told, or it may simply be practically necessary to enable what follows: Patroclus needs to be in the midst of fighting if he is to be killed by Euphorbus and Hector.

711
μῆνιν: 'wrath', the central theme of the whole poem and its very first word. The fact that Patroclus has 'escaped' the wrath of Apollo might give us hope that he will make it back to the Greek camp alive after all.

712–750

Apollo rebukes Hector for withdrawing from the fighting. Hector returns to battle and engages with Patroclus. Patroclus throws a rock at Hector, but ends up killing his charioteer, Cebriones.

AS

712
πύλῃς: plural, but refers to a single gate, the Scaean Gate.

712
ἔχε . . . ἵππους: 'he halted his horses'.

713
δίζε: 'was undecided'.

713–714
ἠὲ . . . ἦ: 'whether . . . or whether'.

713
μάχοιτο: here: 'continue to fight'.

713
ἐλάσσας: aorist participle of ἐλαύνω, 'to steer, drive'; the object of the verb, ἵππους, must be understood from the previous line.

714
ὁμοκλήσειεν: 'called on'; indirect command governing the accusative (**λαοὺς**) and infinitive (**ἀλῆναι**).

714
ἀλῆναι: aorist passive infinitive of εἴλω, 'to crowd together, gather together'.

715
οἱ φρονέοντι παρίστατο Φοῖβος Ἀπόλλων: a sense of anticipation is created by the delaying of the subject to the end of line. If we were to preserve the word order in English, it might read: 'Next to him [Hector], as he was considering [what to do], there stood . . . Phoebus Apollo.'

716
ἀνέρι εἰσάμενος: 'taking the form of a man'; **ἀνέρι** = ἀνδρί; **εἰσάμενος** comes from εἴδομαι, 'to resemble someone, take their form'. Gods appear to mortal characters in this way throughout the poem – taking the form of a close relative or acquaintance. Characters occasionally realize that they have been conversing with 'some god', though they are generally unable to tell which one.

716
αἰζηῷ ... κρατερῷ: 'vigorous and strong'; these two adjectives are basically synonymous, so a good translation might require a bit of imagination! Other translators have offered 'young and strong' (Lattimore), 'a man of strength and power' (Hammond), 'vigorous and strong' (Green).

717
Ἀσίῳ: 'Asius'; the name is emphasized by being placed in the emphatic runover position.

AS

719
Φρυγίῃ: 'in Phrygia'. Homeric Greek can omit the preposition (ἐν) when specifying a location, as here. Phrygia was the land to the east of Troy. Elsewhere in the poem, the Phrygians appear as allies to the Trojans.

719
ναίεσκε: iterative form of ναίω ('to inhabit'), with barely any change in meaning.

719
ῥοῇς ἔπι = ἐπὶ ῥοαῖς; for the positioning and accentuation of **ἔπι**, see note on 45 **νεῶν ἄπο** above.

719
Σαγγαρίοιο: the Sangarius River formed the border between Phrygia and its eastern neighbour, Bithynia.

720
μιν: i.e. Hector, governed by **προσέφη**.

721
τίπτε = τί ποτε, 'why then?'; the word usually signals rebuke or disconcertment.

721
οὐδέ τί σε χρή: the infinitive ἀποπαύεσθαι must be understood from the context; despite the accent, **τί** is actually an indefinite pronoun not an interrogative pronoun; it is accented because of its position before the enclitic **σε**, which has thrown back an accent onto the preceding syllable. In terms of its function here, **τί** strengthens the negative of **οὐδέ**, i.e. 'there's *really* no need for you to do this'.

722
αἴθ᾽ ὅσον . . . εἴην: Apollo is speaking in the character of Asius, which is why he can describe Hector as being much stronger than him. There is more than a hint of irony here.

722
αἴθ(ε) : with the optative, introduces an unrealizable wish, 'would that . . .!'

722
ὅσον ἥσσων εἰμί, τόσον σέο φέρτερος εἴην: 'If only I were so much stronger than you as I am weaker.' Despite the word order that puts **ὅσον** ahead of **τόσον**, the demonstrative **τόσον** needs to be read ahead of the relative **ὅσον**.

723
τώ κε . . . ἀπερωήσειας: literally, 'then you would (**τώ κε**) soon (**τάχα**) refrain from war (**πολέμου ἀπερωήσειας**) to your sorrow (**στυγερῶς**)', i.e. 'then you would soon regret your decision to refrain from the fighting'.

723
τώ: 'then', 'in that case'.

723
κε = ἄν.

723
τάχα: adverb 'soon'.

723
στυγερῶς: 'with grievous results (to yourself)', i.e. 'you would regret it'.

723
ἀπερωήσειας: second person singular aorist optative of ἀπερωέω, 'to refrain from something'.

724
ἔφεπε: the verb ἐφέπω here means 'to steer something (accusative) towards something (dative).'

725
αἴ κέν: 'in the hope that'.

725
μιν: i.e. Patroclus.

725
ἕλῃς: second person singular aorist subjunctive; this word usually means 'to take', but here means 'to overcome, kill'.

725
τοι = σοι.

725
εὖχος: literally, 'something prayed for' (from εὔχομαι, 'to pray'), i.e. 'victory'.

725
Ἀπόλλων: slightly ironic given the speaker, though the question of whether Patroclus lives or dies is ultimately decided by Zeus, not Apollo, as we saw at 647–651.

726
ὁ . . . θεὸς: 'he, the god'.

726
αὖτις: 'farther back'.

726
ἔβη . . . ἂμ: 'to embark upon", tmesis, with **ἂμ** = **ἀνα**.

726
πόνον: literally, 'toil', i.e. 'the fighting'.

727
Κεβριόνη: Cebriones is Hector's half-brother and his third charioteer in the poem after the death of two others in Book 8.

728
ἵππους ἐς πόλεμον πεπληγέμεν: the repetition of 'p' sounds in this line is perhaps an attempt to imitate the beating of hooves.

728
πεπληγέμεν: a redoubled epic aorist infinitive of πλήσσω, 'to strike', here describing the whipping of Hector's horses in action, i.e. 'to spur on'.

729
δύσεθ' ὅμιλον ἰών: 'went away and made his way into the crowd'.

729–730
ἐν . . . ἧκε: tmesis. ἐνίημι here means 'to inject'.

731
ἔα οὐδ' ἐνάριζεν: 'left them alone and did not try to kill them'.

733
ἀφ' ἵππων: 'from the chariot'.

733
ἆλτο: third person singular aorist of ἅλλομαι, 'to leap'; leaping down from one's chariot is a typical action before a duel between two warriors.

734
σκαιῇ . . . ἑτέρηφι: 'in his left (hand) . . . in his other (hand)'; in both cases, we much supply the word χειρί.

734
λάζετο: imperfect with aorist sense, 'he took hold of'.

735
μάρμαρον: stands in apposition to **πέτρον** in the previous line, 'a rock, a jagged white rock . . .'

735
τόν: 'which', relative pronoun.

735
οἱ = αὐτῷ, 'his', i.e. Patroclus'.

AS

735
περὶ . . . ἐκάλυψεν: tmesis. The fact that Patroclus can grasp this rock in one hand suggests it is smaller than the rocks that are usually hurled in battle.

736
ἐρεισάμενος: 'having braced himself'.

736
οὐδὲ δὴν χάζετο φωτός: literally, 'nor did he hold back from the man (i.e. Hector) for long'. This line has been taken to mean that Patroclus did not wait to attack Hector, i.e. he attacked him immediately, but it will be fifteen lines before this happens. The verb χάζομαι governs the genitive.

737
ἁλίωσε: here, 'threw in vain'.

737
βάλε δ' Ἕκτορος ἡνιοχῆα: given the formulaic nature of fighting in the *Iliad*, we are expecting the rock to hit Hector. Nowhere else in the poem does a rock hit a third party like it does here.

738
νόθον υἱὸν: 'illegitimate son'; although the status of extramarital sons was lower than that of legitimate sons, there seems to have been no particular stigma attached to it. In Book 24, for example, Priam will tell Achilles that he had fathered thirty-one sons on 'women of the palace', i.e. not his wife.

739
ἡνί' ἔχοντα: the fact that Cebriones dies whilst 'holding the reins' adds a powerful sense of pathos. Cebriones remains dutiful right to the very end.

739
μετώπιον: 'on the forehead'; predicative adjective going with **ἡνιοχῆα**.

740
ἔσχεν: intransitive, 'withstand'.

741
ὀφθαλμοὶ δὲ χαμαὶ πέσον: it is anatomically impossible for one's eyes to be knocked clean out of one's head in this fashion.

742
αὐτοῦ πρόσθε ποδῶν: 'right there on the spot, in front of his feet'.

742
ἀρνευτῆρι ἐοικὼς: 'like a diver or acrobat'; the imagery in this short simile will be picked up by Patroclus himself at 745–750.

743
εὐεργέος: 'well-built'; the relative fixity of some noun–epithet formulas can lead to epithets appearing in 'inappropriate' contexts, as here.

744
ἐπικερτομέων: 'mocking, sneering'. There are several occasions in the poem where heroes mock their vanquished foes, as Patroclus does here.

744
Πατρόκλεες ἱππεῦ: another vocative; as Patroclus' death approaches, the poet addresses him directly more and more frequently.

745
ὢ πόποι: 'Oh no, what a shame!' Patroclus is being sarcastic.

745
ὡς ῥεῖα κυβιστᾷ: perhaps better read as an exclamation, i.e. 'How easily he turns somersaults!'

746
εἰ δή που . . . γένοιτο: 'assuming he was perhaps . . .'

747
πολλοὺς: 'many people'.

747
κορέσειεν: aorist optative of κορέννυμι, 'to sate, satisfy hunger'.

747
τήθεα: *hapax*, possibly 'oysters' or 'sea-squirts'.

747
διφῶν: another *hapax*, 'searching for something that is deeply hidden'.

745
ὡς ῥεῖα κυβιστᾷ: 'since he leaps so lightly'.

748
δυσπέμφελος: 'dark and stormy'; πόντος must be understood from 746.

749
ὡς νῦν: 'judging by how . . .'

750
ἔασιν = εἰσίν, 'they are'. Patroclus' whole line here is sarcastic.

751–783

Patroclus and Hector and the rest of the Greeks and Trojans fight for possession of the body of Cebriones.

752
οἶμα: 'momentum, vigour'.

753
ἔβλητο: 'has been shot'; third person singular aorist middle of βάλλω, with passive meaning

753
πρὸς: here, 'in'.

753
ἑή: possessive pronoun, 'his own'.

753
ἑή τέ μιν ὤλεσεν ἀλκή: 'and his [i.e. the lion's] own bravery destroys him'. Homeric similes will often have more than points of contact with the main narrative than the explicit point of comparison. In this case, the explicit point of comparison is the fact that both Patroclus and the lion are attacking things. But the fact that the lion dies in the attack also has a connection with the main narrative: this is exactly what is going to happen to Patroclus.

753
ὤλεσεν – gnomic aorist for a simile, cf. **δηρινθήτην** at line 756

754
Πατρόκλεες: another vocative.

756–761
similes that feature two animals of the same kind fighting against one another are rare in Homer, perhaps emphasizing just how evenly balanced Hector and Patroclus are.

756
τὼ: dual, 'both of them', i.e. Patroclus and Hector.

756
ὥς: 'just as, just like'; postposition, governing the word that precedes it. See note on 45 **νεῶν ἄπο** above.

756
δηρινθήτην: third person dual aorist, 'began fighting'; gnomic aorist for a simile.

757
ὥ: dual of the relative pronoun.

757
κορυφῇσι: 'in the high places'; for the omission of the preposition (ἐν), see note on 719 **Φρυγίῃ** above.

757
κταμένης: 'killed', middle aorist of κτείνω, with passive meaning.

758
πεινάοντε . . . φρονέοντε μάχεσθον: these are all duals. The juxtaposition of the latter two participles without any connective is known as asyndeton, and serves to add to the vividness of the description. The parallelism of the two phrases **ἄμφω πεινάοντε** and **μέγα φρονέοντε**, as well as the internal rhyme, may be thought to evoke the back and forth of battle.

758
μέγα φρονέοντε: literally, 'thinking great things', i.e. 'spirited, with great energy'.

759
μήστωρες ἀϋτῆς: 'masters of battle'; ἀυτή is literally a battle cry, though it is often used just to mean 'battle', as here.

761
ἵεντ(ο): 'they strained', main verb, governing the infinitive.

761
ταμέειν χρόα: 'to slice the skin', i.e. 'to cut into the flesh'.

761
νηλέϊ χαλκῷ: 'with pitiless bronze', i.e. 'with his spear'.

762
κεφαλῆφιν . . . λάβεν: genitive singular of κεφαλή; verbs of touching, grasping, holding, etc. govern the genitive case.

763
ἔχεν ποδός: see note on 762 **κεφαλῆφιν . . . λάβεν** above.

765
ὡς: 'just as', introducing a simile.

765
ἐριδαίνετον ἀλλήλοιιν: 'compete with one another', dual, governing the infinitive.

766
βαθέην = βαθεῖαν, which here means 'dense', emphasizing how thickly forested this mountain hollow is.

767
Note how the three species of tree completely fill the line, perhaps representing the thick coverage of the forest.

767
φηγόν: a species of oak.

767
μελίην: 'ash tree'.

767
τανύφλοιόν: the meaning of this word is obscure; it literally means 'with stretched bark', which might suggest that the tree is tall and thin.

767
κράνειαν: 'cornelian cherry'.

768
αἵ τε: 'and they', i.e. the trees described in the previous line.

768
ἔβαλον: gnomic aorist within the simile.

768
τανυήκεας: 'with elongated point'.

769
ἠχῇ . . . πάταγος: **ἠχή** is a dull, resounding thud, whereas **πάταγος** is a high-pitched, piercing crash.

769
θεσπεσίῃ: this word literally means 'spoken by a god', though here must be mean something like 'miraculous, wondrous, awesome'.

769
ἀγνυμενάων: the noun 'trees' must be understood from the context.

769
πάταγος: the verb ἦν must be understood from the context.

770
θορόντες: aorist participle of θρῴσκω, 'to leap, charge'.

771
δῄουν: 'they slay'; the word is placed in the emphatic runover position.

771
οὐδ᾽ ἕτεροι: 'and no one from either side'.

771
μνώοντ᾽ ὀλοοῖο φόβοιο: cf. 697, where 'flight' was exactly what the Trojans had 'turned their minds' to.

772–775
πολλὰ δὲ . . . αὐτόν: the flurry of fighting that takes place over Cebriones' body is reinforced by the repetition of the words **πολλὰ** and **ἀμφ(ί)**, a literary technique known as 'anaphora'. Note also the sheer number of different types of missiles that are involved here: spears, arrows and stones.

772
Κεβριόνην ἀμφ(ί) = ἀμφὶ Κεβριόνην; another postpositional phrase.

772
πεπήγει: pluperfect active used intransitively, 'were stuck fast'.

775
μαρναμένων: this genitive can depend on any of **δοῦρα, ἰοί** or **χερμάδια**.

775
ἀμφ(ί) – here: 'over'

776
μέγας μεγαλωστί: 'great in his greatness'; observe the juxtaposition of two cognate words, a literary device known as a *figura etymologica*.

776
λελασμένος: from (ἐπι)λανθάνομαι, 'no longer thinking of'.

776
ἱπποσυνάων: a plural form, but translate 'horsemanship'.

777–778
ὄφρα . . . τόφρα: 'as long as . . . for so long'.

779
ἦμος: temporal, 'when'.

779
μετενίσετο: 'was about to return', i.e. back to the horizon.

779
βουλυτόνδε: βουλυτός refers to the unyoking (λύω) the oxen (βοῦς), which took place in the afternoon or early evening. Most scholars have taken βουλυτόνδε as a temporal adverb referring to this particular time of day, though it is also possible to read it as a locative adjective, i.e. 'towards the place where the oxen are unyoked'.

780
ὑπὲρ αἶσαν – 'beyond what was fated'. This refers to the 'plan of Zeus' outlined in Book 1 of the poem, in which Zeus agreed to bring the Greeks to the brink of destruction to set up Achilles' glorious return to battle.

781–783
μὲν . . . δὲ: is here used to show the simultaneity of the two actions described in these lines.

782
Τρώων ἐξ ἐνοπῆς: literally, 'from the battle cries of the Trojans', i.e. out of the thick of battle.

784–817

Patroclus is disarmed by Apollo and then run through by Euphorbus.

785
σμερδαλέα: 'terribly'; this is the accusative plural neuter of σμερδαλέος, but here acts as an adverb.

785
ἔπεφνεν: aorist of θείνω, 'he killed'.

786
ἐπέσσυτο: root aorist of ἐπισεύομαι, 'to charge at, fall upon'.

786–867
ὅτε . . . ἔνθ(α): 'when . . . then'; the use of **ἔνθα** in a broad temporal sense ('then') is frequent in battle descriptions.

787
τοι = σοι.

789
This line is as dactylic as it is possible to be.

789
ὁ = οὗτος, i.e. Patroclus.

789
τὸν = τοῦτον, i.e. Apollo.

789
κατὰ κλόνον: 'though the confusion (of the fighting)', governed by ἰόντα.

AS

790
ἠέρι . . . κεκαλυμμένος: 'cloaked in fog', used metaphorically to mean 'invisible'.

791
στῆ δ' ὄπιθεν: 'approached (him) from behind'.

792
χειρὶ καταπρηνεῖ – 'with the flat of the hand'; Apollo need only 'slap' Patroclus to completely disarm him, cf. when Apollo merely 'nudges' Patroclus' shield to throw him back from the walls of Troy.

792
στρεφεδίνηθεν – third person plural aorist passive form, but translate 'he rolled his eyes backwards'.

792
οἱ = αὐτῷ.

792
ὄσσε: nominative dual.

793
κρατὸς: genitive of κάρη.

794
κυλινδομένη καναχὴν ἔχε: the repetition of the 'k' sounds in this line might reflect the rattling of Patroclus' armour as it falls to the ground.

794
ποσσὶν ὑφ' ἵππων: 'beneath the feet of the horses'; **ὑφ'** is postpositive, i.e. governing the word that precedes it.

796
πάρος γε: 'previously', i.e. as long as Achilles had been wearing it.

796
μὲν = μήν.

796
οὐ θέμις ἦεν: θέμις here refers to the natural or divine order of things, though translators tend to translate more simply as 'it was not permitted' (Lattimore) or 'it was not allowed' (Green).

796
ἦεν = ἦν.

799
ῥύετ(ο): durative imperfect of ἔρυμαι/ῥύομαι, 'always protected'.

AS

800
ᾗ: possessive pronominal adjective, 'his'.

800
κεφαλῇ: locative dative without a preposition, 'on his head'.

800
σχεδόθεν δέ οἱ ἦεν ὄλεθρος: just as the description of Hector's death follows closely from that of his greatest triumph, so in real life will Hector die shortly after killing Patroclus.

800
σχεδόθεν = σχεδόν, 'near at hand'.

800
δέ: may have an explanatory sense (≈ γάρ), as at line 90. Zeus allows Hector to wear Achilles' helmet precisely *because* his own death approaches.

801
πᾶν: adverbial, intensifying the sense of ἄγη.

801
ἄγη: 'was shattered', aorist passive of ἄγνυμι, 'to break into pieces, shatter'.

802
βριθὺ μέγα στιβαρὸν κεκορυθμένον – these four adjectives all describe Patroclus' spear. Exactly the same set of adjectives were used earlier in Book 16 (16.141 – not part of the set text) to describe the spear of Achilles, a weapon which Patroclus was emphatically unable to wield. Just as Patroclus came up short then, so he comes up short now.

802
κεκορυθμένον: literally, 'helmeted', i.e. furnished with a bronze tip.

803
τερμιόεσσα: this word is found only here in Homer and its meaning is obscure. The ancient scholars thought the word derived from τέρμις ('foot') and thus meant 'reaching down to the feet', i.e. 'large'. If the word is derived from τέρμα ('end'), however, it might mean something like 'furnished with a rim'.

805
φρένας: accusative of respect.

805
ἄτη: 'confusion'; this word can be used to describe both a physical state, as here, or a mental state, as we saw at line 685.

AS

806
ταφών: 'as if paralyzed'.

807
ὤμων μεσσηγὺς = μεταξὺ ὤμων.

807
σχεδόθεν: 'at close range'.

807
Δάρδανος: 'Dardanian' is here used synonymously with 'Trojan'.

808
Πανθοΐδης Εὔφορβος: the name of Patroclus' killer occupies the emphatic runover position.

808
ἡλικίην ἐκέκαστο: the verb καίνυμαι ('to surpass, excel') governs an accusative of the thing being surpassed. ἡλικίη serves as a collective, i.e. 'a group of people born at the same time', 'a generation'.

810
καὶ γὰρ δὴ: used to introduce a concrete example following a more general statement.

810
βῆσεν: causative, 'caused them to get down', i.e. 'brought them down'. Warriors in Homer usually step down from their chariots before engaging in battle. The fact that Euphorbus defeats no fewer than twenty warriors while still on their chariots might be a sign of a particular eagerness to fight.

811
πρῶτ' ἐλθὼν . . . διδασκόμενος πολέμοιο: 'whereby he first learned the art of war'; verbs of learning often govern the (partitive) genitive.

811
ὄχεσφι: dative plural of ὄχεα, 'chariot'.

813
ἀνέδραμε: 'he ran back', aorist of ἀνατρέχω.

813
μίκτο: middle root aorist of μίσγομαι / μείγνυμαι, 'to mix oneself (among)', 'merge oneself (into)'.

814
χροὸς = χρωτός.

AS

816
πληγῇ: echoes πλῆξεν from line 791.

816
δουρὶ: this is Euphorbus' spear; it was mentioned at line 806.

817
ἂψ: 'back'.

817
ἐχάζετο: conative imperfect, 'attempted to retreat'.

817
ἀλεείνων: conative, 'in an attempt to avoid'.

818–867

Patroclus is finished off by Hector.

820
ἀγχίμολόν: 'close (to him)'.

820
κατὰ στίχας: 'through the lines (of battle)'.

821
νείατον: 'outermost, lowermost'.

821
κενεῶνα: 'the side', imagined as the 'empty space' (κενός) between the ribs and the pelvis.

821
διάπρο: 'all the way through'.

822
δούπησεν δὲ πεσών: 'he fell with a thud'; the verb even sounds like a thud.

822
ἤκαχε: 'was a cause of grief to'.

823–826
ὡς δ' ὅτε . . . βίηφιν: The simile at 756 ff. presented Hector and Patroclus as evenly matched opponents – both were lions. Here, Hector remains a lion, but Patroclus has become a boar.

823
χάρμη: 'aggressiveness, belligerence'.

824
ὥ: 'both of whom', dual of the relative pronoun.

825
πίδακος: 'mountain spring', a word found only here in Homer.

825
ἀμφ(ί): '(fight) over'.

826
πολλὰ: 'a lot', 'heavily'.

826
ἀσθμαίνοντα: the word σῦν must be understood from its previous mention on line 823.

827
ὣς = οὕτως.

827
πολέας = πολλούς.

828
ἀπηύρα: this verb governs two accusatives, 'to take something (accusative) away from someone (accusative)'.

829
οἱ ἐπευχόμενος: 'triumphing over him', i.e. Patroclus.

830–863
This interchange between Hector and Patroclus is closely mirrored later in the poem in the scene between Achilles and Hector in Book 22.

830
ἦ που ἔφησθα: 'you thought . . . didn't you?', 'I bet you thought . . .'

830
ἁμήν: ἡμετέραν.

831

ἐλεύθερον ἦμαρ: '(day of) freedom'; it was customary for the wives and children of a defeated army to be sold into slavery.

833
τάων . . . πρόσθ(ε): 'in front of them'.

834
ποσσὶν ὀρωρέχαται: literally, 'they stretched out with their feet', i.e. 'they galloped'.

835
ὅ = ὅτι, i.e. 'related to the fact that'.

836
ἦμαρ ἀναγκαῖον: '(day of) captivity'.

836
σὲ δέ: 'but as for *you*'; the placement of **σὲ** at the beginning of the clause adds emphasis.

836
ἔδονται: 'will eat'.

837
οὐδέ: 'not once'.

837
τοι = σοι, as in the following line.

837
χραίσμησεν: 'could protect you, save you from harm'.

838
πού: 'I suppose,' Hector is imagining what Achilles said to Patroclus earlier that morning.

838
μάλα πολλὰ . . . ἐπετέλλετ(ο): **μάλα πολλὰ** is strongly emphatic, 'he told you in no uncertain terms', 'he expressly said'.

838
μένων . . . ἰόντι: a neat contrast between what Achilles told Patroclus to do (μένων, 'remain behind') and what Patroclus actually did (ἰόντι, 'go forth').

839
μή . . . ἰέναι: governed by the ἐπετέλλετ(ο) in the previous line, 'he told you not . . .'

839
πρὶν: adverb – 'earlier'.

840
νῆας ἔπι = ἐπὶ νῆας.

840
πρὶν: governs the infinitive, δαίξαι, on line 841.

841
φρένας ἄφρονι πεῖθε: literally, 'he persuaded the mind of you who are a mindless'. Hector ends his speech with a highly alliterative oxymoron.

843
Πατρόκλεες ἱππεῦ: vocative.

844
μεγάλ(α): 'loudly'.

844
εὔχεο: corresponds to **ἐπευχόμενος** at line 829.

846
ῥηιδίως = ῥᾳδίως; the word's placement in the emphatic runover position highlights just how 'easily' Patroclus was brought down by the gods.

847
τοιοῦτοι δ(έ): 'such (people), however'; Patroclus does not deign to mention Hector's name.

847
εἴ πέρ: 'even if'.

848
αὐτόθ(ι): 'on the spot, right here'.

848
δαμέντες: aorist passive participle of δάμνημι / δαμάζω, 'to slay'.

850
ἀνδρῶν: partitive genitive, 'of men', as opposed to 'of gods'.

852
θην: 'certainly'.

852
οὐδ' αὐτὸς: 'nor also you yourself'.

852
βέῃ: 'you will live'; subjunctive in form, but acts as a future.

856
ἐκ ῥεθέων – this expression has traditionally been understood to mean 'from his limbs', though some scholars have suggested 'from his mouth'.

856
πταμένη: aorist participle of πέτομαι, 'to fly'.

856
Ἄιδόσδε: 'into (the house) of Hades'.

856
βεβήκει: 'was already on the way'.

857
πότμον: 'lot', usually in the sense 'death'.

857
γοόωσα: Patroclus' soul 'laments' as it leaves his body.

857
ἀνδροτῆτα: 'physical manhood'.

858
τεθνηῶτα προσηύδα: these two participles lack a connective particle, known as 'asyndeton'.

859
τί νύ: 'but why, for what?'

860
τίς δ' οἶδ' εἴ κ(ε): 'who knows if perhaps?'

861
φθήῃ ... τυπεὶς ... ἀπὸ ... ὀλέσσαι – φθάνω: should be understood with **τυπεὶς** with **ἀπὸ ... ὀλέσσαι** (tmesis) forming a consecutive (or explanatory) infinitive, 'whether Achilles is not struck first so that he loses his life'.

861
φθήῃ: subjunctive of φθάνω, 'to do something first'.

863
προσβάς: aorist participle, 'stepping against'.

863
ὕπτιον: 'onto his back'.

863
ὦσ(ε): aorist of ὠθέω, 'to push'.

864
μετ' ... βεβήκει: 'strode out towards'.

866
ἵετο: 'he was eager'.

867
ἀγλαὰ δῶρα: 'as a gift'; Achilles' horses were wedding gifts to his father, Peleus, on the occasion of his wedding to Thetis. The armour that Patroclus has just lost was also a gift on the same occasion.

Vocabulary

Iliad, Book 16

An asterisk * denotes a word in OCR's Defined Vocabulary List for AS.

ἆ	ah!
ἀάω	to confuse, delude
ἀγακλεής -ές	very famous, glorious
Ἀγαμέμνων -ονος, m.	Agamemnon, son of Atreus
ἄγε, adv.	come on, come now
ἀγέρωχος -ον	high-minded, lordly
ἀγκών -ῶνος, m.	corner (of a wall)
ἀγλαός -ή -όν	splendid, shining, bright
ἄγνυμι, aor. pass. **ἄγην**	to break, shatter
ἄγυρις -ιος, f.	gathering, crowd
ἄγχι, adv.	near, nearby
***ἄγω**	to bring, lead; (mid.) to take as a wife
Ἄδρηστος -ου, m.	Adrestus, a Trojan
***ἀεί**, adv.	ever, always
ἀεικής -ές	unseemly, shameful
ἀείρω	to lift, raise up
ἀήρ, ἠέρος, m.	mist, fog
ἀθάνατος -ον	immortal
αἴ	= εἰ
Αἰακίδης -αο, m.	descendent of Aeacus, i.e. Achilles
Ἄιδης -ου, m.	Hades
Ἀιδόσδε, adv.	to Hades
αἰέν	= ἀεί
αἰζηός	vigorous, strong
αἴθε	(introduces a wish) 'would that . . .!'
αἷμα -ατος, n.	blood
αἱματόεις -εσσα -εν	bloody, bleeding
αἰναρέτης	dreadful in one's valour
αἰνός -ή -όν	dreadful, terrible
αἰπύς -εῖα -ύ	steep, towering; (of work) arduous
***αἱρέω**	to take, grasp; to kill, capture, sack (e.g. a city); (mid.) to take for oneself, to choose
αἶσα -ης, f.	fate
ἀκάμας -αντος	untiring, tireless
ἀκέομαι	to heal, cure
ἀκμής -ῆτος	unwearied
ἀλεείνω	to avoid, shun
ἀλέομαι	to avoid, flee from
ἁλιόω	to do something fruitlessly, to fail at something
ἀλκή -ῆς, f.	strength, might
ἄλκιμος -ον	brave, bold
***ἀλλά**	but
ἀλλήλων	each other, one another
ἅλλομαι	to jump, leap
***ἄλλος -η -ο**	other, another
ἄμ	= ἀνά
***ἅμα** (+ dat.)	at the same time as, together with
ἀμβροσίη -ης, f.	ambrosia, the food of the gods; also used as an ointment for embalming or as perfume
ἄμβροτος -ον	immortal, divine
ἀμείνων -ον	better
ἀμήχανος -ον	impractical, unmanageable
ἀμός -ή -όν	our
ἀμύμων -ον	excellent
***ἀμύνω** (+ acc. and dat.)	to defend someone (dat.) from something (acc.)
ἀμφί (+ dat.)	around, over, on

ἀμφιβαίνω	to stand over or across
ἀμφιπένομαι	to attend (to), tend (the sick or wounded)
ἀμφότερος -α -ον	both
ἄμφω	both
***ἄν**	would, could (indef.)
ἀνά	up, on
ἀναβαίνω	to go up, mount; to embark upon
ἄναξ -ακτος, m.	lord, master
ἀνάπνευσις -εως, f.	respite (from something, gen.)
ἀναπνέω	to catch one's breath
ἀναχάζω	to force back
ἀνδρότης -ῆτος, f.	courage, manliness
ἀνδροφόνος -ον	man-slaying, murderous, epithet of Hector
ἀνήρ, ἀνδρός, m.	an
ἀνίημι	to incite, prompt
ἀντιβολέω	to meet
ἀντίθεος -η -ον	godlike
ἄντομαι (+ dat.)	to meet with, encounter someone (dat.)
ἀγχίμολον, adv.	near, close at hand
ἀπαυράω	to take something (acc.) away from someone (acc.)
ἀπερωέω	to refrain from something
ἀπέχω	to keep off or away from
ἀποθρῴσκω	to leap off from
ἀποπαύω (+ gen.)	to cease from something (gen.)
ἄποπρο, adv.	far away
ἀποστυφελίζω	to drive someone (acc.) away by force from something (gen.)
ἀναγκαῖος -η -ον	binding, constraining
ἄναλκις -ιδος	without strength, feeble
ἀνατρέχω, aor. **ἀνέδραμον**	to run back
***ἀνήρ, ἀνδρός**, m.	man
ἀντίθεος -η -ον	godlike, equal to the gods
***ἄρα**	. . . then . . . (often no recognizable impact on the meaning)
Ἀργεῖος -α -ον	of or from Argos, Argive
ἄριστος -η -ον	best, excellent, noble
ἁρπάζω	to seize, snatch
ἀπαυράω	to take away, rob, deprive
ἀπερωέω	to slink away (from fighting)
ἀπηνής -ές	unfeeling, harsh
***ἀπό** (+ gen.)	from, away from
Ἀπόλλων -ωνος, m.	Apollo
ἅπτομαι (+ gen.)	to take hold of, cling to

ἀρήγω (+ dat.)	to bring aid to, protect in battle
ἀρήιος -α -ον	warlike
ἀρνευτήρ -ῆρος, m.	tumbler, acrobat
Ἄσιος -ου, m.	Asius, a Trojan
ἀσθμαίνω	to breathe heavily, to pant, gasp
ἀσπίς -ίδος, f.	shield
***ἄστυ -εος**, n.	town, city
ἀτάλαντος -ον	equivalent to, like
ἄτη -ης, f.	confusion, bewilderment
***αὖθις**, adv.	again, back again
αὐλῶπις -ιδος, f.	socketed (in order to hold the plume), epithet of helmets
αὐτὰρ	and, but
ἀυτή -ῆς, f.	a battle cry
***αὐτίκα**	immediately, straightaway
αὖτις	= αὖθις
αὐτόθι, adv.	here, on the spot
αὐτοκασίγνητος -ου, m.	brother
Αὐτομέδων -ονος, m.	Automedon, one of the Myrmidons
Αὐτόνοος -ου, m.	Autonous, a Trojan
αὐτοῦ, adv.	there, then
ἀφαιρέω	to take away
ἄφρων -ον	senseless, unfeeling
Ἀχαιοί -ῶν, m. plur.	the Achaeans, i.e. the Greeks
Ἀχιλλεύς -έως, m.	Achilles
ἀχεύω	to cause pain to
ἄχος -εος, n.	pain, distress
ἄψ, adv.	backwards, back again
***βαίνω**	to go
βαθύς -εῖα -ύ	deep
***βάλλω**	to throw; to cast (a javelin), to fire (an arrow); to bear something in mind
βαρύς -εῖα -ύ	heavy, strong, deep
βασιλεύς -ῆος, m.	king
βέλος -εος, n.	missile, shot, anything thrown or shot (e.g. arrow, stone)
βέομαι	to live
βῆσσα -ας, f.	a wooded glen
βιάω, perf. **βεβίηκα**	to overwhelm
***βίη -ης**, feminine	bodily strength, force, might
βίοτος -ου, masculine	life
βλάπτω	to hinder, disable

βουλυτόνδε, adverb	towards evening
βριθύς -εῖα -ύ	heavy, ponderous
γαῖα -ης, f.	land
***γάρ**	for, since
γέρας -αος, n.	prerogative, a mark of honour
***γίγνομαι**	to be, exist
***γιγνώσκω**	to come to know, learn
γλαυκός -ή -όν	gleaming, shimmering, perhaps with a sense of colour, greyish-blue
γλαφυρός -ή -όν	hollow
γοάω	to bewail
γυῖα, γυίων, n. plur.	limbs, legs
γυμνός -ή -όν	naked, unarmed
***γυνή, γυναικός**, f.	woman
γύψ, γυπός, m.	vulture
δαΐζω	to tear, cut through, wound
δαίμων -ονος, m.	god, divinity
δαΐφρων -ον	warlike; skilful, prudent
Δαναοί, -ών, m. plur.	Danaans, i.e. the Greeks
δαμάζω	to overpower, tame, kill
Δάρδανος -ου, m.	Dardanian, i.e. Trojan
***δέ**	and, but
δειλός -ή -όν	cowardly, worthless
δεινὰ, adv.	terribly, dreadfully
***δεινός -ή -όν**	dreadful, terrible
***δή**	(emphasizes preceding word)
δηιοτής -ῆτος, f.	battle
δηιόω	to cut down, slay
δῆμος -ου, m.	country, land
δήν, adv.	long, for a long time
δηριάομαι	to contend, wrangle
δηρὸν, adv.	long
διάπρο, adv.	all the way through
διδάσκω	to instruct, teach
διδυμάων -ονος, m.	twin
***δίδωμι**	to give; to grant, i.e. allow something to happen (+ inf.)
δίζω	to be in doubt, be at a loss
διογενής -έος	Zeus-born, epithet of heroes
Διομήδης -ους, m.	Diomedes
δῖος -α -ον	divine, godlike
διφάω	to search for, dive after
δίφρος -ου, masculine	chariot
δοάσσατο	= Attic ἔδοξε, 'it seemed'
δολιχόσκιος -ον	long-shadowed, epithet of spears
δόρυ, δουρός, n.	spear
δουπέω	to make a heavy or dead sound, to thud
δουρικλειτός -ον	renowned in the use of the spear, spear-famed
Δύμας -αντος, m.	Dymas, father of Hecuba and Asius
δύνω	see δύω
δυσπέμφελος -ον	rough and stormy, epithet of the sea
δύω	to enter, make one's way into, plunge into; to come upon, take possession of
δύω	two
***δῶρον -οῦ**, n.	gift, present
***ἐάω**	to leave alone
ἔγχος -εος, noun	spear
***ἐγώ, ἐγών**	I
ἔδω, future **ἔδομαι**	to eat
ἐείκοσι	twenty
***εἰ**	if
εἴδομαι	to appear
εἶδον	(not used in act. pres.) I saw, perceived
εἷμα -ατος, n.	garment
εἴλω	to crowd together, gather up
***εἰμί**	to be
***εἶμι**	I shall go
εἶπον	I said, spoke
***εἰς** (+ acc.)	to, towards
ἔθειρα -ης, f.	hair
***ἐθέλω**	to be willing, to want (to do something, + inf.); to choose
ἔθνος -εος, n.	a group, company, body of people or things
***ἐκ** or **ἐξ** (+ gen.)	out of, from
Ἑκάβη -ης, f.	Hecuba, Hector's mother
ἑκατηβόλος -ον	far-shooting, shooting from afar, epithet of Apollo
ἐκεῖνος -η -ο	that
Ἕκτωρ -ορος, m.	Hector, the foremost warrior of the Trojans
ἐκφέρω	to carry off
Ἔλασος -ου, m.	Elasus, a Trojan
ἐλαύνω	to drive
ἔλαφος -ου, m.e or f.	deer
ἐλαφρός -ά -όν	light, nimble
***ἐλεύθερος -α -ον**	free
ἕλκος -εος, n.	wound
***ἐμός -ή -όν**	my
***ἐν** (+ dat.)	in, on, onto, among

ἐναρίζω	to kill, slay
***ἔνθα**, adv.	where, there
***ἐνθάδε**, adv.	here
ἐνίημι	to send in; to inspire, inject
ἐννέα	nine
ἐνοπή -ῆς, f.	the cry of battle or the battle itself
ἐνορούω (+ dat.)	to leap upon, spring upon
ἔντεα -έων, n. plur.	amour
ἐξαῦτις, adv.	once more, anew
ἐξεναρίζω	to kill, slay
ἐοικώς, adv.	as, like
ἑός, ἑή, ἑόν	his, her own
***ἐπεί**	when, after (temporal); since, because (causal)
***ἔπειτα**	then, afterwards
ἐπεύχομαι	to boast over, triumph over
***ἐπί** (+ acc.)	to, towards
ἐπιδεύομαι	to lack, be inferior to (+ gen.)
ἐπικερτομέω	to mock, deride
ἐπισεύω	to rush on or at
Ἐπίστωρ -ορος, m.	Epistor, a Trojan
ἐπιτέλλω	to command
ἔπος -εος, n.	word, words, message
ἐποτρύνω	to urge on, prompt, impel
ἐρείδω	(mid.) to support oneself firmly
ἐρέω	to speak, say
ἐριδαίνω	to contend with, dispute with
ἔρις -ιδος, f.	quarrel, strife
ἐρύω	to drag
***ἔρχομαι**	to come, go
ἐς	= εἰς
ἐσθλός -ή -όν	good
ἔται -ῶν, m. plur.	kinsmen, clansmen
***ἑταῖρος -ου**, m.	companion
ἑτέρηφι	with the other (hand)
ἕτερος -α -ον	the other
ἑτέρωθεν, adv.	from or on the other side
***ἔτι**	still, yet (often with neg.)
εὔδμητος -ον	well-built
εὐεργής -ές	well-made, epithet of chariots
Εὖρος -ου, m.	Eurus, the east wind
Εὐρύπυλος -ου, m.	Eurypylus, a Greek hero
***εὐρύς -εῖα -ύ**	wide, broad
εὖτε	when
Εὔφορβος -ου, m.	Euphorbus, a Trojan
εὖχος -εος, n.	glory

ἐφέπω (+ dat.)	to urge something or someone on against; to steer something towards something
ἐφίημι	to let fly (of ranged weapons)
Ἔχεκλος -ου, m.	Echeclus, a Trojan
***ἔχω**	to hold, to hold back
***Ζεύς, Διός**, m.	Zeus
ἤ	or
ἤ . . . ἤ	whether . . . or whether
ἦ, adverb	in truth, surely
ἥβη -ης, feminine	youth
ἠδὲ	and
ἤδη, adverb	already, by this time
ἠέ	= ἤ
ἠέλιος -ου, m.	the sun; (when capitalized) Helios, the sun god
ἠλίβατος -ον	high, steep
ἠλικίη -ης, f.	age cohort, a group of people the same age, a generation
ἦμαρ -ατος, n.	day
ἦμος, adv.	when
ἡνία -ίων, m. plur.	reins
ἡνιοχεύς - ῆος, m.e	charioteer
ἥρως -ωος, m.	hero
ἥσσων -ον	inferior, weaker, lesser
ἦτορ -ορος, n.	heart
ἠΰκομος -ον	lovely haired
ἠΰς -ύ	good, brave, noble
ἠχή -ῆς, f.	a resounding, echoing noise
***θάλασσα -ης**, f.	sea
***θάνατος -ου**, m.	death; (when capitalized) the god Death, brother of Sleep
θεῖος -α -ον	divine, godlike
θέμις ἐστίν	it is right, ordained
θεοπροπία -ης, f.	prophecy, oracle
***θεός -οῦ**, m.	god
θεράπων -οντος, m.	attendant, comrade-at-arms
θεσπέσιος -α -ον	divinely sounding
Θέτις -ιδος, f.	Thetis, mother of Achilles
θήν, adv.	doubtless, surely
θνῄσκω	to die
θοός -ή -όν	swift
θρῴσκω	to leap, spring
θυμός -οῦ, m.	heart, soul
θύω	to rage, surge
θώραξ -ακος, m.	breastplate, cuirass

θωρήσσω	to arm oneself for battle
ἰάχω	to cry, shout
Ἰδαῖος -α -ον	relating to Mount Ida, the mountain that overlooks Troy
***ἵημι**	to throw, let fly; to stretch, strain to do something (+ inf.)
ἰητρός -οῦ, m.	healer, physician, surgeon
ἱππεύς -ῆος, m.	charioteer
ἱππόδαμος -ον	horse-taming, epithet of heroes, esp. Hector
ἱπποκέλευθος -ον	horse-driving, epithet of Patroclus
ἱππόκομος -ον	decked with horse-hair, epithet of helmets
ἱπποσύνη -ης, f.	the art of driving the chariot, horsemanship
***ἵππος -ου**, m.	horse
ἱππότα -ου, m.	driver or rider of horses
ἰός -οῦ, m.	arrow
ἱρός -ά -όν	hallowed, holy
ἴσκω	to make someone equate something (acc.) to something else (dat.)
***ἴσος -η -ον**	equal to, the same as (+ dat.)
ἵστημι	to make to stand, set up; to stand
ἴφθιμος -η -ον	stout, strong
ἰχθυόεις -εσσα -εν	fishy, full of fish
καθαίρω	to cleanse
***καί**	and, even, also
καίνυμαι	to surpass, excel
***κακός -ή -όν**	bad, evil, cowardly
***καλέω**	to call, summon
καλύπτω	to hide, conceal, cover
κάμνω	to grow weary
καναχή -ῆς, f.	the ring or clang of metal
κάρη, κάρητος, n.	head
καρπάλιμος -ον	swift, quick
κασίγνητος -ου, m.	brother
***κατά** (+ acc.)	down, according to, by, in, throughout
καταπίπτω	to fall down
καταπρηνής -ές	down-turned, (of hands) open, i.e. not clenched
κατατίθημι	to put or lay down
κέ, κέν	= ἄν
Κεβριόνης -ου, m.	Cebriones, a Trojan, charioteer of Hector
***κεῖμαι**	to lie down, be dead
κεῖνος -η -ο	= ἐκεῖνος -η -ο
***κελεύω**	to order, command, tell
κελαινεφής -ές	dark
κέλομαι, aor. **κεκλόμην**	to call on, urge
κενεών -ῶνος, m.	the soft part of the body between the ribs and the hips, the side
κεραΐζω	to ravage, despoil, plunder
κερδίων -ον	better, more profitable
κεφαλή -ῆφι, f.	head
κήρ, κηρός, f.	doom, fate
κλισία -ας, f.	tent, hut
κλόνος -ου, m.	confusion, turmoil (of the battlefield)
κοῖλος -η -ον	hollow
κονίη -ης, f.	dust
κορέννυμι	to sate, satiate
κορύσσω	to arm oneself, equip oneself
κορυφή -ῆς, f.	crest, summit
κραιπνός -ή -όν	swift, rushing
κράνεια -ας, f.	the cherry tree
κραταιός -ά -όν	strong, mighty
κρατερός -ά -όν	strong, mighty
κρατερῶνυξ -υχος	strong-hoofed, solid-hoofed
κράτος -εος, n.	strength, might
κρείσσων -ον	strong, mighty
Κρονίδης -ου, m.	son of Cronus, i.e. Zeus
κτείνω	to kill, slay
κυβιστάω	to tumble, somersault
κυβιστητήρ -ῆρος, m.	tumbler, acrobat
κῦδος -εος, n.	glory, renown
κυλίνδω	to roll
κυνέη -ης, f.	helmet
λᾶας -ος, m.	rock
λάζομαι	to take hold of, seize
***λαμβάνω**	to take hold of, seize
λανθάνομαι	to not have knowledge of, not think of
λάξ, adv.	with the foot
λαός -οῦ, m.	the people or men of the army
***λείπω**	to leave
λέων -οντος, m.	lion
Λητώ -οῦς, f.	Leto, mother of Apollo and Artemis
λίθος -ου, m.	stone, rock
λίσσομαι	to pray, beg
λίτομαι	= λίσσομαι
λοιγός -οῦ, m.	destruction, ruin
λούω	to bathe, wash
Λυκίη -ης, f.	Lycia

Λύκιος -α -ον	Lycian
μαντεύομαι	to prophesy
μαρμαίρω	to flash, sparkle, gleam
μάρμαρος -ου, m.	marble; (as adj.) made of marble
μάρναμαι	to fight, do battle
***μάχομαι**	to fight
Μεγάδης	son of Megas, i.e. Perimus
μεγάθυμος -ον	great-hearted
***μέγας, μεγάλη, μέγα**	great
μέγας μεγαλωστί	great in his greatness
μεθίημι	to let go
μείλινος -α -ον	ashen, made of ash wood
Μελάνιππος -ου, m.	Melanippus, a Trojan
μελανός -ή -όν	black
μελίη -ης, f.	the ash tree
***μέλλω**	to be going or about to do something (+ fut. inf.)
μέμαα	to eagerly desire to do something
μέν	in truth, indeed
***μέν ... δέ**	(marks a contrast)
Μενοιτιάδης -ου, m.	the son of Menoetius, i.e. Patroclus
***μένω**	to remain, wait, hold one's ground
μερμηρίζω	to think carefully about something, weigh up the different options
μέσος -η -ον	middle, in the middle
μεσσηγύς, adv.	in the middle, between
μετά (+ acc.)	towards
μετακιάθω	to go after, pursue
μετανίσσομαι	to pass over the meridian (of the sun), i.e. to pass its highest point, to begin setting
μεταπρέπω (+ dat.)	to be conspicuous or prominent among
μετάφρενον -ου, n.	the upper back
μέτωπον -ου, n.	brow, forehead
μετώπιον -ου, n.	forehead
***μή** (and comp.)	see οὐ
μῆνις -ιος, fut.	wrath
μηρός -οῦ, m.	thigh
μήστωρ -ωρος, m.	raiser or author or something, esp. the war-cry
***μήτηρ, -έρος or -ρός**, fut.	mother
μήτρως -ως, m.	maternal uncle, i.e. your mother's brother
μιαίνω	to stain, sully
μίγνυμι	to mix, mingle, come into contact with something
μιμνήσκω	to turn one's mind to, remember
μιν	him, her, it
μνάομαι	to turn one's mind to something
μοῖρα -ας, f.	fate, lot
Μούλιος -ου, m.	Mulius, a Trojan
Μυρμιδόνες -ων, m. plur.	Myrmidons, the Thracian tribe of which Achilles is the leader
μῶνυξ -υχος	single-hoofed, solid-hoofed, epithet of horses
ναίω	to live in, inhabit
νείατος -η -ον	lowest, bottommost
νεκρός -οῦ, m.	corpse
νέκυς -υος, m.	corpse
νεμεσάω	to be indignant or angry
νευρή -ῆφι, f.	bow-string
νεφεληγερέτα -αο, m.	cloud-gatherer (epithet of Zeus)
νηλής -ές	pitiless, ruthless
νήπιος	helpless, unwitting, foolish
νηῦς, νηός, f.	ship
***νίκη -ης**, f.	victory
νοέω	to perceive, notice
νόθος -η -ον	(of children) illegitimate, born out of wedlock
νόος, νοῦ, m.	mind
Νότος -ου, m.	Notus, the south wind
***νῦν**, adv.	now
νύσσω	to prick, pierce
ξύν	= σύν
ὁ, ἡ, τό	he, she, it; who, which; (rarely) the
Ὀδυσσεύς -ῆος, m.	Odysseus, son of Laertes
ὄζος -ου, m.	branch
οἶδα	to know
οἶμα -ατος, n.	spring, swoop
***οἷος, οἵη, οἷον**	such, of such a kind
ὀιστός -οῦ, m.	arrow
ὀκριόεις -εσσα -εν	jagged, with many points or sharp edges
ὄλεθρος -ου, m.	ruin, destruction, death
ὀλιγοδρανέω	to be weak, feeble
***ὀλίγος -η -ον**	little, small
ὄλλυμι	to destroy, kill
ὀλοός -ή -όν	destructive, deadly
ὁμιλέω (+ acc.)	to be in a crowd around something (acc.)

ὅμιλος -ου, m.	an assembled crowd, throng of people
ὁμοκλέω	to call out to, command sharply
ὀνίνημι	to benefit, help
***ὀξύς -εῖα -ύ**	sharp (of weapons), piercing or shrill (of sounds)
ὀπάζω	to send (with); bestow, confer
ὄπιθεν, adv.	behind
ὀπίσσω, adv.	back, backwards
***ὁράω**	to see, behold, look on
ὀρέγομαι	to stretch out
ὄρος -εος, n.	mountain
ὅς, ἥ, ὅ	he, this, that (demonst. pron.); who, that, which (rel. pron.)
***ὅσος or ὅσσος, -η, -ον**	how great, how much, how many, etc.
ὄσσε, n. dual	eyes
ὀστέον -ου, n.	bone
***ὅστις, ἥτις, ὅ τι**	whoever, whichever, whatever
***ὅτε**	when
***οὐ / οὐκ / οὐχ / οὐχί / μή**	not
οὐ . . . οὐδέ	neither . . . nor
οὐδέποτε	never
***οὖν**	so, then
οὐρανός -οῦ, m.	the sky, the heavens
οὖρος -εος, n.	mountain
οὐτάω	to wound (esp. in hand-to-hand combat, as opp. to wounding with a missile)
***οὗτος, αὕτη, τοῦτο**	this
ὀφέλλω	to augment, increase
ὀφθαλμός -οῦ, m.	eye
ὄφρα	in order to; while, so long as
ὄφρα . . . τόφρα	for as long as . . . for that long . . .
ὀφρύς -ος, f.	the brow, eyebrow
ὀψίγονος -ον	late-born
ὄχος -εος, n.	chariot
Πανθοίδης -ου, m.	son of Pathous, i.e. Euphorbus
πάρ	= παρά
παρά (+ gen.)	from (a person)
παρίστημι	to come up to, stand by or near
πάρος, adv.	formerly
***πᾶς, πᾶσα, πᾶν**	every, all
πάταγος -ου, m.	clatter, crash, as of trees falling
πατρίς -ίδος, f.	native land, native country
Πάτροκλος -ῆος, m.	Patroclus, son of Menoetius
***πατήρ, πατέρος**, m.	father
πεδίον -ου, n.	plain, the battlefield between the Greek camp and the city of Troy
πείθω	to persuade
πεινάω	to be hungry, hunger after (+ gen.)
πελεμίζω	to shake, cause to shake
πέλω	to be
***πέμπω**	to send
πέρ	very, at least, even, just
πέρθω	to sack, lay waste, plunder
περί (+ acc.)	around
περί (+ dat.)	around
περιέννυμι	to cloathe
περικαλύπτω	to grasp
Πέριμος -ου, m.	Perimus, a Trojan
πέτομαι	to fly
πέτρη -ης, f.	rock
πέτρος -ου, m.	rock
πήγνυμι	to fix, plant firmly
Πηλείδης -ου, m.	son of Peleus, i.e. Achilles
Πηλεύς -ῆος, m.	Peleus, father of Achilles
πήληξ -ηκος, f.	helmet
πῖδαξ -ακος, f.	spring, fountain
πίνω	to drink
πίπτω, aor. **ἔπεσον**	to fall
πίων, πίειρα, πῖον	fat, fertile
πλείων	more
πλήσσω, inf. **πεπληγέμεν**	to strike, smite
ποδώκης -ες	swift-footed, epithet of Achilles
πολεμίζω	to wage war, fight
πόλεμος -ου, m.	war
***πόλις, -ιος or -ηος**, f.	city
πολλὸν, adv.	by far
***πολύς, πολλή, πολύ**	many
πολυφάρμακος -ον	knowing many drugs or charms
πομπός -οῦ, m.	escort, guide
πόνος -ου, m.	hard work, toil
πόντος -όφιν, m.	the sea
ποταμός -οῦ, m.	river

πότμος -ου, m.	one's fate or destiny (always in a bad sense)
πότνια -ης, f.	revered, honourable (usually used as a title of honour for goddesses or ladies)
πού, adv.	doubtless, perhaps
***πούς, ποδός**, m.	foot
Πρίαμος -ου, m.	Priam, father of Hector and king of Troy
πρίν, adv.	before, previously
πρίν (+ inf.)	before
***πρό** (+ gen.)	before, in front of
προίημι, imperat. **πρόες**	to send on or forward
***πρὸς** (+ acc.)	to, towards
προσαυδάω	to speak to, address
προσβαίνω	to put one's foot against something, to brace oneself with one's foot
πρόσθε (+ gen.)	in front of
πρόσφημι	to speak to, address
προτί	= πρός
πρώτιστος -η -ον	first, foremost
***πρῶτος -η -ον**	first, foremost
πτερόεις -εσσα -εν	winged, feathered
Πυλάρτης -ου, m.	Pylartes, a Trojan
***πύλη -ης**, f.	gate
πύργος -ου, m.	tower
***πως**	in any way, at all, by any means
ῥέθος -εος, n.	limb
ῥεῖα, adv.	easily, lightly
ῥηιδίως, adv.	easily
ῥοή -ῆς, f.	stream
ῥύομαι	to protect, cover
Σαγγάριος -ου, m.	Sangarius, a river that flows through Phrygia
Σαρπηδών -όνος, m.	Sarpedon
Σκαιαί -ών, f. plur.	(usually with πύλαι) the Scaean Gate, the only gate of the city of Troy that Homer mentions by name
σκαιῇ	with or in one's left hand
σμερδαλέος -α -ον	terrible, fearful
σταθμός -οῦ, m.	pen, fold (for animals)
στενάχω	to groan
στῆθος -εος, n.	breast
στήλη -ης, f.	gravestone, grave monument
στιβαρός -ά -όν	strong, stout, sturdy
στίξ, στιχός, f.	row, rank, file of soldiers
στρεφεδινέω	to spin, whirl round
στροφάλιγξ -λιγγος, f.	whirl, eddy (of dust)
στυγερῶς, adv.	to one's sorrow, miserably
στυφελίζω	to strike hard
σός -ή -όν	your
***σύ**	you
***σύν** (+ dat.)	with
συνάγω	to bring together, collect
συναιρέω	to tear away
σφεῖς, σφέων	they, them
σχεδόθεν, adv.	near; nearby, at close range
σχεδόν, adv.	nearby, at close range
τάλαντα, n. plur.	pair of scales, esp. the scales of Zeus in which he weighs the fates of men
τανυήκης -ες	with long point or edge, tapering
τανύφλοιος -ον	lit. with long-stretched bark, i.e. tall and thin (of trees)
τανύω	to arrange
ταρχύω	to bury
***τε**	and; also found in generalizing statements, 'epic τε'
***τέ . . . καί**	both . . . and
τείρω	to oppress, distress, exhaust
***τεῖχος -εος**, n.	wall (of a city or town, or of any fortification)
τέθηπα	(perf. with pres. sense) to be astonished, paralyzed
τελαμών -ῶνος, m.	strap or band for bearing or supporting anything
τελευτή -ῆς, f.	end
***τέλος -εος**, n.	end
τέμνω	to cut
τερμιόεις -εσσα -εν	fringed, rimmed
τέταρτον, adv.	for the fourth time
τεῦχος -εος, n.	(mostly in plur., τεύχεα) armour
τῆθος -εος, n.	oyster
τί	why? how?
τίκτω	to give birth to
τίπτε, adv.	why?
τίς, τί	who? what?
τοι	indeed
τοι	= σοι
τοιοῦτος -αύτη -οῦτο	of such a kind

***τότε**, adv.	at that time, then
τόφρα	see ὄφρα . . . τόφρα
τρέπω	to turn
τρὶς, adv.	three times, thrice
τρίτος	third
τρυφάλεια -ης, f.	helmet
Τρῳάς -άδος, f.	Trojan woman
Τρῶες, Τρώων, m. plur.	the Trojans
Τυδείδης -ους, m.	the son of Tydeus, i.e. Diomedes
τύμβος -ου, m.	funeral mound, barrow
τύπτω	to hit, strike
τῷ	therefore, in this way
φαεινός -ή -όν	shining, radiant
φαίδιμος -ον	shining, radiant
***φαίνω**	to show; (mid. and pass.) to come to light, appear
φένω, aor. **ἔπεφνον**	to kill, slay
φέρτατος -η -ον	bravest, best
***φέρω**	to carry, bear
***φεύγω**	to flee, take flight (from)
φηγός -ου, f.	a species of oak tree with edible acorns
φημί	to say, speak, declare
φθάνω	to overtake; to do something first
φιλοπόλεμος -ον	fond of war, warlike
***φίλος -η -ον**	beloved, dear
φοβέω	to put to flight, cause to flee
φόβος -ου, m.	flight from battle
Φοῖβος -ου, m.	Phoebus (epithet of Apollo)
φόνος -ου, m.	murder, slaughter, death
φορέω	to wear, carry
φόως, n.	light, often used as a metaphor for rescue or deliverance
φράζω, aor. **ἐπέφραδον**	to point out, show; devise, plan
φρήν, φρενός, f.	heart, mind
φρονέω	to have in mind, think, consider
Φρύγιη -ης, f.	Phrygia, a region in Asia Minor
φύγαδε, adv.	in flight
φυλάσσω	to preserve, maintain
φυλοπις -ιδος, f.	the din of battle, battle
φωνέω	to speak

φώς, φωτός, m.	man
***υἱός, υἱοῦ or υἷος**, m.	son
ὕλη -ης, f.	forest, woodland
ὑπεκφεύγω (+ acc.)	to escape from
ὑπέρ (+ acc.)	beyond
ὕπνος -ου, m.	sleep; (when capitalized) Sleep, as a god, brother of Death
***ὑπὸ** (+ dat.)	under; by (a person or thing)
ὑπομένω	to remain, wait
ὕπτιος -α -ον	laid on one's back
ὑσμίνη -ης, f.	battle, combat
ὕστατον, adv.	last of all
ὑψηλός -ή -όν	high, lofty
ὑψίπυλος -ον	high-gated, epithet of the city of Troy
χάζομαι	to fall back, retreat
χαλκοκορυστής -οῦ, m.	in bronze armour, bronze-clad
χαλκός -οῦ, m.	bronze
χαμᾶζε, adv.	to the ground
χαμαί, adv.	to the ground, on the ground
χαρίεις -εσσα -εν	graceful, beautiful
χάρμη -ης, f.	aggressiveness, belligerence
***χείρ, χειρός**, f.	hand
χερμάδιον -ου, n.	large stone, boulder
χιτών -ῶνος, m.	tunic
χόλος -ου, m.	anger
χραισμέω	to help, protect
χρή	it is necessary
χρίω	to anoint (with oil)
χρώς, χροός, m.	the surface of the body, the skin
ψυχή -ῆς, f.	life, soul
ὢ πόποι	alas!
ὧδε, adv.	in this way, thus
ὠθέω	to push, thrust
ὦκα, adv.	quickly
ὠκύς, ὠκεῖα, ὠκύ	swift
ὦμος -ου, m.	shoulder
ὡς	just as (introducing a simile)
ὣς, adv.	so, thus
ὠτειλή -ῆς, f.	wound

Text

Iliad, Book 24

οἳ δ᾽ ἐπεὶ οὖν μέγα σῆμα παρὲξ Ἴλοιο ἔλασσαν,
στῆσαν ἄρ᾽ ἡμιόνους τε καὶ ἵππους ὄφρα πίοιεν
ἐν ποταμῷ: δὴ γὰρ καὶ ἐπὶ κνέφας ἤλυθε γαῖαν.
τὸν δ᾽ ἐξ ἀγχιμόλοιο ἰδὼν ἐφράσσατο κῆρυξ
Ἑρμείαν, ποτὶ δὲ Πρίαμον φάτο φώνησέν τε:
φράζεο Δαρδανίδη: φραδέος νόου ἔργα τέτυκται.
ἄνδρ᾽ ὁρόω, τάχα δ᾽ ἄμμε διαρραίσεσθαι ὀΐω.
ἀλλ᾽ ἄγε δὴ φεύγωμεν ἐφ᾽ ἵππων, ἤ μιν ἔπειτα
γούνων ἁψάμενοι λιτανεύσομεν αἴ κ᾽ ἐλεήσῃ.

ὣς φάτο, σὺν δὲ γέροντι νόος χύτο, δείδιε δ᾽ αἰνῶς,
ὀρθαὶ δὲ τρίχες ἔσταν ἐνὶ γναμπτοῖσι μέλεσσι,
στῆ δὲ ταφών: αὐτὸς δ᾽ ἐριούνιος ἐγγύθεν ἐλθὼν
χεῖρα γέροντος ἑλὼν ἐξείρετο καὶ προσέειπε:
"πῇ πάτερ ὧδ᾽ ἵππους τε καὶ ἡμιόνους ἰθύνεις
νύκτα δι᾽ ἀμβροσίην, ὅτε θ᾽ εὕδουσι βροτοὶ ἄλλοι;
οὐδὲ σύ γ᾽ ἔδεισας μένεα πνείοντας Ἀχαιούς,
οἵ τοι δυσμενέες καὶ ἀνάρσιοι ἐγγὺς ἔασι;
τῶν εἴ τίς σε ἴδοιτο θοὴν διὰ νύκτα μέλαιναν
τοσσάδ᾽ ὀνείατ᾽ ἄγοντα, τίς ἂν δή τοι νόος εἴη;
οὔτ᾽ αὐτὸς νέος ἐσσί, γέρων δέ τοι οὗτος ὀπηδεῖ,
ἄνδρ᾽ ἀπαμύνασθαι, ὅτε τις πρότερος χαλεπήνῃ.
ἀλλ᾽ ἐγὼ οὐδέν σε ῥέξω κακά, καὶ δέ κεν ἄλλον
σεῦ ἀπαλεξήσαιμι: φίλῳ δέ σε πατρὶ ἐΐσκω.

τὸν δ᾽ ἠμείβετ᾽ ἔπειτα γέρων Πρίαμος θεοειδής:
"οὕτω πῃ τάδε γ᾽ ἐστὶ φίλον τέκος ὡς ἀγορεύεις.
ἀλλ᾽ ἔτι τις καὶ ἐμεῖο θεῶν ὑπερέσχεθε χεῖρα,
ὅς μοι τοιόνδ᾽ ἧκεν ὁδοιπόρον ἀντιβολῆσαι
αἴσιον, οἷος δὴ σὺ δέμας καὶ εἶδος ἀγητός,
πέπνυσαί τε νόῳ, μακάρων δ᾽ ἔξεσσι τοκήων.

A Level

τὸν δ᾽ αὖτε προσέειπε διάκτορος ἀργεϊφόντης:
"ναὶ δὴ ταῦτά γε πάντα γέρον κατὰ μοῖραν ἔειπες.
ἀλλ᾽ ἄγε μοι τόδε εἰπὲ καὶ ἀτρεκέως κατάλεξον,
ἠέ πῃ ἐκπέμπεις κειμήλια πολλὰ καὶ ἐσθλὰ
ἄνδρας ἐς ἀλλοδαποὺς ἵνα περ τάδε τοι σόα μίμνῃ,
ἦ ἤδη πάντες καταλείπετε Ἴλιον ἱρὴν
δειδιότες: τοῖος γὰρ ἀνὴρ ὤριστος ὄλωλε
σὸς πάϊς: οὐ μὲν γάρ τι μάχης ἐπιδεύετ᾽ Ἀχαιῶν.'

τὸν δ᾽ ἠμείβετ᾽ ἔπειτα γέρων Πρίαμος θεοειδής:
"τίς δὲ σύ ἐσσι φέριστε τέων δ᾽ ἔξεσσι τοκήων;
ὥς μοι καλὰ τὸν οἶτον ἀπότμου παιδὸς ἔνισπες.'

τὸν δ᾽ αὖτε προσέειπε διάκτορος ἀργεϊφόντης:
"πειρᾷ ἐμεῖο γεραιὲ καὶ εἴρεαι Ἕκτορα δῖον.
τὸν μὲν ἐγὼ μάλα πολλὰ μάχῃ ἔνι κυδιανείρῃ
ὀφθαλμοῖσιν ὄπωπα, καὶ εὖτ᾽ ἐπὶ νηυσὶν ἐλάσσας
Ἀργείους κτείνεσκε δαΐζων ὀξέϊ χαλκῷ:
ἡμεῖς δ᾽ ἑσταότες θαυμάζομεν: οὐ γὰρ Ἀχιλλεὺς
εἴα μάρνασθαι κεχολωμένος Ἀτρεΐωνι.
τοῦ γὰρ ἐγὼ θεράπων, μία δ᾽ ἤγαγε νηῦς εὐεργής:
Μυρμιδόνων δ᾽ ἔξειμι, πατὴρ δέ μοί ἐστι Πολύκτωρ.
ἀφνειὸς μὲν ὅ γ᾽ ἐστί, γέρων δὲ δὴ ὡς σύ περ ὧδε,
ἓξ δέ οἱ υἷες ἔασιν, ἐγὼ δέ οἱ ἕβδομός εἰμι:
τῶν μέτα παλλόμενος κλήρῳ λάχον ἐνθάδ᾽ ἕπεσθαι.
νῦν δ᾽ ἦλθον πεδίονδ᾽ ἀπὸ νηῶν: ἠῶθεν γὰρ
θήσονται περὶ ἄστυ μάχην ἑλίκωπες Ἀχαιοί.
ἀσχαλόωσι γὰρ οἵδε καθήμενοι, οὐδὲ δύνανται
ἴσχειν ἐσσυμένους πολέμου βασιλῆες Ἀχαιῶν.'

τὸν δ᾽ ἠμείβετ᾽ ἔπειτα γέρων Πρίαμος θεοειδής:
"εἰ μὲν δὴ θεράπων Πηληϊάδεω Ἀχιλῆος
εἴς, ἄγε δή μοι πᾶσαν ἀληθείην κατάλεξον,
ἢ ἔτι πὰρ νήεσσιν ἐμὸς πάϊς, ἦέ μιν ἤδη
ᾗσι κυσὶν μελεϊστὶ ταμὼν προὔθηκεν Ἀχιλλεύς.'

τὸν δ᾽ αὖτε προσέειπε διάκτορος ἀργεϊφόντης:
"ὦ γέρον οὔ πω τόν γε κύνες φάγον οὐδ᾽ οἰωνοί,
ἀλλ᾽ ἔτι κεῖνος κεῖται Ἀχιλλῆος παρὰ νηῒ
αὔτως ἐν κλισίῃσι: δυωδεκάτη δέ οἱ ἠὼς
κειμένῳ, οὐδέ τί οἱ χρὼς σήπεται, οὐδέ μιν εὐλαὶ
ἔσθουσ᾽, αἵ ῥά τε φῶτας ἀρηϊφάτους κατέδουσιν.
ἦ μέν μιν περὶ σῆμα ἑοῦ ἑτάροιο φίλοιο
ἕλκει ἀκηδέστως ἠὼς ὅτε δῖα φανήῃ,
οὐδέ μιν αἰσχύνει: θηοῖό κεν αὐτὸς ἐπελθὼν
οἷον ἐερσήεις κεῖται, περὶ δ᾽ αἷμα νένιπται,
οὐδέ ποθι μιαρός: σὺν δ᾽ ἕλκεα πάντα μέμυκεν

A Level

ὅσσ᾽ ἐτύπη: πολέες γὰρ ἐν αὐτῷ χαλκὸν ἔλασσαν.
ὥς τοι κήδονται μάκαρες θεοὶ υἷος ἑῆος
καὶ νέκυός περ ἐόντος, ἐπεί σφι φίλος περὶ κῆρι.᾽

ὣς φάτο, γήθησεν δ᾽ ὁ γέρων, καὶ ἀμείβετο μύθῳ:
"ὦ τέκος, ἦ ῥ᾽ ἀγαθὸν καὶ ἐναίσιμα δῶρα διδοῦναι
ἀθανάτοις, ἐπεὶ οὔ ποτ᾽ ἐμὸς πάϊς, εἴ ποτ᾽ ἔην γε,
λήθετ᾽ ἐνὶ μεγάροισι θεῶν οἳ Ὄλυμπον ἔχουσι:
τώ οἱ ἀπεμνήσαντο καὶ ἐν θανάτοιό περ αἴσῃ.
ἀλλ᾽ ἄγε δὴ τόδε δέξαι ἐμεῦ πάρα καλὸν ἄλεισον,
αὐτόν τε ῥῦσαι, πέμψον δέ με σύν γε θεοῖσιν,
ὄφρά κεν ἐς κλισίην Πηληϊάδεω ἀφίκωμαι.
τὸν δ᾽ αὖτε προσέειπε διάκτορος ἀργεϊφόντης:
"πειρᾷ ἐμεῖο γεραιὲ νεωτέρου, οὐδέ με πείσεις,
ὅς με κέλῃ σέο δῶρα παρὲξ Ἀχιλῆα δέχεσθαι.
τὸν μὲν ἐγὼ δείδοικα καὶ αἰδέομαι περὶ κῆρι
συλεύειν, μή μοί τι κακὸν μετόπισθε γένηται.
σοὶ δ᾽ ἂν ἐγὼ πομπὸς καί κε κλυτὸν Ἄργος ἱκοίμην,
ἐνδυκέως ἐν νηῒ θοῇ ἢ πεζὸς ὁμαρτέων:
οὐκ ἄν τίς τοι πομπὸν ὀνοσσάμενος μαχέσαιτο.

ἦ καὶ ἀναΐξας ἐριούνιος ἅρμα καὶ ἵππους
καρπαλίμως μάστιγα καὶ ἡνία λάζετο χερσίν,
ἐν δ᾽ ἔπνευσ᾽ ἵπποισι καὶ ἡμιόνοις μένος ἠΰ.
ἀλλ᾽ ὅτε δὴ πύργους τε νεῶν καὶ τάφρον ἵκοντο,
οἳ δὲ νέον περὶ δόρπα φυλακτῆρες πονέοντο,
τοῖσι δ᾽ ἐφ᾽ ὕπνον ἔχευε διάκτορος ἀργεϊφόντης
πᾶσιν, ἄφαρ δ᾽ ᾤϊξε πύλας καὶ ἀπῶσεν ὀχῆας,
ἐς δ᾽ ἄγαγε Πρίαμόν τε καὶ ἀγλαὰ δῶρ᾽ ἐπ᾽ ἀπήνης.
ἀλλ᾽ ὅτε δὴ κλισίην Πηληϊάδεω ἀφίκοντο
ὑψηλήν, τὴν Μυρμιδόνες ποίησαν ἄνακτι
δοῦρ᾽ ἐλάτης κέρσαντες: ἀτὰρ καθύπερθεν ἔρεψαν
λαχνήεντ᾽ ὄροφον λειμωνόθεν ἀμήσαντες:
ἀμφὶ δέ οἱ μεγάλην αὐλὴν ποίησαν ἄνακτι
σταυροῖσιν πυκινοῖσι: θύρην δ᾽ ἔχε μοῦνος ἐπιβλὴς
εἰλάτινος, τὸν τρεῖς μὲν ἐπιρρήσσεσκον Ἀχαιοί,
τρεῖς δ᾽ ἀναοίγεσκον μεγάλην κληῖδα θυράων
τῶν ἄλλων: Ἀχιλεὺς δ᾽ ἄρ᾽ ἐπιρρήσσεσκε καὶ οἶος:
δή ῥα τόθ᾽ Ἑρμείας ἐριούνιος ᾧξε γέροντι,
ἐς δ᾽ ἄγαγε κλυτὰ δῶρα ποδώκεϊ Πηλεΐωνι,
ἐξ ἵππων δ᾽ ἀπέβαινεν ἐπὶ χθόνα φώνησέν τε:
"ὦ γέρον ἤτοι ἐγὼ θεὸς ἄμβροτος εἰλήλουθα
Ἑρμείας: σοὶ γάρ με πατὴρ ἅμα πομπὸν ὄπασσεν.
ἀλλ᾽ ἤτοι μὲν ἐγὼ πάλιν εἴσομαι, οὐδ᾽ Ἀχιλῆος
ὀφθαλμοὺς εἴσειμι: νεμεσσητὸν δέ κεν εἴη
ἀθάνατον θεὸν ὧδε βροτοὺς ἀγαπαζέμεν ἄντην:

A Level

τύνη δ᾽ εἰσελθὼν λαβὲ γούνατα Πηλεΐωνος,
καί μιν ὑπὲρ πατρὸς καὶ μητέρος ἠϋκόμοιο
λίσσεο καὶ τέκεος, ἵνα οἱ σὺν θυμὸν ὀρίνῃς.᾽

ὣς ἄρα φωνήσας ἀπέβη πρὸς μακρὸν Ὄλυμπον
Ἑρμείας: Πρίαμος δ᾽ ἐξ ἵππων ἆλτο χαμᾶζε,
Ἰδαῖον δὲ κατ᾽ αὖθι λίπεν: ὃ δὲ μίμνεν ἐρύκων
ἵππους ἡμιόνους τε: γέρων δ᾽ ἰθὺς κίεν οἴκου,
τῇ ῥ᾽ Ἀχιλεὺς ἵζεσκε Διῒ φίλος: ἐν δέ μιν αὐτὸν
εὗρ᾽, ἕταροι δ᾽ ἀπάνευθε καθήατο: τὼ δὲ δύ᾽ οἴω
ἥρως Αὐτομέδων τε καὶ Ἄλκιμος ὄζος Ἄρηος
ποίπνυον παρεόντε: νέον δ᾽ ἀπέληγεν ἐδωδῆς
ἔσθων καὶ πίνων: ἔτι καὶ παρέκειτο τράπεζα.
τοὺς δ᾽ ἔλαθ᾽ εἰσελθὼν Πρίαμος μέγας, ἄγχι δ᾽ ἄρα στὰς
χερσὶν Ἀχιλλῆος λάβε γούνατα καὶ κύσε χεῖρας
δεινὰς ἀνδροφόνους, αἵ οἱ πολέας κτάνον υἷας.
ὡς δ᾽ ὅτ᾽ ἂν ἄνδρ᾽ ἄτη πυκινὴ λάβῃ, ὅς τ᾽ ἐνὶ πάτρῃ
φῶτα κατακτείνας ἄλλων ἐξίκετο δῆμον
ἀνδρὸς ἐς ἀφνειοῦ, θάμβος δ᾽ ἔχει εἰσορόωντας,
ὣς Ἀχιλεὺς θάμβησεν ἰδὼν Πρίαμον θεοειδέα:
θάμβησαν δὲ καὶ ἄλλοι, ἐς ἀλλήλους δὲ ἴδοντο.
τὸν καὶ λισσόμενος Πρίαμος πρὸς μῦθον ἔειπε:
"μνῆσαι πατρὸς σοῖο θεοῖς ἐπιείκελ᾽ Ἀχιλλεῦ,
τηλίκου ὥς περ ἐγών, ὀλοῷ ἐπὶ γήραος οὐδῷ:
καὶ μέν που κεῖνον περιναιέται ἀμφὶς ἐόντες
τείρουσ᾽, οὐδέ τίς ἐστιν ἀρὴν καὶ λοιγὸν ἀμῦναι.
ἀλλ᾽ ἤτοι κεῖνός γε σέθεν ζώοντος ἀκούων
χαίρει τ᾽ ἐν θυμῷ, ἐπί τ᾽ ἔλπεται ἤματα πάντα
ὄψεσθαι φίλον υἱὸν ἀπὸ Τροίηθεν ἰόντα:
αὐτὰρ ἐγὼ πανάποτμος, ἐπεὶ τέκον υἷας ἀρίστους
Τροίῃ ἐν εὐρείῃ, τῶν δ᾽ οὔ τινά φημι λελεῖφθαι.
πεντήκοντά μοι ἦσαν ὅτ᾽ ἤλυθον υἷες Ἀχαιῶν:
ἐννεακαίδεκα μέν μοι ἰῆς ἐκ νηδύος ἦσαν,
τοὺς δ᾽ ἄλλους μοι ἔτικτον ἐνὶ μεγάροισι γυναῖκες.
τῶν μὲν πολλῶν θοῦρος Ἄρης ὑπὸ γούνατ᾽ ἔλυσεν:
ὃς δέ μοι οἶος ἔην, εἴρυτο δὲ ἄστυ καὶ αὐτούς,
τὸν σὺ πρῴην κτεῖνας ἀμυνόμενον περὶ πάτρης
Ἕκτορα: τοῦ νῦν εἵνεχ᾽ ἱκάνω νῆας Ἀχαιῶν
λυσόμενος παρὰ σεῖο, φέρω δ᾽ ἀπερείσι᾽ ἄποινα.
ἀλλ᾽ αἰδεῖο θεοὺς Ἀχιλεῦ, αὐτόν τ᾽ ἐλέησον
μνησάμενος σοῦ πατρός: ἐγὼ δ᾽ ἐλεεινότερός περ,
ἔτλην δ᾽ οἷ᾽ οὔ πώ τις ἐπιχθόνιος βροτὸς ἄλλος,
ἀνδρὸς παιδοφόνοιο ποτὶ στόμα χεῖρ᾽ ὀρέγεσθαι.᾽

ὣς φάτο, τῷ δ᾽ ἄρα πατρὸς ὑφ᾽ ἵμερον ὦρσε γόοιο:
ἁψάμενος δ᾽ ἄρα χειρὸς ἀπώσατο ἦκα γέροντα.

τὼ δὲ μνησαμένω ὃ μὲν Ἕκτορος ἀνδροφόνοιο
κλαῖ᾽ ἁδινὰ προπάροιθε ποδῶν Ἀχιλῆος ἐλυσθείς,
αὐτὰρ Ἀχιλλεὺς κλαῖεν ἑὸν πατέρ᾽, ἄλλοτε δ᾽ αὖτε
Πάτροκλον: τῶν δὲ στοναχὴ κατὰ δώματ᾽ ὀρώρει.
αὐτὰρ ἐπεί ῥα γόοιο τετάρπετο δῖος Ἀχιλλεύς,
καί οἱ ἀπὸ πραπίδων ἦλθ᾽ ἵμερος ἠδ᾽ ἀπὸ γυίων,
αὐτίκ᾽ ἀπὸ θρόνου ὦρτο, γέροντα δὲ χειρὸς ἀνίστη
οἰκτίρων πολιόν τε κάρη πολιόν τε γένειον,
καί μιν φωνήσας ἔπεα πτερόεντα προσηύδα:
"ἆ δείλ᾽, ἦ δὴ πολλὰ κάκ᾽ ἄνσχεο σὸν κατὰ θυμόν.
πῶς ἔτλης ἐπὶ νῆας Ἀχαιῶν ἐλθέμεν οἶος
ἀνδρὸς ἐς ὀφθαλμοὺς ὅς τοι πολέας τε καὶ ἐσθλοὺς
υἱέας ἐξενάριξα; σιδήρειόν νύ τοι ἦτορ.
ἀλλ᾽ ἄγε δὴ κατ᾽ ἄρ᾽ ἕζευ ἐπὶ θρόνου, ἄλγεα δ᾽ ἔμπης
ἐν θυμῷ κατακεῖσθαι ἐάσομεν ἀχνύμενοί περ:
οὐ γάρ τις πρῆξις πέλεται κρυεροῖο γόοιο:
ὡς γὰρ ἐπεκλώσαντο θεοὶ δειλοῖσι βροτοῖσι
ζώειν ἀχνυμένοις: αὐτοὶ δέ τ᾽ ἀκηδέες εἰσί.
δοιοὶ γάρ τε πίθοι κατακείαται ἐν Διὸς οὔδει
δώρων οἷα δίδωσι κακῶν, ἕτερος δὲ ἑάων:
ᾧ μέν κ᾽ ἀμμίξας δώῃ Ζεὺς τερπικέραυνος,
ἄλλοτε μέν τε κακῷ ὅ γε κύρεται, ἄλλοτε δ᾽ ἐσθλῷ:
ᾧ δέ κε τῶν λυγρῶν δώῃ, λωβητὸν ἔθηκε,
καί ἑ κακὴ βούβρωστις ἐπὶ χθόνα δῖαν ἐλαύνει,
φοιτᾷ δ᾽ οὔτε θεοῖσι τετιμένος οὔτε βροτοῖσιν.
ὣς μὲν καὶ Πηλῆϊ θεοὶ δόσαν ἀγλαὰ δῶρα
ἐκ γενετῆς: πάντας γὰρ ἐπ᾽ ἀνθρώπους ἐκέκαστο
ὄλβῳ τε πλούτῳ τε, ἄνασσε δὲ Μυρμιδόνεσσι,
καί οἱ θνητῷ ἐόντι θεὰν ποίησαν ἄκοιτιν.
ἀλλ᾽ ἐπὶ καὶ τῷ θῆκε θεὸς κακόν, ὅττί οἱ οὔ τι
παίδων ἐν μεγάροισι γονὴ γένετο κρειόντων,
ἀλλ᾽ ἕνα παῖδα τέκεν παναώριον: οὐδέ νυ τόν γε
γηράσκοντα κομίζω, ἐπεὶ μάλα τηλόθι πάτρης
ἧμαι ἐνὶ Τροίῃ, σέ τε κήδων ἠδὲ σὰ τέκνα.
καὶ σὲ γέρον τὸ πρὶν μὲν ἀκούομεν ὄλβιον εἶναι:
ὅσσον Λέσβος ἄνω Μάκαρος ἕδος ἐντὸς ἐέργει
καὶ Φρυγίη καθύπερθε καὶ Ἑλλήσποντος ἀπείρων,
τῶν σε γέρον πλούτῳ τε καὶ υἱάσι φασὶ κεκάσθαι.
αὐτὰρ ἐπεί τοι πῆμα τόδ᾽ ἤγαγον Οὐρανίωνες
αἰεί τοι περὶ ἄστυ μάχαι τ᾽ ἀνδροκτασίαι τε.
ἄνσχεο, μὴ δ᾽ ἀλίαστον ὀδύρεο σὸν κατὰ θυμόν:
οὐ γάρ τι πρήξεις ἀκαχήμενος υἷος ἑῆος,
οὐδέ μιν ἀνστήσεις, πρὶν καὶ κακὸν ἄλλο πάθῃσθα.'

τὸν δ᾽ ἠμείβετ᾽ ἔπειτα γέρων Πρίαμος θεοειδής:
'μή πω μ᾽ ἐς θρόνον ἵζε διοτρεφὲς ὄφρά κεν Ἕκτωρ
κεῖται ἐνὶ κλισίῃσιν ἀκηδής, ἀλλὰ τάχιστα

λῦσον ἵν᾽ ὀφθαλμοῖσιν ἴδω: σὺ δὲ δέξαι ἄποινα
πολλά, τά τοι φέρομεν: σὺ δὲ τῶνδ᾽ ἀπόναιο, καὶ ἔλθοις
σὴν ἐς πατρίδα γαῖαν, ἐπεί με πρῶτον ἔασας
αὐτόν τε ζώειν καὶ ὁρᾶν φάος ἠελίοιο.
τὸν δ᾽ ἄρ᾽ ὑπόδρα ἰδὼν προσέφη πόδας ὠκὺς Ἀχιλλεύς:
'μηκέτι νῦν μ᾽ ἐρέθιζε γέρον: νοέω δὲ καὶ αὐτὸς
Ἕκτορά τοι λῦσαι, Διόθεν δέ μοι ἄγγελος ἦλθε
μήτηρ, ἥ μ᾽ ἔτεκεν, θυγάτηρ ἁλίοιο γέροντος.
καὶ δέ σε γιγνώσκω Πρίαμε φρεσίν, οὐδέ με λήθεις,
ὅττι θεῶν τίς σ᾽ ἦγε θοὰς ἐπὶ νῆας Ἀχαιῶν.
οὐ γάρ κε τλαίη βροτὸς ἐλθέμεν, οὐδὲ μάλ᾽ ἡβῶν,
ἐς στρατόν: οὐδὲ γὰρ ἂν φυλάκους λάθοι, οὐδέ κ᾽ ὀχῆα
ῥεῖα μετοχλίσσειε θυράων ἡμετεράων.
τὼ νῦν μή μοι μᾶλλον ἐν ἄλγεσι θυμὸν ὀρίνῃς,
μή σε γέρον οὐδ᾽ αὐτὸν ἐνὶ κλισίῃσιν ἐάσω
καὶ ἱκέτην περ ἐόντα, Διὸς δ᾽ ἀλίτωμαι ἐφετμάς.

ὣς ἔφατ᾽, ἔδεισεν δ᾽ ὃ γέρων καὶ ἐπείθετο μύθῳ.
Πηλεΐδης δ᾽ οἴκοιο λέων ὣς ἆλτο θύραζε
οὐκ οἶος, ἅμα τῷ γε δύω θεράποντες ἕποντο
ἥρως Αὐτομέδων ἠδ᾽ Ἄλκιμος, οὕς ῥα μάλιστα
τῖ᾽ Ἀχιλεὺς ἑτάρων μετὰ Πάτροκλόν γε θανόντα,
οἳ τόθ᾽ ὑπὸ ζυγόφιν λύον ἵππους ἡμιόνους τε,
ἐς δ᾽ ἄγαγον κήρυκα καλήτορα τοῖο γέροντος,
κὰδ δ᾽ ἐπὶ δίφρου εἷσαν: ἐϋξέστου δ᾽ ἀπ᾽ ἀπήνης
ᾕρεον Ἑκτορέης κεφαλῆς ἀπερείσι᾽ ἄποινα.
κὰδ δ᾽ ἔλιπον δύο φάρε᾽ ἐΰννητόν τε χιτῶνα,
ὄφρα νέκυν πυκάσας δοίη οἶκον δὲ φέρεσθαι.
δμῳὰς δ᾽ ἐκκαλέσας λοῦσαι κέλετ᾽ ἀμφί τ᾽ ἀλεῖψαι
νόσφιν ἀειράσας, ὡς μὴ Πρίαμος ἴδοι υἱόν,
μὴ ὃ μὲν ἀχνυμένῃ κραδίῃ χόλον οὐκ ἐρύσαιτο
παῖδα ἰδών, Ἀχιλῆϊ δ᾽ ὀρινθείη φίλον ἦτορ,
καί ἑ κατακτείνειε, Διὸς δ᾽ ἀλίτηται ἐφετμάς.
τὸν δ᾽ ἐπεὶ οὖν δμῳαὶ λοῦσαν καὶ χρῖσαν ἐλαίῳ,
ἀμφὶ δέ μιν φᾶρος καλὸν βάλον ἠδὲ χιτῶνα,
αὐτὸς τόν γ᾽ Ἀχιλεὺς λεχέων ἐπέθηκεν ἀείρας,
σὺν δ᾽ ἕταροι ἤειραν ἐϋξέστην ἐπ᾽ ἀπήνην.
ᾤμωξέν τ᾽ ἄρ᾽ ἔπειτα, φίλον δ᾽ ὀνόμηνεν ἑταῖρον:
μή μοι Πάτροκλε σκυδμαινέμεν, αἴ κε πύθηαι
εἰν Ἄϊδός περ ἐὼν ὅτι Ἕκτορα δῖον ἔλυσα
πατρὶ φίλῳ, ἐπεὶ οὔ μοι ἀεικέα δῶκεν ἄποινα.
σοὶ δ᾽ αὖ ἐγὼ καὶ τῶνδ᾽ ἀποδάσσομαι ὅσσ᾽ ἐπέοικεν.

Commentary Notes

Iliad, Book 24

349–439

Priam and Idaeus make their way across the battlefield towards the Greek camp and Achilles. They meet someone on the battlefield, who claims to be a Greek on a scouting mission. It is actually the god Hermes, sent by Zeus to make sure Priam gets to Achilles' tent safely.

349
οἳ δ(ε): 'they', i.e. Priam and Idaeus. In Homer, ὁ, ἡ, τό, is almost always used as a third-person pronoun, not the definite article as in Attic Greek.

349
μέγα σῆμα . . . Ἴλοιο: 'the great tomb of Ilus'. Ilus is the founding hero of the city of Troy and Priam's grandfather. The tomb is mentioned several times in the preceding narrative: it appears to be relatively close to the city and thus marks the boundary between safety and unsafety. The fact this is a tomb contributes to the prevailing atmosphere of death in this scene, as well as alluding to a time when there was no war.

349
σῆμα παρὲξ Ἴλοιο = πάρεξ σῆμα Ἴλοιο.

349
παρὲξ: 'past'.

349
ἔλασσαν: third person plural aorist of intransitive ἐλαύνω.

350
στῆσαν ἄρ' ἡμιόνους: 'they stayed the mules', i.e. made them come to a halt. **στῆσαν** is transitive.

A
Level

350
ὄφρα: 'so that'.

351
ποταμῷ: the river Scamander does not run across the battlefield but along its edge, so Priam and Idaeus do not need to cross it to reach their destination. This point, like the tomb of Ilus, nevertheless represents a boundary between safety and danger: it is here that Hermes will leave Priam on his way back from the Greek camp.

351
δὴ γὰρ καὶ: 'then indeed also'.

351
ἐπὶ . . . ἤλυθε: in Homeric Greek, it is possible for prepositions to become detached from the main verb, a phenomenon known as 'tmesis' ('cutting'). In these cases, students should translate as if the preposition and the verb formed a single word, i.e. ἐπήλυθε.

351
ἐπὶ κνέφας ἤλυθε γαῖαν: 'darkness had come across the earth'. Priam makes the journey to the Greek camp under the cover of darkness to avoid being detected by the Greeks. His adventure echoes an earlier episode in the poem in which a Trojan ventures out in the middle of the night to spy on the Greeks but ends up being apprehended and executed, a memory that can only add to the sense of foreboding in this scene.

352
ἐξ ἀγχιμόλοιο: 'from nearby'.

352
ἐφράσσατο: 'became aware of'; φράζω usually means 'to recognize', but it is clear that neither man recognizes the figure that emerges out of the darkness.

353–354
Ἑρμείαν, ποτὶ . . . τέτυκται: the high frequency of π- and φ- words in these two lines may be a deliberate attempt to evoke Priam and Idaeus' increasing anxiety as the unknown man approaches.

353
Ἑρμείαν: in apposition to **τὸν δ(έ)** in the previous line. Note its position in the emphatic runover position.

353
ποτὶ . . . φάτο = προσέφη, tmesis; ποτὶ is an alternative form of πρός.

354–355
Idaeus' anxiety is evident from the lack of connective particles in these two lines, a literary technique known an 'asyndeton'.

A
Level

354
φράζεο = φράζου; words can be left uncontracted in Homeric Greek for metrical reasons.

354
Δαρδανίδη: 'Dardanian'; Priam is the great, great, great grandson of Dardanus.

354
φραδέος: 'wary'; this word is a hapax, appearing elsewhere only in compounds; the poet may have been influenced by φράζεο ('beware') earlier in the line, the two words forming a kind of wordplay.

354
ἔργα τέτυκται: the phrase ἔργον (ἔστι) with the genitive means 'it is a matter for', and hence 'there is a need for'.

355
ὁρόω: an example of diectasis, the 'artificial lengthening' of a word via the insertion of a short vowel in the middle for metrical reasons.

355
τάχα: 'soon'.

355
ἄμμε = ἡμᾶς.

355
διαρραίσεσθαι can be construed in one of two ways, active ('to tear into pieces') or passive ('to be torn into pieces'). If construed as an active infinitive, **ἄνδρ(α)** ('he') would serve as the subject and **ἄμμε** ('us') as the object, i.e. 'I think that he will tear us into pieces.' If construed as a passive infinitive **ἄμμε** ('we') would serve as the subject, i.e. 'I think that we will be torn into pieces.' Most scholars favour the latter interpretation.

356
ἐφ' ἵππων: 'with our horses'. Priam and Idaeus are making their way across the plain with a chariot (drawn by horses) and a four-wheeled wagon laden with gifts for Achilles (drawn by mules). A quick getaway would necessitate the abandonment of the slow-moving, heavy wagon.

356
ἤ . . . ἔπειτα: 'or else', with ἔπειτα meaning 'alternatively', 'if not'.

356
μιν = αὐτόν.

357
γούνων = γονάτων.

A Level

357
γούνων ἁψάμενοι: 'clasping his knees', a traditional gesture in the act of supplication.

357
αἴ κ(ε): 'as to whether in fact'.

358
σὺν . . . χύτο: 'became confused', tmesis.

359
ὀρθαὶ δὲ τρίχες ἔσταν: 'his hairs stood on end'. This is the only time in the *Iliad* that a character gets goosebumps.

359
ἔσταν = ἔστησαν, 'stood [on end]'. This use of the verb is intransitive.

359
γναμπτοῖσι: 'bent'; Priam's 'upright' (**ὀρθαὶ**) hairs contrast with his limbs that have been bent by age.

360
ταφών: 'paralyzed (by fear)'; the phrase can refer to both mental and physical incapacitation. The verb may call to mind the word τάφος ('funeral rites'), although the two words are etymologically unrelated.

360
ἐριούνιος: the meaning of this epithet of Hermes is unclear. The most recent scholarship connects it to a dialect term for 'running', hence 'swift runner', or 'one who runs on high', i.e. 'one who can fly'. Alternatively, the Cambridge Greek Lexicon (2021) links it to the verb ὀνίνημι ('to profit, benefit, help'), in which case it would mean something like 'good helper'.

360
ἐγγύθεν: 'nearby'.

361
χεῖρα γέροντος ἑλὼν: 'taking the old man's hand'. Gestures between two people play an important role in Book 24, culminating in Priam's extraordinary gesture of kissing Achilles' hands, 'the hands of the man who killed my son'.

361
ἐξείρετο καὶ προσέειπε: 'he spoke and addressed him'; these are both verbs of speaking.

362–439
This interchange between Priam and Hermes is made up of nine short speeches, making it the most complex interchange in the whole poem. Part of the reason for

this is the peaceful context – conversations between enemy warriors on the battlefield are naturally short – but there is something to be said for Priam's reticence and caution in what he considers an extremely dangerous situation.

362
πῇ: literally, 'on which path?', i.e. 'where?'

362
πάτερ: a deferential address used often in Homer when a younger man is addressing an older one. Priam and the stranger (Hermes) are not literally father and son, of course, though it serves to introduce the father–son relationship, which will be so important when Priam meets Achilles later in the book.

362
ὧδ(ε): 'thus', probably in reference to the unusual circumstances, it being the middle of the night.

363
ἀμβροσίην: 'ambrosial', usually understood in the sense that night is a 'divine gift' of some kind.

363
θ': generalizing statements can feature the particle τε (known as 'epic τε'); there is no discernible impact on the meaning.

364
μένεα πνείοντας: 'breathing out aggression'.

365
τοι = σοι.

365
ἔασι = εἰσίν.

366
θοὴν . . . νύκτα: the night is 'swift' (scholars have suggested) in the sense that the night descends quickly.

367
τοσσάδ' ὀνείατ' ἄγοντα: 'carrying so much treasure'. Priam has a wagonload of gifts that he plans to give to Achilles in order to ransom the body of his son, Hector.

367
ὀνείατ(α): 'treasure', 'valuables'; the word comes from the verb ὀνίνημι ('to profit, benefit, help').

A Level

367
τίς ἂν δή τοι νόος εἴη: literally, 'what would your **νόος** be in that case?', where **νόος** either means 'mental state' (i.e. 'how would you *feel* in that case?') or 'intention' (i.e. 'what would you *do* in that case?').

368
οὔτ᾽ . . . δέ: 'not on the one hand . . . but on the other hand'.

368
ἐσσί = εἶ.

368
γέρων δέ τοι οὗτος ὀπηδεῖ: 'this man who accompanies you is old'; **γέρων** is predicative.

369
ἀπαμύνασθαι: the infinitive strictly depends on the first clause in the previous line (**οὔτ᾽ . . . νέος ἐσσί**, 'you are not young enough to . . .'), though the sentiment really applies to both clauses. In the middle, this verb means 'to ward off something (accusative) from something else (dative)'.

369
ὅτε . . . χαλεπήνῃ: an iterative temporal clause, almost conditional in sense, i.e. 'if anyone were to attack you'.

369
πρότερος χαλεπήνῃ: 'attack you unawares'; the attack is imagined as taking place 'before' (**πρότερος**) any aggressive action by the two old men.

370
ἀλλ᾽ ἐγὼ: 'I, however'.

370
οὐδέν: adverbial, 'in no way'.

370
σε ῥέξω κακά: 'I shall harm you'; verbs of 'doing' or 'performing' govern two accusatives when the sense is 'to treat someone (accusative) in a certain way (accusative)'.

370
καὶ δέ: 'and also'.

370–371
ἄλλον σεῦ ἀπαλεξήσαιμι: 'I would defend you from anyone else'; the verb ἀπαλέξω governs the accusative and genitive, and means 'to ward something (accusative) off from someone (genitive)'. The verb is in the optative since we must understand the words (e.g.) 'if anyone were to threaten you'.

A Level

371
φίλῳ δέ σε πατρὶ ἐίσκω: 'I liken you to my father.' Hermes' speech begins and ends by presenting Priam as a father figure. The father–son relationship will receive its richest and most tragic expression in the meeting between Priam and Achilles later in the book.

373
οὕτω πῃ τάδε γ' ἐστὶ . . . ὡς ἀγορεύεις: 'these things may be more or less as you say . . .', i.e. 'you might be right . . .'; **πῃ**, 'more or less', 'to some extent'.

373
φίλον τέκος: 'dear child', answers the vocative **πάτερ** on line 362. As there, this is merely an affectionate address – the two men are not literally father and son.

374
ἔτι: 'still, furthermore'.

374
τις . . . θεῶν: 'one of the gods'; **θεῶν** is a partitive genitive.

374
ἐμεῖο: ἐμοῦ, genitive dependent on **ὑπερέσχεθε**, which is third person singular of an aorist form of ὑπερέχω ('to hold above something [accusative] over something else [genitive]').

375
ἀντιβολῆσαι: final infinitive dependent on **ἧκεν**, 'who sent such a traveller to meet with me'.

376
αἴσιον: this word, which is used only here in Homer, is related to αἶσα, 'share, lot, fortune'. In this context, it means something like 'timely' or 'auspicious'. The word is given emphasis by its positioning in the emphatic runover position.

376
σὺ: the verb εἶ must be supplied from the context, i.e. 'you are'.

376
δέμας . . . εἶδος: both are accusatives of respect dependant on **ἀγητός**.

377
νόῳ: 'in your intellectual capacity', instrumental dative dependant on **πέπνυσαί**.

377
μακάρων δ' ἔξεσσι τοκήων: literally, 'you are of blessed parents', i.e. 'your parents are blessed in you.' **ἔξεσσι** is second person singular of ἔξειμι.

A Level

378
ἀργεϊφόντης: 'slayer of Argos'. Argos was a hundred-eyed giant who was killed by Hermes during his mission to deliver the nymph Io to Zeus.

380
ἄγε: 'come!'

380
τόδε: 'this' refers to the question that follows.

380
ἀτρεκέως: literally, 'untwistingly', i.e. 'accurately'.

381
ἠέ . . . ἦ: 'whether . . . or'.

381
πῃ: '(to) somewhere'; Hermes has already asked Priam where he is going with his wagonload of treasure, but Priam ignores the question in his reply. He now asks him a second time.

382
ἵνα: 'so that there', in Homer, **ἵνα** can introduce either a relative clause ('where') or a final clause ('so that'); in this case, it seems that we get a bit of both meanings.

382
περ: 'at least'; the wagonload of treasure that Priam is (apparently) sending out of the country for safe-keeping contrasts with everything that he is unable to keep safe; this includes the **κειμήλια πολλὰ καὶ ἐσθλὰ** that still remains within the city and (more pertinently) the lives of his wife and family and the Trojan people in general.

382
σόα: 'in safety'.

383
καταλείπετε: present tense, 'you are (now) leaving'. Earlier in the poem, Achilles had suggested that the death of Hector would precipitate a mass exodus from the city of Troy.

383
ἱρὴν = ἱεράν.

384
δειδιότες: 'because you are scared'; placed in the emphatic runover position.

384
τοῖος γὰρ ἀνὴρ ὤριστος: **τοῖος** is most likely attributive here, 'since such a man, the best, has been killed'.

A Level

385
σὸς πάϊς: 'your son'; the identity of the man Hermes is talking about is delayed until the following line and placed in the emphatic runover position. In English, we might attempt to replicate the effect as follows: 'since so great a man, the best of men, has been killed – your son!'

385
τι: accusative of respect, 'in any respect'.

385
ἐπιδεύετ(ε): means 'to be inferior in something (genitive) (and/or) to someone (genitive)'; in this case, the word might govern two genitives, i.e. 'he was not inferior in battle to the Achaeans', or we might read **Ἀχαιῶν** as being dependant on **μάχης**, i.e. 'he was not inferior in battle against the Achaeans'.

388
ὥς: most likely exclamatory, i.e. 'how well you describe . . .'

388
καλὰ: adverbial, 'well'.

388
τὸν οἶτον: 'the fate', a rare use of the definite article in Homer. The fate that is being referred to here is that of Hector, described at lines 384–385.

388
οἶτον ἀπότμου: note the juxtaposition of related ideas here, 'the fate of the ill-fated (son)'.

388
ἔνισπες: second person singular aorist of ἐνέπω, 'report, describe'.

390
καὶ: 'when', explanatory, introducing the capacity in which Hermes thinks Priam is 'testing' him. The Homeric dictionary of G. Autenrieth and R. P. Keep explains this use of **καὶ** as 'joining to a general sentence a special illustration of truth previously announced'.

390
εἴρεαι: second person singular present of εἴρομαι, 'ask'.

391
πολλὰ: adverbial, 'often'.

391
μάχῃ ἔνι = ἐν μάχῃ.

A
Level

392
καὶ εὖτ’: ‘and especially when’, introduces a concrete example of when Hermes saw in Hector in battle following the vaguer **μάλα πολλὰ** (‘very often’) in the previous line. Hector’s glorious exploits in battle are described in the central books of the *Iliad*.

392
ἐλάσσας: aorist participle of ἐλαύνω, intransitive, ‘drive (a chariot)’.

393
κτείνεσκε: iterative/frequentative imperfect, referring to repeated action in the past.

394–395
Book 1 of the *Iliad* features a quarrel between Agamemnon and Achilles, which results in Achilles’ decision to withdraw from battle. Hermes, who now ‘reveals’ to Priam that he is actually one of Achilles’ men, describes how he and his fellow Myrmidons ‘stood and watched Hector in amazement’.

394
ἑσταότες: ‘standing there’, perfect participle (intransitive) of ἵστημι.

395
εἴα: third person singular imperfect of ἐάω; the object of the verb, ἡμᾶς (‘us’), must be supplied from the context.

395
Ἀτρείωνι: i.e. Agamemnon.

396
τοῦ: ‘his’, i.e. Achilles’.

396
μία . . . νηῦς: ‘one and the same ship’.

397
Μυρμιδόνων: Achilles’ men were known as Myrmidons, so-called because they were said to have been created by Zeus from a colony of ants (μύρμηκες).

398
ὡς σύ περ ὧδε: ‘as you stand before me’.

399
οἱ = αὐτῷ.

399
ἔασιν = εἰσίν.

A
Level

400
There are several occasions in the *Iliad* where the drawing of lots is used to decide who of a group of individuals should do something dangerous or unpleasant. Earlier in the poem, a group of heroes drew lots to see which of them would take Hector on in a one-on-one duel. Here, it looks like Hermes is the only of Polyctor's seven sons to have been sent to war. In both the *Iliad* and (particularly) the *Odyssey*, the lot tends to fall on the person who would have been the natural choice in any case.

400
μέτα: 'among'.

401
νῦν δ(ε): 'but now', Hermes turns from how he first came to Troy to what he is doing here, right now.

401
ἦλθον: i.e. as a scout.

401
ἠῶθεν: 'at daybreak'.

402
θήσονται . . . μάχην: literally, 'they will place/set battle', i.e. 'they will commence battle'. The use of such a matter-of-fact, practical verb as τίθημι ('to put, place') to describe the waging of war has somewhat sinister implications.

403
καθήμενοι: 'sitting there and doing nothing'.

404
ἐσσυμένους: perfect participle of σεύομαι, 'to be eager for', which governs the genitive.

406–407
εἰ μὲν δὴ . . . εἷς: 'if you are in fact, as you say'.

406
θεράπων: Hermes had described himself using this word at line 396.

407
πᾶσαν ἀληθείην: literally, 'the whole truth', i.e. don't leave out any unpleasant details, e.g. those described by Priam himself in line 409.

408
ἦ . . . ἠέ: 'whether . . . or'.

A
Level

408
πὰρ = παρά.

408
μιν = αὐτόν.

409
Priam has one of the most morbid imaginations in the Iliad. When Hector is killed in Book 22, he immediately has a vision of the entire city of Troy on fire. A little later, he imagines his corpse being eaten by his own dogs. Now he offers a vision of Hector's body being eaten by dogs that is (slightly) more brutal than other descriptions in the poem. Elsewhere, it is imagined that the body will be torn to pieces by animals. Here, Priam imagines Achilles cutting up Hector's body in advance of throwing the pieces to the dogs.

409
ᾗσι: 'his', third person singular pronominal adjective.

409
μελειστὶ: 'limb by limb'.

409
προύθηκεν = προέθηκεν; like Hermes earlier (see note on **402 θήσονται . . . μάχην**), Priam uses a 'matter-of-fact' verb in a gruesome context.

413
αὔτως: 'as it was', i.e. undamaged.

413
ἐν κλισίῃσι: 'among the tents', i.e. between them, on the floor outside.

413
δυωδεκάτη δέ οἱ ἠὼς: 'it is the twelfth morning for him'; scholars have puzzled over the mention of 'morning' (**ἠὼς**) in this line when the sun has just gone down.

413
οἱ: the use of the dative of (dis)advantage is grammatically unproblematic, though we might question whether there can be any (dis)advantage for Hector's corpse here.

414
οὐδέ τί: 'and yet in no regard'; **τί** is an accusative of respect of the indefinite pronoun, not the interrogative pronoun. The word is accented because an accent has been thrown back from the following **οἱ**.

414
χρὼς: literally, 'skin', but here stands in for the 'body' as a whole.

A Level

415
ῥά: 'indeed, of course'.

416
ἦ μέν: 'in fact', strongly emphatic.

416
ἑτάροιο = ἑταίρου

417
ἀκηδέστως: 'without pity', i.e. because he is denying the body proper funeral rites.

417
ὅτε δῖα φανήῃ: **ὅτε** + subjunctive carries an iterative meaning, i.e. 'whenever', 'on every occasion that'.

418
αἰσχύνει: '(physically) disfigure'.

418
θηοῖό: 'you may see', second person singular present optative of θηέομαι, 'to observe'.

419
οἷον: 'in which way'.

419
περὶ: adverbial, 'all around'.

419
αἷμα νένιπται: verbs of washing often take an accusative of the substance being washed off, in this case, 'blood'.

420
ποθι: που, 'anywhere'.

420
μιαρός: 'defiled', a word found only here in Homer.

420
σὺν . . . μέμυκεν: tmesis. After Hector is killed by Achilles, several Achaeans run up to him to stab his corpse. These wounds have apparently miraculously 'closed up'.

421
ὅσσ᾽ ἐτύπη: 'all (the wounds) that he received'.

421
πολέες: πολλοί.

A Level

421
ἐν αὐτῷ: 'in his body'.

422
ὥς: 'so'.

422
κήδονται: 'they care', echoes **ἀκηδέστως** ('without care') on line 417; the verb governs the genitive case, who particular use here (i.e. describing someone as the object as someone else's feelings) is known as the objective genitive.

422
υἷος ἑῆος: 'of your good son'.

423
καὶ . . . περ: intensifying rather than concessive, i.e. 'all the more because . . .', not 'even though he is only . . .'

423
ἐόντος = ὄντος.

423
σφι = αὐτοῖς, i.e. the gods.

423
περὶ: adverbial, 'very, extremely'.

423
κῆρι: 'in the heart'.

424
γήθησεν: 'rejoiced'; the verb is given emphasis by its placement at the beginning of the clause.

425
ἦ ῥ(α): 'indeed, surely'.

425
ἀγαθὸν: the verb ἐστιν must be supplied from the context, as is often the case with neuter singular adjectives, 'it is worthwhile'.

425
καὶ: here: 'indeed'.

425
ἐναίσιμα δῶρα: 'appropriate gifts'.

A
Level

426
ἐπεὶ: 'since'.

426
εἴ ποτ᾽ ἔην γε: 'if ever he was', i.e. 'if Hector had ever really existed'; one of the most wistful utterances in the whole poem.

426
ἔην = ἦν.

427
λήθετ᾽ . . . θεῶν: 'forgot the gods'; verbs of remembering and forgetting govern the genitive.

427
ἐνὶ μεγάροισι: 'in our halls'.

428
τῶ: 'therefore'.

428
οἱ: dative of advantage, 'for him'.

428
καὶ . . . περ: has the same intensifying force as **καὶ . . . περ** at line 423, 'even more'.

429
ἐμεῦ πάρα = παρ᾽ ἐμοῦ.

430
αὐτόν: 'me', **αὐτόν** is very occasionally used in place of ἐμέ.

430
ῥῦσαι: imperative of ἔρυμαι, 'protect'.

430
πέμψον: 'escort'.

430
σύν γε θεοῖσιν: 'with the aid of the gods'.

431
ὄφρά . . . ἀφίκωμαι: ὄφρά can either have a temporal ('until') or a final ('so that') sense here.

434
σέο: 'from you', dependant on **δέχεσθαι**.

A Level

434
παρὲξ Ἀχιλῆα: literally, 'along the side of Achilles', i.e. without his knowledge.

436
συλεύειν: infinitive following **δείδοικα** and **αἰδέομαι** on the previous line; note the placement of the verb in the emphatic runover position.

437
ἂν . . . καί κε: 'possibly even'.

437
πομπὸς: predicative, 'as a guide'.

437
Ἄργος: most likely Pelasgian Argos, home of the Myrmidons, rather than the more famous Peloponnesian Argos. Alternatively, 'Argos' might simply mean 'Greece' in the same way that 'Argives' = 'Greeks'.

438
ὁμαρτέων: literally, 'acting together', i.e. 'attending, accompanying'.

439
τοι: governed equally by the participle (**ὀνοσσάμενος**) and the main verb (**μαχέσαιτο**).

439
ὀνοσσάμενος: aorist participle of ὄνομαι, 'disdain'.

439
μαχέσαιτο: 'commence battle' or 'attack'.

440–467

Hermes removes all the obstacles in Priam's path as he leads him to his meeting with Achilles. He takes his leave before the two men meet.

440
ἦ: third person singular imperfect of ἠμί, 'say'.

440
ἀναΐξας: 'having leapt up onto'; the use of ἀναίσσω is transitive here.

440
ἅρμα καὶ ἵππους: hendiadys, 'horse-drawn chariot'.

441
λάζετο: third person singular imperfect of λάζομαι, 'seize, take'.

A Level

442
ἐν . . . ἔπνευσ᾽: tmesis.

443
πύργους . . . τάφρον: accusatives following verbs of motion express the idea of movement to or towards without the need for a preposition.

443
νεῶν: literally, 'of the ships', i.e. 'of the Greek encampment', which has been set up beside the ships.

443
ἠύ = ἐύ.

444
νέον: 'just now'; the guards had just begun to prepare their evening meal.

445
ἐφ᾽ . . . ἔχευε: tmesis.

446
πᾶσιν: the word is stressed by its placement in the emphatic runover position.

446
ἀπῶσεν: third person singular aorist of ἀπωθέω, 'shove, push away'.

446
ὀχῆας: accusative plural of ὀχεύς, 'bar, bolt'.

447
ἐς . . . ἄγαγε: tmesis.

447
ἐπ᾽ ἀπήνης: 'on the wagon'; Hermes drives the horse-drawn chariot, Priam follows with the mule-drawn wagon, which is laden with gifts for Achilles.

448
κλισίην: the word κλισίη is used both of tents and more solid constructions made of wood. As we shall see in the next few lines, Achilles' 'hut' is actually quite elaborate, featuring wooden walls, a thatched roof, and a fenced enclosure.

449
ὑψηλήν: the word is stressed by its placement in the emphatic runover position.

449
τὴν: 'which'.

450
δοῦρ(α): 'beams, planks'; accusative plural of **δόρυ**, which can denote both wood itself and things made out of wood, e.g. 'spear', 'boat', etc.

450
κέρσαντες: from κείρω, 'cut'; it is unclear whether this refers to the felling of trees or the later preparation of the wood for use in building Achilles' hut, e.g. removing branches, sawing it into planks, etc.

450
ἀτὰρ: 'but'.

450
ἔρεψαν: from ἐρέφω, 'to cover, roof'.

452
ἀμφὶ: adverbial, 'all around'.

452
οἱ . . . ἄνακτι: 'for him, their lord', i.e. Achilles.

452
αὐλὴν: refers specifically to the courtyard wall, rather than the space enclosed by the wall; hence **μεγάλην** refers to the height or thickness of the wall itself, rather than the amount of space that has been enclosed by it.

453
θύρην δ᾽ ἔχε: literally, 'held the door', i.e. kept it locked shut.

454–456
τὸν τρεῖς . . . οἶος: it is common in the *Iliad* for a hero to be distinguished by doing alone what it takes several other men to achieve.

454
τὸν: 'which'.

454
ἐπιρρήσσεσκον: iterative form of the third person plural imperfect of ἐπιρρήσσω, 'to drive home, push shut'.

455
ἀναοίγεσκον: another iterative form, cf. **ἐπιρρήσσεσκον** in the preceding line.

456
τῶν ἄλλων: the word Ἀχαιῶν must be understood from the context; this genitive phrase is dependant on **τρεῖς** in the previous line.

A Level

456
οἶος: 'by himself', i.e. without anyone else's help.

457
ᾦξε: aorist of οἴγω (which later becomes οἴγνυμι), 'to open'.

459
ἵππων: 'chariot'.

461
Ἑρμείας: in the emphatic runover position.

461
πατὴρ: i.e. Zeus.

461
ὄπασσεν: 'appointed'.

462
πάλιν: 'back', i.e. to Olympus.

462
εἴσομαι: 'I will hasten,' an epic form related to ἵημι.

463
ὀφθαλμοὺς εἴσειμι: literally, 'I will enter the eyes [of Achilles],' i.e. 'I will come within Achilles' sight.'

463–464
νεμεσσητὸν δέ . . . ἄντην. There are two ways of reading this line. The first takes **βροτοὺς** as dependant on **νεμεσσητὸν** and **θεὸν** as the object of **ἀγαπαζέμεν** ('it would be a matter of indignation for mortal men to welcome an immortal god in this way'). The second sees **βροτοὺς** as the object of **ἀγαπαζέμεν** and **θεὸν** dependent on **νεμεσσητὸν** (i.e. 'it would be a matter of indignation for an immortal god to show favour to mortal men in this way'). Perhaps in this 'social' context the first reading is the more likely.

463
νεμεσσητὸν: 'it would be a matter of indignation'.

464
ὧδε: 'in this way'.

466–467
πατρὸς . . . μητέρος . . . τέκεος: a mini tricolon. Achilles' sense of yearning for his family, especially for his aged father back in Greece, is more pronounced than in any other hero in the *Iliad*.

A
Level

467
σὺν . . . ὀρίνῃς: tmesis.

468–512

Priam enters Achilles' hut and entreats him to return the body of his son. Both men weep as they remember their relatives.

469
Ἑρμείας: once again in the emphatic runover position.

469
ἆλτο: third person singular aorist of ἅλλομαι, 'leap, jump'.

470
κατ' . . . λίπεν: tmesis.

470
αὖθι: 'on the spot, there'.

472
τῇ: 'where'.

472
ἵζεσκε: iterative, 'he usually sat'.

472
ἐν: adverbial, 'inside, within'.

472
μιν αὐτὸν: 'him in person', 'the man himself'.

473
ἕταροι = ἑταῖροι.

473
ἀπάνευθε: 'apart, at a distance'.

473
καθήατο = ἐκάθηντο.

475
ποίπνυον παρεόντε: an alliterative and slightly comical phrase; ποιπνύω has connotations of panting with effort.

475
νέον: adverbial, 'just now'.

A Level

476
ἔσθων = ἐσθίων.

476
ἔτι καὶ παρέκειτο τράπεζα: an almost intimate domestic image.

477
μέγας: the description of Priam as 'great' contrasts with his actual situation, which is that of a supplicant.

478
κύσε: third person singular aorist of κυνέω, 'kiss'. This is only the second kiss in the whole poem; the first was when Hector bent down to kiss his son, Astyanax, in Book 6.

479
ἀνδροφόνους: 'man-slaughtering'; this epithet is mostly use of Hector, the killer of Patroclus. Its transfer here to Achilles, Hector's killer, links Achilles' loss (Patroclus) with Priam's (Hector).

480–482
The world of a simile is a reversal of the action of the *Iliad*: in the simile, a killer comes to a foreign land to supplicate a rich man, whereas in the action of the *Iliad*, a rich man (Priam) supplicates a killer (Achilles) in his own country.

480
πυκινὴ: literally, 'dense, thick', i.e. 'strong, heavy'.

481
δῆμον: 'community'.

482
ἀνδρὸς ἐς ἀφνειοῦ: 'into a rich man's (house)'; the omission of the word for 'house' in this context is common in Homer.

483
ὣς: 'so'.

485
πρὸς . . . ἔειπε: tmesis.

486
μνῆσαι πατρὸς σοῖο: 'remember your father'; verbs of remembering and forgetting govern the genitive case. Throughout the poem, people have appealed to Achilles by asking him to remember his father, especially by people who are of a similar age to the aged Peleus.

A Level

487
τηλίκου ὥς περ ἐγών: 'who is of such an age as I am', i.e. who is just as old as me. **τηλίκου** is genitive because it is in agreement with **πατρὸς** in the previous line.

487
ὀλοῷ ἐπὶ γήραος οὐδῷ: literally, 'at the destructive threshold of old age', i.e. the threshold between old age and death.

488
καὶ μέν που κεῖνον: 'indeed he, too, . . . probably'.

488
που: ('no doubt', 'I am sure') is used of statements that the speaker believes is true but cannot strictly know for certain. In this case, Priam speculates what life must be like for Peleus back in Phthia.

488
περιναιέται: 'inhabitants of the surrounding region', i.e. neighbours.

489
τείρουσ': occupies the emphatic runover position.

489
τίς ἐστιν . . . ἀμῦναι: 'there is someone to ward off . . .'; **ἀμῦναι** is aorist infinitive.

490
σέθεν ζώοντος ἀκούων: 'hearing that you are (still) alive'; ἀκούω with a genitive object and a participle means 'to hear of someone being (or doing) something'.

491
ἐν θυμῷ: perhaps 'in secret'.

491
ἐπί . . . ἔλπεται: tmesis.

491
ἤματα πάντα: 'each day, day by day'; lengths of time are denoted in the accusative case.

492
φίλον: in Homeric Greek, this word most often means 'one's own' rather than 'dear'.

493
ἐγὼ: the verb εἰμι must be understood from the context.

493
πανάποτμος: this word has a double prefix, i.e. 'wholly-un-fortunate'.

A
Level

494
τῶν: 'of whom', relative pronoun referring to **υἷας** in the previous line.

494
οὔ . . . φημι: as in Attic prose, used when it is a positive denial, i.e. 'I say that . . . not.'

495
μοι ἦσαν: literally, 'there were to me' , i.e. 'I had'.

495
ὅτ᾽ ἤλυθον υἷες Ἀχαιῶν: 'when the sons of the Achaeans came'; in the *Iliad* this phrase is occasionally used ruefully to remind the reader/listener that there have been no happy times since the Greeks arrived at Troy.

496
ἰῆς ἐκ νηδύος ἦσαν: literally, 'they were from one womb', i.e. they all had the same mother. ἰῆς must here be understood in the sense 'one and the same'.

498
τῶν . . . πολλῶν: 'the majority of them', dependant on **γούνατ(α)**.

498
Ἄρης: 'war' or 'battle' in general, rather than Ares himself.

498
ὑπὸ . . .᾽ ἔλυσεν: tmesis.

499
ὃς δέ . . . δὲ: 'and he who . . . and'.

499
οἶος: 'only'.

499
ἄστυ καὶ αὐτούς: 'the city and its inhabitants'.

500
πρῴην: 'recently'.

503
αἰδεῖο . . . ἐλέησον: 'respect . . . pity'; earlier in the book, Apollo had named these two qualities as something Achilles lacked.

503
αὐτόν: 'me', as at line 430.

A Level

504
μνησάμενος σοῦ πατρός: 'remembering your father'. Priam ends his speech as he began it (**μνῆσαι πατρὸς σοῖο**), a technique known as ring composition.

504
ἐλεεινότερός περ: 'more pitiful', i.e. more pitiful even than Peleus.

505
ἔτλην: 'I have brought it upon myself . . .'

506
ἀνδρὸς παιδοφόνοιο ποτὶ στόμα χεῖρ' ὀρέγεσθαι: grammatically speaking, the most natural reading of this line is '[I have suffered] to reach out with my hand to the mouth of the man who killed my son'. In other words, Priam is stretching his hand towards Achilles' face in the typical gesture of supplication. In lines 477-78, however, we were told that Priam 'kissed' (**κύσε**) Achilles' 'terrible, man-slaying hands' (**χεῖρας δεινὰς ἀνδροφόνους**), which suggests, contrary to the above, that Priam brought *Achilles'* hands towards *his own* mouth, hence the line would mean (e.g.) '[I have suffered] to stretch the hands of the man who killed my son to my lips.'

506
παιδοφόνοιο: 'child-killing'; a *hapax legomenon.*

507
πατρὸς . . . ἵμερον . . . γόοιο: 'the desire to grieve for his father'; **πατρὸς** is an objective genitive.

507
ὑφ' . . . ὦρσε: tmesis; ὦρσε is third person singular aorist of ὄρνυμι, 'rouse'.

508
χειρὸς: genitive following a verb of touching (**ἁψάμενος**).

508
ἀπώσατο: from ἀπωθέομαι (middle), 'to push away from oneself'.

508
ἦκα: 'gently'.

509
τὼ δὲ μνησαμένω: 'and they both remembered', dual.

509
ὁ μὲν: 'one of them' i.e. Priam, as **αὐτὰρ Ἀχιλλεὺς** on line 511 makes clear.

509
Ἕκτορος: genitive with an understood μνησάμενος, taken from **μνησαμένω** earlier in the line.

A Level

510
ἐλυσθείς: from εἰλύω, 'to roll', but here signifying either 'rolling around on the floor' or 'curling up into a ball on the floor'.

511
ἄλλοτε δ' αὖτε: 'then again'.

512
Πάτροκλον: stressed by its placement in the emphatic runover position.

512
κατὰ δώματ(α): 'throughout the house'; the plural **δώματ(α)** is used simply for metrical convenience. The depth of grief is emphasized by the size of the space that the sound of grieving fills.

512
ὀρώρει: 'arose', intransitive pluperfect of ὄρνυμι.

513–595

Achilles raises Priam to his feet makes a great speech of consolation, explaining why human suffering exists in the world in the famous allegory of the jars of Zeus.

513
αὐτὰρ: 'but'.

513
γόοιο τετάρπετο: literally, 'he made himself satisfied with mourning', i.e. he had his fill of it.

514
ἀπὸ . . . ἦλθ(ε): 'departed'; in Homer, fading emotions are imagined as physically departing from the parts of the body they were imagined to affect.

514
πραπίδων: variously glossed as 'diaphragm', 'lungs', or 'chest', although the mention of **γυίων** later in the line might suggest a sense of 'core' and 'extremities', i.e. the whole body.

514
ἠδ(έ): 'and'.

514
γυίων: literally, 'limbs', i.e. 'body'.

515
αὐτίκ(α): Achilles' emotional state might be suggested by the quickness with which he gets up out of his seat.

A Level

515
θρόνου: the θρόνος is the most prestigious chair in Homer, usually reserved for the master of the house or his guests. Later on, we will encounter the δίφρος, which was a 'stool' usually used only by servants and enslaved people.

515
ὦρτο: aorist from ὄρνυμαι, here intransitive, literally 'he raised himself', i.e. 'he got up'.

515
χειρὸς: a verb of 'taking' must be understood here, i.e. '(taking him) by the hand'. Verbs of 'taking' (as with verbs of 'touching' and 'holding') govern the genitive case.

515
ἀνίστη: imperfect and transitive, 'he raised [Priam]'.

516
κάρη: literally, 'head' but the use of the adjective πολιός ('grey') suggests this refers to Priam's hair rather than his head.

517
μιν . . . ἔπεα . . . προσηύδα: the verb προσαυδάω governs two accusative objects, one of the words being said (**ἔπεα**), the other of the person being addressed (**μιν**).

517
μιν = αὐτόν.

518
ἆ δείλ᾽: an expression of genuine pity, e.g. 'Oh, you poor man!'

518
ἦ δὴ: 'yes, indeed'.

518
ἄνσχεο: second person singular aorist of ἀνέχομαι, 'suffer, endure'.

519
πῶς ἔτλης: 'have did you have the courage . . .?'

519
ἐλθέμεν: infinitive.

519
οἶος: 'alone'. At lines 563–567, however, Achilles tells Priam that he knows he must have help getting into the camp, and that he could not have possibly made it alone.

A Level

520
τοι = σοι.

522
κατ᾽ . . . ἕζευ: aorist imperative, tmesis, 'sit!'

522
ἔμπης: 'although'.

523
ἐν θυμῷ κατακεῖσθαι ἐάσομεν: literally, 'let (your grief) rest in your heart', i.e. do not make any outward show of it.

523
ἐάσομεν: aorist subjunctive, denoting a polite instruction; the verb ἐάω governs the infinitive.

523
περ = καίπερ.

524
πρῆξις: 'profit, benefit'.

524
πέλεται: 'there is'.

524
κρυεροῖο: literally, 'cold', though the word is only ever used metaphorically in Homer in reference to (negative) emotions, so perhaps 'chilling' is a better translation here.

525
ὡς: 'thus, in this way'.

525
ἐπεκλώσαντο: literally, 'spun out', i.e. 'ordained'. The metaphor is that of the thread of life, spun out at one's birth and cut at one's death. The verb governs the dative and the infinitive, i.e. 'they have ordained for X (dative) to do Y (infinitive)'.

526
ἀχνυμένοις: adverbial, 'in unhappiness'.

526
αὐτοὶ: 'they', i.e. the gods.

526
ἀκηδέες: 'without care', i.e. they do not have any worries.

A
Level

527
πίθοι: a 'pithos' was a large urn used to store oil or grain. Pandora's 'box' (which contained all the evils in the world) was also a 'pithos' in the original version by Hesiod.

527
κατακείαται = κατάκεινται, literally 'there lie in stock', i.e. 'there are'.

527
ἐν Διὸς οὔδει: 'on the floor of Zeus' (palace)'; note that **οὔδει** comes from οὖδας, 'floor', not οὐδός, 'threshold', which we saw at line 487.

528
δώρων: governed by **πίθοι** in the previous line, 'jars . . . of gifts'.

528
οἷα δίδωσι: 'which he gives', i.e. which Zeus hands to people.

528
κακῶν, ἕτερος δὲ ἑάων: a highly condensed phrase, which in full would read ἕτερος (πίθος) μὲν κακῶν, ἕτερος δὲ ἑάων, 'one (is a jar) of evils, the other (a jar) of good things'.

528
ἑάων: genitive neuter plural of ἐύς, 'noble, good', i.e. 'good things'.

529–531
ᾧ μέν . . . ᾧ δέ: literally, 'to one man . . . but to another', i.e. 'to some people . . . to others'.

529
ἀμμίξας = ἀναμείξας, 'having mixed . . . together'; the object of the participle must be understood from the context, since the poet does not mention it explicitly. What Zeus is 'mixing together' is gifts from each of the urns. Note that whatever noun we supply must be understood as being governed *both* by the participle (**ἀμμίξας**) and the main verb (**δώῃ**). The line as a whole can be translated: 'To some people, Zeus gives a mixture of good and evil . . .'

529
δώῃ: third person singular aorist subjunctive of δίδωμι.

530
κύρεται: literally, 'encounters, meets with'; the subject of the verb is not Zeus, but the man to whom Zeus has handed out these gifts; the verb governs the dative.

531
τῶν λυγρῶν: partitive genitive, 'from the evils'. The word 'only' must be understood from the context, i.e. not giving out any gifts from the 'good' urn.

A Level

531
λωβητὸν: 'an object of shame, bereft of honour'; it is in keeping with the ethos of the poem as a whole that a life of unadulterated evil is a life without honour. The same concern is repeated two lines later.

531
ἔθηκε: gnomic aorist, which should be translated as if present tense; the subject is either Zeus (i.e. 'and he renders him. . .') or the fact of the man being given 'gifts' from the jar of evils only (i.e. 'which renders him . . .').

532
καί: 'and so'.

532
ἑ = αὐτόν.

532
βούβρωστις: there is some debate over the precise meaning of this word, though it most likely means 'hunger' or 'famine'.

532
ἐπὶ χθόνα: 'across the land'.

533
δῖαν: literally, 'fine, splendid, noble', but in this context we might say 'fertile', contrasting with the hunger of the man who wanders across it.

533
φοιτᾷ: 'he walks to and fro'.

533
οὔτε θεοῖσι . . . οὔτε βροτοῖσιν: 'neither by gods nor by humans', i.e. by no one.

534
ἀγλαὰ δῶρα: the 'shining gifts' given to Peleus might refer generally to his fortunate lot, although the poem equally contains numerous references to specific items given to Peleus to the gods, e.g. his horses, the armour initially worn by Achilles (lent to Patroclus and then lost to Hector in Book 16) and the famous spear (which Patroclus is symbolically unable to wield in Book 16).

535
ἐκ γενετῆς: 'from birth'.

535
πάντας . . . ἐπ᾽ ἀνθρώπους: 'among all men'.

535
ἐκέκαστο: from κέκασμαι, 'excel, stand out'; the epic pluperfect is here used in an imperfect sense.

A
Level

536

ὄλβῳ . . . πλούτῳ: the contrast is between happiness or fortune (**ὄλβῳ**) and wealth (**πλούτῳ**).

537

θνητῷ ἐόντι: concessive, 'though a mortal'.

537

θεὰν . . . ἄκοιτιν: i.e. Thetis.

537

ποίησαν: the subject is 'the gods'.

538

ἐπὶ καὶ τῷ θῆκε = καὶ τούτῳ ἐπέθηκε, 'but he gave to this man in addition'.

538

ὅττί: 'namely that'.

538–539

οὔ τι . . . γονὴ γένετο: 'there was no birth of children at all'; γονὴ γένετο is a *figura etymologica*, a phrase containing two words that derive from the same root.

539

κρειόντων: lierally, 'mighty', though probably meant in the sense of children who are 'able (to inherit the estate).'

540

παναώριον: literally, 'altogether untimely', i.e. 'doomed to die prematurely'.

540

οὐδέ νυ . . . γε: 'not so much as', 'not even'; the sense is that Achilles is 'not even' able to look after his father in his old age, the bare minimum duty that a son owes to his father.

540

τόν γε: i.e. Peleus.

541

κομίζω: 'look after'.

542

ἧμαι: 'I sit here doing nothing'. Achilles has refused to enter the fighting since the very beginning of the poem following a quarrel with the commander-in-chief of the Greek forces, Agamemnon. The pathos derives from the fact that not only is Achilles not at home looking after his father, he is not even doing anything useful in Troy.

A
Level

542
σέ τε . . . τέκνα: **κήδων** literally means 'creating cares for', i.e. 'causing suffering to'. The idea of 'caring' is a key theme in this part of the poem. Achilles has created unnecessary 'cares' for Priam, while other people – Hector and Peleus – have been left unnecessarily 'uncared for' (**ἀκηδής**, 554) Meanwhile the gods live 'free from care' (**ἀκηδέες**, 526) altogether.
Note the stark contrast between what Achilles ought to be doing and what he is in fact doing is absolute: Achilles 'is not caring for' (**οὐδέ νυ . . . κομίζω**, 540–541) his own father, but is 'creating cares' for Priam and his sons (**σέ . . . σὰ τέκνα**).

542
ἠδὲ: 'and'.

543
καὶ: 'also'; the words 'like Peleus' must be understood from the context. The situation in Phthia and Troy has a few points of comparison at least: both Peleus and Priam are old men, and both have fallen on hard times.

543
γέρον: the vocative form is used respectfully by Achilles.

543
τὸ πρὶν: 'then', the contrasting 'but now' comes with **αὐτὰρ** on line 547.

543
ἀκούομεν: literally, 'we hear', i.e. 'it is widely known'.

544–545: Achilles define the extent of Priam's kingdom: Lesbos to the south, Phrygia to the east and the Hellespont to the north.

544
ὅσσον: 'all that which . . .'

544
Λέσβος: 'Lesbos', large island to the west of the Troad.

544
ἄνω: an unusual use of the adverb, which occurs only here in the poem. It appears to mean 'out there' or 'out to sea'.

544
Μάκαρος ἕδος: in apposition to **Λέσβος**; 'Macar' was a legendary king and law-giver of Lesbos.

544
ἐέργει = εἴργει, 'encloses', the verb is singular, though the subject has to be all three kingdoms mentioned in this and the following line; they collectively 'enclose' or 'surround' (i.e. form the borders of) Priam's kingdom.

A
Level

545
Φρυγίη: Phrygia was the land to the east of Troy. Elsewhere in the poem, the Phrygians appear as allies to the Trojans.

545
καθύπερθε: 'inland', another unusual use of the adverb.

545
Ἑλλήσποντος: 'Hellespont', the body of water to the north of the Troad, now known as the Dardanelles.

546
τῶν . . . κεκάσθαι: 'to excel, be pre-eminent', echoing **ἐκέκαστο** in line 535. The verb usually governs the dative, but here governs the genitive, **τῶν**, at the beginning of the line. The verb is a perfect infinitive with present meaning.

546
πλούτῳ . . . υἱάσι: datives of respect, 'in terms of your wealth and your sons'.

547
πῆμα τόδ(ε): 'this current suffering', i.e. the Trojan War.

547
Οὐρανίωνες: 'gods'; Achilles continues with the conceit that it is the gods that are responsible for all this suffering.

548
The word εἰσίν must be understood in this line, i.e. 'there are ever battles and man-slayings around the city'.

549
ἀλίαστον: literally, 'inescapably', i.e. 'endlessly'.

550
πρήξεις: second person singular future indicative of πρήσσω, 'be able to achieve'.

550
ἀκαχήμενος υἷος ἑῆος: 'in mourning for your noble son'; **ἀκαχήμενος** is perfect participle with present sense from ἄχνυμαι.

551
ἀνστήσεις: from ἀνίστημι, 'bring back to life'.

551
πρὶν καὶ κακὸν ἄλλο πάθησθα: literally, 'before you suffer another ill', i.e. you will be dead before you bring Hector back to life. Achilles' tone is strangely threatening here. At 559, we get an even clearer indication of just how angry Achilles remains.

A Level

553
ἵζε: transitive, 'make sit down'.

553
ὄφρά: 'so long as'.

554
ἀκηδής: 'uncared for', i.e. without having received proper burial rites.

555
λῦσον: the object of this verb, Hector's body, is not stated explicitly, but must be understood from the context; second person aorist imperative.

556
πολλά: stressed by its placement in the emphatic runover position. To achieve the same effect in English, we might translate: 'And please take the ransom money – which is huge'.

556
τά τοι φέρομεν: 'which I have brought'; plural for singular, as happens occasionally in Homer.

556
τῶνδ(ε): i.e. the gifts that Priam has brought to give to Achilles.

556
ἀπόναιο: second person singular aorist optative middle of ἀπονίνημι, 'make use of', expressing a wish: 'may you make use of it (i.e. the ransom money)'. Achilles knows that this wish will never be fulfilled.

557
πρῶτον: 'from the very beginning'.

558
ζώειν καὶ ὁρᾶν φάος ἠελίοιο: 'to live and to see the light of the son'; two ways of saying the same thing, the technical term for which is pleonasm.

559
ὑπόδρα ἰδὼν: 'looking darkly at him'. This flash of anger from Achilles is the result of Priam not doing what he has been asked, i.e. to sit down, and emphasizes the fragility of the temporary entente between the two men.

559
ὑπόδρα: this word derives from **δέρκομαι** ('to look on, at'), the **ὑπό** prefix implying a particularly sinister or baleful look.

560
μηκέτι . . . μ' ἐρέθιζε: 'do not irritate me any further'.

A Level

560
νοέω: 'I intend to, plan'.

562
μήτηρ: placed in the emphatic runover position; we might render the effect in English as follows: 'A messenger came to me from Zeus – my mother.'

562
ἁλίοιο γέροντος: literally, 'of the old man of the sea', i.e. Nereus.

563
καὶ δέ: 'and what is more'.

563
γιγνώσκω Πρίαμε φρεσίν, οὐδέ με λήθεις: throughout the poem, Achilles has shown himself highly sensitive to being 'deceived'. This particular line evokes his stinging rebuke to Odysseus in Book 9, where he says he 'hates like the gates of Hades the man who hides one thing in his chest and says another'.

563
λήθεις = λανθάνεις.

565
οὐ γάρ . . . ἐλθέμεν: the words 'without the assistance of the gods' must be understood from the context.

565
οὐδὲ μάλ' ἡβῶν: 'not even if he were in the bloom of youth'. Achilles makes the *a fortiori* argument that if a young man would not have dared come to the camp, an old man certainly would not have done.

566
ἐς στρατόν: i.e. the Greek encampment.

566
οὐδὲ . . . οὐδέ: 'neither . . . nor also'.

567
ῥεῖα: adverbial, 'easily'. At lines 454–456, we were told that this bar required three men to shift into place.

568
τῷ: 'therefore'.

569
μή: 'lest'.

569
σε . . . οὐδ' . . . ἐάσω: 'I shall not spare you,' i.e. 'I shall kill you.'

A Level

596
σε is emphasized by **αὐτὸν**, 'even you'.

570
καὶ . . . περ = καίπερ, 'even though'.

570
Διὸς . . . ἐφετμάς: 'Zeus's orders' – while Zeus was felt to guarantee the rights of suppliants in a general sense, the 'orders' that Achilles refers to here are the orders he received from Zeus earlier in the book (lines 133–137, not part of the set text) to release Hector's body to Priam.

572
οἴκοιο . . . θύραζε: 'out of the house, to the door'.

572
λέων ὣς: the image of Achilles leaping up 'like a lion' contributes to the tension of the scene. Achilles has already threatened Priam at lines 569–570; the image of the lion is emphasized by being placed ahead of ὣς, which serves as a postpositive, i.e. governing the word that precedes it.

572
ὣς: accented thus because it stands as a postpositive, governing the word that precedes it rather than the word that follows.

574
ῥα: 'indeed, as is well known'.

576
ὑπὸ ζυγόφιν: 'out from under the yoke'.

577
ἐς . . . ἄγαγον: tmesis.

578
κὰδ . . . εἷσαν: aorist active of καθίζω, 'let one sit'; **κὰδ** = κατά.

580
κὰδ . . . ἔλιπον: the words 'on the wagon' must be understood from the context.

581
ὄφρα: 'so that'.

582
ἐκκαλέσας: the words 'from out of the house' must be understood from the context.

582
κέλετ(ο): 'ordered'.

A
Level

582
ἀμφί: adverbial, 'all around'.

583
ἀειράσας: aorist part of ἀείρω.

584
χόλον οὐκ ἐρύσαιτο: the verb is best taken as meaning 'to watch out for, beware'.

586
κατακτείνειε: the subject here is Achilles.

588
ἀμφὶ δέ . . . χιτῶνα: the δμωαὶ dress Hector's body in a χιτών ('tunic') and then wrap his body in one of the φάρεα ('shrouds').

589
λεχέων: genitive dependant on **ἐπέθηκεν**, 'lay upon'. **λεχέων** is plural for metrical reasons.

590
σὺν: adverbial, 'together (with Achilles)'.

592
σκυδμαινέμεν: infinitive for imperative, 'be angry with'; Achilles says this because he promised the ghost of Patroclus he would not do exactly what he is doing, i.e. releasing the body of Hector.

593
εἰν Ἄιδός: 'in (the house of) Hades'.

593
περ: concessive, 'although'.

594
οὔ . . . ἀεικέα: the use of two negatives here ('not unseemly') adds up to a strong positive, a rhetorical technique known as 'litotes'.

595
καὶ τῶνδ(ε): 'also from these'.

595
ἀποδάσσομαι: Achilles presumably plans to burn a portion of the ransom gifts in honour of (the dead) Patroclus.

595
ὅσσ' ἐπέοικεν: 'all that is fitting'; the word **ὅσσα** always stresses amount.

A Level

Vocabulary

Iliad, Book 24

While there is no Defined Vocabulary List for A level, words in the OCR Defined Vocabulary List for AS are marked with * so that students can quickly see the vocabulary with which they should be particularly familiar.

ἆ	ah!
***ἀγαθός -ή -όν**	good, noble, excellent
ἀγαπάζω	to treat with affection
ἄγγελος -ου, m.	messenger
ἄγε, adv.	come on, come now
ἀγητός -ή -όν	admirable, wonderful
ἀγλαός -ή -όν	splendid, shining, bright
ἀγορεύω	to speak, say
ἄγχι, adv.	nearby
***ἄγω**	to bring, bear
ἀγχίμολος -ον	coming near, close by
ἀδινά, adv.	loudly, vehemently
***ἀεί**, adv.	ever, always
ἀεικής -ές	meagre (of gifts)
ἀείρω	to raise up, lift
ἀθάνατοι -ων, m. plur.	the immortals, i.e. the gods
ἀθάνατος -η -ον	immortal, undying
αἴ	= εἰ
αἰδέομαι	to be ashamed, feel shame; have regard for, respect
Ἀιδης -ου, m.	Hades
αἰεί	= ἀεί
αἷμα -ατος, n.	blood
αἰνός -ή -όν	dreadful, terrible
***αἱρέω**	to grasp, seize
αἶσα, f.	one's appointed lot, destiny
αἴσιος -ον	auspicious, opportune
αἰσχύνω	to disfigure, disgrace
ἀκηδέστως, adv.	pitilessly
ἀκηδής -ές	free from care; uncared for
ἄκοιτις -ιος, f.	wife
***ἀκούω**	to hear of something (+ gen.); to hear
ἄλγος -εος, n.	pain
ἄλεισον -ου, n.	cup, goblet
ἀλείφω	to anoint with oil
ἀληθείη -ης, f.	truth
ἀλίαστον, adv.	incessantly
ἅλιος -α -ον	of the sea
ἀλιταίνω	to transgress (a law)
Ἄλκιμος -ου, m.	Alcimus, one of the Myrmidons
***ἀλλά**	but
***ἀλλήλους -α**	each other, one another
ἀλλοδαπός -ή -όν	foreign
ἅλλομαι	to jump, leap
***ἄλλος -η -ο**	other, another
ἄλλοτε, adv.	at another time
ἀμάω	to reap, gather
ἀμβρόσιος -η -ον	ambrosial, divine
ἄμβροτος -ον	immortal, divine
ἀμείβω	to answer, reply
ἀμύνω	to ward off; (mid.) to ward off from oneself, i.e. to defend oneself
ἀμφί, adv.	around, about; all over
ἀμφίς, adv.	all around
***ἄν**	would, could (indef.)
ἀναίσσω, aor. **ἀνήιξα**	to dart up, spring up onto something (acc.)
ἀναμίσγω	to mix
ἄναξ -ακτος, m.	lord, master
ἀνάρσιος -ον	unfriendly, hostile
ἀνάσσω	to be king or master of, rule over

ἀνδροκτασία -ης, f.	slaughter of men (in battle)
ἀνδροφόνος -ον	man-slaying, murderous
ἀνέχω	to endure, tolerate
***ἀνήρ, ἀνδρός**, m.	man
***ἄνθρωπος -ου**, m.	man, (plur.) mankind
ἀνίστημι	to make someone get up; to bring someone back from the dead
ἀνοίγνυμι	to open
ἄντην, adv.	openly
ἀντιβολέω	to meet, encounter
ἄνω, adv.	(locative) upper
ἀπαλέξω	to protect someone or something (gen.)
ἀπαμύνω	to defend, protect oneself
ἀπάνευθε, adv.	away, apart from
ἄπειμι	to come or go away from
ἀπείρων -ον	boundless, endless
ἀπερείσιος -ον	countless
ἀπήνη -ης, f.	four-wheeled wagon
***ἀπό** (+ gen.)	from
ἀποβαίνω	to dismount; to depart
ἀποδατέομαι	to apportion something (acc.) out to someone (dat.)
ἄποινα -ων, n. plur.	ransom
ἀπολήγω	to cease from something (+ gen.)
ἀπομιμνήσκομαι	to remember something fully
ἀπονίναμαι	to have to the use or enjoyment of a thing (gen.)
ἄποτμος -ον	unhappy, ill-starred
ἅπτομαι	to take hold of (+ gen.)
ἀπωθέω	to push back, push away
***ἄρα**	. . . then . . . (often no recognizable impact on the meaning)
Ἀργεῖος -α -ον	of or from Argos, Argive
Ἀργειφόντης -ου, m.	slayer of Argus, epithet of Hermes
Ἄργος -εος, n.	the city of Argos
ἀρείφατος -ον	slain by Ares, i.e. slain in war
ἀρή -ῆς, f.	calamity, destruction
Ἄρης -ηος, m.	Ares, the god of war
ἄριστος -η -ον	best
ἅρμα -ατος, n.	chariot
***ἄστυ -εος**, n.	city
ἀσχαλάω	to be distressed, grieved
ἀτάρ	but, nevertheless
ἄτη -ης, f.	bewilderment, confusion, delusion or blindness sent by the gods
Ἀτρείδης, -αο or -εω, m.	son of Atreus
ἀτρεκέως, adv.	exactly, precisely
αὖ, adv.	again, once more
αὖθι, adv.	right there, on the spot
αὐλή -ῆς, f.	courtyard, enclosure
αὐτὰρ	and, but
αὖτε, adv.	again; on the other hand, however
***αὐτίκα**, adv.	straightaway, immediately
Αὐτομέδων -οντος, m.	Automedon, one of the Myrmidons
***αὐτός -ή -ό**	self, myself, yourself, etc. (refl. pron.; him, her, it (in obl. cases, used for pers. pron.)
αὔτως, adv.	in the same way, all the same
ἄφαρ, adv.	instantly, at once
ἀφικνέομαι	to arrive at, come to, reach
ἀφνειός -όν	rich, wealthy
Ἀχαιοί -ών, m. plur.	the Achaeans, i.e. the Greeks
ἀχεύω	to grieve, mourn
Ἀχιλλεύς -έως, m.	Achilles
***βάλλω**	to throw
***βασιλεύς -ῆος**, m.	king, noble, chief
βούβρωστις -εως, f.	ravenous hunger
βροτός -οῦ, m.	a mortal man (with or without **ἀνήρ**)
γαῖα, γαίης, f.	land, country
***γάρ**	for, since
***γε**	at least, at any rate
γένειον -ου, n.	chin, beard
γενετή -ῆς, f.	birth
γεραιός -ά -όν	old
***γέρων -οντος**, m.	old man
γηθέω	to rejoice, be glad
γῆρας -αος, n.	old age
γηράσκω	to grow old
***γίγνομαι**	to be, exist
γιγνώσκω	to know, understand
γναμπτός -ή -όν	curved, bent
γονή -ής, f.	child, son
γόνυ -ατος, n.	knee
γόος -ου, m.	weeping, wailing, lamentation

γυῖα -ων, n. plur. limbs
***γυνή, γυναικός**, f. woman

δαΐζω to tear, cut through, wound
Δαρδανίδης -ου, m. descendant of Dardanus, i.e. Priam
***δέ** and, but
δείδω to be afraid
δειλός -ή -όν miserable, wretched
δεινός -ή -όν terrible, dreadful
δέμας, n. bodily frame, build
δέχομαι to take, accept, receive
***δή** (emphasizes preceding word)
δῆμος -ου, m. country, land
δμωή -ῆς, f. female captured in war and enslaved, slave-woman
διά (+ acc.) during (temporal)
διάκτορος -ου, m. epithet of Hermes, guide, minister
διαρραίω to tear into pieces
***δίδωμι** to give
Διόθεν, adv. from Zeus, by command of Zeus
δῖος -α -ον divine, godlike, heavenly
διοτρεφής -ές fostered, cherished by Zeus
δίφρος -ου, m. chariot-board
δοιοί -αί -ά = δύο
δόρπον -ου, n. evening meal
δόρυ, δουρός, n. wood
***δύναμαι** to be able (to do something, + inf.)
δύο two
δυωδέκατος -η -ον twelfth
δυσμενής -έος hostile
δῶμα -ατος, n. room
***δῶρον -ου**, n. gift

***ἐάω** to let something go, give it up; to allow, permit (+ inf.)
ἕβδομος -η -ον seventh
ἐγγύθεν, adv. near
***ἐγγύς**, adv. near, nearby
***ἐγώ, ἐγών** I
ἕδος -εος, n. abode, dwelling-place
ἐδωδή -ῆς, f. food, meal
ἐερσήεις -εσσα -εν fresh
ἕζομαι to sit, take a seat
***εἰ** if
εἶδον (not used in act. pres.) I saw, perceived
εἶδος -εος, n. appearance, look
εἰλύω to roll
εἰμί to be
εἶμι I shall go
εἵνεκα = ἕνεκα, ἕνεκεν
εἶπον I said, spoke
εἴργω = ἔργω
εἴρομαι to ask, inquire about (+ acc.)
εἷς, μία, ἕν one; one and the same
εἰσάγω to lead or bring in
εἴσειμι to go into, enter
ἐΐσκω to liken, compare something (acc.) to something (dat.)
εἰσοράω to look upon, behold
***ἐκ** or **ἐξ** (+ gen.) out of, from
***ἐκεῖνος -η -ο** that
ἐκκαλέω to call out or forth
ἐκπέμπω to send away
Ἕκτωρ -ορος, m. Hector
ἔλαιον -ου, n. olive oil
ἐλάτινος -η -ον made of fir or pine-wood
ἐλάτη -ης, f. silver fir
ἐλαύνω to drive
ἐλεεινός -ή -όν pitiful
ἐλεέω to show mercy to, have pity on
ἑλίκωψ -ωπος, m. with rolling eyes, quick-glancing
ἑλκέω to drag about, tear asunder
ἕλκος -εος, n. wound
Ἑλλήσποντος -ου, m. the Hellespont, the narrow strait that links the Propontis to the Aegean Sea; now known as the Dardanelles
ἔλπομαι to hope
ἐλύω to writhe, roll on the ground
***ἐμός -ή -όν** my
ἔμπης, adv. alike, the same
***ἐν or ἐνί** (+ dat.) in, on, onto, among
ἐναίσιμος -ον ominous, fateful
ἐνδυκέως, adv. kindly, attentively
ἕνεκα (+ gen.) on account of, for the sake of
ἐνέπω to relate, talk about
***ἐνθάδε**, adv. here
ἐννεακαίδεκα nineteen
ἐντός, adv. within, inside
ἕξ six
ἐξεναρίζω to kill, slay

ἐξέρομαι	to inquire of someone (acc.)
ἔξειμι	to be one of (+ gen.)
ἐξικνέομαι	to reach, come to, arrive at
ἑός, ἑή, ἑόν	his own, her own, its own
***ἐπεί**	when, after (temporal); since, because (causal)
***ἔπειτα**	then, afterwards; alternatively
ἐπέοικε	to be suitable
ἐπέρχομαι	to come upon, arrive, approach
***ἐπί** (+ acc.)	to, towards
***ἐπί** (+ dat.)	at, to, towards
***ἐπί** (+ gen.)	on
ἐπιβλής -ῆτος, m.	bar, bolt (used to secure a gate or door)
ἐπιδεύομαι	to be inferior in something (gen.) to someone (gen.)
ἐπιείκελος -ον	like (+ dat.)
ἐπικλώθω	to allot to, grant (+ inf.)
ἐπιρρήσσω	to drive home, push shut (of the bar that locks a gate or door)
ἐπιτίθημι	to add; to place or put upon
ἐπιχέω	to pour over
ἐπιχθόνιος -ον	earthly, mortal
ἕπομαι	to follow
ἔπος -εος, n.	word
ἔργα -ων, n. plur.	matters, affairs
ἔργω	to enclose
ἐρεθίζω	to rouse or provoke to anger
ἐρέφω, aor. **ἔρεψα**	to cover with a roof, roof over
ἐριούνιος -ου, m.	helper, epithet of Hermes
Ἑρμείας -αο, m.	Hermes
ἐρύκω	to hold back, restrain
ἔρυμαι	to protect
ἐρύω	to protect, guard; check, curb; to watch out for
***ἔρχομαι**, perf. **εἰλήλουθα**	to come, go
ἐσθίω, aor. **ἔφαγον**	to eat
ἐσθλός -ή -όν	good
ἔσθω	= ἐσθίω
***ἑταῖρος -ου**, m.	companion
ἕτερος -η -ον	the other (of two)
***ἔτι**	still, yet (often with neg.)
εὕδω	to sleep
εὐεργής -ές	well-wrought, well-made
εὐλή, -ῆς, f.	worm, maggot
ἐΰννητος -ον	well-spun
ἐΰξεστος -η -ον	well-polished, well-planned
εὑρίσκω	to find
εὐρύς -εῖα -ύ	broad, wide
ἐΰς, ἐΰ	good, brave, noble
εὖτε	when
ἐφετμή -ῆς, f.	command
***ἔχω**	to have, hold; to inhabit (a place)
***Ζεύς, Διός**, m.	Zeus
ζυγόν -όφιν, m.	yoke
ζώω	to live
ἤ . . . ἤ	whether . . . or whether
ἥβη -ης, f.	youth, young man
ἠδέ	and
ἤδη	immediately, already
ἠέλιος, -ου or **-οιο**, m.	sun
ἦκα, adv.	gently, softly, slightly
ἥκω	to have come, i.e. to be present
ἧμαι	to sit
ἦμαρ -ατος, n.	day
ἡμέτερος -α -ον	our
ἡμίονος -ου, m.	mule
ἡνία -ίων, m. plur.	reins
ἥρως, ἥρωος, m.	hero
ἤτοι	to be sure, indeed
ἦτορ -ορος, n.	heart
ἠΰς, ἠΰ	= ἐΰς, ἐΰ
ἠῶθεν, adv.	in the morning
ἠώς, ἠοῦς, f.	dawn, morning
θαμβέω	to be astonished or wonder at
θάμβος -εος, n.	amazement
***θάνατος -ου**, m.	death
θαυμάζω	to marvel at, admire
θεάομαι	to gaze at, behold
θεοειδής -ές	godlike
θεά -ῆς, f.	goddess
***θεός -οῦ**. m.	god
θεράπων -οντος, m.	companion, attendant
θηέομαι	to observe, see with amazement
θνήσκω, aor. **ἔθανον**	to die
θνητός -ή -όν	liable to death, mortal
θοός -ή -όν	swift
θοῦρος -ον	impetuous, furious
θρίξ, τριχός, f.	hair
θρόνος -ου, m.	seat, chair

***θυγάτηρ, -έρος**, f.	daughter
θυμός -οῦ, m.	heart
θύραζε, adv.	to the door
θύρη -ης, f.	door
Ἰδαῖος -ου, m.	Idaeus, the man who drives Priam's wagon
ἵζω	to sit
ἰθύνω	to guide, direct
ἰθύς (+ gen.)	straight at, straight towards
ἱκάνω	= ἱκνέομαι
ἱκέτης -ου, m.	suppliant
ἱκνέομαι	to come to, arrive at, reach
Ἴλιος -ου, f.	Ilium, the city of Troy
Ἶλος -οιο, m.	Ilus
ἵμερος -ου, m.	longing, yearning after (+ gen.)
ἵνα	where; so that, in order that
***ἵππος -ου**, m.	horse
ἱρός -ή -όν	sacred, holy
ἵστημι	to make to stand, set up; to stand
ἴσχω	to check, restrain
κάδ	= κατά
κάθημαι	to be seated, sit, esp. of sitting quietly
καθύπερθ⊠, adv.	above, over
***καί**	and, even, also
καίνυμαι	to surpass, excel
***κακός -ή -όν**	bad, evil, cowardly
καλήτωρ -ορος, m.	crier
***καλός -ή -όν**	beautiful
κάρη -ης, n.	head
καρπαλίμως, adv.	swiftly, speedily
***κατά** (+ acc.)	down, according to, by, in, throughout
κατάκειμαι	to rest (line 523); to be set down (line 527)
κατακτείνω	to kill, slay
καταλέγω	to recount, tell at length
καταλείπω	to leave behind
κατέδω	to eat up, devour
κέ, κέν	= ἄν
***κεῖμαι**	to lie, be placed or situated
κειμήλιον -ου, n.	treasure
κεῖνος -η -ο	= ἐκεῖνος
κείρω	to cut, cut down
κέλομαι	to urge, command
***κεφαλή -ῆς**, f.	head
κήδω	to cause pain or distress to; (pass.) to be concerned for something, care for it (gen.)
κῆρ, κῆρος, n.	heart
κῆρυξ -υκος, m.	herald
κίω	to go
κλαίω	to cry, lament
κλείς, κλειδός, f.	bar, bolt (used to secure a gate or door)
κλῆρος -ου, m.	a lot
κλισίη -ής, f.	hut, tent
κλυτός -ή -όν	famous, illustrious, renowned
κνέφας -ους, n.	evening darkness, dusk
κομίζω	to care for, wait upon
κραδίη -ης, f.	heart
κρείων -οντος, m.	ruler, lord, master
κρυερός -ά -όν	icy, cold, chilling
κτείνω	to kill, slay
κυδιάνειρα	bringing men glory or renown, epithet of battle
κυνέω	to kiss
κυρέω	to chance upon something (dat.)
κύων, κυνός, m.	dog
λαγχάνω	to obtain by lot (to do something, + inf.)
λάζομαι	to grasp, seize
***λαμβάνω**	to take hold of, seize
λανθάνω, aor. **ἔλαθον**	to not think or care about something (gen.); to escape someone's (acc.) notice
λαχνήεις -εσσα -εν	downy, soft (of roofing materials)
λειμωνόθεν	from a meadow
λείπω	(pass.) to be left, remain, survive
Λέσβος -ου, f.	the island of Lesbos
λέχος -εος, n.	bed, bedstead
λέων -οντος, m.	lion
λιτανεύω	to pray to, entreat
λοιγός -οῦ, m.	ruin, destruction
λούω	to wash
λυγρός -ά -όν	baneful, mournful
***λύω**	to release, set free
λωβητός -ή -όν	maltreated, outraged
Μάκαρ -ος, m.	Macar, son of Aeolus, who lives in Lesbos

μάκαρ -αιρα -ον	blest, fortunate
μακρός -ά -όν	high, lofty (of mountains)
***μάλα**, adv.	very, exceedingly
μάρναμαι	to fight, do battle
μάστιξ -ῖγος, f.	whip
μάχη -ης, f.	battle, combat
***μάχομαι**	to fight
μέγαρον -ου, n.	house, home
***μέγας, μεγάλη, μέγα**	great
μελειστί, adv.	limb from limb
μέλας -αινα -αν	black
μέλος -εος, n.	limb
μέν	in truth, indeed, certainly
***μέν . . . δέ**	(marks a contrast)
μένος -εος, n.	strength, force
μετόπισθε, adv.	afterwards, in the future
μετοχλίζω	to push back or away
***μή** (and comp.)	see οὐ
μηκέτι, adv.	no longer, no more
μήπω, adv.	not yet
***μήτηρ, -έρος** or **-ρός**, f.	mother
μιαρός -ά -όν	stained with blood
μιμνήσκω	to call to mind, remember
μίμνω	to remain, be left
μιν	him, her, it
μοῖρα -ας, feminine	part, portion; one's lot, destiny, fate
μοῦνος -η -ον	alone, solitary
μῦθος -ου, m.	anything delivered by word of mouth, word, speech
Μυρμιδόνες -ων, m. plur.	Myrmidons, the Thracian tribe of which Achilles is the leader
μύω	to close, shut
ναί	yes, indeed
νέκυς -υος, m.	corpse
νεμεσσητός -ή -όν	worthy of indignation or wrath
νέον, adv.	just now, lately
νέος -ου, m.	young, youthful
νεώτερος -α -ον	younger
νηδύς -ύος, f.	belly, womb
νηῦς, νηός, f.	ship
νοέω	to plan or intend to do something (inf.)
νόος, νοῦ, m.	mind
νόσφι, adv.	apart, afar, away
νύ	(part. of emphasis)

***νῦν**, adv.	now
***νύξ, νυκτός**, f.	night
ὁ, ἡ, τό	he, she, it; who, which
ὅδε, ἥδε, τόδε	this
ὁδοίπορος -ου, m.	traveller, wanderer
ὀδύρομαι	to grieve, lament
ὄζος -ου, m.	offshoot
οἴγω, aor. **ᾦξα**	to open
οἶκος -ου, m.	dwelling
οἰκτείρω	to pity
οἰμώζω	to cry out in grief, lament
***οἷος, οἵη, οἷον**	such, of such a kind
οἶος - η -ον	alone, by oneself
οἶτος -ου, m.	fate, doom
ὀΐω	to think, suspect
οἰωνός -οῦ, m.	a large bird of prey
ὄλβιος -ον	happy, blessed
ὄλβος -ου, m.	happiness, bliss
ὄλλυμι	to kill, destroy
ὀλοός -ή -όν	destructive, deadly
Ὄλυμπος -ου, m.	Mount Olympus, the dwelling-place of the gods
ὁμαρτέω	to attend, accompany
ὄνειαρ -ατος, n.	anything that is helpful, benefit, boon
ὄνομαι	to find fault with
ὀνομαίνω	to call by name
***ὀξύς -εῖα -ύ**	sharp (of weapons), piercing or shrill (of sounds)
ὀπάζω	to tell someone (acc.), to accompany someone (dat.); to appoint
ὀπηδέω	to accompany, attend (+ dat.)
***ὁράω**	to see, behold, look on
ὀρέγω	to stretch out
ὀρθός -ή -όν	straight, upright
ὀρίνω	to rouse, move
ὄρνυμι	to rouse, excite, awake
ὄροφος -ου, m.	reed used for thatching houses
ὅς, ἥ, ὅ	he, this, that (demonst. pron.); who, that, which (rel. pron.)
ὅσσος -η -ον	as great as, how great
***ὅτε**	when
***οὐ / οὐκ / οὐχ / οὐχί / μή**	not
οὐδέ	but not
οὐδείς -εμία -έν	no one, nothing
οὐδός -οῦ, m.	threshold

***οὖν**	so, then
Οὐρανίωνες -ων, m. plur.	the gods
οὔτε	and not
οὕτω, adv.	in this way
ὀφθαλμός -οῦ, m.	eye
ὄφρα	in order to; while, so long as
ὀχεύς -ῆος, m.	the door-bolt
παιδοφόνος -ον	child-killing
***παῖς** or **πάϊς, παιδός**, com.	child
πάλλω	to cast a lot
πανάποτμος -ον	completely luckless, entirely wretched
παναώριος -ον	doomed to an untimely end
πάρ	= παρὰ
***παρὰ** (+ dat.)	beside, next to
***παρὰ** (+ gen.)	from (a person)
παράκειμαι	to lie or be placed nearby, at one's side
πάρειμι	to be present, to be at hand
παρέκ or **παρέξ** (+ gen.)	past
παρέκ or **παρέξ** (+ acc.)	without the knowledge of
***πᾶς, πᾶσα, πᾶν**	every, all
πάσχω	to suffer
***πατήρ, πατέρος**, m.	father
πάτρη -ης, f.	fatherland, native land
πατρίς -ίδος, f.	of one's father, native
Πάτροκλος -ου, m.	Patroclus
πέδιον -ου, n.	battlefield
πεζός -ή -όν	on foot, walking
***πείθω**	to persuade
πειράω	to make a trial of, test
πέλω	to be
***πέμπω**	to send
πεντήκοντα	fifty
πέπνυμαι	to be clever, intelligent
πέρ	very, at least, even, just; though
περί (+ acc.)	around; with
περιναιέτης -ου, m.	neighbour
περινίζω	to wash off all round
πῆ, adv.	where; somehow, approximately
Πηλείδης -ου, m.	son of Peleus, i.e. Achilles
Πηλείων	= Πηλείδης
Πηλεύς -έως, m.	Peleus, Achilles' father
πῆμα -ατος, n.	misery, calamity

πίθος -ου, m.	large earthen jar, for wine or oil
πίνω	to drink
πλοῦτος -ου, m.	wealth, riches
πνέω	to blow
ποδώκης -ες	swift-footed, epithet of Achilles
ποθι	probably, perhaps
***ποιέω**	to make, build
ποιπνύω	to bustle about
πόλεμος -ου, m.	war
πολιός -ά -όν	grey
Πολύκτωρ -ορος, m.	Polyctor
πολύς, πολλή, πολύ	much, many
πομπός, -οῦ, m.	conductor, escort, guide
πονέομαι	to busy oneself with something (περί + acc.)
***ποταμός -οῦ**, m.	river
ποτί	= πρός
πού	doubtless, perhaps
πούς, ποδός, m.	foot
πραπίδες -ων, f. plur.	mind, heart
πρῆξις -ιος, f.	a good result, success
Πρίαμος -ου, m.	Priam, father of Hector and king of Troy
πρὶν, adv.	previously, in the past
προπάροιθε (+ gen.)	before, in front of
***πρὸς** (+ acc.)	to, towards
προσαυδάω	to speak to, address
πρόσφημι	to speak to, address
πρότερος -η -ον	previous
προτίθημι	to throw something (acc.) in front of something (dat.)
πρώιος -η -ον	early in the day, at early morn
πτερόεις -εσσα -εν	winged, feathered
πυκάζω	to wrap closely
πυκινός -ή -όν	compact, dense, close-packed; great, strong (of pain or delusion)
***πύλη -ης**, f.	gate
πυνθάνομαι	to learn, find out
πύργος -ου, m.	(in plur.) defensive wall, rampart
πω	up to this time, yet (always with **οὔ**)
πῶς	how?
ῥά	= ἄρα
ῥέζω	do, work, perform

ῥεῖα, adv. — easily
ῥύομαι — to rescue, save, deliver

σεύω — to put in quick motion, drive
σῆμα -ατος, n. — tomb
σήπω — to rot, moulder (of flesh)
σιδήρειος -η -ον — iron
σκυδμαίνω — to be angry
σόος -η -ον — safe, sound
σός, σή, σόν — your
σταυρός -οῦ, m. — upright stake or pale (used for constructing walls)
στόμα -ατος, n. — mouth
στοναχή -ῆς, f. — groaning, wailing
στρατός -οῦ, m. — military encampment
***σύ** — you
συγχέω — to confuse, confound
συλεύω — to trick, cheat
συμμύω — to shut up, close (of wounds)
***σύν** (+ dat.) — with
σφεῖς, σφέων — they, them

τάμνω — to cut, slice
τάφρος -ου, f. — ditch, trench
τάχα, adv. — quickly
ταχύς -εῖα -ύ — quick
***τέ** — and
τείρω — to wear down, exhaust, distress
τέκνον -ου, n. — child
τέκος -εος, n. — child
τέθηπα — (perf. with pres. sense) to be astonished, paralyzed
τερπικέραυνος -ον — delighting in thunder, epithet of Zeus
τέρπω — to have one's fill of something (gen.)
τεύχω — to make, render; (pass.) to be, become, take place
τῇ — where
τηλίκος -η -ον — of such an age, so old or so young
τηλόθι (+ gen.) — far from
τίθημι — to put, place
τίκτω — to beget, father
***τις, τι** — someone, something; anyone, anything
τίς, τί — who? what?
τίω — to show honour to, respect
τλάω — to suffer, endure
τοι — indeed
τοι — = σοι
τοῖος, τοίη, τοῖον — of such a kind, such
τοιόσδε -ήδε -όνδε — such as this
τοκεύς -έως, m. — parent
τοσσόσδε -ήδε -όνδε — = τόσσος
τόσσος -η -ον — so great, so vast
τράπεζα -ης, f. — table
***τρεῖς** — three
Τροίη -ης, f. — Troy, either the city itself or the surrounding area (also known as the Troad)
Τροίηθεν, adv. — from Troy
τύνη — = σύ
τύπτω — to strike, hit, esp. in hand-to-hand combat
τῷ, adv. — therefore, in this way

***υἱός, υἱοῦ or υἷος**, m.e — son
ὑπέρ (+ gen.) — (with v. of entreaty) by, for the sake of
ὑπερέχω — to hold something (acc.) over something (gen.), i.e. cover it, protect it
ὕπνος -ου, m. — sleep, slumber
ὑπόδρα, adv. — sternly, darkly, angrily
ὑπολύω — to loosen from underneath, make to sink or fail (of limbs)
ὑπόρνυμι — to rouse gradually
ὑψηλός -ή -όν — high, lofty

φαίνομαι — to come to light, appear, shine
φάος -εος, n. — light
φᾶρος -εος, n. — large piece of cloth, a shroud
φέριστος -η -ον — bravest, best
***φέρω** — to carry, bear
***φεύγω** — to take flight, run away
***φημί** — to say, speak, declare
***φίλος -η -ον** — one's own; beloved
φοιτάω — to go or hurry to and fro, roam around
φραδής -ές — prudent, clear
φράζω, aor. **ἐπέφραδον** — to perceive, become aware; devise, plan
φρήν, φρενός, f. — heart, mind
Φρύγιη -ης, f. — Phrygia, a region in Asia Minor
φυλακός -οῦ, m. — guard
φυλακτήρ -ῆρος, m. — guard
φωνέω — to speak

φώς, φωτός, m.	man
χαίρω	to rejoice, be glad
χαλεπαίνω	to act antagonistically, to show aggression
χαλκός -οῦ, m.	bronze
χαμᾶζε, adv.	to the ground
***χείρ, χειρός**, f.	hand
χθών -ονός, f.	ground
χιτών -ῶνος, m.	tunic
χόλος -ου, m.	anger
χολόω	to anger, enrage
χρίω	to anoint, smear with oil
χρώς, χροός, m.	the surface of the body, the skin
ὧδε, adv.	in this way, thus
ὠκύς, ὠκεῖα, ὠκύ	swift
ὤριστος	= ὁ ἄριστος, best, most excellent
ὣς, adv.	so, thus
ὡς	just as, like (introducing a simile)

Euripides, *Hippolytus*

Introduction, Commentary Notes and Vocabulary by Benedict Gravell

AS: 284–361, 391–524

A Level: 601–624, 627–633, 638–662, 664–668, 682–731, 885–911, 914–1028, 1030–1035

Introduction

Powerful and of great renown among mortals

πολλὴ μὲν ἐν βροτοῖσι κοὐκ ἀνώνυμος (1)

The goddess of desire, Aphrodite, speaks the first line of Euripides' *Hippolytus*, confidently and terrifyingly asserting her authority over humanity. Her divinity has been slighted by Hippolytus, who calls her the worst of the gods, spurns sex and marriage, and worships only Artemis, the goddess of virginity and hunting. In revenge, she has inflamed his stepmother Phaedra with a destructive passion for him. This passion will set in motion the events which will lead to both their deaths over the course of the play.

However, despite the play's framework of divine retribution and its stark affirmation of Aphrodite's power, it is human speech and action which dominate the drama and there is something which feels strikingly modern about *Hippolytus*. Even though her influence continues to be felt, Aphrodite does not return after the opening scene, and while Artemis does appear at the end of the play, she leaves the stage before its final moments. The play, instead, closes with Hippolytus' death in his father's arms after a moving reconciliation, a scene of real human emotion which provides some consolation for the ruthlessness of the gods and the tragic events of the rest of the play. The play's exploration of gender, sexuality, shame, family relationships and failed communication also contributes to its contemporary feel and helps to explain its enduring popularity and relevance.

Nevertheless, it is still important to remember that there are significant differences between ancient Greek drama and modern theatre. This introduction will therefore begin by outlining the context, function and key conventions of Athenian tragedy, before considering the plot, characters and themes of *Hippolytus* in greater detail.

Euripides

Euripides was born around 480 BCE and died in 406 BCE. He was younger than Aeschylus (*c.* 525–456 BCE) and Sophocles (*c.* 496–405 BCE), the two other most important Athenian tragedians. While a hugely celebrated playwright, and according to Aristotle the 'most tragic' ('τραγικώτατος') in terms of emotional impact, he was not quite as successful as them, winning fewer first prizes in dramatic competitions (although *Hippolytus* did receive first prize). However, more of his work has survived.

Of the 92 plays originally attributed to him, 19 have survived under his name (although one is of disputed authorship), compared to only 7 each for Aeschylus and Sophocles. Perhaps as a result of the sample size, Euripides' work appears to have a greater variety and is harder to categorize. Plays like *Hippolytus*, *Medea* and the *Bacchae* are masterpieces of tragic theatre, while others such as *Helen* and *Iphigenia in Tauris* have happy endings and sometimes seem more akin to romantic drama. There are also elements of humour throughout the Euripidean corpus and *Cyclops* provides our only complete example of a bawdy satyr play.

Although he is difficult to categorize, we can get a sense of contemporary opinion from a play called *Frogs* (a work also included in this Anthology) written by the comic playwright Aristophanes after Euripides' death. Much of the play is set in the Underworld, where Euripides competes with Aeschylus for the title of best tragic poet. As they debate, Aeschylus is presented as an old-fashioned literary purist, whose output is concerned with the presentation of traditional morality, and whose music is monotonous and uninteresting. Euripides, on the other hand, is portrayed as trendy, intellectual and innovative, but at the same time pretentious and potentially dangerous due to his focus on low-born characters and women, who use rhetoric to justify their immoral actions.

Of course, these are comic caricatures, and it would certainly be wrong to cast Euripides as a modernist playwright breaking completely with all convention. His plays are still relatively conservative in their observation of tragic form and continue to be based on traditional mythological plots and characters. Aphrodite's punishment of Hippolytus is also an example of Euripides employing the established tragic motif of divine vengeance. It is also important to note that Sophocles and Aeschylus were innovators in their own way. That said, his plays do show a real freshness, inquiring outlook and faculty for defying expectations. His ability to make us feel pity for a character like Phaedra, who harbours a shameful lust for her own stepson, or to present Medea, who kills her own children, as possessing a certain heroic nobility, would have provided a radically new perspective on traditional myth.

Euripides' presentation of characters is often based on a real sensitivity to human psychology which sometimes approaches a realism often lacking in ancient theatre. This was noted in ancient times: according to Aristotle, Sophocles is supposed to have claimed that he portrayed people as they ought to be, but that Euripides portrayed people as they actually were (*Poetics* 1460b). There is also an increased focus on lower-status characters such as women, slaves (e.g. the Nurse in *Hippolytus*) and non-Greeks. Focusing on characters on the margins of the Athenian *polis* expands the world of tragedy, and at times Euripides challenges his audience to reconsider conventional assumptions about characters based on status.

Euripides also shows a real interest in clever rhetoric and argument. This questioning spirit even extends to his presentation of the gods. Many of his prologues are delivered by gods and Euripides is particularly fond of the *deux ex machina*, where a powerful god arrives at the end of a play to help resolve the situation. Equally, though, human characters offer scepticism about the gods or criticize them for being so excessively heartless and vindictive. In general, Euripides' work reveals a dynamic mind keen to look at stories from new perspectives, reconsider assumptions and ask complex questions of his audience without simplifying issues, all within the established frameworks of tragedy.

While impossible to reconstruct fully, the poetry and musicality of his work also deserves mention. He introduced new and varied melodies and rhythms which enhanced the emotional impact of his choral odes and increased the importance of solo arias. Testament to the power of his music and poetry is Plutarch's story that Athenians roaming the countryside of Sicily after a colossal defeat in 413 were offered food and drink after singing sections from his odes, and that prisoners of war were even released after reciting passages.

Euripides' Athens

Euripides life stretched across the majority of the fifth century BCE, a period generally seen as the heyday of Classical Athens. Greece at the time was not a country per se, but a collection of various city states, or *poleis*, held in a network of alliances and rivalries. During the two Persian invasions of 490 BCE and 480–479 BCE, many of these city states had joined forces to drive out the Persians, and Athens had been instrumentally important at battles such as Marathon (490 BCE) and Salamis (480 BCE). There is even a tradition that Euripides was born on the day of Salamis, but this is probably apocryphal. Although Athens suffered huge damage, including the evacuation of its population and the destruction of the Acropolis, it became the head of an anti-Persian alliance known as the Delian League. This developed into an empire with most of the states giving up their navies and paying Athens tribute in return for protection. The imposing Parthenon which was built on the ruined Acropolis is testament to Athens' wealth and power at the time. This growth in Athenian might, however, led to tension with Sparta and the Peloponnesian states (see Figure 3) which resulted in the Peloponnesian War (431–404 BCE), a conflict which Athens ultimately lost. *Hippolytus* was produced in 428 BCE, three years into the war, and the year after the famous Athenian general Pericles was killed by a devastating plague.

Since the end of the sixth century, Athens had been a democracy. It differed, however, from modern representative democracies in which we elect politicians, because all adult male citizens were eligible to attend, vote and speak at meetings of the Assembly (the *Ekklesia*). The Assembly held sovereign power and 6,000 people were required for some important votes, out of a total citizen population of 30,000–60,000. There were also more than three times as many non-citizens who were not enfranchised (e.g. women, slaves, foreigners, children). There was also a smaller group called the Council (the *Boule*) which was made up of 500 citizens over the age of thirty selected by lot each year to oversee daily affairs in the city. For a tenth of the year, in groups of fifty, each member of the Council served in the *Prytany*, the body in charge of calling meetings of the Assembly and the Council. Each day a different member of the *Prytany*, selected by lot, was selected to chair meetings. In addition to the Council, over 500 other political offices were decided by lottery each year. One of these was the Eponymous Archon, who gave his name to the year, performed certain legal duties and arranged dramatic festivals. The selection of officials by lot meant that most Athenian citizens would have performed a duty for the state at some point in their lives, revealing how radically state management was divided. Ten generals each year, however, were elected by the Assembly rather than chosen by lot. This provided an opportunity for individuals to gain more permanent influence and allowed a figure like Pericles to gain huge power. Alongside tribute from other cities, state activities were partly funded by wealthy individuals who were assigned an item of public expenditure (called a 'liturgy') according to their wealth, for example funding a trireme or a tragic performance. Courts were managed by magistrates but decisions were made by citizen juries, at their smallest comprised of 200 people, but sometimes numbering over 1,000.

An appreciation of the special characteristics of Athenian political organization is fundamental to building up an understanding of Athenian tragedy. Attendance at dramatic performances was a communal activity and an important part of the political life of the city. Many citizens even participated more actively, as members of the chorus for example. Poets were seen to hold an important role in terms of the collective instruction and improvement of the city. In *Frogs* Euripides claims that a poet should be admired for 'cleverness and giving good advice and for making the men in the cities better' (*Frogs* 1009–1010). Athenian citizens were used to listening to, evaluating and collectively participating in political debate. Tragedy, too, puts special emphasis on speech, persuasion and argument in order to subject principles and ideas to scrutiny in a public arena.

The wealth and power of Athens also led to it becoming a melting pot of new ideas and a centre of learning and culture in the Greek world. Athens was a favoured location of a number of travelling intellectuals and teachers, known as 'sophist's. They each had their own specialisms and were concerned with a huge variety of subjects including science, maths, ethics, grammar and philosophy. The study of rhetoric as a discipline *per se* is said to have developed in mid-fifth-century Sicily under two men called Corax and Tisias, and many sophists were particularly interested in the power of language and argumentation. We still possess the work of a sophist called Gorgias whose *Encomium of Helen*, for example, revels in displaying clever argumentative techniques to further a seemingly weak position. Euripides' plays share the questioning intellectualism of the sophists and their interest in the power of language. However, while they were hugely influential in the development of Greek thought, some sources criticize the sophists for advancing potentially dangerous moral positions and for being concerned with clever persuasion and deception rather than truth-seeking. Similar criticisms were levelled at Euripides and his characters by Aristophanes. Indeed, characters like the Nurse in *Hippolytus*, who is condemned for her 'overly fine words' (487) can be understood better when viewed in the context of this intellectual culture.

Athenian tragedy

Hippolytus was first performed at a five-day long festival in March called the City Dionysia, in honour of Dionysus, the god of theatre and wine. Business was put on hold, people from the countryside travelled in and camped near the city, all crimes were treated as sacrilege, law courts were closed and some prisoners were even released. Its position at the start of the sailing season may have allowed even more to attend. The excitement was even greater given that, unlike now, theatre could only be watched at certain times in the year.

Before the festival, the *Eponymous Archon* (see 'Euripides' Athens') selected playwrights based on their proposed plays, hired actors, and chose a *choregos* for each playwright. The *choregos* was a wealthy individual who took on the cost of the plays (an example of a liturgy) and was responsible for organizing the training the chorus. The professional actors were trained by the playwright himself. Citizens chosen by lot voted on which set of plays was the best. An ivy crown was given jointly to the winning playwright and the *choregos* and their names were put on official lists and monuments, showing the huge honour in which they were held.

When it comes to the sequence of events at the festival, it is important to note that much of our evidence comes from the fourth century and many of the details are disputed (see Csapo and Slater 1995). On the first day of the festival there was probably a ceremony announcing the poets and plays and a procession through Athens to the theatre of Dionysus carrying sacred objects (including phalluses) and offerings which ended with a huge sacrifice to the god and celebratory revels. Men and boys also competed singing ecstatic choral hymns to Dionysus in groups of fifty (the dithyramb). The following three days may have been devoted to tragic performances, while the final day may have been reserved for comedy. Each day of tragedy was devoted to one dramatist who presented three tragedies followed by a satyr play. This was a lighter form of entertainment which presented a mythological story with a chorus of satyrs, faun-like followers of Dionysus who were often drunk and lecherous. Before the plays began on day two there was a grand opening ceremony. The ten generals poured a libation to Dionysus, names were read out of citizens who had performed outstanding services to the state, the tribute provided by states in the Athenian empire was displayed and there was a parade of war orphans who were being brought up at state expense. All these rituals combine civic, religious, martial and imperial symbolism underlining yet again the centrality of the Athenian *polis* to Greek tragedy.

The theatre of Dionysus was in the open air on the slopes of the Acropolis (see Figure 1). Seating was on wooden benches and the audience may have numbered around 15,000 which makes it one of the biggest gatherings in the Greek world. The atmosphere would have been more similar to that of a music festival or a football match than that of a modern theatre. Seating may have been divided into the ten different Athenian tribes (an administrative division of the population), and special seating was provided for the members of the Council, war orphans brought up by the state, certain priests and officials and foreign ambassadors. The arrangement of the audience highlighted the sense that it represented the whole of the *demos* and its values, and it was a shared, communal experience at heart.

The main performance space where the chorus danced and sang was an area called the *orchestra*. Later the *orchestra* became circular but some scholars now think it was more rectangular in the fifth century (see Figures 1 and 2). At the back of the *orchestra* there was a painted wooden structure (the *skene)* with a door in the centre. It often represented a palace and inside actors could change and props and costumes could be stored. The location represented was usually fixed for the duration of the play. There was also a ladder and trap door which allowed actors to perform from the roof of the *skene*. At some point a small raised stage (*logeion*) for the actors was added, but before this they would have performed in the *orchestra* with the chorus. There were entrances on both sides called *eisodoi*, allowing the chorus and actors to enter and exit. There were also two pieces of stage machinery: the *ekkyklema*

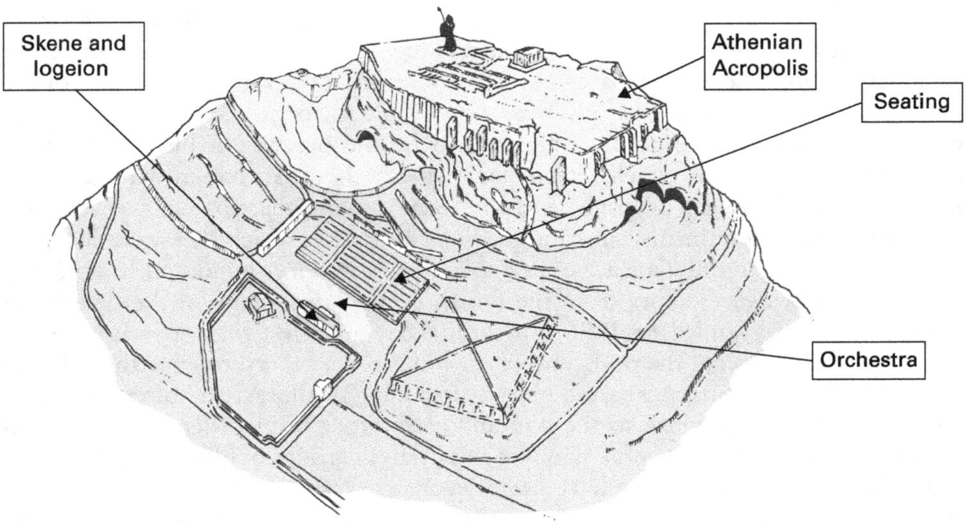

FIGURE 1 *An artist's impression of the Theatre of Dionysus as it might have looked in the fifth century.*

was a wheeled platform which was often used to bring out dead bodies (including Phaedra's corpse in *Hippolytus*) or other tableaux, and a crane-like device called a *mechane* allowed actors, often those playing gods, to be suspended. The text does not contain any stage directions but as you read the text, try to think beyond the words on the page by considering how one might stage the action of the play.

Tragedies began with a *prologue*, in which one or two characters established the context of the play, providing background information and introducing the characters. After this, the chorus entered by the sides singing an ode called the *parodos* and usually remained in the *orchestra* until the end of the play. Then sections of dialogue between characters (*episodes*) alternated with choral songs called *stasima*. The action portrayed in tragedy usually lasted for no longer than one day (Aeschylus' *Eumenides* is an exception to this), but the choral odes allowed for the passing of time within this. The final section was the *exodos* which concluded the drama. During one of the episodes, there was a messenger speech which brought news or reported (often violent) off-stage action. There was also often a section called the *agon*, a formal debate speech between two characters with a law-court feel.

At the time of Euripides, only three actors with speaking roles were used, so actors would sometimes have to double up parts. However, mute actors could be employed as children or attendants, for example. All actors were men, and they wore masks and costumes to aid character identification. Due to the size of the audience, they had to be able to project their voices effectively as well as employ large gestures to express visual meaning. Most of the actors' lines were spoken in poetic metre but they also had solo passages of singing (*monodies*) or sung exchanges with the chorus. Dialogue could be in a long set speech (*rhesis*) or in shorter exchanges between characters. *Stichomythia*, when characters exchange one line of verse each, is often employed in particularly dramatic or tense sections.

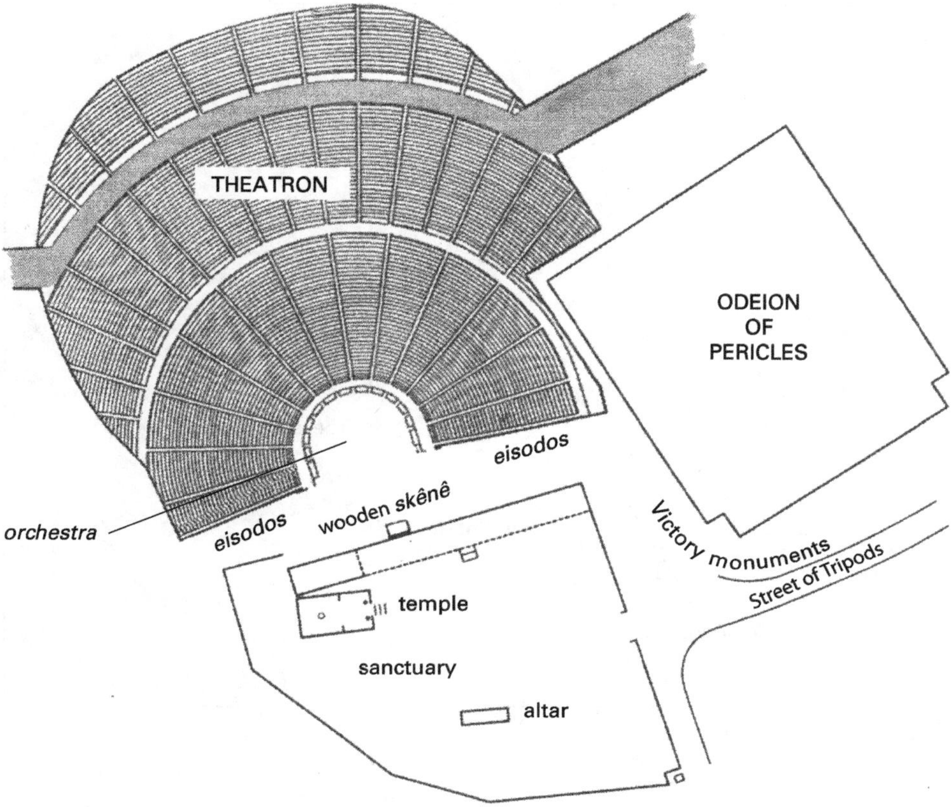

FIGURE 2 *A plan of the Theatre of Dionysus in the late fourth century.*

The chorus was a hugely important part of tragedy and one of the most challenging features of ancient dramas for modern audiences. Choral performance was a hugely important part of ancient culture and fundamental to civic identity. In addition to the 600 or so people required for the dithyrambs and tragic choruses at each *City Dionysia*, group singing and dancing was also part of funerals, weddings, military training, celebration of athletic victories and religious processions. In his *Laws*, Plato even describes the uneducated man as someone without experience of choral singing. Tragedy itself probably developed out of choral singing and a herald proclaimed, 'Bring on your chorus!' to signal the start of each day's plays.

Each tragic chorus comprised fifteen male citizens who remained in the orchestra for most of the play. They represented a group of characters who could engage in dialogue with the actors but could only participate in the action to a limited extent. The main chorus in *Hippolytus* was a group of fifteen married women of the city of Troezen (see Figure 3), but there was also an (atypical) secondary chorus of Hippolytus' attendants who appear at the beginning and end of the play. As well as providing scene breaks and time for the actors to change, the choral odes were a huge part of the spectacle. They were accompanied as they sang and danced by an instrument called the *aulos*, a reed instrument with two pipes which sounded a bit

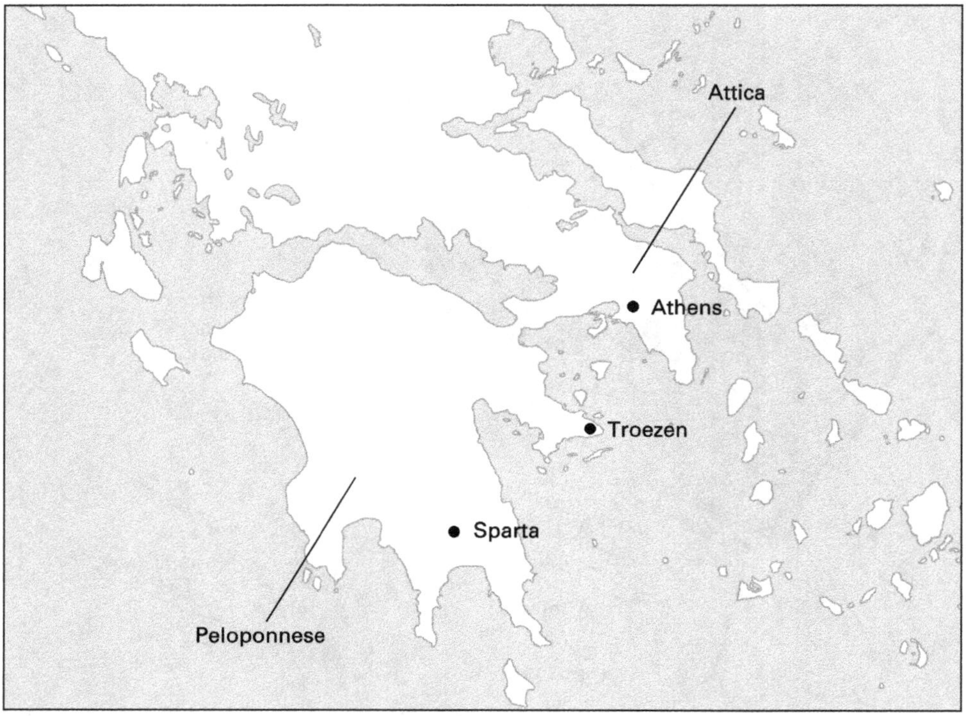

FIGURE 3 *Map of Greece.*

like a bagpipe. The complex metres give us some clue as to the rhythm but melody and dance steps are harder to reconstruct. However, each ode was made up of pairs of stanzas (the *strophe* and the *antistrophe*) which correspond with the chorus' movement in one direction across the stage, and then a retracing of their steps. The choral odes also contained more poetic language and use the Doric dialect of Greek (the dialogue is in Attic Greek, the dialect used by Athenians), perhaps because of the Peloponnesian origins of choral song.

However, the tragic chorus provides more than mere spectacle. A playwright was able to change the focus of a play based on his choice of chorus. If the primary chorus in *Hippolytus* had been Hippolytus' attendants, for example, pity for Phaedra's situation may have been far less natural a response. They were able to help set the scene, refer to wider events which put things in context, commentate on the action and characters' arguments, provide collective moral insight, help change the atmosphere, or heighten the dramatic tension. They are no 'ideal audience' and should not be viewed as a window into the playwright's opinions or the mindset of the Athenian spectators. Choruses have their own agenda and morality, and their knowledge is sometimes limited. However, they can provide another filter and viewpoint on the events of the play for the audience to consider and examine critically as they form their own judgments.

Synopsis

Background

Theseus is the King of Athens. His mother is the mortal Aethra, but tradition assigns him both a mortal (Aegeus) and divine (Poseidon) father. To atone for killing his uncle Pallas and his fifty sons, Theseus and his wife Phaedra have gone into exile for a year in Troezen. Here Hippolytus, the product of Theseus' rape of an Amazon named Antiope, is being raised by Pittheus (Aethra's father). The play is set outside the palace in Troezen (see Figure 3), and on stage there may have been statues of Artemis and Aphrodite on either side of the central door.

1–120 Prologue

Aphrodite explains how Hippolytus has shown her dishonour by calling her the worst of the gods and rejecting sex and marriage. In revenge, she has filled Phaedra with passion for her stepson. Phaedra is currently suffering in silence, but Aphrodite will soon be reveal all to Theseus, who will cause his son's death by invoking a curse given to him by his father Poseidon. Phaedra will maintain her good reputation but will also die. To Aphrodite, she is nothing but collateral damage.

Hippolytus and a band of attendants return from the hunt, singing a hymn to Artemis. Hippolytus offers a garland and a personal prayer to Artemis which underlines his devotion to her but also his arrogant belief in his own superiority.

A servant tries to persuade Hippolytus to honour Aphrodite, but he is tersely rejected. The servant prays that Aphrodite will overlook Hippolytus' youthful rashness.

121–169 Parode

The chorus, fifteen Troezenian women, enter singing the first choral ode. They explain how, while washing clothes, they heard a rumour of Phaedra's sickness and speculate on its causes. The domestic, female tone of the ode contrasts with the earlier religious song of Hippolytus' band of male followers.

170–524 First Episode

Phaedra is brought from the palace on a couch by the Nurse. The Nurse laments Phaedra's changeable condition and her inability to help. Phaedra frantically cries out that she wants to be taken hunting, but suddenly shows embarrassment, asks to be covered and falls silent again. The Nurse begs Phaedra to explain her illness and eventually pressures Phaedra into revealing her love for Hippolytus through a ritual supplication (see note on line 324).

Phaedra's tone becomes rational and she explains her decision to commit suicide in order to save her reputation. While the Nurse's initial reaction to hearing of Phaedra's love was to dramatically wish for death, she now pulls herself together, and by arguing that such feelings are not extraordinary or without remedy, she undermines Phaedra's resolve. The Nurse cryptically suggests she has a love potion which will solve the issue and Phaedra passively accepts the Nurse's help.

525–564 First Stasimon

The Chorus sing of the destructive power of Eros and Aphrodite.

565–731 Second Episode

Through the palace doors Phaedra overhears Hippolytus' angry reaction as the Nurse reveals her passion. When Hippolytus and the Nurse enter, Phaedra remains cowering at the side of the stage but invisible to them. Hippolytus reveals that he has sworn an oath not to reveal Phaedra's feelings to anyone, makes a strong speech in which he wishes women did not exist, and then storms off.

Phaedra, fearing that Hippolytus will tell Theseus, laments her fate. She condemns the Nurse and sends her away despite her protestations. Phaedra makes the Chorus promise to conceal everything they have witnessed, then reveals that she has a solution which will keep her reputation intact and teach Hippolytus moderation.

732–775 Second Stasimon

The chorus express a desire to escape, reminisce about Phaedra's ill-fated marriage and lament her imminent suicide.

776–1101 Third Episode

From within the Nurse cries that Phaedra has been found hanged. Suddenly, Theseus returns from the oracle wearing a wreath and expecting a happy welcome. Phaedra's suicide is revealed to him and the corpse is wheeled out on the *ekkyklema*. Theseus laments her death but discovers a tablet hanging from her hand which claims that Hippolytus has raped her. Theseus prays to Poseidon that Hippolytus will not see another day, using one of the curses Poseidon has granted him. He also proclaims that Hippolytus is to be exiled from the land, in case the curse does not work.

Hippolytus enters and is shocked to see Phaedra's corpse. In the play's *agon* Theseus accuses him of the crime and Hippolytus attempts to refute his father's arguments. However, he is restricted in what he can say by his honourable desire not to break the oath of silence he swore to the Nurse. Hippolytus realizes that Theseus is fixed in his decision, and bids farewell to the land of Troezen.

1102–1150 Third Stasimon

The chorus, in alternation with Hippolytus' followers, express their angst at the unpredictability of human fate, as well as grief and anger at Hippolytus' exile.

1151–1267 Fourth Episode

The messenger, one of Hippolytus' companions, enters and Theseus is summoned. He describes how Hippolytus' friends gathered, readied their horses and accompanied him into exile. Suddenly they heard a roar and a bull burst out of the sea, pursuing Hippolytus' chariot until its wheels were smashed. Hippolytus, tangled in the reins, was violently dragged along the ground by his own horses. The bull and horses then magically disappeared. Hippolytus has been freed from the wreckage, but he is now on the point of death.

1268–1282 Fourth Stasimon

The chorus briefly sing of the power of Aphrodite and Eros.

1283–1466 Exodos

Artemis appears and explains to Theseus the truth of Hippolytus' innocence. Hippolytus is then brought in, delirious and writhing in pain. He recognizes Artemis, who reveals to him that his destruction was Aphrodite's plan. Artemis says she will punish one of Aphrodite's favourites in return and promises that Hippolytus will become a cult hero for young women to venerate before their marriages. However, Artemis claims that she will not be defiled by witnessing his death and coldly leaves him to his suffering. After expressing forgiveness for his father, and a moving exchange of tender words between the two of them, Hippolytus dies in Theseus' arms.

The other Hippolytus

Our *Hippolytus* was actually the second play which Euripides wrote on the same myth and is the only example of an Athenian playwright revisiting earlier material. According to Aristophanes of Byzantium (writing around 200 BCE) the play was unsuccessful due to its portrayal of 'unseemly material'. We possess only small fragments of the play, which is usually called *Hippolytus Kalyptomenos (Hippolytus Veiled)*. Its name derives from a scene in which Hippolytus attempted to hide his face as Phaedra declared her intentions to him. Nowhere in our *Hippolytus* is Phaedra so direct, and it appears that the biggest difference between the two plays was its presentation of Phaedra as immorally lustful, rather than torn by her desire to act correctly and maintain her reputation. When Euripides is criticized in Aristophanes' *Frogs* (see 'Euripides') for including 'whores like Phaedra' in his work it is a presentation presumably coloured by this earlier play.

While details are unclear, the overall plot seems to have been relatively similar with the main difference being that Phaedra directly revealed the information to Hippolytus rather than the Nurse taking matters into her own hands on Phaedra's behalf. Fragments reveal that Phaedra may even have suggested that Hippolytus should oust his father and declare himself ruler. However, it is not clear how Phaedra communicated to Theseus that Hippolytus had raped her or how she killed herself, although she probably committed suicide after Hippolytus' death. The exact role of the Nurse is very uncertain, and the function of the gods is also unclear, but the chorus was still comprised of women of Troezen. Theseus' presentation also may have been even less sympathetic. His willingness to believe a character as brazen as the original Phaedra cannot have worked in his favour. While Theseus in our version cursed Hippolytus with the first of his three wishes from Poseidon, it is likely that Theseus used his third wish in *Hippolytus Kalyptomenos*, which would have made him far more certain of its efficacy. Furthermore, at the start of our version play Theseus was absent on a visit to the Oracle, whereas in the earlier play he may have been in Hades attempting to abduct the Queen of the Underworld (in line with earlier traditions), a far less pious activity.

While we cannot reconstruct the earlier play completely, the difference between the plays does reveal the extent to which tragedians possessed real flexibility even when presenting traditional mythological stories, which allowed them to present characters differently, emphasize certain ideas and even invent or adapt details of the plot. Traditional versions of the myth also presented Phaedra in a far more negative light, so it is important to remember that the more nuanced and sympathetic portrayal of her in our *Hippolytus*, and the more complex moral picture in general, is very much a Euripidean invention and one which may have subverted audience expectations.

Characters

Hippolytus is striking in that the lines are shared almost equally between the four main characters. Part of what makes *Hippolytus* such an engaging piece of drama is that each character exhibits a mixture of positive and negative traits and motivations, and none is truly innocent. What follows is a brief character sketch of each figure, but it should not be seen as an exhaustive summary. It should be remembered that each person who engages with the text will form a different impression of each character and Greek audiences too would have left the theatre with a whole range of responses. It is advisable to read the play first so that you can form your own judgments before reading what follows.

Hippolytus is presented as an incredibly pious young man. His speech to Artemis (73–87) shows an impressive devotion to the goddess and his refusal to break his oath of silence to Phaedra, even when it leads to his own exile and death, also shows a commitment to right action. He also shows a forgiveness for his father at the end of the play. However, balanced against this piety is a rigidity and a belief in his own superiority. He claims that he 'alone of mortals' (84) is pure enough to associate and converse with Artemis and tells Theseus that there is 'no man more virtuous' (994–995) than he. The selectivity of his worship and belief in his own purity is taken to an extreme as he arrogantly rejects Aphrodite and vows celibacy, claiming that 'no god which is worshipped at night is pleasing' (106) to him. Although male celibacy is part of the Christian religious tradition, it was not really a feature of ancient Greek religion. Marriage and procreation were seen as essential citizen duties. While he believes he is showing self-control and virtue through his celibacy, Hippolytus' refusal to come to terms with his own sexuality, and his denial of such an important part of human experience, is an extreme position which reveals a lack of moderation and self-control. His furious attack on women, delivered after the audience have been conditioned to sympathize with Phaedra, provides another example of a character lacking in moderation.

Hippolytus' youth is also an important part of his character. His attendant links his age to his inability to see nuance and balance in the world when he claims that 'the young should not be imitated when they think in this way' (114–115). Hippolytus is also shown as unwilling to make the transition into the adult world, which for the Greeks involved marriage to a woman and the production of a family, even if there may be a hint at 640–641 that he desires to marry eventually. Hippolytus' love of sport and hunting, as well as his company of young male followers, is reminiscent of the sorts of communal exercise undertaken by young Athenian men, but his tragic death leaves him frozen forever in this liminal stage. The third choral ode, sung in alternation between the male and female choruses, enacts an interaction between the two sexes which draws attention to Hippolytus' failure to reconcile himself to the existence of women. However, Hippolytus' failure to enter adulthood also provides an example which benefits the wider community: Artemis promises that in death Hippolytus will become a cult hero and that girls before their weddings will offer locks of their hair to him (1423–1429) as they lament the passing of the previous stage of their lives and look forward to the next step.

The presentation of **Phaedra** focuses on her desire to act virtuously and preserve her reputation, in contrast with her characterization in *Hippolytus Kalyptomenos*. While she is inflamed by shameful love for her stepson, her feelings are caused by Aphrodite and out of her control, and she resolves to die rather than act on her passion. She is a chaste and virtuous Greek wife and mother who clearly loves her children (315) and is keen not to be seen doing harm to Theseus (321). Although at the start of the play she is presented as thrashing wildly and out of her mind, she regains control of herself and refuses to speak. While she does eventually reveal the truth, this is only after the Nurse applies force through a ritual supplication and weakens her resolve through clever and ambiguous arguments. Hippolytus himself describes her as having 'acted virtuously' (1034) even after she has indicted him, and Artemis acknowledges that Phaedra was 'destroyed by the nurse's machinations' (1304–1305) and retained her honour despite her passion (1300–1301).

Part of Phaedra's virtue comes from the huge importance she attaches to reputation, both for her and her children, and for how she is seen by others. She expresses a wish 'neither to be unnoticed when doing good things nor have many witnesses when doing disgraceful things' (403–404) although the Nurse is of the opinion that her 'overly-exacting conduct in life' (261–263) is what damages her. Phaedra also shows that she is a calm, rational thinker of real rhetorical skill when she initially outlines her decision to kill herself and explores the reasons why humans commit immoral actions in her first speech (373–430). However, she shows deception, vindictiveness, and a willingness to sacrifice Hippolytus to save her own reputation when she leaves her dishonest message to Theseus. Her final words show an almost sadistic pleasure as she hopes that Hippolytus will 'share in her disease and learn to be moderate' (729–730). When she does this, her actions are perhaps more understandable given that she has just heard Hippolytus' misogynistic tirade and is working on the (misplaced) assumption that he will not keep his oath of silence.

The **Nurse** is a fantastic example of Euripides giving more focus to low-born characters (she has the second-highest number of lines in the play after Hippolytus himself), and her flexible pragmatism is a brilliant foil for both Phaedra's virtuousness and Hippolytus' inflexibility. She is persistent and manipulative, using a combination of ritual supplication and sophistic arguments to sway Phaedra (see 'Euripides' Athens'). Her speech uses poetic language (447–450) as well as references to literature and mythology (451–458) in order to prevail upon Phaedra, who describes her words as 'overly fine' (487). When she convinces Phaedra by ambiguous talk of love potions it is unclear whether even she herself actually has something in mind (517). She is also untrustworthy, as despite Phaedra's direct request not to mention her passion to Hippolytus (520) she betrays her confidence.

She does, however, love and want to help her mistress and expresses real distress when she is unable to assist (176–177) and her decision to tell Hippolytus is founded on her belief that she can remedy the situation. She is pragmatically focused on finding a solution with less concern for moral standards, claiming that Phaedra should yield to her desires (501). This is linked to her belief that perfectionism in life is unattainable (467) and that Phaedra is destroying herself by setting unrealistic standards (439). She also shows a degree of flexibility and is able to adapt her approach quickly. Her initial reaction when Phaedra admits her love for Hippolytus is hugely emotional, claiming she will jump off a cliff (356–357). However, she subsequently notes that 'second thoughts are wiser' (436) and claims that Phaedra's love is nothing remarkable' (437). However, it is also possible to interpret this flexibility as a dangerously impulsive volatility.

Theseus shows real love and grief for his wife at her death, crashing into despair after his return from the oracle joyfully wearing a garland. He is a man of decisive action and is proud of his reputation for administering justice based on his killing of dangerous brigands such as Sinis and Sciron (976–980). However, he is rash and hasty in his denunciation of Hippolytus when he discovers Phaedra's letter, claiming that he has been 'clearly convicted by the dead woman' (945) even before Hippolytus has made his case. He angrily curses his son with death and then exiles him even when Hippolytus protests that he deserves more time (1051) and a fairer trial (1056). The debate (*agon*) over Hippolytus' guilt is highly dysfunctional, with Theseus showing little real knowledge of his son's personality by claiming that Aphrodite must have 'stirred up [his] young mind' (969) to passion. As he casts his son out, he shows no love and 'no pity' (1089) for his exile, and Hippolytus later says that Theseus' anger was so great he could have killed him (1413). When he hears about his son's death at first, he jokingly speculates that he was killed by another man whose wife he had raped (1164–1165) which again shows little real understanding of his son's character. That said, the play's final scene does show his ability to repent and express remorse. As Hippolytus dies he laments that there is no more pleasure in life for him (1408) and he praises Hippolytus for his 'pious and noble mind' (1454).

Considerations

What follows is a quick rundown of some of the major ideas explored in the play. It is not intended to be a complete summary, but more a springboard for consideration and class discussion.

Gods

Aphrodite's opening speech predicts much of the action of the play, and it would be easy to see this as diminishing its dramatic power. However, the key features of the story would have been familiar to the audience and Aphrodite's revelation is only partial. She does not even mention the Nurse and is even incorrect when she states that she will reveal the truth to Theseus (42) when it is actually Artemis who appears at the end of the play. In fact, this partial revelation creates excitement as the play opens and contributes to much of the dramatic irony which heightens its tension. It would also be possible to see Aphrodite's orchestration of events as lessening the importance of the human actions which make up the majority of the drama. Of course, the play is concerned with the punishment of a mortal for their excessive pride towards a goddess. However, it is not just the gods who impact the action. Hippolytus' narcissism, Phaedra's desire for her reputation, the Nurse taking matters into her own hands and Theseus' rashness are all part of the play's machinery. Artemis herself claims that 'it is likely that men will make mistakes when the gods bring it about' (1433–1434). This combination of supernatural forces and human motivations and actions in shaping the drama is sometimes known as double determinism.

The play also explores the morality of the gods and whether their behaviour should conform to human standards. Hippolytus is criticized by his attendant for being 'arrogant' (93) because he does not show enough respect to a 'proud goddess' (99); on each of these occasions the word *semnos* (holy, proud, arrogant) is used which suggests that the same quality which is acceptable in Aphrodite is not permitted for a mortal. His attendant also believes that Aphrodite 'should have forgiveness' (117) for Hippolytus and that 'gods should be wiser than mortals' (120) but his hopes do not seem to be borne out. Aphrodite is horrifically vindictive in her destruction of Hippolytus and treats Phaedra as collateral damage (48–50). Poseidon, by fulfilling Theseus' wish, brings about Hippolytus' painful death. Although Artemis reveals the truth to Theseus and urges him to forgive his son, she still vows that she will get revenge on Aphrodite by punishing her favourite mortal Adonis (1420–1422), and her relationship with Hippolytus is so one-sided that she can leave their 'long friendship' (1441) with ease before he dies. After Artemis' departure, as Hippolytus dies in his father's arms we are ultimately left with a picture of human love and tenderness in contrast to the ruthlessness and unforgiving nature of the gods.

Moderation

The concept of *sophrosyne* (σωφροσύνη) is important in *Hippolytus*. It can literally be translated as 'safe-mindedness' but there is not really a direct English translation.

It mixes together ideas of 'good sense', 'moderation', 'self-control' (often over physical desires), but also 'virtue' in general. The play explores the concept by presenting the characters' different understandings of the idea. Hippolytus tells Theseus that 'there is no man more *sophron* (σώφρων)' than him (994–995) because of his piety, the virtuous company he keeps and his virginity. However, he fails to see that his excessive devotion to Artemis and rejection of Aphrodite are far from moderate, and that his absolute hatred of sex and women is an extreme position. There is a paradox here as it is Hippolytus' excessive commitment to being *sophron* which means he is unable to see the balance in the world and is therefore lacking in *sophrosyne*. He condemns women for lacking *sophrosyne* (667) but at the same time shows little self-control of his furious emotions as he wishes he can 'always trample on' women (668).

Phaedra seems to show little self-control when she first appears, frantically begging the Nurse to allow her to run through the woods. Her passion is described by the Nurse as a disease (294) and it is out of her control. However, in her refusal to give into temptation or reveal her passion, and her reasoned defence of her decision to commit suicide, it is possible to see self-control. Phaedra herself also says that she conquered her passion with moderation (399) and even Hippolytus admits that she paradoxically behaved with virtue in killing herself even though she was not a virtuous person (1034–1035). The Nurse criticizes Phaedra for being overly concerned with her reputation and acting virtuously (261–266), claiming that it is this excessiveness which is destroying her. She states the common Greek maxim 'μηδὲν ἄγαν' ('nothing in excess' – 265) suggesting the importance of balance and sees sex as a natural part of life. However, her understanding of moderation is also problematic as she uses this argument to encourage Phaedra to give into her passion and temptation, and she later admits that in telling Hippolytus she did not show *sophrosyne* (704). The gods too do not show a huge amount of moderation, but as we have discussed, the play explores the degree to which we should expect them to act according to human morality.

Women and reputation

It has been argued that ancient societies were usually 'shame cultures', in which negative behaviour was discouraged by societal pressure and the fear of the judgment of others, while modern society is more often an example of 'guilt culture', in which one's own conscience and internalized belief system hinder immoral actions. Clearly it is far more complex than this, but it is true that many characters in *Hippolytus* express concern for how they are seen by others. Phaedra, most obviously, is concerned with not damaging the reputation of her and her children. She is first introduced by Aphrodite as possessing a 'good reputation' ('εὐκλεής' – 26) and she is afraid of the consequences of damaging this, claiming that if she gets a bad reputation it will 'enslave' (424) her sons. Her decision to commit suicide is based on preserving this, and when the Nurse tells Hippolytus about her passion, she fears that she will 'no longer die with a good reputation' (687–688). Hippolytus is also concerned with his reputation for virtue. The chorus refer to him as the 'brightest star' of Greece (1123) and Artemis reveals the truth so that Hippolytus will die with a 'good reputation' (1299). Theseus is concerned that the reputation he has built up by ridding the land of brigands like Sinis and Sciron (976–980) will be destroyed if he doesn't bring justice on Hippolytus. The Nurse too talks about the reputation for intelligence which she would have won if her plan had succeeded (700–701). As has already been mentioned, the Nurse also acknowledges the damaging potential of putting too much store on others' perception (261–266). When she encourages Phaedra to give in to her passion provided it is done in secret (462–466) she draws attention to one of the tensions in shame culture: one's reputation is based on external appearance, but appearances can be deceiving.

Phaedra also acknowledges the societal double standards and entrenched misogyny which mean her reputation is far more susceptible to damage than that of men. She claims that as a woman she is 'an object of hatred for everyone' (407) revealing the difficulty of retaining a good reputation. Theseus too suggests that men who give free rein to their lust suffer less disapproval due to their gender (970) and the double standards are perhaps confirmed when the messenger tells Theseus that even if every woman was hanged and the forest was filled with writing, he would not believe Hippolytus was bad (1250–1254). The very fact that the first version of the play was deemed so shocking because of Phaedra's forwardness also gives a sense of the male anxiety about female sexuality.

While it is difficult to summarize, this anxiety is partly due to the fact that when a woman married a man, she brought a foreign and unknown influence into her new family. She might have loyalties to her old family, the paternity of her children could never be confirmed, and it was felt that women could be a drain on resources and offer little. Women were also seen as less in control of their feelings (lacking σωφροσύνη). Many of these attitudes are echoed in Hippolytus' rant and this anxiety might also help explain the number of dangerous female figures in Greek literature, such as Medea or Clytemnestra in tragedy, or the Sirens and Circe in the *Odyssey*. Women in Athens were very limited in freedoms: as well as being politically disenfranchised, they also spent their lives under the legal power of the male head of their household (usually a father or husband). It would certainly not be true to call Euripides a feminist, but his plays often explore the status and position of women in a society which was theoretically based on the equality and freedom of its male citizens.

Communication and knowledge

Characters' different levels of knowledge affect their ability to bring about positive outcomes. Theseus most clearly acts based on the false information in Phaedra's tablet, and his failure to understand his son's unbending chastity leads him to accuse him of rape. The Nurse is ignorant of Phaedra's situation at the beginning of the play, and her lack of understanding about Hippolytus' nature also causes her to believe he will reciprocate Phaedra's feelings. Hippolytus also fails to recognize Phaedra's virtue because he never communicates with her directly. The audience is also often in a position of superior knowledge when compared to the characters. Aphrodite's prologue contributes to this, but we are also privy to conversations which are hidden from other characters. While the audience is not omniscient and can still be surprised by unexpected events such as Theseus' return, such dramatic irony adds to the plays tension and heightens its emphasis on knowledge and judgement.

Deceit and ineffective communication are also a cause of many of the problems. The Nurse's arguments are clever and manipulative, and her ambiguous words about love potions also lead to Phaedra foolishly putting herself in the Nurse's hands. Phaedra's tablet is another example of deceitful communication and the *agon* between Theseus and Hippolytus lacks vital information which makes it dysfunctional and ineffective. Hippolytus' misogynistic tirade also leads to Phaedra believing he will break his oath of silence. Hippolytus wishes that women's attendants were beasts who could not talk (646–648) because of the damaging power of their words. He also acknowledges the difficulty of ever knowing a person's true intentions when he tells the Nurse that although his 'tongue swore' his 'mind is not bound by oath' (612).

The interplay of speech and silence is also important and the consequences of not speaking are often as bad as speaking. At first Phaedra is dying in silence and the Nurse has to force her to speak. Phaedra directly tells the Nurse not to speak to Hippolytus, but the Nurse does so anyway. Phaedra and Hippolytus never speak directly to each other. Theseus pays more attention to Phaedra's silent corpse and the mute tablet which seems to be 'crying out' (877) than he does to his own son's words. The oaths of silence taken by Hippolytus and the chorus (712–713) prevent Theseus from realizing the truth of Hippolytus' actions, and Hippolytus wishes that the palace itself could speak and reveal the truth (1074–1075).

Constructive communication is only really seen at the end of the play. Artemis' words bring about the resolution between Theseus and his father and predict the cult of Hippolytus which provides some consolation for his death. The words of forgiveness and love between Hippolytus and Theseus at the end of the play, even if they cannot avert his death, do lead to reconciliation and closure.

Language and metre

Athenian tragedy is a verse form whose language differs from that of Attic prose such as history writing or oratory. Most grammar will be the same as the Greek you have been learning, but some of the important differences are listed here:

- Less strictness with the use of the definite article. When translating into English, the word 'the' may be used when it does not appear in the Greek.
- The dative plural endings -αισι(ν) and -οισι(ν) may be used instead of -αις and -οις.
- The pronoun νιν is used instead of αὐτόν or αὐτήν.
- Two-syllable prepositions may sometimes come after their nouns. When this happens the accent moves onto the first syllable, a phenomenon called antistrophe (e.g. περὶ ἀνδρός becomes ἀνδρὸς πέρι).
- Frequent use of elision (e.g. παρ' οἷσι instead of παρὰ οἷσι).
- Crasis, where two words merge vowel sounds to form one word (e.g. κοὐδέν for καὶ οὐδὲν), often starting with καί or the definite article.
- Simple verb forms used rather than compound forms (e.g. θνήσκω rather than ἀποθνήσκω).
- Poetic and unusual choices of vocabulary.

The choral odes and sung sections of tragedy are more poetic in style than the spoken sections. They also employ a huge range of different metres such as dochmiacs, for moments of high emotion, or anapaests, which give the feel of a march. They also differ from spoken sections as they are usually written in the Doric dialect, rather than the Attic dialect spoken by Athenians.

The whole of this prescription is in dialogue form rather than sung. Dialogue in tragedy is written in a metre called **iambic trimeter**, which was supposed to capture best the rhythms of normal speech. There is no rhyme in Greek poetry. Instead, the rhythm is provided by an interplay between heavy (marked by –) and light (marked by ∪) syllables. Its basic unit is the iamb, a combination of a light and a heavy syllable (∪–), although there is variation too. Two iambs make up one iambic metron, and iambic trimeter is made of three iambic metra (hence tri‌meter). Therefore, even though it is called 'trimeter' the line is usually seen as having six feet. Even though English poetry tends to use stressed syllables rather than length of syllable, Shakespearean iambic pentameter (Shall *I* com*pare* thee *to* a *sum*mer's *day*?) uses the iamb as its basic unit too, so the feel of Greek iambic trimeter is not too alien to an English ear. While you are not expected to comment closely on the metrical features of the text at A Level, it is worth trying to read the Greek out loud as much as possible and as you become more practised you will begin to hear the iambic rhythm coming through. You will need to learn to scan (work out which syllables are heavy and light) iambic trimeter for the A Level language paper and if you are more interested in getting to grips with this feature of tragedy, a good summary is provided in the chapter on Aristophanes' *Frogs* in this edition.

Further reading

Barrett, W. S. (1964), *Euripides: Hippolytos*, Oxford: Oxford University Press.

Csapo, E. and W. J. Slater, eds (1995), *The Context of Ancient Drama*, An Arbor, MI: University of Michigan Press.

Easterling, P., ed. (1997), *Cambridge Companion to Greek Tragedy*, Cambridge: Cambridge University Press.

Ferguson, J. (1991), *Hippolytus*, London: Bloomsbury.

Halleran, M. R. (1995), *Euripides: Hippolytus*, Liverpool: Aris & Phillips.

Hancock, R., J. Renshaw and L. Swift (2017), *Greek Theatre and Imperial Image*, London: Bloomsbury.

Mills, S. (2002), *Euripides: Hippolytus*, London: Bloomsbury.

Morwood, J. (2016), *The Plays of Euripides*, London: Bloomsbury.

A note on the text

The text here has been taken from Diggle (1984) *Oxford Classical Texts: Euripidis Fabulae, Vol. 1* (Oxford University Press). The text produced here does not include a number of disputed lines which have been provided and translated in an appendix to the Commentary Notes.

Text

Τροφός ἐς πάντ᾽ ἀφῖγμαι κοὐδὲν εἴργασμαι πλέον.
οὐ μὴν ἀνήσω γ᾽ οὐδὲ νῦν προθυμίας,
ὡς ἂν παροῦσα καὶ σύ μοι ξυμμαρτυρῇς
οἵα πέφυκα δυστυχοῦσι δεσπόταις.
ἄγ᾽, ὦ φίλη παῖ, τῶν πάροιθε μὲν λόγων
λαθώμεθ᾽ ἄμφω, καὶ σύ θ᾽ ἡδίων γενοῦ
στυγνὴν ὀφρὺν λύσασα καὶ γνώμης ὁδόν,
ἐγώ θ᾽ ὅπῃ σοι μὴ καλῶς τόθ᾽ εἱπόμην
μεθεῖσ᾽ ἐπ᾽ ἄλλον εἶμι βελτίω λόγον.
κεἰ μὲν νοσεῖς τι τῶν ἀπορρήτων κακῶν,
γυναῖκες αἵδε συγκαθιστάναι νόσον·
εἰ δ᾽ ἔκφορός σοι συμφορὰ πρὸς ἄρσενας,
λέγ᾽, ὡς ἰατροῖς πρᾶγμα μηνυθῇ τόδε.
εἶέν, τί σιγᾷς; οὐκ ἐχρῆν σιγᾶν, τέκνον,
ἀλλ᾽ ἤ μ᾽ ἐλέγχειν, εἴ τι μὴ καλῶς λέγω,
ἢ τοῖσιν εὖ λεχθεῖσι συγχωρεῖν λόγοις.
φθέγξαι τι, δεῦρ᾽ ἄθρησον. ὦ τάλαιν᾽ ἐγώ,
γυναῖκες, ἄλλως τούσδε μοχθοῦμεν πόνους,
ἴσον δ᾽ ἄπεσμεν τῷ πρίν· οὔτε γὰρ τότε
λόγοις ἐτέγγεθ᾽ ἥδε νῦν τ᾽ οὐ πείθεται.
ἀλλ᾽ ἴσθι μέντοι – πρὸς τάδ᾽ αὐθαδεστέρα
γίγνου θαλάσσης – εἰ θανῇ, προδοῦσα σοὺς
παῖδας, πατρῴων μὴ μεθέξοντας δόμων,
μὰ τὴν ἄνασσαν ἱππίαν Ἀμαζόνα,
ἣ σοῖς τέκνοισι δεσπότην ἐγείνατο,
νόθον φρονοῦντα γνήσι᾽, οἶσθά νιν καλῶς,
Ἱππόλυτον. . .   Φα.   οἴμοι.   Τρ. θιγγάνει σέθεν τόδε;
Φαίδρα ἀπώλεσάς με, μαῖα, καί σε πρὸς θεῶν
τοῦδ᾽ ἀνδρὸς αὖθις λίσσομαι σιγᾶν πέρι.
Τροφός ὁρᾷς; φρονεῖς μὲν εὖ, φρονοῦσα δ᾽ οὐ θέλεις
παῖδάς τ᾽ ὀνῆσαι καὶ σὸν ἐκσῶσαι βίον.
Φαίδρα φιλῶ τέκν᾽· ἄλλῃ δ᾽ ἐν τύχῃ χειμάζομαι.
Τροφός ἁγνὰς μέν, ὦ παῖ, χεῖρας αἵματος φορεῖς;
Φαίδρα χεῖρες μὲν ἁγναί, φρὴν δ᾽ ἔχει μίασμά τι.
Τροφός μῶν ἐξ ἐπακτοῦ πημονῆς ἐχθρῶν τινος;

AS

Φαίδρα φίλος μ᾽ ἀπόλλυσ᾽ οὐχ ἑκοῦσαν οὐχ ἑκών.
Τροφός Θησεύς τιν᾽ ἡμάρτηκεν ἐς σ᾽ ἁμαρτίαν;
Φαίδρα μὴ δρῶσ᾽ ἔγωγ᾽ ἐκεῖνον ὀφθείην κακῶς.
Τροφός τί γὰρ τὸ δεινὸν τοῦθ᾽ ὅ σ᾽ ἐξαίρει θανεῖν;
Φαίδρα ἔα μ᾽ ἁμαρτεῖν· οὐ γὰρ ἐς σ᾽ ἁμαρτάνω.
Τροφός οὐ δῆθ᾽ ἑκοῦσά γ᾽, ἐν δὲ σοὶ λελείψομαι.
Φαίδρα τί δρᾷς; βιάζῃ χειρὸς ἐξαρτωμένη;
Τροφός καὶ σῶν γε γονάτων, κοὐ μεθήσομαί ποτε.
Φαίδρα κάκ᾽ ὦ τάλαινά σοι τάδ᾽, εἰ πεύσῃ, κακά.
Τροφός μεῖζον γὰρ ἤ σου μὴ τυχεῖν τί μοι κακόν;
Φαίδρα ὀλῇ. τὸ μέντοι πρᾶγμ᾽ ἐμοὶ τιμὴν φέρει.
Τροφός κἄπειτα κρύπτεις, χρήσθ᾽ ἱκνουμένης ἐμοῦ;
Φαίδρα ἐκ τῶν γὰρ αἰσχρῶν ἐσθλὰ μηχανώμεθα.
Τροφός οὔκουν λέγουσα τιμιωτέρα φανῇ;
Φαίδρα ἄπελθε πρὸς θεῶν δεξιάν τ᾽ ἐμὴν μέθες.
Τροφός οὐ δῆτ᾽, ἐπεί μοι δῶρον οὐ δίδως ὃ χρῆν.
Φαίδρα δώσω· σέβας γὰρ χειρὸς αἰδοῦμαι τὸ σόν.
Τροφός σιγῷμ᾽ ἂν ἤδη· σὸς γὰρ οὑντεῦθεν λόγος.
Φαίδρα ὦ τλῆμον, οἷον, μῆτερ, ἠράσθης ἔρον.
Τροφός ὃν ἔσχε ταύρου, τέκνον; ἢ τί φῂς τόδε;
Φαίδρα σύ τ᾽, ὦ τάλαιν᾽ ὅμαιμε, Διονύσου δάμαρ.
Τροφός τέκνον, τί πάσχεις; συγγόνους κακορροθεῖς;
Φαίδρα τρίτη δ᾽ ἐγὼ δύστηνος ὡς ἀπόλλυμαι.
Τροφός ἔκ τοι πέπληγμαι· ποῖ προβήσεται λόγος;
Φαίδρα ἐκεῖθεν ἡμεῖς, οὐ νεωστί, δυστυχεῖς.
Τροφός οὐδέν τι μᾶλλον οἶδ᾽ ἃ βούλομαι κλύειν.
Φαίδρα φεῦ·
πῶς ἂν σύ μοι λέξειας ἁμὲ χρὴ λέγειν;
Τροφός οὐ μάντις εἰμὶ τἀφανῆ γνῶναι σαφῶς.
Φαίδρα τί τοῦθ᾽ ὃ δὴ λέγουσιν ἀνθρώπους ἐρᾶν;
Τροφός ἥδιστον, ὦ παῖ, ταὐτὸν ἀλγεινόν θ᾽ ἅμα.
Φαίδρα ἡμεῖς ἂν εἶμεν θατέρῳ κεχρημένοι.
Τροφός τί φῄς; ἐρᾷς, ὦ τέκνον; ἀνθρώπων τίνος;
Φαίδρα ὅστις ποθ᾽ οὗτός ἐσθ᾽, ὁ τῆς Ἀμαζόνος . . .
Τροφός Ἱππόλυτον αὐδᾷς; Φα. σοῦ τάδ᾽, οὐκ ἐμοῦ, κλύεις.
Τροφός οἴμοι, τί λέξεις, τέκνον; ὥς μ᾽ ἀπώλεσας.
γυναῖκες, οὐκ ἀνασχέτ᾽, οὐκ ἀνέξομαι
ζῶσ᾽· ἐχθρὸν ἦμαρ, ἐχθρὸν εἰσορῶ φάος.
ῥίψω μεθήσω σῶμ᾽, ἀπαλλαχθήσομαι
βίου θανοῦσα· χαίρετ᾽, οὐκέτ᾽ εἴμ᾽ ἐγώ.
οἱ σώφρονες γάρ, οὐχ ἑκόντες ἀλλ᾽ ὅμως,
κακῶν ἐρῶσι. Κύπρις οὐκ ἄρ᾽ ἦν θεός,
ἀλλ᾽ εἴ τι μεῖζον ἄλλο γίγνεται θεοῦ,
ἣ τήνδε κἀμὲ καὶ δόμους ἀπώλεσεν.

362–390: The Nurse throws herself onto the floor and the chorus lament Phaedra's fate. Phaedra then begins a long speech, explaining her actions in far more considered and rational language. She claims that people usually know what is right but fail to act virtuously because of laziness or prioritisation of other pleasures. Phaedra also suggests that αἰδώς *or shame (see Introduction) can have negative effects.*

Φαίδρα
λέξω δὲ καί σοι τῆς ἐμῆς γνώμης ὁδόν.
ἐπεί μ᾽ ἔρως ἔτρωσεν, ἐσκόπουν ὅπως
κάλλιστ᾽ ἐνέγκαιμ᾽ αὐτόν. ἠρξάμην μὲν οὖν
ἐκ τοῦδε, σιγᾶν τήνδε καὶ κρύπτειν νόσον·
γλώσσῃ γὰρ οὐδὲν πιστόν, ἣ θυραῖα μὲν
φρονήματ᾽ ἀνδρῶν νουθετεῖν ἐπίσταται,
αὐτὴ δ᾽ ὑφ᾽ αὑτῆς πλεῖστα κέκτηται κακά.
τὸ δεύτερον δὲ τὴν ἄνοιαν εὖ φέρειν
τῷ σωφρονεῖν νικῶσα προυνοησάμην.
τρίτον δ᾽, ἐπειδὴ τοισίδ᾽ οὐκ ἐξήνυτον
Κύπριν κρατῆσαι, κατθανεῖν ἔδοξέ μοι,
κράτιστον (οὐδεὶς ἀντερεῖ) βουλευμάτων.
ἐμοὶ γὰρ εἴη μήτε λανθάνειν καλὰ
μήτ᾽ αἰσχρὰ δρώσῃ μάρτυρας πολλοὺς ἔχειν.
τὸ δ᾽ ἔργον ᾔδη τὴν νόσον τε δυσκλεᾶ,
γυνή τε πρὸς τοῖσδ᾽ οὖσ᾽ ἐγίγνωσκον καλῶς,
μίσημα πᾶσιν· ὡς ὄλοιτο παγκάκως
ἥτις πρὸς ἄνδρας ἤρξατ᾽ αἰσχύνειν λέχη
πρώτη θυραίους. ἐκ δὲ γενναίων δόμων
τόδ᾽ ἦρξε θηλείαισι γίγνεσθαι κακόν·
ὅταν γὰρ αἰσχρὰ τοῖσιν ἐσθλοῖσιν δοκῇ,
ἦ κάρτα δόξει τοῖς κακοῖς γ᾽ εἶναι καλά.
μισῶ δὲ καὶ τὰς σώφρονας μὲν ἐν λόγοις,
λάθρᾳ δὲ τόλμας οὐ καλὰς κεκτημένας·
αἳ πῶς ποτ᾽, ὦ δέσποινα ποντία Κύπρι,
βλέπουσιν ἐς πρόσωπα τῶν ξυνευνετῶν
οὐδὲ σκότον φρίσσουσι τὸν ξυνεργάτην
τέραμνά τ᾽ οἴκων μή ποτε φθογγὴν ἀφῇ;
ἡμᾶς γὰρ αὐτὸ τοῦτ᾽ ἀποκτείνει, φίλαι,
ὡς μήποτ᾽ ἄνδρα τὸν ἐμὸν αἰσχύνασ᾽ ἁλῶ,
μὴ παῖδας οὓς ἔτικτον· ἀλλ᾽ ἐλεύθεροι
παρρησίᾳ θάλλοντες οἰκοῖεν πόλιν
κλεινῶν Ἀθηνῶν, μητρὸς οὕνεκ᾽ εὐκλεεῖς.
δουλοῖ γὰρ ἄνδρα, κἂν θρασύσπλαγχνός τις ᾖ,
ὅταν ξυνειδῇ μητρὸς ἢ πατρὸς κακά.
μόνον δὲ τοῦτό φασ᾽ ἁμιλλᾶσθαι βίῳ,
γνώμην δικαίαν κἀγαθήν ὅτῳ παρῇ.
κακοὺς δὲ θνητῶν ἐξέφην᾽ ὅταν τύχῃ,
προθεὶς κάτοπτρον ὥστε παρθένῳ νέᾳ,
χρόνος· παρ᾽ οἷσι μήποτ᾽ ὀφθείην ἐγώ.

Χορός φεῦ φεῦ, τὸ σῶφρον ὡς ἁπανταχοῦ καλὸν
καὶ δόξαν ἐσθλὴν ἐν βροτοῖς καρπίζεται.

Τροφός δέσποιν᾽, ἐμοί τοι συμφορὰ μὲν ἀρτίως
ἡ σὴ παρέσχε δεινὸν ἐξαίφνης φόβον·
νῦν δ᾽ ἐννοοῦμαι φαῦλος οὖσα, κἀν βροτοῖς
αἱ δεύτεραί πως φροντίδες σοφώτεραι.
οὐ γὰρ περισσὸν οὐδὲν οὐδ᾽ ἔξω λόγου
πέπονθας, ὀργαὶ δ᾽ ἐς σ᾽ ἀπέσκηψαν θεᾶς.
ἐρᾷς (τί τοῦτο θαῦμα;) σὺν πολλοῖς βροτῶν·
κἄπειτ᾽ ἔρωτος οὕνεκα ψυχὴν ὀλεῖς;
οὔ τἄρα λύει τοῖς ἐρῶσι τῶν πέλας,
ὅσοι τε μέλλουσ᾽, εἰ θανεῖν αὐτοὺς χρεών.
Κύπρις γὰρ οὐ φορητὸν ἢν πολλὴ ῥυῇ,
ἣ τὸν μὲν εἴκονθ᾽ ἡσυχῇ μετέρχεται,
ὃν δ᾽ ἂν περισσὸν καὶ φρονοῦνθ᾽ εὕρῃ μέγα,
τοῦτον λαβοῦσα πῶς δοκεῖς καθύβρισεν.
φοιτᾷ δ᾽ ἀν᾽ αἰθέρ᾽, ἔστι δ᾽ ἐν θαλασσίῳ
κλύδωνι Κύπρις, πάντα δ᾽ ἐκ ταύτης ἔφυ·
ἥδ᾽ ἐστὶν ἡ σπείρουσα καὶ διδοῦσ᾽ ἔρον,
οὗ πάντες ἐσμὲν οἱ κατὰ χθόν᾽ ἔκγονοι.
ὅσοι μὲν οὖν γραφάς τε τῶν παλαιτέρων
ἔχουσιν αὐτοί τ᾽ εἰσὶν ἐν μούσαις ἀεὶ
ἴσασι μὲν Ζεὺς ὥς ποτ᾽ ἠράσθη γάμων
Σεμέλης, ἴσασι δ᾽ ὡς ἀνήρπασέν ποτε
ἡ καλλιφεγγὴς Κέφαλον ἐς θεοὺς Ἕως
ἔρωτος οὕνεκ᾽· ἀλλ᾽ ὅμως ἐν οὐρανῷ
ναίουσι κοὐ φεύγουσιν ἐκποδὼν θεούς,
στέργουσι δ᾽, οἶμαι, ξυμφορᾷ νικώμενοι.
σὺ δ᾽ οὐκ ἀνέξῃ; χρῆν σ᾽ ἐπὶ ῥητοῖς ἄρα
πατέρα φυτεύειν, ἢ ᾽πὶ δεσπόταις θεοῖς
ἄλλοισιν, εἰ μὴ τούσδε γε στέρξεις νόμους.
πόσους δοκεῖς δὴ κάρτ᾽ ἔχοντας εὖ φρενῶν
νοσοῦνθ᾽ ὁρῶντας λέκτρα μὴ δοκεῖν ὁρᾶν;
πόσους δὲ παισὶ πατέρας ἡμαρτηκόσι
συνεκκομίζειν Κύπριν; ἐν σοφοῖσι γὰρ
τάδ᾽ ἐστὶ θνητῶν, λανθάνειν τὰ μὴ καλά.
οὐδ᾽ ἐκπονεῖν τοι χρὴ βίον λίαν βροτούς·
οὐδὲ στέγην γὰρ ἧ κατηρεφεῖς δόμοι
καλῶς ἀκριβώσαις ἄν· ἐς δὲ τὴν τύχην
πεσοῦσ᾽ ὅσην σύ, πῶς ἂν ἐκνεῦσαι δοκεῖς;
ἀλλ᾽ εἰ τὰ πλείω χρηστὰ τῶν κακῶν ἔχεις,
ἄνθρωπος οὖσα κάρτα γ᾽ εὖ πράξειας ἄν.
ἀλλ᾽, ὦ φίλη παῖ, λῆγε μὲν κακῶν φρενῶν,
λῆξον δ᾽ ὑβρίζουσ᾽, οὐ γὰρ ἄλλο πλὴν ὕβρις
τάδ᾽ ἐστί, κρείσσω δαιμόνων εἶναι θέλειν,
τόλμα δ᾽ ἐρῶσα· θεὸς ἐβουλήθη τάδε·
νοσοῦσα δ᾽ εὖ πως τὴν νόσον καταστρέφου.

εἰσὶν δ᾽ ἐπῳδαὶ καὶ λόγοι θελκτήριοι·
φανήσεταί τι τῆσδε φάρμακον νόσου.
ἦ τἄρ᾽ ἂν ὀψέ γ᾽ ἄνδρες ἐξεύροιεν ἄν,
εἰ μὴ γυναῖκες μηχανὰς εὑρήσομεν.

Χορός Φαίδρα, λέγει μὲν ἥδε χρησιμώτερα
πρὸς τὴν παροῦσαν ξυμφοράν, αἰνῶ δὲ σέ.
ὁ δ᾽ αἶνος οὗτος δυσχερέστερος λόγων
τῶν τῆσδε καί σοι μᾶλλον ἀλγίων κλύειν.

Φαίδρα τοῦτ᾽ ἔσθ᾽ ὃ θνητῶν εὖ πόλεις οἰκουμένας
δόμους τ᾽ ἀπόλλυσ᾽, οἱ καλοὶ λίαν λόγοι.
οὐ γάρ τι τοῖσιν ὠσὶ τερπνὰ χρὴ λέγειν
ἀλλ᾽ ἐξ ὅτου τις εὐκλεὴς γενήσεται.

Τροφός τί σεμνομυθεῖς; οὐ λόγων εὐσχημόνων
δεῖ σ᾽ ἀλλὰ τἀνδρός. ὡς τάχος διιστέον,
τὸν εὐθὺν ἐξειπόντας ἀμφὶ σοῦ λόγον.
εἰ μὲν γὰρ ἦν σοι μὴ ᾽πὶ συμφοραῖς βίος
τοιαῖσδε, σώφρων δ᾽ οὖσ᾽ ἐτύγχανες γυνή,
οὐκ ἄν ποτ᾽ εὐνῆς οὕνεχ᾽ ἡδονῆς τε σῆς
προῆγον ἄν σε δεῦρο· νῦν δ᾽ ἀγὼν μέγας,
σῶσαι βίον σόν, κοὐκ ἐπίφθονον τόδε.

Φαίδρα ὦ δεινὰ λέξασ᾽, οὐχὶ συγκλῄσεις στόμα
καὶ μὴ μεθήσεις αὖθις αἰσχίστους λόγους;

Τροφός αἴσχρ᾽, ἀλλ᾽ ἀμείνω τῶν καλῶν τάδ᾽ ἐστί σοι·
κρεῖσσον δὲ τοὔργον, εἴπερ ἐκσώσει γέ σε,
ἢ τοὔνομ᾽, ᾧ σὺ κατθανῇ γαυρουμένη.

Φαίδρα ἆ μή σε πρὸς θεῶν, εὖ λέγεις γὰρ αἰσχρὰ δέ,
πέρα προβῇς τῶνδ᾽· ὡς ὑπείργασμαι μὲν εὖ
ψυχὴν ἔρωτι, τᾀσχρὰ δ᾽ ἢν λέγῃς καλῶς
ἐς τοῦθ᾽ ὃ φεύγω νῦν ἀναλωθήσομαι.

Τροφός εἴ τοι δοκεῖ σοι, χρῆν μὲν οὔ σ᾽ ἁμαρτάνειν,
εἰ δ᾽ οὖν, πιθοῦ μοι· δευτέρα γὰρ ἡ χάρις.
ἔστιν κατ᾽ οἴκους φίλτρα μοι θελκτήρια
ἔρωτος, ἦλθε δ᾽ ἄρτι μοι γνώμης ἔσω,
ἅ σ᾽ οὔτ᾽ επ᾽ αἰσχροῖς οὔτ᾽ ἐπὶ βλάβῃ φρενῶν
παύσει νόσου τῆσδ᾽, ἢν σὺ μὴ γένῃ κακή.
δεῖ δ᾽ ἐξ ἐκείνου δή τι τοῦ ποθουμένου
σημεῖον, ἢ πλόκον τιν᾽ ἢ πέπλων ἄπο,
λαβεῖν, συνάψαι τ᾽ ἐκ δυοῖν μίαν χάριν.

Φαίδρα πότερα δὲ χριστὸν ἢ ποτὸν τὸ φάρμακον;

Τροφός οὐκ οἶδ᾽· ὀνάσθαι, μὴ μαθεῖν, βούλου, τέκνον.

Φαίδρα δέδοιχ᾽ ὅπως μοι μὴ λίαν φανῇς σοφή.

Τροφός πάντ᾽ ἂν φοβηθεῖσ᾽ ἴσθι. δειμαίνεις δὲ τί;

Φαίδρα μή μοί τι Θησέως τῶνδε μηνύσῃς τόκῳ.

Τροφός ἔασον, ὦ παῖ· ταῦτ᾽ ἐγὼ θήσω καλῶς.
μόνον σύ μοι, δέσποινα ποντία Κύπρι,
συνεργὸς εἴης· τἄλλα δ᾽ οἷ᾽ ἐγὼ φρονῶ
τοῖς ἔνδον ἡμῖν ἀρκέσει λέξαι φίλοις.

*525–600: In the **First Stasimon** (525–564) the Chorus sing of the destructive power of Eros and Aphrodite. The **Second Episode** (565–731) begins when Phaedra, at the door to the palace, overhears Hippolytus inside angrily rebuking the Nurse for revealing Phaedra's feelings for him.*

Ἱππόλυτος ὦ γαῖα μῆτερ ἡλίου τ᾽ ἀναπτυχαί,
οἵων λόγων ἄρρητον εἰσήκουσ᾽ ὄπα.
Τροφός σίγησον, ὦ παῖ, πρίν τιν᾽ αἰσθέσθαι βοῆς.
Ἱππόλυτος οὐκ ἔστ᾽ ἀκούσας δείν᾽ ὅπως σιγήσομαι.
Τροφός ναί, πρός σε τῆς σῆς δεξιᾶς εὐωλένου.
Ἱππόλυτος οὐ μὴ προσοίσεις χεῖρα μηδ᾽ ἅψῃ πέπλων;
Τροφός ὦ πρός σε γονάτων, μηδαμῶς μ᾽ ἐξεργάσῃ.
Ἱππόλυτος τί δ᾽, εἴπερ, ὡς φῄς, μηδὲν εἴρηκας κακόν;
Τροφός ὁ μῦθος, ὦ παῖ, κοινὸς οὐδαμῶς ὅδε.
Ἱππόλυτος τά τοι κάλ᾽ ἐν πολλοῖσι κάλλιον λέγειν.
Τροφός ὦ τέκνον, ὅρκους μηδαμῶς ἀτιμάσῃς.
Ἱππόλυτος ἡ γλῶσσ᾽ ὀμώμοχ᾽, ἡ δὲ φρὴν ἀνώμοτος.
Τροφός ὦ παῖ, τί δράσεις; σοὺς φίλους διεργάσῃ;
Ἱππόλυτος ἀπέπτυσ᾽· οὐδεὶς ἄδικός ἐστί μοι φίλος.
Τροφός σύγγνωθ᾽· ἁμαρτεῖν εἰκὸς ἀνθρώπους, τέκνον.
Ἱππόλυτος ὦ Ζεῦ, τί δὴ κίβδηλον ἀνθρώποις κακὸν
γυναῖκας ἐς φῶς ἡλίου κατῴκισας;
εἰ γὰρ βρότειον ἤθελες σπεῖραι γένος,
οὐκ ἐκ γυναικῶν χρῆν παρασχέσθαι τόδε,
ἀλλ᾽ ἀντιθέντας σοῖσιν ἐν ναοῖς βροτοὺς
ἢ χαλκὸν ἢ σίδηρον ἢ χρυσοῦ βάρος
παίδων πρίασθαι σπέρμα του τιμήματος,
τῆς ἀξίας ἕκαστον, ἐν δὲ δώμασιν
ναίειν ἐλευθέροισι θηλειῶν ἄτερ. 624
τούτῳ δὲ δῆλον ὡς γυνὴ κακὸν μέγα· 627
προσθεὶς γὰρ ὁ σπείρας τε καὶ θρέψας πατὴρ
φερνὰς ἀπῴκισ᾽, ὡς ἀπαλλαχθῇ κακοῦ.
ὁ δ᾽ αὖ λαβὼν ἀτηρὸν ἐς δόμους φυτὸν
γέγηθε κόσμον προστιθεὶς ἀγάλματι
καλὸν κακίστῳ καὶ πέπλοισιν ἐκπονεῖ
δύστηνος, ὄλβον δωμάτων ὑπεξελών. 633
ῥᾷστον δ᾽ ὅτῳ τὸ μηδέν· ἀλλ᾽ ἀνωφελὴς 638
εὐηθίᾳ κατ᾽ οἶκον ἵδρυται γυνή.
σοφὴν δὲ μισῶ· μὴ γὰρ ἔν γ᾽ ἐμοῖς δόμοις
εἴη φρονοῦσα πλεῖον᾽ ἢ γυναῖκα χρή.
τὸ γὰρ κακοῦργον μᾶλλον ἐντίκτει Κύπρις
ἐν ταῖς σοφαῖσιν· ἡ δ᾽ ἀμήχανος γυνὴ
γνώμῃ βραχείᾳ μωρίαν ἀφῃρέθη.
χρῆν δ᾽ ἐς γυναῖκα πρόσπολον μὲν οὐ περᾶν,
ἄφθογγα δ᾽ αὐταῖς συγκατοικίζειν δάκη
θηρῶν, ἵν᾽ εἶχον μήτε προσφωνεῖν τινα

A Level

μήτ᾽ ἐξ ἐκείνων φθέγμα δέξασθαι πάλιν.
νῦν δ᾽ †αἱ μὲν ἔνδον δρῶσιν αἱ κακαὶ† κακὰ
βουλεύματ᾽, ἔξω δ᾽ ἐκφέρουσι πρόσπολοι.
ὡς καὶ σύ γ᾽ ἡμῖν πατρός, ὦ κακὸν κάρα,
λέκτρων ἀθίκτων ἦλθες ἐς συναλλαγάς·
ἁγὼ ῥυτοῖς νασμοῖσιν ἐξομόρξομαι
ἐς ὦτα κλύζων. πῶς ἂν οὖν εἴην κακός,
ὃς οὐδ᾽ ἀκούσας τοιάδ᾽ ἁγνεύειν δοκῶ;
εὖ δ᾽ ἴσθι, τοὐμόν σ᾽ εὐσεβὲς σῴζει, γύναι·
εἰ μὴ γὰρ ὅρκοις θεῶν ἄφαρκτος ᾑρέθην,
οὐκ ἄν ποτ᾽ ἔσχον μὴ οὐ τάδ᾽ ἐξειπεῖν πατρί.
νῦν δ᾽ ἐκ δόμων μέν, ἔστ᾽ ἂν ἔκδημῃ χθονὸς
Θησεύς, ἄπειμι, σῖγα δ᾽ ἕξομεν στόμα·
θεάσομαι δὲ σὺν πατρὸς μολὼν ποδὶ
πῶς νιν προσόψῃ, καὶ σὺ καὶ δέσποινα σή.
ὄλοισθε. μισῶν δ᾽ οὔποτ᾽ ἐμπλησθήσομαι
γυναῖκας, οὐδ᾽ εἴ φησί τίς μ᾽ ἀεὶ λέγειν·
ἀεὶ γὰρ οὖν πώς εἰσι κἀκεῖναι κακαί.
ἤ νύν τις αὐτὰς σωφρονεῖν διδαξάτω
ἢ κἄμ᾽ ἐάτω ταῖσδ᾽ ἐπεμβαίνειν ἀεί.

669–681: Hippolytus exits and Phaedra laments her fate in lyric metre.

Φαίδρα ὦ παγκακίστη καὶ φίλων διαφθορεῦ,
οἷ᾽ εἰργάσω με. Ζεύς σε γεννήτωρ ἐμὸς
πρόρριζον ἐκτρίψειεν οὐτάσας πυρί.
οὐκ εἶπον, οὐ σῆς προυνοησάμην φρενός,
σιγᾶν ἐφ᾽ οἷσι νῦν ἐγὼ κακύνομαι;
σὺ δ᾽ οὐκ ἀνέσχου· τοιγὰρ οὐκέτ᾽ εὐκλεεῖς
θανούμεθ᾽. ἀλλὰ δεῖ με δὴ καινῶν λόγων·
οὗτος γὰρ ὀργῇ συντεθηγμένος φρένας
ἐρεῖ καθ᾽ ἡμῶν πατρὶ σὰς ἁμαρτίας,
ἐρεῖ δὲ Πιτθεῖ τῷ γέροντι συμφοράς,
πλήσει τε πᾶσαν γαῖαν αἰσχίστων λόγων.
ὄλοιο καὶ σὺ χὤστις ἄκοντας φίλους
πρόθυμός ἐστι μὴ καλῶς εὐεργετεῖν.

Τροφός δέσποιν᾽, ἔχεις μὲν τἀμὰ μέμψασθαι κακά,
τὸ γὰρ δάκνον σου τὴν διάγνωσιν κρατεῖ·
ἔχω δὲ κἀγὼ πρὸς τάδ᾽, εἰ δέξῃ, λέγειν.
ἔθρεψά σ᾽ εὔνους τ᾽ εἰμί· τῆς νόσου δέ σοι
ζητοῦσα φάρμαχ᾽ ηὗρον οὐχ ἁβουλόμην.
εἰ δ᾽ εὖ γ᾽ ἔπραξα, κάρτ᾽ ἂν ἐν σοφοῖσιν ἦ·
πρὸς τὰς τύχας γὰρ τὰς φρένας κεκτήμεθα.

Φαίδρα ἦ γὰρ δίκαια ταῦτα κἀξαρκοῦντά μοι,
τρώσασαν ἡμᾶς εἶτα συγχωρεῖν λόγοις;

Τροφός μακρηγοροῦμεν· οὐκ ἐσωφρόνουν ἐγώ.
ἀλλ᾽ ἔστι κἀκ τῶνδ᾽ ὥστε σωθῆναι, τέκνον.

A
Level

Φαίδρα παῦσαι λέγουσα· καὶ τὰ πρὶν γὰρ οὐ καλῶς
παρῄνεσάς μοι κἀπεχείρησας κακά.
ἀλλ᾽ ἐκποδὼν ἄπελθε καὶ σαυτῆς πέρι
φρόντιζ᾽· ἐγὼ γὰρ τἀμὰ θήσομαι καλῶς.
ὑμεῖς δέ, παῖδες εὐγενεῖς Τροζήνιαι,
τοσόνδε μοι παράσχετ᾽ ἐξαιτουμένῃ·
σιγῇ καλύψαθ᾽ ἁνθάδ᾽ εἰσηκούσατε.

Χορός ὄμνυμι σεμνὴν Ἄρτεμιν, Διὸς κόρην,
μηδὲν κακῶν σῶν ἐς φάος δείξειν ποτέ.

Φαίδρα καλῶς ἔλεξαθ᾽· ἓν δὲ †προτρέπουσ᾽† ἐγὼ
εὕρημα δή τι τῆσδε συμφορᾶς ἔχω
ὥστ᾽ εὐκλεᾶ μὲν παισὶ προσθεῖναι βίον
αὐτή τ᾽ ὀνάσθαι πρὸς τὰ νῦν πεπτωκότα.
οὐ γάρ ποτ᾽ αἰσχυνῶ γε Κρησίους δόμους
οὐδ᾽ ἐς πρόσωπον Θησέως ἀφίξομαι
αἰσχροῖς ἐπ᾽ ἔργοις οὕνεκα ψυχῆς μιᾶς.

Χορός μέλλεις δὲ δὴ τί δρᾶν ἀνήκεστον κακόν;

Φαίδρα θανεῖν· ὅπως δέ, τοῦτ᾽ ἐγὼ βουλεύσομαι.

Χορός εὔφημος ἴσθι. Φα. καὶ σύ γ᾽ εὖ με νουθέτει.
ἐγὼ δὲ Κύπριν, ἥπερ ἐξόλλυσί με,
ψυχῆς ἀπαλλαχθεῖσα τῇδ᾽ ἐν ἡμέρᾳ
τέρψω· πικροῦ δ᾽ ἔρωτος ἡσσηθήσομαι.
ἀτὰρ κακόν γε χἀτέρῳ γενήσομαι
θανοῦσ᾽, ἵν᾽ εἰδῇ μὴ ᾽πὶ τοῖς ἐμοῖς κακοῖς
ὑψηλὸς εἶναι· τῆς νόσου δὲ τῆσδέ μοι
κοινῇ μετασχὼν σωφρονεῖν μαθήσεται.

732–884: In the ***Second Stasimon*** *(732–775) the chorus express a desire to escape, reminisce about Phaedra's ill-fated marriage and lament her imminent suicide.*

The ***Third Episode*** *(776–1101) begins with the Nurse crying from off-stage that Phaedra has hanged herself. Theseus returns from the oracle and is informed of Phaedra's suicide. Phaedra's corpse is wheeled out on the ekkyklema and Theseus laments her death. Theseus notices a tablet attached to her wrist, and upon reading it he bursts into a fit of despair and rage.*

Θησεύς Ἱππόλυτος εὐνῆς τῆς ἐμῆς ἔτλη θιγεῖν
βίᾳ, τὸ σεμνὸν Ζηνὸς ὄμμ᾽ ἀτιμάσας.
ἀλλ᾽, ὦ πάτερ Πόσειδον, ἃς ἐμοί ποτε
ἀρὰς ὑπέσχου τρεῖς, μιᾷ κατέργασαι
τούτων ἐμὸν παῖδ᾽, ἡμέραν δὲ μὴ φύγοι
τήνδ᾽, εἴπερ ἡμῖν ὤπασας σαφεῖς ἀράς.

Χορός ἄναξ, ἀπεύχου ταῦτα πρὸς θεῶν πάλιν,
γνώσῃ γὰρ αὖθις ἀμπλακών· ἐμοὶ πιθοῦ.

Θησεύς οὐκ ἔστι. καὶ πρός γ᾽ ἐξελῶ σφε τῆσδε γῆς,
δυοῖν δὲ μοίραιν θατέρᾳ πεπλήξεται·
ἢ γὰρ Ποσειδῶν αὐτὸν εἰς Ἅιδου δόμους

A Level

θανόντα πέμψει τὰς ἐμὰς ἀρὰς σέβων
ἢ τῆσδε χώρας ἐκπεσὼν ἀλώμενος
ξένην ἐπ᾽ αἶαν λυπρὸν ἀντλήσει βίον.
Χορός καὶ μὴν ὅδ᾽ αὐτὸς παῖς σὸς ἐς καιρὸν πάρα
Ἱππόλυτος· ὀργῆς δ᾽ ἐξανεὶς κακῆς, ἄναξ
Θησεῦ, τὸ λῷστον σοῖσι βούλευσαι δόμοις.
Ἱππόλυτος κραυγῆς ἀκούσας σῆς ἀφικόμην, πάτερ,
σπουδῇ· τὸ μέντοι πρᾶγμ᾽ ὅτῳ στένεις ἔπι
οὐκ οἶδα, βουλοίμην δ᾽ ἂν ἐκ σέθεν κλύειν.
ἔα, τί χρῆμα; σὴν δάμαρθ᾽ ὁρῶ, πάτερ,
νεκρόν· μεγίστου θαύματος τόδ᾽ ἄξιον·
ἣν ἀρτίως ἔλειπον, ἣ φάος τόδε
οὔπω χρόνος παλαιὸς εἰσεδέρκετο.
τί χρῆμα πάσχει; τῷ τρόπῳ διόλλυται;
πάτερ, πυθέσθαι βούλομαι σέθεν πάρα.
σιγᾷς; σιωπῆς δ᾽ οὐδὲν ἔργον ἐν κακοῖς.
οὐ μὴν φίλους γε, κἄτι μᾶλλον ἢ φίλους,
κρύπτειν δίκαιον σάς, πάτερ, δυσπραξίας.
Θησεύς ὦ πόλλ᾽ ἁμαρτάνοντες ἄνθρωποι μάτην,
τί δὴ τέχνας μὲν μυρίας διδάσκετε
καὶ πάντα μηχανᾶσθε κἀξευρίσκετε,
ἓν δ᾽ οὐκ ἐπίστασθ᾽ οὐδ᾽ ἐθηράσασθέ πω,
φρονεῖν διδάσκειν οἷσιν οὐκ ἔνεστι νοῦς;
Ἱππόλυτος δεινὸν σοφιστὴν εἶπας, ὅστις εὖ φρονεῖν
τοὺς μὴ φρονοῦντας δυνατός ἐστ᾽ ἀναγκάσαι.
ἀλλ᾽ οὐ γὰρ ἐν δέοντι λεπτουργεῖς, πάτερ,
δέδοικα μή σου γλῶσσ᾽ ὑπερβάλλῃ κακοῖς.
Θησεύς φεῦ, χρῆν βροτοῖσι τῶν φίλων τεκμήριον
σαφές τι κεῖσθαι καὶ διάγνωσιν φρενῶν,
ὅστις τ᾽ ἀληθής ἐστιν ὅς τε μὴ φίλος,
δισσάς τε φωνὰς πάντας ἀνθρώπους ἔχειν,
τὴν μὲν δικαίαν τὴν δ᾽ ὅπως ἐτύγχανεν,
ὡς ἡ φρονοῦσα τἄδικ᾽ ἐξηλέγχετο
πρὸς τῆς δικαίας, κοὐκ ἂν ἠπατώμεθα.
Ἱππόλυτος ἀλλ᾽ ἦ τις ἐς σὸν οὖς με διαβαλὼν ἔχει
φίλων, νοσοῦμεν δ᾽ οὐδὲν ὄντες αἴτιοι;
ἔκ τοι πέπληγμαι· σοὶ γὰρ ἐκπλήσσουσί με
λόγοι, παραλλάσσοντες ἔξεδροι φρενῶν.
Θησεύς φεῦ τῆς βροτείας – ποῖ προβήσεται; – φρενός.
τί τέρμα τόλμης καὶ θράσους γενήσεται;
εἰ γὰρ κατ᾽ ἀνδρὸς βίοτον ἐξογκώσεται,
ὁ δ᾽ ὕστερος τοῦ πρόσθεν εἰς ὑπερβολὴν
πανοῦργος ἔσται, θεοῖσι προσβαλεῖν χθονὶ
ἄλλην δεήσει γαῖαν ἣ χωρήσεται
τοὺς μὴ δικαίους καὶ κακοὺς πεφυκότας.
σκέψασθε δ᾽ ἐς τόνδ᾽, ὅστις ἐξ ἐμοῦ γεγὼς
ᾔσχυνε τἀμὰ λέκτρα κἀξελέγχεται

A Level

πρὸς τῆς θανούσης ἐμφανῶς κάκιστος ὤν.
δεῖξον δ᾽, ἐπειδή γ᾽ ἐς μίασμ᾽ ἐλήλυθα,
τὸ σὸν πρόσωπον δεῦρ᾽ ἐναντίον πατρί.
σὺ δὴ θεοῖσιν ὡς περισσὸς ὢν ἀνὴρ
ξύνει; σὺ σώφρων καὶ κακῶν ἀκήρατος;
οὐκ ἂν πιθοίμην τοῖσι σοῖς κόμποις ἐγὼ
θεοῖσι προσθεὶς ἀμαθίαν φρονεῖν κακῶς.
ἤδη νυν αὔχει καὶ δι᾽ ἀψύχου βορᾶς
σίτοις καπήλευ᾽ Ὀρφέα τ᾽ ἄνακτ᾽ ἔχων
βάκχευε πολλῶν γραμμάτων τιμῶν καπνούς·
ἐπεί γ᾽ ἐλήφθης. τοὺς δὲ τοιούτους ἐγὼ
φεύγειν προφωνῶ πᾶσι· θηρεύουσι γὰρ
σεμνοῖς λόγοισιν, αἰσχρὰ μηχανώμενοι.
τέθνηκεν ἥδε· τοῦτό σ᾽ ἐκσώσειν δοκεῖς;
ἐν τῷδ᾽ ἁλίσκῃ πλεῖστον, ὦ κάκιστε σύ·
ποῖοι γὰρ ὅρκοι κρείσσονες, τίνες λόγοι
τῆσδ᾽ ἂν γένοιντ᾽ ἄν, ὥστε σ᾽ αἰτίαν φυγεῖν;
μισεῖν σε φήσεις τήνδε, καὶ τὸ δὴ νόθον
τοῖς γνησίοισι πολέμιον πεφυκέναι;
κακὴν ἄρ᾽ αὐτὴν ἔμπορον βίου λέγεις
εἰ δυσμενείᾳ σῇ τὰ φίλτατ᾽ ὤλεσεν.
ἀλλ᾽ ὡς τὸ μῶρον ἀνδράσιν μὲν οὐκ ἔνι,
γυναιξὶ δ᾽ ἐμπέφυκεν; οἶδ᾽ ἐγὼ νέους
οὐδὲν γυναικῶν ὄντας ἀσφαλεστέρους,
ὅταν ταράξῃ Κύπρις ἡβῶσαν φρένα·
τὸ δ᾽ ἄρσεν αὐτοὺς ὠφελεῖ προσκείμενον.
νῦν οὖν – τί ταῦτα σοῖς ἁμιλλῶμαι λόγοις
νεκροῦ παρόντος μάρτυρος σαφεστάτου;
ἔξερρε γαίας τῆσδ᾽ ὅσον τάχος φυγάς,
καὶ μήτ᾽ Ἀθήνας τὰς θεοδμήτους μόλῃς
μήτ᾽ εἰς ὅρους γῆς ἧς ἐμὸν κρατεῖ δόρυ.
εἰ γὰρ παθών γε σοῦ τάδ᾽ ἡσσηθήσομαι,
οὐ μαρτυρήσει μ᾽ Ἴσθμιος Σίνις ποτὲ
κτανεῖν ἑαυτὸν ἀλλὰ κομπάζειν μάτην,
οὐδ᾽ αἱ θαλάσσῃ σύννομοι Σκιρωνίδες
φήσουσι πέτραι τοῖς κακοῖς μ᾽ εἶναι βαρύν.

Χορός οὐκ οἶδ᾽ ὅπως εἴποιμ᾽ ἂν εὐτυχεῖν τινα
θνητῶν· τὰ γὰρ δὴ πρῶτ᾽ ἀνέστραπται πάλιν.

Ἱππόλυτος πάτερ, μένος μὲν ξύντασίς τε σῶν φρενῶν
δεινή· τὸ μέντοι πρᾶγμ᾽, ἔχον καλοὺς λόγους,
εἴ τις διαπτύξειεν οὐ καλὸν τόδε.
ἐγὼ δ᾽ ἄκομψος εἰς ὄχλον δοῦναι λόγον,
ἐς ἥλικας δὲ κὠλίγους σοφώτερος·
ἔχει δὲ μοῖραν καὶ τόδ᾽· οἱ γὰρ ἐν σοφοῖς
φαῦλοι παρ᾽ ὄχλῳ μουσικώτεροι λέγειν.
ὅμως δ᾽ ἀνάγκη, ξυμφορᾶς ἀφιγμένης,
γλῶσσάν μ᾽ ἀφεῖναι. πρῶτα δ᾽ ἄρξομαι λέγειν

ὅθεν μ᾽ ὑπῆλθες πρῶτον ὡς διαφθερῶν
οὐκ ἀντιλέξοντ᾽. εἰσορᾷς φάος τόδε
καὶ γαῖαν· ἐν τοῖσδ᾽ οὐκ ἔνεστ᾽ ἀνὴρ ἐμοῦ,
οὐδ᾽ ἢν σὺ μὴ φῇς, σωφρονέστερος γεγώς.
ἐπίσταμαι γὰρ πρῶτα μὲν θεοὺς σέβειν
φίλοις τε χρῆσθαι μὴ ἀδικεῖν πειρωμένοις
ἀλλ᾽ οἷσιν αἰδὼς μήτ᾽ ἐπαγγέλλειν κακὰ
μήτ᾽ ἀνθυπουργεῖν αἰσχρὰ τοῖσι χρωμένοις,
οὐκ ἐγγελαστὴς τῶν ὁμιλούντων, πάτερ,
ἀλλ᾽ αὑτὸς οὐ παροῦσι κἀγγὺς ὢν φίλοις.
ἑνὸς δ᾽ ἄθικτος, ᾧ με νῦν ἔχειν δοκεῖς·
λέχους γὰρ ἐς τόδ᾽ ἡμέρας ἁγνὸν δέμας.
οὐκ οἶδα πρᾶξιν τήνδε πλὴν λόγῳ κλύων
γραφῇ τε λεύσσων· οὐδὲ ταῦτα γὰρ σκοπεῖν
πρόθυμός εἰμι, παρθένον ψυχὴν ἔχων.
καὶ δὴ τὸ σῶφρον τοὐμὸν οὐ πείθει σ᾽· ἴτω·
δεῖ δή σε δεῖξαι τῷ τρόπῳ διεφθάρην.
πότερα τὸ τῆσδε σῶμ᾽ ἐκαλλιστεύετο
πασῶν γυναικῶν; ἢ σὸν οἰκήσειν δόμον
ἔγκληρον εὐνὴν προσλαβὼν ἐπήλπισα;
μάταιος ἆρ᾽ ἦν, οὐδαμοῦ μὲν οὖν φρενῶν.
ἀλλ᾽ ὡς τυραννεῖν ἡδὺ τοῖσι σώφροσιν;
†ἥκιστα γ᾽, εἰ μὴ† τὰς φρένας διέφθορεν
θνητῶν ὅσοισιν ἁνδάνει μοναρχία.
ἐγὼ δ᾽ ἀγῶνας μὲν κρατεῖν Ἑλληνικοὺς
πρῶτος θέλοιμ᾽ ἄν, ἐν πόλει δὲ δεύτερος
σὺν τοῖς ἀρίστοις εὐτυχεῖν ἀεὶ φίλοις·
πράσσειν τε γὰρ πάρεστι, κίνδυνός τ᾽ ἀπὼν
κρείσσω δίδωσι τῆς τυραννίδος χάριν.
ἓν οὐ λέλεκται τῶν ἐμῶν, τὰ δ᾽ ἄλλ᾽ ἔχεις·
εἰ μὲν γὰρ ἦν μοι μάρτυς οἷός εἰμ᾽ ἐγὼ
καὶ τῆσδ᾽ ὁρώσης φέγγος ἠγωνιζόμην,
ἔργοις ἂν εἶδες τοὺς κακοὺς διεξιών·
νῦν δ᾽ ὅρκιόν σοι Ζῆνα καὶ πέδον χθονὸς
ὄμνυμι τῶν σῶν μήποθ᾽ ἅψασθαι γάμων
μηδ᾽ ἂν θελῆσαι μηδ᾽ ἂν ἔννοιαν λαβεῖν.
ἦ τἄρ᾽ ὀλοίμην ἀκλεὴς ἀνώνυμος
καὶ μήτε πόντος μήτε γῆ δέξαιτό μου
σάρκας θανόντος, εἰ κακὸς πέφυκ᾽ ἀνήρ.
τί δ᾽ ἥδε δειμαίνουσ᾽ ἀπώλεσεν βίον
οὐκ οἶδ᾽, ἐμοὶ γὰρ οὐ θέμις πέρα λέγειν·
ἐσωφρόνησε δ᾽ οὐκ ἔχουσα σωφρονεῖν,
ἡμεῖς δ᾽ ἔχοντες οὐ καλῶς ἐχρώμεθα.

1036–1466: For a summary of the rest of the play, see the Introduction.

A Level

Commentary Notes

For a summary of the ***Prologue (1–120)*** *and the* ***Parode (121–169)*** *see the Introduction.*

The set text begins part way through the ***First Episode (170–524)****. The Nurse brings Phaedra out from the palace and laments her pitiful condition. Phaedra deliriously expresses her desire to go hunting but suddenly shows embarrassment and suggests that death is preferable to her current plight. The Chorus Leader questions the Nurse about the nature of Phaedra's illness and where our text begins the Chorus Leader has just asked whether the Nurse has tried anything to get Phaedra to explain why she is suffering.*

284

ἐς πάντ' ἀφῖγμαι: 'I have gone to all lengths.'

κοὐδὲν: the breathing mark in the middle of the word (properly called a 'coronis') is a sign that two vowel sounds have merged to create one word from two (καὶ οὐδὲν), a phenomenon called 'crasis'. It is common in tragedy (293, 326, 330, 361, etc.) and only more difficult examples will be pointed out in future.

285

οὐ μὴν . . . γ': 'not even so'.

ἀνήσω: future indicative of ἀνίημι.

οὐδὲ: 'not even'. οὐδέ may be a conjunction ('and not') or adverb ('not even'). The use of the negative here emphasizes the previous negative οὐ to make the Nurse's refusal more forceful, rather than cancelling it out. Simple negative (οὐ, μή) before compound negative (οὐδέ, οὐδέποτε, μηδέ, etc.) is reinforced, while simple negative after compound negative is a double negative.

286

ὡς ἂν . . . ξυμμαρτυρῇς: purpose clause where ὡς ἂν is equivalent to ἵνα.

καὶ σύ: 'you also'. The Nurse addresses the chorus leader here, before turning to Phaedra in 288. Like οὐδέ (n. 285), καί may be conjunction ('and') or adverb ('indeed, even, also').

μοι ξυμμαρτυρῇς/οἵα πέφυκα: 'bear witness to what sort of woman I am'. This is an example of prolepsis, where the subject of the subordinate clause is brought into the main clause for emphasis (literally, 'bear witness to me, what sort of woman I am'). Even though she cannot achieve the desired results, reputation is clearly important to the Nurse.

AS

287

πέφυκα: 'I am (by nature)', perfect indicative of φύομαι. Literally, 'I have been born as,' but as the perfect describes a present state resulting from a past action, the present is often best in English.

δυστυχοῦσι δεσπόταις: the Nurse generalizes to stress her devotion to anyone in her care. Greek uses the masculine to generalize, but given the context 'mistresses' works better in English.

289

λαθώμεθ᾽: 'let's forget (+ genitive)', exhortative subjunctive (aorist by aspect).

θ᾽: elision of τε where the next word begins with a rough breathing.

γενοῦ: aorist imperative from γίγνομαι.

290

λύσασα: an example of zeugma, where a verb is applied to two nouns in different senses. Here it refers to Phaedra's expression ('στυγνὴν ὀφρὺν') in a literal sense, but to the passage of her thoughts ('γνώμης ὁδόν') metaphorically to suggest she needs to be less constricted in her thinking. The definite article would be used in prose with each accusative but tragedy is less strict with its inclusion.

291

ὅπῃ . . . λόγον: 'wherever I didn't follow you well before, putting that aside, I'll now move onto better words'. The Nurse suggests that she has been unsympathetic previously and now intends to take a different approach. The Nurse's speech contains numerous references to words and silence, a major theme in the play (see Introduction). There is also a focus on the idea of movement (ἀφῖγμαι, ὁδόν, εἱπόμην, εἶμι) which perhaps suggests the idea that speech can bring forward progress. The action of the play testifies to the power of speech, but usually with destructive consequences (see Introduction).

μὴ: used here instead of οὐ (negative of facts) due to the indefinite ('wherever') nature of ὅπῃ.

τόθ᾽: elision of τότε (n. 289).

εἱπόμην: imperfect of ἕπομαι.

292

μεθεῖσ᾽: aorist active participle (nominative feminine singular) from μεθίημι.

βελτίω: contracted form of βελτίονα, masculine accusative singular.

293

τι τῶν ἀπορρήτων κακῶν: 'with one of the problems which should be kept secret'. τι is accusative of respect ('with respect to . . .'). The Nurse means a female problem which cannot be talked about with male doctors, but there is dramatic irony as the audience already know that it is desire which consumes her. The word ἀπορρήτων also relates to the theme of speech/silence (n. 291).

294

γυναῖκες αἵδε συγκαθιστάναι: 'these people here are women, to help treat', with εἰσί supplied. συγκαθιστάναι is present infinitive of συγκαθίστημι, literally to

'help (συν-) set in order'. Forms of ὅδε are often used in tragedy to point out something visible on stage, maybe even accompanied with a gesture (deictic).
νόσον: the imagery of disease is ubiquitous in the play to describe the power of desire and its effects. It is worth saying that not every example of this, and other imagery, will be drawn attention to. Part of the fun is making these discoveries for yourself!

295
ἔκφορός σοι συμφορά: supply ἐστί. Translate σοι as 'your' (possessive dative).
ὡς: introducing purpose clause (this time without ἄν as at 286).

297
οὐκ ἐχρῆν: 'you shouldn't'. The imperfects of χρή (ἐχρῆν or χρῆν) and δεῖ sometimes refer to present time but imply that the obligation is not fulfilled.

298
ἐλέγχειν . . . συγχωρεῖν: infinitives with implied ἐχρῆν ('but you should either . . .'). The Nurse draws attention to the difficulty of determining the truth of words, even when spoken by herself.

299
τοῖσιν: -οισι and -αισι are poetic alternatives for -οις and -αις.

300
φθέγξαι . . . ἄθρησον: the imperatives help to convey the Nurse's frustration at the silent Phaedra. This frustration leads the Nurse to turn away from Phaedra and address the chorus.

302
ἴσον δ' ἄπεσμεν τῷ πρίν: 'but we are as far away as before', literally 'we are absent equally to the before thing'.

303
ἐτέγγεθ': elision of ἐτέγγετο.

304
ἴσθι: imperative of οἶδα, addressing Phaedra again.
πρὸς τάδ': 'and then'.
αὐθαδεστέρα: 'stubborn'. The word literally means 'self-pleasing' (αὐτο-άδης, related to ἥδομαι) referring to someone who does things for their own pleasure and ignores others. This is ironic given that Phaedra's current desire to die is based on anxiety about her reputation in the eyes of others and a concern for the future of her children.

305
θαλάσσης: genitive of comparison.
εἰ θανῇ: unusual use of εἰ + subjunctive (rather than ἐάν) for metrical reasons.

προδοῦσα: the participle picks up an indirect statement after ἴσθι. The aorist tense stresses the Nurse's certainty in the outcome of Phaedra's death.

306

μὴ μεθέξοντας: 'as they will not have a share'. μή is sometimes used in indirect statements with verbs of knowing.

307

μὰ: 'in the name of'. The Nurse uses the language of oaths to dramatically point out that Phaedra's children will be usurped by Hippolytus if she is not there to insist on their inheritance.

Ἀμαζόνα: 'the Amazon'. Euripides does not explicitly name Hippolytus' mother, but she is elsewhere identified as Antiope or Hippolyte. By referring to her the Nurse highlights the competing claims of lineage and birthright, but it also increases the tension by delaying the direct mention of Hippolytus' name.

309

φρονοῦντα γνήσι': 'with thoughts of legitimacy', literally 'thinking legitimate things'.

νιν: poetic alternative for αὐτον.

310

Ἱππόλυτον . . .: Hippolytus' name has been delayed until now and finally causes Phaedra to break her silence, although the Nurse believes that it is anxiety over her children's future which has got through to her. The height of the drama here is emphasized by the change of speakers within the line (antilabe). The next time antilabe occurs is also when Hippolytus' name is mentioned again (line 352).

σέθεν: poetic genitive of σύ depending on θιγγάνει.

311

ἀπώλεσάς: aorist indicative of ἀπόλλυμι.

312

τοῦδ' ἀνδρὸς . . . πέρι: the preposition περί is usually placed before its noun, but in verse two syllable prepositions may come after with the accent moved onto the first syllable (antistrophe). Phaedra cannot bear to use Hippolytus' name. It is ironic that Phaedra breaks her silence only to ask the Nurse to be silent.

313

φρονεῖς . . . εὖ: 'you are in your right mind'.

φρονοῦσα: 'despite being in your right mind', participle used concessively.

315

Now begins a long section of dramatic stichomythia, where each character speaks a line in turn.

τέκν': elision of τέκνα.

316

ἁγνὰς μέν . . . χεῖρας αἵματος φορεῖς;: 'are your hands undefiled by blood?'. The Nurse asks whether Phaedra has killed to clear it as a possibility, with the word μέν suggesting this will be the first question in a series.

317

χεῖρες μὲν ἁγναί: supply εἰσί.

μίασμά τι: this refers to the idea that someone who committed a crime became stained by a contagious pollution which could affect others. This phenomenon can also be seen in Sophocles' *Oedipus Rex* where the community is affected by a plague until the killer of Laius, the previous King of Thebes, is discovered. Phaedra contrasts this traditional notion of external, physical pollution with her own internal, mental miasma. The Nurse fails to understand her words.

318

μῶν ἐξ ἐπακτοῦ πημονῆς ἐχθρῶν τινος: 'surely it's not from harm conjured up by one of your enemies?'

319

φίλος: 'someone dear to me', contrasting with ἐχθρῶν. The clear dichotomy between φίλοι (who one should help) and ἐχθροί (who one should harm) is common in tragedy. Phaedra is paradoxically being harmed by someone who should be on her side, but both parties are unwilling victims of Aphrodite. See n. 613 for more on the word φίλος.

320

τιν' ἡμάρτηκεν . . . ἁμαρτίαν: 'has committed some fault'. This is an example of a cognate accusative, where the object is etymologically related to its verb (literally, 'has erred some error').

321

μὴ . . . ὀφθείην: 'may I not be seen'. The optative as main verb without ἄν expresses a wish. The phrasing here reveals Phaedra's focus on her reputation and how she is seen by others.

322

τί γὰρ τὸ δεινὸν τοῦθ': 'well what is this terrible thing'. ἐστί should be supplied and τοῦθ' is elision of τοῦτο. γάρ ('well') is used when an initial suggestion is rejected and a question is restated. Phaedra ignores this question as communication breaks down.

θανεῖν: tragedy often uses the simple version of verbs which are more common in compounds in prose (ἀποθανεῖν).

324

οὐ δῆθ' ἑκοῦσά γ': supply ἐάσω σε

ἐν δὲ σοὶ λελείψομαι: 'I will fail because of you'. λελείψομαι is future perfect laying stress on the future state of failure. The Nurse means that she will go to all lengths to save Phaedra, and it is only her mistress' resistance which will stand in her way. She backs up these words with the ritual act of supplication, whereby a person in need makes a request kneeling at another's feet while grasping their chin, knees or hand (actions described in the following lines). The person being supplicated was compelled by religious and moral obligations to fulfil the request. Supplication is ordinarily only used in desperate circumstances such as when safety is at risk, so for the Nurse to resort to it here is a shock to Phaedra. The use of supplication also serves to exculpate Phaedra somewhat when she finally reveals her love for Hippolytus. Euripides subverts expectation by making a ritual which was supposed to lead to positive results have destructive consequences. The same is true when Hippolytus keeps his oath but is destroyed is a result.

325

βιάζῃ χειρὸς ἐξαρτωμένη: 'are you using force, fastening yourself onto my hand?'. Phaedra describes the supplication as tantamount to physical force. γονάτων in the next line is also genitive because of ἐξαρτωμένη.

326

μεθήσομαί: middle future of μεθίημι.

327

Part of 'to be' should be supplied in this line and the next.

328

ἢ σου μὴ τυχεῖν: 'than not succeeding with you'.

329

ὀλῇ: 'it will be the death of you', future middle of ὄλλυμι. The hyperbole here is indicative of Phaedra's turmoil, and ironic given that supplication usually leads to safety for the suppliant.

330

κρύπτεις: supply τὸ πρᾶγμα from previous line. The theme of silence/speech is often linked to the language of concealment and revelation.

χρήσθ': 'things which are good for you', elision of χρήστα.

331

γὰρ: 'yes, for'. In a response to a question, γάρ gives the answer 'yes' or 'no' followed by a reason.

μηχανώμεθα: 'I am contriving', poetic royal we. Phaedra means that her concealment of her shameful feelings is noble. The Nurse, misunderstanding, replies that if she is doing something good she should speak out about it.

332

φανῇ: future second singular of φαίνομαι. Again, the emphasis is on appearance and reputation.

333
μέθες: aorist imperative of μέθιημι.

335
σέβας γὰρ χειρὸς αἰδοῦμαι τὸ σόν: 'I respect the sanctity of your supplication', but, literally, 'I respect your sanctity of hand'. Phaedra promises that she will tell the Nurse but presents it as a virtuous obedience to the Nurse's supplication.

336
σιγῷμ' ἂν: 'I shall be quiet,' a reversal of roles. The unelided form would be σιγῷμι. Optative + ἄν = potential optative, usually translated 'would' or 'could', but here a polite alternative to the future tense.
σὸς: supply ἐστί ('is yours').

337
τλῆμον, οἷον . . . ἠράσθης ἔρον: 'what a miserable love you had', another example of a cognate accusative. Phaedra's mother was Pasiphae, the Queen of Crete and wife of King Minos. God-sent lust drives Pasiphae to have sex with a bull and she gives birth to the Minotaur. Phaedra is presenting shameful love as a hereditary part of her nature.

338
ὃν ἔσχε ταύρου: 'the one which she had for the bull'. The Nurse makes explicit what Phaedra was alluding to obliquely.

339
ὅμαιμε: Phaedra's sister Ariadne helps Theseus escape from the Labyrinth but is abandoned by him on the island of Naxos. In some accounts of the myth, Dionysus then appears and marries Ariadne. In other versions Dionysus, who was already married to Ariadne, arrives and punishes her with death for her infidelity. Given that Phaedra represents the love as ill-fated, the second version is probably referred to here.

341
Τρίτη δ' ἐγὼ δύστηνος: 'and I, the third unfortunate one'. δύστηνος is a two-termination adjective, so the masculine and feminine forms are identical.
ὡς: 'how' (also at 353).

342
ἐκ . . . πέπληγμαι: an example of tmesis, where one word splits another in half (like English 'a-whole-nother thing').

343
ἐκεῖθεν ἡμεῖς: 'it was then that I became . . .', another example of the royal 'we', with a verb to be supplied. Phaedra means her own problems have been inevitable for a long time, since the fates of her mother and sister.

344

οὐδέν τι μᾶλλον οἶδ': 'I'm no closer to knowing at all,' literally 'no more with respect to a bit do I know'. οἶδ' = οἶδα.

345

φεῦ: the stichomythia is dramatically interrupted by an emotional cry which breaks the metre (extrametrical).

ἂν . . . λέξειας: 'could you say', potential optative. Phaedra's wish is fulfilled in line 352.

346

τἀφανῆ γνῶναι: 'who can know what is unclear'.

347

τοῦθ': = τοῦτο. Supply ἐστί.

λέγουσιν ἀνθρώπους ἐρᾶν: 'they call people being in love'.

348

ταὐτὸν: alternative to τὸ αὐτό (literally, 'the same thing'). Supply ἐστί and translate as 'both'.

349

ἡμεῖς ἂν εἶμεν θατέρῳ κεχρημένοι: 'I must be experiencing the latter'. The potential optative here expresses likelihood. εἰμί + perfect participle is another way of expressing the perfect tense (periphrastic perfect), best translated as a present. θατέρῳ is crasis of τῷ ἑτέρῳ and the masculine (κεχρημένοι) is common for the royal we even when a woman is speaking.

351

ὅστις ποθ' οὗτός ἐσθ': 'whoever on earth he is'. Phaedra cannot bear to say his name and feigns ignorance. Even more vagueness is added by the word ποθ' = ποτε ('ever'/'on earth'). Note the lack of accent differentiating it from πότε ('when').

ὁ τῆς Ἀμαζόνος: supply the word 'son'.

353

λέξεις: translate as present. The future implies the words need to be repeated to be believed.

354

οὐκ ἀνασχέτ': 'this is unendurable', elision of ἀνασχέτα. The quick flurry of words here adds drama.

356

ῥίψω μεθήσω σῶμ': 'I will throw down, cast aside my body', as if she intends to jump off a cliff. Note the distressed asyndeton and tautology indicating her distress.

358

οἱ σώφρονες: see Introduction.

ἀλλ' ὅμως: 'but they still do'.

359

Κύπρις . . . ἄρ' ἦν: 'so Kypris is', the imperfect is used for a fact just recognized ('was all along'). Be careful to distinguish ἄρα ('indeed', 'so') from ἆρα (question word). Kypris is another name for Aphrodite, who was associated with the island of Cyprus.

360

εἴ τι μεῖζον ἄλλο γίγνεται: 'whatever else there is which is greater'. εἴ τις ('if anyone'/'whoever') is equivalent to si quis in Latin.

362–390: The Nurse throws herself onto the floor and the chorus lament Phaedra's fate. Phaedra then begins a long speech, explaining her actions in far more considered and rational language. She claims that people usually know what is right but fail to act virtuously because of laziness or prioritization of other pleasures. Phaedra also suggests that αἰδώς or shame (see Introduction) can have negative effects.

392

ἔτρωσεν: the power of Aphrodite is compared to a physical wound (compare with the imagery of disease elsewhere).

393

κάλλιστ' ἐνέγκαιμ' αὐτόν: 'how best I should bear it'. In direct speech, ἐνέγκαιμι would have been deliberative subjunctive ('how should I . . .?') but in Phaedra's indirect question it is replaced by an optative (historic sequence).

394

ἐκ τοῦδε: 'with this', explained by the infinitives. Phaedra first tries to deal with the problem through silence and concealment.

395

οὐδὲν πιστόν: 'there is no trusting (+ dative)'.

θυραῖα . . . φρονήματ' ἀνδρῶν: 'other people's thoughts'. θυραῖα literally means 'out of doors' but can also mean 'someone else's'. The literal meaning captures a sense of Phaedra's preoccupation with reputation and the divide between public and private realms.

397

ὑφ' αὑτῆς . . . κέκτηται: 'it possesses . . . by its own doing'. The perfect tense puts stress on the present effect of a past action, so 'it has obtained' = 'it possesses'.

398

τὸ δεύτερον: 'secondly', adverbial accusative. Phaedra then attempts to subdue and moderate her feelings with sophrosyne (see Introduction).

ἄνοιαν . . . προυνοησάμην: note the related words. If Phaedra was suffering from ἄ-νοια ('without mindedness') how effective was προ-νοεῖν ('using one's mind in advance') ever going to be?

399
τῷ σωφρονεῖν: 'by being sensible' or 'by getting control over myself', an articular infinitive (like a Latin gerund).

400
τρίτον: Phaedra's third option is death.

403
ἐμοὶ . . . εἴη μήτε λανθάνειν καλὰ . . . δρώσῃ: 'may I neither go unnoticed when I do good things', literally 'may it neither be to me to . . .' δρώσῃ is feminine agreeing with ἐμοὶ and for the optative, see n. 321. Again, Phaedra's focus is all on reputation.

405
ᾔδη: 'I knew' (from οἶδα). This takes an indirect statement, with εἰμί to be supplied.

406
γυνή . . . οὖσ᾽ ἐγίγνωσκον . . . μίσημα: 'I was aware that I was a woman, an object of hatred,' another indirect statement.

407
ὡς ὄλοιτο: 'may she perish'. The word ὡς sometimes accompanies an optative of wish. Phaedra now curses the first woman to commit adultery.

408
πρὸς ἄνδρας . . . θυραίους: 'with other men'.
λέχη: 'her bed'. Poetic plural for singular.

410
ἦρξε θηλείαισι γίγνεσθαι: 'began for women', literally 'began to happen to women'.

411
ὅταν: 'whenever'. ἄν + subjunctive (here ὅτ<u>αν</u>) is the indefinite (-ever) construction. In historic sequence the optative is used without ἄν.
τοῖσιν ἐσθλοῖσιν . . . τοῖς κακοῖς: 'to the nobles . . . to the commoners'. Note how the ancient words describing different social classes are heavily charged with moral connotations. Phaedra claims that upper class morality has a 'trickle-down' effect.
δοκῇ . . . εἶναι καλά: take εἶναι καλά with both lines.

413
τόλμας οὐ καλὰς κεκτημένας: 'who have engaged in reckless activities which are not good'. Phaedra is keen to stress her virtue in contrast with these women who

fraudulently appear chaste. The relationship between deed/reality and words/ appearance is a key concern of the play.

415
αἳ: 'they' (connecting relative).
ποντία: Aphrodite was said to have been born from the foam (ἀφρός) which accumulated around the genitals of Ouranos when they were cut off and thrown into the sea by Kronos.

417
οὐδὲ σκότον φρίσσουσι . . . μή ποτε φθογγὴν ἀφῇ: 'and they don't shudder that the darkness, their accomplice, and the timbers of the house might at some point speak ', literally 'shudder at the darkness . . . lest it let loose a voice'. An example of prolepsis (n. 286) where the accusatives in the main clause (σκότον and τέραμνά) are best translated as part of the fear clause. ἀφῇ is the third singular aorist active subjunctive of ἀφίημι. The theme of speech/silence in the play is often linked to what happens inside and outside the house. Compare Phaedra's words here with Hippolytus' wishes that the palace itself could speak (1074–1075).

419
ἡμᾶς: royal we.
αὐτὸ τοῦτ': 'this is the very thing which', i.e. Phaedra's feeling of shame, not shared by the brazen women she detests, which motivates her decision to commit suicide.

420
ἁλῶ: first singular aorist subjunctive of ἁλίσκομαι as part of the purpose clause.

421
μὴ: 'nor'. Literally, 'not', but the striking asyndeton does not work well in English.

422
παρρησίᾳ θάλλοντες: 'blooming with freedom of speech', an important idea in democratic Athens. The implication is that Phaedra's disgrace will diminish her children's value in society and render their speech less effectual.
οἰκοῖεν: optative of wish (n. 321).

423
Ἀθηνῶν: Athens was Phaedra's permanent home, but she and Theseus have been exiled to Troezen for a year to atone for Theseus' killing of his cousins, the Pallantids.

424
δουλοῖ: from the verb δουλόω.
κἂν: 'even if', crasis for καὶ ἐὰν.

426
φασ': = φασί, 'they say'.

ἁμιλλᾶσθαι βίῳ: 'competes in value with life'. Having reflected on the impact of infidelity on her sons, Phaedra now considers the idea that preservation of virtue is more valuable than life itself.

427

γνώμην δικαίαν κἀγαθήν ὅτῳ παρῇ: 'for someone to possess a just and good mind', literally 'a just and good mind for whoever it is present'. ὅτῳ is used in tragedy for ᾧτινι, and παρῇ is subjunctive due to the indefinite construction. Usually ἄν would be required (n. 411) but it can be omitted in poetry. The whole phrase is in apposition to (describes) τοῦτό.

428

θνητῶν: 'among mortals'.

ἐξέφην': = ἐξέφηνε, 'reveals'. The aorist is used sometimes for general truths (gnomic aorist), best translated as present.

ὅταν τύχῃ: 'sooner or later', literally 'whenever it happens to' (indefinite construction).

429

προθεὶς κάτοπτρον ὥστε παρθένῳ νέᾳ: 'placing a mirror before them, like before a young girl'. προθεὶς is aorist participle from προτίθημι. A mirror can reveal things which are otherwise hidden (i.e. which people are really bad) as well as reflect a person's image back at themselves for self-examination (like the girl inspecting her appearance). The imagery of the mirror continues the play's exploration of appearance and reality, while the girl evokes the themes of youth and sexuality.

430

παρ' οἷσι: 'in company with them' (i.e. the κακοὺς in line 428). οἷσι is connecting relative.

ὀφθείην: optative of wish (n. 321).

431

τὸ σῶφρον: 'self-control', neuter article + adjective equivalent to abstract noun.

ὡς . . . καλὸν: 'how fine a thing is', ἐστί supplied.

435

κἀν: crasis of καὶ ἐν (compare with κἄν, n. 424).

436

σοφώτεραι: supply εἰσί. The Nurse's original response had been to lament melodramatically and wish for death but she is far more circumspect here. While she does try to explain her change of approach, there is some inconsistency and unreliability in her characterization, which reinforces the sophistic character of her speech.

437

περισσὸν οὐδὲν οὐδ' ἔξω λόγου: 'anything remarkable or even beyond reason'. See n. 285 for the emphatic negatives. The Nurse pragmatically tries to normalize

Phaedra's desire, but does not mention the fact that Phaedra's love (being for her step-son) is far from normal. The sophism of her argument is underlined by the claim that Phaedra's desire is not ἔξω λόγου, implying that words and reason can find a solution.

438
πέπονθας: perfect from πάσχω.
ὀργαὶ: translate as singular.

439
τί τοῦτο θαῦμα;: 'what's so amazing about that?', literally, 'what is this wonder?' (ἐστί supplied).
σὺν: 'it's something you share with . . .'

440
ὀλεῖς: 'will you destroy', future of ὄλλυμι.

441
οὔ τἄρα λύει . . . αὐτοὺς χρεών: 'It's certainly not a profitable thing then for people in love with others, and anyone who is in love in the future, if they have to die!' λύει is equivalent to λυσιτελεῖ, 'it is profitable (+ dative)'. τῶν πέλας is, literally, 'those nearby' but simply means 'other people', and χρεών (ἐστί supplied) is equivalent to χρή. The Nurse means it would be absurd if everyone who fell in love had to kill themselves. The word λύει employs exaggerated understatement (litotes) to add a touch of humour and highlight the absurdity of killing oneself because of love. Through this tone she tries to lighten the mood, underscoring her point that Phaedra's desire is completely normal.

443
οὐ φορητὸν: 'is something which cannot be endured'. φορητὸν is a gerundive ('to be endured') and ἐστί should be supplied. Against such a force Phaedra should not try to resist.
ἢν πολλὴ ῥυῇ: 'if she flows in full force'. ῥυῇ is aorist (deponent) passive subjunctive of ῥέω after ἢν (= ἐάν).

444
ἣ: technically 'who', but best to start a new sentence with 'she'.
εἴκονθ': εἴκοντα.

445
ὃν δ' ἂν . . . εὕρῃ: indefinite construction (n. 411).
φρονοῦνθ' . . . μέγα: 'with proud thoughts', literally 'thinking big'. The language here echoes the words of Aphrodite in the Prologue.

446
πῶς δοκεῖς: 'ever so badly'. A colloquial expression, literally 'how do you think?'
καθύβρισεν: gnomic aorist (n. 428).

AS

448
ἔφυ: 'is born'. The root aorist from φύομαι often has a present sense.

450
οὗ . . . ἔκγονοι: 'from which . . . are sprung'. As all living beings are the product of sexual desire, Kypris is the root of everything and Phaedra should not try to resist. The Nurse here underlines the importance of love and sexuality, rejected so strongly by Hippolytus, to human experience.

451
παλαιτέρων: 'of the ancient poets'.

452
ἐν μούσαις ἀεὶ: 'constantly occupied with poetry', literally 'among the Muses'.

453
ὥς: 'that'. The accent here comes from the word ποτε ('once') which is an enclitic, a small word which attaches itself to the word before and often passes over its accent. Compare with unaccented ὡς (also 'that') in line 454.
ἠράσθη γάμων/Σεμέλης: 'lusted after a union with Semele'. The point is that even the gods are subject to Aphrodite's power and are not ashamed of it. The mythological exemplum used is that of Zeus' affair with the Theban princess Semele. While pregnant with their son (Dionysus), Semele begs Zeus to reveal his true divine form and she is burnt to a crisp as a result. This is hardly a reassuring example for a woman in Phaedra's position!

455
Κέφαλον . . . Ἕως: Cephalus was a young man abducted by Eos (Dawn).

457
κοὐ φεύγουσιν ἐκποδὼν θεούς: 'and they don't flee out of the way of the other gods'. This is the equivalent of suicide for the gods, who cannot die. There is Euripidean irony here: as the Nurse is trying to suggest the applicability of the gods' situation to Phaedra, we are reminded of the fundamental difference between them. Equally, in both stories it is mortals, not the gods, who suffer the consequences of love.

459
ἐπὶ ῥητοῖς . . . ἢ 'πὶ δεσπόταις θεοῖς/ἄλλοισιν: 'under fixed terms or under other gods as masters'. The point is that individual people cannot live under separate terms, and there is only one set of gods under whose laws humans can live.

462
κάρτ' ἔχοντας εὖ φρενῶν: 'who are very sensible'. ἔχω + adverb = εἰμί + adjective, literally 'who are very good of/in their senses'.

463
νοσοῦνθ': νοσοῦντα agreeing with λέκτρα.

μὴ δοκεῖν ὁρᾶν: 'pretend not to see it', literally 'seem not to see it'. Sensible people ignore infidelities. The Nurse here advances a morality rooted in pragmatism.

464

πόσους . . . πατέρας: supply δοκεῖς ('do you think?') from the previous question.

ἡμαρτηκόσι: 'who have committed some indiscretion', perfect participle from ἁμαρτάνω. The examples are carefully chosen to fit Theseus who will be affected as husband (of Phaedra) and father (of Hippolytus).

465

ἐν σοφοῖσι τάδ' ἐστὶ θνητῶν: 'this is a wise principle for mortals to follow', literally 'this is among wise things of mortals'.

466

λανθάνειν τὰ μὴ καλά: 'what is not good lies hidden', accusative + infinitive in apposition to τάδ' (n. 427). The Nurse again uses sophistic techniques by repeating Phaedra's language at 403, where she prays that she will be conspicuous for virtuous actions. The Nurse here claims that if she acts unvirtuously no one will notice. For μὴ here, see n. 291.

468

οὐδὲ . . . καλῶς ἀκριβώσαις ἄν: 'you wouldn't make perfectly exact', potential optative. The point is that a roof cannot be seen so there is no need for it to be perfect.

κατηρεφεῖς δόμοι: supply part of εἰμί.

469

τὴν τύχην . . . ὅσην σύ: 'as much misfortune as you have'.

470

ἂν ἐκνεῦσαι: 'could swim out'. The potential optative has become an infinitive in indirect statement. The metaphor presents Phaedra in a sea of troubles.

471

πλείω: contracted form of πλείονα, neuter accusative plural.

472

ἄνθρωπος οὖσα: 'being human'. Phaedra would be doing very well if her life had more good than bad as only gods can hope for perfect lives.

πράξειας ἄν: potential optative.

475

κρείσσω: contracted form of κρείσσονα, feminine accusative singular.

θέλειν: infinitive in apposition (n. 427) to τάδ'. Again sophistic argument is at play as the Nurse argues that Phaedra, by trying to behave with sexual self-control and moderation, is in fact committing hubris, a lack of self-control and moderation, against the gods.

477

εὖ πως: 'in some good way'. The Nurse is vague here in euphemistically referring to Phaedra consummating her passion with Hippolytus (who is not even mentioned in the speech). This is a clever tactic as she does not give the principled Phaedra anything concrete to object to.

479

φανήσεταί: 'will show up', future of φαίνομαι. Again, the Nurse is vague and does not explicitly explain that the magic is intended to make Hippolytus reciprocate Phaedra's advances, leaving open the possibility that it could remove Phaedra's love instead. The passive verb also suggests that the potion will spring out of nowhere, rather than be provided by the Nurse.

480

τἄρ': n. 441.

ἂν ὀψέ . . . μηχανὰς εὑρήσομεν: 'men would be slow to develop such tactics if we women didn't come up with them'. The Nurse optimistically states how resourceful women are, trying to create a sense of solidarity and involve Phaedra in the plan.

483

αἰνῶ δὲ σέ: the chorus leader is balanced. Even though the Nurse's words are useful in the circumstances, Phaedra's behaviour is still more praiseworthy.

484

δυσχερέστερος λόγων/τῶν τῆσδε: 'is harder to bear than her speech', with ἐστί supplied. Any praise of Phaedra's actions is double-edged as it will lead to her death, causing distress to the chorus and pain to Phaedra.

487

οἱ καλοὶ λίαν λόγοι: 'words that are too well spoken'. The Nurse's sophistry has not gone unnoticed.

488

οὐ . . . τι: 'not at all' (n. 344).

τοῖσιν ὠσὶ: dative plural of οὖς, ὠτός, τό (ear).

489

ἐξ ὅτου τις εὐκλεὴς γενήσεται.: 'anything as a result of which a person can gain good repute'. ὅτου is an alternative for οὗτινος.

491

τἀνδρός: 'the man', i.e. Hippolytus. The Nurse has had enough and speaks brusquely, acknowledging that the time for discussion has past.

ὡς τάχος: = ὡς τάχιστα.

διιστέον: 'we must make things clear'. Gerundive from διοῖδα, with εἰμί supplied, literally 'it to be known through and through'.

492

τὸν εὐθὺν ἐξειπόντας . . . λόγον: 'telling the direct truth'. ἐξειπόντας refers to the Nurse and Phaedra, but the masculine gender gives the statement a more generalizing feel.

494

σώφρων δ' οὖσ' ἐτύγχανες γυνή: 'and you happened to be a woman with self-control'. Harsh words from the Nurse who had promised to speak directly.

495

οὐκ ἄν . . . προῆγον ἄν: 'I wouldn't be leading.' ἄν is often repeated when separated from the verb. Imperfect + ἄν is used in the apodosis of a closed present conditional.

εὐνῆς οὕνεχ' ἡδονῆς τε σῆς: 'for your sexual pleasure'. An example of hendiadys, where two words joined by 'and' express one concept. Literally, 'for your bed and pleasure'.

497

κοὐκ ἐπίφθονον τόδε: 'this course is not something to be resented'. Supply ἐστι here and with ἀγών.

499

μεθήσεις: future of μεθίημι ('you will utter'). The tone of the conversation has degenerated somewhat.

500

αἴσχρα . . . σοι: the characterization of shameful things as better is a sophistic paradox.

501

τοὔργον: supply ἐστί. The contrast is between the Nurse's plan of action (again referred to vaguely) and Phaedra's destructive obsession with her reputation, evoking the common distinction between word and deed.

503

μη . . . πέρα προβῇς τῶνδ': 'don't go any further than this'. The broken syntax here indicates Phaedra's desperation.

σε: supply 'I beg'.

αἰσχρὰ: 'shamefully', translate as adverb contrasting with εὖ.

504

ὡς ὑπείργασμαι μὲν εὖ/ψυχὴν: 'since my soul is well ploughed'. ψυχὴν is accusative of respect, literally, 'I am well ploughed with respect to my soul.' Desire has ground down Phaedra so much that she is ready to acquiesce to the Nurse's proposals.

505

ἢν: ἐάν.

506

ἐς τοῦθ᾽ . . . ἀναλωθήσομαι: 'I will be all used up on the thing.' ἀναλωθήσομαι is future passive of ἀναλίσκω. Phaedra means that her energy will be fully spent as she will give way completely to her passion.

507

εἴ τοι δοκεῖ σοι: 'very well, if that is your decision . . .' The Nurse takes Phaedra's words to mean she is submitting to her, even though Phaedra did not make this clear.

χρῆν . . . οὔ σ᾽ ἁμαρτάνειν: for χρῆν, see n. 297. Translate ἁμαρτάνειν as 'be going astray', but it really refers to her being in love with Hippolytus. The Nurse reminds Phaedra that this is not the ideal situation, but to listen to her is the best choice in the circumstances.

508

εἰ δ᾽ οὖν: 'but since you are . . .'

δευτέρα γὰρ ἡ χάρις: 'for this favour is second best', an ambiguous phrase. The Nurse may simply mean that for Phaedra to do her a favour by obeying her instructions is second best to her never having fallen in love at all. However, Phaedra could also take it to imply that the Nurse has shelved her first plan (i.e. Phaedra satisfying her sexual desire with Hippolytus) in favour of the second best option (the drug mentioned in the next sentence).

510

ἔρωτος: 'for love'. The ambiguity continues as we are still unsure whether this means to create love in Hippolytus or to get rid of it for Phaedra.

ἦλθε δ᾽ ἄρτι μοι γνώμης ἔσω: 'it has just come into my mind', the Nurse was earlier talking about magic in general and has just remembered a particular spell which she can use.

511

σ᾽ . . . παύσει νόσου τῆσδ᾽: 'will free you from this disease'.

ἐπ᾽ αἰσχροῖς: 'accompanied by disgrace'.

512

ἢν: ἐὰν.

κακή: 'a coward'. The Nurse presents this is the brave, heroic course of action, but it remains unclear whether the bravery is required for merely taking a dangerous potion which will cure her of love, or approaching Hippolytus.

514

ἢ πέπλων ἄπο: 'or a piece from his clothing'.

515

συνάψαι τ᾽ ἐκ δυοῖν μίαν χάριν: 'and by uniting two things to produce a single gratifying outcome', literally 'to join together one gratification from two things'. The Nurse means to mix the potion with the token for it to have its desired outcome (χάριν), but the words have sexual undertones.

516

πότερα . . . ἢ . . .: πότερα is used in alternative questions (whether . . . or . . .) and can be left out in translation. ἐστί should be supplied. Phaedra's interest is piqued, and the tension is increased by stichomythia. The Nurse's answer suggests that even she doesn't really have anything in mind.

518

ὅπως . . . μὴ φανῇς: 'that you'll prove'. φανῇς is aorist subjunctive of φαίνομαι in the fear clause introduced by ὅπως μὴ. Although Phaedra has sanctioned the Nurse's actions she is still suspicious of her, and we do not know whether she thinks the drug will remove her love, or fire up Hippolytus' desire. The danger of σοφία is acknowledged here.

519

ἂν φοβηθεῖσ᾽: the potential optative has become a participle in indirect statement after ἴσθι, the imperative of οἶδα ('be aware').

521

ἔασον: 'let it be'. The Nurse dismisses Phaedra's worries.
θήσω: future of τίθημι.

523

εἴης: 'may you be', optative of wish. The Nurse asks Aphrodite to be her accomplice as she moves offstage and passes her statue, but really the Nurse is Aphrodite's instrument of vengeance.
τἄλλα δ᾽ οἷ᾽ ἐγὼ φρονῶ: 'the other sorts of things which I have in mind'. Again, the Nurse speaks in very vague terms.

524

τοῖς ἔνδον . . . φίλοις: another ambiguous reference which could refer to more servants inside, or Hippolytus himself.
ἡμῖν ἀρκέσει: 'it will be enough for me', royal we.

525–600: First Stasimon (525–564). The Chorus sing of the destructive power of Eros and Aphrodite. Start of the Second Episode (565–731) Phaedra, at the door to the palace, overhears Hippolytus inside angrily rebuking the Nurse for revealing Phaedra's feelings for him.

601
ἡλίου τ' ἀναπτυχαί: 'the wide expanse of land under the sun', literally 'unfoldings of the sun'. Hippolytus escapes the enclosed, contaminated domestic space and openly calls on the land to witness what he has heard. As Hippolytus and the Nurse come on stage, Phaedra may have remained on stage cowering at the side (if so, this would be the only time in the play when they are on stage together). Line 907 suggests that Hippolytus is aware of her presence but contemptuously refuses to address her directly, but as always with staging we cannot be sur, so she may even have left the stage completely here. The theme of speech and silence is bound up with what goes on inside the house and what goes on outside.

602
οἵων λόγων ἄρρητον εἰσήκουσ' ὄπα: 'what unspeakable words I have heard', literally 'of what sort of words is the unspeakable utterance which I have heard'. The number of words to do with communication emphasizes Hippolytus' disgust.

604
οὐκ ἔστ' . . . ὅπως σιγήσομαι: 'it is not possible for me to be silent', literally 'there is not a way in which I will be silent'.

605
πρός σε τῆς σῆς . . .: 'I beg you by your . . .,' πρός + genitive, with σε accusative after the implicit verb 'I beg' (also in line 607). The Nurse attempts to supplicate Hippolytus just as she had Phaedra (n. 324).

606
οὐ μὴ προσοίσεις: οὐ μή + future indicative = strong prohibition ('don't you dare'). οἴσω is future indicative from φέρω. Hippolytus refuses to her to touch his hand, the desperate Nurse now tries to grab his knees.

608
τί: 'why (do you say that)?'
εἴρηκας: perfect indicative of λέγω.

610
κάλλιον: supply ἐστί ('it is'). Hippolytus' words here are perhaps condescendingly sarcastic.

611
ὅρκους: the Nurse made Hippolytus swear an oath of silence before she revealed Phaedra's feeling.

A Level

612

ἡ γλῶσσ᾽ ὀμώμοχ᾽, ἡ δὲ φρὴν ἀνώμοτος: a very famous line quoted by Aristophanes (*Frogs* 101–102 and 1471) to satirize Euripides' amorality. Although Hippolytus angrily threatens that he will break his oath, his steadfast refusal to reveal the truth to Theseus later is important both for the plot and the presentation of Hippolytus' character. His comment here keeps the tension high as we are not sure whether he will keep it, but it also encapsulates many of the difficulties inherent in human communication which are so central to the play.

613

φίλους: 'those close to you'. φίλοι were not just friends but those in a wider network of close relationships including family members, business associates and dependents. The Nurse implicitly refers to Phaedra and herself, but Hippolytus angrily rejects her appeal and redefines the concept of φιλία, basing it on moral criteria rather than those of mutual social responsibilities.

614

ἀπέπτυσ᾽: 'I spit on your words' or less liteally, 'Pah! How dare you?' The aorist is sometimes used for actions in dramatic situations with reference to things so recent that English finds the present more natural. The act of spitting indicates Hippolytus' disgust, but it was also thought to avert (literally, 'spit *away*') the bad effects of offensive words. Note the harsh onomatopoeia.

615

σύγγνωθ᾽: = σύγγνωθι, second singular aorist active imperative of συγγιγνώσκω.

616

τί: 'why?'

κίβδηλον . . . κακὸν: in apposition to γυναῖκας ('as a . . .'). The word κίβδηλον ('counterfeit') uses the metaphor of fake coins to stress women's untrustworthy nature and inherent lack of value. Economic images occur throughout the speech as Hippolytus portrays women as costly commodities. The harsh misogyny in this speech, which begins with a wish that women did not exist, goes even further than his arrogant rejection of sex/Aphrodite earlier in the play. Even though many of these criticisms of women were not new (see *Medea* 573–575 and Hesiod's *Theogony* 570–612) and he is not criticized in the play for articulating them, the vehemence with which they are expressed would surely have been extreme even to an ancient ear, especially after such focus on Phaedra's suffering. It should still be remembered, however, that his words are an immediate response to the news that his step-mother wishes to sleep with him.

619

χρῆν: supply σε in this line ('you should not have . . .') but take with βροτοὺς in the following line ('but men should . . .'). For the tense of χρῆν in line 620 see n. 297.

A Level

620

ἀντιθέντας ... πρίασθαι: 'place in exchange and buy'. ἀντιθέντας is aorist participle of ἀντιτίθημι agreeing with βροτοὺς, but it is easiest to treat as two verbs joined by 'and'. πρίασθαι is aorist infinitive of ὠνέομαι.

622

παίδων . . . σπέρμα: translate as 'offspring' but, literally, 'the seed of offspring'.

του τιμήματος: 'at a valuation', genitive of price (also ἀξίας in the next line). Note that it is του (another form of indefinite τινος) and not τοῦ (definite article).

623

τῆς ἀξίας ἕκαστον: 'each child for its price'. Poor men without gold will only be able to afford lower quality children.

625–626: Some editors have deleted these lines, considering them to be interpolations, and they are not included in the A Level text. See the Appendix for Greek and translations of all missed lines here and in future.

627

τούτῳ: 'for the following reason'.

628

προσθεὶς: aorist active participle from προστίθημι. Dowries were customary in fifth-century Athens, but Hippolytus claims that fathers pay them merely to escape from their daughters. Compare this with Medea's inverse contention that women are forced to pay exorbitant prices for husbands just so they can become masters of their bodies (*Medea* 232–233).

630

φυτὸν: Hippolytus even denies women human status.

631

γέγηθε: 'rejoices in', perfect form with present meaning. Hippolytus describes women as statues and nothing but expensive decoration.

633

ὑπεξελών: aorist participle from ὑπεξαιρέω. The prefix ὑπο- often means 'gradually' or 'in secret' and underlines the sense of the husband's naivety.

634–637: lines omitted.

638

ῥᾷστον δ᾽ ὅτῳ τὸ μηδέν: 'it's easiest for the man whose wife is a nonentity'. For ὅτῳ, see n. 427. μηδέν is used as it is an indefinite statement.

ἀλλ᾽ ἀνωφελὴς εὐηθίᾳ κατ᾽ οἶκον ἵδρυται γυνή: 'but even a simple woman is set up in a household as a harmful thing'. εὐηθίᾳ is technically a dative noun ('set up with her simplicity') but an adjective captures the sense better. ἵδρυται is perfect passive (n. 287) and is often used of setting up statues, continuing the

A Level

earlier metaphor. So that he might not be misconstrued Hippolytus emphasizes that an unintelligent woman, although the lesser of two evils, is still dreadful.

641

εἴη: optative wish.

φρονοῦσα πλείον': 'a woman who is more intelligent', literally 'thinking more things'. Hippolytus moves from general misogyny to cases more appropriate to his situation. Some see evidence here that Hippolytus does intend to marry eventually (just not to a clever woman).

642

τὸ . . . κακοῦργον: n. 431. Hippolytus here envisages a destructive alliance between Kypris and clever women.

644

μωρίαν ἀφηρέθη: 'is kept from foolish action', gnomic aorist (n. 428) passive of ἀφαιρέομαι. μωρία is a euphemism for sexual misconduct, which allows Hippolytus to paradoxically and scornfully state that stupid women are too stupid to be stupid.

645

χρῆν: followed by πρόσπολον ('a servant should not . . .'), but reused in the next line with an indefinite subject ('but we should . . .').

646

ἄφθογγα: again, the theme of speech/silence. Hippolytus' ideal is that women are reduced to silence in the company of animals.

δάκη/θηρῶν: 'ravenous beasts', literally 'biting beasts of beasts'.

647

ἵν' εἶχον: ἵνα + indicative is used because the situation imagined is not real.

649

†αἱ μὲν ἔνδον δρῶσιν αἱ κακαὶ†: 'these evil women inside their own homes devise'. The obelus (†) marks enclose text which is probably corrupt but the editor cannot offer an adequate emendation. Hippolytus means that servants carry out women's plans without them even having to leave the house. These words touch on some of the male anxieties about women inside the home, and the greater fear that these issues will leave the domestic sphere and enter the public realm.

651

ὡς καὶ σύ γ': 'so you too'. Hippolytus finally addresses the current situation directly.

ἡμῖν πατρός . . . λέκτρων ἀθίκτων . . . ἐς συναλλαγάς: 'to do dealings with me over my father's chaste bed'. Hippolytus' disgust is shown by the juxtaposition of σύ and ἡμῖν, as well as the emphatic placement of πατρός, and the harsh alliterative address to the Nurse.

A
Level

653
ἁγὼ: crasis of ἅ ('these things') + ἐγώ.

655
οὐδ' ἀκούσας . . . δοκῶ: 'even hearing . . . do not think . . .', evidence of Hippolytus' obsession with his own purity.

656
τοὐμόν . . . εὐσεβές: see n. 431.

658
ἔσχον μὴ οὐ . . .: 'have held back from . . .' After negative verbs of prevention, redundant μὴ οὐ is often used.

659
ἔστ' ἂν: 'as long as', ἔστ' = ἔστε.

661
σὺν πατρὸς μολὼν ποδὶ: 'returning when my father does', literally 'having come with the foot of my father'. μολὼν is aorist participle from βλώσκω.

662
καὶ δέσποινα σή: this is the first direct reference to Phaedra, scornfully added almost as an afterthought.

663: line omitted.

664
ὄλοισθε: 'may you both perish'. Optative wish from ὠλόμην, the intransitive aorist of ὄλλυμι ('I die, I perish'). The words which follow further indicate that Hippolytus' sentiments go beyond conventional misogyny.

666
γὰρ οὖν: 'for indeed'.
πώς: πως ('in some way') takes an accent here as it is followed by the enclitic εἰσι (n. 453).

667
νύν: not νῦν ('now') but the emphatic enclitic νυν ('then', 'so'). Its accent here comes from τις, which is also enclitic. In Hippolytus' eyes all women lack sophrosyne.

669–681: Hippolytus exits and Phaedra laments her fate in lyric metre.

683
οἵ': = οἷα.
γεννήτωρ: Phaedra's father, Minos, was the son of Zeus.

685
οὐκ εἶπον: 'didn't I tell you', followed by infinitive σιγᾶν.

A
Level

686
ἐφ' οἷσι: 'about things owing to which', with antecedent (ταῦτα) omitted.

687
οὐκ ἀνέσχου: 'you couldn't hold yourself back'.

688
θανούμεθ': royal we.
καινῶν λόγων: Phaedra assumes Hippolytus will break his oath of silence, so needs a 'a new story' to counter his words.

689
συντεθηγμένος φρένας: 'his mind fully sharpened'. φρένας is accusative of respect, literally 'sharpened fully with respect to his mind'. The imagery evokes Hippolytus' fierce desire for vengeance.

690
καθ' ἡμῶν: 'against me' or 'to my discredit'.

691
Πιτθεῖ: Pittheus was Theseus' maternal grandfather.

693
ὄλοιο καὶ σὺ χὤστις: 'may you perish, both you and whoever'. For ὄλοιο, see n. 664.

694
μὴ καλῶς: 'dishonourably'.

696
τὸ . . . δάκνον: 'your biting agony', literally 'the thing biting'.

697
πρὸς τάδ' . . . λέγειν: 'speak in reply to this'.

699
οὐχ ἁβουλόμην: 'which were not what I wished for', crasis of ἃ ἐβουλόμην.

700
ἂν ἐν σοφοῖσιν ἦ: 'I would be counted among the wise'.

701
πρὸς τὰς τύχας γὰρ τὰς φρένας κεκτήμεθα: 'for we gain a reputation for good sense according to our fortunes'. The pragmatic Nurse believes that ends justify means, but that even ends are subject to the whims of fate (τύχη). She admits that things did not go to plan, but not that she was wrong.

A Level

702

ἦ γὰρ . . . ταῦτα: 'What? Is this really . . .' The particles suggest surprise and frustration.

κἀξαρκοῦντά: 'and satisfactory'.

703

τρώσασαν ἡμᾶς εἶτα συγχωρεῖν λόγοις: 'that you, after wounding me, then acquiesce in your words?' Supply σε with τρώσασαν and the resulting accusative + infinitive is in apposition to ταῦτα. ἡμᾶς is royal we.

704

οὐκ ἐσωφρόνουν ἐγώ: the Nurse finally admits she was wrong but undercuts this by immediately trying to suggest a new plan. A link here is made between talking too much, and lacking *sophrosyne*.

705

ἔστι: 'it is possible'. ὥστε can be ignored in translation.

706

τὰ πρὶν: 'before'.

708

πέρι: see n. 312.

709

τἀμὰ θήσομαι: 'I will arrange my affairs', θήσομαι = future middle of τίθημι. After this sentence, the Nurse leaves and is not seen again.

711

τοσόνδε: 'this much'.

713

Ἄρτεμιν: the goddess traditionally sworn to by women. The oath may have been accompanied by a gesture towards her statue. Ironically, their oath will seal the fate of her favourite, Hippolytus.

715

ἔλεξαθ': although the chorus leader swore in the first person singular, she represented the whole group.

†προτρέπουσ'† . . . ἔχω: 'I have discovered.' ἔχω + aorist participle is another way of expressing the perfect tense (periphrastic perfect). This is like English, which also uses an auxiliary verb. For the obeli, see n. 649.

717

προσθεῖναι: aorist infinitive of προστίθημι after ὥστε. Phaedra's main concerns are crystallized here: her children and her reputation.

A Level

718

πρὸς τὰ νῦν πεπτωκότα: 'in light of how things have now fallen out', using the metaphor of dice.

721

αἰσχροῖς ἐπ᾽ ἔργοις: 'after committing disgraceful deeds'.

οὕνεκα ψυχῆς μιᾶς: ambiguous as it is applicable both to herself and Hippolytus.

723

ὅπως: 'as for how'.

724

εὔφημος ἴσθι: 'don't say such inauspicious words'. ἴσθι is imperative of εἰμί, so, literally, 'be well-omened in your speech'.

728

κακόν γε χἀτέρῳ: 'the ruin of another, too'.

729

'πὶ: 'in response to'.

732–775: Second Stasimon: The chorus express a desire to escape, reminisce about Phaedra's ill-fated marriage and lament her imminent suicide.

Start of the Third Episode (776–1101): The Nurse cries from off-stage that Phaedra has hanged herself. Theseus returns from the oracle and is informed of Phaedra's suicide. Phaedra's corpse is wheeled out on the ekkyklema and Theseus laments her death. Theseus notices a tablet attached to her wrist, and upon reading it he bursts into a fit of despair and rage.

885

εὐνῆς: 'marriage bed'. This refers to Phaedra by metonymy (use of a related noun to refer to something, rather than direct reference), emphasizing the sexual perversity of the disgrace.

886

τὸ σεμνὸν Ζηνὸς ὄμμ᾽: Zeus was witness to all things (hence 'eye') and, as god of justice, likely to be offended by Hippolytus' supposed action.

887

Πόσειδον: mythological tradition ascribes to Theseus both a mortal (Aegeus) and immortal father (Poseidon).

ἃς . . . ἀρὰς . . . τρεῖς, μιᾷ . . . τούτων: 'as for those three curses which . . . with one of them'. Equivalent to μιᾷ τούτων ἀρῶν τριῶν ἃς but the curses are emphasized by being incorporated into the relative clause. In other versions of the story Theseus uses his last wish here; Euripides' decision to make it his first softens Theseus' characterization as he curses Hippolytus without certainty that it will be effective.

A Level

889
μὴ φύγοι: optative of wish.

890
ἡμῖν: royal we.

893
ἔστι: 'it is possible'.
καὶ πρός γ': 'and in addition, too'.

894
θατέρᾳ: 'by one'. By adding exile as a punishment, Theseus reveals his uncertainty about the effectiveness of the curse. All focus now moves onto this punishment, and the curse is not mentioned again until Hippolytus' death is announced. In lines 1045–1049 Theseus even defends his choice of exile over death. As well as softening Theseus' character, this also makes Hippolytus' death more unexpected when it occurs.
πεπλήξεται: 'he will find himself stricken'. Future perfect passive, focusing, like the perfect (n. 287), on the resultant state.

898
λυπρὸν ἀντλήσει βίον: 'he will sap out the dregs of a miserable life'. The verb originally means to bale out the dirty water from the bottom of a ship.

899
πάρα: = πάρεστι. Hippolytus now comes on stage in readiness for the agon (debate scene).

900
ἐξανεὶς: aorist participle from ἐξανίημι.

903
τὸ . . . πρᾶγμ' ὅτῳ στένεις ἔπι: 'what matter you are groaning about', with examples of antistrophe (n. 312) and prolepsis (n. 286). For ὅτῳ, see n. 427. The text here is disputed.

905
τί χρῆμα;: 'what's this?', literally, 'what thing?'. χρῆμα can often be omitted in translation (see also 909).
δάμαρθ': = δάμαρτα.

907
ἣν: 'her'.
ἔλειπον: the imperfect stresses how recently. This passage is evidence that Hippolytus was aware of Phaedra's presence when he made his misogynistic speech.

908
οὔπω χρόνος παλαιὸς: 'not long ago', literally 'it isn't yet a long time ago'.

A
Level

909

πάσχει: vivid present, translate this and διόλλυται as past.

τῷ: = τίνι. Hippolytus desperately tries to engage his father with questions, but Theseus refuses to answer him. Compare this with the Nurse's desperate attempts to make Phaedra speak earlier in the play.

912–913: lines omitted.

914

κἄτι μᾶλλον ἢ φίλους: 'and from those who are even more than friends', i.e. his own son.

916

ὦ . . . ἄνθρωποι: Theseus apostrophizes humankind in general rather than replying to Hippolytus, whom he only addresses directly at 946. These generalizations have a lot in common with the opening of Hippolytus' misogynistic speech.

πόλλ': it may help to translate this as 'so often'.

919

ἐθηράσασθέ: 'tracked down'. An interesting choice of word, evoking human resourcefulness and dominance over animals. It also calls to mind the hunter Hippolytus, whose senseless actions Theseus is referencing indirectly.

920

διδάσκειν: 'how to teach', in apposition to ἓν ('one thing').

οἷσιν οὐκ ἔνεστι νοῦς: 'those who have no sense', literally 'whom there is no sense in'. The antecedent τούτους ('those'), object of διδάσκειν, is omitted.

921

εἶπας: 'you are speaking about'. For the tense, see n. 614.

δεινὸν σοφιστὴν: 'a clever expert' (see Introduction for more on the word σοφιστὴν). Hippolytus is humouring his father's cryptic words.

εὖ φρονεῖν: 'to be sensible'.

922

μὴ: used as this refers to a type of person (indefinite).

923

ἀλλ' . . . γὰρ: 'but, since you are . . .', giving a reason for the main verb.

οὐ . . . ἐν δέοντι: 'at a time when it is not necessary', with a noun like καιρῷ supplied.

924

ὑπερβάλλῃ κακοῖς: 'may prove to be overreaching itself as a result of your troubles'. μή + subjunctive can be used for a fear for the future ('that x will happen') or for future ascertainment of a present fact ('that x will prove to be the case'). The dative κακοῖς is causal.

A Level

925
χρῆν βροτοῖσι τῶν φίλων σαφές τι κεῖσθαι: 'humans should have some sort of clear proof as to who their friends are', literally 'it is necessary that a proof of friends is established for men'. Medea makes a similar point about how there should be an external marker of a person's moral character (*Medea* 516–519).

927
ὅστις ἀληθής ἐστιν ὅς τε μὴ φίλος: 'to tell who is a true friend and who is not', indirect question. ὅς is used in place of ὅστις, and for μή, see n. 922.

928
πάντας ἀνθρώπους: 'all men should have', with χρῆν repeated.

929
τὴν δ᾽ ὅπως ἐτύγχανεν: 'the other however it happened to be'. Theseus means a person's normal voice which could tell the truth or lie. The voice of justice would interrupt whenever the normal voice lied. This thought experiment resembles Hippolytus' wish that children could be bought in temples, and is interesting in the context of the play's exploration of speech and communication.

930
ὡς . . . ἐξηλέγχετο: for the indicative with the purpose clause, see n. 647.
ἡ φρονοῦσα τἄδικ᾽: 'the one with unjust thoughts'.

931
κοὐκ ἂν ἠπατώμεθα: 'and we wouldn't be deceived'. ἄν + imperfect indicative is used to express a hypothetical situation in the present, as if it were half of a conditional ('it that were the case . . .').

932
ἀλλ᾽ ἦ: 'What? Can it be the case that . . .?' The particles suggest Hippolytus' surprised realization.
διαβαλὼν ἔχει: periphrastic perfect (n. 715).

933
νοσοῦμεν: 'I am suffering,' royal we.

934
ἔκ τοι πέπληγμαι: see n. 342 for this exact phrase.

935
ἔξεδροι φρενῶν: 'beyond all sense'. ἔξεδρος literally means 'out of place' carrying on the metaphor of παραλλάσσοντες.

936
φεῦ τῆς βροτείας . . . φρενός: 'oh the mortal mind'. φεῦ is often followed by a genitive denoting the reason behind the emotion.
ποῖ προβήσεται;: 'how far will it go?'

A Level

938
κατ᾽ ἀνδρὸς βίοτον: 'generation after generation', literally 'through the life of man'.

939
ὁ δ᾽ ὕστερος: 'the next generation.'
εἰς ὑπερβολὴν: 'far more than', literally 'in excess of', followed by the genitive.

940
θεοῖσι προσβαλεῖν . . . δεήσει: 'the gods will need to attach', rare example of δεῖ + dative.

941
ἣ χωρήσεται: 'to make room for', relative pronoun + future equivalent to purpose clause.

943
ὅστις: virtually equivalent to ὅς.

946
ἐς μίασμ᾽: see n. 317. Theseus tells Hippolytus that there is no need for him to turn his face away as he has already been exposed to his contagious pollution.

948
σὺ δὴ: 'are you the one who . . .', with δὴ expressing contempt. For Hippolytus' special relationship with Artemis and his perceived superiority to others see lines 73–87 where Hippolytus offers a wreath to Artemis' statue. That passage is evoked here particularly by shared vocabulary (ξύνει, σώφρων and ἀκήρατος).

949
οὐκ ἂν πιθοίμην . . . φρονεῖν κακῶς: 'I couldn't be persuaded by your boasts to think so incorrectly and attribute the gods with ignorance.' προσθεὶς is aorist participle from προστίθημι. Theseus means it would be wrong to think the gods stupid enough not to see through Hippolytus' arrogant claims.

952
νυν: n. 667.
αὔχει: 'carry on feeling proud'. The present imperatives suggest ongoing action (aspect).
δι᾽ ἀψύχου βορᾶς: 'through your vegetarian diet', literally 'lifeless food'. The keen huntsman Hippolytus was hardly a vegetarian, but Theseus is mockingly comparing him to a virtue-signalling follower of Orpheus (see n. 953).

953
σίτοις καπήλευ᾽: 'keep peddling your eating habits', literally 'be a peddler with food'. A κάπηλος is a market trader who convinces people of the value of cheap goods. Theseus means Hippolytus is presenting his way of life as honourable, when it is not in fact.

A Level

Ὀρφέα: Orpheus was a legendary musician around whom a religious cult, called Orphism, formed. Evidence is patchy, but its followers believed in an immortal soul which was reincarnated upon death but could be liberated by ascetic practices such as vegetarianism and secretive ritual acts. Its followers also had a reputation for charlatanism. Theseus is taunting Hippolytus' deeply held personal religion by comparing him to a fanatical, and hypocritical, follower of such an eccentric cult.

954

βάκχευε: 'keep engaging in your Bacchic rites'. Bacchic rituals consisted of drinking, music and dancing with the aim of entering a trance-like state. It is unclear how related Orphism was to Bacchus but the verb adds to the exaggerated image of Hippolytus' fanaticism.

πολλῶν γραμμάτων . . . καπνούς: 'many hazy writings', literally 'the smokes of many writings'. καπνός ('smoke') can refer to anything trivial or worthless. Orphism relied on a body of poetry ascribed to Orpheus himself, and his follower Musaeus.

956

θηρεύουσι: 'they hunt down their prey'. Theseus continues his characterization of these religious fanatics as shameful hypocrites. The hunting metaphor is also contained in the word ἐλήφθης.

958

ἥδε: n. 294.

τοῦτο: i.e. the fact that Phaedra cannot speak to convict him. Theseus imagines Hippolytus' defence but in 959 claims that her dead body is evidence enough.

959

ἁλίσκῃ . . . αἰτίαν φυγεῖν: the forensic nature of Theseus' speech is marked by legal vocabulary.

962

μισεῖν . . . τήνδε: 'that she hated'. In indirect statement the present infinitive may represent the imperfect of direct speech. This is the second defence Theseus predicts and quashes.

καὶ τὸ δὴ νόθον: 'and indeed that the bastard'. The neuter adjective is used to refer to bastards as a collective.

964

κακὴν ἄρ' αὐτὴν ἔμπορον βίου: 'that she traded her life in so badly', literally 'that indeed she was a bad trader of her life'. Theseus means it is preposterous to think that she would have killed herself just to frame you. In fact, Phaedra did trade in her life in exchange for her reputation.

965

σῆ: 'of you' (not possessive 'your').

τὰ φίλτατ': i.e. her life.

A Level

966
ὡς: 'will you say that'. The third predicted defence is the argument (appropriate given Hippolytus' earlier speech) that it is always women who are responsible for crimes based on lust.
τὸ μῶρον: 'stupidity', n. 431.
ἔνι: = ἔνεστι.

968
ἀσφαλεστέρους: 'more liable to trip up'. ἀσφαλής (often 'safe') is literally 'untrippupable', from σφάλλω ('I trip up').

970
τὸ δ' ἄρσεν αὐτοὺς ὠφελεῖ προσκείμενον: 'the fact that they are male makes it easier for them', literally 'the maleness assigned to them helps them'. Theseus acknowledges that societal double-standards allow men to get away with things which women would be criticized for.

971
ταῦτα σοῖς ἁμιλλῶμαι λόγοις: 'do I contend with your words in this way'. ταῦτα is technically an internal accusative ('I make these contentions'), one which refers to the action of the verb itself rather than the external object acted upon. Consider the difference between 'I strike a blow' and 'I strike the pupil.'

973
ὅσον τάχος: = ὡς τάχιστα.

974
μόλῃς: aorist subjunctive of βλώσκω, followed by accusative with no preposition ('go to').

977
Ἴσθμιος Σίνις: Sinis was an outlaw killed by Theseus at the Isthmus (the strip of land which connects the Peloponnese to the rest of Greece) in his youth. Sinis used to get travellers to help him bend down trees to the ground, but would then let go, flinging the travellers to their death. Theseus means that if he lets Hippolytus go, all his previous heroic deeds will count for nothing. Like Phaedra, reputation is important to Theseus.

978
κομπάζειν: 'but (will bear witness that I) boast'.

979
Σκιρωνίδες . . . πέτραι: 'the rocks of Sciron'. Sciron was another bandit killed by Theseus at Megara north of the Isthmus. Sciron made travellers wash his feet near the cliffs before kicking them off the edge.

980
βαρύν: 'harsh to'.

A Level

982
τὰ . . . πρῶτ᾽ ἀνέστραπται πάλιν: 'what was most noble has been turned over upside down'. ἀνέστραπται is perfect passive of ἀναστρέφω, and πάλιν emphasizes the idea already present in ἀνα- (here translated as 'over').

984
ἔχον: 'although it provides an opportunity for fine words', concessive participle.

985
τόδε: supply part of εἰμί.

986
ἄκομψος εἰς ὄχλον δοῦναι λόγον: 'unaccomplished in making speeches before a crowd'. δοῦναι is an epexegetic infinitive, one which explains or defines the meaning of an adjective, adverb or noun (see also λέγειν in 989). ὄχλος refers to the chorus, and perhaps a few other silent attendants and citizens on stage. This is a relatively conventional introduction to what is a self-consciously rhetorical speech.

987
ἐς ἥλικας δὲ κὠλίγους: 'at speaking to a small number of my peers'. Athenians on trial would often begin by acknowledging their lack of rhetorical skill to win the jurors over. Hippolytus, however, uses the opportunity to express contempt for the common people and stress his own superiority.

988
ἔχει δὲ μοῖραν: 'is right and proper'. μοῖρα can mean 'what is fated' , and therefore also 'what is right'.
οἱ γὰρ ἐν σοφοῖς/φαῦλοι: 'those who are considered worthless by the wise'.

991
γλῶσσάν . . . ἀφεῖναι: 'to speak', literally 'to let loose my tongue'. ἀφεῖναι is aorist infinitive of ἀφίημι.

992
μ᾽ ὑπῆλθες: 'you tried to catch me out', literally 'you came upon me stealthily' (n. 633).

993
οὐκ ἀντιλέξοντ᾽: 'without me being able to reply'.

995
ἢν: = ἐὰν.
σωφρονέστερος: Hippolytus' arrogant claim counters Theseus' assertion that he was unable to restrain his lust for Phaedra and is central to his own view of himself.

A
Level

997

φίλοις . . . χρῆσθαι: 'to treat as friends those who . . .' See n. 613 for Hippolytus' definition of φιλία as based on moral purity.

998

οἷσιν αἰδὼς μήτ᾽ ἐπαγγέλλειν κακὰ/μήτ᾽ ἀνθυπουργεῖν αἰσχρὰ τοῖσι χρωμένοις: 'who would be ashamed either to give evil instructions or to render in return shameful services to their companions'. More literally, 'but to whom (there is) a sense of shame (such as) neither to order bad things nor render shameful services to those treating (them as friends)'. Hippolytus can only reference the actions of Phaedra and the Nurse implicitly due to his oath of silence.

1001

αὑτὸς οὐ παροῦσι κἀγγὺς ὢν φίλοις: 'being the same to my friends whether they are not present or nearby', αὑτὸς = crasis of ὁ αὐτὸς. Hippolytus means he would not treat his father badly behind his back by sleeping with Phaedra.

1002

ᾧ με νῦν ἔχειν δοκεῖς: 'the thing with which you think you now have hold of me'.

1003

λέχους . . . ἁγνὸν: 'pure of sex'.

ἐς τόδ᾽ ἡμέρας: 'to this very moment', literally 'to this point of day'.

1005

γραφῇ: 'in paintings', such as explicit sexual images on vases.

1007

καὶ δὴ τὸ σῶφρον τοὐμὸν οὐ πείθει σ᾽: 'and I suppose the idea of my chastity isn't convincing you'.

ἴτω: 'drop it'. Literally, 'let it go', third person imperative.

1008

τῷ: = τίνι.

διεφθάρην: 'I was corrupted'. Hippolytus says that Theseus needs to explain logically why Hippolytus would have thrown away the chastity which he valued so much. Hippolytus shows his lack of understanding here, as lust does not often have a logical explanation.

1009

ἐκαλλιστεύετο: Hippolytus, like Theseus earlier, now imagines and refutes his father's potential arguments. He first implies that Phaedra was not even the most beautiful woman, a contention which is hardly going to win over Theseus.

1010

σὸν οἰκήσειν δόμον ἔγκληρον εὐνὴν προσλαβὼν: 'that I would become lord of your household by securing a marriage with inheritance attached'. οἰκήσειν

A Level

δόμον can mean 'dwell in a house as master' rather than just 'dwell in a house'. The second imagined argument is that Hippolytus could get hold of Theseus' property by marrying Phaedra, who would inherit his wealth upon his death (presumably at Hippolytus' hands).

1012
ἆρ': 'then'.
οὐδαμοῦ μὲν οὖν φρενῶν: 'or even completely out of my mind', literally 'nowhere of senses'. μὲν οὖν can be used to correct a previous statement. Hippolytus suggests that the argument is so absurd that it does not need explanation: the plan would mean killing his own father, which was unthinkable; the inheritance might in fact go to Theseus' legitimate male heirs, Phaedra's children; raping Phaedra was not a likely way to gain a marriage. Hippolytus continues assessing the absurdity of this idea in the next lines, by explaining how he has no wish for Theseus' wealth and position.

1013
ἀλλ' ὡς: 'but will you say that', used also by Theseus at 966.

1014
εἰ μὴ . . . ὅσοισιν ἁνδάνει μοναρχία: 'unless monarchy makes the minds of all men whom it pleases corrupt'. διέφθορεν is perfect of διαφθείρω. The obeli show that the Greek is suspect here (perhaps 'unless' should be replaced by 'since'?), but the general idea is clear: Hippolytus refutes the idea that sensible people enjoy kingship by claiming that power corrupts. This is not the most tactful argument to use to Theseus, a man who exercises μοναρχία.

1016
ἀγῶνας . . . κρατεῖν Ἑλληνικοὺς . . . πρῶτος: 'to win first place at the Hellenic games'. In keeping with his youth and love of horses, Hippolytus wishes for success in athletic competitions rather than power.

1018
εὐτυχεῖν ἀεὶ: 'to continue living a prosperous life'.

1019
πράσσειν: 'for me to exercise political power'. In 'second place in the city', Hippolytus gets the benefits of power without the fear of assassination.
κίνδυνός . . . ἀπὼν: 'the absence of danger', literally 'absent danger'.

1020
κρείσσω . . . χάριν: 'greater pleasure', see n. 475.

1021
τῶν ἐμῶν: 'of my points'.

1022
οἷός εἰμ' ἐγὼ: 'as to what sort of person I am'.

A Level

1024
ἔργοις ἂν εἶδες τοὺς κακοὺς διεξιών: 'you would have seen from the facts who was in the wrong by examining things in detail'. Hippolytus implies that this is not a fair trial and draws a distinction between ἔργα ('deeds', 'facts') and the λόγοι ('words', 'arguments') which their debate has relied upon.

1025
ὅρκιόν . . . Ζῆνα: 'by Zeus the protector of oaths'.

1026
μήποθ': = μήποτε. μή is the negative used with the infinitive in oaths.

1027
μηδ' ἂν ἔννοιαν λαβεῖν: 'nor would I have conceived the idea'. The aorist infinitives with ἄν represent aorist indicatives with ἄν ('would have', the aorist of lost opportunity) which would have been used in direct speech.

1028
τἄρ': n. 441.

1029: line omitted.

1034
ἐσωφρόνησε δ' οὐκ ἔχουσα σωφρονεῖν: 'she acted virtuously when she could not be virtuous', ἔχω + infinitive = I am able to. Hippolytus' oath limits him to these cryptic words, which might lead Theseus to suspect Hippolytus of knowing more than he is letting on. Phaedra's virtuous act was her suicide when her passion made her unable to live virtuously. Hippolytus' words also lead us to question the difference between a person's general moral character and their individual moral decisions.

1035
ἡμεῖς δ' ἔχοντες οὐ καλῶς ἐχρώμεθα: 'but I, despite being able to be virtuous, I didn't make good use of it'. Hippolytus means that he received no benefit from acting virtuously (both by refusing Phaedra and keeping his oath of silence).
1036–1466: For a summary of the rest of the play, see the Introduction.

A
Level

Appendix: Deleted lines

For discussion of each deletion, see the commentary of W. S. Barrett (1964).

625–626
νῦν δ᾽ εἰς δόμους μὲν πρῶτον ἄξεσθαι κακὸν
μέλλοντες ὄλβον δωμάτων ἐκτίνομεν.

But as it is, intending to bring an evil into our house, we first pay out the wealth of our homes.

634–637
ἔχει δ᾽ ἀνάγκην: ὥστε κηδεύσας καλῶς
γαμβροῖσι χαίρων σῴζεται πικρὸν λέχος,
ἢ χρηστὰ λέκτρα πενθεροὺς δ᾽ ἀνωφελεῖς
λαβὼν πιέζει τἀγαθῷ τὸ δυστυχές.

But he cannot escape this: as a result, if he marries into a good family, he is pleased with his in-laws but keeps a marriage bed which is bitter to him, or if he acquires a good marriage but unprofitable in-laws he suppresses his ill-fortune with what is good.

663
τῆς σῆς δὲ τόλμης εἴσομαι γεγευμένος.

And I will know that I have tasted your daring.

912–913
ἡ γὰρ ποθοῦσα πάντα καρδία κλύειν
κἀν τοῖς κακοῖσι λίχνος οὖσ᾽ ἁλίσκεται.

For the heart which desires to hear everything even in troubles is convicted of being greedy.

1029
ἄπολις ἄοικος, φυγὰς ἀλητεύων χθόνα

without city, without house, an exile wandering over the land

A Level

Vocabulary

An asterisk * denotes a word in OCR's Defined Vocabulary List for AS.

ἆ	alas
ἀβουλόμην	crasis of ἆ ἐβουλόμην
*ἀγαθός, ἀγαθή, ἀγαθόν	good
ἄγαλμα, ἀγάλματος, τό	statue
ἄγε	come!
ἁγνεύω	I am pure
ἁγνός, ἁγνή, ἁγνόν	pure, undefiled
ἀγὼ	crasis of ἆ ἐγὼ
*ἀγών, ἀγῶνος, ὁ	contest, struggle
ἀγωνίζομαι	I plead my case
*ἀδικέω	I do wrong
*ἄδικος, ἄδικον	unjust
*ἀεί	always
*Ἀθῆναι, Ἀθηνῶν, αἱ	Athens
ἄθικτος, ἄθικτον	chaste, inviolable; untouched by (+ gen.)
ἀθρέω	I look
αἶα, αἴας, ἡ	land
*αἰδέομαι	I respect, I feel shame before
Ἅιδης, Ἅιδου, ὁ	Hades
αἰδώς, αἰδοῦς, ἡ	shame
αἰθήρ, αἰθέρος, ὁ	air
*αἷμα, αἵματος, τό	blood
αἰνέω	I praise
αἶνος, αἴνου, ὁ	praise
*αἱρέω, aor. pass. ᾑρέθην	I take, I catch
*αἰσθάνομαι, aor. ᾐσθόμην	I perceive (+ gen.)
*αἴσχιστος, αἰσχίστη, αἴσχιστον	most shameful (superl. of αἰσχρός)
*αἰσχρός, αἰσχρά, αἰσχρόν	shameful
*αἰσχύνω, fut. αἰσχυνῶ, aor. ᾔσχυνα	I shame, I disgrace
*αἰτία, αἰτίας, ἡ	charge
*αἴτιος, αἰτία, αἴτιον	guilty
ἀκήρατος, ἀκήρατον	untainted by (+ gen.)
ἀκλεής, ἀκλεές	without glory
ἄκομψος, ἄκομψον	unadorned, unaccomplished
*ἀκούω	I hear; I hear (+ gen.)
ἀκριβόω	I make exact
*ἄκων, ἄκουσα, ἆκον	unwilling
ἀλάομαι	I wander
ἀλγεινός, ἀλγεινή, ἀλγεινόν	painful
ἀλγίων, ἄλγιον	more painful (compar. of ἀλγεινός)
*ἀληθής, ἀληθές	true
ἁλίσκομαι, aor. ἑάλων	I am caught, I am found guilty, I am convicted
*ἀλλά	but
*ἄλλος, ἄλλη, ἄλλο	other, another
ἄλλως	in vain
*ἅμα	at the same time
Ἀμαζών, Ἀμαζόνος, ἡ	Amazon
ἀμαθία, ἀμαθίας, ἡ	ignorance
ἁμαρτάνω, aor. ἥμαρτον, pf. *ἡμάρτηκα	I go astray, I make a mistake, I commit a fault
ἁμαρτία, ἁμαρτίας, ἡ	fault, error
ἀμὲ	crasis of ἆ ἐμε
ἀμείνων, ἀμείνον	better
ἀμήχανος, ἀμήχανον	incompetent, helpless
ἁμιλλάομαι	I compete with (+ dat.) I contend with (+ dat.)
*ἀμπλακών	participle of ἤμπλακον
*ἀμφί	about (+ gen.)
ἄμφω	both
*ἄν	would, could (indef.)
*ἀνά	through (+ acc.)

***ἀναγκάζω**, aor. **ἠνάγκασα**	I force
***ἀνάγκη**	necessary; (+ **ἐστί** = it is necessary)
ἀναλίσκω, fut. pass. **ἀναλωθήσομαι**	I spend
ἄναξ, ἄνακτος, ὁ	lord
ἀναπτυχή, ἀναπτυχῆς, ἡ	ray
ἀναρπάζω	I snatch up
ἄνασσα, ἀνάσσης, ἡ	queen
ἀναστρέφω, perf. mid./pass. **ἀνέστραμμαι**	I turn upside down
ἀνασχετός, ἀνασχετόν	endurable
ἁνδάνω	I delight (+ dat.)
ἀνέχομαι, fut. **ἀνέξομαι**, aor. **ἀνεσχόμην**	I endure, I hold myself back
ἀνήκεστος, ἀνήκεστον	incurable
***ἀνήρ, ἀνδρός, ὁ**	man, husband
ἁνθάδε	crasis of **ἃ ἐνθάδε**
***ἄνθρωπος, ἀνθρώπου, ὁ**	human, man
ἀνθυπουργέω	I render a service in return
ἀνίημι, fut. **ἀνήσω**	I cease from, I give up (+ gen.)
ἄνοια, ἀνοίας, ἡ	foolishness, lack of thought
ἀντερῶ (fut. only)	I will deny
ἀντιθέντας	aor. ppl. of **ἀντιτίθημι**
ἀντιλέγω, fut. **ἀντιλέξω**	I speak in reply
ἀντιτίθημι	I place in return
ἀντλέω	I use up, I sap out
ἀνώμοτος, ἀνώμοτον	unsworn, not bound by oath
ἀνώνυμος, ἀνώνυμον	without name
ἀνωφελής, ἀνωφελές	harmful
ἀξία, ἀξίας, ἡ	price, worth
***ἄξιος, ἀξία, ἄξιον**	worthy of (+ gen.)
ἀπαλλάσσω, aor. pass. **ἀπηλλάχθην**	I free from, I release from (+ gen.)
ἁπανταχοῦ	everywhere
ἀπατάω	I deceive
ἄπειμι	fut. of **ἀπέρχομαι**
ἄπειμι	I am absent
ἀπερχομαι, fut. **ἄπειμι**, aor. **ἀπῆλθον**	I go away
ἀπεύχομαι	I pray that x may not happen
***ἀπό**	from (+ gen.)
ἀποικίζω	I send away from home
***ἀποκτείνω**	I kill
***ἀπολλυμι**, aor. **ἀπώλεσα**	I destroy, I lose; (mid.) I am destroyed
ἀποπτυω	I spit away, I loathe
ἀπόρρητος, ἀπόρρητον	not fit to be spoken of
ἀποσκήπτω	I sweep down upon
***ἅπτομαι**	I touch (+ gen.)
***ἄρα**	so, then, indeed, surely
ἀρά, ἀρᾶς, ἡ	curse
ἄριστος, ἀρίστη, ἄριστον	best (superl. of **ἀγαθός**)
ἀρκέω, fut. **ἀρκέσω**	I am enough, I am sufficient
ἄρρητος, ἄρρητον	unspeakable
ἄρσην, ἄρσεν	male
ἄρσην, ἄρσενος, ὁ	man
Ἄρτεμις, Ἀρτέμιδος, ἡ	Artemis
***ἄρτι**	just, recently
ἀρτίως	just, recently
***ἄρχω**	(act. and mid.) I begin, I am first to
***ἀσφαλής, ἀσφαλές**	safe, liable to trip up
ἀτάρ	but
ἄτερ	without (+ gen.)
ἀτηρός, ἀτηρά, ἀτηρόν	ruinous
ἀτιμάζω	I dishonour
***αὖ**	in turn
αὐδάω	I talk about
αὐθάδης, αὔθαδες	stubborn
***αὖθις**	again, later, from now on
αὑτός	crasis of **ὁ αὐτός**
***αὐτός, αὐτή, αὐτό**	him, her, it; -self; (after art.) the same
αὐχέω	I feel proud
ἀφαιρέομαι, aor. pass. **ἀφηρέθην**	I hold someone (acc.) back from something (ac.)
ἀφανής, ἀφανές	unclear
ἄφαρκτος, ἄφαρκτον	off guard
ἀφεῖναι	aor. infinitive of **ἀφίημι**
ἀφῇ	aor. subjunc. of **ἀφίημι**
ἄφθογγος, ἄφθογγον	speechless
ἀφίημι, aor. **ἀφῆκα**	I release, I let loose
ἀφικνεομαι, fut. **ἀφίξομαι**, aor. ***ἀφικόμην**, perf. **ἀφῖγμαι**	I arrive, I approach, I come upon
ἄψυχος, ἄψυχον	lifeless, vegetarian
βακχεύω	I engage in Bacchic rites
βάρος, βάρους, τό	weight

***βαρύς, βαρεῖα, βαρύ**	heavy, harsh
βελτίων, βέλτιον	better (compar. of **ἀγαθός**)
***βίᾳ**	by force
βιάζομαι	I use force
***βίος, βίου, ὁ**	life
βίοτος, βιότου, ὁ	life
βλάβη, βλάβης, ἡ	harm
***βλέπω**	I look
βλώσκω, aor. **ἔμολον**	I go, I come
***βοή, βοῆς, ἡ**	shout
βορά, βορῆς, ἡ	food
βούλευμα, βουλεύματος, τό	plan
***βουλεύομαι**	I deliberate, I determine, I think about
βουλοίμην ἄν	I would like
***βούλομαι**, aor. **ἐβουλήθην**	I want, I desire
βραχύς, βραχεῖα, βραχύ	small, insignificant
βρότειος, βρότειον	mortal
βροτός, βροτοῦ, ὁ	mortal
γαῖα, γαίας, ἡ	earth, land
γάμος, γάμου, ὁ	marriage, union
***γάρ**	for, yes/no for . . .
γαυρόομαι	I pride myself on (+ dat.)
***γε**	indeed, at any rate, at least (emphasis)
γέγηθα (perf. used for pres.)	I rejoice in (+ ppl.)
γεγώς, γεγῶσα, γεγώς	perf. ppl. from **γίγνομαι**
γείνομαι	I give birth to
γενναῖος, γενναία, γενναῖον	noble
γεννήτωρ, γεννήτορος, ὁ	ancestor
***γένος, γένους, τό**	race
γέρων, γέρον	aged
***γῆ, γῆς, ἡ**	land
***γίγνομαι**, fut. **γενήσομαι**, aor. **ἐγενόμην**	I become, I am, I am born; (perf.) I am by nature
***γιγνώσκω**, fut. **γνώσομαι**, aor. **ἔγνων**	I get to know, I know
***γλῶσσα, γλώσσης, ἡ**	tongue
γνήσιος, γνήσια, γνήσιον	legitimate
***γνώμη, γνώμης, ἡ**	mind, intelligence, thoughts
γονύ, γόνατος, τό	knee

γράμμα, γράμματος, τό	letter; (plur.) writings
γραφή, γραφῆς, ἡ	writing, painting
***γυνή, γυναικός, ἡ**	woman, wife
δαιμών, δαιμόνος, ὁ	god
δάκνω	I bite
δάκος, δάκους, τό	biting beast
δάμαρ, δάμαρτος, ἡ	wife
***δέ**	and, but
δέδοικα (perf. used for pres.)	I fear
***δεῖ**, fut. **δεήσει**	it is necessary (+ acc. + inf., rarely + dat. + inf.), there is need of x (gen.) for y (acc.)
***δείκνυμι**, aor. **ἔδειξα**	I show, I reveal
δειμαίνω	I fear
δεινός, δεινή, δεινόν	terrible, clever
δέμας, τό (nom./acc. only)	body
***δεξιά, δεξιᾶς, ἡ**	right hand
***δέσποινα, δεσποίνης, ἡ**	mistress
***δεσπότης, δεσπότου, ὁ**	master
***δεῦρο**	here
δεύτερος, δευτέρα, δεύτερον	second
***δέχομαι**	I receive, I hear, I listen
***δή**	indeed
***δῆλος, δήλη, δῆλον**	clear
***δῆτα**	indeed
***διά**	through (+ gen.)
διαβάλλω, aor. **διέβαλον**	I slander
διάγνωσις, διαγνώσεως, ἡ	judgement, way of understanding
διαπτύσσω	I unfold, I examine closely
διαφθείρω, fut. **διαφθερῶ**, perf. ***διέφθορα**, aor. pass. **διεφθάρην**	I destroy, I corrupt
διαφθορεύς, -έως, ἡ	destroyer
***διδάσκω**	I teach
***δίδωμι**, fut. **δώσω**, aor. **ἔδωκα**	I give
διεξέρχομαι	I go through in detail
διεξιών	pres. ppl. of **διεξέρχομαι**
διεργάζομαι	I destroy
διιστέος, διιστέα, διιστέον	to be known through and through

*δίκαιος, δικαία, δίκαιον	just
διόλλυμι	I destroy; (pass.) I perish
Διόνυσος, Διονύσου, ὁ	Dionysus
δισσός, δισσή, δισσόν	two
*δοκεῖ	it seems good to (+ dat.), x (dat.) decides
*δοκέω, fut. δόξω	I seem, I think
δόμος, δόμου, ὁ	house (freq. in plur. for sing.)
*δόξα, δόξης, ἡ	reputation
δόρυ, δόρατος, τό	spear
*δουλόω	I enslave
δοῦναι	aor. inf. of δίδωμι
*δράω, fut. δράσω	I do, I devise
*δυνατός, δυνατή, δυνατόν	able
δυό, δυοῖν	two
δυσκλεής, δυσκλεές	shameful
δυσμενεία, δυσμενείας, ἡ	hatred
δυσπραξία, δυσπραξίας, ἡ	misfortune
δύστηνος, δύστηνον	miserable, wretched, unlucky
δυστυχέω	I am unfortunate
δυσχερής, δυσχερές	hard to bear
δῶμα, δώματος, τό	house (freq. in plur. for sing.)
*δῶρον, δώρου, τό	gift
ἔα	ah!
*ἐάν	if
*ἑαυτόν, ἑαυτήν, ἑαυτό	himself, herself, itself
*ἐαω, aor. εἴασα	I allow, I let be
ἐγγελαστής, ἐγγελαστοῦ, ὁ	mocker, one who mocks
*ἐγγύς	near
ἔγκληρος, ἔγκληρον	with inheritance attached
*ἐγώ, ἐμοῦ/μου	I
*ἔγωγε	I at any rate
*ἐθέλω, ἠθέλησα	I want
*εἰ	if
εἰ μή	unless, if not
εἴ τις, εἴ τι	if anyone, if anything, whoever, whatever
εἰδῇ	subjunctive of οἶδα
εἶέν	so, well then
*εἰκός, εἰκότος, τό	likelihood; (+ ἐστί) it is reasonable, expected
εἴκω	I yield

*εἶμι	I will go
*εἰμί, fut. ἔσομαι	I am
εἴπερ	if really, if indeed
*εἰς	to, into, on, in, at, for, against (+ acc.)
εἷς, μία, ἕν	one
εἰσακούω, εἰσήκουσα	I hear
εἰσδέρκομαι	I look at
εἰσοράω	I see, I look upon
εἶτα	then
*ἐκ, ἐξ	from, because of (+ gen.)
*ἕκαστος, ἑκάστη, ἕκαστον	each
ἔκγονος, ἔκγονον	born from, sprung from (+ gen.)
ἐκδημέω	I am out of the country
*ἐκεῖθεν	then, from there
*ἐκεῖνος, ἐκείνη, ἐκεῖνο	that, he, she, it
ἐκνεω, aor. ἐξένευσα	I swim out
ἐκπίπτω, aor. ἐξέπεσον	I am exiled
ἐκπλήσσω, perf. pass. ἐκπέπληγμαι	I amaze, I strike with panic; (perf. pass.) I am alarmed
ἐκποδών	out of the way (adv.)
ἐκπονέω	I finish off, I perfect
ἐκσῴζω	I save
ἐκφαίνω, aor. ἐξέφηνα	I reveal
ἐκφέρω	I bring out, I accomplish
ἔκφορος, ἔκφορον	can be divulged
ἑκών, ἑκοῦσα, ἑκόν	willing
ἐλέγχω	I refute, I examine
*ἐλεύθερος, ἐλευθέρα, ἐλεύθερον	free
Ἑλληνικός, Ἑλληνική, Ἑλληνικόν	Hellenic
*ἐμός, ἐμή, ἐμόν	my, of mine
ἐμπιμπλημι, fut. pass. ἐμπλησθήσομαι	I fill; (pass.) I have my fill of
ἔμπορος, ἐμπόρου, ὁ/ἡ	merchant
ἐμφανής, ἐμφανές	clear
ἐμφύομαι, perf. ἐμπέφυκα	I am born in (+ dat.); (perf. with pres. sense) I am by nature in, I am inherent to (+ dat.)
*ἐν	in, on, among, engaged with, because of (+ dat.)

***ἐναντίος, ἐναντία, ἐναντίον**	opposite, in front of (+ dat.)
ἔνδον	inside
ἔνειμι	I am in (+ dat.)
***ἐνθάδε**	here
ἔνι	= **ἔνεστι**
ἐννοέομαι	I realize
ἔννοια, ἐννοίας, ἡ	plan
***ἐντεῦθεν**	from here on
ἐντίκτω	I engender
ἐξαγορεύω, aor. **ἐξεῖπον**	I say, I tell, I declare
ἐξαίρω	I raise up, I incite
ἐξαιτέομαι	I request
***ἐξαίφνης**	suddenly
ἐξανείς	aor. part. of **ἐξανίημι**
ἐξανίημι, aor. **ἐξανῆκα**	I slacken off from (+ gen.)
ἐξανύτω	I manage
ἐξαρτάομαι	I fasten to, I hang off (+ gen.)
ἔξεδρος, ἔξεδρον	beyond (+ gen.)
ἐξεῖπον	aor. of **ἐξαγορεύω**
ἐξελαύνω, fut. **ἐξελῶ**	I exile
ἐξελεγχω	I refute, I convict
ἐξεργάζομαι	I destroy
ἔξερρε	get away! (only in imperat.)
ἐξευρίσκω ἐξηῦρον	I discover, I invent
ἐξογκόομαι	I swell up
ἐξόλλυμι	I destroy
ἐξομόργνυμι, mid. fut. **ἐξομόρξομαι**	I wipe off, I wash away
ἔξω	outside, beyond (+ gen.)
ἐπαγγέλλω	I order
ἐπακτός, ἐκαπτόν	conjured
***ἐπεί**	when, since
***ἐπειδή**	when, since
***ἔπειτα**	then
ἐπελπίζω	I hope
ἐπεμβαίνω	I trample on (+ dat.)
***ἐπί**	on, over, in, to, owing to, about, under, accompanied by (+ dat.)
***ἐπίσταμαι**	I know, I know how to (+ inf.)
ἐπίφθονος, ἐπίφθονον	to be resented
ἐπιχειρέω	I attempt
***ἕπομαι**, imperf. **είπόμην**, aor. **έσπόμην**	I follow (+ dat.)
ἐπῳδή, ἐπῳδῆς, ἡ	incantation

ἔραμαι, aor. **ἠράσθην**	I love, I lust after (+ gen.)
ἐράω	I love, I am in love (+ gen.)
***ἐργάζομαι**, aor. **εἰργασάμην**, perf. **εἴργασμαι**	I do x (acc.) to y (acc.), I accomplish
ἔργον ἐστί	there is need of (+ gen.)
***ἔργον, ἔργου, τό**	deed
ἔρος, ἔρου, ὁ	passion, desire
***ἔρχομαι**, aor. **ἦλθον**, pf. **ἐλήλυθα**	I go, I come
ἔρως, ἔρωτος, ὁ	love, passion
ἐς	= **εἰς**
ἐσθλός, ἐσθλή, ἐσθλόν	good, noble
ἔστε	as long as
ἔστι	it is possible
ἔσω	inside, into (+ gen.)
***ἕτερος, ἑτέρα, ἕτερον**	other
***ἔτι**	still, even
***εὖ**	well
***εὐγενής, εὐγενές**	noble
εὐεργετέω	I help
εὐηθία, εὐηθίας, ἡ	simplicity
εὐθύς, εὐθεία, εὐθύ	straight, direct
εὐκλεής, εὐκλεές	respectable, with a good reputation, of good repute
εὐνή, εὐνῆς, ἡ	bed, marriage
εὔνους, εὔνουν	well-disposed, friendly
εὕρημα, εὑρήματος, τό	remedy
***εὑρίσκω**, fut. **εὑρήσω**, aor. **ηὗρον**	I find, I come up with
***εὐσεβής, εὐσεβές**	pious
εὐσχήμων, εὐσχήμον	fine, elegant
εὐτυχέω	I am happy, I live a prosperous life
εὔφημος, εὔφημον	well-omened in speech
εὐώλενος, εὐώλενον	fair-armed, fair
***ἐχθρός, ἐχθρά, ἐχθρόν**	hateful
ἐχθρός, ἐχθροῦ, ὁ	enemy
***ἔχω**, fut. **ἕξω**, imperf. **εἶχον**, aor. ***ἔσχον**	I have, I keep, I hold back; I am (+ adv.); I am able to (+ inf.)
Ἕως, Ἕω, ἡ	Dawn
***ζάω**	I live
***Ζεύς, Διός, ὁ**	Zeus
Ζῆν, Ζηνός, ὁ	Zeus
***ζητέω**	I seek

*ἤ	than, or
ἦ	certainly, indeed, surely
*ἤ . . . ἤ . . .	either . . . or . . .
ἡβάω	I am young
*ἤδη	now
ᾔδη	imperfect of **οἶδα**
ἥδιστος, ἡδίστη, ἥδιστον	sweetest (superl. of **ἡδύς**)
ἡδίων, ἥδιον	sweeter (compar. of **ἡδύς**)
ἡδονή, ἡδονῆς, ἡ	pleasure
*ἡδύς, ἡδεῖα, ἡδύ	pleasant, sweet
*ἥκιστα	not at all
ἧλιξ, ἥλικος, ὁ	peer
*ἥλιος, ἡλίου, ὁ	sun
ἦμαρ, ἤματος, τό	day
*ἡμεῖς, ἡμῶν	we; (royal we) I
*ἡμέρα, ἡμέρας, ἡ	day
ἤμπλακον (aor. only)	I have made a mistake
ἤν	if (= **ἐάν**)
ἡσσάομαι, fut. ἡσσηθήσομαι	I give way to (+ gen.)
ἡσυχῇ	gently, peacefully
θ᾽	= **τε**
*θάλασσα, θαλάσσης, ἡ	sea
θαλάσσιος, θαλασσία, θαλάσσιον	of the sea
θάλλω	I bloom
θατέρᾳ	crasis of **τῇ ἑτέρᾳ**
θαῦμα, θαύματος, τό	wonder
*θεά, θεᾶς, ἡ	goddess
*θεάομαι	I watch
θελκτήριος, θελκτήριον	enchanting, of enchantment
θέλω	= **ἐθέλω**
θέμις, θέμιστος, ἡ	right
θεόδμητος, θεόδμητον	god-built
*θεός, θεοῦ, ὁ	god
θήλεια, θηλείας, ἡ	woman
θῆλυς, θήλεια, θῆλυ	female
θήρ, θηρός, ὁ	beast
θηράομαι, aor. ἐθηρασάμην	I track down
*θηρεύω	I hunt
Θησεύς, Θησέως, ὁ	Theseus
θήσομαι	fut. mid. of **τίθημι**
θιγγάνω, aor. ἔθιγον	I touch, I get through to (+ gen.)

θνῄσκω, fut. θανοῦμαι, aor. ἔθανον, perf. τέθνηκα	I die; (perf.) I am dead
θνητός, θνητοῦ, ὁ	mortal
θράσος, θράσους, τό	boldness
θρασύσπλαγχνος, θρασύσπλαγχνον	bold-hearted
θυραῖος, θυραία, θυραῖον	of someone else, other
*ἰατρός, ἰατροῦ, ὁ	doctor
ἱδρύω	I set up
ἱκνέομαι	I supplicate
*ἵνα	in order that, so that (+ subjunc./opt.)
ἵππιος, ἱππία, ἵππιον	horse-riding
Ἱππόλυτος, Ἱππολύτου, ὁ	Hippolytus
ἴσθι	imperat. of **εἰμί** or **οἶδα**
Ἴσθμιος, Ἰσθμία, Ἴσθμιον	Isthmian
*ἴσος, ἴση, ἴσον	equal
ἴτω	let it go, drop it (third sing. imperative of εἶμι)
κἀγαθήν	crasis of **καὶ ἀγαθήν**
κἀγγὺς	crasis of **καὶ ἐγγὺς**
κἀγὼ	crasis of **καὶ ἐγὼ**
καθυβρίζω	I abuse, I violate
*καί	and, also, actually
καινός, καινή, καινόν	new
*καιρός, καιροῦ, ὁ	right time
κἀκ	crasis of **καὶ ἐκ**
κἀκεῖναι	crasis of **καὶ ἐκεῖναι**
κάκιστος, κακίστη, κάκιστον	very bad, worst (superl. of **κακός**)
κακόν, κακοῦ, τό	evil, misfortune, trouble
κακορροθέω	I revile, I condemn
κακός, κακή, κακόν	bad, evil, base, morally corrupt, cowardly
κακοῦργος, κακοῦργον	wicked
κακύνω	I disgrace
καλλιστεύομαι	I am most beautiful
κάλλιστος, καλλίστη, κάλλιστον	most fine (superl. of **καλός**)
καλλιφεγγής, καλλιφεγγές	beautiful-shining
καλλίων, κάλλιον	more fine (compar. of **καλός**)

***καλός, καλή, καλόν**	fine, good, honourable, well-spoken
καλύπτω	I conceal
κἀμὲ	crasis of **καὶ ἐμὲ**
κἀν	crasis of **καὶ ἐν**
κἂν	crasis of **καὶ ἐὰν**
κἀξαρκοῦντά	crasis of **καὶ ἐξαρκοῦντα**
κἀξελέγχεται	crasis of **καὶ ἐξελέγχεται**
κἀξευρίσκετε	crasis of **καὶ ἐξευρίσκετε**
κἄπειτα	crasis of **καὶ ἔπειτα**
κἀπεχείρησας	crasis of **καὶ ἐπεχείρησας**
καπηλεύω	I am a huckster, hawker of goods
καπνός, καπνοῦ, ὁ	smoke
κάρα, κάρατος, τό	head, person
καρπίζομαι	I harvest
κάρτα	very much, surely
***κατά**	in, over, throughout (+ acc.); against (+ gen.)
καταθνῄσκω, κατέθανον	I die
καταστρέφομαι	I subdue
κατεργάζομαι	I finish off, I kill
κατηρεφής, κατηρεφές	covered
κατθανεῖν	aor. inf. of **καταθνῄσκω**
κἄτι	crasis of **καὶ ἔτι**
κατοικίζω	I settle
κάτοπτρον, κατόπτρου, τό	mirror
***κεῖμαι**	I am established
Κέφαλος, Κεφάλου, ὁ	Cephalus
κίβδηλος, κίβδηλον	false, counterfeit
***κίνδυνος, κινδύνου, ὁ**	danger
κλεινός, κλεινή, κλεινόν	famous
κλύδων, κλύδωνος, ὁ	waves, surge
κλύζω	I dash over, I wash with water to cleanse
κλύω	I hear; I hear from (+ gen.)
κοινῇ	together with (+ dat.)
***κοινός, κοινή, κοινόν**	shared, for all ears
κομπάζω	I boast
κόμπος, κόμπου, ὁ	boast
***κόρη, κόρης, ἡ**	girl, daughter
κόσμος, κόσμου, ὁ	decoration
κοὐ(κ)	crasis of **καὶ οὐ(κ)**
***κρατέω**	I conquer, I win; I control (+ genitive)
κράτιστος, κρατίστη, κράτιστον	best
κραυγή, κραυγῆς, ἡ	shout
κρείσσων, κρεῖσσον	better, stronger, mightier
Κρήσιος, Κρησία, Κρήσιον	Cretan
***κρύπτω**	I hide; I hide x (acc.) from y (acc.)
***κτάομαι**, perf. **κέκτημαι**	I possess, I obtain, I engage in
κτείνω, ἔκτανον	I kill
Κύπρις, Κύπριδος, ἡ	Kypris, passion
κὠλίγους	crasis of **καὶ ὀλίγους**
***λάθρᾳ**	in secret
λαμβάνω, aor ἔλαβον, aor. pass. ***ἐλήφθην**	I take, I catch
***λανθάνω**, aor. **ἔλαθον**	I go unnoticed, I lie hidden; (mid.) I forget (+ gen.)
λέγω, fut. **λέξω/ἐρῶ**, aor. **ἔλεξα/εἶπα/εἶπον**, perf. εἴρηκα, perf. mid. **λέλεγμαι**, aor. pass. **ἐλέχθην**	I speak, I say, I tell, I speak about
***λείπω**	I leave; (mid.) I fall short, I fail
λέκτρον, λέκτρου, τό	bed
λεπτουργέω	I speak eloquently, subtly
λεύσσω	I see
λέχος, λέχους, τό	bed, sex
λήγω, aor. **ἔληξα**	I cease, I put an end to (+ gen.)
λίαν	too
λίσσομαι	I beg
***λόγος, λόγου, ὁ**	word, speech, story, reason, truth
λύει	it is profitable (= **λυσιτελεῖ**)
λυπρός, λυπρά, λυπρόν	miserable
λύω	I release, I slacken
λῷστος, λῴστη, λῷστον	best
μά	in the name of (+ acc.)
μαῖα, μαίας, ἡ	nurse
μακρηγορέω	I talk too much
***μᾶλλον**	more, rather
μανθάνω, fut. **μαθήσομαι**, aor. ***ἔμαθον**	I learn, I understand

*μάντις, μάντεως, ὁ	prophet
μαρτυρέω	I bear witness
μάρτυς, μάρτυρος, ὁ	witness
μάταιος, ματαία, μάταιον	foolish
*μάτην	in vain, to no avail
*μέγας, μεγάλη, μέγα	big, great, important
μέγιστος, μεγίστη, μέγιστον	biggest, greatest (superl. of μέγας)
μεθεῖσα	aor. participle of μεθίημι
μέθες	aor. imperative of μεθίημι
μεθίημι, fut. μεθήσω	I cast aside, I put aside, I let go of, I utter
μείζων, μεῖζον	bigger, greater (compar. of μέγας)
*μέλλω	I intend to, I am going to
μέμφομαι	I blame
μὲν οὖν	nay, rather
*μέν ... δέ ...	(marks contrast)
μένος, μένους, τό	power, strength
μέντοι	however
μετέρχομαι	I come after, I pursue
μετεχω, fut. μεθέξω, aor. μετέσχον	I have a share in (+ gen.)
*μή [NTS: Please align with: not; (+ imper./ aor. subjunc.) don't; (fear clause) that]	not; (+ imper./aor. subjunc.) don't; (fear clause) that
*μηδαμῶς	in no way
*μηδέ	and not, nor, not even
*μηδείς, μηδέν	no one, nothing
μήν	indeed
μηνύω	I mention
*μήποτε	never
μήτε ... μήτε ...	neither ... nor ...
*μήτηρ, μητρός, ἡ	mother
μηχανάομαι	I devise
*μηχανή, μηχανῆς, ἡ	device, tactic
μίασμα, μιάσματος, τό	pollution
*μισέω	I hate
μίσημα, μισήματος, τό	an object of hatred
μοῖρα, μοίρας, ἡ	fate, what is right
μοναρχία, μοναρχίας, ἡ	monarchy
*μόνον	only
μούσα, μούσης, ἡ	muse, poetry
μουσικός, μουσική, μουσικόν	eloquent
μοχθέω	I labour at
*μῦθος, μύθου, ὁ	conversation, tale
μυρίος, μυρία, μυρίον	countless
μῶν	surely ... not?
μωρία, μωρίας, ἡ	foolish action
*μῶρος, μώρα, μῶρον	stupid
*ναί	yes
ναίω	I live
ναός, ναοῦ, ὁ	temple
νασμός, νασμοῦ, ὁ	water
νεκρός, νεκρά, νεκρόν	dead
*νεκρός, νεκροῦ, ὁ	corpse
*νέος, νέα, νέον	young
*νικάω	I conquer
νιν	him, her, it
νόθος, νόθη, νόθον	bastard
*νόμος, νόμου, ὁ	law
*νοσέω	I am ill, I am sick, I am suffering
*νόσος, νόσου, ἡ	disease, illness
νουθετέω	I advise, I rebuke
*νοῦς, νοῦ, ὁ	sense
νυν	then, so
*νῦν	now
νῦν δέ	but as it is
*ξένος, ξένη, ξένον	foreign
ξυμμαρτυρέω	I bear witness
ξυμφορά, ξυμφορᾶς, ἡ	= συμφορά
ξυνειδῇ	subjunctive of ξύνοιδα
ξύνειμι	I associate with (+ dat.)
ξυνεργάτης, ξυνεργάτου, ὁ	accomplice
ξυνευνέτης, ξυνευνέτου, ὁ	bed-fellow, husband
ξύνοιδα	I am conscious of something (acc.) in someone (dat.)
ξύντασις, ξυντάσεως, ἡ	intensity
ὁ, ἡ, τό	the
*ὅδε, ἥδε, τόδε	this (here), the following, he, she, it
*ὁδός, ὁδοῦ, ἡ	path
*ὅθεν	from where
*οἶδα	I know, I am aware of, I know about
*οἰκέω	I live in, I inhabit, I govern
*οἶκος, οἴκου, ὁ	house
οἶμαι	I think

οἴμοι	alas, oh no!
οἷος, οἵα, οἷον	of the sort which, what sort of, what
ὄλβος, ὄλβου, ὁ	wealth
***ὀλίγοι, ὀλίγαι, ὀλίγα**	few
ὄλλυμαι, fut. **ὀλοῦμαι**, aor. **ὠλόμην**	I perish, I die (mid./intrans. of **ὄλλυμι**)
ὄλλυμι, fut. **ὀλῶ**, aor. **ὤλεσα**	I destroy, I lose
ὅμαιμος, ὁμαίμου, ἡ	sister
ὁμιλέω	I associate with (+ dat.)
ὄμμα, ὄμματος, τό	eye
***ὄμνυμι**, perf. **ὀμώμοκα**	I swear, I swear by
***ὅμως**	nevertheless
ὀνίνημι, aor. ὤνησα	I help; (mid.) I benefit
***ὄνομα, ὀνόματος, τό**	name, reputation
ὀπάζω	I grant
ὅπῃ	where, wherever
***ὅπως**	how
ὅπως μὴ	(fear clause) that
***ὁράω**, aor. **εἶδον**, aor. pass. **ὤφθην**	I see
***ὀργή, ὀργῆς, ἡ**	anger
ὅρκιος, ὅρκιον	of oaths
***ὅρκος, ὅρκου, ὁ**	oath
ὅρος, ὅρου, ὁ	boundary
Ὀρφεύς, Ὀρφέως, ὁ	Orpheus
***ὅς, ἥ, ὅ**	who, which, what; (connecting rel.) he, she, it, this, that
***ὅσοι, ὅσαι, ὅσα**	as many as, all who
ὅσον τάχος	as quickly as possible
***ὅσος, ὅση, ὅσον**	as much as
ὅσπερ, ἥπερ, ὅπερ	who, the very man who
ὅστις, ὅ τι	(indef. rel.) whoever, whatever; (indir. interrog.) who, what
***ὅταν**	when, whenever
ὅτου	= **οὗτινος**
ὅτῳ	= **ᾧτινι**
οὐ μὴν . . . γε	not even so
***οὐ, οὐκ, οὐχ, οὐχί**	not
οὐ . . . τι	not at all
***οὐδαμοῦ**	nowhere
***οὐδαμῶς**	in no way
***οὐδέ**	and not, nor, not even
***οὐδείς, οὐδέν**	no one, nothing, no
οὐδέν	not at all, in no way
***οὐκέτι**	no longer
***οὔκουν**	therefore . . . not
***οὖν**	and so
οὕνεκα	because of, for the sake of (+ gen.)
οὑντεῦθεν	crasis of **ὁ ἐντεῦθεν**
οὔποτε	never
οὔπω	not yet
***οὐρανός, οὐρανοῦ, ὁ**	heaven
οὖς, ὠτός, τό	ear
οὐτάζω	I wound
***οὔτε . . . οὔτε**	neither
***οὗτος, αὕτη, τοῦτο**	this, he, she, it
ὀφρύς, ὀφρύος, ἡ	brow
ὄχλος, ὄχλου, ὁ	crowd, the masses
ὄψ, ὀπός, ἡ	utterance, words
ὀψέ	late
πάγκακος, πάγκακον; superl. **παγκακίστ**	utterly bad, utterly evil
***παῖς, παιδός, ὁ/ἡ**	child, son
***παλαιός, παλαιά, παλαιόν**	long ago
παλαίτερος, παλαιτέρα, παλαίτερον	ancient (compar. of **παλαιός**)
***πάλιν**	back, in turn
πανοῦργος, πανοῦργον	wicked
***παρά**	from (+ gen.); before, in company with (+ dat.)
πάρα	= **πάρεστι**
***παραινέω**, aor. **παρῄνεσα**	I advise (+ dat.)
παραλλάσσω	I go astray
***πάρειμι**	I am present
***πάρεστι**	it is possible
***παρέχω**, aor. **παρέσχον**	(act. and mid.) I provide, I grant, I produce
παρθένος, παρθένον	virgin, chaste
***παρθένος, παρθένου, ἡ**	virgin, maiden
πάροιθε	previous
παρρησία, παρρησίας, ἡ	freedom of speech
***πᾶς, πᾶσα, πᾶν**	all, every, whole
***πάσχω**, aor. **ἔπαθον**, perf. **πέπονθα**	I suffer, I experience
***πατήρ, πατρός, ὁ**	father
***πατρῷος, πατρῴα, πατρῷον**	father's, ancestral
***παύω**	I stop, I end; (mid.) I cease
πέδον, πέδου, τό	earth
πείθω, aor. **ἔπεισα**, aor. mid. ***ἐπιθόμην**	I persuade; (mid.) I obey, I listen

***πειράομαι**	I try
πέλας	near
***πέμπω**	I send
πέπλος, πέπλου, ὁ	robe, cloak, clothes
πέρα	further; further than (+ gen..)
περάω	I pass through, I go inside
***πέρι**	about (+ gen.)
περισσός, περισσή, περισσόν	unusual, remarkable, excessive, proud
πέτρα, πέτρας, ἡ	rock
πημονή, πημονῆς, ἡ	harm
πικρός, πικρά, πικρόν	bitter
πιμπλημι, fut. **πλήσω**	I fill x (acc.) with y (gen.)
***πίπτω**, aor. **ἔπεσον**, perf. **πέπτωκα**	I fall
***πιστός, πιστή, πιστόν**	trusted, faithful
Πιτθεύς, Πιτθέως, ὁ	Pittheus
πλεῖστον	most of all (adv.)
πλεῖστος, πλείστη, πλεῖστον	very many, most (superl. of **πολύς**)
πλείων, πλεῖον	more (compar. of **πολύς**)
πλέον	more, further (adv.)
πλήν	except, other than
πλησσω, perf. mid./pass. **πέπληγμαι**	I strike with panic
πλόκος, πλόκου, ὁ	lock of hair
ποθ᾽	= **ποτε**
ποθέω	I desire
ποῖ	(to) where, to what point
***ποῖος, ποία, ποῖον**	what sort of
***πολέμιος, πολεμία, πολέμιον**	hostile to (+ dat.)
***πόλις, πόλεως, ἡ**	city
***πολύς, πολλή, πολύ**	much, many, in full force
***πόνος, πόνου, ὁ**	toil
πόντιος, ποντία, πόντιον	of the sea
πόντος, πόντου, ὁ	sea
Ποσειδῶν, Ποσειδῶνος, ὁ	Poseidon
***πόσοι, πόσαι, πόσα**	how many
***ποτε**	once, ever, at some point
πότερα . . . ἤ	(whether) . . . or
ποτός, ποτοῦ, ὁ	drink
***πούς, ποδός, ὁ**	foot
***πρᾶγμα, πράγματος, τό**	matter, affair, situation, deed, thing
πρᾶξις, πράξεως, ἡ	deed
***πράσσω**	I fare, I exercise political power
πρίασθαι	aor. inf. of **ὠνέομαι**
***πρίν**	before (**τὰ πρίν** = previously)
προάγω	I lead on
προβαίνω, fut. **προβήσομαι**, aor. **προὔβην**	I go, I advance, I proceed
προβῇς	aor. subjunctive of **προβαίνω**
***προδίδωμι**, aor. **προὔδωκα**	I betray
προδοῦσα	aor. ppl. of **προδίδωμι**
προθείς	aor. ppl. of **προτίθημι**
***προθυμία, προθυμίας, ἡ**	eagerness
***πρόθυμος, προθυμον**	eager
προνόεομαι, aor. **προὐνοησάμην**	I plan, I take precautions; I anticipate (+ gen.)
πρόρριζος, πρόρριζον	root and branch, utterly
***πρός**	to, in reply to, with regard to, according to, with (+ acc.); by (+ gen.); in addition (+ dat.)
προσβάλλω, aor. **προσέβαλον**	I attach x (acc.) to y (dat.)
προσθεῖναι	aor. inf. of **προστίθημι**
***πρόσθεν**	before
πρόσκειμαι	I am assigned to
προσλαμβάνω, aor. **προσέλαβον**	I take hold of, I secure
προσοράω, fut. **προσόψομαι**	I look upon
πρόσπολος, προσπόλου, ὁ/ἡ	servant
προστίθημι, aor. **προσέθηκα**	I hand over, I attribute, I place in addition, I add
προσφέρω, fut. **προσοίσω**	I bring near, I lay on
προσφωνέω	I speak to
πρόσωπον, προσώπου, τό	face
προτίθημι	I place before
προτρέπω	I discover
προφωνέω	I order (+ dat.)
πρῶτα	first of all (adv.)
***πρῶτος, πρώτη, πρῶτον**	first, noblest

πυνθάνομαι, fut. **πεύσομαι**, aor. ***ἐπυθόμην**	I find out, I learn
***πῦρ, πυρός, τό**	fire
πω	yet
***πως**	somehow, I suppose
***πῶς**	how
***ῥᾴδιος, ῥᾳδία, ῥᾴδιον**	easy
ῥᾷστος, ῥᾴστη, ῥᾷστον	easiest (superl. of **ῥᾴδιος**)
ῥέω, deponent aor. **ἐρρύην**	I flow
ῥητός, ῥητή, ῥητόν	fixed (**ἐπὶ ῥητοῖς** = on fixed terms)
***ῥίπτω**	I throw down
ῥυτός, ῥυτή, ῥυτόν	flowing
σάρξ, σαρκός, ἡ	flesh
σαυτοῦ, σαυτῆς	of yourself
***σαφής, σαφές**	sure, reliable, clear
σέβας, τό (nom./voc./acc. only)	reverence, sanctity, pride
σέβω	I revere, I honour
σέθεν	poetic genitive of **σύ**
Σεμέλη, Σεμέλης, ἡ	Semele
σεμνομυθέω	I speak haughtily
σεμνός, σεμνή, σεμνόν	reverent, proud, holy
σημεῖον, σημείου, τό	token
σῖγα	silently
***σιγάω**, fut. **σιγήσομαι**	I am silent, I keep silent, I am silent about
σιγῇ	in silence
σίδηρος, σιδήρου, ὁ	iron
Σίνις, Σίνιδος, ὁ	Sinis
***σῖτος, σίτου, ὁ**	food
σιωπή, σιωπῆς, ἡ	silence
σκέπτομαι	I look at
Σκιρωνίς, Σκιρωνίδος	Scironian
***σκοπέω**	I consider, I look at
***σκότος, σκότου, ὁ**	darkness
***σός, σή, σόν**	your, of you, of yours
σοφιστής, σοφιστοῦ, ὁ	expert, sophist
***σοφός, σοφή, σοφόν**	wise, skilled
σπείρω, aor. **ἔσπειρα**	I sow, I propagate, I beget
σπέρμα, σπέρματος, τό	seed
σπουδῇ	with haste (adv.)
στέγη, στέγης, ἡ	roof
στένω	I groan
στέργω	I put up with, I am content
***στόμα, στόματος, τό**	mouth
στυγνός, στυγνή, στυγνόν	sullen
***σύ, σοῦ/σου**	you
συγγιγνώσκω	I forgive
σύγγνωθι	aor. imperat. of **συγγιγνώσκω**
σύγγονος, συγγόνου, ὁ/ἡ	relative
συγκαθίστημι	I help treat
συγκατοικίζω	I settle; I pair up x (acc.) with y (dat.)
συγκλῄω	I shut
***συγχωρέω**	I give way to, I acquiesce to, I agree with (+ dat.)
***συμφορά, συμφορᾶς, ἡ**	misfortune, circumstance, disaster
***σύν**	with (+ dat.)
συναλλαγή, συναλλαγῆς, ἡ	dealing
συνάπτω	I join together
συνεκκομίζω	I help x (dat.) in bearing y (acc.)
συνεργός, συνεργοῦ, ὁ/ἡ	accomplice
συνθήγω, perf. pass. **συντέθηγμαι**	I sharpen completely
σύννομος, σύννομον	lying next to (+ dat.)
σφε	him
σῴζω, aor. **ἔσωσα**, aor. pass. **ἐσώθην**	I save
***σῶμα, σώματος, τό**	body
σωφρονέω	I am sensible, I am right-minded, I am moderate, I act virtuously
***σώφρων, σῶφρον**	modest, sensible, virtuous, chaste, with self-control
τἄδικα	crasis of **τὰ ἄδικα**
τάλας, τάλαινα, τάλαν	poor, long-suffering, wretched
τἄλλα	crasis of **τὰ ἄλλα**
τἀμὰ	crasis of **τὰ ἐμὰ**
τἀνδρός	crasis of **τοῦ ἀνδρός**
τἄρα	crasis of **τοι ἄρα**
***ταράσσω**, aor. **ἐτάραξα**	I throw into confusion, I stir up
τᾀσχρὰ	crasis of **τὰ αἰσχρὰ**
ταῦρος, ταύρου, ὁ	bull
ταὐτόν	= **τὸ αὐτό**
τἀφανῆ	crasis of **τὰ ἀφανῆ**

τάχος, τάχους, τό speed (**ὡς τάχος** = as quickly as possible)
τ*ε and
***τε . . . καί** both . . . and
τέγγω I soften
τεκμήριον, τεκμηρίου, τό evidence, proof
τέκνον, τέκνου, τό child
τέραμνα, τεράμνων, τά timbers
τέρμα, τέρματος, τό end
τερπνός, τερπνή, τερπνόν pleasant
τέρπω I delight
***τέχνη, τέχνης, ἡ** craft
***τίθημι**, fut. **θήσω** (act. and mid.) I place, I arrange
τίκτω I bear
***τιμάω** I honour
***τιμή, τιμῆς, ἡ** honour
τίμημα, τιμήματος, τό valuation
τίμιος, τιμία, τίμιον honourable
***τις, τι** a, any, anyone, anything, some, something, some sort of
***τίς, τί** who, what, which; **τί** = why
τιτρώσκω, aor. ἔτρωσα I wound
τλάω, aor. **ἔτλην** I dare
τλήμων, τλῆμον poor, long-suffering, wretched
τόθ᾽ = **τότε**
***τοι** you know, indeed, let me tell you, well
τοιγάρ therefore
τοιόσδε, τοιάδε, τοιόνδε such, such as this
***τοιοῦτος, τοιαύτη, τοιοῦτο** such
τόκος, τόκου, ὁ child
***τόλμα, τόλμης, ἡ** daring, daring act
***τολμάω** I endure
τοσόσδε, τοσήδε, τοσόνδε so much, this much
***τότε** then
του = **τινος**
τοὐμόν crasis of **τὸ ἐμόν**
τοὔνομα crasis of **τὸ ὄνομα**
τοὔργον crasis of **τό ἔργον**
τρεῖς, τρία three
τρέφω, aor. **ἔθρεψα** I raise
τρίτον thirdly (adv.)
τρίτος, τρίτη, τρίτον third
Τροζήνιος, Τροζηνία, Τροζήνιον of Trozen
***τρόπος, τρόπου, ὁ** way
Τροφός, Τροφοῦ, ἡ Nurse
***τυγχάνω**, aor. **ἔτυχον** I succeed with (+ gen.); I happen to (+ ppl.)
τυραννέω I rule
τυραννίς, τυραννίδος, ἡ monarchy, tyranny
***τύχη, τύχης, ἡ** fate, fortune, success, misfortune
τῷ = **τίνι**

***ὑβρίζω** I act outrageously
ὕβρις, ὕβρεως, ἡ immoderate behaviour, outrageous behaviour, pride
* **ὑμεῖς, ὑμῶν** you
ὑπεξαιρέω, aor. **ὑπεξεῖλον** I destroy gradually
ὑπερβάλλω I overreach myself, I go too far
ὑπερβολή, ὑπερβολῆς, ἡ excess
ὑπεργάζομαι, perf. **ὑπείργασμαι** I plough up, I prepare the ground
ὑπέρχομαι, aor. **ὑπῆλθον** I catch out
* **ὑπισχνέομαι**, aor. **ὑπεσχόμην** I promise
* **ὑπό** by (+ gen.)
* **ὕστερος, ὑστέρα, ὕστερον** later
* **ὑψηλός, ὑψηλή, ὑψηλόν** haughty

Φαίδρα, Φαίδρας, ἡ Phaedra
***φαίνομαι**, fut. **φανήσομαι**, aor. **ἐφάνην** I appear
φάος, φάους, τό light, light of day
φάρμακον, φαρμάκου, τό drug
φαῦλος, φαῦλον worthless, inferior, foolish
φέγγος, φέγγους, τό light
φερνή, φερνῆς, ἡ dowry
***φέρω**, aor. **ἤνεγκα** I bring, I carry, I bear
φεῦ alas; oh, for (+ gen.)
***φεύγω**, aor. **ἔφυγον** I flee, I avoid, I flee from
***φημί**, fut. **φήσω** I say (**οὔ φημι** = I say . . . not, I deny)
φθέγγομαι, aor. **ἐφθεγξάμην** I say

φθέγμα, φθέγματος, τό	word, utterance
φθογγή, φθογγῆς, ἡ	voice
***φιλέω**	I love
φίλη, φίλης, ἡ	friend
φίλος, φίλη, φίλον	dear
***φίλος, φίλου, ὁ**	friend
φίλτατος, φιλτάτη, φίλτατον	dearest (superl. of **φίλος**)
φίλτρον, φίλτρου, τό	charm
***φοβέομαι, aor. ἐφοβήθην**	I fear
***φόβος, φόβου, ὁ**	fear
φοιτάω	I go, I travel
φορέω	I bear, I endure, I wear, I have
φορητός, φορητή, φορητόν	to be borne, to be endured
φρήν, φρενός, ἡ	heart, mind, thought, sense, purpose
φρίσσω	I shudder at
φρονέω	I think, I have in mind, I am sensible, I am in my senses
φρονέω μέγα	I have proud thoughts, I am arrogant
φρόνημα, φρονήματος, τό	thought
φροντίζω	I think
φροντίς, φροντίδος, ἡ	thought
***φυγάς, φυγάδος, ὁ**	exile
φύομαι, aor. **ἔφυν**, perf. **πέφυκα**	I am born; (aor. and perf. with pres. sense) I am by nature
φυτεύω	I father, I beget
φυτόν, φυτοῦ, τό	creature
***φωνή, φωνῆς, ἡ**	voice
φῶς, φωτός, τό	light
χαῖρε, χαίρετε	farewell
χαλκός, χαλκοῦ, ὁ	bronze

χάρις, χάριτος, ἡ	favour, pleasure, gratification
χἀτέρῳ	crasis of **καὶ ἑτέρῳ**
χειμάζομαι	I am storm-tossed, I am tormented
***χείρ, χειρός, ἡ**	hand
χθών, χθονός, ἡ	land, country, earth
χορός, χοροῦ, ὁ	chorus
***χράομαι**, perf. **κέχρημαι**	I use, I experience, I treat (+ dat.)
χρεών, χρεών, τό	necessity; (+ **ἐστί**) it is necessary
***χρη**, imperf. **ἐχρην**/χρῆν	it is necessary
***χρῆμα, χρήματος, τό**	thing
***χρήσιμος, χρησίμη, χρήσιμον**	useful, helpful
χρηστός, χρηστή, χρηστόν	good
χριστός, χριστή, χριστόν	used as ointment
***χρόνος, χρόνου, ὁ**	time
***χρυσός, χρυσοῦ, ὁ**	gold
***χώρα, χώρας, ἡ**	land
***χωρέω**, fut. **χωρήσομαι**	I give way, I make room for
χὤστις	crasis of **καὶ ὅστις**
ψυχή, ψυχῆς, ἡ	life, soul
ὦ	o
ὠνέομαι, aor. **ἐπριάμην**	I buy
***ὡς**	as, how, that; in order to (+ subjunc. or opt.); introducing wish (+ opt.); on the grounds of (+ ppl.); in order to (+ fut. ppl.)
***ὥστε**	like, (so as) to, such that
***ὠφελέω**	I help

Aristophanes, *Frogs*

Introduction, Commentary Notes and Vocabulary by Charlie Paterson

A Level: 1–208, 830–874

Introduction

Aristophanes and Old Comedy

Any discussion of Aristophanes must begin with a caveat: we have little reliable information about the man behind the plays. Our evidence is limited to the ancient summaries of the plays, known as 'hypotheses', and Hellenistic commentaries, referred to as the 'scholia'. There is also a *Life of Aristophanes* preserved in the Suda, a Byzantine encyclopedia of the ancient world. In reality, much of this comes back to the plays: the Hellenistic scholars mainly infer biographical information from Aristophanes' scripts. In particular, biographers look to the *parabases*, in which the chorus seems to speak on behalf of the playwright, for information on Aristophanes' motive for writing and his political views; yet, there is nothing to suggest that comic poets tell the truth about themselves. Aristophanes is also found in Plato's *Symposium*, where he gives a brilliant speech on love and sexuality. However, he is very much a caricature.

The exact year of his birth is unknown, but an ancient scholar on *Clouds* tells us that Aristophanes felt he was too young to produce his first play, *Banqueters*, which was produced on his behalf by Callistratus in 427. This would suggest he was born during the 450s. Thus, as a young man, he experienced the rise of the Athenian Empire and, as a late teenager, the development of the Peloponnesian War. His death was probably in the 380s. His father was a certain Philippus and he came from Cydathenaeus deme in central Athens, where he had an affluent upbringing. His plays show an interest in politics and the workings of the democracy, and he is likely to have been involved in politics in some way, probably as a councillor. He had three sons who followed him into comedy writing. His son Araros acted in his last extant play, *Wealth*, in 388 and went on to produce his father's final two plays.

Aristophanes' career is rather better documented thanks to the official state records of plays performed at the dramatic festivals. *Banqueters* received second prize – a very promising start to his career – and it was only one year until he was awarded first prize for his *Babylonians*. During his very successful career, he was awarded first prize at least six times. At the Lenaea festival, he won the first prize at least three times for his *Acharnians* (425), *Knights* (424) and *Frogs* (405), which was such a popular play that Aristophanes was awarded an honorific crown of olive leaves and the play was given the extraordinary honour of being reperformed in Athens. He appears to have been the most popular comic playwright in antiquity, as shown by the wealth of his work that has survived: we have 11 of his plays as well as around 32 potential titles and nearly 1,000 short fragments, either on papyrus or in the form of citations in the works of other authors. In contrast, no single complete play has survived from the fifty or so other comic poets we are aware of who were writing at the same time.

The plays are a collection of speeches, spoken dialogue, chanting, singing and dancing. The audience would have expected grotesque costumes, fantastical storylines, a distorted treatment of the reality of Athens, rude jokes, wild physical comedy, attacks on authority, jibes at intellectual or cultural fads and acerbic political commentary. Old Comedy was extremely self-aware and would parody other theatrical works, particularly Tragedy, as well as the conventions of the theatre, frequently breaking the fourth wall with references to the audience, props, costume and rivals. In comparison to Tragedy, which mainly used characters and settings from elsewhere and other times, Comedy was explicitly about contemporary Athens, but an Athens in which strange things could happen: men could fly on giant dung beetles to the heavens or be returned to life in Athens from the underworld. Politicians and public figures were frequently satirized and attacked; gods and heroes, such as Dionysus and Heracles in *Frogs*, were ridiculed.

The play: Plot and structure

Prologue – an introduction to the theme and hero of the play, as well as an opportunity to really get the audience laughing so that they are warmed up for the rest of the play.

Lines 1–37: Dionysus enters with his slave, Xanthias, who is riding a donkey while also carrying a heavy pack on a porter's pole. Dionysus is dressed in his feminine apparel as well as a Heracles costume. They begin as actors arguing over the type of joke to make: Dionysus wants to avoid the overused toilet humour about slaves carrying heavy loads that Xanthias wishes to deploy. This moves into a parody of sophistic argument. Dionysus announces they have reached the house he is aiming for and calls for a slave.

Lines 38–166: Heracles opens his own door to come face to face with his brother dressed as him. Dionysus at last begins to explain his dress and plan: he has been overcome by a great passion for Euripides, which he explains with a comparison to a craving for soup, and he wishes to go to the underworld to bring him back because there are no good poets left in Athens. Heracles teases his brother for his appearance, the nature of his desire, his choice of poet and the quality of his literary criticism. Dionysus reveals that he wants Heracles' advice (as Heracles famously visited the underworld on his twelfth labour to capture the three-headed guard dog Cerberus), particularly on where to stay and how to get there. Heracles continues to tease his brother by offering various forms of suicide before giving a description of his route into the Underworld: Charon, monsters, muddy punishments and the pure light reserved for those initiated into the Eleusinian Mysteries, a secretive cult. He tells Dionysus that the initiates will take him the rest of the way.

Lines 167–179: Xanthias begs Dionysus to hire a corpse to carry their luggage to the Underworld. A funeral party appears and Dionysus barters with the corpse for its labour but the corpse refuses the nine-obol pay.

Lines 180–208: Dionysus and Xanthias have now reached the lake and Charon punts his boat into the orchestra, calling off points of disembarkation. He refuses to take Xanthias, who will have to run around the lake.

Pseudo-Parodos – the chorus sing and dance. This is also the first agon (contest) of the comedy.

Lines 209–268: the chorus of frogs sing a song for Dionysus (unaware that it is actually Dionysus in the boat). The speed of their rhythms forces Dionysus to row at an increasingly fast pace which he cannot cope with and this leads to a shouting match between the god and the frogs until Dionysus eventually works out their metre, gets to grips with rowing, and wins the contest with the last word.

The Prologue continues

Lines 269–315: Dionysus and Xanthias reunite. Both are terrified by beasts and the Empusa, a shape-shifting monster. Dionysus ducks behind Xanthias and even turns to the priest of Dionysus in the front row for protection. Xanthias jokes that Dionysus has lost control of his bowels. At last they hear some pipe music as they approach the initiates.

Parodos – the chorus enters the theatre from the sides, singing and dancing.

Lines 316–353: the chorus sings to Iacchus, the god who led the Eleusinian initiates in the procession from Athens to Eleusis, inviting him to dance in their meadow. They then sing briefly to Demeter and call on Iacchus again to light up their festivities with his torch.

Lines 354–371: the leader parodies the proclamation made at the beginning of the festival of the Mysteries warning those who are unwelcome at the initiations to keep away, but the list is comically extended.

Lines 372–396: the chorus comes back together and sings to Demeter with great playful energy. They call for her to keep them safe and wish that they be both funny and serious.

Lines 397–415: the chorus members sing to Iacchus to accompany them on their journey towards initiation. As the chorus starts to sing about spotting a beautiful girl, Dionysus and Xanthias can no longer remain silent observers and want to cavort with the girl, too.

Lines 416–459: the chorus ridicules Archedemus, Cleisthenes, and Callias in increasingly crude attacks. Dionysus interrupts to ask for directions to Pluto's house and is told he has already reached it. The chorus concludes with a song of celebration.

Episodes – short scenes of dialogue with choral interjections.

Lines 460–502: Dionysus is unsure how to proceed when he gets to the door; Xanthias is forced to remind him to play the part of Heracles. An angry doorkeeper (sometimes assumed to be Aeacus, one of the judges of the Underworld) attacks the fake Heracles and threatens him with monstrous punishments for his past crime of stealing Cerberus. The doorkeeper goes back inside and Dionysus reveals he has fouled himself by wiping himself with a sponge Xanthias handed him to mop his brow. Xanthias impresses with his bravery and Dionysus quickly persuades him to take his Heracles costume. Dionysus picks up the luggage.

Lines 503–533: A maid appears from the house to tell Heracles (now actually Xanthias) that Persephone has excitedly started cooking for her gluttonous guest. As Xanthias tries to refuse, she tells him of roast meats, wine and a beautiful girl, who piques Xanthias' interest. As Xanthias is about to enter the house, Dionysus ruins his act and demands his Heracles costume back from the understandably peeved Xanthias.

Lines 534–548: the chorus ironically praises Dionysus with an attack on the politician Theramenes. Dionysus responds with an outrageous scenario in which Xanthias, lying with the girl, spots his master masturbating and punches his teeth out.

Lines 549–589: a female innkeeper and her maid come out to berate Heracles (now Dionysus again) for all the food he stole from them on his last visit. The two women threaten him with various punishments and then depart for their patrons Cleon and Hyperbolus, both dead politicians whom Aristophanes satirizes. Dionysus has to charm Xanthias to take back his Heracles costume and swears an oath to be utterly destroyed if he takes it back from Xanthias again. Xanthias accepts the costume and the oath.

Lines 590–604: the chorus encourage Xanthias to be bold now that he is Heracles again and warn him that Dionysus is likely to give him the luggage again if he makes a mistake. Xanthias agrees with their advice.

Lines 605–673: the doorkeeper returns in full force, but Xanthias channels the anger and bravery of the character he plays. Dionysus shows his full cowardice by backing the doorkeeper and not his slave. Xanthias swears an oath of innocence and offers the doorkeeper his slave (Dionysus) for him to torture as proof. Dionysus is terrified and reveals himself as a god. This leads to the second *agon* of the play: the doorkeeper intends to beat them both in the knowledge that the first to cry out will be mortal. However, in a contest in which Dionysus should have an upper hand, there is no result: both cry out. Xanthias manages to avoid his final blow by distracting the doorkeeper and redirecting the blow onto Dionysus. The doorkeeper decides that Pluto and Persephone can decide the matter.

Parabasis – the actors clear the stage and the chorus come forward to chant and sing an interlude in which they step out of character and the leader speaks to the audience as if Aristophanes himself.

Ode (sung)
Lines 674–685: the chorus calls on the muse and flatters the audience while also attacking Cleophon, the most prominent demagogue of the time, who was known for resisting peace with Sparta.

Epirrhema (chanted)
Lines 686–705: in a very serious tone, the chorus leader advises the city to treat all citizens equally and advocates clemency for all those involved in the rule of the Four Hundred in 411. He goes on to argue that no citizens should be without rights, particularly when the state has awarded freedom to slaves at Arginusae, something the speaker fully supports.

Antode (sung)
Lines 706–716: the chorus attack Cleigenes, a politician who was involved in many unjust attacks on those involved in the Four Hundred, presenting him as an ugly drunkard.

Antepirrhema (chanted)
Lines 718–737: the chorus leader uses an analogy which compares the quality of the city's politicians to its coinage. The best politicians are equated with the famous Athenian silver as well as the recent gold coins made from melting the statues from temples. Current politicians are equated with the debased coinage of bronze plated with silver. He accuses Athens of rejecting traditional politicians of aristocratic background and relying on base foreigners and criminals. He encourages them to use the gold coinage but is far from confident that all will work out for Athens.

Episodes – a series of spoken dialogues with choral interjections.

Lines 738–813: Xanthias and a fellow slave from the palace of Pluto enter, sharing ways in which they take pleasure in undermining or betraying their masters. Xanthias asks about the noise coming from behind the door and the unnamed slave reveals that there is a great argument between Aeschylus and Euripides for the Chair of Tragedy, which sits next to Pluto's throne. Aeschylus holds the Chair but Euripides has been performing to the worst of men in the Underworld and their praise has encouraged him to claim the Chair for himself. Sophocles is said to have ruled himself out of the contest. The plan is to weigh their poetry in scales but they are having difficulty finding a judge as Aeschylus does not trust the Athenians. It is Dionysus who has been chosen.

Lines 814–829: the chorus describes the upcoming contest in terms of a Homeric duel. Aeschylus, the Thunderer, is scowling and bellowing his vast linguistic constructions; Euripides, sharpening his tusk, hurls fast-paced words of attack and plays with language until it loses all meaning.

Lines 830–894: Aeschylus, Euripides, Pluto and Dionysus appear on the stage set out for the contest. The two tragedians trade insults. Euripides mocks Aeschylus' use of silent characters and self-indulgent language. Aeschylus mocks Euripides for creating idle chatter, dressing his characters in rags and filling his plays was sexual outrages. Dionysus plays the role of referee, indicating Euripides' weakness in the face of Aeschylus' roaring attack.

Lines 895–904: the chorus invokes the muses as Dionysus silently prays and burns incense to mark the beginning of the contest. Aeschylus prays to Demeter and Euripides prays to his own invented gods.

The Agon – a contest between two characters with some comments from the chorus and Dionysus.

Lines 905–991: Euripides speaks first (a sign in Aristophanes' plays that he is to lose the contest) in the style of a lawyer. He attacks Aeschylus' silent characters as a deceptive play on his audience and then moves on to critique his long words and lack of clarity. Euripides claims that he himself put the bloated tragedy he took over from Aeschylus on a diet, introduced monodies (songs sung by a single actor), removed nonsense, made his prologues a clear introduction to the play, let all types of character speak in a democratic fashion and taught the Athenians to speak and think for themselves.

Lines 992–1003: the chorus calls upon Aeschylus to respond, reminding him to control his temper. He is called Achilles by the chorus.

Lines 1004–1098: Aeschylus begins by getting Euripides to agree that a poet should give citizens good advice. From this starting point, he argues that he produced noble characters and filled his plays with war. In contrast, Euripides created bad examples, such as sexually promiscuous women who offended the noble women of Athens and kings in rags who encouraged men to pretend to be poor to avoid taxes. He also accuses Euripides of teaching Athenians to chatter and be idle.

Lines 1099–1118: the chorus describes the contest as even so far and encourages the competitors to be bold and trust in the audience.

Lines 1119–1247: Euripides attacks Aeschylus' prologues by claiming that they lack clarity. He picks at small linguistic issues of Aeschylus' style, such as his use of synonyms, in a few lines of his *Libation Bearers*. As Aeschylus takes control, Euripides can barely say half a line before his opponent starts questioning his choice of vocabulary. He soon changes his approach and ridicules Euripides' prologues by finishing each line with 'my little oil flask'.

Lines 1248–1363: the poets turn from spoken lines to sung lyrics. After a short introduction by the chorus, Euripides parodies Aeschylus, drawing attention to his odes accompanied by aulos and then those accompanied by cithara. Aeschylus responds by parodying Euripides' lyrics to the accompaniment of a dancing girl with castanets and then attacks his love of monodies with an outrageously banal performance which includes the daily matters of normal people.

Lines 1364–1410: Aeschylus asks to take Euripides to the scales and to test the weight of their poetry. Euripides starts with the opening of his *Medea* but it is beaten by Aeschylus' weighty scene with the river Sepercheius. Aeschylus then wins a contest of abstract terms by using death in contrast to Euripides' use of persuasion, which Dionysus calls specious. Aeschylus wins a final round with a line of two chariots and two corpses which easily beats Euripides' wooden stick weighed down with metal.

Lines 1411–1481: Dionysus cannot judge (even though he came down to find Euripides) as he finds one of them clever and enjoys the other, without being completely clear as to which tragedian he refers to in each case. Pluto intervenes and allows Dionysus to take back the one he chooses. Dionysus designs a final round: who is most likely to give the city good advice? His first question is what each poet advises about Alcibiades. Euripides's response shows his hatred for the selfishness of Alcibiades; Aeschylus' lion cub analogy is more balanced and suggests careful management of this difficult figure. Dionysus asks a second question: how do Athenians keep the city safe? Euripides answers that Athens needs to trust the politicians it currently rejects. Aeschylus delays a little then speaks in an oracular style, which appears to advise the people of Athens to avoid factionalism, trust in the navy, invade the Peloponnese and accept Peloponnesian invasion of Attica as part of the process. Dionysus decides that Aeschylus is the winner; Euripides loses his temper.

Lines 1482–1499: the chorus sings of Aeschylus as a wise man and a good thing for the city of Athens. Euripides is described as ignoring the greatness of Tragedy and wasting time on chatter and nit-picking.

Exodos – the final scene of the play and the exit of the chorus to music.

Lines 1500–1533: Pluto, Dionysus and Aeschylus return to the stage. Pluto wishes Aeschylus well and asks him to hurry the arrival of particular politicians into the Underworld. Aeschylus asks for Sophocles to take the Chair of Tragedy in his absence and demands that Euripides goes nowhere near it. Pluto orders that torches, songs and dance accompany Aeschylus into the upper world while the chorus sing for his safety and peace in Athens. The final words attack Cleophon and other warmongers in Athens.

War and politics

The Peloponnesian War, fought between Athens, Sparta and their allies, had dominated the Greek world since 431 and would come to its dramatic conclusion in the year following *Frogs*' first production. To gain a fuller sense of the situation for

Athens in 405 it is worth briefly going back to the start. The first ten years of the war, which lead to a fragile peace treaty in 421, revealed that the two sides were awkwardly matched: Sparta and her allies were unrivaled by land, while Athens relied on the prowess of its navy. This incompatibility led to little that could be called a decisive victory for either side. During this period, the Spartan king Archidamus initiated yearly summer invasions of Attica, significantly disrupting the rural economy and food supply. Pericles, the Athenian general and politician, responded with a defensive strategy, which Aeschylus seems to recommend for Athens at the end of the play (lines 1461–1466). The Athenians in the countryside were forced to move into the Long Walls, which connected the city of Athens to its harbour, the Piraeus. This meant that the countryside of Attica was lost, but the Athenians still had access to the sea and thus were able to have access to their empire and the Peloponnese.

Although arms dealers and politicians had much to gain in terms of wealth and prestige from the ongoing war, the majority of the citizens, particularly those who came from the countryside, suffered greatly. Athens quickly ate into its vast resources building ships, training soldiers and importing food across the sea. Huge demands were made on wealthy citizens who then became embittered at their personal loss. For many of these men, their wealth was based on land ownership overseas, which was now losing rental income due to the war. The overcrowding of the city and land within the Long Walls, as well as the increased contact between the states of the empire, led to the outbreak of a terrible plague in 430, which killed a significant proportion of the population, including the leading politician, Pericles. As the population shrank through disease and military failure, men with insufficient training or expertise were sent off as both basic soldiers and senior leaders.

Athens did enjoy some success and a short peace treaty along the way but the Athenians in the audience of *Frogs* were well aware of the dire financial and military situation Athens was in by 405. In 413, the Spartans took control of Decelea in Attica and the Spartan incursions into rural Attica could now take place throughout the year, not just the summer. As a result of this, the Athenians struggled to continue to access the silver mines at Laurium which had been so vital for developing and maintaining their navy. The situation was exacerbated in 407, when the Athenians suffered a significant defeat at the hands of the Spartan general Lysander. The Athenians were forced to melt down the gold plating of religious statuary to finance the war. The pure silver coinage, for which Athens was famed, was reduced in value or debased, as is lamented by the frogs (lines 718–737), and increasingly used up. While Athens struggled financially, Sparta had gained the support of Darius II and the almost unlimited resources of the Persian Empire. It was now the case that Sparta could build a navy to threaten the Athenians and afford to draw out the war. The coffers allowed Sparta to absorb significant losses, while Athens was increasingly a small loss away from bankruptcy and disaster.

Despite suffering defeat at Notium (a naval battle on the coast of modern Turkey) and then finding themselves blockaded by the Spartan general Callicratidas, the Athenians managed a surprise victory in 406 at the Arginusae islands (near the island of Lesbos, on the coast of modern Turkey). The Athenians were forced to send out boats with inexperienced crews, including a large number of slaves and metics (resident aliens with limited citizen rights), with the promise of freedom and even citizenship. This policy was clearly on the mind of Athenians in 405: Xanthias wishes he had rowed at Arginusae so he could abuse his master (line 34); the chorus leader calls this policy one of the most sensible things Athens has done (line 696). A storm and conflict among the generals following the battle impeded the rescue mission for the 25 triremes that had been lost, which resulted in the death of many thousands of men. This military disaster quickly became political: the eight generals (two of whom fled) were illegally tried by the Assembly on a single vote and put to death. Socrates happened to be the president of the council on the day of the trial and refused to go against the law; however, this did not stop the vote. This was a remarkable act of self-harm and led to regret and recriminations. Aristophanes would have been writing the play in October 406 when this trial took place and it is no surprise to find references to these events: Dionysus makes a joke that Oedipus was in some ways lucky – at least he was not commanding with Erasinides, one of the generals at Arginusae (lines 1195–1196); Theramenes (lines 534–541) and Archedemos (lines 416–421), both leaders of the charge against the generals, are fiercely attacked by the comedian.

There was growing political mistrust. The development of a radical democracy and the rise of demagogic politicians who flattered the people and turned against the elites had ruffled many aristocratic feathers. Characters like Cleon and Hyperbolus, both demagogues who were previously satirized by Aristophanes but were long dead by 405, appropriately appear in Aristophanes' underworld (lines 546–570), where they remain aggressive prosecutors and populist figures. In the face of such figures, conservatives sought refuge from the radical democracy in aristocratic clubs where oligarchic views in support of a small aristocratic ruling body were promoted. For these groups, any failure in foreign policy was considered a failure of the democracy itself and confirmed the belief held by these oligarchs that the general public could not control an empire or lead the Athenians to victory. By 411, the extreme oligarchs saw an opportunity to act: they murdered democrats, took control of key institutions of the democracy and created their own powerful council of 400 men, known as the Four Hundred, disenfranchising large numbers of the poor and establishing a commission to ensure a return to the laws of their forefathers. Factionalism among the oligarchs led to significant instability: the moderates soon overcame the extremists and eventually democracy returned in 410.

The aftermath of this oligarchic revolution is significant in *Frogs*. Emotions were raw in Athens after 411 and many of those involved in the oligarchy lost their homes, property and rights as citizens. Aristophanes directly addresses this through the chorus leader in the parabasis, calling for an amnesty and a return of the many moderate men who had been caught up in events and were now unable to help their state in a time of need: just as the city was short of good sailors and generals, it was also short of good politicians and there was, according to the chorus, an obvious solution to this. The chorus refer to those wrestled by Phrynicus (line 689), one of the leaders of the Four Hundred, and Theramenes is mocked (lines 534–541) for his U-turns and ability to come out of every political scandal on the winning side. He had been a leading figure in the establishment of the Four Hundred but then also its removal in 410; he was also embroiled in the Arginusae scandal. Cleophon, a leading politician of the time who opposed the peace treaty proposed by Sparta after Arginusae, is satirized several times as an example of the debased sort of politician that Athens now relies on: he is described as ambitious and duplicitous (lines 675–

685) and in the final lines he is bunched together with non-Athenians. He was tried and put to death in the months after the play as opinion turned against the warmongering politicians.

One further figure who is lurking behind many of the significant events of this period and certainly contributed to the feeling of political mistrust is Alcibiades. This talented but unscrupulous Athenian politician was in voluntary exile on the Hellespont when the play was performed and is another example of Athenian talent that was not being employed at a time of need. In the play, Euripides wants nothing to do with him; Aeschylus appears to encourage a cautious approach. There is no doubt that he would have split opinions in the audience. From 421 he undermined the peace treaty by unilaterally forming an alliance of states against Sparta; in 415, he was elected as general for the Sicilian expedition, but was recalled on the politically motivated charge of mutilating the herms (sacred statues) and profaning the Eleusinian Mysteries; he fled prosecution and defected to Sparta and then Persia before joining the rebel Athenian fleet at Samos and planning to return to Athens as leader of the 411 oligarchic coup; he was then elected general of the fleet, which had become democratic once again, and his success led to him being recalled to Athens in 407 without fear of prosecution; while in Athens he was the first leader to provide the military cover to allow the festival of the Eleusinian Mysteries, which included a march from Athens to Eleusis beyond the city walls; political enemies then made the most of his failure at Notium and he fled to Thrace. When Athens was on its last legs, this unscrupulous but remarkable figure was a potential route to salvation.

Overall, the audience was, to various extents, suffering from the stress of constant political intrigues, financial losses, harsh living conditions and the emotional strains of recent years. Six months after the production, the Athenians lost at Aegospotami; in 404 Athens was surrendered to Sparta and the democracy fell to a regime called the Thirty Tyrants. The Athenians survived, but submitted to a humiliating peace treaty. The audience may not have known that loss in the Peloponnesian War was inevitable, but it was worryingly possible and hopes of making peace seemed slim with the recent Spartan offers rejected thanks to the rhetoric of Cleophon. The potential for loss brought with it the fear of being treated in the way they had treated others: the death of all men and enslavement of women and children.

The Lenaea

It should not be forgotten how different the experience of drama was for the Athenians in comparison to modern theatre-goers. Dramatic performances in Athens were put on not only as entertainment but also as part of a competition within a religious festival to the god Dionysus. The two main festivals in the year were the Lenaea in the month Gamelion (January) and the City Dionysia in Elaphebolion (end of March into April).

The Lenaea began with a procession which was led by the Archon Basileus, a senior magistrate, and officials of the Eleusinian Mysteries. This cult is significant not only to the festival but to the play itself. The Eleusinian Mysteries were celebrated annually with a 22 kilometre procession from Athens to the sanctuary at Eleusis. The mystery cult was based on the stages of the myth of Demeter and Persephone:

Persephone was abducted into the underworld, Demeter searched for her daughter, and eventually Persephone returned to the mortal world to be reunited with her mother.

Originally held in the Lenaion, which does not survive, by the 440s the Lenaea possibly made use of the theatre of Dionysus on the south slope of the Acropolis in central Athens. It was a much smaller festival than the City Dionysia and, given the time of year, it did not host foreign dignitaries in the audience. The Comedy competition seems to have been highly regarded. Traditionally five comedies were performed; this may have been reduced to three during the war. There were prizes for best tragedy and best comedy, which were awarded by the panel of ten judges, all selected by lot from a shortlist compiled by the Athenian Council. Winning poets were awarded a crown of ivy and paraded through the streets of Athens. Each comedy performed at the Lenaea was funded by the *choregos*, a wealthy citizen who paid for the actors, chorus, costumes, scenery and musicians. There was also a director, the *didaskalos*, who would either be a professional or the poet himself.

The audience would have been made up of free Athenians and the theatre of Dionysus at the time of *Frogs* could have held 10,000 people. There is some debate over the presence of women, but it is quite possible that they did attend performances. The front rows were reserved for the magistrates of the democracy and priests. Dionysus notably attempts to hide behind his own priest in *Frogs* (lines 274-276). The audience would have consisted of a large number of lower middle-class and wealthier citizens from the city itself. Pericles did introduce a fund to make the theatre more affordable, but this would not have helped many of the poor rural workers to leave their land and travel to the city. The range of jokes in Aristophanes' plays and the ways in which his characters characterize the audience can also suggest the range of people present: politicians (like Cleophon and Theramenes), playwrights, labourers, business men, craftsmen, philosophers, and intellectuals. Even Dionysus himself is a spectator: his cult statue was present in the theatre.

Staging

Before turning to the practicalities of staging, it is worth first considering the limitations of the scripts that survive to us. The very original texts, which do not survive, did not mark how the lines were divided by characters and provided no stage directions. The surviving manuscripts do indicate the speaker with small symbols, *sigla*, but these are based on the assumptions of the early scholars who commented on the text, and could often be unclear and miscopied, particularly in sections of *stichomythia* (a dialogue in which speakers take alternate lines of verse) and *antilabe* (the sharing of a metrical line among several speakers). Some stage directions do appear on the manuscripts: in *Frogs* the playing of pipes is marked at lines 315–316, for example. However, these were included far later than Aristophanes' time and are rare. Modern editors continue to debate over the allocation of lines and the stage directions using the same methods as ancient commentators: what makes the best sense given the context and the restrictions of the theatre. Reperformance of the play allowed for editing and three passages have surviving alternative versions which are likely to have arisen from this process.

At the centre of the theatre was the *orchestra*, a circular space from which the rows of seating rose upwards around just over half of the circumference. At either side of the orchestra there were two entry passageways known as *parodoi* and at the back of the orchestra was the *skene*, which would have been a simple wooden building. The roof of this building was flat and accessible from backstage, allowing actors to appear before the audience at a height. Although it is a matter of some debate, it is unlikely that there was a high stage in front of the *skene* as the plays that survive suggest the actors were not cut off from the chorus. The *skene* is likely to have had three doors: one larger central door and smaller doors on each side of this. There were two significant theatrical devices in the theatre. The first was the crane, which was used to fly characters across the orchestra. The second was the *ekkyklema*, a platform which could be wheeled through the central doors of the *skene*.

Many of the effects of ancient theatre rely on the words of the script. The play was performed in bright sunlight, so any changes in lighting, such as the shifts from Heracles' house to the dark realms of punishment, and then to the bright light of the meadow of the initiated, needed to be created with words. However, the *Frogs* did also make good use of props and theatrical devices: Heracles' club, Xanthias' luggage pole, the funeral bier, the doorkeeper's whip, torches for procession, and measuring instruments, to list a few. Xanthias opens the play on a donkey which could well have been a real animal or made up of actors like in a modern pantomime. It is worth remembering that the way these props are carried and used, as well as their appearance, could be central to the humour in a scene. At times, the play spills into the audience: Dionysus' smoke and incense would have drifted around the theatre as he prepares for the contest (lines 871–874) and drawn even greater attention to the ridiculous scene of a god saying a prayer in the context of his own religious festival.

Two aspects of the play's staging are particularly memorable. The first is Charon's arrival in a boat. There are several ways in which this could have been achieved. Did he punt a boat on wheels across the stage in an amusingly haphazard fashion? Did he simply walk on as hidden stage hands moved a fake side of a boat across the stage? It is quite possible that a wheeled trolley, like the *ekkyklema*, was pulled on a rope across the orchestra. Without curtains, stagehands would have been visible to the audience throughout. Some comentators would argue that Charon calls his rowing commands to the stagehands as they pull him across in the sort of metatheatrical joke that comedy revels in. The second memorable element of the play would have been the giant scales used to weigh poetry. It is tempting to think that the crane could have been cleverly used to create scales big enough to dominate the orchestra and take the weight of the actors. This is, of course, highly conjectural.

Actors

Most comedies had three male actors, although there are some extant that required four. There could also be a number of silent parts. For *Frogs*, there would have been four main actors for the major characters (Xanthias, Dionysus, Heracles, the Corpse, Charon, the Doorkeeper (Aeacus), Pandoceutria, Plathane, Pluto's Slave, Euripides and Aeschylus), and several silent actors (Funeral Goers, Maids, Slaves, Scythian Archers, Persephone). Actors wore grotesque masks that depicted their character in a fixed facial expression. The use of masks meant that actors would have made significant use of noises and physical comedy to convey changes in emotion. Costumes were often worn over padding, which gave the actors fat bellies and bottoms: when Charon calls Dionysus a fatso, we should imagine his giant padded belly (line 200). There is potential for significant visual humour here if old Charon is unpadded and providing a strong contrast to the fat god. Actors also wore a large artificial penis made out of red leather. These phalluses could be used as props in the play: consider how Dionysus' attempt at rowing could be enhanced by the use of his phallus as an oar. Most characters would have been obvious from their costume and *Frogs* plays with this idea from the very beginning: Dionysus is an actor dressed as Dionysus but is also wearing the lionskin and carrying the club of Heracles.

The chorus

The chorus was essential to Athenian drama, but it is hard to fully appreciate this when reading the play in a classroom. Made up of twenty-four male Athenian citizens, the chorus sang and danced to choral odes accompanied by music, providing commentary on the action of the play, varying the performance and giving events a festive atmosphere. From within the chorus a leader who would step forward to engage in dialogue with the main actors. The chorus that arrives in the *parados* of *Frogs* is a group of men and women who were initiated into the mysteries while alive and, now dead, they dwell in the bright light near the palace of Pluto. Their dual role as a comic chorus and a group of initiates is most clear from line 340 where they blur their choral role with the proclamation given before a religious ceremony to remove those who are impure. As the literary contest begins, the chorus somewhat lose their initial identity until their final procession exits from the stage.

However, the initiates are not the only chorus in the play. *Frogs* is remarkable in that it seems to have two different choruses: before we even learn about the initiates, Dionysus hears the frog chorus and battles with them. It is much debated whether the frog chorus was intended to be visible. It would seem rather a shame for the audience, if the play was advertised as *Frogs*, not to get to see this chorus. It is, after all, an obvious opportunity for bright, bold costuming and physical comedy. It would be an expensive chorus at a time when even the wealthy of Athens were struggling due to the war; however, it could be argued that the costumes of rags for the initiates would have been very cheap and left plenty of budget for the frogs.

Speaking, chanting and singing

While visualizing the play, the modern reader also needs to hear it. We do not need to doubt that the audience could hear the actors clearly in the theatre of Dionysus. In fact, excellent evidence of this is found in this play itself: in lines 303–304 Xanthias refers to the famous error of an actor named Hegelochus whose mispronunciation in his performance of Euripides' *Orestes* changed the sense from 'I see calm again' to 'I see a weasel again' and set the audience rolling in the aisles. Poor Hegelochus has survived to the modern day as excellent evidence of the audience's ability to pick up the slightest accentual changes. It is hard to believe that comic actors are ever that subtle, but it is certainly important for a modern reader to be aware of the ways in which actors would have manipulated their voices to develop characterization or act out emotions, particularly when their masks limited the use of facial expressions.

Metre matters for experiencing the play. Iambic trimeter was most commonly used for spoken lines and all the lines in the set Greek text are in this metre. It is formed of three iambic metra, each of which is made up of two two-syllable feet. In a basic iambic metron, the first and last syllable can be either heavy or light (×) and is called an anceps, the second and fourth are heavy (–), and the third is light (∪). This provides the fundamental structure:

× – ∪ –   × – ∪ –   × – ∪ ×

This simple form of the metre could easily become rather tedious, so the comic poet had various ways in which these metra could be varied by resolution, which is the substitution of one heavy with two light syllables. Two light syllables could also replace an anceps or a single light syllable in certain positions, thus introducing a range of metrical units into the line: anapaests (∪ ∪ –), tribrachs (∪ ∪ ∪), and dactyls (– ∪ ∪). To keep metre intelligible, the final syllables adhere to the fundamental structure above and there was a natural word break in the line, called the caesura, which is often found in the middle of either the 3rd or the 4th foot. The many variations available to the poet meant that comic iambic trimeter could closely create the sounds and rhythms of natural, conversational speech. The freedom of comic iambic trimeter also means that the more restricted trimeter employed for the dialogue and speeches of tragedy is often noticeable. Thus, the metre can often signal where the author is parodying tragedy (e.g. line 59) and so prompt the reader to imagine where the actor may ham up his performance for a laugh.

Beyond parody, the different metres used can highlight other aspects of the performance or develop meaning, while also allowing Aristophanes to show off his versatility and flair. Lyric metres indicate that the chorus is dancing as well as singing to the music of the *aulos*, pipes with a double reed. Specific metres can bring certain colouring to the poetry. For example, dactylic hexameter, the metre of epic poetry, is used to describe Aeschylus (e.g. lines 814–816). It is not only one of a number of metres commonly found in Aeschylus' choral odes, but it also recalls the archaic world of Homeric heroes which Aeschylus represents. The oil-flask scene (lines 1201–1250) is another good example where metre plays a role: part of the humour here is that Euripides is too predictable in his use of metre and so Aeschylus can easily jump in with a metrical unit now known as the *Lekythion* or Little Oil Flask. Another memorable moment is Dionysus' battle with the frogs, where two conflicting metres fight it out: Dionysus shouts in iambics until line 250, where he finally gets the rhythm of the Frog's trochees.

Aeschylus, Sophocles and Euripides

Aeschylus first took a tragedy to the stage in 499 and went on to claim 13 victories across his career. His final production in Athens was the *Oresteia*, and the lost satyr play, *Proteus*. Following this, he went to the court of Hieron at Syracuse until his death on Sicily in 456/5. Despite his illustrious career as a tragedian, composing upwards of 90 tragedies (of which 6 or 7 survive), his epitaph made no mention of this career, only his military service at the battle of Marathon in 490 BCE against the Persian forces. By the performance of *Frogs* Aeschylus had been dead for half a century, but his tragedies went on to be reperformed and lived on after his death. A reputation for being devoted to the city and the grand, traditional style of his poetry is what Aristophanes relies on to contrast this early tragedian with Euripides, who is characterized in the play as a modern renegade and innovator, willing to question everything and encourage this in his audience. Euripides was born in the 480s and his career began the year after Aeschylus' death. He was the least successful of the three famous tragedians in terms of prizes, achieving only 4 victories, but of around 95 plays, 17 or 18 of his works survive. Euripides' final victory at the City Dionysia would not come until the spring following *Frogs*: his trilogy which included *Bacchae* won posthumously.

Where is Sophocles? It seems surprising that a search for the best tragedian to teach the city did not find the most successful of the big three. Born in the 490s, his career stretched from the last decade of Aeschylus' life to his own death, only a few months after Euripides', in 406. He achieved 18 victories at the City Dionysia and never slipped below second place. It is very likely that *Frogs* was being written while Sophocles was still alive and then edited quickly on his death. Within the text set for examination, lines 71–88 are a noticeable addition which acknowledge the poet's death. It is worth considering whether Sophocles would have been included in the play if he had been dead from the start. Despite being a tragedian and holding public offices, Sophocles is treated incredibly fairly by Aristophanes. It could well be that he was just too popular and uncontroversial to provide good comic material. More importantly, the contrasting characterization of Aeschylus and Euripides that Aristophanes employs is what matters to the play and Sophocles was not useful in this.

Serious comedy?

There are two central thematic strands to the play that are significantly intertwined. One is the extended criticism of drama in Athens. The other is the salvation of Athens from its current crisis. The seriousness with which Aristophanes approaches these ideas is much debated. For some, the play is simply escapist literature at its best. For others, it is Aristophanes' most serious and powerful work, one in which he gives a thoughtful assessment of the power of theatre and provides genuine advice to the Athenians.

Several critics have written about the inconsistencies and structural problems of the play, and these are worth bearing in mind. The purpose of the play as a whole and individual scenes within it appears to shift: Dionysus' role is particularly problematic as he sets out initially to bring back Euripides, but returns in the end with Aeschylus; the literary competition begins for the Chair of Tragedy, but ends up becoming one concerning the salvation of Athens. Characterization is also inconsistent: the presentation of Aeschylus and Euripides has truth to it at times, but often relies on stereotypes and selective approaches to their work. The political advice is contradictory: Euripides seems to put forward the same advice as the *parabasis* to recall the oligarchs but it is rejected; Aeschylus wants to keep attacking Sparta while defending Athens, but the chorus want peace. One way to account for these inconsistencies is to say that Aristophanes' driving motivation is to win the prize at the festival by making the audience laugh. To look for a single consistent structure or message may well be to miss the point of Comedy and how a comic plot develops. However, this does not completely undermine the argument that there is something serious about this play and there certainly are significant political and artistic themes that deserve attention.

The theme of the salvation of Athens is certainly prominent from early in the play and the choral odes that deal directly with current politics (lines 354–371 and 686–705) are persistent and remarkably free from jokes: Aristophanes presents the exiled oligarchs as victims and calls upon the Athenians to restore their rights, seek unity, and reject the advice of current demagogues; in the contest, Dionysus all of a sudden asks the poets for their opinions on Alcibiades and how to save Athens, questions which are answered with relative seriousness, albeit still in character; the play ends with the chorus praying for peace and the rejection of warmongers like Cleophon. The characterization also provides some insight into recent politics: the dominance of Xanthias over his master in the first half plays on Athenian anxieties stemming from Arginusae and their reliance on slaves to row in the fleet. The decree that allowed a second performance of *Frogs* has been seen as support for the political message in the play and it could well be that the play was influential: Cleophon went on to be prosecuted and executed; many oligarchs were given their rights back.

Frogs is also obsessed with drama. This goes beyond Comedy's usual interest in breaking the fourth wall for comic effect to reflections on the truth of drama and its power to educate. From the beginning, costume is exploited: Dionysus hopes by dressing as Heracles he will take on Heracles' character, but he fails miserably; the swapping of costume between Xanthias and Dionysus draws further attention to the power of costume in drama. The literary contest in the second half is a significant piece of literary or theatrical criticism. The playwrights take on the characters of their plays, or at least a particular perception of their plays that might well have been common among regular theatre-goers in the audience.

One thing that both tragedians and Dionysus agree on is the role of the poets in educating the people of Athens. How to do it is an important question: strong moral characters and traditional values, or questioning the status quo and making the audience think? In many ways, the literary contest represents the political sentiments expressed by the chorus: Aeschylus, the poet of the period in which Athens defeated Persia and took control of the Mediterranean, is the champion of traditionalism and morality, a great patriot, and a representative of the old families now in exile; Euripides is presented as a dangerous atheist, sceptic and corrupting influence. This might suggest that Aristophanes takes the educative power of poets seriously, but it is worth remembering that neither tragedian really shines in most rounds of the literary contest, as both raise significant issues with each other. If there is any real winner here, it is Comedy which trumps Tragedy and reveals itself to be the most significant educator of the Athenian people.

One further point to consider is the significance of the mystery cults. The mystery cults of the Greek world were secretive religions accessible only to those who had been initiated. With some awareness of these cults, readers will quickly realize how much they pervade the play. The chorus is a group of initiates and Dionysus' journey to bring back a dead poet is a literal enactment of the initiate's metaphorical journey to the underworld. Furthermore, Dionysus goes dressed as Heracles, who was initiated into the mysteries before his journey to and from the underworld for his twelfth labour. The terrifying Empusa in the underworld is associated with the Eleusinian Mysteries and might also represent the moment of the initiation at which initiates were terrified so that they would be open to new experiences; in the parados, the chorus call on Iacchus (lines 316 ff.), probably parodying the official call of the Eleusinian procession; in lines 354–370, the chorus parody the proclamation of restrictions on those who could attend the rituals; the abuse and scandal at the end of the parados (lines 404–431) may well represent the abuse hurled at the initiates as they crossed a bridge on the way to Eleusis. On a larger scale, the presentation of the underworld combines the depressing vision seen in Homeric epic with the Eleusinian vision of a meadow with pipe music and beautiful light. Within the play there are also elements of the rituals of Orpheus, a poet famous for unsuccessfully visiting the underworld to retrieve his dead wife, and Dionysus.

Why so much parody of the rituals of the mystery cults? The Lenaea's connection to mystery cult is one reason. It may also have a political purpose: the audience would be reminded of Alcibiades, a native of Eleusis, who was charged with profaning the mysteries but later attempted to restore the Eleusinian festival when he first returned to Athens after his exile. The positive presentation of an Athenian exile certainly fits with the apparent political message of the play. The theme of exclusion is particularly significant and it is possible to see parallels between those who are excluded from the mysteries by the chorus and the exiled Athenian politicians. As the Athenians had only had the opportunity to celebrate the Eleusinian Mysteries once since 413, the whole state had become the outsiders, barred from the ecstatic joy and happiness promised by initiation. The significance of rebirth and light from darkness in the mystery cults seems very fitting for a play concerned with salvation of Athens from dark times. It is perhaps possible to explain the split structure of the play and the many foibles of Dionysus' character as an attempt to recreate the process of initiation. Dionysus is an everyman of the Athenian polis who is initiated into the mysteries: he starts as a boastful, selfish, sophistic, cowardly (but likeable) incompetent, and transforms into a patriot, active citizen and good judge. Like the audience, one could say, he begins with an uncritical love of Euripides' sophistry and realism, but ends as an enlightened supporter of Aeschylus. Dionysus, the god of theatre, turns from the popular Euripides, whom he still admits to enjoying at the end, and rediscovers Aeschylus, much as the dramatic festivals of Athens need to do if they are to genuinely teach the people and fulfil their purpose.

Comic writing

There are vast numbers of terms for the devices employed by Aristophanes. This list provides some elements of his comic writing along with a few examples from the set Greek and English text:

- **Surrealism and selective reality:** the idea of Dionysus, the god of theatre, going to the underworld to bring back a dead playwright is an obvious example of surrealism. Within this fantastical plot, there are moments that are grounded in an Athenian reality: Xanthias laments his failure to fight at Arginusae (line 33); Dionysus expects Heracles to have a slave like a wealthy Athenian (line 40). Scenes within the play also manage to balance surrealism and reality to great effect: the poetic contest includes realistic points of criticism with parody and the surreal idea of weighing poetry on scales; the bartering scene in the underworld has a god and a slave try to employ a dead man. The character of Dionysus is another example of this comic approach, as he is both god of theatre and a flawed Athenian: he has been at sea on a trireme where he managed to read tragedy (lines 48–54); he struggles to remember quotations from his favourite tragedian (lines 100–106); he revels in sophistic arguments (lines 21–37). Inverted reality is commonly found: Xanthias' power over his master throughout the first half of the play is a notable example.
- **Farce:** scenes of slapstick comedy are common, combining skilful writing with physical movement, voice, song and costume. The most notable is Dionysus annoying Charon and then trying to row across the lake while competing with the frogs (lines 200–268).
- **Delayed revelation:** Aristophanes likes to mystify his audiences by delaying the revelation of key information. For example, it is not clear what Dionysus is doing at the start of the play until he finally explains his plan to Heracles.
- **Inversion of expectation:** much humour relies on defying what the audience may expect. Dionysus calls himself υἱὸς Σταμνίου (line 22) when we would have expected him to be the son of Zeus; σμικρός, ἡλίκος Μόλων (line 55) unexpectedly juxtaposes a famously large man with σμικρός.
- **Metatheatre:** this play is particularly aware of its dramatic nature and provides an extended criticism of theatre. The opening scene is an excellent example: the two men enter as comic actors rather than their dramatic personae and reveal Aristophanes' competitive relationship with fellow comedians Phyrnicus, Lycis and Ameipsias (lines 1–15). Much of the first half prominently plays with the concept of theatrical costume and the nature of theatre as Dionysus and Xanthias keep swapping costumes.
- **Parody:** the most extensive parody in the play is of tragic poetry. Often lines are composed in the style of tragedy, recreating the grand style of language and restricted metre of the tragedians. For example, the grandeur of line 59 is overblown and then seems ridiculous as Dionysus goes on to compare his passion to an urge for soup. Real tragedy is frequently quoted, often with amusing errors or distortions, or paraphrased ludicrously. In lines 101–102, Dionysus shows his love of Euripides by offering one quotation that has been altered to make his poetry sound ridiculous, and one that makes little sense out of context; he then paraphrases one of Euripides' most famous lines in a pedestrian prose style while revealing a significant misunderstanding of the play. There is other parody, too: Dionysus presents an argument that parodies

the style of the Sophists (lines 21–37); Charon is a parody of a ferryman (lines 185–208).

- **Political and topical satire:** *Frogs* contains a significant number of politicians who are attacked: most notably, Cleisthenes, Archedemos, Cleophon, and Theramenes. In the section set for examination in Greek, Cleisthenes, a common target for Aristophanes, is mocked as a passive homosexual (lines 48–51).
- **Teasing and abuse:** the characters of *Frogs* enjoy abusing each other and even the audience. Dionysus and Xanthias curse each other throughout the first half; Charon calls Dionysus a fatso (line 199). Much of the abuse is designed to appeal to the majority of the audience and so often focuses on underrepresented groups: women, foreigners, homosexual men (see note on line 56).
- **Sexual and scatological jokes:** the sorts of bodily functions that are not normally mentioned in polite company are prominent in comedy. The luggage-carrying jokes that dominate the prologue are all related to bowels.
- **Linguistic devices:**
    - **Asyndeton,** the omission of conjunctions, is often found with lists to emphasize the extent of something, e.g. sinners in the mud (lines 145–151).
    - **Alliteration and word play** bring the drama to life, highlight an idea, and provide humorous moments: e.g. πόθος; πόσος τις (line 55) and χαῖρ᾽, ὦ Χάρων, χαῖρ᾽, ὦ Χάρων, χαῖρ᾽, ὦ Χάρων (line 184).
    - **Comic distortions** of common phrases create vivid images and humour: ἀποσοβῆσαι τὸν γέλων (line 45).
    - **Comic exclamations** create drama, e.g. βαβαιάξ (line 63).
    - **Diminutives** such as ὦδελφίδιον (line 60) and μειρακύλλια (line 89), are found in normal conversation and often reveal arrogance or affection.
    - **Lists** that cover multiple lines (often combined with asyndeton) draw out a joke or emphasize an idea, e.g. the exhaustive list of the needs of a traveller to the Underworld (lines 112–115).
    - **Metaphorical language** is vivid, e.g. κωδωνίσω (line 79) suggests that testing poetry is like testing metal and begins the idea of physically examining poetry.
    - **Polyptoton,** the repetition of a word in different grammatical forms, is used to highlight wordplay. This often refers to nouns but has come to apply to any inflected part of speech, e.g. φέρω during the pseudo-sophistic argument in lines 25–37.
    - **Tricolons,** three parallel words, clauses or phrases, are used to emphasize a point, such as Dionysus' lack of sea legs in line 204: ἄπειρος ἀθαλάττωτος ἀσαλαμίνιος.
    - **Words invented by Aristophanes** are often used to satirize individuals and groups of people, e.g. Aeschylus' grandiose language: ὦ στωμυλιοσυλλεκτάδη / καὶ πτωχοποιὲ καὶ ῥακιοσυρραπτάδη (lines 841–842).

Further reading

This brief bibliography provides a range of commentaries, translations and books which have all been of significant help in preparing this edition.

Texts and commentaries

Dover, K. J. (1993), *Aristophanes: Frogs*, Oxford: Oxford University Press.
Merry, W. W. (1905), *Aristophanis Ranae*, Oxford: Oxford University Press.
Sommerstein, A. H. (1996), *The Comedies of Aristophanes: Frogs*, Warminster: Aris & Phillips.
Stanford, W. B. (1958), *Aristophanes: The Frogs*, London: Macmillan.

Translations

Affleck, J. and C. Letchford (2014), *Aristophanes Frogs*, Cambridge: Cambridge University Press.
Halliwell, S. (2016), *Aristophanes: Frogs and Other Plays*, Oxford: Oxford University Press.

Aristophanes, *Frogs* and Greek comedy

Bowie, A. M. (1993), *Aristophanes: Myth, Ritual and Comedy*, Cambridge: Cambridge University Press.
Dover, K. J. (1972), *Aristophanic Comedy*, London: B. T. Batsford.
Goldhill, S. (1990), 'The Great Dionysia and Civic Ideology', in J. Winkler and F. Zeitlin (eds), *Nothing to Do with Dionysus*, 97–129, Princeton, NJ: Princeton University Press.
Griffith, M. (2012), *Aristophanes' Frogs*, Oxford: Oxford University Press.
MacDowell, D. M. (1995), *Aristophanes and Athens: An Introduction to the Plays*. Oxford: Oxford University Press.
McLeish, K. (1980), *The Theatre of Aristophanes*, London: Thames & Hudson.
Silk, M. S. (2000), *Aristophanes and the Definition of Comedy*, Oxford: Oxford University Press.

The Peloponnesian War

de Ste Croix, G. E. M. (1972), *The Origins of the Peloponnesian War*, London: Duckworth.
Rhodes, P. J. (2006), *A History of the Classical Greek World*, Oxford: Blackwell Publishing.

The text

The text used in this edition is that of the Oxford Classical Text, *Aristophanis Fabvlae*, edited by N. G. Wilson (Oxford: Oxford University Press, 2007) bar lines 167–168, where Hamaker's deletion of 168 is ignored and the full stop at the end of 167 has been moved to the end of 168.

Text

ΞΑΝΘΙΑΣ
εἴπω τι τῶν εἰωθότων, ὦ δέσποτα,
ἐφ᾿ οἷς ἀεὶ γελῶσιν οἱ θεώμενοι;

ΔΙΟΝΥΣΟΣ
νὴ τὸν Δί᾿ ὅ τι βούλει γε, πλὴν "πιέζομαι,"
τοῦτο δὲ φύλαξαι· πάνυ γάρ ἐστ᾿ ἤδη χολή.
Ξα. μηδ᾿ ἕτερον ἀστεῖόν τι;
Δι. πλήν γ᾿ "ὡς θλίβομαι."
Ξα. τί δαί; τὸ πάνυ γέλοιον εἴπω;
Δι. νὴ Δία
θαρρῶν γε· μόνον ἐκεῖν᾿ ὅπως μὴ ᾿ρεῖς —
Ξα. τὸ τί;
Δι. μεταβαλλόμενος τἀνάφορον ὅτι χεζητιᾷς.
Ξα. μηδ᾿ ὅτι τοσοῦτον ἄχθος ἐπ᾿ ἐμαυτῷ φέρων,
εἰ μὴ καθαιρήσει τις, ἀποπαρδήσομαι;
Δι. μὴ δῆθ᾿, ἱκετεύω, πλήν γ᾿ ὅταν μέλλω ᾿ξεμεῖν.
Ξα. τί δῆτ᾿ ἔδει με ταῦτα τὰ σκεύη φέρειν,
εἴπερ ποιήσω μηδὲν ὧνπερ Φρύνιχος
εἴωθε ποιεῖν; καὶ Λύκις κἀμειψίας
σκεύη φέρουσ᾿ ἑκάστοτ᾿ ἐν κωμῳδίᾳ.
Δι. μή νυν ποιήσῃς· ὡς ἐγὼ θεώμενος,
ὅταν τι τούτων τῶν σοφισμάτων ἴδω,
πλεῖν ἢ ᾿νιαυτῷ πρεσβύτερος ἀπέρχομαι.
Ξα. ὦ τρισκακοδαίμων ἄρ᾿ ὁ τράχηλος οὑτοσί,
ὅτι θλίβεται μέν, τὸ δὲ γέλοιον οὐκ ἐρεῖ.
Δι. εἶτ᾿ οὐχ ὕβρις ταῦτ᾿ ἐστὶ καὶ πολλὴ τρυφή,
ὅτ᾿ ἐγὼ μὲν ὢν Διόνυσος, υἱὸς Σταμνίου,
αὐτὸς βαδίζω καὶ πονῶ, τοῦτον δ᾿ ὀχῶ,
ἵνα μὴ ταλαιπωροῖτο μηδ᾿ ἄχθος φέροι;
Ξα. οὐ γὰρ φέρω ᾿γώ;
Δι. πῶς φέρεις γάρ, ὅς γ᾿ ὀχεῖ;
Ξα. φέρων γε ταυτί.
Δι. τίνα τρόπον;
Ξα. βαρέως πάνυ.

Δι. οὔκουν τὸ βάρος τοῦθ᾽, ὃ σὺ φέρεις, οὕνος φέρει;
Ξα. οὐ δῆθ᾽ ὅ γ᾽ ἔχω ᾽γὼ καὶ φέρω, μὰ τὸν Δί᾽ οὔ.
Δι. πῶς γὰρ φέρεις, ὅς γ᾽ αὐτὸς ὑφ᾽ ἑτέρου φέρει;
Ξα. οὐκ οἶδ᾽· ὁ δ᾽ ὦμος οὑτοσὶ πιέζεται.
Δι. σὺ δ᾽ οὖν ἐπειδὴ τὸν ὄνον οὐ φῄς σ᾽ ὠφελεῖν,
ἐν τῷ μέρει σὺ τὸν ὄνον ἀράμενος φέρε.
Ξα. οἴμοι κακοδαίμων· τί γὰρ ἐγὼ οὐκ ἐναυμάχουν;
ἦ τἄν σε κωκύειν ἂν ἐκέλευον μακρά.
Δι. κατάβα, πανοῦργε. καὶ γὰρ ἐγγὺς τῆς θύρας
ἤδη βαδίζων εἰμὶ τῆσδ᾽, οἷ πρῶτά με
ἔδει τραπέσθαι. παιδίον, παῖ, ἠμί, παῖ.

ΗΡΑΚΛΗΣ
τίς τὴν θύραν ἐπάταξεν; ὡς κενταυρικῶς
ἐνήλαθ᾽, ὅστις — εἰπέ μοι, τουτὶ τί ἦν;
Δι. ὁ παῖς.
Ξα. τί ἔστιν;
Δι. οὐκ ἐνεθυμήθης;
Ξα. τὸ τί;
Δι. ὡς σφόδρα μ᾽ ἔδεισε.
Ξα. νὴ Δία, μὴ μαίνοιό γε.
Ηρ. οὔτοι μὰ τὴν Δήμητρα δύναμαι μὴ γελᾶν·
καίτοι δάκνω γ᾽ ἐμαυτόν· ἀλλ᾽ ὅμως γελῶ.
Δι. ὦ δαιμόνιε, πρόσελθε· δέομαι γάρ τί σου.
Ηρ. ἀλλ᾽ οὐχ οἷός τ᾽ εἴμ᾽ ἀποσοβῆσαι τὸν γέλων,
ὁρῶν λεοντῆν ἐπὶ κροκωτῷ κειμένην.
τίς ὁ νοῦς; τί κόθορνος καὶ ῥόπαλον ξυνηλθέτην;
ποῖ γῆς ἀπεδήμεις;
Δι. ἐπεβάτευον Κλεισθένει.
Ηρ. κἀναυμάχησας;
Δι. καὶ κατεδύσαμέν γε ναῦς
τῶν πολεμίων ἢ δώδεκ᾽ ἢ τρεῖς καὶ δέκα.
Ηρ. σφώ;
Δι. νὴ τὸν Ἀπόλλω.
Ξα. κᾆτ᾽ ἔγωγ᾽ ἐξηγρόμην.
Δι. καὶ δῆτ᾽ ἐπὶ τῆς νεὼς ἀναγιγνώσκοντί μοι
τὴν Ἀνδρομέδαν πρὸς ἐμαυτὸν ἐξαίφνης πόθος
τὴν καρδίαν ἐπάταξε πῶς οἴει σφόδρα.
Ηρ. πόθος; πόσος τις;
Δι. σμικρός, ἡλίκος Μόλων.
Ηρ. γυναικός;
Δι. οὐ δῆτ᾽.
Ηρ. ἀλλὰ παιδός;
Δι. οὐδαμῶς.
Ηρ. ἀλλ᾽ ἀνδρός;
Δι. ἀπαπαῖ.
Ηρ. ξυνεγένου τῷ Κλεισθένει;

Δι. μὴ σκῶπτέ μ᾽, ὦδέλφ᾽· οὐ γὰρ ἀλλ᾽ ἔχω κακῶς·
τοιοῦτος ἵμερός με διαλυμαίνεται.
Ηρ. ποῖός τις, ὦδελφίδιον;
Δι. οὐκ ἔχω φράσαι.
ὅμως γε μέντοι σοι δι᾽ αἰνιγμῶν ἐρῶ.
ἤδη ποτ᾽ ἐπεθύμησας ἐξαίφνης ἔτνους;
Ηρ. ἔτνους; βαβαιάξ, μυριάκις γ᾽ ἐν τῷ βίῳ.
Δι. ἆρ᾽ ἐκδιδάσκω τὸ σαφές, ἢ ᾽τέρᾳ φράσω;
Ηρ. μὴ δῆτα περὶ ἔτνους γε· πάνυ γὰρ μανθάνω.
Δι. τοιουτοσὶ τοίνυν με δαρδάπτει πόθος
Εὐριπίδου.
Ηρ. καὶ ταῦτα τοῦ τεθνηκότος;
Δι. κοὐδείς γέ μ᾽ ἂν πείσειεν ἀνθρώπων τὸ μὴ οὐκ
ἐλθεῖν ἐπ᾽ ἐκεῖνον.
Ηρ. πότερον εἰς Ἅιδου κάτω;
Δι. καὶ νὴ Δί᾽ εἴ τί γ᾽ ἔστιν ἔτι κατωτέρω.
Ηρ. τί βουλόμενος;
Δι. δέομαι ποιητοῦ δεξιοῦ.
οἱ μὲν γὰρ οὐκέτ᾽ εἰσίν, οἱ δ᾽ ὄντες κακοί.
Ηρ. τί δ᾽; οὐκ Ἰοφῶν ζῇ;
Δι. τοῦτο γάρ τοι καὶ μόνον
ἔτ᾽ ἐστὶ λοιπὸν ἀγαθόν, εἰ καὶ τοῦτ᾽ ἄρα·
οὐ γὰρ σάφ᾽ οἶδ᾽ οὐδ᾽ αὐτὸ τοῦθ᾽ ὅπως ἔχει.
Ηρ. εἶτ᾽ οὐ Σοφοκλέα πρότερον ὄντ᾽ Εὐριπίδου
μέλλεις ἀναγαγεῖν, εἴπερ ἐκεῖθεν δεῖ σ᾽ ἄγειν;
Δι. οὔ πρίν γ᾽ ἂν Ἰοφῶντ᾽, ἀπολαβὼν αὐτὸν μόνον,
ἄνευ Σοφοκλέους ὅ τι ποιεῖ κωδωνίσω.
κἄλλως ὁ μέν γ᾽ Εὐριπίδης πανοῦργος ὢν
κἂν ξυναποδρᾶναι δεῦρ᾽ ἐπιχειρήσειέ μοι·
ὁ δ᾽ εὔκολος μὲν ἐνθάδ᾽, εὔκολος δ᾽ ἐκεῖ.
Ηρ. Ἀγάθων δὲ ποῦ ᾽στιν;
Δι. ἀπολιπών μ᾽ ἀποίχεται,
ἀγαθὸς ποιητὴς καὶ ποθεινὸς τοῖς φίλοις.
Ηρ. ποῖ γῆς ὁ τλήμων;
Δι. εἰς μακάρων εὐωχίαν.
Ηρ. ὁ δὲ Ξενοκλέης;
Δι. ἐξόλοιτο νὴ Δία.
Ηρ. Πυθάγγελος δέ;
Ξα. περὶ ἐμοῦ δ᾽ οὐδεὶς λόγος
ἐπιτριβομένου τὸν ὦμον οὑτωσὶ σφόδρα.
Ηρ. οὔκουν ἕτερ᾽ ἔστ᾽ ἐνταῦθα μειρακύλλια
τραγῳδίας ποιοῦντα πλεῖν ἢ μύρια,
Εὐριπίδου πλεῖν ἢ σταδίῳ λαλίστερα;
Δι. ἐπιφυλλίδες ταῦτ᾽ ἐστὶ καὶ στωμύλματα,
χελιδόνων μουσεῖα, λωβηταὶ τέχνης,
ἃ φροῦδα θᾶττον, ἢν ἅπαξ χορὸν λάβῃ,
μόνον προσουρήσαντα τῇ τραγῳδίᾳ.

γόνιμον δὲ ποιητὴν ἂν οὐχ εὕροις ἔτι
ζητῶν ἄν, ὅστις ῥῆμα γενναῖον λάκοι.
Ηρ. πῶς γόνιμον;
Δι. ὡδὶ γόνιμον, ὅστις φθέγξεται
τοιουτονί τι παρακεκινδυνευμένον,
"αἰθέρα Διὸς δωμάτιον" ἢ "χρόνου πόδα",
ἢ "φρένα μὲν οὐκ ἐθέλουσαν ὀμόσαι καθ᾽ ἱερῶν,
γλῶτταν δ᾽ ἐπιορκήσασαν ἰδίᾳ τῆς φρενός".
Ηρ. σὲ δὲ ταῦτ᾽ ἀρέσκει;
Δι. μάλλὰ πλεῖν ἢ μαίνομαι.
Ηρ. ἦ μὴν κόβαλά γ᾽ ἐστίν, ὡς καὶ σοὶ δοκεῖ.
Δι. μὴ τὸν ἐμὸν οἴκει νοῦν· ἔχεις γὰρ οἰκίαν.
Ηρ. καὶ μὴν ἀτεχνῶς γε παμπόνηρα φαίνεται.
Δι. δειπνεῖν με δίδασκε.
Ξα. περὶ ἐμοῦ δ᾽ οὐδεὶς λόγος.
Δι. ἀλλ᾽ ὧνπερ ἕνεκα τήνδε τὴν σκευὴν ἔχων
ἦλθον κατὰ σὴν μίμησιν, ἵνα μοι τοὺς ξένους
τοὺς σοὺς φράσειας, εἰ δεοίμην, οἷσι σὺ
ἐχρῶ τόθ᾽, ἡνίκ᾽ ἦλθες ἐπὶ τὸν Κέρβερον,
τούτους φράσον μοι, λιμένας, ἀρτοπώλια,
πορνεῖ᾽, ἀναπαύλας, ἐκτροπάς, κρήνας, ὁδούς,
πόλεις, διαίτας, πανδοκευτρίας, ὅπου
κόρεις ὀλίγιστοι.
Ξα. περὶ ἐμοῦ δ᾽ οὐδεὶς λόγος.
Ηρ. ὦ σχέτλιε, τολμήσεις γὰρ ἰέναι καὶ σύ γε;
Δι. μηδὲν ἔτι πρὸς ταῦτ᾽, ἀλλὰ φράζε τῶν ὁδῶν
ὅπῃ τάχιστ᾽ ἀφίξομ᾽ εἰς Ἅιδου κάτω·
καὶ μήτε θερμὴν μήτ᾽ ἄγαν ψυχρὰν φράσῃς.
Ηρ. φέρε δή, τίν᾽ αὐτῶν σοι φράσω πρώτην; τίνα;
μία μὲν γάρ ἐστιν ἀπὸ κάλω καὶ θρανίου,
κρεμάσαντι σαυτόν.
Δι. παῦε, πνιγηρὰν λέγεις.
Ηρ. ἀλλ᾽ ἔστιν ἀτραπὸς ξύντομος τετριμμένη,
ἡ διὰ θυείας.
Δι. ἆρα κώνειον λέγεις;
Ηρ. μάλιστά γε.
Δι. ψυχράν γε καὶ δυσχείμερον·
εὐθὺς γὰρ ἀποπήγνυσι τἀντικνήμια.
Ηρ. βούλει ταχεῖαν καὶ κατάντη σοι φράσω;
Δι. νὴ τὸν Δί᾽, ὡς ὄντος γε μὴ βαδιστικοῦ.
Ηρ. καθέρπυσόν νυν εἰς Κεραμεικόν.
Δι. κᾆτα τί;
Ηρ. ἀναβὰς ἐπὶ τὸν πύργον τὸν ὑψηλόν —
Δι. τί δρῶ;
Ηρ. ἀφιεμένην τὴν λαμπάδ᾽ ἐντεῦθεν θεῶ,
κἄπειτ᾽ ἐπειδὰν φῶσιν οἱ θεώμενοι
"εἶνται," τόθ᾽ εἶναι καὶ σὺ σαυτόν.

Δι. ποῖ;
Ηρ. κάτω.
Δι. ἀλλ᾽ ἀπολέσαιμ᾽ ἂν ἐγκεφάλου θρίω δύο.
οὐκ ἂν βαδίσαιμι τὴν ὁδὸν ταύτην.
Ηρ. τί δαί;
Δι. ἥνπερ σὺ τότε κατῆλθες.
Ηρ. ἀλλ᾽ ὁ πλοῦς πολύς.
εὐθὺς γὰρ ἐπὶ λίμνην μεγάλην ἥξεις πάνυ
ἄβυσσον.
Δι. εἶτα πῶς περαιωθήσομαι;
Ηρ. ἐν πλοιαρίῳ τυννουτῳί σ᾽ ἀνὴρ γέρων
ναύτης διάξει δύ᾽ ὀβολὼ μισθὸν λαβών.
Δι. φεῦ,
ὡς μέγα δύνασθον πανταχοῦ τὼ δύ᾽ ὀβολώ.
πῶς ἠλθέτην κἀκεῖσε;
Ηρ. Θησεὺς ἤγαγεν.
μετὰ τοῦτ᾽ ὄφεις καὶ θηρί᾽ ὄψει μυρία
δεινότατα.
Δι. μή μ᾽ ἔκπληττε μηδὲ δειμάτου·
οὐ γάρ μ᾽ ἀποτρέψεις.
Ηρ. εἶτα βόρβορον πολὺν
καὶ σκῶρ ἀείνων· ἐν δὲ τούτῳ κειμένους,
εἴ που ξένον τις ἠδίκησε πώποτε,
ἢ παῖδα κινῶν τἀργύριον ὑφείλετο,
ἢ μητέρ᾽ ἠλόησεν, ἢ πατρὸς γνάθον
ἐπάταξεν, ἢ ᾽πίορκον ὅρκον ὤμοσεν,
ἢ Μορσίμου τις ῥῆσιν ἐξεγράψατο.
Δι. νὴ τοὺς θεοὺς ἐχρῆν γε πρὸς τούτοισι κεἰ
τὴν πυρρίχην τις ἔμαθε τὴν Κινησίου.
Ηρ. ἐντεῦθεν αὐλῶν τίς σε περίεισιν πνοή,
ὄψει τε φῶς κάλλιστον ὥσπερ ἐνθάδε,
καὶ μυρρινῶνας καὶ θιάσους εὐδαίμονας
ἀνδρῶν γυναικῶν καὶ κρότον χειρῶν πολύν.
Δι. οὗτοι δὲ δὴ τίνες εἰσίν;
Ηρ. οἱ μεμυημένοι —
Ξα. νὴ τὸν Δί᾽ ἐγὼ γοῦν ὄνος ἄγω μυστήρια.
ἀτὰρ οὐ καθέξω ταῦτα τὸν πλείω χρόνον.
Ηρ. οἵ σοι φράσουσ᾽ ἁπαξάπανθ᾽ ὧν ἂν δέῃ.
οὗτοι γὰρ ἐγγύτατα παρ᾽ αὐτὴν τὴν ὁδὸν
ἐπὶ ταῖσι τοῦ Πλούτωνος οἰκοῦσιν θύραις.
καὶ χαῖρε πόλλ᾽, ὦδελφέ.
Δι. νὴ Δία καὶ σύ γε
ὑγίαινε. σὺ δὲ τὰ στρώματ᾽ αὖθις λάμβανε.
Ξα. πρὶν καὶ καταθέσθαι;
Δι. καὶ ταχέως μέντοι πάνυ.
Ξα. μὴ δῆθ᾽, ἱκετεύω σ᾽, ἀλλὰ μίσθωσαί τινα
τῶν ἐκφερομένων, ὅστις ἐπὶ τοῦτ᾽ ἔρχεται.

Δι. ἐὰν δὲ μὴ εὕρω;
Ξα. τότ᾽ ἔμ᾽ ἄγειν.
Δι. καλῶς λέγεις.
καὶ γάρ τιν᾽ ἐκφέρουσι τουτονὶ νεκρόν.
οὗτος, σὲ λέγω μέντοι, σὲ τὸν τεθνηκότα·
ἄνθρωπε, βούλει σκευάρι᾽ εἰς Ἅιδου φέρειν;

ΝΕΚΡΟΣ
πόσ᾽ ἄττα;
Δι. ταυτί.
Νε. δύο δραχμὰς μισθὸν τελεῖς;
Δι. μὰ Δί᾽, ἀλλ᾽ ἔλαττον.
Νε. ὑπάγεθ᾽ ὑμεῖς τῆς ὁδοῦ.
Δι. ἀνάμεινον, ὦ δαιμόνι᾽, ἐὰν ξυμβῶ τί σοι.
Νε. εἰ μὴ καταθήσεις δύο δραχμάς, μὴ διαλέγου.
Δι. λάβ᾽ ἐννέ᾽ ὀβολούς.
Νε. ἀναβιῴην νυν πάλιν.
Ξα. ὡς σεμνὸς ὁ κατάρατος· οὐκ οἰμώξεται;
ἐγὼ βαδιοῦμαι.
Δι. χρηστὸς εἶ καὶ γεννάδας.
χωρῶμεν ἐπὶ τὸ πλοῖον.

ΧΑΡΩΝ
ὢ ὄπ· παραβαλοῦ.
Δι. τουτὶ τί ἔστι;
Ξα. τοῦτο; λίμνη.
Δι. νὴ Δία
αὑτή ᾽στὶν ἣν ἔφραζε, καὶ πλοῖόν γ᾽ ὁρῶ.
Ξα. νὴ τὸν Ποσειδῶ, κἄστι γ᾽ ὁ Χάρων οὑτοσί.
Δι. χαῖρ᾽, ὦ Χάρων, χαῖρ᾽, ὦ Χάρων, χαῖρ᾽, ὦ Χάρων.
Χα. τίς εἰς ἀναπαύλας ἐκ κακῶν καὶ πραγμάτων;
τίς εἰς τὸ Λήθης πεδίον, ἢ ᾽ς Ὄκνου πλοκάς,
ἢ ᾽ς Κερβερίους, ἢ ᾽ς κόρακας, ἢ ᾽πὶ Ταίναρον;
Δι. ἐγώ.
Χα. ταχέως ἔμβαινε.
Δι. ποῦ σχήσειν δοκεῖς;
Χα. ἐς κόρακας.
Δι. ὄντως;
Χα. ναὶ μὰ Δία. σοῦ γ᾽ οὕνεκα.
εἴσβαινε δή.
Δι. παῖ, δεῦρο.
Χα. δοῦλον οὐκ ἄγω,
εἰ μὴ νεναυμάχηκε τὴν περὶ τῶν κρεῶν.
Ξα. μὰ τὸν Δί᾽ οὐ γάρ, ἀλλ᾽ ἔτυχον ὀφθαλμιῶν.
Χα. οὔκουν περιθρέξει δῆτα τὴν λίμνην κύκλῳ;
Ξα. ποῦ δῆτ᾽ ἀναμενῶ;
Χα. παρὰ τὸν Αὑαίνου λίθον,

ἐπὶ ταῖς ἀναπαύλαις.
Δι. μανθάνεις;
Ξα. πάνυ μανθάνω.
οἴμοι κακοδαίμων, τῷ ξυνέτυχον ἐξιών;
Χα. κάθιζ᾽ ἐπὶ κώπην. εἴ τις ἔτι πλεῖ, σπευδέτω.
οὗτος, τί ποιεῖς;
Δι. ὅ τι ποιῶ; τί δ᾽ ἄλλο γ᾽ ἢ
ἵζω ᾽πὶ κώπην, οὗπερ ἐκέλευές με σύ;
Χα. οὔκουν καθεδεῖ δῆτ᾽ ἐνθαδί, γάστρων;
Δι. ἰδού.
Χα. οὔκουν προβαλεῖ τὼ χεῖρε κἀκτενεῖς;
Δι. ἰδού.
Χα. οὐ μὴ φλυαρήσεις ἔχων, ἀλλ᾽ ἀντιβὰς
ἐλᾷς προθύμως.
Δι. κᾆτα πῶς δυνήσομαι
ἄπειρος, ἀθαλάττωτος, ἀσαλαμίνιος
ὢν εἶτ᾽ ἐλαύνειν;
Χα. ῥᾷστ᾽· ἀκούσει γὰρ μέλη
κάλλιστ᾽, ἐπειδὰν ἐμβάλῃς ἅπαξ.
Δι. τίνων;
Χα. βατράχων κύκνων θαυμαστά.
Δι. κατακέλευε δή.
Χα. ὢ ὄπ· ὄπ. ὢ ὄπ· ὄπ.

The set text now moves from the prologue to what might be considered the third episode of the play. See the Introduction for a detailed summary of the play.

ΕΥΡΙΠΙΔΗΣ
οὐκ ἂν μεθείμην τοῦ θρόνου, μὴ νουθέτει·
κρείττων γὰρ εἶναί φημι τούτου τὴν τέχνην.
Δι. Αἰσχύλε, τί σιγᾷς; αἰσθάνει γὰρ τοῦ λόγου.
Ευ. ἀποσεμνυνεῖται πρῶτον, ἅπερ ἑκάστοτε
ἐν ταῖς τραγῳδίαισιν ἐτερατεύετο.
Δι. ὦ δαιμόνι᾽ ἀνδρῶν, μὴ μεγάλα λίαν λέγε.
Ευ. ἐγᾦδα τοῦτον καὶ διέσκεμμαι πάλαι,
ἄνθρωπον ἀγριοποιόν, αὐθαδόστομον,
ἔχοντ᾽ ἀχάλινον ἀκρατὲς ἀπύλωτον στόμα,
ἀπεριλάλητον, κομποφακελορρήμονα.

ΑΙΣΧΥΛΟΣ
ἄληθες, ὦ παῖ τῆς ἀρουραίας θεοῦ;
σὺ δή με ταῦτ᾽, ὦ στωμυλιοσυλλεκτάδη
καὶ πτωχοποιὲ καὶ ῥακιοσυρραπτάδη;
ἀλλ᾽ οὔ τι χαίρων αὔτ᾽ ἐρεῖς.
Δι. παῦ᾽, Αἰσχύλε,
καὶ μὴ πρὸς ὀργὴν σπλάγχνα θερμήνῃς κότῳ.

Αι. οὐ δῆτα, πρίν γ᾽ ἂν τοῦτον ἀποφήνω σαφῶς
τὸν χωλοποιὸν οἷος ὢν θρασύνεται.
Δι. ἄρν᾽ ἄρνα μέλανα, παῖδες, ἐξενέγκατε·
τυφὼς γὰρ ἐκβαίνειν παρασκευάζεται.
Αι. ὦ Κρητικὰς μὲν συλλέγων μονῳδίας,
γάμους δ᾽ ἀνοσίους εἰσφέρων εἰς τὴν τέχνην —
Δι. ἐπίσχες οὗτος, ὦ πολυτίμητ᾽ Αἰσχύλε.
ἀπὸ τῶν χαλαζῶν δ᾽, ὦ πόνηρ᾽ Εὐριπίδη,
ἄναγε σεαυτὸν ἐκποδών, εἰ σωφρονεῖς,
ἵνα μὴ κεφαλαίῳ τὸν κρόταφόν σου ῥήματι
θενὼν ὑπ᾽ ὀργῆς ἐκχέῃ τὸν Τήλεφον·
σὺ δὲ μὴ πρὸς ὀργήν, Αἰσχύλ᾽, ἀλλὰ πραόνως
ἔλεγχ᾽, ἐλέγχου· λοιδορεῖσθαι δ᾽ οὐ πρέπει
ἄνδρας ποιητὰς ὥσπερ ἀρτοπώλιδας·
σὺ δ᾽ εὐθὺς ὥσπερ πρῖνος ἐμπρησθεὶς βοᾷς.
Ευ. ἕτοιμός εἰμ᾽ ἔγωγε, κοὐκ ἀναδύομαι,
δάκνειν, δάκνεσθαι πρότερος, εἰ τούτῳ δοκεῖ,
τἄπη, τὰ μέλη, τὰ νεῦρα τῆς τραγῳδίας,
καὶ νὴ Δία τὸν Πηλέα γε καὶ τὸν Αἴολον
καὶ τὸν Μελέαγρον κἄτι μάλα τὸν Τήλεφον.
Δι. σὺ δὲ δὴ τί βουλεύει ποιεῖν; λέγ᾽, Αἰσχύλε.
Αι. ἐβουλόμην μὲν οὐκ ἐρίζειν ἐνθάδε·
οὐκ ἐξ ἴσου γάρ ἐστιν ἀγὼν νῷν.
Δι. τί δαί;
Αι. ὅτι ἡ ποίησις οὐχὶ συντέθνηκέ μοι,
τούτῳ δὲ συντέθνηκεν, ὥσθ᾽ ἕξει λέγειν.
ὅμως δ᾽, ἐπειδή σοι δοκεῖ, δρᾶν ταῦτα χρή.
Δι. ἴθι νυν, λιβανωτὸν δεῦρό τις καὶ πῦρ δότω,
ὅπως ἂν εὔξωμαι πρὸ τῶν σοφισμάτων
ἀγῶνα κρῖναι τόνδε μουσικώτατα·
ὑμεῖς δὲ ταῖς Μούσαις τι μέλος ὑπᾴσατε.

Commentary Notes

1

εἴπω: 'should I say?' – deliberative subjunctive. This is seen again in line 6.

τῶν εἰωθότων: 'of the usual ones' – a partitive genitive following τι, referring to the stale jokes of Aristophanes' rivals about slaves carrying luggage.

ὦ δέσποτα: the audience are used to Aristophanic plays starting with a prologue between two slaves (e.g. *Knights*, *Wasps*, and *Peace*), so this is a novel opening.

2

ἐφ' = ἐπί.

οἱ θεώμενοι: 'the audience'. Aristophanes not only has a dig at his rivals, but jokes at the expense of his audience as well.

3

νὴ τὸν Δί': 'yes by Zeus'. Oaths like this are used throughout the set text.

ὅ τι βούλει: assume the imperative 'say . . .!' to introduce this indefinite clause.

γε: this particle strengthens the oath.

πλὴν πιέζομαι: Dionysus' taste in jokes is more refined than that of his slave and he bans from this point on any vocabulary that would allow his slave to make a typical slave-carrying-luggage joke. The very act of forbidding these words would have set the audience laughing. The list of banned words becomes increasingly scatological: πιέζομαι and θλίβομαι (line 5) could refer to both the strain on the neck of carrying as well as strain on ones' bowels; χεζητιᾷς (line 8) is a little more to the point.

4

φύλαξαι: 'guard yourself against . . .!' – aorist middle imperative.

χολή: 'there is already excessive bile *to me*' – assume a dative of possession here. This is not an idiom commonly used in English and so needs to be rephrased. An excess of bile was considered to cause melancholy (note the clear derivation from Greek to English) or anger.

5

μηδ': 'should I not say . . .?' – this negative form is a reminder to supply another deliberative subjunctive (εἴπω).

ἀστεῖόν: note that this word implies a contrast between the clever wit of the city and the boorishness of the countryside. Xanthias clearly misuses this term: the joke he has in mind is something rather unsophisticated.

ὡς θλίβομαι: another forbidden verb. Note how the speakers start to share metrical lines as they become more impatient with each other.

6

τί δαί: 'All right, what then?' δαί is a colloquial form of δή which expresses wonder or impatience.

τὸ πάνυ γέλοιον: his description of what will turn out to be a scatological joke as the height of humour is another reminder that Xanthias (and the audience) is not particularly refined.

7

θαρρῶν γε: 'yes, say it without fear' – assume another imperative.

ἐκεῖν᾽ = ἐκεῖνο.

ὅπως μὴ ᾽ρεῖς: ὅπως + future indicative is a colloquial idiom which omits the imperative form of a verb of caution – 'take care you don't . . .!' 'ρεῖς = ἐρεῖς, future tense of λέγω.

τὸ τί: 'which one?' – a colloquial question.

8

μεταβαλλόμενος τἀνάφορον: this presumably refers to shifting the heavy porter's pole from one shoulder to another and back again as he struggles under the weight. τἀνάφορον = τὸ ἀνάφορον.

ὅτι: 'you say that . . .' – the verb of speaking is implied from line 7.

χεζητιᾷς: once again, Dionysus gains a laugh by forbidding the joke.

9

μηδ᾽ ὅτι: supply the deliberative subjunctive εἴπω.

10

ἀποπαρδήσομαι: an impressive polysyllabic compound verb which requires some imagination to translate. The uncompounded form means 'I will fart.' With the compound, it must cap Dionysus' use of χεζητιᾷς in line 8 and imply a noisy loss of bowel control: 'I will fart it all out.'

11

μὴ δῆθ᾽ = μὴ δῆτα – 'no way' or 'please don't'.

ἱκετεύω: the strange relationship between the god and his slave develops with the master begging the slave rather than ordering him.

ὅταν μέλλω: the indefinite construction – ὅταν + subjunctive in the primary sequence.

᾽ξεμεῖν = ἐξεμεῖν. The sense here is that Dionysus will only allow the joke to be told if he requires an emetic to make him sick, such is the physical response that it brings out in him.

12

τί δῆτ᾽ ἔδει με: the imperfect of impersonal verbs expressing obligation can be translated in the present and imply the obligation has not yet been fulfilled.

13

ὧνπερ = τούτων ἅ. The genitive antecedent and accusative relative pronoun have been telescoped into one.

Φρύνιχος: Phrynichus was a rival comic poet who is not to be confused with the early tragic poet of the same name. We know of eleven plays written by Phrynichus but they only survive in fragments. He may well be in the front of the audience's minds at this point because his play, *Muses*, was performed in this same Lenaea and eventually took second place to *Frogs*.

14

Λύκις: Lycis was another comic poet. He may be the poet to whom a victory at the City Dionysia in *c.* 410 BCE is attributed in a fragmentary inscription. An ancient commentator notes on these lines that Lycis was often satirized for being boring.

κἀμειψίας = καὶ Ἀμειψίας. Ameipsias was also a comic poet. He took first place with *Konnos* in 423 BCE, beating Aristophanes' first version of *Clouds*. His play *Revellers* also took the first prize in 414 BCE, beating Aristophanes' Birds, which took second place.

15

φέρουσ᾽ = φέρουσι(ν). The sense cannot be that the authors themselves carry baggage, but that they introduce characters carrying baggage.

16

μή νυν ποιήσῃς: μή + aorist subjunctive forms a one-off negative command.

θεώμενος: 'as a member of the audience'. See line 2. There would have been a statue of Dionysus in the theatre, so the god could be considered a spectator. However, the speaker has not yet identified himself to the audience as Dionysus.

17

ὅταν . . . ἴδω: an indefinite construction (see line 11).

σοφισμάτων: '*wise*cracks'. This may well be a subtle attack on the Sophists, travelling teachers who were often negatively characterized as subversive for their teaching on morality, religion and argumentation. It might amuse an Athenian to hear these hackneyed jokes described with pretentious vocabulary.

18

πλεῖν = πλεῖον, the neuter comparative form of πόλυς.

᾽νιαυτῷ = ἐνιαυτῷ. A dative of manner or measure of difference used with the comparative adjective πρεσβύτερος. The sense here is that watching these sorts of jokes takes a year off his life.

19

ὦ τρισκακοδαίμων: the register here becomes very lofty, much like that of tragedy. This polysyllabic exclamation particularly draws attention to this parody and the overly dramatic reaction of the slave to being banned from the jokes for which he is prepared.

οὑτοσί: the final iota here is an example of the deictic iota, which is commonly added to pronouns in comedy to indicate something that is close at hand.

20

ὅτι: 'because' – causal clause.

θλίβεται: Xanthias dares a verb forbidden in line 5.

οὐκ ἐρεῖ: his neck is personified here as not being able to complain about its treatment.

21

εἶτ' = εἶτα. This adds an angry tone to the question – 'and yet ?' or 'now . . .?'

ὕβρις . . . τρυφή: Dionysus suddenly notices that he is being treated unfairly by his own slave and finally points out the odd slave–master dynamic that some members of the audience will have wondered about from the start.

22

ὅτ' = ὅτε.

ἐγὼ μὲν ὢν Διόνυσος: this is the first time that the speaker confirms his identity as Dionysus; it seems most impactful to reveal himself as the god as he reveals his outrage at his slave's hubristic behaviour.

υἱὸς Σταμνίου: an excellent example of a *παρὰ προσδοκίαν* joke which defies the expectation of the listener or reader. We would expect Dionysus to say he is the son of Zeus, an unbeatable claim to gravitas but instead he presents himself as the son of a Mr Wine-Jar, which plays on the metonymy of Dionysus for wine.

24

ἵνα μὴ ταλαιπωροῖτο . . . φέροι: the optative is unexpected in a purpose clause in primary sequence (i.e. after a present tense main verb). This optative implies that the present tense main verb refers to the past as well as the present: Dionysus initially allowed him to ride and continues to do so. A good way to translate this is 'as it was my intention . . .'

25

οὐ γάρ: 'What? You mean I am not . . .'

'γώ = ἐγώ.

πῶς φέρεις γάρ: here the particle gives confirmation – 'Yes (that is what I mean), how are you carrying . . .'

ὅς γ': the relative clause is best translated as 'when indeed . . .' At this point, the comedy lurches from the groaning slave routine to a parody of the sorts of arguments that were considered stereotypical of the Sophists (see line 17). Here the argument revolves around the use of an active or passive verb: if the slave is on the donkey, is he carrying the load still or is he in fact being carried? Note the various forms of φέρω throughout these lines.

26

ταυτί = ταῦτα with the deictic iota.

τίνα τρόπον: φέρεις is assumed here.

βαρέως: a comic confusion which puns on the meaning of φέρω. Xanthias interprets τίνα τρόπον as 'how are you coping?' rather than as it was intended by Dionysus: 'how exactly are you *carrying*?' Thus, Xanthias replies with the idiomatic use of βαρέως φέρω – 'I'm doing badly.' The confusion continues as Dionysus goes on to interpret this as a comment on the weight of Xanthias' load rather than his condition. Overall, Dionysus seems to outsmart his slave or the slave purposefully misunderstands to further annoy his master.

27

οὔκουν: 'well then . . .' – used in replies when the speaker seizes an opening offered by the previous speaker.

τοῦθ' = τοῦτο.

οὔνος = ὁ ὄνος.

28

οὐ . . . οὔ: the emphatically placed negatives framing the line, the particles δῆτα and γε, and the negative oath all make this a particularly strong denial.

30

οὑτοσὶ: deictic iota (see line 19).

πιέζεται: Xanthias breaks Dionysus' rules again and thus Aristophanes manages to use one of the stale jokes for a second time.

31

οὐ φῄς: 'you say that . . . not . . .' – when introducing indirect statement, the negative with φήμι is translated in the indirect statement.

σ' = σέ.

32

ἐν τῷ μέρει: 'in turn'.

ἀράμενος φέρε: a participle followed by the imperative in Greek is best translated as two imperatives joined by a conjunction ('and') in English: 'pick up and carry!'

33

οἴμοι κακοδαίμων: this dramatic exclamation shows that Xanthias realizes he is being mocked but cannot work out how to win the argument. It is worth considering who Xanthias is talking to here. Is it just to himself or is this an aside to the audience?

τί . . . ἐναυμάχουν: this could be translated as a conative imperfect: 'why did I not try to . . .' or 'why was I unwilling to . . .' Xanthias wishes he had fought for the Athenians at the battle of Arginusae in 406 BCE as he would now be free and thus able to be rude to his master. Although he does not name the battle, the reference would be very clear to the audience. This victorious fleet was manned by both free men and slaves. The slaves who fought were rewarded with their freedom.

34

ἦ τἄν = ἤτοι ἄν – 'Then, I can tell you . . .' or 'Then, in actual fact . . .'

ἄν: this particle is often repeated without effect.

κωκύειν ἄν ἐκέλευον μακρά: literally, 'I would tell you to wail aloud.' ἄν with the imperfect indicative is a past potential, much like the apodosis of a present closed condition (e.g. If I were a free man, I would tell you to wail aloud). This is a comic parody of the colloquial phrase χαίρειν κελευω πολλα which essentially means 'farewell'. Rather than a positive farewell, the phrase becomes a hostile dismissal: 'I would tell you to go to hell.'

35

κατάβα: aorist singular imperative. The donkey is not involved in the play again from this point.

πανοῦργε: 'you villain' – often a term of abuse in Comedy.

τῆς θύρας: the actors now approach a stage door at the front of the scenery. The audience still have no idea where they are going or who will be behind this door.

36

βαδίζων: 'on my walk'. Dionysus emphasizes that he is walking and not riding.

37

ἔδει: 'it was my plan'. This impersonal verb takes the accusative με on the previous line.

τραπέσθαι: literally, 'to turn one's steps to' but better translated as 'to head to'.

παιδίον, παῖ, ἡμί, παῖ: Dionysus assumes that the owner of the house would have a slave boy open the door for them. In fact, Heracles opens the door himself and is faced with his lookalike.

38–166: Heracles

38

ὡς κενταυρικῶς: 'just like a centaur' or 'how savagely'. The half man, half horse centaurs were strong and violent. Heracles knew them well as he had fought and killed the famous centaur Nessus, who had attempted to rape Heracles' wife, Deianira. In addition, he fought and killed the centaur Eurytion and a whole band of anonymous centaurs.

39

ἐνήλαθ': ἐνήλατε from ἐνάλλομαι. the choice of vocabulary here suggests that Dionysus has knocked unreasonably loudly, perhaps even by kicking the door.

ὅστις: at this point, Heracles breaks off from what he is about to say in astonishment at finding himself face-to-face with a strange version of himself.

τουτὶ τί ἦν: 'what's this?' – an exclamation of astonishment.

40

ὁ παῖς: 'o slave' – the nominative address is more imperious than the vocative. Note the antilabe (distribution of a line of verse between multiple characters): one metrical line divided into four between two characters. This starts to build excitement and interest.

τὸ τί: 'what exactly?'

41

ἔδεισε: Dionysus has misinterpreted Heracles' astonishment as fear.

μὴ μαίνοιό γε: 'yes, afraid that you might be mad' – μὴ introduces a fear clause with the optative in historic sequence. The introductory verb of fearing is assumed from ἔδεισε earlier in the line and this is highlighted by the particle γε, which is best translated as 'yes'. This is probably spoken as an aside to the audience.

42

Δήμητρα: commonly women would swear oaths to Demeter, so it is amusing for Heracles to say this. Dionysus' femininity seems to be rubbing off on him!

μὴ γελᾶν: the actor needs to make the sounds of someone struggling to suppress laughter here as the mask he is wearing blocks the use of facial expressions.

43

δάκνω γ' ἐμαυτόν: 'I am biting my lip.'

44

ὦ δαιμόνιε: 'my good man' – this form of address can be very deferential and Aristophanes employs it when a character is asking for something from someone they respect.

πρόσελθε: aorist singular imperative.

45

ἀποσοβῆσαι: from ἀποσοβέω – 'I scare away', a verb often used in the context of shooing animals. It seems rather odd to scare away one's laughter. This may well be comic word play: Heracles may have intended to say ἀποσβέσαι from the verb ἀποσβέννυμι – 'I quench.' This would make more sense given that the laughter of the gods in the Iliad is described as unquenchable (see *Iliad* 1.599). The confusion not only adds a vivid image to the script but also parodies the grandeur of epic.

46

λεοντῆν ἐπὶ κροκωτῷ: the lion skin, along with a club, is an essential part of any Heracles costume. It represents the skin of the Nemean lion which Heracles killed and then skinned using its own claws during his first labour. The might and violence that it represents contrasts significantly with the feminine saffron coloured dress which is associated with Dionysus.

47

τίς ὁ νοῦς: 'what's the big idea?'

κόθορνος καὶ ῥόπαλον: the masculine violence of Heraclean costume is again juxtaposed with the effeminate clothing of Dionysus. A cothurnus was a thick-soled boot for women that later became the customary footwear of tragic actors. It was clearly associated with Dionysus, too. A club is the weapon most characteristic of Heracles.

ξυνηλθέτην: 'the two of them came together' – an example of the active historic dual form. The dual draws even more attention to the incongruity emphasized here.

48

ἀπεδήμεις: note the imperfect tense. The sense of this question is 'where in the world have you learnt to dress in this style?'

ἐπεβάτευον Κλεισθένει: an ἐπιβάτης was a hoplite on a trireme, a warship with three banks of oars. Each trireme was captained by a trierarch, often a wealthy citizen who paid to maintain and man the boat as a form of taxation. Cleisthenes was a prominent Athenian politician and ambassador who is mercilessly mocked in all but one of Aristophanes' surviving plays, being described as effeminate and a passive homosexual. Without realizing it, Dionysus has spoken euphemistically: ἐπιβατεύω can mean 'to mount' and is very close to ἐπιβαίνω which is used of male horses mounting the female.

49

κἀναυμάχησας = καὶ ἀναυμάχησας. The sexual vocabulary continues: 'to fight a sea battle' is used as a euphemism for sex in line 430 of the play: κύσθου . . . ναυμαχεῖν (literally, 'to fight a sea battle with a vagina'). This must come from the idea of one ship ramming another. The two speakers are now on different wave lengths: Heracles is trying to work out if Dionysus had sex with Cleisthenes while Dionysus thinks he is being asked whether he fought at Arginusae.

γε: highlights a positive response – 'yes . . .'

50

ἢ δώδεκ᾽ ἢ τρεῖς καὶ δέκα: this would be an impressive number for a single trireme given that the forces of the Peloponnesians lost 77 ships in total during the battle of Arginusae. Dionysus presumably intends to impress Heracles with his nonchalance over the exact number of boats, but in fact sounds ridiculous.

51

σφώ: 'the both of you?' – another dual ending. Heracles is referring to Dionysus and Cleisthenes.

Ἀπόλλω: accusative singular alternative form of Ἀπόλλωνα.

κᾆτ᾽ = καὶ εἶτα.

ἔγωγ᾽ ἐξηγρόμην: Xanthias implies in this aside to the audience that this is all a dream and that the next words Dionysus should utter are these if he is to tell the truth.

52

ἀναγιγνώσκοντί μοι: a dative of possession with τὴν καρδίαν in line 54, best translated as a temporal clause 'when I was reading, . . . my heart . . .' Reading books was a strange pastime for an Athenian, suggestive of wealth and private interests which could conflict with the Athenian ideal of taking an active role in the war and democracy.

53

τὴν Ἀνδρομέδαν: Euripides' *Andromeda* was produced at the City Dionysia of 412 BCE. The play survives in fragments and in the extended parody it suffers in Aristophanes' *Thesmophoriazusae*. The story of Perseus saving Andromeda from a terrible sea monster and then claiming her as his bride made a romantic play similar to the other later Euripidean tragedies, sometimes called the escape tragedies, which are mocked within the contest in the second half of the play.

πρὸς ἐμαυτὸν: the common practice was to read aloud to oneself.

πόθος: the personification of this desire emphasizes the overwhelming nature of this feeling.

54

πῶς οἴει σφόδρα: 'you can't imagine how seriously.' πῶς οἴει is an idiomatic interjection.

55

πόθος πόσος: note the entertaining wordplay.

σμικρός: used ironically as he has already made clear the significance of this desire.

ἡλίκος Μόλων: 'as small as Molon.' Little is known about Molon other than that he was a tragic actor who had taken to the stage in Euripidean tragedy. We might like to imagine that he played Perseus in *Andromeda*. According to an ancient commentator on the text, he was a very large man. The unexpected shift from large to small is designed to get a laugh.

56

γυναικός: genitive after πόθος for the object of desire. Heracles, known for his promiscuity, still has sex on the brain rather than literary criticism.

οὐ δῆτ' . . . οὐδαμῶς: 'Incorrect! . . . Way off the mark!' This is not said with indignation. Both women and boys were acceptable objects of desire for Athenian men.

57

ἀλλ' ἀνδρός: this would have been insulting as homosexuality between adult males was rare. The passive lover was open to harsh ridicule, much like Cleisthenes was in this and other plays by Aristophanes.

ἀπαπαῖ: the nature of this outburst can be interpreted in several ways, each of which impacts our understanding of Heracles' response at the end of the line. One interpretation is that it is the cry of a distressed lover as Heracles touches on the somewhat shameful or tortured nature of his passion.

ξυνεγένου τῷ Κλεισθένει: Heracles' euphemism shows he continues to misunderstand the nature of this desire.

58

μὴ σκῶπτέ: negative direct command.

ὦδέλφ' = ὦ ἀδέλφε. Dionysus and Heracles are both sons of Zeus.
οὐ γὰρ ἀλλ': 'for . . . really . . .'
ἔχω κακῶς: 'I am in a bad state' – ἔχω + adverb is translated as if εἰμί + adjective.

59
τοιοῦτος ἵμερός με διαλυμαίνεται: parody, in terms of metre and vocabulary, of a typical line of tragedy, which would no doubt be hammed up by the actor.

60
ὦδελφίδιον: 'little brother' – the diminutive can show care while also being patronizing. Heracles is actually younger than Dionysus in order of birth in mythology.
οὐκ ἔχω φράσαι: ἔχω + infinitive = I am able to.

61
ὅμως γε μέντοι: 'but nonetheless . . .'
δι' αἰνιγμῶν: 'by analogy'.

62
ἔτνους: a soup made from vegetables, in the genitive as the object of desire following ἐπεθύμησας. Dionysus uses a simple analogy that is appropriate for his gluttonous interlocutor. The comparison of this desire for literature with that of a desire for soup is another comic element that relies on a sudden change of direction.

63
ἔτνους: genitive assumes the verb – 'a desire for . . .?'
βαβαιάξ: 'goodness me!' – this time it is Heracles who lets out an inarticulate noise, showing that the mention of soup has led to a craving for some.

64
ἆρ' ἐκδιδάσκω τὸ σαφές: 'am I explaining myself clearly?' A quotation from Euripides' lost play *Hypsipyle,* according to an ancient commentator. Dionysus starts to speak in the manner of his literary hero. There is some wordplay here as τὸ σαφὲς is the complete opposition of αἰνιγμῶν (line 61).
'τέρᾳ = ἑτέρᾳ – 'in another way'.

66
τοιουτοσὶ: deictic iota (see line 19).
δαρδάπτει: this verb, found in epic poetry to describe wild animals devouring their prey, personifies the desire for a second time.

67
Εὐριπίδου: delayed to the end of the sentence, presumably with a dramatic pause between this and the last word of the previous line. The longing was first introduced in line 53 and has taken until now for the object to be made clear.
καὶ ταῦτα: 'even though' – this takes a participle, here a genitive absolute. Heracles continues to have sex on the mind and shows his shock at what he interprets as necrophilia. Euripides is likely to have died in early 406 BCE.

68–69

κοὐδείς = καὶ οὐδείς – followed by the partitive genitive ἀνθρώπων – 'no man on earth'.

γέ: marking an affirmative response.

ἂν πείσειεν: the potential optative is often found after negative formulations along the line of 'there is no one who . . .' Translate with 'could'.

τὸ μὴ οὐκ ἐλθεῖν: the simple infinitive or (as here) the articular infinitive can be used with μὴ οὐκ to express prevention, particularly when the introductory or main clause is negative. Translate μὴ οὐκ as 'from'.

69

ἐπ' ἐκεῖνον: 'in search of him'.

πότερον: simply introduces a question and does not require translation.

εἰς Ἅιδου: a common phrase in which the word for house (such as οἰκίαν) must be assumed to follow εἰς and thus Ἅιδου is a genitive of possession. Hades is king of the dead and his home is the underworld.

70

κατωτέρω: for the best sense here, translate this comparative in both the main clause and the subordinate εἴ clause – 'Yes, by Zeus, even lower, if . . .'

71

δέομαι ποιητοῦ δεξιοῦ: δέομαι is followed by the genitive. While reading the following lines, it is useful to consider how Dionysus might define δεξιός in this context. He seems most interested in the poet's skill with words to excite the audience.

72

οἱ μὲν . . . οἱ δ': 'some . . . and those . . .' εἰμί here means 'to live' or 'be alive'. This line is quoted from Euripides' play *Oineus*, which has only survived in fragments.

73

τί δ': 'what?'

Ἰοφῶν: successful tragic playwright and also a son of Sophocles. He gained the first prize at the City Dionysia of 435 BCE and came second place to Euripides' *Hippolytus* in 428 BCE. These lines suggest that his father helped to write his plays.

ζῇ: as the *α* of *ζάω* is long before contraction, it contracts to η where you would expect *α*.

καὶ μόνον: 'just the only' – the adverbial καί serves to increase the force of μόνον.

74

εἰ καὶ τοῦτ' ἄρα: 'if that really is so'.

75

σάφ' οἶδ' οὐδ' . . . τοῦθ' = σάφα οἶδα οὐδε . . . τοῦτο.

αὐτὸ τοῦθ' ὅπως ἔχει: an indirect question following οἶδ' where the subject of the indirect question has been put before the question – literally, 'I don't know clearly this matter how it is' which needs to be rephrased into better English – 'I don't know clearly where the truth lies in this matter'. ὅπως ἔχει is another example of ἔχω having the same sense as εἰμι with an adverb. A compound negative following a simple negative simply confirms the negative: οὐδ' emphasizes οὐ.

76

πρότερον: 'superior'.

ὄντ': causal participle – 'since he is'.

Εὐριπίδου: genitive of comparison.

77

εἴπερ: a strengthened form of εἴ – 'if you really need . . .'

ἄγειν: assume object 'someone' or 'a poet'.

78–79

οὐ πρίν γ' ἂν . . . κωδωνίσω: temporal clause with the indefinite construction in primary sequence (ἂν + subjunctive) – 'not until I test . . .' The main verb is implied from Heracles' line ('I do not intend to bring back Sophocles until . . .'). κωδωνίζω is metaphorical: its basic meaning is to test metal objects by hitting them and making them ring. This plays with the idea of poetry being something that can be physically tested, a metaphor that is developed in the later contest when the lines of Aeschylus and Euripides are weighed.

μόνον: sense here is 'to one side' or 'on his own'.

80

κἄλλως = καὶ ἄλλως.

πανοῦργος ὢν: causal participle – 'since he is . . .'

81

κἂν = καὶ ἄν

ξυναποδρᾶναι: a derogatory verb used for deserters and runaways.

ἐπιχειρήσειέ: 'he might really try . . .' – potential optative following ἄν.

μοι: 'with me'.

82

εὔκολος . . . εὔκολος: the emphasis is on Sophocles' good nature. See the Introduction for a discussion of why Sophocles does not feature significantly in this play.

83

Ἀγάθων: Agathon was a renowned tragedian. He won first prize at the Lenaea in 416 BCE. According to Aristotle, Agathon was the first to write choral parts that were not linked to the drama of each scene and to compose tales that were not taken from existing myth or history. He is mercilessly mocked in Aristophanes' *Thesmophoriazusae* for the style of his poetry as well as his beauty and homosexuality. He also appears in Plato's *Symposium*.

ʼστιν = ἐστίν.

ἀπολιπών μʼ ἀποίχεται: best translated as two indicative verbs joined by 'and' in English. Agathon left Athens for the court of Archelaos in Macedonia around 407 BCE.

84

ἀγαθὸς . . . φίλοις: the line reads a little like a Greek epitaph. Since he has left for Macedonia, he is now as good as dead to the Athenians. As well as honouring Agathon's success and popularity, this line could also make a comic jibe at the poet's sex life: φίλοις can mean both 'friends' and 'lovers'.

85

ποῖ γῆς: 'where on earth?'

εἰς μακάρων εὐωχίαν: another example of Aristophanes inverting audience expectation. You would expect Agathon to be at the feasts of the Macedonians (Μακεδόνες), who were famed for their big appetites and extravagant banquets. 'The blessed' (μάκαρες) are the dead heroes.

86

ὁ δὲ Ξενοκλέης: Xenocles was another tragedian who was mocked in Comedy for being a second-rate poet. However, he did have some success, beating Euripides' *Trojan Women* to first place in 415 BCE. He is also ridiculed in Aristophanes' *Thesmophoriazusae*.

ἐξόλοιτο: optative of wish for the future.

87

Πυθάγγελος: Pythangelus is not known to us from any other source. He must be another tragedian ridiculed by Comedy.

οὐδεὶς λόγος: assume a form of εἰμί – 'there is . . .' Xanthias speaks to the audience and reminds them of the baggage which had been so prominent at the start of the play.

88

ἐπιτριβομένου: agrees with ἐμοῦ on the previous line.

τὸν ὦμον: accusative of respect – initially translate the noun with 'in respect to' before it and then develop a more idiomatic English translation.

οὑτωσὶ: deictic iota (see line 19).

89

ἕτερʼ ἔστʼ = ἕτερα ἔστι. A neuter plural nominative takes a singular verb.

μειρακύλλια: 'little lads'. This diminutive form is rather patronizing to the next generation of tragedians: a μεῖραξ is a young girl or little boy.

90

πλεῖν ἢ μύρια: hyperbolic and delayed for effect. πλεῖν = πλεῖον – see line 18.

91

Εὐριπίδου: genitive of comparison.

πλεῖν ἢ σταδίῳ: the sense is 'by a country mile.' For πλεῖν, see line 18. A stade was the measure of the 607 foot (185 metres) running track for Greek athletics. There were various lengths of foot in the ancient world, but it equates to around 200 metres. To be a stade ahead in a race would be a significant lead.

92

ἐπιφυλλίδες: this is likely to refer to the small grapes on the vine that have been stunted. The sense is that although these young lads are prolific, they produce very little fruit. A metaphor from the vineyard seems very suitable in the theatre of Dionysus.

ταῦτ᾽ ἐστὶ: nominative neuter plural takes a singular verb.

στωμύλματα: this word was probably coined by Aristophanes.

93

χελιδόνων μουσεῖα: 'concert halls of swallows.' A μούσειον was a sanctuary to the muses and so a place for gathering and performing. The noise of swallows twittering together, considered endless and harsh on the ear, was often used to describe barbarian speech.

94

ἃ: nominative neuter plural relative pronoun with ταῦτ᾽ in line 92 as its antecedent (which itself refers back to μειρακύλλια in line 89).

φροῦδα: 'they vanish' – this is in the apodosis of a conditional clause and requires a main verb to be supplied.

θᾶττον: 'rather quickly' – a common translation of the comparative.

ἢν ἅπαξ χορὸν λάβῃ: ἢν = ἐάν and is followed by the subjunctive to form the protasis of a future open conditional. This is best translated in the present in English. A chorus was granted to a tragedian when he was approved to take part in a dramatic festival by the Eponymous Archon.

95

προσουρήσαντα τῇ τραγῳδίᾳ: the initial sense is that their plays are so bad that they are an insult to the art of tragedy and so can be described as pissing over her.

96

γόνιμον δὲ ποιητὴν: 'an original poet' – the idea of a good poet being γόνιμον (sexually potent) encourages a reassessment of the image of other tragedians pissing on tragedy: those young lads get a shot with Tragedy and can only piss on her. A vulgar expression of their inability to go all the way to a proper climax.

ἂν . . . εὕροις: ἂν + optative indicates the apodosis of a future remote conditional.

οὐχ . . . ἔτι = 'no longer'.

97

ζητῶν: 'if you were to go looking' – the participle represents the protasis of the future remote conditional.

ὅστις . . . λάκοι: 'who could say . . .' The verb λάσκω is taken from the lofty vocabulary of epic and tragedy to match the grand concept of the ῥῆμα γενναῖον.

98

πῶς γόνιμον: Heracles does not understand what he really means with this medical term (and the audience might well feel sympathy for him).

ὡδὶ γόνιμον ὅστις: 'this is what I mean by original, someone who . . .' ὡδὶ = ὧδε with the deictic iota (see line 19). Dionysus offers a tricolon of examples.

99

τοιουτονί τι παρακεκινδυνευμένον: 'something daring like this'. τοιουτονί = τοιουτον with the deictic iota (see line 19).

100

αἰθέρα Διὸς δωμάτιον: Dionysus' first example of a ῥῆμα γενναῖον is a misremembered oath from Euripides' *Melanippe*: αἰθέρ' οἴκησιν Διός (by the sky, the home of Zeus). What started as a tragic oath is rendered ridiculous by Dionysus' poor memory: he replaces οἴκησιν with the diminutive δωμάτιον (little bedroom), which is a form not found in extant tragedy.

χρόνου πόδα: this appears in Euripides' *Alexandros* and *Bacchae* (line 888). The implication here is that Euripides was rather novel in giving feet to personified Time.

101–102

φρένα . . . φρενός: the syntax here is that of an indirect statement using participles. Dionysus attempts to remember one of Euripides' most famous lines (*Hippolytus* line 612): ἡ γλῶσσ᾽ ὀμώμοχ᾽, ἡ δὲ φρὴν ἀνώμοτος (my tongue has sworn it but my heart is not bound by oath). Dionysus appears ridiculous on two counts. Firstly, he mangles the line, reproducing it over two lines in the style of prose rather than high poetry. Second, he reveals that he has misunderstood the Euripidean original. It is not the case that these lines justify perjury because Hippolytus keeps his oath. However, the line was commonly misremembered as such and Dionysus' version follows this popular misunderstanding.

καθ᾽ ἱερῶν = κατὰ ἱερῶν – 'by the sacrificial victims'.

ἰδίᾳ: 'separate from' – followed by the genitive.

103

ταῦτ᾽ ἀρέσκει: nominative neuter plural followed by a singular verb. ἀρέσκει here takes an accusative object σὲ which is emphasized at the start of the line.

μάλλὰ = μή, ἀλλὰ. An imperative should be assumed following the μὴ – 'Don't say that but . . .'

πλεῖν ἢ μαίνομαι: 'I am more than crazy.' πλεῖν = πλεῖον – see line 18.

104

ἦ μὴν: 'in truth' or 'I swear that' – these particles are used to indicate a strong oath.

κόβαλά: 'garbage' (literally, 'something carried by a porter').

ὡς καὶ σοὶ δοκεῖ: Heracles thinks better of Dionysus or assumes that everyone must see things the way he does. In fact, Dionysus will conclude the play in agreement with him.

105

μὴ . . . οἴκει νοῦν: negative direct command. The ancient commentators suggest this is a quotation of Euripides.

οἰκίαν: 'your own house'. Note the wordplay in this line: οἴκει means both 'manage' and 'live in'.

106

καὶ μὴν: 'Yes, and what's more . . .'

φαίνεται: 'it is obviously . . .' – assume a participle of εἰμί.

107

δειπνεῖν με δίδασκε: gluttony is clearly Heracles' only area of expertise.

περὶ ἐμοῦ δ' οὐδεὶς λόγος: Xanthias speaks up again at the mention of food!

108

ὧνπερ ἕνεκα: 'because of this' or 'for this reason'.

τήνδε τὴν σκευὴν: the audience still do not know why Dionysus is dressed as Heracles.

ἔχων: 'with'.

109–110

κατὰ σὴν μίμησιν: 'in imitation of you'.

ἵνα . . . φράσειας: purpose clause with an optative in historic sequence.

εἰ δεοίμην: 'if I were to need them'.

111

ἐχρῶ: second person singular of the imperfect tense (α contract) of deponent verb χράομαι.

τόθ' = τότε.

ἡνίκ' = ἡνίκα.

ἐπὶ τὸν Κέρβερον: 'in search of Cerberus' or 'to fetch Cerberus'. This refers to Heracles' twelfth and last labour. Cerberus is the huge three-headed dog that guards the underworld; Heracles was sent to fetch it and show it to Eurystheus, King of Tiryns.

112

τούτους: refers back to τοὺς ξένους on line 109.

φράσον: aorist singular imperative.

112–115

λιμένας . . . ὀλίγιστοι: an expansive and disordered asyndetic list of all the information a traveller could need. Much humour is created from the idea that the Underworld functions much like the real world.

ὀλίγιστοι: assume εἰσίν as the main verb in this relative clause. There is huge bathos at the end of this list: bedbugs seem such a minor concern for a journey to Hades and it is incongruous for a god to be expecting the fewest rather than none at all!

115
περὶ ἐμοῦ δ' οὐδεὶς λόγος: repetition of line 107. This time Xanthias seems to have been prompted by the thought of poor conditions.

116
ὦ σχέτλιε: 'o you bold fool' – this adjective is used by Homer to refer to valour, bravery or stubbornness. It can be used between comrades rather amicably or to reproach and abuse someone. It seems rather mock-heroic when used to refer to Dionysus.
καὶ σύ γε: 'you, too'.

117
μηδὲν ἔτι πρὸς ταῦτ': 'nothing more about that' – assume the imperative φράζε applies to this clause as well as the next.
φράζε τῶν ὁδῶν: 'tell of . . .' – φράζω can take a genitive.

118
ἀφίξόμ': ἀφίξόμαι.
εἰς Ἅιδου: see line 69.

119
μήτε . . . φράσῃς: negative command using a form of μή with the aorist subjunctive.
ἄγαν: most likely applies to both θερμὴν and ψυχρὰν. The adjectives are feminine to agree with an assumed ὁδόν. This line sets up a series of jokes on 'the best route to Hades.'

120
τίν' = τίνα. Heracles repeats this in the line as he deliberates.
πρώτην: the feminine form agrees with an assumed ὁδόν. As a response to Dionysus' three examples of Euripides' noble statements, Heracles now offers his immortal brother three forms of suicide as routes to the underworld.

121–122
ἀπὸ κάλω καὶ θρανίου: 'by rope and bench'. This at first sounds like Heracles is suggesting that Dionysus travel to the underworld by boat, perhaps as Odysseus did in Book 11 of Homer's Odyssey. However, it is made clear on line 122 that Heracles means suicide: the rope is to make a noose and the bench is to be kicked away to allow the body to fall and hang.

122
κρεμάσαντι: dative singular aorist patriciple – 'for you . . .'
σαυτόν = σεαυτόν.
πνιγηρὰν: the adjective can refer to 'stifling' heat, reminding us of the instruction to avoid a route that is too hot, but also means 'choking'.

123
ἀτραπὸς ξύντομος τετριμμένη: a path can be cut short (ξύντομος) and well-trodden (τετριμμένη) but also hemlock, famously used as the poison to kill Socrates in 399 BCE, needs to be cut up (ξύντομος) and pounded (τετριμμένη).

124

ἡ: refers to ἀτραπός.

θυείας: the mortar used with a pestle to crush hemlock to form the poison. Heracles' language continues the play on the journey with διὰ + genitive – 'through' or 'by means of'.

125

μάλιστά γε: 'I certainly do' or 'spot on'.

ψυχράν γε καὶ δυσχείμερον: Heracles' first suggestion was too stifling, this one is too cold, still breaking Dionysus' request on line 119. As previously, adjectives suitable to a physical journey are used only to be reinterpreted on the next line.

126

ἀποπήγνυσι τἀντικνήμια: the coldness is the working of the poison. According to Plato's *Phaedo*, Socrates experienced this coldness when paralysis started in his feet.

τἀντικνήμια = τα ἀντικνήμια.

127

βούλει . . . φράσω: 'do you want me to . . .' – followed by the deliberative subjunctive.

ταχεῖαν καὶ κατάντη: the same joke continues as this vocabulary is suitable for the description of a journey and its terrain as well as a suicidal jump from a tower. This climax in the tricolon of suicides is extended and the full explanation delayed until line 133.

128

ὡς ὄντος γε μὴ βαδιστικοῦ: a genitive absolute for which ἐμοῦ or μου needs to be assumed – 'since I am not . . .' μὴ is used instead of οὐ because it is a generic participle: Dionysus is not the sort of man to like walking. βαδιστικοῦ is probably a word coined by Aristophanes, perhaps to parody the Sophists who may have been fond of technical terms that ended in – ικός.

129

καθέρπυσόν: aorist singular imperative.

Κεραμεικόν: the Cerameicus or potters' quarter, just to the north-west of the Agora.

κᾆτα = καὶ εἶτα.

130

ἀναβὰς: an aorist participle, but best translated as another imperative.

τὸν πύργον τὸν ὑψηλόν: the tower has not been definitively identified but it could be a tower mentioned by Pausanias, the Greek travel writer of the second century CE, which by that time was known as the tower of Timon. It is clear from line 131 that the top of the tower offers a view of the festival torch races that took place at night during some of the major Athenian festivals.

131

ἀφιεμένην: 'being set off'.

θεῶ: present singular imperative of θεάομαι.

132

κἄπειτ᾽: καὶ ἔπειτα.

ἐπειδὰν φῶσιν: indefinite construction in the primary sequence (ἐπειδὰν + subjunctive) but best translated as 'when' rather than 'whenever'.

οἱ θεώμενοι: see line 2.

133

εἶνται: perfect passive form of ἵημι, best translated in the present – 'they are off'.

τόθ᾽ = τότε.

εἶναι: the aorist infinitive is used in place of the imperative.

σαυτόν = σεαυτόν.

134

ἀπολέσαιμ᾽ ἄν: 'I would destroy' or 'I would spoil' – the apodosis of a future remote conditional with the assumed protasis 'if I were to do this'.

ἐγκεφάλου θρίω δύο: 'the two rissoles of my brain'. θρίω is an accusative dual form. θρῖον (a fig leaf) could refer to the wrinkled membrane around the brain, but also to a popular meal of a fig leaf stuffed with meat and herbs. There are two because Greek doctors believed that the brain was formed of two parts. Thus, the line can be read in two ways: either Dionysus would ruin his snack, presumably something he could buy to eat while watching the torch races, or he would smash his brains out by jumping off the tower.

135

ἂν βαδίσαιμι: potential optative, best translated as the future indicative.

136

ἥνπερ: refers back to ὁδὸν.

τότε: best translated as 'before' as it refers to when Heracles went to the underworld on his 12th labour (see line 111).

ὁ πλοῦς πολύς: assume ἐστί. The assonance helps to emphasize the length of the journey ahead.

137

ἥξεις: 'you will come'.

λίμνην: the Acherusian lake.

πάνυ: this modifies μεγάλην. Note the way in which Heracles builds up the size of the lake with μεγάλην, πάνυ and then ἄβυσσον.

139

πλοιαρίῳ: 'a little boat' – note the diminutive form.

τυννουτῳί: 'this little' – with its deictic iota this word suggests an accompanying hand gesture to emphasize the size of the boat. Heracles attempts to scare Dionysus by contrasting the enormous lake with the tiny boat.

ἀνὴρ γέρων: Charon, the boatman, enters the play at line 183.

140

δύ' ὀβολὼ μισθὸν λαβών: ὀβολὼ is another example of the accusative dual. It was a Greek death ritual to place an obol in the mouth of the deceased as payment for Charon. The cost was normally a single obol not two. Commentators have been ingenious in explaining why Aristophanes doubles the fee here: it is a double ticket for Dionysus and Xanthias; the ticket includes a return journey; inflation towards the end of the Peloponnesian War has doubled the cost.

141

φεῦ: this exclamation stands outside of the metrical structure of the poetry. It is an 'ah' of recognition rather than 'alas'.

δύνασθον . . . τὼ δύ' ὀβολώ: dual forms. This may refer to the διωβελία, a daily dole of 2 obols introduced by Cleophon in 410 BCE. It might also refer to the 2-obol charge for entry to the theatre. Sommerstein convincingly argues that the second is the more likely as the line refers to the power of the 2 obols: in the theatre, the spectators in the 2-obol seats have all the power over a playwright's victory.

142

ἠλθέτην: dual form.

κἀκεῖσε = καὶ ἐκεῖσε – 'down there, too'.

Θησεὺς ἤγαγεν: Theseus was the mythical founder of Athens who had gone down to the underworld to abduct Persephone. As the only living Athenian to enter the underworld, he is assumed to have introduced the 2-obol custom to Charon.

143

τοῦτ' = τοῦτο.

θηρί' = θηρία.

ὄψει: second person singular of the deponent future form of ὁράω.

144

μή μ' ἔκπληττε μηδὲ δειμάτου: two pleonastic present imperative forms. The use of the present tense (by aspect) emphasizes the number of times Heracles has tried to frighten Dionysus – 'don't keep on trying to terrifying me!'

145

εἶτα βόρβορον: assume the verb ὄψει from line 142. The punishment of lying in mud seems to be a feature of the Eleusinian Mysteries. There are many elements of this underworld scene that might make the audience aware of the Eleusinian Mysteries.

146

σκῶρ ἀείνων: shit is a typical comic development from mud.

κειμένους: accusative governed by ὄψει.

147

ξένον: this marks the beginning of a list of sins which lead the perpetrators to a muddy punishment. Three of the sins would be recognized as serious: harming a guest, one's parents or the gods. This particular grouping of crimes appears to be significant to the Eleusinian Mysteries. This is another example of a long, asyndetic list.

148

τἀργύριον = τὸ ἀργύριον.

παῖδα: 'rent-boy' – in this scenario, the boy has been paid but then the client takes back the money during the act. Among the serious sins are ones that appeal to course humour.

150

'πίορκον = ἐπίορκον. Note the repeated sound in the line.

151

Μορσίμου: Morsimus was a tragic poet whom Aristophanes mocks in several of his plays for being second rate. It would be a crime against literary taste to have this work copied!

ῥῆσιν ἐξεγράψατο: 'got a speech copied out' – the middle is used when the nominative gets something done.

152

ἐχρῆν γε πρὸς τούτοισι: 'one ought to add to these men (you have listed)'.

κεἰ = καὶ εἰ. Dionysus uses the same construction with εἰ and τις as Heracles uses in lines 147–151 to list offenders.

153

τὴν πυρρίχην . . . τὴν Κινησίου: Cinesias was a successful dithyrambic poet (a dithyramb was a hymn that was sung and accompanied by a dance). He was mocked by Aristophanes, among other things, for his thin frame and sickly nature, as well as his innovative approach to his art. The πυρρίχη was a dance in which naked men carrying a shield and spear and wearing a helmet turned in a circle imitating the movements of a hoplite in war. It was a very popular competition dance that formed part of Athens' celebrations of the Panathenaea, a major festival in honour of Athena. This crime is another one against artistic taste: Cinesias must have recently choreographed a particularly avant-garde performance!

154

τίς: the indefinite pronoun in agreement with πνοή.

περίεισιν: compound of the future form εἶμι (I shall go).

155

φῶς κάλλιστον: Heracles turns to the nicer parts of the underworld at this point. Here, the bright light is reserved for those who have been initiated.

ὥσπερ ἐνθάδε: i.e. just like the brightness of Athens in the upper world.

156

μυρρινῶνας: myrtle was associated with religious festivals, particularly the Eleusinian Mysteries. It not only provides the lush vegetation expected of somewhere like the Elysian fields in the underworld, but was also known for its sweet fragrance.

157

ἀνδρῶν γυναικῶν: supply a conjunction when translating this asyndetic couplet. Men and women could be initiated into the Eleusinian Mysteries.

κρότον χειρῶν πολύν: the clapping is a natural part of the θιάσους in line 156 – people are clapping the time for dancers. Aristophanes is also hinting to his audience that he hopes this play will achieve a huge round of applause.

158

οἱ μεμυημένοι: 'the initiates'. Our first introduction to the main chorus of the play.

159

ἐγὼ γοῦν: 'and so *I*' – the particle both emphasizes ἐγὼ and leads to a conclusion.

ὄνος: to be the donkey at the mysteries was to have the least enviable role: all the hard work and none of the benefits. The donkey would carry all the equipment and baggage on the march from Athens to Eleusis but receive none of the rewards that the mystery cult offered its initiates.

ἄγω μυστήρια: 'I am celebrating the Mysteries.'

160

τὸν πλείω χρόνον: accusative of time. πλείω = πλείονα. The donkey departed from the scene at line 35 and Xanthias has not been acknowledged by Dionysus since line 42. He starts to put down the luggage very slowly.

161

οἵ: Xanthias' lines have interrupted Heracles' syntax which continues here with a relative clause referring back to the antecedent οἱ μεμυημένοι in line 158.

φράσουσ᾽ = φράσουσιν.

ἁπαξάπανθ᾽ = ἁπαξάπαντα.

ὧν ἂν δέῃ: 'which you need to know.' The relative pronoun is genitive following δέομαι.

162

οὗτοι: refers to the initiates. The main verb is found on the next line: οἰκοῦσιν.

παρ᾽ = παρά.

163

Πλούτωνος: by this time Pluto or Pluton was a common name for Hades, god of the underworld. This name is closely associated with Plutus, god of abundance and good harvests, who had an important role in the Eleusinian Mysteries. This starts to prepare the audience for the scenery later in the play: from line 460, the scenery at the back of the orchestra will represent Pluto's palace and the chorus of initiates will cluster around it.

164

χαῖρε πόλλ': πόλλα refers to an internal accusative of the verb (literally, 'farewell many farewells), which is best translated along the lines of 'a huge farewell'. The emphasis put on these good wishes suggest that Heracles sees a dangerous journey ahead for Dionysus.

ὦδελφέ = ὦ ἀδελφέ. Heracles departs back through his door at the end of this line, leaving Dionysus and Xanthias on stage.

165

σύ: Xanthias. The pronoun is a rather authoritative addition to the imperative λάμβανε.

166

πρὶν καὶ καταθέσθαι: πρὶν followed by the infinitive means 'before'. καταθέσθαι is the aorist middle infinitive of κατατίθημι. καὶ is best translated as 'even'. Since line 160, Xanthias has been very slowly putting down the luggage and the comfort he hopes for is suddenly snatched away from him.

καὶ: 'yes and . . .'

167–179: The Corpse

167

δῆθ' = δῆτα.

σ' = σέ.

μίσθωσαί: aorist middle (deponent) singular imperative.

168

τῶν ἐκφερομένων: 'one of those being carried out for burial' – partitive genitive following τινα on the previous line.

ὅστις: 'who' – no need for the indefinite '-ever' in English.

ἐπὶ τοῦτ': 'to this place (i.e. Hades)' or 'for this reason (i.e. to carry baggage)' – the sense of this is disputed among modern commentators.

169

ἐὰν δὲ μὴ εὕρω: ἐὰν + subjunctive is used for the protasis of a future open conditional (negative μὴ), best translated with the present indicative in English.

ἔμ' = ἔμε

ἄγειν: infinitive used as an imperative (see line 133).

170

καὶ γάρ: 'yes, for . . .'

τιν' . . . τουτονὶ νεκρόν: τινα agrees with νεκρόν. τουτονὶ with its deictic iota draws attention to the anonymous corpse – 'here's a corpse'. The ridiculous argument in lines 21–32 about carrying while being carried comes back to mind as a corpse being carried is asked to carry the luggage.

171

οὗτος: 'you there'.

λέγω μέντοι: 'Yes, I mean . . .' There is obvious comic value in addressing a dead man in this colloquial style in expectation of a response.

172

σκευάρι' = σκευάρια. Note the use of a diminutive to underplay the weight of the load and thus reach a cheaper price for labour.

εἰς Ἅιδου: see line 69.

173

πόσ' ἄττα = πόσα ἅτινα – 'about how many?'

ταυτί = ταῦτα with a deictic iota suggesting a gesture towards the luggage Xanthias is still holding.

δύο δραχμὰς μισθὸν: 'two drachmas as my wage' – all accusative in apposition. A single drachma was roughly the wage for a full day's hard labour, so this seems quite a significant demand.

τελεῖς: future tense.

174

μὰ Δί': a negative oath here.

ἔλαττον: in agreement with μισθὸν on the previous line.

ὑπάγεθ' = ὑπάγετε – the corpse is speaking to the silent actors carrying his bier.

τῆς ὁδοῦ: the genitive is used to mean 'along'.

175

ἀνάμεινον: aorist singular imperative.

ὦ δαιμόνι' = ὦ δαιμόνιε – 'my good man' or similar.

ἐὰν: 'in case' is the best translation for this protasis of a future open conditional.

ξυμβῶ τί: τί refers to an internal accusative of the verb – 'come to some arrangement'.

176

μὴ διαλέγου: negative command. The present imperative implies an ongoing action – 'don't keep on . . .'

177

λάβ' ἐννέ = λάβε ἐννέα.

ἐννέ' ὀβολούς: 9 obols amount to a drachma and a half, so Dionysus is starting to barter downwards.

ἀναβιῴην: optative wish for the future. This is a witty reversal of the standard 'strike me dead' in the face of something unwelcome. Here the dead man wishes to be alive again: amusingly the terrible fate of being alive is better than receiving only 9 obols for his labour. It is possible that conditions of Athens in these final years of the Peloponnesian Wars really had made death and Hades a more pleasing prospect.

178

οὐκ οἰμώξεται: this negative future tense has the same sense as the imperative or iussive subjunctive – 'let him wail!'

179

εἶ: second person singular present tense of εἰμί.

γεννάδας: rather oxymoronic to call a slave 'noble'. It also has the sense of 'generous' or 'brave'.

180–208: Charon

180

ἐπὶ: 'in search of'.

ὢ ὄπ παραβαλοῦ: heard from offstage, these are the commands of a captain ordering his crew to row a boat into land – 'easy there, bring her alongside!' Charon traditionally punts his boat, so who he is giving orders to? They are probably to himself, highlighting to the audience that he is a boatman, but they could also be to imagined rowers or even to the stage hands who are helping to move the boat.

181

τουτὶ = τοῦτο with a deictic iota.

182

'στὶν = ἐστὶν.

ἔφραζε: Heracles is the assumed nominative in this relative clause.

πλοῖόν γ' ὁρῶ: at this point Charon's boat must wheel into view in the orchestra.

183

νὴ τὸν Ποσειδῶ: an appropriate oath to Poseidon, god of the sea and sailors, for a scene with a boat.

κἄστι = καὶ ἐστί.

οὑτοσί: the deictic iota suggests wild hand gestures. Note the excitement in these lines created by the oaths and particles.

184

χαῖρ' = χαῖρε. Further wild gesturing was likely to accompany this triplet of welcomes. The repetition is for comic effect. Some commentators have suggested that a rather deaf Charon (the ἀνὴρ γέρων of line 139) needed to be called upon several times. He does not appear to notice them until line 188. The comic use of similar sounds in the line creates bathos at the arrival of one of the Underworld's most significant figures. One manuscript suggests that this is a quotation from the satyr play, *Aithon*, by Achaeus; however, the significance of this is unclear.

185

τίς εἰς: 'who is for . . .?' – these lines parody the way ferrymen (or modern bus and train announcers) list their destinations.

ἀναπαύλας ἐκ κακῶν καὶ πραγμάτων: this aspect of Hades may seem appealing to the audience of 405 BCE who are suffering hugely because of the war.

186

τὸ Λήθης πεδίον: 'the plain of Oblivion' – a barren plain surrounded by a river.

'ς = ἐς – similarly on line 187.

Ὄκνου πλοκάς: 'The Rope of Ocnus' – Ocnus, a name which translates as 'Lethargy', was depicted in a detailed painting by the fifth-century-BCE painter Polygnotus which only survives in a description given by Pausanius in his 'Guide to Greece' 10.25 ff. (see line 130). He is depicted in the eternal punishment of plaiting a rope while a mule stands next to him eating the rope he has produced.

187

Κερβερίους: 'the Cerberians' remind us of Cerberus, the three-headed dog guarding the underworld (see line 111). This refers to a group of people living near the entrance to the underworld.

'ς κόρακας: literally, 'to the ravens', which was a common idiom for 'go to hell'.

'πὶ Ταίναρον = ἐπὶ Ταίναρον. Tainaros was an actual place in the far south of the Peloponnese. It was believed that there was an entrance to the underworld there. The ferryman's list becomes more ridiculous as it turns from places in the underworld to ravens and then a place in the world above. Some commentators have read into Tainaros the implication that the theatre of the Peloponnesian War was much like the underworld.

188

σχήσειν: future infinitive (formed with the aorist stem) with assumed nominative to create an indirect statement. Sense of ἔχω here is 'land' or 'steer'. Dionysus does not seem to have understood where the boat is actually going.

189

ἐς κόρακας: see line 187. Here it is an exclamation of annoyance.

ὄντως: 'really?' – Dionysus in confusion has taken Charon's exclamation literally.

σοῦ γ' οὕνεκα: 'as far as you are concerned' – the sense is that this is exactly where Charon would like to take Dionysus.

190

παῖ: Dionysus turns to Xanthias.

191

εἰ μὴ: 'unless'.

τὴν: assume μάχην.

περὶ τῶν κρεῶν: literally, 'about the flesh' which is used to refer to a life or death situation. He means Arginusae (see line 33).

192

οὐ γὰρ: 'not me, I tell you'.

ἔτυχον ὀφθαλμιῶν: τυγχάνω + participle means 'I happen to . . .' but is best translated with the participle as the main verb and τυγχάνω as 'by chance' or something similar.

193
οὔκουν περιθρέξει: this negative future tense has the same sense as the imperative – 'so get running around . . .'

194
ποῦ δῆτ᾽ ἀναμενῶ: it is ridiculous that the slave who is to run around the lake will make it to the other side before Dionysus in his boat.
τὸν Αὑαίνου λίθον: 'the stone of Hauainos' – this seems to be a distortion of the usual sort of title given to landmarks. Haiainos is not the name of a hero, as an Athenian might expect, but it is to do with withering or dryness. It presumably plays on the idea of dead bodies withering in Hades.

195
μανθάνεις: 'do you understand?'

196
τῷ = τινί.
ξυνέτυχον ἐξιών: the Greeks were superstitious and believed that meeting certain people or animals could be ominous.

197
κάθιζ᾽ = κάθιζε.
ἐπὶ κώπην: 'at an oar' (i.e. 'ready to row') but the phrase is open to comic misinterpretation. Dionysus' performance in the boat is perfectly judged comedy given Athenian naval prowess. Comedy needs to make its audience laugh early and this slapstick scene is very much the hook that draws in the spectators.
πλεῖ: 'is making the crossing'. Charon calls out for any further passengers.
σπευδέτω: third person singular imperative.

198
οὗτος: 'you there'.

199
᾽πὶ = ἐπὶ.
οὗπερ: 'where'.

200
οὔκουν καθεδεῖ: see line 193.
ἐνθαδί = ἐνθάδε.
γάστρων: 'fatso' – a comic term of abuse. The actor would have worn padding to look fatter than he was and this probably contrasted visually with a skinny Charon.
ἰδού: aorist middle singular imperative of ὁράω. Dionysus points out that he is doing what he is told.

201
οὔκουν προβαλεῖ: see line 193.
τὼ χεῖρε: dual endings, here the accusative.

κἀκτενεῖς = καὶ ἐκτενεῖς.
ἰδού: see line 200.

202
οὐ μὴ φλυαρήσεις ... ἀλλ' ... ἐλᾷς: οὐ μὴ followed by the future indicative creates a negative command. The ἀλλ' then introduces a positive command. Note how Charon speaks to Dionysus like he is a child.
ἔχων: this participle accompanies the main verb φλυαρήσεις to give the sense 'constantly' or 'keep on . . .-ing'.
ἀντιβὰς: 'set your feet against the stretcher' – a technical rowing term. The participle is best translated as another command and a conjunction should then be supplied.

203
κᾆτα = καὶ εἶτα.
δυνήσομαι: followed by the infinitive ἐλαύνειν on line 205.

204
ἄπειρος ἀθαλάττωτος ἀσαλαμίνιος: a remarkable asyndetic tricolon of pleonastic negatives that fill the line; these alpha-privative forms are a clear parody of tragic diction and present ideas that would be shameful for any self-respecting Athenian citizen.
ἀθαλάττωτος: there is wordplay here as the form could mean 'unseaworthy' but also 'undiluted by seawater'. Wine was sometimes diluted with seawater to make it keep longer and Dionysus himself represents wine.
ἀσαλαμίνιος: the men from the island of Salamis were famed for being excellent seamen.

205
εἶτ'= εἶτα – repeated from line 203 to bring out a self-pitying tone.
ῥᾷστ' = ῥᾷστα.
μέλη: the music will presumably help Dionysus to keep time.

206
κάλλιστ' = κάλλιστα.
ἐπειδὰν ἐμβάλῃς ἅπαξ: see line 132 for the construction. ἐμβάλῃς refers to the act of rowing the oar through the water.

207
βατράχων κύκνων: 'frog swans' – genitive following θαυμαστά with μέλη understood. In the Greek world, Swans were considered to be beautiful singers, so the real sense is 'frogs who can sing beautifully'. There is something comic in the juxtaposition of the beauty of swans and the ugliness of frogs.

208
ὦ ὄπ ὄπ: calls for rowers: it has been suggested that ὦ is the drive phase of the stroke, while ὄπ is used for the release of the oar from the water and the recovery before the next stroke.

The set text now moves from the prologue to what might be considered the third episode of the play. See the Introduction for a detailed summary of the play.

830–874: Euripides and Aeschylus

830

οὐκ ἂν μεθείμην: 'I will not let go of . . .' – potential optative.

τοῦ θρόνου: genitive following μεθείμην. This refers to the Chair of Tragedy.

μὴ νουθέτει: negative direct command. The present imperative gives the sense 'don't keep on . . .'

831

εἶναί φημι: indirect statement with the main nominative as subject of the infinitive.

τούτου: genitive of comparison. Note the derogatory use of this pronoun, presumably accompanied by a hand gesture.

τὴν τέχνην: accusative of respect (see line 88).

832

τοῦ λόγου: αἰσθάνει is followed by the genitive.

833

ἅπερ: 'which pretentious acts' – this agrees with the internal accusative of ἐτερατεύετο and its antecedent is all the actions implied by the verb ἀποσεμνυνεῖται.

834

ἐτερατεύετο: this verb is used to describe puffed up and pretentious forms of speech. The particular act being mocked here is Aeschylus' use of silence which is attacked by Euripides more fully later in the agon (lines 911 ff). Note that is Pluto is on stage at this point then he remains silent for an awfully long time in a rather Aeschylean fashion!

835

ὦ δαιμόνι᾽ ἀνδρῶν: 'oh, my good man'.

μὴ μεγάλα λίαν λέγε: 'don't speak too proudly'. Euripides has indeed been over confident up to this point. Dionysus takes on the role of referee as well as judge.

836

ἐγῷδα: ἐγὼ οἶδα.

διέσκεμμαι: perfect middle of διασκέπτομαι.

837

ἀγριοποιόν: many commentators take this to mean that Aeschylus is being accused of producing savage characters; however, it might make more sense in the context that he writes in a savage style. Evidence in support of this reading is that the line itself is a three-word trimeter, a common feature of Aeschylus' work given his love of long compounds. Note also the assonance in the line.

αὐθαδόστομον: another polysyllabic compound verb which emphasizes' Aeschylus' daring (or reckless) diction in his plays. From this point begins a run of polysyllabic words coined by Aristophanes to parody Aeschylus' sesquipedalian (polysyllabic) style.

838

ἔχοντ᾽ = ἔχοντα.

ἀχάλινον ἀκρατὲς ἀπύλωτον: another tricolon with assonance, this time made up of negative compound forms. They are expressions used by Euripides in his own plays.

839

ἀπεριλάλητον: 'unable to chatter'. Euripides is proud of the fact that he taught the people of Athens to talk freely (see lines 954ff in the English section of the text), whereas Aeschylus' obscure and complex diction has had the opposite effect.

κομποφακελορρήμονα: a remarkable compound of three forms – 'boast + bundle + phrased'. This parodies the style of Aeschylus in an excessive way: no triple compound is recorded in tragedy, nor is a trimeter of tragedy ever made up of only two words.

840

ἄληθες: 'Is that so?'

τῆς ἀρουραίας θεοῦ: in Old Comedy, Euripides' mother was derisively called a grower or seller of vegetables, even though she was from a noble family. This attack on Euripides and his family is a parody of tragedy, specifically a line that survives in a fragment of Euripidean tragedy in which Achilles is being addressed. It is interesting that Aeschylus' opening line is very much Aristophanic.

841

σὺ δή με ταῦτ᾽: assume a verb like λέγεις here.

στωμυλιοσυλλεκτάδη: further sesquipedalian parody.

842

πτωχοποιὲ . . . ῥακιοσυρραπτάδη: further coined words develop the parody of Aeschylus. Aeschylus attacks Euripides for his love of producing heroes in rags. Euripides had already been mocked for this in Aristophanes' *Acharnians* in which Dicaeopolis intends to borrow rags from Euripides. In *Acharnians*, Aristophanes lists a number of examples from Euripidean tragedy: Oeneus, Phoenix, Philoctetes, Bellerophon, Telephus, Thyestes, and Ino.

843

οὔ τι χαίρων: literally, 'not rejoicing in any way', which when combined with the main verb ἐρεῖς comes to mean 'you will regret saying . . .'

αὔτ᾽ = αὔτα.

παῦ᾽ = παῦε.

844

μὴ . . . θερμήνῃς: negative command using μὴ and the aorist subjunctive.

πρὸς ὀργὴν: 'angrily'.

κότῳ: the line as a whole is in the style of tragedy and this word is particularly Aeschylean. It is quite possible that the line is from one of Aeschylus' plays that do not survive.

845

πρίν . . . ἂν . . . ἀποφήνω: πρίν means 'until' when followed by the indefinite construction.

846

τὸν χωλοποιὸν: a similar attack as discussed on line 842. Bellerophon and Philoctetes are good examples of characters in Euripidean tragedy that are lame.

οἷος ὢν: 'who despite being such a man . . .'

847

ἄρν᾽ ἄρνα: Aeschylus' anger is similar to a whirlwind, so Dionysus jokingly calls for the sacrifice of a black lamb to assuage the storm god. The repetition shows eagerness.

ἐξενέγκατε: aorist plural imperative. The command may well be to the stagehands as this verb is used for the bringing on of props and scenery.

849

Κρητικὰς . . . μονῳδίας: monodies were songs sung by a single actor and they became a distinctive feature of Euripides' later tragedies. Cretan is likely used here to refer to the style of music and dancing that accompanied the songs as well as the notorious nature of the Cretan characters such as Pasiphae, who slept with a bull, and Phaedra, who fell in love with her stepson. From line 1331 in the English section of the text, Aeschylus performs a parody of a Euripidean monody.

συλλέγων: 'collector'.

850

γάμους δ᾽ ἀνοσίους: the audience are likely to think of Euripides' *Cretans* (fragmentary) in which Pasiphae sleeps with a bull and gives birth to the minotaur, or his *Aeolus* (also fragmentary), in which Aeolus' son, Macareus, falls in love with his own sister, Canace.

851

ἐπίσχες: aorist singular imperative.

οὗτος: 'you there' is perhaps best translated together with the imperative – 'hold it right there, you!'

πολυτίμητ᾽ = πολυτίμητε. A hint at Dionysus' great respect for Aeschylus as this term is normally reserved for gods.

852

τῶν χαλαζῶν: the storm imagery for Aeschylus' anger continues.

πόνηρ᾽ = πόνηρε – the adjective is meant sympathetically but the more negative sense would also make sense given the earlier characterization of Euripides. This double meaning acts as another hint at the outcome of this contest.

854

ἵνα μὴ: negative purpose clause with the subjunctive ἐκχέῃ in line 855.

κεφαλαίῳ . . . ῥήματι: a much-debated phrase but probably a παρὰ προσδοκίαν joke which defies the expectation of the listener or reader. In architectural terms κεφαλαίος describes a stone that was suitable for the top of a column or to go over a doorway. When we would expect 'stone' or similar, we get 'word': Aeschylus' wording will hit Euripides like a block of stone. It could also be that κεφαλαίος is used with 'word' to create a sense along the lines of 'an argument that caps another' but with the possible secondary meaning of 'an argument that hits you on the head'.

855

θενὼν: translate this participle as if it were a main subjunctive of the purpose clause and supply a conjunction.

τὸν Τήλεφον: another παρὰ προσδοκίαν as we would expect his brains to pour out after a whack on the head, not his Telephus. Euripides' *Telephus* was produced in 438 BCE and seems to be one of Aristophanes' favourite plays to parody. It told the story of the wounded Telephus going to Argos dressed as a beggar to get a cure for his wound. The idea of being hit on the head and giving birth to something is a parody of Zeus giving birth to Athena from a knock on the head.

856

μὴ: 'don't question . . . but question . . .' – negative followed by the imperative ἔλεγχ᾽ (ἔλεγχε) on line 857 which requires repetition as a positive command after ἀλλὰ.

πρὸς ὀργήν: 'angrily'.

Αἰσχύλ᾽ = Αἰσχύλε.

857

ἐλέγχου: passive imperative – 'be questioned'.

πρέπει: impersonal verb followed by an accusative (ἄνδρας ποιητὰς) and an infinitive (λοιδορεῖσθαι).

858

ἄνδρας: no need to translate this word into English.

ἀρτοπώλιδας: female bakers are here imagined as argumentative and loud. Dover points out that people who sell things or offer a service are often, in Comedy, seen as if through the eyes of a dissatisfied customer. There is humour in comparing male tragedians to female market-sellers.

859

πρῖνος: not only is fire imagery suitable for Aeschylus' temper, but the holm-oak is apt for the volume of his shouting: the tree roars as it burns.

860

κοὐκ: καί οὐκ.

861

δάκνειν, δάκνεσθαι: the translation 'to peck and be pecked' is perhaps best here as an ancient commentator points out that this contest is being described as a cock fight.

πρότερος: there is dramatic irony here as the first character to speak in an Aristophanic agon or contest is always the loser.

τούτῳ: Aeschylus.

862

τἄπη = τα ἔπη. The accusatives that follow are accusatives of respect after δάκνεσθαι (see line 88).

τὰ μέλη: double-meaning of 'music' as well as 'limbs'.

τὰ νεῦρα: the anatomical description of his art (following the cock fighting image established on line 861) becomes most obvious here.

863

τὸν Πηλέα: Euripides seems to play into Aeschylus' hands here by listing plays that may have been considered controversial. Euripides' *Peleus* only survives in very few small fragments but it is likely that the plot involved Peleus being falsely accused of seducing his host's wife and then being left out on Mt. Pelion as punishment. It seems likely that Peleus would have been dressed in rags when he was rescued by centaurs.

τὸν Αἴολον: see line 850.

864

τὸν Μελέαγρον: in Euripides' *Meleager*, the eponymous hero kills his maternal uncles in a dispute over whom should be awarded the hide of the Calydonian Boar, a monstrous animal which Meleager pursued and killed along with a band of other heroes. In response to this, Althaea, Meleager's mother, arranges her son's death. Euripides' version of this play may have been controversial for developing a story of war into one of love as in Euripides' version of the myth Meleager falls out with his uncles in a personal dispute because he is in love with Atalanta, who helped to hunt the boar, and wishes to give its hide to her.

κἄτι = καὶ ἔτι.

τὸν Τήλεφον: see line 855.

865

λέγ' = λέγε.

866

ἐβουλόμην: 'I would prefer.'

867

ἐξ ἴσου: 'fair' or 'on equal terms'.

νῷν: dative dual form of ἐγώ / ἡμεῖς.

868

οὐχὶ = οὐ.

μοι: 'with me' – following the compound συντέθνηκέ. The proud boast that his poetry did not die with him stems from a state decree following his death that allowed his plays to be reperformed at the dramatic festivals. The amusing problem for Aeschylus then is that he does not have his plays to recite from in the underworld because they are not there yet.

869

τούτῳ δὲ συντέθνηκεν: in reality, Euripides' plays went on to be extremely popular long after his death and became a central part of the school curriculum.

ὥσθ' = ὥστε – introducing a result clause.

871

ἴθι: 'go' – imperative of εἶμι (I shall go).

λιβανωτὸν . . . πῦρ: burning incense and then praying is an invocation to the gods before an important event. This signifies the start of the agon or contest, and highlights its importance.

δότω: 'bring' third person aorist imperative.

872

ὅπως ἂν εὔξωμαι: purpose clause.

σοφισμάτων: see line 17. This refers to the arguments to follow in the agon.

873

κρῖναι: an infinitive follows εὔξωμαι on line 872.

874

ὑμεῖς: Dionysus speaks to the chorus of initiates.

ταῖς Μούσαις: 'the Muses' – traditionally a group of nine goddesses on whom poets and artists depended for inspiration: Calliope, Clio, Euterpe, Terpsichore, Erato, Melpomene, Thalia, Polyhymnia and Urania.

ὑπᾴσατε: aorist plural imperative.

Vocabulary

While there is no Defined Vocabulary List for A Level, words in the OCR Defined Vocabulary List for AS are marked with * so that students can quickly see the vocabulary with which they should be particularly familiar.

ἄβυσσος -ον	bottomless
***ἀγαθός -ή -όν**	good
Ἀγάθων -ωνος m.	Agathon
***ἄγαν**	too, excessively
ἀγριοποιός -όν	savage
***ἄγω**	to bring
***ἀγών -ῶνος** m.	contest
ἀδελφίδιον -ου n.	little brother, brother dear
***ἀδελφός -οῦ** m.	brother
***ἀδικέω**	to wrong, injure
***ἀεί**	always
ἀέναος -ον	ever-flowing
ἀθαλάττωτος -ον	unused to the sea
Ἅιδης -ου m.	Hades, the underworld
αἰθήρ -έρος m.	sky
αἰνιγμός -οῦ m.	riddle, analogy
Αἴολος -ου m.	Aeolus
***αἴρω**	to lift up
***αἰσθάνομαι** + gen.	to hear
Αἰσχύλος -ου m.	Aeschylus
***ἀκούω**, fut. **ἀκούσομαι**	to hear
ἀκρατής -ές	uncontrolled
***ἀληθής -ές**	true
***ἀλλά**	but
ἄλλως	besides
ἀλοάω, aor. **ἠλόησα**	to hit, strike
Ἀμειψίας, Ἀμειψίου m.	Ameipsias
***ἄν**	particle used in indef. const./cond.
ἀναβαίνω, aor. **ἀνέβην**	to go up, climb up
ἀναβιόω	to come to life again
***ἀναγιγνώσκω**	to read
ἀνάγω, aor. **ἀνήγαγον**	to bring up
ἀναδύομαι	to back out of
ἀναμένω, fut. **ἀναμενέω**, aor. **ἀνέμεινα**	to wait
ἀνάπαυλα -ης f.	rest, resting-place, inn
ἀνάφορον -ου n.	pole
Ἀνδρομέδα -ας f.	Andromeda
***ἄνευ** + gen.	without
***ἀνήρ, ἀνδρός** m.	man
***ἄνθρωπος -ου** m.	human, mortal, man
ἀνόσιος -ον	unholy, profane
ἀντιβαίνω	to set against
ἀντικνήμιον -ου n.	shin
ἅπαξ	once, one time
ἁπαξάπας -ασα -αν	absolutely all
ἀπαπαῖ	aaaah!
ἄπειρος -ον	inexperienced
ἀπεριλάλητος -ον	not able to chatter
ἀπέρχομαι	to depart
***ἀπό** + gen.	by means of, from
ἀποδημέω	to be on one's travels
***ἀποθνήσκω**, perf. **τέθνηκα**	to die
ἀποίχομαι	to go away, depart
ἀπολαμβάνω, aor. **ἀπέλαβον**	to take aside
ἀπολείπω, aor. **ἀπέλιπον**	to abandon, desert
***ἀπόλλυμι**, aor. **ἀπώλεσα**	to destroy
Ἀπόλλων -ωνος m.	Apollo
ἀποπέρδομαι, fut. **ἀποπαρδήσομαι**	to fart it all out
ἀποπήγνυμι	to freeze

ἀποσεμνύνομαι, fut. **ἀποσεμνυνέομαι**	to give oneself solemn airs, become haughty
ἀποσοβέω	to scare away
ἀποτρέπω	to put off
ἀποφαίνω	to denounce, show up
ἀπύλωτος -ον	ungated
***ἄρα**	then, after all
***ἆρα**	particle introducing a question
***ἀργύριον -ου** n.	money
ἀρέσκω	to please
ἀρήν, ἀρνός m.	lamb
ἀρουραῖος -α -ον	rustic, agricultural
ἀρτοπώλιον -ου n.	bakery
ἀρτόπωλις -ιδος f.	female baker
ἀσαλαμίνιος -ον	not from Salamis
ἀστεῖος -α -ον	witty, clever
ἀτάρ	but
ἀτέχνως	absolutely
ἀτραπός -οῦ f.	path
Αὑαίνος -ου m.	Hauaenus, lit. 'Withering'
αὐθαδόστομος -ον	of a self-indulgent style
***αὖθις**	again
αὐλός -οῦ m.	pipe
***αὐτός -ή -ό**	self; (not in nom.) him, her, it
ἀφίημι, pres. pass. ppl. **ἀφιεμένος**	to send forth, start
***ἀφικνέομαι**, fut.**ἀφίξομαι**	to arrive
ἀχάλινος -ον	unbridled
ἄχθος -εος n.	load, burden
βαβαιάξ	goodness me!
***βαδίζω**, fut. **βαδιοῦμαι**	to walk, go
βαδιστικός -ή -όν	good at walking
***βαρέως φέρω**	to take something badly
βάρος -ους n.	load, weight
βάτραχος -ου m.	frog
***βίος -ου** m.	life
***βοάω**	to shout
βόρβορος -ου m.	mud
***βουλεύομαι**	to plan
***βούλομαι**	to want, wish
γάμος -ου m.	marriage, union
***γάρ**	for
γάστρων -ωνος m.	pot-belly, fatso, fatty
***γε**	indeed, certainly
***γελάω**	to laugh
γέλοιος -α -ον	funny, amusing
γέλως -ωτος m.	laughter
γεννάδας -ου m.	noble

γενναῖος -α -ον	noble
***γέρων -οντος** m.	old man
***γῆ -ῆς** f.	land
***γλῶττα -ης** f.	tongue
γνάθος -ου f.	jaw
γόνιμος -η -ον	fertile, creative
***γοῦν**	at any rate
***γυνή, γυναικός** f.	woman
δαί	(after interrog.) then
δαιμόνιος -α -ον	(voc.) good sir, dear man
δάκνω	to bite, peck
δαρδάπτω	to devour
***δέ**	and, but
***δεῖ**, imp. **ἔδει** + acc. + inf.	it is necessary
δείδω, aor. **ἔδεισα**	to fear
δειματόω	to frighten, scare
***δεινός -ή -όν**	terrible, fearful
δειπνέω	to feast, dine
***δέκα**	ten
***δεξιός -ά -όν**	talented, skilful
***δέομαι** + acc. + gen.	to ask for X from Y
+ gen.	to need
***δεσπότης -ου** m.	master
***δεῦρο**	to here
***δή**	in truth, indeed, then
Δημήτηρ -τρος f.	Demeter
***δῆτα**	(answer) to be sure, certainly (question) then?
***διά** + gen.	through, by
διάγω, fut. **διάξω**	to carry across
δίαιτα -ης f.	accommodation
***διαλέγομαι**	to discuss, converse
διαλυμαίνομαι	to mistreat, ravage
διασκέπτομαι, perf. **διέσκεμμαι**	to examine thoroughly
***διδάσκω**	to teach, instruct
Διόνυσος – ου m.	Dionysus
***δίδωμι**	to give
***δοκεῖ** + dat. + inf.	it seems good to X, X decides
***δοκέω**	to expect, intend
δραχμή -ῆς f.	drachma (silver coin)
***δράω**	to do
***δύναμαι**, fut. **δυνήσομαι**	to be able
***δύο**	two
δυσχείμερος -ον	wintry
***δώδεκα**	twelve
δωμάτιον -ου n.	bedroom
***ἐάν** + subjunc.	if (in fut. open conditions)

*ἐγγύς + gen	near
ἐγκέφαλος -ου m.	brain
*ἐγώ	I
*ἔγωγε	I for my part
*ἐθέλω	to want
ἔθω, perf. εἴωθα	to be accustomed to
*εἰ	if
*εἰμί, imperf. ἦ(ν)	to be
*εἶμι, inf. ἰέναι	to go
εἴπερ	if really
*εἰς + acc.	into, to
εἶτα	then, and then, and yet
εἰωθότα -ων n.	the usual things
ἑκάστοτε	each time
ἐκβαίνω	to go out
ἐκγράφω	to copy, write out
ἐκδιδάσκω	to explain, spell out
*ἐκεῖ	there
*ἐκεῖθεν	from there
*ἐκεῖνος -η -ο	that, plur. those
*ἐκεῖσε	to that place
ἐκπλήττω	to frighten
ἐκποδών	out of the way
ἐκτείνω, fut. ἐκτενῶ	to stretch out
ἐκτροπή -ῆς f.	fork (in the road), turning
ἐκφέρω, aor. ἐξήνεγκα	to bring out, to carry out for burial
ἐκχέω	to pour out
*ἐλάττων -ον	smaller, less
*ἐλαύνω	to row
ἐλάω	to row
ἐλέγχω	to question, cross-examine
*ἐμαυτόν -ήν	myself
ἐμβαίνω	to get on board
ἐμβάλλω, aor. ἐνέβαλον	to lay to
*ἐμός -ή -όν	my, mine
ἐμπίμπρημι, aor. pass. ἐνεπρήσθην	to set on fire
*ἐν + dat.	in
ἐνάλλομαι, aor. ἐνηλάμην	to leap at, charge
*ἕνεκα + gen.	on account of, because of
*ἐνθάδε	here
ἐνθυμέομαι, aor. ἐνεθυμήθην	to notice
*ἐνιαυτός -οῦ m.	year
*ἐννέα	nine
*ἐνταῦθα	here
*ἐντεῦθεν	from there
ἐξ ἴσου	on equal terms

*ἐξαίφνης	suddenly
ἐξεγείρομαι, aor. ἐξηγρόμην	to wake up
ἔξειμι	to go out
ἐξεμέω	to vomit
ἐξόλλυμι, fut. ἐξολῶ	to completely destroy
*ἐπειδάν + subjunc.	when(ever)
*ἐπειδή	since
*ἔπειτα	then, next
ἐπέχω, aor. imperat. ἐπίσχες	to stop, hold it
*ἐπί + acc.	to, onto, in search of, to fetch
*ἐπί + gen.	on
*ἐπί + dat.	at, on
ἐπιβατεύω	to serve as a marine on a trireme
ἐπιθυμέω, aor. ἐπεθύμησα	to desire
ἐπιορκέω	to swear falsely
ἐπίορκος -ον	sworn falsely
ἐπιτρίβω	to crush
ἐπιφυλλίς -ίδος f.	left-over grapes, small grapes
ἐπιχειρέω, aor. ἐπεχειρήσα	to try, attempt
ἔπος -ους n.	word
ἐρίζω	to compete
*ἔρχομαι, aor. ἦλθον	to go, come
*ἐς + acc.	into, to
ἐσφέρω	to bring in
*ἕτερος -α -ον	another
*ἔτι	still, further, in addition (with neg.) any longer
ἔτνος -ους n.	soup
*ἑτοῖμος -ον	ready
*εὐδαίμων -ον	happy
*εὐθύς	at once, immediately
εὔκολος -ον	good natured
Εὐριπίδης -ου m.	Euripides
*εὑρίσκω, aor. ηὗρον	to find
*εὔχομαι, aor. εὐξάμην	to pray
εὐωχία -ης f.	feast, banquet
*ἔχω, fut. ἕξω *or* σχήσω	to hold, to steer, land
*ἔχω + inf.	to be able
*ζάω	to live
*Ζεύς, Διός m.	Zeus
*ζητέω	to seek, look for
*ἤ	or, than
*ἤ . . . ἤ	either . . . or

ἦ μήν (introducing a strong oath) in truth
ἤ τοι I can tell you
***ἤδη** already, by now
***ἥκω**, fut. **ἥξω** to have come
ἡλίκος -η -ον as big as
ἠμί I say!
***ἤν** if
ἡνίκα when

***θαρρέω** to not fear, have courage
θαυμαστός -ή -όν wonderful, marvellous
***θεάομαι** to watch
θείνω, aor. **ἔθενον** to strike
***θεός -οῦ** m./f. god
θερμαίνω, aor. **ἐθέρμηνα** to heat
θερμός -ή -όν hot
***θηρίον -ου** n. wild animal, beast
Θησεύς -έως m. Theseus
θίασος -ου m. Bacchic revel, troupe
θλίβομαι to be squeezed, to chafe
θνῄσκω, perf. **τέθνηκα** to die
θρανίον -ου n. rower's bench
θρασύνομαι to be over-confident
θρῖον -ου n. rissole wrapped in a fig leaf
θρόνος -ου m. chair
θυεία -ας f. mortar (for grinding herbs, etc.)
***θύρα -ας** f. door

ἰδίᾳ + gen. apart from, separate from
ἰδού see for yourself, as you please!
ἱερά -ῶν n. plur. sacrificial victims
ἵζω to sit
***ἵημι**, aor. act. inf. **εἶναι**, perf. pass. **εἵμην** to send, to start
ἱκετεύω to beg
ἵμερος -ου m. longing, desire
***ἵνα** so that, in order that
Ἰοφῶν -ῶντος m. Iophon

καθαιρέω to take down
καθέζομαι, fut. **καθεδοῦμαι** to sit down
καθέρπω, aor. **καθείρπυσα** to stroll, creep, toddle
***καθίζω** to sit down
***καί** and, even, also
καὶ μήν and what's more
***καίτοι** and yet
κακοδαίμων -ον miserable, unlucky
***κακός -ή -όν** bad
***καλός -ή -όν** fine, right
κάλως -ω m. rope
καρδία -ας f. heart
***κατά** + acc. for the purpose of
κατά + gen. by
καταβαίνω to get down, dismount
καταδύω, aor. **κατεδυσάμην** to sink (trans.)
κατακελεύω to give the time (in rowing)
κατάντης -ες downhill
κατάρατος -ον accursed, abominable
κατατίθημι, fut. **καταθήσω** to put down, pay
κατέρχομαι, aor.**κατῆλθον** to go down
κατέχω, fut. **καθέξω** to hold onto
κάτω down below
κατώτερω lower
***κεῖμαι** to lie, be strewn
***κελεύω** to order, tell
κενταυρικός -ή -όν like a centaur, savage, brutal
Κεραμεικός -οῦ m. Cerameicus, the potters' quarter
Κερβέριοι -ων m. plur. Cerberians
κεφάλαιος -α -ον of the head, chief, principal
***κινέω** to have sex
Κινησίος -ου m. Cinesias
Κλεισθένης -ους m. Cleisthenes
κόβαλα -ων n. plur. garbage
κόθορνος -ου m. boot, buskin
κομποφακελορρήμων -ον spouting bundles of pompous bluster
κόραξ -ακος m. raven
κόρις -εως m. bedbug
κότος -ου m. rage, rancour
κρέας -ως n. flesh, body
κρείττων -ον superior, stronger
κρεμάννυμι, aor. **ἐκρέμασα** to hang
κρήνη -ης f. spring
Κρητικός -ή -όν Cretan
***κρίνω** to judge
κροκωτός -οῦ m. saffron-coloured robe
κρόταφος -ου m. temple, side of forehead
κρότος -ου m. clapping
***κύκλος -ου** m. circle
κύκνος -ου m. swan

κωδωνίζω	to test (the mettle of)
κωκύω	to wail
κωμῳδία -ας f.	comedy
κώνειον -ου n.	hemlock
κώπη -ης f.	oar
λάλος -ον	talkative, babbling
***λαμβάνω**, aor. **ἔλαβον**	to get, pick up
λαμπάς -άδος f.	torch-race
λάσκω, aor. **ἔλακον**	to utter, declaim
***λέγω**, fut.**ἐρῶ**, aor. **εἶπον**	to speak, say, mean
λεοντῆ -ῆς f.	lion-skin
Λήθη -ης f.	Oblivion
λίαν	excessively
λιβανωτός -οῦ m.	incense
***λίθος -ου** m.	stone
***λιμήν -ένος** m.	harbour
***λίμνη -ης** f.	lake
***λόγος -ου** m.	word
λοιδορέομαι	to rail at one another
***λοιπός -ή -όν**	left over, remaining
Λύκις -ιος m.	Lycis
λωβητής -οῦ m.	debaucher, damager
μὰ + acc.	by X, for X's sake (often referring to a god)
μαίνομαι	to be mad
μάκαρες -ων m.	the blessed
***μακρός -ά -όν**	long
***μάλα**	especially
***μάλιστα**	very much, yes
***μανθάνω**, aor. **ἔμαθον**	to understand
***μέγας, μεγάλη, μέγα**	big
μεθίημι + gen.	to let go of
μειρακύλλιον -ου n.	lad, kid
μέλας, μέλαινα, μέλαν	black
Μελέαγρος -ου m.	Meleager
***μέλλω**	to intend to
μέλος -εος n.	music, singing
***μέν . . . δέ . . .**	on the one hand . . . on the other . . .
***μέντοι**	however, certainly, indeed
***μέρος -εος** n.	turn
μεταβάλλομαι	to shift
***μή**	not
***μή** + aor. subjunc.	don't!
***μηδέ**	and not

***μηδείς, μηδεμία, μηδέν**	no-one, nothing
μήν	indeed, truly
***μητηρ -τρος** f.	mother
μίμησις -εως f.	imitation
μισθόομαι	to hire
***μισθός -οῦ** m.	fee
Μόλων -ωνος m.	Molon
***μόνος -η -ον**	alone
μονῳδία -ας f.	monody, ode
Μορσίμος -ου m.	Morsimus
Μοῦσα -ης f.	Muse
μούσειον -ου n.	sanctuary of the muses, music-halls
μουσικός -ή -όν	skilled in music, cultivated, elegant
μυέομαι, perf.**μεμύημαι**	to be initiated into the mysteries
μυριάκις	thousands of times
μυρίος -α -ον	countless, plur. 10,000
μυρρινών -ῶνος m.	myrtle-grove
μυστήριον -ου n.	mystery, secret rite
***ναυμαχέω**	to fight in a sea battle
***ναῦς, νεώς** f.	ship
***ναύτης -ου** m.	sailor
***νεκρός -οῦ** m.	corpse
νεῦρον -ου n.	sinew
νή + acc.	yes by X
νή (τὸν) Δία	yes by Zeus (str. affirm.)
νουθετέω	to instruct
***νοῦς, νοῦ** m.	mind, purpose, idea
***νῦν**	now
Ξενοκλέης -ους m.	Xenocles
***ξένος -ου** m.	host, guest
ξυγγίγνομαι, aor. **ξυνεγενόμην**	to meet; have sex with
ξυμ-	see συμ-
ξυναποδιδράσκω, aor. **ξυναπέδραμον**	to run away together with
ξυνέρχομαι, aor. **ξυνῆλθον**	to come together
ξύντομος -ον	cut short
ξυντυγχάνω, aor. **ξυνέτυχον** + dat.	to meet
ὀβολός -οῦ m.	obol (coin)
***ὅδε, ἥδε, τόδε**	this
***ὁδός -οῦ** f.	road
***οἷ**	to where
***οἶδα**	to know
***οἰκέω**	to manage, direct
***οἰκία -ας** f.	house
οἴμοι	alas!

οἰμώζω	to wail
οἴομαι	to think
***οἷος -α -ον**	what sort of
***οἷός τ'εἰμί**	to be able
Ὄκνος -ου m.	Ocnus, lit. 'Lethargy'
***ὀλίγος -η -ον**	few
***ὄμνυμι**, aor. **ὤμοσα**	to swear, take an oath
***ὅμως**	still, nevertheless
ὄνος -ου m.	donkey, ass
ὄντως	really
ὅπῃ	by which
ὅπου	where
***ὅπως** + fut. indic.	take care that, so that
***ὅπως**	how
***ὁράω**, fut. **ὄψομαι**, aor. **εἶδον**	to see
***ὀργή -ῆν** f.	anger
***ὅρκος -ου** m.	oath
***ὅς, ἥ, ὅ**	who, which
ὅσπερ, ἥπερ, ὅπερ	who, which
***ὅστις, ἥτις, ὅ τι**	whoever, whichever
***ὅταν**	whenever, when
***ὅτε**	when, since
***ὅτι**	because, that
***οὐ (οὐκ, οὐχ)**	not
***οὐδαμῶς**	in no way
***οὐδείς, οὐδεμία, οὐδέν**	no one, nothing
***οὐκέτι**	no longer
***οὔκουν**	(speaker seizes an opportunity) well . . . not, (impatient question) not
***οὖν**	and so, then
οὕνεκα + gen.	on account of
οὗπερ	where
οὔτοι	indeed not
***οὗτος, αὕτη, τοῦτο**	this, plur.these
οὑτοσί, αὑτηί, τουτί	this, plur. these
***οὕτως**	in this way
ὀφθαλμιάω	to have conjunctivitis
ὄφις -εως m.	serpent
ὀχέω	to let someone ride; (pass.) to ride
παιδίον -ου n.	slave-boy, boy
***παῖς, παιδός** m.	boy
***πάλιν**	back, again
παμπόνηρος -ον	thoroughly depraved
πανδοκεύτρια -ας f.	landlady
πανοῦργος -ον	wicked, villainous
πανταχοῦ	everywhere
πάνυ	really, altogether, completely
***παρά** + acc.	beside
παραβάλλομαι	to bring alongside
παρακινδυνεύω, perf. pass. ppl. **παρακεκινδυνευμένος**	to be bold
***παρασκευάζω**	to prepare, get ready
πατάσσω, aor.**ἐπάταξα**	to knock, strike
***πατήρ -τρός** m	father
***παύω**	to stop
***πεδίον -ου** n.	plain
***πείθω**, aor. **ἔπεισα**	to persuade
περαιόομαι	to cross
***περί** + gen.	about
περίειμι	to go around
περιτρέχω, fut.**περιθρέξομαι**	to run about
Πηλεύς -έως m.	Peleus
***πιέζομαι**	to be weighed down
***πλέω**	to sail
***πλήν** + gen.	except, save
πλοιάριον -ου n.	skiff, boat
***πλοῖον -ου** n.	boat
πλοκή -ῆς f.	rope
***πλοῦς -οῦ** m.	voyage, journey
Πλούτων -ωνος m.	Pluto
πνιγηρός -ά -ό	stifling, choking
πνοή -ῆς f.	breath, blast
ποθεινός -ή -όν	missed, longed for
πόθος -ου m.	longing, desire
ποῖ	to where?
ποιέω, fut. **ποιήσω**	to do, make, compose poetry
ποίησις -εως f.	poetry
ποιητής -οῦ m.	poet
***ποῖος -α -ον**	what kind of?
***πολέμιοι -ων** m. plur.	enemy
***πόλις -εως** f.	city
***πολύς, πολλή, πολύ**	much, many
πολυτίμητος -ον	most honourable
***πονέω**	to toil, work hard
πονηρός -ά -όν	poor, wicked
πορνεῖον -ου n.	brothel
Ποσειδῶν -ῶνος m.	Poseidon
***πόσος -η -ον**	how big?, plur. how many?
***ποτέ**	ever
***πότερον**	introduces a question
***πού**	perhaps
***ποῦ**	where?
***πούς, ποδός** m.	foot
***πρᾶγμα -ατος** n.	affair, trouble
πραόνως	calmly
πρέπει + acc. + inf.	it is fitting for X to Y
***πρεσβύτερος -α -ον**	older

***πρίν** before, until
πρῖνος -ου f. holm-oak
***πρό** + gen. before
προβάλλω, fut. **Προβαλῶ** to put out
***πρόθυμως** eagerly
***πρός** + acc. to, about, in relation to
πρός + dat. in addition to
προσέρχομαι, aor. **προσῆλθον** to approach, come near
προσουρέω + dat. to urinate on
πρότερος -α -ον superior, better
***πρῶτος -η -ον** first
πτωχοποιός -όν creator of beggars
Πυθάγγελος -ου m. Pythangelus
***πῦρ, πυρός** n. fire
πύργος -ου m. tower
πυρρίχη -ης f. war-dance
πώποτε ever
πῶς how

***ῥᾴδιος -α -ον** easy
ῥακιοσυρραπτάδης -ου m. rag-stitcher
ῥῆμα -ατος n. word, phrase, line
ῥῆσις -εως f. speech
ῥόπαλον -ου n. club

***σαυτόν, σαυτήν** yourself
***σαφής -ές** clear
σεμνός -ή -όν proud, haughty
***σιγάω** to be quiet
σκευάριον -ου n. little piece of baggage
σκευή -ῆς f. costume
***σκεύη -ων** n. plur. luggage
σκώπτω to mock, make fun of
σκῶρ, σκατος n. dung
σμικρός -ά -όν small
σός -ή -όν your
σόφισμα -ατος n. stage-trick, clever device
Σοφοκλῆς -έους m. Sophocles
σπεύδω to hurry, press on
σπλάγχνον -ου n. guts
***στάδιον -ου** n. stade (distance of *c.* 607 feet, 185 metres)
σταμνίον -ου n. wine jar
στρῶμα -ατος n. bedding
στωμυλιοσυλλεκτάδης -ου m. gossip-gleaner
στώμυλμα -ατος n. chatterbox
***σύ** you sing.
συλλέγω to collect, gather
συμβαίνω, aor. **συνέβην** to agree
συνθνήσκω + dat. to die with

***σφόδρα** very much, greatly, thoroughly
σχέτλιος -α -ον stubborn, wretched
σωφρονέω to be of sound mind, have good sense

Ταίναρος -ου f. Tainarus
ταλαιπωρέω to work hard, suffer
***ταχύς -εῖα -ύ** quick
τελέω, fut. **τελέω** to pay
τερατεύομαι to act pretentiously
***τέχνη -ης** f. skill, art
Τήλεφος -ου m. Telephus
τί δαί; what then?
***τίς, τί** who? what? which?
***τις, τι** someone, something
τλήμων -ονος wretched, miserable
***τοι** in truth, indeed
τοίνυν well then
***τοιοῦτος -αύτη -οῦτο** such
***τολμάω** to dare
***τοσοῦτος -αύτη -οῦτο** so much
***τότε** then
τραγῳδία -ας f. tragedy
τράχηλος -ου m. neck
***τρεῖς, τρία** three
***τρέπω**, aor. **ἔτραπον** to turn towards
τρίβω, perf. pass. ppl. **τετριμμένος** to knead, pound
τρισκακοδαίμων -ον three times unlucky
***τρόπος -ου** m. way, manner
τρυφή -ῆς f. wantonness
***τυγχάνω**, aor. **ἔτυχον** + ppl. to happen to be
τυννουτοσί -ονί so small, so little
τυφώς -ῶ m. whirlwind

ὕβρις -εως f. outrageous behaviour
ὑγιαίνω to have good health, to fare well
***υἱός -οῦ** m. son
***ὑμεῖς** you plur.
ὑπάγω to go
ὑπαείδω, aor.**ὕπᾳσα** to sing in accompaniment
***ὑπό** + gen. by
ὑφαιρέομαι, aor. **ὑφειλάμην** to steal
***ὑψηλός -ή -όν** high

***φαίνομαι** + ppl. to clearly be
***φέρε** come on!
***φέρω** to carry

φεῦ	ah!
***φημί**	to say
φθέγγομαι, fut. **φθέγξομαι**	to say
***φίλος -ου** m.	friend
φλυαρέω	to play the fool
φράζω, fut. **φράσω**, aor. **ἔφρασα**	to say
φρήν, φρενός f.	heart
φροῦδος -η -ον	vanished, gone
Φρύνιχος -ου m.	Phrynicus
***φυλάσσομαι**	to watch for, look out for
φῶς φωτός n.	light
***χαίρω**	to have good health, to fare well
χάλαζα -ης f.	hail
Χάρων -ωνος m.	Charon
χεζητιάω	to need to defecate
***χείρ χειρός** f.	hand
χελιδών -όνος f.	swallow
χολή -ῆς f.	gall, something that makes one sick
χορός -οῦ m.	chorus
***χράομαι** + dat.	to make use of
***χρή**, imp. **ἐχρῆν** + inf.	it is necessary
χρηστός -ή -όν	valiant, worthy, kind
***χρόνος -ου** m.	time
χωλοποιός -όν	creator of cripples
***χωρέω**	to go
ψυχρός -ά -όν	cold
ὤ	oh!
ὦ + voc.	o *(addressing someone)*
ὦ ὄπ	calls for rowers
ὡδί	in this way
ὦμος -ου m.	shoulder
***ὡς**	how, since, just as
ὥσπερ	as if, just as
***ὥστε**	with the result that
***ὠφελέω**	to help